AMSCO®

ADVANCED PLACEMENT® EDITION

UNITED STATES
GOVERNMENT & POLITICS

DAVID WOLFFORD

PERFECTION LEARNING®

David Wolfford teaches Advanced Placement® U.S. Government and Politics at Mariemont High School in Cincinnati, Ohio, and has served as an AP® Reader. He has a B.A. in Secondary Education and an M.A. in Constitutional and Legal History, both from the University of Kentucky. He has conducted historical research projects on school desegregation and American political history. David has published in historical journals, such as *Ohio Valley History* and *Kentucky Humanities*. He has written on government, politics, and campaigns for national magazines and Cincinnati newspapers. He is a James Madison Fellow, a National Board certified teacher, and a regular contributor to *Social Education*. David is editor of *By George: Articles from the Ashland Daily Independent* (Jesse Stuart Foundation) and editor of *Ohio Social Studies Review*. He has reported on government, politics, and campaigns for national magazines and newspapers, including the *Cincinnati Enquirer, Columbus Dispatch,* and *Lexington Herald-Leader.*

Reviewers and Consultants

Bryan J. Henry, M.A.
Lone Star College-UP
AP® U.S. Government and Politics
Houston, Texas

Jenifer A. Hitchcock, M.Ed., NBCT
AP® U.S Government and Politics
    Question Leader
James Madison Fellow '16 (VA)
Thomas Jefferson High School for Science
    and Technology
Alexandria, Virginia

Jennifer A. Jolley, NBCT, M.A.
James Madison Fellow '10 (FL)
Palm Bay Magnet High School
Melbourne, Florida

David LaShomb, M.S.
College Board Consultant
AP® U.S. Government and Politics
Georgetown, Texas

Louis Magnon, M.A.T., M.Ed.
Department of History and Political
    Science
San Antonio College
San Antonio, Texas

Melanie J. Pavlides, M.Ed.
AP® U.S. Government and Politics
Silverado High School
Las Vegas, Nevada

Eric Ruff, M.S.
AP® U.S. Government and Politics
Bishop Denis J. O'Connell High School
Arlington, Virginia

Rachael A. Ryan, MLA
College Board Consultant
The Taft School
Watertown, Connecticut

David M. Seiter, M.Ed.
AP® U.S. Government and Politics
Northridge High School
Layton, Utah

Eileen Sheehy
AP® U.S. Government and Politics
Billings West High School
Billings, Montana

Brian Stevens, B.A., M.A.
College Board Consultant
AP® U.S. Government and Politics
Coldwater High School
Coldwater, Michigan

Benwari Singh
AP® U.S Government and Politics
    Question Leader
Former Co-Chair A.P.® Government and
    Politics Test Development Committee
Cherry Creek High School
Greenwood Village, Colorado

Barry L. Tadlock, Ph.D.
AP® Government and Politics Reader
Associate Professor of Political Science
Ohio University
Athens, Ohio

AMSCO®

ADVANCED PLACEMENT® EDITION

UNITED STATES
GOVERNMENT & POLITICS

DAVID WOLFFORD

PERFECTION LEARNING®

Contents

UNIT 2—Interactions Among Branches of Government

UNIT 4—American Political Ideologies and Beliefs

UNIT 5—Political Participation

Preface

AMSCO® United States Government and Politics: Advanced Placement® Edition explains the American political system and will enhance student performance on the Advanced Placement® U.S. Government and Politics exam. This edition reflects the College Board's redesigned course and national exam and the most recent topics-based updates to the new Course and Examination Description.

The text includes a mix of colorful history, modern politics, and relevant statistics. Political personalities and memorable events aid understanding and provide examples for students to answer the exam's questions. The free-response and multiple-choice practice questions parallel those on the national exam.

This redesigned and updated book reflects contemporary trends in Congress, the presidency, and the courts, and it includes data from the 2018 federal elections. I draw from my research projects, political reporting, and years of teaching the AP® Government course. When necessary or useful, sources are cited in a simple manner and a bibliography is provided for those who want more information and insights.

This book fills the gap between a test-prep handbook and a costly, heavy political science textbook. It is thorough enough to be a student's go-to book, especially if used in conjunction with other print and online resources. One can read it gradually over an entire term or during a thorough review period.

I would like to thank for their inspiration and good counsel my dad George Wolfford, a noted journalist, historian, and storyteller; history professor David Hamilton; and colleagues Luke Wiseman, Dan Ruff, and Matt Litton. Special thanks go to Brian Stevens, a reviewer of this volume and my first source for how to teach AP® Government and Politics. Thanks to all my reviewers of this revision: Bryan Henry, Jenifer Hitchcock, Melanie Pavlides, Eric Ruff, Rachel Ryan, Ben Singh, and Brian Stevens.

A special thanks to editorial director Carol Francis and supervising editor Joe Bianchi. They kick-started the project, guided it, and have contributed much to the book. And, of course, thanks to AMSCO/Perfection Learning and Steve Keay for believing in me and for publishing my work. To more than any, thanks to Mika, Maya, and Miki for their sacrifices to allow this book to become a reality.

David Wolfford, May 2020

Introduction

Congratulations on accepting the challenge to learn United States government and politics at an accelerated level. *AMSCO® United States Government and Politics: Advanced Placement® Edition*, revised to align with the College Board's latest Course and Exam Description (CED), will help you master the fundamental government concepts as well as political science disciplinary practices. This introduction explains the redesigned course and test format. Twenty content and skills-building chapters, with extensive information, examples, and practice questions bring to life the required foundational documents, Supreme Court cases, and fundamental concepts.

The College Board's Advanced Placement® program started in 1955. The U.S. Government and Politics course began in 1987. In 2019, nearly 10,000 high schools offered this course, and nearly 315,000 students took the national exam. Most took this class in their senior year. More than 3,000 colleges accepted these scores and awarded credit in place of course work.

Taking an Advanced Placement® course and exam in government and politics has many benefits. The depth and rigor will help you gain deep understanding of this relevant subject. The course will also help prepare you for college, sharpening your skills in analyzing and interpreting information from a variety of sources. These courses may save time and money by awarding credit for college courses. Colleges also consider your enrollment and performance in these courses as they determine admissions and award scholarships. One College Board study found that 85 percent of colleges view students' AP® experience favorably as they consider admissions decisions, and 31 percent report considering it when determining scholarship awards.

The exam is given in early May, but you must register early in the school year. Check your school's guidance department or the College Board's website for details, fees, and deadlines.

Please note: This book focuses on the U.S. Government and Politics course, not the separate Comparative Government and Politics course, which compares various national governments.

The Course

The AP® United States Government and Politics course "provides a college-level, nonpartisan introduction," states the College Board, "that characterizes the constitutional system and the political culture of the United States" focuses on depth rather than breadth, and concepts rather than rote learning. Five "Big Ideas" that animate American government—(1) Constitutionalism, (2) Liberty and Order, (3) Civic Participation in a Representative Democracy, (4) Competing Policymaking Interests, and (5) Methods of Political Analysis—are woven throughout the book. Interactions among the three branches of government, between the federal and state governments, and between citizens and their government are highlighted.

The new course has less emphasis on content and more on skills. The College Board expects that students be well versed in 15 landmark Supreme Court cases—the only ones on which students might be explicitly tested. The law emanating from other Court precedents may also appear, but students and teacher will no longer have to predict which nonrequired cases might appear somewhere on the exam.

Eight of the nine foundational documents are from the U.S. founding; the ninth is Dr. Martin Luther King Jr.'s "Letter from a Birmingham Jail." A feature introduces each document, focusing on the key concepts with questions to get you thinking about the documents and providing opportunities to develop and apply political science disciplinary skills and practices.

Since policy and policymaking are necessary to understanding government, the policymaking process has been interwoven throughout the course. In this way, policymaking is tied directly to the concepts in the course instead of in separate chapters.

The course also develops **political science disciplinary practices**, such as analyzing arguments and relating concepts to political institutions, behavior, or policies. In addition, the course provides many opportunities to develop and strengthen **reasoning processes**—defining, understanding stages in processes, comparing, and understanding causation.

Finally, the program requires the completion of **a project** through which students will make a civic connection. Several examples appear in "Think Tank," a supplement after the content chapters starting on p. 667. The course emphasizes citizen participation as the bedrock of American representative democracy and the project promotes that.

Government and Politics Content

This course is like a college-level introductory course in government and politics. The key themes include the creation and design of government, the three branches, civil rights and liberties, political ideology, and how the citizens interact with government. Overarching questions include the following: How do elections work and how are they won? How do the three branches interact to create law and policy? How are people in this democracy linked to government institutions?

Enduring Understandings The course content is developed from enduring understandings—statements that synthesize the important concepts in a discipline area and have lasting value even beyond that discipline area. For example, the College Board has articulated this enduring understanding derived from the big idea of constitutionalism:

A balance between governmental power and individual rights has been a hallmark of American political development.

Why is that an enduring understanding? It highlights a fundamental tension in American government between the individual liberties our culture cherishes and the recognition that to live in society, we must turn over some power to the government so that it can keep order and provide public safety. Exactly where to draw the line between government power and individual liberties has been debated and clarified. Each unit in this book begins with a listing of the enduring understandings relevant to that unit.

Learning Objectives To help students fully develop those enduring understandings, the College Board has also articulated learning objectives—the expected outcomes of study that can be demonstrated through student action. For example, this is a learning objective related to the enduring understanding listed on the previous page:

> Explain how democratic ideals are reflected in the Declaration of Independence and the U.S. Constitution.

This learning objective ties to the enduring understanding by providing specific examples for study—the Declaration of Independence and the U.S. Constitution—and then clearly identifies how a student can demonstrate this understanding: "Explain how democratic ideals are reflected . . ." Each chapter ends with a list of the learning objectives and the key terms and names to associate with each learning objective.

Essential Knowledge Being able to fulfill the learning objectives requires content knowledge. The College Board has homed in on what it considers essential knowledge to achieve that purpose. For example:

> The U.S. government is based on ideas of limited government, including natural rights, popular sovereignty, republicanism, and social contract.

This essential knowledge statement outlines what you need to know to fulfill the learning objective, so you can focus your study on the truly relevant information. The College Board has boiled down this essential knowledge point to one concept, limited government, and the elements that contribute to it: natural rights, popular sovereignty (people's power), republicanism, and social contract. This book provides all the essential knowledge you will need to fulfill the learning objectives and develop enduring understandings.

Understanding Political History If you've already taken a high school U.S. history course, you will recognize some important eras and their relevance to politics. For example, the American founding included an intense dispute between the American colonists and Great Britain about a lack of democratic representation and liberty. This course focuses on the American Revolution's legal and political (not military) history, the ideas in the Declaration of Independence, and the creation and ratification of the Constitution.

Knowing something about a few leading presidents—their terms in office, impact, and accomplishments—will help you cement your understanding of key political events and forces. Other key historical personalities are also relevant to shaping the American government. Federalists James Madison and

Alexander Hamilton promoted a strong national government. Chief Justice John Marshall became the father of the Supreme Court, serving during its formative era, 1801–1837. During the 1950s civil rights movement, civil rights attorney Thurgood Marshall helped forge the legal path for desegregating America. Such historic individuals' names could appear on the exam, but you will not need to fully recall them. However, knowing historical figures provides you with strong examples to answer the free-response questions.

Understanding Modern Politics This course focuses on the three branches of federal government and how people and groups interact with these institutions to create public policy. However, the relationship between the federal and state governments is also a recurring theme in understanding the challenges of federalism.

Most high-level federal government decisions are made "inside the Beltway"—the Washington, D.C., area encircled by Interstate 495. Congress convenes on Capitol Hill, the president lives and works in the White House, and the Supreme Court justices hear cases in their building nearby. These institutions and the vast federal bureaucracy are the policymaking bodies that create, shape, and carry out the law. The press, or media, report to citizens on the work of these branches. Interest groups and political parties try to influence all three branches in different ways. These different entities work together, and at odds with one another, to accomplish their separate goals.

In addition to the federal government, which includes hundreds of agencies and well over two million employees, each state has a legislature, a governor and state administration, and a court system. Countless municipal or city governments and school boards create a massive web of policies. This complex system addresses a variety of viewpoints while ultimately adopting only those few ideas on which the masses can largely agree. This is the basis of pluralism, a system of public policies resulting from compromise among competing groups. With pluralism, we create a consensus government to satisfy most participants most of the time.

Where Does the Power Lie? This course repeatedly asks that question. Officially, national political power and authority rests with "We the people" as introduced in the Preamble of the Constitution. To ensure the ideals of a government by the people, the Constitution defines the structure of delegated power from the people to Congress, the qualifications for president, and the jurisdiction of the courts. Actual government policies, however, depend on who holds these offices and how they approach their duties. In many instances, public policy is forged after a competition between the political elites (upper-level politicians and policymakers) and the rank-and-file citizens (voters).

Those who subscribe to the elite theory of government claim that big businesses, political leaders, and those with money and resources overly dominate the policymaking process. But pluralists counter that because such political resources and access to the media are so widely scattered, no single elite group has a monopoly on power. Pluralists also argue that the many levels of government and the officials within each branch bring a variety of views and divide the power to prevent one sector of society or one view from dominating.

This Book

This book explains American government in straightforward terms and with many memorable examples for understanding. The author's experiences in teaching AP® Government and Politics, serving as a Reader for the College Board, and engaging with real-world government and researching political history has resulted in a plainspoken yet colorful version of American government while aligning the presentation with the College Board's Course and Examination Description (CED).

The College Board recently reorganized the content of AP® Government and Politics into 60 **topics**. The approach of this book mirrors the College Board's CED and presents manageable lessons that provide essential knowledge for students to complete each learning objective. At the same time, it groups related topics into chapters so that shared overarching concepts can be tied together. As with other government books, there is overlap among the chapters, so the text includes cross-references to related topics. Multiple-choice questions and free-response questions follow each chapter and unit review.

To balance accuracy with clarity, historical quotes have been occasionally altered to eliminate archaic spellings or errors and language has been inserted parenthetically to aid reader's understanding.

Five Units

This book contains 5 units and a total of 20 chapters.

Unit One: Foundations of American Democracy The first unit focuses on the historical creation of the United States government. It includes the struggle between the American colonists and the British government, the infant U.S. government under the failed Articles of Confederation, and the creation of the Constitution and the Bill of Rights. It also explains the divisions of federalism. The full text of the Constitution and Declaration of Independence are provided in the back of this book.

Unit Two: Interactions Among Branches of Government Unit Two covers the legislative, executive, and judicial branches defined in Articles I, II, and III of the Constitution. The major national governing institutions— Congress, the presidency, the judiciary, and the bureaucracy of government agencies and departments that carry out the nation's laws are covered. The bureaucracy is the president's administration, from Cabinet-level advisors down to national park rangers. Government sub-institutions include the House and Senate, congressional committees, federal departments and agencies, and the lower U.S. courts. These institutions have relationships with one another, and this unit explores their interactions.

Unit Three: Civil Liberties and Civil Rights This unit focuses on civil liberties—a person's political freedoms, such as the right to free speech or fair trials. The chapters in this unit will help you understand the division of church and state, the limits of free speech in the public square, and the line between an individual's liberty and societal order.

Civil rights generally refer to a person's basic rights to freedom and to equal treatment under the law. Civil rights quests usually involve the struggle for certain groups—African Americans, other ethnic minorities, women, or gays and lesbians—seeking equality under the law. Understanding civil rights and liberties requires solid knowledge of the Supreme Court's role and landmark decisions.

Unit Four: American Political Ideologies and Beliefs Unit Four examines why Americans hold different political ideologies and what forces or experiences cause people to develop their beliefs. Family, demographics, religion, school, geographic location, race, and countless other factors shape how a voter votes and affect the relationship between citizens and government. This unit also discusses the science of polling and the differing ideologies on government's role in the economy and in social programs.

Unit Five: Political Participation The final unit focuses on the linkage institutions—political parties, campaigns, elections, interest groups, and the mass media—that connect voters to the government. The chapter on voting and voter behavior will help you understand how individual characteristics and government action influences voter turnout. Those on political parties and interest groups explain their structure, function, and impact on policy. Presidential and congressional elections, the campaigns to win these contests, and the money game are analyzed. The role of the media and its relationship to government appear in the final topics.

Updated Content

Besides covering every item in the College Board's materials and including standard terms and concepts for any American government course, this volume addresses an array of current and sometimes controversial topics, new voting trends, major news stories, and changes in modern communication.

The quest to legalize marijuana and same-sex marriage have recently crossed new milestones. Several states now allow medical or recreational use of cannabis after state-wide votes or legislative action. The gay rights movement and the quest for marriage equality has also crossed new thresholds. In 2015, the Supreme Court announced its *Obergefell v. Hodges* ruling, legalizing same sex marriage. And a host of states have outlawed discrimination against members of the LGBTQ community.

Social media has taken on a major role in linking people with government and in political campaigns. The White House is operating under new media relations. And the federal government plans to regulate political advertising on social media platforms for transparency and accountability. President Trump's impeachment and acquittal, the Democrats' 2020 presidential nomination quest, and recent legislation appears in this edition.

Features based on the College Board's CED

To support the in-depth learning promoted by the College Board course, this book includes a number of special features. These features include Foundational Documents, Must-Know Supreme Court Decisions, and a section on the civic connection project.

Foundational Documents You must become familiar with the nine foundational documents the College Board has selected. These include the charters of freedom that created the national republic, four of the *Federalist Papers*, one Anti-Federalist essay, and Dr. Martin Luther King Jr.'s "Letter from a Birmingham Jail." For each featured document, you will find a selected passage or excerpt and a few questions for understanding. The Declaration of Independence and Constitution of the United States are reprinted in their entirety at the end of the book.

Must-Know Supreme Court Decisions Though you will read about a number of Supreme Court cases and how these shaped the law, the course requires you to know 15 landmark decisions in depth. These range from the early *Marbury v. Madison* (1803) through the recent *McDonald v. Chicago* (2010) decisions. These cases cover an array of disputes, such as the limits of government action and the level of citizens' rights. For each Must-Know Decision, you will read an introduction and selected passages from the Court's opinions. Questions will follow each case for further analysis.

The Civic Engagement Project In an effort to encourage political science research and civic engagement, the College Board requires that all students taking this course complete a project. This project can take several forms and is meant to show how you can affect, and how you are affected by, government and politics throughout your life. In "Think Tank: Making a Civic Connection" (pages 667–671) you will find several suitable examples of such projects. The project must be research-oriented or applied civics tied to the AP® U.S. Government and Politics Course CED. Your government teacher must be involved and likely has a project or options already planned.

The Exam

You can earn college credit for your work in the course upon your successful performance on the national AP® U.S. Government and Politics exam given in early May. This three-hour test consists of 55 four-option multiple-choice questions and 4 free-response questions. You will have 80 minutes (1:20) to complete the multiple-choice questions and then 100 minutes (1:40) for the free-response questions. Each section is worth half of the total test. A talented team of college faculty and experienced AP® teachers draft the questions and create the exam each year. A parallel practice exam is included at the end of this book. On the test, you can earn a score of 1 through 5. The College Board considers a score of 3 as "qualified." To learn more about how colleges regard the exam, check out this website: https://apstudent.collegeboard.org/creditandplacement/search-credit-policies.

Multiple-Choice Questions

The 55 multiple-choice questions take different forms, have four options, and only one correct answer. Many of the multiple-choice questions require you to examine a graph, text passage, table, map, or political cartoon. Many questions compare governmental terms or concepts. Some parallel the classic multiple-choice questions that require deep conceptual understandings. Others are simple definitions to test your knowledge of terminology. In this book, you will find specific questions related to the content of the chapter at the end of each chapter, while questions covering a broader range of topics will be in the unit reviews and on the practice exam.

As with most multiple-choice tests, determine what exactly the question is asking and then select the best answer. If an early option in (A) or (B) looks extremely obvious, continue to read and consider the remaining options to confirm or reconsider your first impressions. For questions you cannot immediately answer, use the process of elimination. Rule out and actually mark through the unlikely options to narrow your choices. Since there is no added penalty for guessing, if you do not know the answer, your teacher has access to an answer key.

If you're just beginning your preparation, the example questions that follow may be challenging but will expose you to the question formats.

Quantitative Analysis These questions will have a quantitative (numbers-based) presentation—chart, table, or graph—that measures some facet of government or politics, followed by two questions. The first question will call for you to recognize or identify data or trends. The second will dig deeper and ask you to demonstrate your understanding of an accurate comparison, conclusion, limitations, implication, or likely outcome based on the data. These will also test your understanding of how the data imply or illustrate political principles, institutions, processes, and behaviors. In other words, be ready to read, interpret, and explain the significance of a graph, table, or chart.

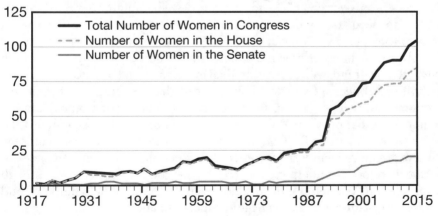

Number of Women in Congress: 1917–2015

— Total Number of Women in Congress
- - - Number of Women in the House
— Number of Women in the Senate

Source: Congressional Research Service

Questions 1 and 2 refer to the graph.

1. Which of the following statements reflects the data in the chart?
   (A) The number of women serving in Congress is on the decline.
   (B) More women have served in the House than in the Senate.
   (C) About half of the members of the past two Congresses have been women.
   (D) There are more African Americans than women in Congress.

2. Which of the following might be a potential consequence of the trend illustrated in the chart?
   (A) More men will run for office in the upcoming election cycles.
   (B) Congress will have a greater number of members as democracy broadens.
   (C) Congress is more likely to address issues of health, education, and family.
   (D) The Republican Party will gain seats in both house of Congress.

The answer to question 1 is B. This question requires you to recognize the information a graphic conveys—the title, the symbols, and the key that explains them and, in this case, the meaning of the *x*- and *y*-axes. To answer the first question, you need to ask yourself exactly what information is represented in the graph. You can eliminate answer A because the trend is upward, not downward. You can eliminate answer C because the figures in the graph refer to numbers, not percentages, and they do not refer to men at all, so there is no way to know that women might make up 50 percent. You can eliminate D because there is likewise no mention of African Americans in the graph.

The answer to question 2 is C. To answer this question, you need to ask yourself, "Given that the number of women serving in the House and Senate has risen—the answer you chose in question 1—what might be a result of this trend?" You need to use critical reasoning processes to choose the correct answer to this question. You can eliminate A because the trend in the graphic clearly shows the number of women increasing—there is nothing in the graph to suggest that trend will change or that more men will run for office. You can eliminate B because you will have learned that the number of members of Congress was capped at 435 in 1929, and the number of women running does not affect that number. You can eliminate D because there's no indication that the women running for Congress are Republicans. In fact, you will learn that there are more Democratic women than Republican women in Congress. You can therefore confidently choose C as the correct answer, even though it is speculation. Women politicians, however, have traditionally initiated and supported legislation addressing health, education, and family.

The national exam will have five quantitative stimuli, with two multiple-choice questions each, for a total of ten]questions (18 percent of the multiple-choice questions) using a quantitative stimulus.

Text-Based Analysis These questions require you to read a short passage and then analyze and apply what you have read. Expect a paragraph-length excerpt, about 100–200 words, from one of the *Federalist Papers*, a notable presidential speech, a government memo, or perhaps a news report. The passages, which you likely will not have seen before, could come from primary or secondary sources. They will be attributed with author, title, and year for context.

On the exam, three or four multiple-choice questions will follow, designed to test your ability to identify or describe the author's perspective, assumptions, claims, and reasoning. These questions will also focus on considering implications of the arguments and their effects on political principles, institutions, processes, and behaviors.

Both in this introduction and at the end of chapters, you will find two questions after each text passage. On the practice exam on page 672 you will see three or four questions following the text-based stimulus questions, which mirrors what you will encounter on the exam.

Example

Questions 3 and 4 refer to the passage below

"The friends and adversaries of the plan of the convention, if they agree in nothing else, concur at least in the value they set upon the trial by jury . . . . the more the operation of the institution has fallen under my observation, [T]he more reason I have discovered for holding it in high estimation . . . as a defense against the oppressions of a hereditary monarch, . . . [and] a barrier to the tyranny of popular magistrates in a popular government. Discussions of this kind would be more curious than beneficial, as all are satisfied of the utility of the institution, and of its friendly aspect to liberty."

—Alexander Hamilton, *Federalist No. 83*, 1788

3. Which of the following statements is most consistent with the author's argument in this passage?
   (A) Judicial panels in cases on appeal will assure fairness in the adjudication of laws.
   (B) A citizen-jury in our judicial branch will serve to prevent tyranny and safeguard liberty from other officials in government.
   (C) The jury system is about the only proposal in the Constitution that is worthy because both sides agree on it.
   (D) Juries are common in state courts and therefore unnecessary in federal courts.

4. Which governmental concept is the author most likely trying to protect or guarantee?

(A) Sovereignty

(B) Representative lawmaking

(C) Equality

(D) Rights of the accused

The answer for question 3 is B. Answer A can be eliminated because there is no mention of appeals in the text. Answer C can be eliminated because it does not follow that other proposals in the Constitution are not worthy or not agreed on by both sides. Answer D can be eliminated both because state courts are not mentioned and, far from saying they are unnecessary in federal courts, Hamilton argues that they are necessary. Answer B is an accurate summary of the main idea of the text.

The correct answer for question 4 is D. A jury, Hamilton suggests, is a protector of liberty, assuring that accused defendants are not put away without this check on runaway prosecution. Of the four concepts listed as choices, only D is "the most likely" concept Hamilton is protecting.

The national exam will have three or four questions with text passages, so six to eight questions of this type, or about 10-15 percent of the multiple-choice section.

Visual Source Analysis These multiple-choice questions call for you to analyze qualitative visual information. An image—a map, political cartoon, or information graphic (or "infographic")—will be followed by two questions. One will focus on identifying the topic and perspective that the image conveys. The second question will focus on explaining the elements of the image; relating the depiction to political principles, institutions, processes, and behaviors; or understanding what consequences may come based on arguments or depictions within the cartoon, map, or graphic.

Example

Questions 5 and 6 refer to the political cartoon below

Source: CartoonStock

5. Which of the following most accurately describes the message in the political cartoon?

(A) Fundraisers and reception dinners are ineffective at influencing candidates.

(B) Candidates are influenced by big campaign donors more than by those who cannot afford to donate.

(C) Political fundraisers for all offices should be open to the general public.

(D) Political fundraising takes too much time away from officials' other duties.

6. Which of the following is a potential consequence of the message in the cartoon?

(A) Fundraisers will lose popularity.

(B) Third-party candidates will follow the fundraising conventions of the major party.

(C) Greater and greater amounts of money will be spent to influence candidates.

(D) Letter-writing campaigns by citizens will become more influential.

The answer to question 5 is B. Answer A can be eliminated because the words express the opposite view—that politicians listen only to the big donors. You can eliminate answer C because it is not logical—the woman represents someone who cannot make a big donation, so she or others like her would have no more influence even if they attended a fundraiser. Answer D, while it is likely true, can be eliminated because there is nothing in the cartoon that supports the idea.

The answer to question 6 is C. Nothing in the cartoon, not words or images, supports the idea that fundraisers will become less popular or that third-party candidates will follow suit. D can be eliminated because the woman states that candidates are not influenced by people's "two cents' worth," so letter writing is unlikely to have much of an effect. Answer C is a reasonable consequence because the woman says politicians won't listen for "less than $10,000," suggesting that the more money offered, the more carefully they will listen.

The national exam will have three of these visuals, each with two questions, making a total of six questions accompanying a map, cartoon, or infographic, a little over 10 percent of the multiple-choice section.

Individual Questions Stand-alone multiple-choice questions will surface on the exam in different forms. One common format will test your understanding of two connected or related political concepts, institutions, groups, or policies via two lists in a table. A question will introduce the two terms. They will appear in the top row of the table. In each column under each term will appear four descriptions, each in its own row and each aligned with the letter answer option A through D. Where you see two true and accurate statements or descriptions that correspond with the item atop the corresponding column, you have your answer. These questions are likely to compare laws, documents, constitutional provisions and principles, Supreme Court decisions, and political terms.

Example

7. Which of the following is an accurate comparison of the Declaration of Independence and the U.S. Constitution?

	DECLARATION OF INDEPENDENCE	CONSTITUTION
(A)	Reflects Enlightenment thought	Set up the framework for national government
(B)	Contains seven articles	Included a bill of rights as a priority
(C)	Justifies the need for an executive	Takes most powers from the state governments
(D)	Outlines the nation's first government	Was ratified with unanimous votes within states

The answer to question 7 is A. It is the only answer that makes an accurate statement about both the Declaration of Independence and the Constitution.

Knowledge The largest category of multiple-choice questions focuses on your acquisition of essential knowledge. These text-only, single questions require you to recall terms, concepts, functions, and processes. These questions will require you to classify concepts and identify stages in a process, such as how candidates get elected or how a bill becomes a law. These will require you to know how the three branches interact and to identify recent political trends. They will also test your recall of changes in policy and policymaking approaches over time, how the Supreme Court overturned a prior precedent, or how a particular voting bloc changed its loyalties from one political party to another. The questions will also test your knowledge of Supreme Court cases, notable laws, foundational documents, and terms.

Some of these are lengthy and could include complex definitions or even analysis within the question. Others are short with one-word answer choices. Common, too, in this type of question will be the real-world scenario question. A sentence or short paragraph will describe a situation that involves government officials, citizens, an issue, or an interaction, and you must determine the likely scenario to follow, the action one or more of the parties can take, or perhaps the cause(s) of the scenario.

Examples

8. Which of the following statements about the Electoral College is accurate?

   (A) The Electoral College votes for members of the House of Representatives.

   (B) The Electoral College votes for state governors.

   (C) The Electoral College votes for the president.

   (D) The Electoral College votes for senators.

9. Which of the following principles protects a citizen from imprisonment without fair procedures?

   (A) Due process

   (B) Separation of powers

   (C) Representative government

   (D) Checks and balances

10. Searching a person's car without a warrant or consent to search, a local police officer finds an illegal firearm. Which of the following concepts might prevent the firearm from being introduced as evidence at a trial?

    (A) Exclusionary rule

    (B) Probable cause

    (C) Freedom of speech

    (D) Right to remain silent

The answer to question 8 is C. The answer to question 9 is A and to question 10, A. The actual exam will have about 30 of these individual questions, a little over 50 percent of the multiple-choice questions.

Free-Response Questions

The free-response section of the exam consists of four questions you must answer in 100 minutes. These questions draw from multiple topics within the course. The College Board recommends you spend 20 minutes on the first three questions and 40 minutes on the fourth question, since it is more complex than the others.

There are four types of free-response questions on the exam.

Concept Application This question asks you to respond to a political scenario that often takes the form of a quoted passage from a news report or other document. The task is to explain how the scenario relates to political principles, institutions, process, policy, or behavior, using substantive examples to back up your answers.

Example Concept Application Question

"Every day, more than 115 people in the United States die after overdosing on opioids. The misuse of and addiction to opioids—including prescription pain relievers, heroin, and synthetic opioids such as fentanyl—is a serious national crisis that affects public health as well as social and economic welfare. The Centers for Disease Control and Prevention estimates that the total "economic burden" of prescription opioid misuse alone in the United States is $78.5 billion a year, including the costs of healthcare, lost productivity, addiction treatment, and criminal justice involvement."

—National Institute on Drug Abuse, March 2018

After reading the scenario, respond to A, B, and C below:

(A) Describe a power Congress could use to address the issues outlined in the scenario.
(B) In the context of the scenario, explain how the use of congressional power described in Part A can affect interaction with special interest groups.
(C) In the context of the scenario, explain how the media can affect the interaction between Congress and special interest groups.

The scoring guides are specific to each question, but they can be generalized as follows:

Scoring the Concept Application Question

A good response should:
- ☐ Describe a political institution, behavior, or process connected with the scenario (0–1 point)
- ☐ Explain how the response in part (A) affects or is affected by a political process, government entity, or citizen behavior as related to the scenario (0–1 point)
- ☐ Explain how the scenario relates to a political institution, behavior, or process in the course (0–1 point)

As you can see, the maximum number of points you can earn on this free-response question is 3. A response earning 3 points might resemble the following:

SAMPLE ANSWER

The opioid crisis has been serious for several years. However, Congress could pass legislation restricting the way opioids are prescribed and, through its power of the purse, appropriate more money for opioid education and addiction treatment. (This part addresses the first point, 1 point.)

Unfortunately, these efforts may run into challenges. For example, special interest groups representing the pharmaceutical companies that manufacture opioids tend to donate to congressional campaigns and have a sizable number of well-connected lobbyists pressing their agendas in Congress. (Addresses the second point and is continued with elaboration—1 point.) The reelection of officials requires both campaign contributions and the support of the public, so officials try to balance those needs in a reasonable way.

If the balance tips too much in favor of the drug companies at the expense of public safety, the media can play a role to tip the balance back the other direction. Among the many roles media play is that of watchdog, keeping a close eye on government practices and investigating areas of concern and then bringing these matters out in public, where people can see for themselves what is taking place. (This addresses the third point with a substantive example—1 point.)

Quantitative Analysis A second type of free-response accompanies a statistical table or graph. This type of question asks you to analyze data, identify trends or patterns, draw a conclusion from those trends, and then explain how the data relates to a political principle, institution, process, policy, or behavior.

Example Quantitative Analysis Question

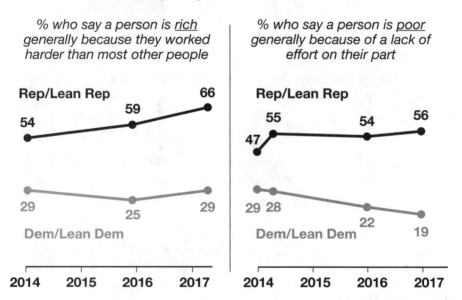

Differences between Republicans and Democrats on Why People are Rich or Poor

% who say a person is rich generally because they worked harder than most other people

Rep/Lean Rep
54 → 59 → 66

29 → 25 → 29
Dem/Lean Dem

% who say a person is poor generally because of a lack of effort on their part

Rep/Lean Rep
47 → 55 → 54 → 56

29 28 → 22 → 19
Dem/Lean Dem

2014   2015   2016   2017   2014   2015   2016   2017

Source: Pew Research Center

Surveys conducted Nov. 30–Dec. 5, 2016 and April 5–11, 2017.

(A) Identify the year in which Republicans/Lean Republican and Democrats/Lean Democrat were closest in their opinions on why people are poor.

(B) Describe a trend in the graph.

(C) Draw a conclusion about the possible causes of that trend.

(D) Explain how the attitudes shown in the information graphic demonstrate differences between Republicans and Democrats in Congress on social policy.

A generalized scoring guide for the Quantitative Analysis Questions appears below.

Scoring the Quantitative Analysis Question

A good response should:

- ❏ Identify or describe the data in the quantitative visual (0–1 point)
- ❏ Describe a pattern, trend, or similarity/difference as prompted in the question (0–1 point)
- ❏ Draw a conclusion for that pattern, trend, or similarity/difference (0–1 point)
- ❏ Explain how specific data in the quantitative visual demonstrates a principle in the prompt (0–1 point)

The maximum number of points you can earn on this free-response question is 4. A response earning 4 points might resemble the following:

Sample Answer

The graph shows how Republican attitudes differ from Democrat attitudes on reasons people are rich or poor. The two groups were closest in their opinions in 2014, when 29 percent of Democrats or those leaning Democrat believed people are poor because of a lack of effort on their part, while 47 percent of Republicans and leaning Republicans held that view. The difference in opinions between the two groups widened after that. (1 point.)

One trend visible in the data is that attitudes about the reasons for poverty are moving in opposite directions for the two groups. In 2014, 47 percent of Republican and Republican-leaning people believed people were poor because of a lack of effort on their part. In 2017, that percentage had risen to 56 percent. In the same years, Democrats and Democratic-leaning people view on the issue moved from 29 percent to 19 percent. (1 point.) One possible conclusion from this trend is that Americans are becoming more polarized, just as the Congress that represents them. (This sentence offers a possible conclusion— 1 point.) These attitudes demonstrate a difference in how Republicans and Democrats in Congress approach social policy. Republicans are less supportive than Democrats of government-sponsored social programs, such as health care subsidies, welfare, and food stamps, believing that people are poor because they do not exert enough effort. Democrats, on the other hand, believing that poverty more often results from circumstances beyond people's control, tend to support programs that help people overcome some of the limitations of their environments to try to rise out of poverty. (1 point.)

SCOTUS Comparison This type of free-response question asks you to compare a non-required Supreme Court case to one of the 15 Must-Know Cases in this book. For this question you will need to know important details, the decision, and relevant constitutional principles for each required case. The prompt will offer details of an unknown, or lesser-known case for your comparison.

Example Scotus Comparison Question

In 1942, the Supreme Court heard an appeal from Smith Betts, a poor person indicted on burglary in Maryland. He had no money to hire a lawyer, so he requested the state to provide one. A previous case had concluded that poor or indigent defendants had the right to an attorney, but only in death penalty cases. So, the judge refused. Betts pleaded not guilty, served as his own counsel, and was found guilty. He appealed the case claiming the lack of legal counsel resulted in his unfair trial and unfair conviction. The Supreme Court ruled that it did not, that the state could not prevent a defendant from using an attorney, but it was not obligated to provide one in non-capital cases.

(A) Identify the constitutional clause that is common to both *Betts v. Brady* and *Gideon v. Wainwright* (1963).

(B) Based on the constitutional clause identified in (A), explain why the *Gideon v. Wainwright* holding differed from the holding in *Betts v. Brady*.

(C) Explain how the holding in either case impacted the process of selective incorporation.

The following page has a generalized scoring guide for the SCOTUS comparison question.

Scoring the SCOTUS Comparison Question

A good response should:

- ❏ Identify a similarity or difference between the two Supreme Court cases, as specified in the question (0–1 point)
- ❏ Provide prompted factual information from the specified required Supreme Court case (0–1 point) and explain how or why that information from the specified required Supreme Court case is relevant to the non-required Supreme Court case described in the question (0–1 point)
- ❏ Describe or explain an interaction between the holding in the non-required Supreme Court case and a relevant political institution, behavior, or process (0–1 point)

This type of question has a maximum of 4 points. A response earning 4 points might resemble the following.

Sample Answer

The constitutional clause common to both *Betts v. Brady* and *Gideon v. Wainwright* is the Sixth Amendment's guarantee of an accused defendant's right to counsel, specifically whether this right applies to state courts as well as federal courts and to general crimes as well as more serious capital offences. (1 point.)

The facts of both cases are similar. Both defendants stood trial for a non-capital offence, and both made the same argument that under the Sixth Amendment, which provides the right to counsel in a federal court, they had the right to counsel in a state court as well and, as poor people, they should be provided counsel by the government. (1 point.) Time had passed and the makeup of the Supreme Court had changed. By the time Gideon's case came before the Court, the chief justice was Earl Warren, whose Court was known for taking a stand for individual liberties. (1 point.)

The holding in *Betts v. Brady* denied incorporation of the Sixth Amendment through the due process clause of the Fourteenth Amendment. The landmark case of *Gideon v. Wainwright*, however, reversed that holding and incorporated the Sixth Amendment so that poor or indigent defendants in state courts had the same right to an attorney as defendants in federal courts and, further, that states now had to provide an attorney to people who could not afford one. (This scores 1 point.)

Argument Essay The final free-response question type, the argument essay, requires developing an argument in the form of an essay and using evidence from one or more foundational documents to back up your claim.

Example Argument Essay Question

Develop an argument that explains whether or not breaking the law in the course of civil disobedience is acceptable.

Use at least one piece of evidence from one of the following foundational documents:

- First Amendment
- Fourteenth Amendment
- "Letter from a Birmingham Jail"

In your response, you should do the following:

- Respond to the prompt with a defensible claim or thesis that establishes a line of reasoning.
- Support your claim or thesis with at least TWO pieces of specific and relevant evidence:
  - One piece of evidence must come from one of the foundational documents listed above.
  - A second piece of evidence can come from any other foundational document not used as your first piece of evidence, or it may be from your knowledge of course concepts.
- Use reasoning to explain why your evidence supports your claim or thesis.
- Respond to an opposing or alternative perspective using refutation, concession, or rebuttal.

The College Board provides a scoring guide for the argument essay. Check the College Board website for the most up-to-date scoring guide.

The argument essay is worth 6 points. A response earning all six points might resemble the following.

Sample Answer

As Americans, we value the rule of law. It sets the U.S. apart from autocracies and dictatorships because it binds everyone, even those holding the highest offices in the nation, to the same legal limits. However, there are times when the importance of following the law may be outweighed by the importance of breaking it if breaking the law can help bring about a needed social change. The due process clause of the Fourteenth Amendment has motivated many social changes, and if groups of people are denied the protection of due process, civil disobedience may be the best way to bring the matter to the attention of the American people, who can then pressure their representatives in government for meaningful change. (The highlighted portion is a defensible claim, the rest lays out a line of reasoning—1 point.)

The Fourteenth Amendment was developed to protect freed slaves. It made equal treatment under the law a fundamental governing principle. The ideal of the Fourteenth Amendment, however, is not always easy to achieve. The amendment, with its promises of life, liberty, and property and the equal protection of the laws, did not automatically enforce itself. (Description of how one piece of evidence from a required document accurately links to topic—1 point.) For example, African Americans, especially in the South, were routinely denied rights exercised by white citizens—the right to vote, the right to equal access to public accommodations, the right to non-segregated schools, even in many cases the right to their lives. Without any reason to change, life in the South may have continued that way for another century, depriving more generations of African Americans the rights that many other Americans take for granted. (Demonstration of how the evidence in the first required document you used connects to the claim—1 point.)

Dr. Martin Luther King, Jr. recognized this possibility in his "Letter from Birmingham Jail." He responded to the white clergy of Birmingham who criticized him for staging a protest over the Easter weekend by listing a long series of reasons African Americans have waited in the past based on promises from whites that never materialized. King knew that without a bold start, change would never come. He recognized that negotiations were, as the white clergy stated, the best way to work toward progress, but King knew that no negotiations would actually happen unless they were forced. (Description or explanation of how an additional piece of evidence connects to the claim—1 point.)

King also recognized and pointed out to his readers that Jim Crow laws kept African Americans from equal protection of the laws. The law that Dr. King decided to break was not of that type. The law he broke was a court order not to hold a protest in the business district of Birmingham, where King had planned it, because it would have the biggest economic effect on local businesses. It was a nonviolent protest, and when the police came to arrest him and Rev. Ralph Abernathy, they went to jail without resistance. (Explanation of how the evidence supports the claim—1 point.)

Those who oppose civil disobedience, as the white clergy in Birmingham did, argue that civil disobedience will only increase hostilities and that progress comes with patience and good will. As Dr. King points out, blaming nonviolent protesters for any violence that breaks out in response to it is like blaming the robbed man for having the money that led to the robbery. And the South had decades of good will and patience from African Americans with no progress to show for it. (Rebuttal consistent with the argument—1 point)

Both Dr. King's actions and his words in "Letter from Birmingham Jail" show the value and necessity of civil disobedience. While much remained to be done after the Birmingham protests, his actions there were no doubt an example of courage for others to follow—not just African Americans, but in later decades war protesters, women, members of the LGBT community, and people with disabilities. And his words laid out a careful argument for the necessity of civil disobedience tied to moral principles, tied to the growth that follows from tension over the injustice of laws when it is brought to light.

Exam Day

Wake up in time to relax and eat a normal breakfast. Bring two #2 pencils for the multiple-choice section, two black or blue ink pens for the free-response section, and a watch. Wear comfortable clothing suitable for a cold or hot testing room. Do not bring any government books, laptops, cell phones, iWatches, or any other connective device. Follow the general advice below to make the most of your testing experience.

Overall Scoring and Credit

The exams are scored in early June and reported back to you and your high school in mid-summer. You can earn between 0 and 5 points. "Most private colleges and universities award credit and/or advanced placement for AP scores of 3 or higher," states the College Board's CED, and "most states in the U.S. have adopted policies that ensure college credit for scores of 3 or higher at public colleges and universities."

The College Board equates a score of 5 to an A in a college-level class, a 4 to an A−, B+, or B, and a 3 to roughly a B−, C+, or C. In 2019, nearly 13 percent of those taking the exam earned a score of 5. More than 12 percent received a 4 and almost 30 percent earned a 3. About 25 percent earned a 2, and roughly another 20 percent earned a 1. So, considering a score of 3 as "qualified," over 55 percent passed, many who could then by-pass an introduction to American government course or Political Science 101. For more on how your college regards the exam and what score they require see: www.collegeboard.com/ap/creditpolicy.

A Final Note

Large numbers of Americans, especially political independents and young adults, mistrust politicians and the partisan talking heads on cable TV and are turned off by the political process. It is normal to feel this way. However, don't let an understandable irritation with polarizing partisans hamper your chances for success as a student or diminish your performance on the exam. You are primarily a student observer. Observe and analyze politics as you would watch or study a ball game where your team was not playing. As you begin your in-depth study of the course, though, you may find that as you learn more about the United States government, you can move from observer to participant.

Review Schedule

Set up a review schedule as you prepare for the exam in the weeks prior to the test date. Studying with a group of fellow students can be helpful. Below is a sample of an eight-week review schedule, including information on the chapters in this book that cover the content to review. Because AP® tests are given during the first two full weeks of May, this review schedule assumes you begin your review in mid-March.

PROPOSED REVIEW SCHEDULE		
Week	Content	Chapters
1	Foundations of American Democracy	1, 2, 3
2	Interactions Among Branches of Government	4, 5
3	Interactions Among Branches of Government	6, 7
4	Civil Liberties and Civil Rights	8, 9
5	Civil Liberties and Civil Rights	10, 11
6	American Political Ideologies and Beliefs	12, 13, 14
7	Political Participation	15, 16, 17
8	Political Participation	18, 19, 20

You should also plan to review the information in this introduction. The suggestions and ideas about answering multiple-choice questions and free-response items will be helpful to you.

RESEARCH-BASED LEARNING STRATEGIES	
Distributed Practice	Spread out your studying over the entire course in manageable amounts.
Retrieval	After every class, or on another regular schedule, close your book and try to recall the important points, using a practice called retrieval. You can use the Reflect on the Essential Question feature at the end of each topic as a framework. Write whatever you can't retrieve from memory alone by going back into the book for the missing pieces. Whether you use sample multiple-choice questions, flash cards, or an online program such as Quizlet, take the time to test yourself.
Elaboration	When studying, ask yourself questions about what you are reading. How does this material connect to other material in the unit? As you learn material, elaborate on it by connecting it to what you are experiencing in your daily life.
Interleaving	Few exams go in the order of how topics are presented in the text. The AP® Government and Politics exam certainly does not. When you study, interleave the material. Switch up the order of your review. For example, when reviewing Units 1–3, change the order of your study. Switch it up to 2, 1, and 3. Then during your next review session, follow a different order—3, 2, and 1, for example. Use this technique only occasionally.
Concrete Examples	Write down all concrete examples your teacher uses in class. Note the examples given in this book. Use these examples to understand the application of the abstract concepts and ideas you are studying.
Dual Coding	Use dual coding, different ways of representing the information. Take notes or write reflections on a segment of text. Then create a visual representation of the same knowledge using graphic organizers, concept maps, drawings with labels, or other graphics.

UNIT 1

Foundations of American Democracy

After suffering years of imposed tax laws, such as the Sugar Act, Stamp Act, and the rights violations that followed, the American colonists presented the Declaration of Independence to the British Crown in 1776. Breaking away from British control and claiming sovereignty, the new states fought a war to establish their independence. The 1783 Treaty of Paris spelled out the peace terms and brought the war to an end. The new United States government at first operated under the Articles of Confederation, a loose association of the 13 states. However, the Articles provided insufficient structure to bind the states together, and its weaknesses were revealed. In 1787, delegates convened in Philadelphia to draft a new constitution. After a public debate between Federalists, who endorsed the plan, and Anti-Federalists, who opposed the plan, citizens of the states ratified it.

The Constitution defined the three branches of government, relations among states, national and state powers, and the process to amend the document. Among its provisions is the system of checks and balances, which keeps any one branch from becoming too powerful. The amendment process also allowed for the addition of the Bill of Rights and, eventually, a total of 27 amendments.

The Constitution established *federalism*, a two-tiered system of government that divides the power between the national and state governments. As new national concerns have surfaced, Congress has used its power to set policies to address these issues consistently throughout the states. Yet states use their power to maintain jurisdiction over schools, marriages and divorces, criminal law enforcement, motor-vehicle law, and other areas. Through state referenda, citizens have recently made changes on family leave, gambling, and the legalization of marijuana.

ENDURING UNDERSTANDINGS: FOUNDATIONS OF AMERICAN DEMOCRACY

LOR-1: A balance between governmental power and individual rights has been a hallmark of American political development.

CON-1: The Constitution emerged from the debate about weaknesses in the Articles of Confederation as a blueprint for limited government.

PMI-1: The Constitution created a competitive policymaking process to ensure the people's will is represented and that freedom is preserved.

CON-2: Federalism reflects the dynamic distribution of power between national and state governments.

Source: AP® United States Government and Politics Course and Exam Description

CHAPTER 1

Founding Principles

Topics 1.1–1.3

Topic 1.1 Ideals of Democracy

LOR-1.A: Explain how democratic ideals are reflected in the Declaration of Independence and the U.S. Constitution.

- – Required Foundational Document:
  - • Declaration of Independence

Topic 1.2 Types of Democracy

LOR-1.B: Explain how models of representative democracy are visible in major institutions, policies, events, or debates in the U.S.

- – Required Foundational Documents:
  - • *Federalist No. 10*
  - • *Brutus No. 1*

Topic 1.3 Government Power and Individual Rights

CON-1.A: Explain how Federalist and Anti-Federalist views on central government and democracy are reflected in U.S. foundational documents.

- – Required Foundational Documents:
  - • *Federalist No. 10*
  - • *Brutus No. 1*

Source: Wellcome Library, London
The Signers of the Declaration of Independence

Ideals of Democracy

"Britain is the parent country, say some. Then the more shame upon her conduct. Even brutes do not devour their young, nor savages make war upon their families . . . Every thing that is right or natural pleads for separation. The blood of the slain, the weeping voice of nature cries, 'TIS TIME TO PART."

—Thomas Paine, *Common Sense*, 1776

Essential Question: How are democratic ideals reflected in the Declaration of Independence and the U.S. Constitution?

The ideals of American democracy are firmly rooted in the establishment of the United States after the Revolution of the late 1700s. More than a century before, however, American settlers began to define democracy and self-governance. When the Pilgrims landed in Massachusetts in 1620, they knew their survival depended on working together and forming a "civil body politic," so they drafted a governing document, the Mayflower Compact. This agreement was grounded in Christian morals and the God-given right to self-rule, even while the Pilgrims remained British subjects. More than 150 years later, the Declaration of Independence, applying the principles of Enlightenment philosophy, provided a foundation for a government in which the people with protected rights, not monarchs, were the true source of governmental power. A decade later, the United States Constitution codified the ideals of self-government, consent of the governed, and representation into guidelines for a new nation.

Influence of Enlightenment Thought

The leading revolutionaries were inspired by Enlightenment thinkers who championed natural, God-given rights and a social contract between a representative government and the people, the true source of power. They argued that if a government violated the understood compact, then the people could take that power back.

Enlightenment Philosophers

Advocates for freedom from British rule drew on Enlightenment political theory. It had been developed when the principles of rationalism that had unlocked doors to the natural world during the Scientific Revolution were applied to the social world as well. Especially influential were the writings of English philosophers Thomas Hobbes (1588–1679) and John Locke (1632–1704), Swiss-born philosopher Jean-Jacques Rousseau (1712–1778), and French philosopher Montesquieu (1689–1755).

Thomas Hobbes and *The Leviathan* In his famous work *The Leviathan*, Hobbes argues that when humans live in "a state of nature" rather than in a governed state, the result is anarchy and war, and human life is "solitary, poor, nasty, brutish, and short." A modern example is Somalia after the collapse of its repressive government in 1991. The resulting stateless society endured a long series of bloody civil wars.

The remedy for this condition, according to Hobbes, was for people to give up some of their rights, as long as others did so as well, and agree to live in peace. In his view, an absolute sovereign—the Leviathan referred to in the title—would hold society together, yet still honor a social contract, as long as the sovereign's rule took the good of society into account.

John Locke and Natural Law John Locke, a British philosopher, argued in *Second Treatise of Civil Government* (1690) that **natural law** is the law of God and that this law is acknowledged through human sense and reason. In contrast to Hobbes, he proposed that under natural law—in a state of nature—people were born free and equal. According to this law, Locke reasoned, "No one can be . . . subjected to the political power of another, without his own consent." Locke argued further that natural law not only entitled but actually obligated people to rebel when the rule of kings did not respect the consent of the governed.

Jean-Jacques Rousseau and *The Social Contract* Rousseau was much influenced by Locke. He spoke for those "intending their minds" away from an irrational and oppressive political order, away from a governmental theory that rested in the divine right of kings and clergy to rule and misrule. The opening sentence of his influential treatise, *The Social Contract*, dramatically lays out a key human problem: "Man was born free, and he is everywhere in chains." The social contract Rousseau describes is the agreement of free and equal people to abandon certain natural rights in order to find secure protections for society and to find freedom in a single body politic committed to the general good. He envisioned **popular sovereignty**—the people as the ultimate ruling authority—and a government of officials to carry out the laws.

Baron de Montesquieu and *The Spirit of the Laws* French philosopher Montesquieu (1689–1755), like Rousseau, recognized in *The Spirit of the Laws* (1748) both the sovereign and administrative aspects of governmental power. He saw a republican form of government as one having defined and limited power while granting political liberty to citizens. Montesquieu argued for the separation of powers in the administrative government, comprised of the executive, legislative, and judicial branches.

Enlightenment thought was well known among English colonists in North America. According to historian Carl Becker, "Most Americans had absorbed

Locke's works as a kind of political gospel." The American revolutionaries believed that men were entitled to "life, liberty, and property" and that these cannot be taken away except under laws created through the consent of the governed. These beliefs formed the bedrock of the political ideology known as **republicanism**. In a republic, citizens elect leaders for a limited period of time; the leaders' job is to make and execute laws in the public interest. The lack of colonial representation in Parliament, such as taxation without consent and subsequent infringements of liberty, violated fundamental rights and the values of republicanism. These violations were remedied by the creation of an independent, limited, and representative government based on the ideas of natural rights, popular sovereignty, republicanism, and the social contract.

THINK AS A POLITICAL SCIENTIST: *DESCRIBE POLITICAL PRINCIPLES IN DIFFERENT SCENARIOS*

The United States is a **limited government**—one kept under control by law, checks and balances, and separation of powers. For example, although the government uses taxpayer money to fund large public projects, such as transportation systems and social safety nets, it cannot make those commitments unless representatives duly elected by the people agree on them. In a monarchy, in contrast, the government uses taxpayer money as it sees fit.

A limited government also respects people's individual liberties and steps in only when necessary to resolve conflicts when individual liberties collide with some opposing force—another individual's liberties or the public interest, for example.

Practice: Describe how the principle of limited government applies to each of the following scenarios.

1. The state government establishes laws governing the legal age to drive.

2. A case before the Supreme Court determines whether a person can be fired for being LGBTQ.

3. The United States Department of Agriculture issues nutritional guidelines.

Declaring Independence

American-British tensions rose to new heights in the early 1770s. Colonists protested Parliament's taxing them without consent or representation. To enforce the tax laws and to quiet the discontent in America, the British government sent a military force to the colonies. Friction between the soldiers, trying to instill order, and the colonists, trying to enjoy their liberty, resulted in a decade of conflict that further divided the two sides.

British suppression of self-rule, economic punishments, and unfair trials and imprisonments finally brought the two sides to blows. In fact, the battles of

Lexington and Concord had already taken place by the summer of 1776 when the Second Continental Congress met in Philadelphia. Virginia delegate Richard Henry Lee offered a short motion declaring American independence and the authority of this Congress to vote to officially end the relationship with Great Britain. Delegates from the colonies debated the motion for days before breaking the session to allow some delegations to travel back to their legislatures to make sure they were adequately representing them. The same gathering, before it temporarily adjourned, commissioned a committee of five men—**Thomas Jefferson**, **John Adams**, **Benjamin Franklin**, Roger Sherman, and Robert Livingston—to draft a full, more official statement to summarize the colonists' views.

On June 11, the five men met at Franklin's lodgings and planned the document's content and shape. When Franklin declined the invitation to draft it because of his shaky health, they handed the assignment to Thomas Jefferson. The Second Continental Congress reconvened on July 1 to debate the enhanced resolution. Over the next two days, Jefferson and the committee made 85 revisions or deletions. The full body debated and then voted on July 4, 1776, to approve the document, which became the **Declaration of Independence**. It provided a moral and legal justification for the rebellion.

FOUNDATIONAL DOCUMENTS: *DECLARATION OF INDEPENDENCE*

The Declaration of Independence drew from Locke and other Enlightenment philosophers, upholding popular sovereignty. It explained how abuses by the too powerful British Crown violated natural rights and self-rule, justified the colonists' separation from Britain, and defined the newly independent states' relationship. Following are key excerpts from the Declaration.

> When in the course of human events, it becomes necessary for one people to dissolve the political bands which have connected them with another . . . they should declare the causes which impel them to the separation. We hold these truths to be self-evident, that all men are created equal, that they are endowed by their creator with certain unalienable Rights, that among these are Life, Liberty and the pursuit of Happiness.—That to secure these rights, Governments are instituted among Men, deriving their just powers from the consent of the governed, —That whenever any Form of Government becomes destructive of these ends, it is the Right of the People to alter or to abolish it. . . .
>
> The history of the present King of Great Britain is a history of repeated injuries and usurpations . . . he has refused his Assent to Laws, the most wholesome and necessary for the public good . . . he has called together legislative bodies at places unusual, uncomfortable, and distant . . . he has dissolved Representative Houses repeatedly, for opposing with manly firmness his invasions on the rights of the people . . . he has plundered our seas, ravaged our coasts, burnt our towns, and destroyed the lives of our people. . . .
>
> [For these reasons], these united colonies are, and of Right ought to be Free and Independent States. . . . And for the support of this Declaration, with a firm reliance on the protection of divine Providence, we mutually pledge to each other our Lives, our Fortunes and our sacred honor.

The Revolutionary War intensified, and the Continental Congress sent diplomats to foreign countries and military generals to lead the fight. The colonies-turned-states created a more official government under the Articles of Confederation, the nation's first constitution. (See Topic 1.4.) The war raged on until General George Washington's army defeated the British at Yorktown, Virginia, in 1781. In 1783, the Treaty of Paris officially ended the war.

Source: Library of Congress

Declaration Committee (left to right): Thomas Jefferson, Roger Sherman, Benjamin Franklin, Robert R. Livingston, and John Adams

The U.S. Constitution: A Blueprint for Government

After experimenting with a decentralized federal government under the Articles of Confederation, the Confederation Congress called a convention in Philadelphia for the sole purpose of revising the Articles of Confederation. In May 1787, delegates began to arrive at Independence Hall (the Pennsylvania State House) to get an early start on improving national governance. Thirty-six-year-old **James Madison** was among the first to arrive. The Virginia lawyer was well prepared for the deliberations. His friend Thomas Jefferson served in Paris as the U.S. ambassador to France and sent Madison books on successful and unsuccessful governments. Madison's influence in creating the plan for the new government and his stalwart support of it during the ratification process (see Topic 1.5) earned him the nickname "Father of the Constitution."

The delegates elected **George Washington** as president of the Convention. He presided as a calming force during heated debate. In fact, Washington's participation alone elevated the validity of the endeavor. **Alexander Hamilton's** intellect, drive, and quest to elevate the nation made him instrumental in shaping the new design. Benjamin Franklin, the elder statesman at age 81, offered his experience as one who had participated in the drafting of the Declaration of Independence, the Articles of Confederation, and the Treaty of Paris with Britain. He also held distinction in discovery, invention, and civic endeavors, embodying Enlightenment ideals.

In addition to these leading statesmen, states sent representatives with significant experience in public affairs—some who became future Supreme Court justices, Cabinet members, and notable congressmen—intent on creating outcomes beneficial to their state. All were well versed in Enlightenment political thought and had served the Revolutionary cause.

The delegation decided on procedural matters and formed the **Grand Committee**. The committee was made up of one delegate from each of the states represented at the convention. George Mason, William Paterson, and Benjamin Franklin were among those on the Grand Committee. The Grand Committee was instrumental in forging the compromises needed to work out the many conflicting interests as the new form of government took shape. (See Topic 1.5 for more about the constitutional compromises.)

An Enlightened Constitution

When the delegates completed their work on September 17, 1787, they had created a blueprint for a unique form of political democracy. They recognized, as did Hobbes, the need for a strong executive, but they discarded his idea that such a person should have absolute power, as a monarch would. Instead, they created an executive branch headed by an elected president, ultimately subject to the will of the people. Like Locke and Rousseau, they believed that people committed to a social contract by giving up some individual rights in exchange for the benefits of a government that sought justice and preserved fairness. Like Montesquieu, they supported the separation of powers.

BIG IDEA The U.S. Constitution establishes a system of checks and balances among branches of government and allocates power between federal and state governments. This system is based on the rule of law and the balance between majority rule and minority rights. The plan for government under the new constitution included three separate branches—legislative, executive, and judicial—each having unique powers and each able to block the others from gaining too much power. Congress as the legislative branch could tax, borrow money, and regulate commerce. The president would serve as commander in chief. The judicial branch included a Supreme Court and a plan to create lower courts. The Constitution also outlined a system to elect the president.

A Representative Republic

The framers wanted the citizen representation of a democracy, but on a national level, so they created a **representative republic**, a collection of sovereign states gathered for the national interest, national needs, and national defense. To promote popular sovereignty, the framers required popular elections every two years for members of the House of Representatives, but those were the only popular elections they put in the original Constitution. State legislatures elected their senators until 1913. The state legislatures named their electors (done today by citizen voters), and then the Electoral College elects the president.

REFLECT ON THE ESSENTIAL QUESTION

Essential Question: *How are democratic ideals reflected in the Declaration of Independence and the U.S. Constitution? On separate paper, complete a chart like the one below.*

Democratic Ideals	Examples in the Founding Documents

KEY TERMS AND NAMES

Adams, John
Declaration of Independence
Franklin, Benjamin
Grand Committee
Hamilton, Alexander
Hobbes, Thomas (*The Leviathan*)
Jefferson, Thomas
limited government
Locke, John (*Second Treatise of Civil Government*)
Madison, James
Montesquieu, Baron de (*The Spirit of the Laws*)
natural law
popular sovereignty
representative republic
republicanism
Rousseau, Jean-Jacques (*The Social Contract*)
U.S. Constitution
Washington, George

Types of Democracy

"To secure [our inherent and inalienable] rights, governments are instituted among men, deriving their just powers from the consent of the governed."
—Declaration of Independence, 1776

Essential Question: How are models of representative democracy visible in U.S. institutions, policies, events, and debates?

The Declaration of Independence laid the foundation for a new government to replace Britain's oppressive rule. The Constitution, formally adopted in 1788, became the permanent plan for government with a workable balance between the states and the federal government and between individual freedoms and government power. The result was a **representative democracy**—a government in which the people entrust elected officials to represent their concerns.

Three Forms of Representative Democracies

Representative democracies can take a number of forms. The structure and principles of the Constitution allow for the following types, among others.

Participatory Democracy

In its purist form, a **participatory democracy** depends on the direct participation of many, if not most, people in a society, not only in government but in public life as well. Participatory democracy emphasizes broad involvement of citizens in politics. Most important, citizens vote directly for laws and other matters that affect them instead of voting for people to represent their interests.

However, a pure form of participatory democracy is unwieldy. Even in Ancient Greece, the birthplace of democracy, only those who had the time and resources took an active part in government. The larger the population, the more difficult it is to involve everyone in decision making in a timely manner.

The framers believed that such a large, diverse country as the United States was too big to function as a participatory democracy. Yet they left room for the individual to exercise self-representation at state and local levels. Small towns and villages hold town hall meetings with occasional votes to establish local policy. Cities and school districts hold votes among the entire local electorate to determine property tax rates and whether or not to construct new public buildings. In many states, the voting populace can establish state law or alter state constitutions.

Source: David Shankbone, 2011, Wikimedia Commons

The Occupy Wall Street movement (2011), modeled on a participatory approach, used bottom-up rather than top-down policymaking. However, its participatory nature made decision making slow and action agendas hard to develop.

Pluralist Democracy

In a **pluralist democracy**, people with widely varying interests find others who share their interests and organize and unite into nongovernmental groups to exert influence on political decision making. These **interest groups** (see Topic 5.6) compete in the "marketplace of ideas" and look for access points at the local, state, and federal levels to persuade policymakers. Groups form along a spectrum of interests, from associations of business executives pressuring the government to reduce environmental regulations on business to associations of environmentalists pressuring the government to preserve natural resources and combat climate change. Because of the competition among interests and the need for bargaining, the process of changing policy is usually slow. However, a pluralist democracy allows many people to voice their interests, preventing the wealthy and elite from grabbing all the power.

The founders knew such varying interests would dominate government, so they created structures to limit their influence. For example, they assumed each state would constitute an interest. In the House and Senate, states have representatives, yet these bodies are composed of so many members from across a broad geography and diversity of views that factions within these bodies often limit the dominance of any single interest. The system of the Electoral College—having electors vote independently while isolated in their state capitals on the same day—would prevent an overpowering influence fueled by interest.

Elite Democracy

The Electoral College demonstrates an elite element in the United States government. In an **elite democracy**, elected representatives make decisions and act as trustees for the people who elected them. Elite democracy recognizes an inequity in the spread of power among the general populace and the elites: People with resources and influence dominate. Despite the inequality of power, some people argue that the elected representatives are well equipped to secure the rights of the individual. They tend to have the necessary skills and education to represent the governed. Proponents of an elite democracy argue that elite leaders can prevent popular but possibly unwise positions from forcing their way into policy.

Elite democratic models are in all three branches of government. The most democratic of them, the House of Representatives, is composed of members elected directly by the people. They have short, two-year terms and represent a geographic constituency. The Senate, originally elected by state legislators, was another step removed from the citizenry, still representative, but more elite. And several appointees in the federal government—Cabinet officials and judges, for example—are appointed, the latter for life.

Tension Over the Models of Democracy

The Constitution and the subsequent spirited ratification debate reflected the tension between the broad participatory model and the more filtered participation of the pluralist and elite models. The central question was, "What is the best way for citizens to participate in government?"

Tensions Within the Constitution The Constitution reflects a balance between citizen participation and a strong central government of representatives. The document and the national policies properly created under it are the supreme law of the land, but it also allows states to retain rights that are not in conflict with federal law. The strong central government reflects an elite model of democracy, since elected representatives have the power to represent their constituents. In fact, in the original Constitution, elected members of the state legislatures elected their U.S. senators. They are now elected directly by the people.

At the same time, the freedom of states to make their own decisions (as long as they are not in conflict with federal law) reflects the possibility for participatory democracy. Elected representatives serve at all levels of state and local governments, but states and the cities and towns that comprise them have the freedom to encourage widespread participation.

The lawmaking process outlined in the Constitution recognizes the necessity of finding agreement within pluralism. Representatives and senators from all regions of the country, representing a wide variety of views, negotiate agreements to pass laws.

Tensions Between Political Beliefs Those who supported the proposed constitutional structure, a strong federal government, and full ratification became known as **Federalists**. Federalist Alexander Hamilton, aware of anti-Constitution sentiment in his home state of New York, recruited James Madison and John Jay to help write and publish 85 essays supporting the Constitution and explaining the government it created. These authors adopted the pen name "Publius" after an ancient Roman who toppled a king and set up a republic. The *Federalist Papers* were the most comprehensive commentary designed to sell ratification. Their influence peaked as Virginia and New York ratified with slim margins. One of the more celebrated arguments is found in *Federalist No. 10*.

"By enlarging too much the number of electors, you render the representatives too little acquainted with all their local circumstances and lesser interests; as by reducing it too much, you render him unduly attached to these, and too little fit

to comprehend and pursue great and national objects. The federal Constitution forms a happy combination in this respect; the great and aggregate interests being referred to the national, the local and particular to the State legislatures."
—*Federalist No. 10* (See Topic 1.3 for a more in-depth look at *Federalist No. 10*.)

Strong, vocal opposition to the Constitution came about as quickly as the document was unveiled. Those who opposed the consolidation of the states under a federal government were known as **Anti-Federalists**. They, too, had well educated leaders, including New York delegates Robert Yates and William Lansing, who wrote newspaper articles to sway people's decisions to adopt or reject the Constitution. Anti-Federalists described what they saw as the impossibility of truly representing constituents' views in a large republic. A series of essays appeared in the *New York Journal* from October 1787 until April 1788 under the pseudonym Brutus, which evoked images of the heroic Roman republican who killed the tyrant Caesar. Brutus wrote 16 total essays, which in many ways paralleled the meticulous analysis of the Federalists from the other side.

"In every free government, the people must give their assent to the laws by which they are governed. This is the true criterion between a free government and an arbitrary one. The former are ruled by the will of the whole, expressed in any manner they may agree upon; the latter by the will of one, or a few . . . Now, in a large extended country, it is impossible to have a representation, possessing the sentiments, and of integrity, to declare the minds of the people, without having it so numerous and unwieldy, as to be subject in great measure to the inconveniency of a democratic government." —*Brutus No. 1* (See Topic 1.3 for a more in-depth look at *Brutus No. 1*.)

MODELS OF REPRESENTATIVE DEMOCRACY		
	Reflected in the Constitution	**Reflected in Ratification Debates**
Participatory	States are free to determine how to allow for direct citizen involvement.	Anti-Federalists feared in the large United States too many people with too many different views to be adequately represented, so they favored smaller units of government more responsive to local needs.
Pluralist	The lawmaking process requires compromise within a wide range of competing interests.	Federalists argued competing interests are unavoidable, but they prevent one single viewpoint from dominating.
Elite	Elected representatives are charged with representing their constituencies. The Electoral College enables elites to determine the president.	Federalists desired representative government and trusted the process of regular elections to remove representatives when they do not meet the needs of their constituents. Anti-Federalists argued only smaller units of government can represent their constituents.

Representative Democracy in the United States Today

The three models of representative democracy continue to be reflected in contemporary institutions and political behavior.

Examples of Participatory Democracy One way in which citizens can participate directly is through state and local ballot initiatives. **Initiatives** give the people the power to place a measure on the ballot for a popular vote. Another is the **referendum**, which allows citizens to contest the work of the legislature. If the legislature passes an unpopular law, the public can gather support, usually through signatures on a petition, to call for a vote to defeat or uphold the law. Twenty-six states allow some form of ballot initiatives. On Election Day 2020, some of the issues voters were deciding through ballot measures related to the minimum wage, exemptions from vaccination requirements for students and health care employees, the use of renewable resources for energy, and gender-neutral language.

Examples of Pluralist Democracy Different interests form special interest groups in a pluralist democracy that allows for the sharing of political power. They interact with government officials searching for consensus among competing interests. They raise and spend money to elect people friendly to their ideas. These groups send professional researchers and experts to testify at congressional committee hearings in hopes of shaping or stopping a bill. They monitor the government as it enforces existing law, and they buy ads to influence public opinion. (See Topic 5.6.) So many policymakers put into effect so many rules and procedures at the local, state, and federal levels that no single force shapes our body of law. As an ethnically and ideologically diverse nation, the United States includes a large variety of viewpoints and public policy usually established and accepted by a consensus.

Several types of interest groups function within the United States today. Some of the strongest exert exceptional influence on policymaking. These groups include civil rights groups, such as the National Association for the Advancement of Colored People (NAACP) and the National Organization for Women (NOW), and economic interest groups that represent labor, such as the American Federation of Labor and Congress of Industrial Organizations (AFL-CIO). Single-interest groups, such as the National Rifle Association (NRA), can also have a strong influence on laws and society.

THINK AS A POLITICAL SCIENTIST: *DESCRIBE THE AUTHOR'S CLAIM*

The debate over the proposed form of government was spirited. Each argument rested on a claim—a statement asserted to be true—and attempted to provide evidence to back up that claim. Some of the most spirited debate was carried on through private letters between Thomas Jefferson, who was serving in Europe as a U.S. minister to France, and James Madison, a key proponent of the Constitution.

Practice: Read the excerpt of a letter from Jefferson to Madison about what Jefferson does not like about the Constitution. Then answer the questions.

"First [it omits] a bill of rights providing clearly . . . for freedom of religion, freedom of the press, protection against standing armies, restriction against monopolies, the eternal & unremitting force of the habeas corpus laws, and trials by jury . . . . To say . . . that a bill of rights was not necessary because all is reserved [by the states and people] in the case of the general government which is not given, while in the particular ones all is given [to the states and people] which is not reserved . . . . [contradicts inferences in the Constitution] . . . . [A] bill of rights is what the people are entitled to against every government on earth, general or particular, & what no just government should refuse or rest on inference."

1. What is Jefferson's chief claim in this passage?
2. What opposing claim is Jefferson arguing against?

Examples of Elitism in Government The Constitution's elite government model was weakened somewhat after Progressive Era reforms (1890–1920), when the masses became more involved in politics. Yet in many ways, elite-dominated politics prevail today. Individuals with the most time, education, money, and access to government will take more action than the less privileged, and because of their resources, they will be heard. People who serve in the leadership of a political party, whether on the local or national level, are usually from a higher socioeconomic level, better known, and better educated than the rank and file, the many members of a group who constitute the group's body.

REFLECT ON THE ESSENTIAL QUESTION

Essential Question: *How are models of representative democracy visible in U.S. institutions, policies, events, and debates? On separate paper, complete a chart like the one below.*

Examples of Participatory	Examples of Pluralist	Examples of Elite

---

KEY TERMS AND NAMES

Anti-Federalists

elite democracy

Federalists

initiative

interest group

participatory democracy

pluralist democracy

referendum

representative democracy

Government Power and Individual Rights

"Different laws, customs, and opinions exist in the different states, which by a uniform system of laws would be unreasonably invaded."

—Federal Farmer, *Poughkeepsie Country Journal*, 1787

Essential Question: How are Federalist and Anti-Federalist views on central government and democracy reflected in America's foundational documents?

Under the Articles of Confederation (see Topic 1.4), political power belonged largely to state governments, with a weaker national government. The delegates at the Constitutional Convention worked to design a stronger national government, yet not as overbearing as the British monarchy had been to the colonies. By 1787, a draft of the Constitution was sent to all 13 state legislatures, which created ratifying conventions to debate and vote for or against the plan. For the Constitution to go into effect, nine states needed to ratify it.

The Constitution was also published in local newspapers. The reaction of many Americans showed a nation divided over opposing beliefs about which level of government should hold more power.

Opposing Beliefs

The differences between the beliefs of Federalists and Anti-Federalists regarding national government were vast. Intense debates over ratification of the Constitution took place between members of these groups. Some of the most substantive arguments appeared in widely circulated newspapers and were read and discussed by many Americans.

The *Federalist Papers* were published in three New York newspapers from 1787 to 1788.

Federalist Support for the Constitution

With the insistence of fellow pro-Constitution Virginians, **James Madison** named himself a candidate for his state's ratifying convention to be held in Richmond. Federalists argued that a strong national government and the diversity of America's large population would protect the rights of all citizens from the elite and would protect the units of states from the collective whole. The Federalists also wanted to allay fears that their plan would subject people in the states to abuses by this new national government. Madison, in *Federalist No. 10*, addressed the concern that a few powerful individuals might unite into a **faction**, or interest group (see Topic 1.2), to dominate political decisions. He believed the Constitution was designed to limit the influence of factions.

FOUNDATIONAL DOCUMENTS: *FEDERALIST NO. 10*

Of the 85 essays that Madison, Hamilton, and Jay penned, one of the most cited is *Federalist No. 10* because it addresses the concern over special interests. *Federalist No. 10* speaks of the "mischiefs of faction," or interest groups in government, whether a majority or a minority, "united and actuated by some common impulse of passion, or of interest, adversed to the rights of other citizens." Publius, the "voice" of the Federalist authors, stated that men of like mind might begin to dominate government for their own ends rather than for the public good. He explained how no plan for government can eliminate factions entirely but noted that the framers had created a system to stall and frustrate factions and thus limit their effects. They created not a pure, participatory democracy at the national level but rather a representative and pluralist republic that had to consider the interests of varied people from across many miles of land. America even at its birth was one of the most expansive countries in the world, and varied factions arriving at the nation's capital from New England and Georgia would neutralize one another.

Following are some key quotes from *Federalist No. 10*.

> A zeal for different opinions concerning religion, concerning government, and many other points, . . . [and] an attachment to different leaders ambitiously contending for pre-eminence and power . . . have . . . divided mankind into parties, inflamed them with mutual animosity, and rendered them much more disposed to vex and oppress each other than to co-operate for their common good . . . .
> The inference to which we are brought is, that the causes of faction cannot be removed, and that relief is only to be sought in the means of controlling its effects. . . . hence, it clearly appears, that the same advantage a republic has over a democracy, in controlling the effects of faction, is enjoyed by a large over a small republic, and is enjoyed by the Union over the States composing it.

Political Science Disciplinary Practices and Reasoning Processes: Analyze
Federalist No. 10

Publius addresses a key concern of many colonists—that a majority could sweep away the will of the minority by their sheer numbers. To answer that in part, he writes, "The influence of factious leaders may kindle a flame within their particular States but will be unable to spread a general conflagration through the other States." Keep that quote in mind as you complete the activity below.

Apply: Publius identifies an inference in the second paragraph of the quote on page 17. Rewrite that inference in your own words and explain how Publius uses it to advance the cause of adopting a republican government. You can read *Federalist No. 10* and all the *Federalist Papers* online.

Anti-Federalist Opposition to the Constitution

Opponents of the Constitution, including Virginia's Patrick Henry and George Mason, desired a federal government more like the confederation under the Articles. These Anti-Federalist concerns came from the recent experience with an autocratic ruling country. Some feared the proposed single executive might replicate a monarchical king, potentially limiting state and individual rights. Congress's power to tax, to control a standing army, and to do anything else it felt "necessary and proper" made the Anti-Federalists wary. The Anti-Federalists suspected foul play and pointed to the thick veil of secrecy in which designing men had conspired to draft the document.

THINK AS A POLITICAL SCIENTIST: *DESCRIBE POLITICAL PRINCIPLES*

Once the united colonies won their freedom from Britain, the nation needed to decide which democratic principles would be at its foundation. One principle centered on the role and importance of **factions** as the framers defined the government of the young nation.

Practice: Complete the following directions.

1. Define faction, or interest group.

2. Give an example of a faction.

3. Describe the opposing views on the role and importance of factions. Be sure to include:

   - Who would have supported and who would have opposed factions?
   - Why was there support for and opposition to factions?

Anti-Federalist Patrick Henry

Anti-Federalists and Federalists differed in their views about a large republic. The *New York Journal* and *Weekly Register* published a series of 16 Anti-Federalist articles written under the pseudonym Brutus. In fact, the first Anti-Federalist article appeared a few weeks before *Federalist No. 1*.

FOUNDATIONAL DOCUMENTS: *BRUTUS NO. 1*

"Brutus" writes for the purpose of dissuading readers from supporting the new Constitution. *Brutus No. 1* is a commentary on the dangers of too large and too consolidated a government. Brutus argues that rarely would the citizens of a large nation know of the workings of government or know their elected representative.

He argues that the necessary and proper clause and the supremacy clause give the federal government unlimited power, risking personal liberty. He argues that in a free republic, people have confidence in their rulers because they know them, and the rulers are accountable to the people who have the power to displace them. He posits that "in a republic of the extent of this continent, the people . . . would be acquainted with very few of their rulers: [they] would know little of their proceedings, and it would be extremely difficult to change them." He also specifically counters the Federalists' view that a large country and government prevent the rise of controlling factions.

... if respect is to be paid to the opinion of the greatest and wisest men who have ever thought or wrote on the science of government, we shall be constrained to conclude, that a free republic cannot succeed over a country of such immense extent, containing such a number of inhabitants, and these increasing in such rapid progression as that of the whole United States. ... in a republic, the manners, sentiments, and interests of the people should be similar. If this be not the case, there will be a constant clashing of opinions; and the representatives of one part will be continually striving against those of the other. This will retard the operations of government, and prevent such conclusions as will promote the public good. If we apply this remark to the condition of the united states, we shall be convinced that it forbids that we should be one government.

Political Science Disciplinary Practices and Reasoning Processes: Compare *Brutus No. 1* and *Federalist No. 10*

Both Brutus and Publius convey the conviction that factions and constant clashing are givens in a large country, yet the two sides come to nearly opposite conclusions.

Apply: Identify and explain the similarities and differences in the political beliefs, ideologies, and principles of Brutus and Publius based on the implications conveyed in their writing. Also, explain how each position may have affected the ratification of the Constitution.

Read the full text of *Brutus No. 1* online.

Newspapers published the text of the Constitution and essays for and against it, such as the *Federalist Papers* and the articles by Brutus, giving citizens of the newly independent nation the opportunity to read and digest views for and against the ratification of the Constitution. Debate was passionate and heated not only at the national level over the Constitution but also within states. The debate in Rhode Island nearly resulted in bloodshed when almost 1,000 Anti-Federalists organized and marched to Providence to prevent ratification. Other states, such as Massachusetts, New York, and Virginia, offered strongly worded responses regarding their fear of the federal power proposed in the Constitution.

Source: National Gallery of Art, Portrait by Gilbert Stuart

John Jay wrote five of the *Federalist Papers* and was the second governor of New York and the first Chief Justice of the Supreme Court. He was also an abolitionist.

OPPOSING VIEWS REGARDING GOVERNMENT AND DEMOCRACY	
Federalists	• Supported the strong national government created by the Constitution • Believed existing Constitutional provisions would protect the rights of states and individuals • Believed qualified representatives were best suited to lead the nation • Believed unchecked factions would put the interests of a few above the interests of the nation
Anti-Federalists	• Wanted states to have more power • Believed a bill of rights was needed to guarantee protection of the rights of states and individuals • Believed many should have a voice in government to prevent the elite from having too much power

REFLECT ON THE ESSENTIAL QUESTION

Essential Question: *How are Federalist and Anti-Federalist views on central government and democracy reflected in America's foundational documents? On separate paper, complete a chart like the one below.*

	View on Central Government	Evidence from Foundational Document
Federalists		
Anti-Federalists		

KEY TERMS AND NAMES

Anti-Federalists   Federalists
Brutus No. 1   *Federalist No. 10*
faction   Madison, James

CHAPTER 1 Review:
Learning Objectives and Key Terms

TOPIC 1.1: Explain how democratic ideals are reflected in the Declaration of Independence. (LOR-1.A)

Democratic Ideals and Philosophers (LOR-1.A.1)

Hobbes, Thomas (*The Leviathan*)

limited government

Locke, John (*Second Treatise of Civil Government*)

Montesquieu, Baron de (*The Spirit of the Laws*)

natural rights

popular sovereignty

representative republic

republicanism

Rousseau, Jean-Jacques (*The Social Contract*)

Foundational Documents and Founders (LOR-1.A.2)

Adams, John

Declaration of Independence

Franklin, Benjamin

Hamilton, Alexander

Jefferson, Thomas

Madison, James

U.S. Constitution

Washington, George

TOPIC 1.2: Explain how models of representative democracy are visible in major institutions, policies, events, or debates in the U.S. (LOR-1.B)

Types of Representative Democracies (LOR-1.B.1)

elite democracy

interest group

participatory democracy

pluralist democracy

representative democracy

Tension Between Models of Democracy (LOR-1.B.2)

Anti-Federalists

Federalists

Representative Democracies Today (LOR-1.B.3)

initiative

referendum

TOPIC 1.3: Explain how Federalist and Anti-Federalist views on central government and democracy are reflected in U.S. foundational documents. (CON-1.A)

Arguments for Federal Power (CON-1.A.1)

factions

Federalists

Federalist No. 10

Madison, James

Arguments for States' Power (CON-1.A.2)

Anti-Federalists

Brutus No. 1

CHAPTER 1 Checkpoint:
Founding Principles

Topics 1.1–1.3

MULTIPLE-CHOICE QUESTIONS

1. Which is the most democratic institution of government that represents the framers' commitment to a limited republic?

   (A) U.S. Senate

   (B) Supreme Court

   (C) U.S. House of Representatives

   (D) Electoral College

2. Which of the following is an accurate comparison of political philosophies of John Locke and Thomas Hobbes?

	Locke	Hobbes
(A)	Was instrumental in drafting the Articles of Confederation	Wrote *Second Treatise of Civil Government*
(B)	Claimed citizens should not be subject to another's political power without their consent	Argued that in a state of nature, the result is anarchy and war
(C)	Wrote *Leviathan*	Believed in the social contract theory
(D)	Was a French philosopher	Argued for separation of powers in government

3. Which of the following is a chief argument in James Madison's *Federalist No. 10*?

   (A) A bill of rights is necessary to secure liberty.

   (B) Free speech should be added to the Constitution.

   (C) Judicial review will prevent harsh laws against the citizenry.

   (D) A large, diverse republic will tame the mischiefs of factions.

Questions 4 and 5 refer to the passage below.

"We . . . [d]o by these presents, solemnly and mutually, in the presence of God and one another, covenant and combine ourselves together into a civil body politic, for our better ordering and preservation . . . [and] do enact, constitute, and frame, such just and equal laws, ordinances, acts, constitutions, and officers, from time to time, as shall be thought most meet and convenient for the general good of the colony."

—The Mayflower Compact, 1620

4. Which of the following statements best reflects the authors' perspective?

   (A) The authors believed faith is the strongest guiding principle to maintain social order.

   (B) The authors recognized their right to collective self-rule even as British subjects.

   (C) The authors created their pact in order to break away from British religious persecution.

   (D) The authors believed that everyone in the colony should share the same religion.

5. Which of the Enlightenment philosophies is most consistent with the ideas in the passage?

   (A) Hobbes's state of nature

   (B) Locke's consent of the governed

   (C) Rousseau's refusal to accept a social contract

   (D) Montesquieu's belief in limited government

6. Which of the following was the basis of one Anti-Federalist concern about the proposed form of government?

   (A) Dissatisfaction with power the states had in the Articles of Confederation

   (B) Fear that large states would have more power than the federal government

   (C) Suspicion of the "necessary and proper" clause and federal power

   (D) Doubts about the need for the separation of powers

FREE-RESPONSE QUESTIONS

Concept Application

1. "I know the name of liberty is dear to . . . us; but have we not enjoyed liberty even under the English monarchy? Shall we . . . renounce that to go and seek it in I know not what form of republic, which will soon change into a licentious anarchy and popular tyranny? In the human body the head only sustains and governs all the members, directing them . . . to the same object, which is self-preservation and happiness; so the head of the body politic, that is the king, in concert with the Parliament, can alone maintain the union of the members of this Empire . . . and prevent civil war by obviating all the evils produced by variety of opinions and diversity of interests."

            —John Dickinson, Continental Congress, July 1, 1776

After reading the excerpt, respond to A, B, and C below:

   (A) Describe the political institution Dickinson wanted to maintain.

   (B) In the context of the passage, explain how the political institution identified in part A affected the behavior of the colonists.

   (C) Explain how the passage relates to representative democracy.

Population Density
of Colonial America, 1775

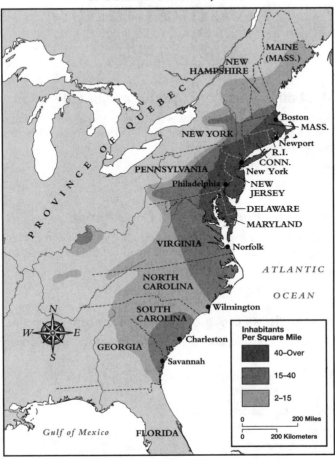

2. Use the map above to answer the following questions.

   (A) Identify an American colony with a colony-wide population density of 40 or more inhabitants per square mile across the entire colony.

   (B) Describe a difference in population density between two colonies.

   (C) Explain how this difference might affect citizen representation in a new government.

   (D) Explain which form of democracy—participatory, pluralist, or elite—might be most effective in governing this population.

CHAPTER 2

The Constitution

Topics 1.4–1.6

Topic 1.4 Challenges of the Articles of Confederation

CON-1.B: Explain the relationship between key provisions of the Articles of Confederation and the debate over granting the federal government greater power formerly reserved to the states.

- Required Foundational Document:
  - Articles of Confederation

Topic 1.5 Ratification of the U.S. Constitution

LOR-1.A: Explain the ongoing impact of political negotiation and compromise at the Constitutional Convention on the development of the constitutional system.

- Required Foundational Document:
  - The Constitution of the United States

Topic 1.6 Principles of American Government

PMI-1.A: Explain the constitutional principles of separation of powers and "checks and balances."

PMI-1.B: Explain the implications of separation of powers and "checks and balances" for the U.S. political system.

- Required Foundational Documents:
  - *Federalist No. 51*
  - The Constitution of the United States

Source: National Archives and Records Administration

The Constitution of the United States

Challenges of the Articles of Confederation

"But the confederation itself is defective and requires to be altered. It is neither fit for war nor peace. The idea of an uncontrollable sovereignty in each state over its internal police [militia] will defeat the other powers given to Congress and make our union feeble and precarious."

—Alexander Hamilton, to New York Mayor James Duane
on the Articles of Confederation, 1780

Essential Question: How did the provisions of the Articles of Confederation lead to debates over granting powers formerly reserved for states to the federal government?

It took five drafts of the Articles of Confederation (formally known as the Articles of Confederation and Perpetual Union) before delegates agreed on the sixth version and sent it to the states for approval in 1777. The colonies had recently declared independence, and the Revolutionary War was underway, presenting an urgent need for a formal government. Disagreements over land charters between states slowed ratification of the Articles. Thomas Jefferson finally persuaded the thirteenth state to ratify in 1781.

The difficulties in ratifying the Articles of Confederation foreshadowed governing problems. A lack of national unity and a struggle for power were only two of many challenges the United States would face under the Articles.

The Articles of Confederation

The Continental Congress created a committee of 13 men to draft the **Articles of Confederation**, the document that laid out the first form of government for the new nation. The Articles redefined the former colonies as states and loosely united them as a confederation or alliance under one governing authority. Each state wrote its own constitution, many of which were pointedly in response to the injustices the colonists had experienced under British rule. The state constitutions shared other features as well: they provided for different branches of government, they protected individual freedoms, and they affirmed that the ruling power came from the people.

John Dickinson wrote the 1776 draft of the Articles, which after revisions was submitted to the states for approval. This document defined "the firm league of friendship" that existed among the states, which had delegated a few powers to the national government.

The question of how to apportion states' representation in the newly designed Confederation Congress was beset with controversy. Some leaders recognized the merits of giving greater representation to the more populated states, something the Virginia delegation advocated. Leaders from smaller states opposed representation based on population. After a furious debate, the authors of the Articles created an equal representation system—each state received one vote in the new Confederation Congress.

The Confederation Congress met in New York. States appointed delegations of up to seven men who voted as a unit. National legislation required the votes of at least nine states. A unanimous vote was required to alter or amend the Articles of Confederation themselves or to alter the format of government. The Articles entitled the Congress to engage in international diplomacy, declare war, and acquire territory. They provided protection of religion and speech. They provided for extradition—the return of criminal fugitives and runaway slaves back to states they had fled. The Articles encouraged a free flow of commerce among the states. They required that states provide a public, fair government and that Congress could sit as a court in disputes between states.

FOUNDATIONAL DOCUMENTS: *ARTICLES OF CONFEDERATION*

The Articles of Confederation provide that "each state retains its sovereignty, freedom, and independence." This provision was essential, since the states were wary of a centralized power that might wield the same influence over them that the British government wielded. Following are some of the key provisions of the Articles of Confederation.

> . . . each state retains its sovereignty, freedom, and independence, and every Power, [not] . . . expressly delegated to the United States, in Congress assembled. . . . in determining questions in the United States, in Congress assembled, each State shall have one vote. . . .
>
> The United States in Congress assembled, shall have the sole and exclusive right and power of determining on peace and war. . . .
>
> Full faith and credit shall be given in each of these States to the records, acts, and judicial proceedings of the courts and magistrates of every other State. . . . congress assembled shall also be the last resort on appeal in all disputes and differences now subsisting or that hereafter may arise between two or more States.

Political Science Disciplinary Practices: Relate the Articles of Confederation to Political Principles and Institutions

Apply: Review the three types of democracies described in Topic 1.2. Based on the provisions above, identify the type of democracy that the Articles of Confederation created. Describe two provisions of the Articles of Confederation that demonstrate that type of democracy.

Then read the full Articles of Confederation online.

An Ineffective Confederation

The people of the confederation feared a strong national government, having just suffered the abuses of the British crown as colonists. Yet, they wanted a structure to keep them organized and united, especially for the economic success of all. Many Americans felt the best way to achieve this outcome was to tip the power in favor of states over a national authority. States, which many felt a sense of loyalty to above the nation, had a wide variety of characteristics and needs to be accommodated by this new form of government.

The Articles of Confederation provided a weak system for the new United States and prevented leaders from making much domestic progress. The system had rendered the Confederation Congress ineffective. In fact, the stagnation and a degree of anarchy threatened the health of the nation.

The following chart summarizes some of the weaknesses.

WEAKNESSES IN THE ARTICLES OF CONFEDERATION
• The requirements that at least nine states must agree in order to enact national law.
• The requirement that all states must agree in order to amend the system of government proved daunting.
• The Congress could not tax the people directly.
• The national government could not raise or maintain an army.
• There was no national court system or national currency.
• The Congress encouraged but could not regulate commerce among the states.

Financial Problems and Inability to Tax

The national government under the Articles lacked the power to mandate taxes, forcing it to rely on voluntary assistance from states to meet its financial needs. States did not lack the funds to pay those taxes, but they did harbor disdain for taxes imposed by a more remote authority after having fought a long war over the issue. One Massachusetts legislator wrote his member of Congress, stating citizens "seem to think that independency being obtained, their liberty is secured without paying the cost, or bestowing any more care upon it." Without taxes, the new government couldn't pay foreign creditors and lost foreign nations' faith and potential loans.

For six years, the Confederation Congress and the infant country wrestled with how it would pay for the independence it had earned while remaining skeptical of giving too much taxing power to its national government. By January 1782, 11 states had approved a resolution to empower Congress to adopt a 5 percent import tax. But Rhode Island's unanimous rejection of the bill and Virginia's less-united "no" vote killed the plan. In 1783, Virginia Congressman James Madison tried again with a tax formula based on state populations (slaves would count as three-fifths a person). For four years, it had the popularity of a strong majority but not the unanimous vote necessary. Many already feared Congress's power to make war and did not want to bestow it with the power to tax. After final defeat of the 1783 tax proposal, no one believed that the states would ever adopt serious tax reform under the Confederation.

Shays' Rebellion

The lack of a centralized military power and readiness to respond to a violent uprising became the closing argument of the need for a strong central government. In western Massachusetts in 1786, a large group of impoverished farmers, including many Revolutionary War veterans, lost their farms to mortgage foreclosures and their failure to pay higher than average state taxes. They organized, disrupted government, and obstructed court claims. The insurgents demanded the government ease financial pressures by printing more money, lowering taxes, and suspending mortgages. In early 1787, Daniel Shays, a former captain in the Continental army, led a band of violent insurgents to the federal arsenal in Springfield. Local authorities had difficulty raising a militia and only did so from private funds. Massachusetts general William Shepard blocked Shays' army. Artillery fire after a standoff killed four and wounded about 20 of Shays' men. The protesting squads retreated, but additional face-offs, skirmishes, and sporadic guerrilla warfare followed. By February, the rebellion was largely suppressed.

Even if quashed, Shays' Rebellion demonstrated to the nation's leaders that the lack of a centralized military power posed a threat to America's security.

Source: Wikimedia Commons

Federal troops defend the armory in Springfield, Massachusetts, from Shays' forces.

A small group convened in Annapolis, Maryland, to discuss the economic drawbacks of the Confederation and how to preserve order. This convention addressed trade and the untapped economic potential of the new United States. Nothing was finalized, except to secure a recommendation for Congress to call a more comprehensive convention. Congress did so: It was to meet in Philadelphia in May 1787. By then few Americans viewed the Articles of Confederation as sufficient. John Adams, who was serving in Congress, argued that a man's "country" was still his state and, for his Massachusetts delegation, the Congress was "our embassy." There was little sense of national unity.

THINK AS A POLITICAL SCIENTIST: *EXPLAIN HOW THE AUTHOR'S ARGUMENT AND PERSPECTIVE RELATE TO POLITICAL PRINCIPLES*

Many Americans had strong beliefs about Daniel Shays' efforts to force the Massachusetts government to provide economic relief to farmers. Some considered Shays to be a traitor for taking up arms against the government, while others supported him for standing up to an unresponsive government.

Practice: Read the excerpts below about Shays' Rebellion and explain the author's argument. Also, explain the political principles of the authors that would have influenced their opinion.

1. "The spirit of resistance to government is so valuable on certain occasions, that I wish it to be always kept alive. It will often be exercised when wrong, but better so than not to be exercised at all. I like a little rebellion now and then. It is like a storm in the atmosphere."

    —Thomas Jefferson, letter to Abigail Adams, 1787

2. I am mortified beyond expression when I view the clouds that have spread over the brightest morn that ever dawned upon any Country. In a word, I am lost in amazement when I behold what intrigue, the interested views of desperate characters, ignorance and jealousy of the minor part, are capable of effecting, as a scourge on the major part of our fellow Citizens of the Union."

    —George Washington, letter to Henry Lee, 1786

REFLECT ON THE ESSENTIAL QUESTION

Essential Question: *How did the provisions of the Articles of Confederation lead to debates over granting powers formerly reserved for states to the federal government? On separate paper, complete a chart like the one below.*

Provision from the Articles of Confederation	How the Provision Proved to be a Weakness

---

KEY TERMS AND NAMES

Articles of Confederation

Shays' Rebellion

Ratification of the U.S. Constitution

"Only twelve of over ninety American newspapers and magazines published . . . essays critical of the Constitution during the ratification controversy."

—Pauline Maier, *Ratification: The People Debate the Constitution, 1787–1788*, 2010

Essential Question: What was the ongoing impact of political negotiation and compromise at the Constitutional Convention on the development of the constitutional system?

The Constitutional Convention's quest for an improved government required countless compromises. The 55 delegates from the states had the difficult task of finding common ground for all of these interests under one governing body. In addition to uniting these diverse groups within the new nation, the delegates demonstrated a willingness to compromise to design a government that could meet the needs of the nation in years to come. In fact, the Constitution is a "bundle of compromises."

Competing Interests

Sharp differences arose between groups in the new nation. Each group wanted what they perceived as fair representation as the delegates at the **Constitutional Convention** hammered out a plan. They also had differing views on slavery, the nature of the executive, and the relationship of the states to the national government.

Constitutional Compromises

During the summer of 1787, intense negotiations at the convention produced a number of compromises that resulted in a lasting document of governance.

Differing Plans Different delegates presented different plans at the convention. Virginia Governor Edmund Randolph proposed the **Virginia Plan** which called for a three-branch system with a national executive, a judiciary, and a **bicameral**—or two-house—legislature. The people would elect the lower house whose members would, in turn, elect the members of the upper house. This plan also made the national government supreme over the states and set clear limits for each of the branches. The comprehensive Virginia Plan, authored largely by James Madison, created the blueprint or first draft of the Constitution.

Small states feared the overwhelming representation of larger states and supported the plan of New Jersey governor William Patterson. The **New Jersey Plan** assured states their sovereignty through a national government with limited and defined powers. This plan also had no national court system and each state would have one vote in a legislative body.

COMPETING INTERESTS IN EARLY AMERICA		
Issue	**Questions to Answer**	**Groups Interested**
Representation	Should a state's representation be based on population or equal representation for a state regardless of size?	Large states vs. small states
Slavery	Should enslaved individuals count toward a state's representation?	Southern states vs. Northern states
Office of the President	Should there be an executive and should the executive be chosen by a small elite or by a popular vote?	Privileged citizens vs. citizens of lower socioeconomic status
Federalism	What is a fair division of power among the levels of government?	Federal government vs. state government

The Great Compromise Representation had been the frustration of the colonists since they began seeking independence. The more populated states believed they deserved a stronger voice in making national policy decisions. The smaller states sought to retain an equal footing. The matter was referred to the Grand Committee (see Topic 1.1) made up of one delegate from each of the 12 states present (Rhode Island did not attend). When Roger Sherman of Connecticut joined the committee, taking the place of Oliver Ellsworth who became ill, he took the lead in forging a compromise that became known as the **Great Compromise** (or the Connecticut Compromise). Sherman's proposal created a two-house Congress composed of a House of Representatives and a Senate. His plan satisfied both those wanting population as the criteria for awarding seats in a legislature, because House seats would be awarded based on population, and those wanting equal representation, because the Senate would receive two senators from each state, regardless of the state's size.

Slavery and the Three-Fifths Compromise The House's design required another compromise. Delegates from non-slave states questioned how enslaved people would be counted in determining representation. Since enslaved people did not have the right to vote, others who were able to vote in slave states would have more sway than voters in non-slave states if enslaved people were counted in the population. Roger Sherman once more put forward a compromise, this time with Pennsylvania delegate James Wilson. Using the formula from Madison's proposed-but-failed tax bill, they introduced and the convention accepted the **Three-Fifths Compromise**—the northern and southern delegates agreed to count only three of every five enslaved persons to determine representation in the House for those states with slaves.

Importation of Enslaved People Two other issues regarding slavery were addressed: whether the federal government could regulate slavery and whether non-slave states would be required to extradite escaped slaves. Delegates resolved the first matter by prohibiting Congress from stopping the international slave trade for twenty years after ratification of the Constitution (which it did). They also debated how to handle slave insurrections, or runaways. They resolved the second debate with an extradition clause that addressed how states should handle runaway enslaved persons and fugitive criminals.

SUMMARY OF MAJOR COMPROMISES	
Virginia Plan	Three branches, bicameral legislature, supremacy of national government, separation of powers
New Jersey Plan	Sovereignty of states, limited and defined powers of national legislature
Great Compromise	House membership apportioned by population; each state given two senators
Three-Fifths Compromise and Importation of Slaves	Only three of every five enslaved persons would be counted to determine representation Congress could not stop the importation of slaves for 20 years after ratification
Electoral College	States decide how their electors are chosen, with each state having the same number of electors as they have representatives in Congress

Other compromises would be necessary during the summer-long convention in Philadelphia. For example, delegates debated whether or not the United States needed a president or chief executive and how to elect such an officer. Some argued Congress should elect the president. Others argued for the states to choose the president, and some thought the people themselves should directly elect the president. The **Electoral College** was the compromise solution. Under this plan, states could decide how their electors would be chosen. Each state would have the same number of electors that they had representatives in Congress, and the people would vote for the electors. Having electors rather than the citizenry choose the president represents one way in which the elite model of democracy helps shape government today.

Source: Wikimedia Commons

George Washington speaks at the Constitutional Convention. Painting by
Junius Brutus Stearns (1787)

THINK AS A POLITICAL SCIENTIST: *EXPLAIN HOW POLITICAL*
PROCESSES APPLY TO DIFFERENT SCENARIOS

The compromise that resulted in the Electoral College has had a great impact
on presidential elections. At several points in the nation's history, many people
have called for changes to or abolition of the Electoral College. Their argument
has focused on how modern politics makes the Electoral College unnecessary.

Practice: Read the following scenarios and determine if the electoral process
functioned as the framers intended. If not, identify where the breakdown occurred.

1. In the early years of the republic, the electoral process called for the candidate
   with the most votes to be elected president and the runner-up to be named vice
   president. In the 1800 election, fellow Democratic-Republicans Thomas Jefferson
   and Aaron Burr ran for president, as did John Adams and others. Jefferson and
   Burr tied, each with 73 electoral votes. The House eventually decided on Jefferson
   for president.

2. In the 1824 election, out of a total of 261 electoral votes, Andrew Jackson received
   99 votes, John Quincy Adams took 84 votes, and the remaining two candidates
   split 78 votes. No candidate had a majority of the electoral votes, so the House of
   Representatives again ended up deciding the winner of the election. The House,
   with the influence of the eventual Secretary of State, Henry Clay, chose Adams in
   what Jackson called the "Corrupt Bargain."

3. In 2016, after a number of scandals leading up to the election, Donald Trump
   won 46.4% of the popular vote to Hillary Clinton's 48.5%. Trump was still able to
   secure 304 electoral votes by winning key states, such as Florida, Wisconsin, and
   Pennsylvania.

Still other compromises were needed to resolve what powers the federal government would have and what powers the states would retain. *A confederal system*—a loose gathering of sovereign states for a common purpose—was the very relationship defined under the Articles of Confederation. A national government, however, would make the national lawmaking body supreme and create a stronger union than the confederal system. Delegates also considered what types of laws Congress could make and what citizen rights to protect.

They addressed the remaining issue with the Commerce Compromise. This agreement appealed to both sides by allowing the government to impose a tariff on imports but not exports. This compromise gave the federal government the ability to regulate trade between states, a power it lacked under the Articles.

FOUNDATIONAL DOCUMENTS: *THE CONSTITUTION OF THE UNITED STATES*

The Constitution, written in the hot summer of 1787, emerged from the debate about the weak Articles of Confederation and created the legislative, executive, and judicial branches defined in the first three articles, a separation of powers among the branches, and the qualifications and terms for offices. It also included articles regarding the relations among the states, the amendment process, national supremacy, and the procedure for ratification. Below, key excerpts from each of the articles are followed by explanatory text.

Article I

All legislative powers herein granted shall be vested in a Congress of the United States, which shall consist of a Senate and House of Representatives . . . . each house may determine the rules of its proceedings . . . .

Article I defines the basic setup and operation of Congress. House members are elected by the people every two years. In contrast, state legislatures would elect senators, who were then beholden to state governments (this provision was later changed by the Seventeenth Amendment). The House became the more representative, or more democratic, institution. Article I has ten sections and is the longest article—about half of the entire Constitution—revealing the framers' concern for representative lawmaking.

Article II

The President shall be commander in chief of the army and navy . . . . He shall from time to time give to the Congress information of the state of the Union . . . . He shall take care that the laws be faithfully executed . . . .

How to create and define the office of president in Article II stirred one of the more heated discussions in Philadelphia. The rebellion against a monarch made the populace concerned about one-person rule. However, the lack of leadership under the Articles of Confederation and the need for an executive to take care of the nation's business made the creation of the presidency inevitable. Article II lays out the requirements to assume this office and the executive's role. As Commander in Chief, the president oversees and manages the U.S. military. As head of state, the president receives foreign ambassadors and sends U.S. ambassadors abroad.

Article III

The judges, both of the supreme and inferior courts, shall hold their offices during good behavior, and shall, at stated times, receive for their services a compensation, which shall not be diminished during their continuance in office.

The need for national courts led to Article III, which defines the judiciary. The framers mentioned only one actual court, the Supreme Court, but they empowered Congress to create inferior courts. The federal courts have jurisdiction over cases involving federal law, disputes between states, and concerns that involve government officials. The president appoints Supreme Court justices and other federal judges, with approval of the Senate. These judges serve "during good behavior," which in practice means for life.

Article IV

Full faith and credit shall be given in each state to the public acts, records, and judicial proceedings of every other state . . . . A person charged in any . . . crime, who shall flee from justice, and be found in another state, shall . . . be delivered up, to be removed to the state having jurisdiction of the crime.

Article IV defines relations among the states. It includes the full faith and credit clause that requires states to be open about their laws and encourages states to respect one another's laws. It also requires that "the citizens of each state shall be entitled to all privileges and immunities of citizens in the several states." In other words, on most issues states cannot play favorites with their own citizens or exclude outsiders from basic privileges and immunities.

Article V

[W]henever two-thirds of both houses shall deem it necessary, [they] shall propose amendments to this constitution . . . which . . . shall be valid to all intents and purposes, as part of this Constitution, when ratified by the legislatures of three-fourths of the several states . . . .

To amend the Articles of Confederation, all thirteen states had to agree. The challenges of that requirement led the framers to establish a high standard for an amendment so that it could not be passed lightly, but not unanimity. A two-thirds vote in both houses of Congress or a proposal from two-thirds of the states, followed by ratification from three-fourths of the states, became the process in Article V to amend the Constitution.

Article VI

> This Constitution, and the laws of the United States which shall be made in pursuance thereof . . . shall be the supreme law of the land . . . .

To avoid the lack of unification experienced under the Articles of Confederation and to unite the nation under stronger national policy, Article VI was included to establish national supremacy. The supremacy clause quoted above makes certain that all states must adhere to the Constitution. Article VI also states that no religious test will be required for a person to take a government office.

Article VII

> The Congress . . . shall propose amendments to this Constitution, or . . . legislatures . . . shall call a convention for proposing amendments . . . .

In this article, the framers outlined the amendment proposal process and declared that the Constitution would go into effect when the ninth state convention approved it.

THE ORIGINAL U.S. CONSTITUTION	
Article I	The Legislative Branch
Article II	The Executive Branch
Article III	The Judiciary
Article IV	Relations Among States
Article V	Amendment Process
Article VI	National Supremacy
Article VII	Ratification Process

Political Science Reasoning Processes: Compare the Articles of Confederation with the U.S. Constitution

Often, comparing documents aids understanding of the political concepts of each of them. When you compare, you look for similarities and differences.

Apply: Based on the information on the previous pages, write an essay in which you compare political principles as you identify and explain similarities and differences between the Articles of Confederation and the Constitution. To help you gather your thoughts, you may want to make a chart for the Articles of Confederation like the one above for the Constitution. Then read the full text of the Constitution on pages 700–719, and answer the questions within it.

The Amendment Process

Amid all the compromises was the realization that the framers would not get everything right or design the perfect system, so they included the amendment process in **Article V**. The Constitution can be altered or amended in a two-stage process. Stage one is a proposal from either two-thirds of the House and Senate, or with a two-thirds vote at a convention initiated by the states and called by Congress. Stage two, ratification, is completed by a vote of three-fourths of the state legislatures or three-fourths of state ratifying conventions. Every proposal was passed through Congress, and all but one, the repeal of the Twenty-first Amendment, was ratified via conventions.

The process offers a balance between rigid standards to change the operating system and flexibility if overwhelmingly desired by the populace. Initially, the framers were prone to allowing only Congress to initiate amendments, but in the later days of the conventions delegate George Mason pointed to the need for a path that didn't require Congress, so the formula to ratify was widened to a different constituency. In a recent count, since 1789, more than 5,000 bills to amend have been introduced in Congress. Thirty-three have been passed and sent to the states, with only 27 being ratified by the required number of states and added to the Constitution, including the Bill of Rights.

Constitutional System

The framers included several governing principles. They ensured a level of democracy by mandating elections for members of Congress and the president. Yet instead of creating a democracy, the Constitution creates a representative republic that limits government and tempers hasty, even if popular, ideas. Under federalism, the national and state governments divide and share power as well, though the principle of national supremacy gives the federal government full authority within its defined sphere. The Constitution's necessary and proper clause gave the government the flexibility to face unforeseen circumstances.

Articles Of Confederation	Debate About State Powers	Resolution In Constitution
"Each state retains its sovereignty, freedom, and independence, and every Power, [not] ... expressly delegated to the United States, in Congress assembled."	After their struggle with the British government, the founders were reluctant to turn over any but the most essential powers to the national government.	States retain sovereignty; the powers of national legislature are limited and defined. (New Jersey Plan)
"In determining questions in the United States, in Congress assembled, each State shall have one vote."	Leaders of populous states wanted representation based on population. Leaders from smaller states did not.	Members of the House of Representatives are apportioned by population; each state is given two senators. (The Great Compromise)

(continued)

Articles Of Confederation	Debate About State Powers	Resolution In Constitution
"Full faith and credit shall be given in each of these States to the records, acts, and judicial proceedings of the courts and magistrates of every other State."	The states were unsure how their records, laws, and judgments would be regarded in other states and how they would regard those of other states.	Article IV's "full faith and credit" clause guarantees that "the citizens of each state shall be entitled to all privileges and immunities of citizens in the several states."
"Congress assembled shall also be the last resort on appeal in all disputes and differences now subsisting or that hereafter may arise between two or more States."	To resolve differences among states, leaders at the Constitutional Convention determined the federal government would have the final word.	Article VI's "supremacy clause" establishes the Constitution and the laws of the United States as the "supreme law of the land."

Unforseen Issues The framers could not have anticipated how the population of the United States would grow when they gave all states equal representation in the Senate. Both the populous states and the less populous states have two votes in the Senate. This disparity also results in unequal representation in the electoral process. The vote of an elector from a state with a small population has a disproportionately large influence on an election compared to that of an electoral vote from a state with a high population.

Ratification

When the framers finished the final draft, the Constitution went out to states for **ratification**, or formal consent. Article VII called for states to hold ratifying conventions to approve it and for the document to go into effect when the ninth state ratified. Most framers signed the final document, though three refused. Among them was George Mason, who was concerned that the document did not go far enough to protect individual rights.

A Bill of Rights

George Mason was not the only one disturbed by the document's lack of rights. Those who fought for independence argued that a bill of rights was necessary to secure the liberties earned through the revolution. The document framed in Philadelphia lacked a guarantee of free speech and press. There were few protections against aggressive prosecution, and no promise against cruel and unusual punishments. The Constitution did, however, include a few basic rights.

The Anti-Federalists and some pro-Constitution leaders believed a list of rights necessary to complete the Philadelphia mission. James Madison and others opposed. He called bills of rights "parchment barriers," mere paper blocks to injustices and tyranny that could prevail if the government design itself did not have provisions to prevent such tyranny. He pointed to abuses by majorities in states that did in fact have bills of rights. He also believed that by listing all the rights the federal government could not take away, a right could be inadvertently overlooked, and the new federal government *could* later take it away. He believed the Constitution never entitled the new federal government to take away any rights in the first place, so why was it necessary to list those that could not be taken way in the future? This final concern was the impetus for the Ninth Amendment.

The debate about adding a bill of rights overlapped the series of ratifying conventions that occurred throughout 1787–1790. With the Federalists' efforts and assurances that amendments protecting personal rights would be added, the reluctant states ratified and joined the Union. Additionally, as the new Congress began meeting in 1789, delegates petitioned for these rights. James Madison, now a House member, was persuaded that a bill of rights would complete the new government. He compiled the many suggestions into the amendments that became the **Bill of Rights**. The Bill of Rights was fully ratified by 1791.

The list includes the essential rights understood at the time and several temporarily lost under the oppressive British regime. The First Amendment declares freedoms of religion, speech, press, peaceable assembly, and the right to petition the government. Congress and the people put a high priority on the right to express political ideas, even if unpopular. (See Topic 3.1.) Other amendments protect private property, due process, fair trials, and prevent cruel and unusual punishments. The Tenth Amendment prevents the federal government from taking any powers that are reserved to the states. The text of the Bill of Rights begins on page 711.

SELECTED RIGHTS IN THE BILL OF RIGHTS	
Amendment I	Freedoms of religion, speech, press, assembly, and petition
Amendment II	Right to bear arms
Amendment III	No quartering of troops
Amendment IV	No unreasonable searches or seizures
Amendment V	Indictment, double jeopardy, protection against self-incrimination, due process
Amendment VI	Speedy and public trial by jury of peers, cross examination of adverse witnesses, to call favorable witnesses to testify, right to defense counsel, to be informed of the crime accused
Amendment VII	Lawsuits and juries
Amendment VIII	No cruel or unusual punishments, no excessive fines and bail
Amendment IX	Listing rights in the Constitution doesn't deny others
Amendment X	Delegated and reserved powers

Constitutional Debates Today

The Constitution has been the governing document of the United States for more than 230 years. Some of the same discussions that took place at the Constitutional Convention are relevant in the 21st century. Protections for the rights of individuals and the role of the federal government in relationship to that of state governments are topics still debated today.

Individual Rights and September 11

Like states' rights, the individual rights guaranteed by the Bill of Rights have sometimes seemed in conflict with federal law. Knowing where individual rights end and governmental authority begins has been the subject of many legal cases and will be covered in depth in Unit 3. One vivid example here—surveillance resulting from the federal government's response to the 9/11/2001 terrorist attacks that killed nearly 3,000 Americans and brought down the twin towers of the World Trade Center—will illuminate a key constitutional issue about democracy and governmental power. **BIG IDEA** Governmental laws and policies balancing order and liberty are based on the U.S. Constitution and have been interpreted differently over time.

Not long after al-Qaeda terrorists hijacked four U.S. commercial aircraft to fly them into selected targets in New York and Washington, President George W. Bush addressed a joint session of Congress, stating, "Whether we bring our enemies to justice or bring justice to our enemies, justice will be done." Faced with an adversary that generally operated underground and not under the flag of any sovereign nation, the United States modified its laws and defense operations to create a series of federal policies to eradicate threats. These policies fueled an ongoing debate about proper recognition of the Bill of Rights.

USA PATRIOT Act Administration officials began to consider a response to the September 11 attacks and, further, how to prevent future attacks. By late October 2001, the Congress passed the **USA PATRIOT Act** (**U**niting and **S**trengthening **A**merica by **P**roviding **A**ppropriate **T**ools **R**equired to **I**ntercept and **O**bstruct **T**errorism). The law covered intelligence gathering and sharing by executive branch agencies, points of criminal procedure, and border protection. It allowed government agencies to share information about significant suspects, and it widened authority on tapping suspects' phones. Government can now share grand jury testimony and proceedings, detain illegal immigrants for longer periods, and monitor email communications. The new bipartisan law passed with strong majorities in both houses.

Soon after its passage, however, people began to question the law's constitutionality and its threat to civil liberties, especially the rights protected by the Fourth Amendment. Muslim communities were especially affected, but every American experienced a loss of some degree of privacy. Many communities and states passed resolutions opposing sections of the Act, but supporters argued that the ability to tap phones and seize information was critical to the prevention of future terrorist attacks. Until 2013, when Edward

Snowden leaked a document that proved the government was engaged in widespread collection of information, many Americans were unaware of the extent of the government's reach. Protests against what were believed to be incursions into rights guaranteed in the Bill of Rights kept the practice in the spotlight. In 2015, after evidence showed that the bulk call record collection was not necessary to prevent terrorist attacks, Congress passed the USA Freedom Act, which upheld certain portions of the USA PATRIOT Act but phased out bulk collection of phone and Internet data and set limits for its collection in certain circumstances.

Education: National Goals, State Management

Protection of civil liberties and the right to privacy are not the only examples of central power still contested today. For most of America's past, education policy has been mostly left to the states, based on the Tenth Amendment's granting jurisdiction to the states in matters not reserved for federal authority. That began to change in the 20th century as the federal government began to take a larger role in education.

The Constitution and the federal government left the creation and management of schools largely to the states until the 1960s. There has always been a national concern for an educated citizenry, but the racial desegregation of public schools and the Cold War competition with the Soviet Union in the 1950s caused education to move up the national agenda. President Lyndon Johnson (a former teacher) and Congress passed the Elementary and Secondary Education Act in 1965. The law was as much an assault on poverty as it was reform of education, ensuring that lesser-funded schools received adequate resources. State officials generally welcomed the law because of the federal government's hands-off approach to school management and the broad discretion it gave local authorities on how to spend federal monies.

Additional significant changes in federal education law have occurred in the last two decades. The **No Child Left Behind Act (NCLB),** passed in 2002, called for improvements in teaching methods, testing to measure progress, and sanctions for underperforming schools. To implement these changes, the federal government increased its role and level of oversight in education. Nearly 80 percent of U.S. schools could not meet the unrealistic standards of NCLB and the law received widespread criticism.

President Obama's **Race to the Top** initiative offered incentives, rather than the sanctions of NCLB, for states to adopt new national standards or develop their own that require students to be college- and career-ready at graduation. In 2015, Congress passed and President Obama signed a new education law—the **Every Student Succeeds Act (ESSA).** Under this law, states are free to determine their own standards for educational achievement, while still upholding protections for disadvantaged students. However, the federal Department of Education must still approve each state's plan, assuring that the states live up to the requirements in the federal law.

REFLECT ON THE ESSENTIAL QUESTION

Essential Question: *What impacts of political negotiation and compromise at the Constitutional Convention are seen in the development of the constitutional system? On separate paper, complete a chart like the one below.*

Constitutional Compromise	Impact (Historically or Currently)

KEY TERMS AND NAMES

Article V

bicameral

Bill of Rights

Constitutional Convention

Electoral College

Every Student Succeeds Act (2015)

Great (Connecticut) Compromise

New Jersey Plan

No Child Left Behind (2002)

Race to the Top

ratification

Three-Fifths Compromise

USA PATRIOT Act (2001)

Virginia Plan

Source: Allyn Cox, Architect of the Capitol

Patrick Henry addresses the First Continental Congress. At that Congress, he proclaimed, "The distinctions between Virginians, Pennsylvanians, New Yorkers, and New Englanders are no more. I am not a Virginian; I am an American." Yet his concerns about individual liberties led him to oppose ratification of the new government's Constitution because it had no Bill of Rights. Even when amendments were added to secure individual rights, Henry opposed them, believing they did not go far enough.

Principles of American Government

"In framing a government which is to be administered by men over men, the great difficulty lies in this: you must first enable the government to control the governed; and in the next place oblige it to control itself."

—James Madison, *Federalist No. 51*, 1788

Essential Question: What do the principles of separation of powers and "checks and balances" mean to the U.S. political system?

The framers structured the United States government to deliver the people's will and to preserve the democratic process. The separation of powers among the three branches of government and the division between federal and state governments dilute the power and prevent abuses by majorities. Additionally, each branch can limit the others under the system of checks and balances. These types of political divisions derive from Enlightenment philosophies dating back to the 16th century. (See Topic 1.1.)

The Three Branches in Practice

The legislative, executive, and judicial branches are headquartered in the nation's capital and remain busy creating and refining national policy. A busy and divisive Congress, a president and the executive's large administration, and a court system stretched across the land are all part of the policymaking process. The federal branches, as well as the three branches in state governments, provide multiple access points for citizens and special interests to voice views and shape policy.

Legislative

Congress operates on Capitol Hill, where 435 House representatives and 100 senators make the nation's laws, determine how to fund government, and shape the nation's foreign policy. On opposite sides of the Capitol, the House and Senate operate in separate chambers and with different rules of procedure. Both the House and Senate have an array of committees, usually between 10 and 40 members on each, that oversee certain topics of law or policymaking. Congress has thousands of employees who write the bills, gather research data, take the pulse of the citizens in each district, and let the voters know about all the good things their Congress member has done, especially near election time.

Legislative Access Points The legislative branch provides one access point for people to influence U.S. policy. One way **stakeholders**—people or groups who will be affected by the policies—exert their influence is through special interest groups. (See Topics 5.6 and 5.7.) These groups pay professionals to lobby lawmakers—meet face-to-face with them and provide them with information and reasons to support or reject certain proposed legislation. In 2020, for example, for every person in Congress, there were two lobbyists representing the interests of big pharmaceutical companies.

Individual citizens also have access to their representatives and senators. They can contact lawmakers by mail or email to make their voices heard. In addition to contacting their legislators, citizens can gain understanding of proposed bills through the Congressional Research Service through the Library of Congress, where they can read synopses of bills. Also, the media report on and analyze proposed laws and critique laws after they have taken effect. The House and Senate proceedings are aired live on C-SPAN television. An informed citizenry can use this knowledge on public policy to exert influence on lawmakers. Participation in town hall meetings sends a message to lawmakers about the population's stance on key issues.

Executive

Article II lays out the requirements for president and the executive's role. The presidency has grown in both scope and power. President George Washington had a four-person Cabinet and no more than a few hundred government employees. Today, the Cabinet has grown to about 20 members, and the federal executive branch has more than 2.7 million employees to carry out the nation's laws.

Executive Access Points People also have access to their government through the executive branch and its many agencies. Some agencies exist to protect citizens, who can file a complaint to assure enforcement of or fairness in the law. For example, the Equal Employment Opportunity Commission investigates complaints of discrimination in the workplace. Of course, citizens can also report federal crimes to the FBI or the Drug Enforcement Administration. And a voter can find where a federal candidate's donations come from at the Federal Election Commission's website.

Judicial

The U.S. Supreme Court, a series of lower appeals courts, and even more trial courts below them form the structure of the court system. The Supreme Court and lower courts have exercised judicial review (see Topic 2.8) to protect liberties and to properly initiate policy. Courts can use this power to check the legislature, the executive, or state actions. Courts can refuse to enforce a poorly written law and can disallow evidence obtained unlawfully by the police.

Judicial Access Points The judicial system offers additional access points for representation and justice. Citizens use the federal courts to challenge unfair government action, to appeal wrongful convictions, and to question public policies. Because of citizen lawsuits in these courts and authoritative Supreme Court decisions, Americans can now say and print unpopular and even antigovernment ideas, challenge convictions made in unfair trials, attend equal schools without limitations based on race, and marry whom they want.

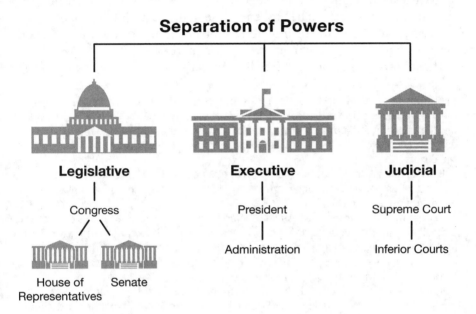

Separation of Powers

The framers assigned the legislative, executive, and judicial branches distinct responsibilities to dilute power among the three branches. Earlier in school, you might have learned that "the legislature makes the law, the executive branch enforces the law, and the judicial branch interprets the law." This simplification highlights the basic function of each branch but overlooks the fact that all three branches can establish law and policy. The legislature is the most representative branch and makes the public's will become public policy. The powers of Congress are further separated between the two chambers. Neither house can pass a bill into law without the consent of the other chamber. The president is ultimately the authority to enforce the law and to carry out Congress's policies, so the president and his administration shape policy in doing so. Members of the Supreme Court and the federal courts, appointed by the president and confirmed by the Senate, hear disputes and interpret laws and their application.

In *Federalist No. 51*, Publius writes, "If men were angels, no government would be necessary." He points to the separation of powers outlined in the Constitution as a guard against tyranny. He also states that the best protection of the minority is that "the society itself will be broken into so many parts, interests, and classes of citizens, that the rights of individuals, or of the minority, will be in little danger from interested combinations of the majority."

The following excerpt addresses the separation of powers.

> In order to lay a due foundation for that separate and distinct exercise of the different powers of government . . . it is evident that each department should have a will of its own; and consequently should be so constituted, that the members of each should have as little agency as possible in the appointment of the members of the others. . . .
>
> It is equally evident, that the members of each department should be as little dependent as possible on those of the others, for the emoluments [earnings] annexed to their offices. . . .
>
> In framing a government which is to be administered by men over men, the great difficulty lies in this: you must first enable the government to control the governed; and in the next place oblige it to control itself. A dependence on the people is, no doubt, the primary control on the government; but experience has taught mankind the necessity of auxiliary precautions. . . .
>
> In republican government, the legislative authority necessarily predominates. The remedy for this inconveniency is to divide the legislature into different branches; and to render them, by different modes of election and different principles of action, as little connected with each other as the nature of their common functions and their common dependence on the society will admit.

Political Science Disciplinary Practices: Explain how the Source Relates to Political Institutions

When you explain how a source relates to political institutions (or principles, processes, and behaviors), you test the degree to which the source accurately describes those features of government. When *Federalist No. 51* was published, the institutions referred to in this article—the executive, legislative, and judicial branches and the two chambers of Congress—had not yet been formed. Now, however, the nation has more than two centuries' experience with these institutions, and the ideas expressed in *Federalist No. 51* can be related to actual government institutions.

Apply: Research the 2017 efforts by members of the Republican Party to "repeal and replace" the Affordable Care Act, President Obama's signature accomplishment. Explain how *Federalist No. 51* relates to those efforts and the various institutions of government involved in them. Then read the full text of *Federalist No. 51* online.

Checks and Balances

Each branch can limit the others with **checks and balances**. These are especially clear in the lawmaking process. A bill (a proposed law) can originate in either the House or Senate and must pass both bodies with a simple majority (50 percent plus 1). Then the bill is presented to the president, who may sign it into law if he agrees with the proposal. Or, exercising executive checks and balances, the president may reject it with a **veto** based on power granted in Article I, Section 7, of the Constitution. Routinely, if after ten days (excluding Sundays) the president has done neither, the bill becomes law. If the president receives the bill at the end of a legislative session, however, refusal to sign is known as a **pocket veto** and kills the bill.

After the president consents to a law, it is entered into the United States Code, the nation's body of federal statutes. If the president vetoes a bill, the Congress, each house acting separately, can overcome the veto with a **two-thirds override**, a super majority vote in each house.

The framers placed additional checks on power, such as the Senate's right to provide **advice and consent**. The Senate can suggest appointees and must formally approve most presidential appointments. Appointed Cabinet secretaries and Supreme Court judges sit before a Senate committee for their confirmation hearings.

The framers assigned to the House of Representatives the power of **impeachment**, an accusation of wrongdoing. Article I, Section 2 claims the House "shall have the sole power of impeachment" and can impeach the president, a federal judge, or another official of wrongdoing. The Senate then holds a trial for the accused official. The Chief Justice presides as the judge at the trial. The Senate must vote by a two-thirds majority to find an official guilty and remove him or her. **BIG IDEA** The U.S. Constitution establishes a system of checks and balances among branches of government and allocates power between federal and state governments. This system is based on the rule of law and the balance between majority rule and minority rights.

Three presidents have been impeached, Andrew Johnson, Bill Clinton, and Donald Trump, variously accused for abuse of power or breaking the law. In each case, the Senate did not remove the president because they determined the charges did not reach the standard for "treason, bribery, or other high crimes or misdemeanors."

THINK AS A POLITICAL SCIENTIST: *EXPLAIN HOW THE AUTHOR'S ARGUMENT RELATES TO POLITICAL PRINCIPLES*

The Constitution was created to ensure the people's will is represented and that freedom is preserved through numerous principles. The principle of checks and balances prevents the concentration of too much power in a single branch of government. The separation of powers spreads authority among the three branches of government. Federalism is the sharing of powers among a national and state governments.

Practice: Read the excerpts below and explain how the argument in each relates to the principle of separation of powers, checks and balances, or federalism.

1. **Religious Freedom Restoration Act, 1993**

   "(a) Government shall not substantially burden a person's exercise of religion even if the burden results from a rule of general applicability, except as provided in subsection (b).

   (b) Government may substantially burden a person's exercise of religion only if it demonstrates that application of the burden to the person—
   (1) is in furtherance of a compelling governmental interest; and
   (2) is the least restrictive means of furthering that compelling governmental interest."

2. **President Barack Obama's executive action on immigration, 2014**

   "Now, I continue to believe that the best way to solve this problem is by working together to pass that kind of common sense law. But until that happens, there are actions I have the legal authority to take as President—the same kinds of actions taken by Democratic and Republican presidents before me—that will help make our immigration system more fair and more just."

3. **Rep. Jerry Nadler (D-NY) on the impeachment of President Bill Clinton, 1998**

   "It is not an abuse of uniquely presidential power. It does not threaten our form of government. It is not an impeachable offense."

REFLECT ON THE ESSENTIAL QUESTION

Essential Question: *What do the principles of separation of powers and "checks and balances" mean to the U.S. political system? On separate paper, complete a chart like the one below.*

Examples of Separation of Powers	Examples of Checks and Balances

KEY TERMS AND NAMES

advice and consent	impeachment	stakeholders
checks and balances	pocket veto	two-thirds override
Federalist No. 51	separation of power	veto

CHAPTER 2 Review:
Learning Objectives and Key Terms

TOPIC 1.4: Explain the relationship between key provisions of the Articles of Confederation and the debate over granting the federal government greater power formerly reserved to the states. (CON-1.B)

Economic and Military Struggles Under the Articles (CON-1.B.1)

Articles of Confederation	Shays' Rebellion

TOPIC 1.5: Explain the ongoing impact of political negotiation and compromise at the Constitutional Convention on the development of the constitutional system. (CON-1.C)

Constitutional Compromises (CON-1.C.1)	**Amendment Process** (CON-1.C.2)	**Constitutional Issues Today** (CON-1.C.3)
bicameral	Article V	Every Student Succeeds Act (ESSA) (2015)
Bill of Rights		No Child Left Behind (NCLB) (2002)
Constitutional Convention		Race to the Top
Electoral College		USA PATRIOT Act (2001)
Great Compromise		
New Jersey Plan		
ratification		
Three-Fifths Compromise		
Virginia Plan		

TOPIC 1.6: Explain the principles of separation of powers and "checks and balances" and their implication for the U.S. political system. (PMI-1.A, PMI-1.B)

Defining Separation of Powers and Checks and Balances (PMI-1.A.1, PMI-1.A.2)	**Examples of Separation of Powers and Checks and Balances** (PMI-1.B.1, PMI-1.B.2)
checks and balances	advice and consent
Federalist No. 51	impeachment
separation of powers	pocket veto
stakeholders	two-thirds override
	veto

CHAPTER 2 Checkpoint:
The Constitution

Topics 1.4–1.6

MULTIPLE-CHOICE QUESTIONS

1. Which of the following is an accurate comparison of the New Jersey Plan and the Virginia Plan?

	New Jersey Plan	Virginia Plan
(A)	Included a layered system of national courts	Made the states supreme over the national government
(B)	Created a bicameral legislature	Assured states would retain sovereignty
(C)	Gave the national legislature only defined and limited powers	Included a three-branch system and a bicameral legislature
(D)	Made the national government supreme over the states	Allowed importation of slaves for 20 years after ratification

Questions 2 and 3 refer to the table below.

RATIFICATION OF CONSTITUTION, 1787–1790 VOTES IN RATIFYING CONVENTIONS				
State	Date	Yes	No	Percent
Delaware	Dec. 7, 1787	30	0	100%
Pennsylvania	Dec. 12, 1787	30	0	100%
New Jersey	Dec. 18, 1787	38	23	66%
Georgia	Jan. 2, 1788	26	0	100%
Connecticut	Jan. 9, 1788	128	40	76%
Massachusetts	Feb. 6, 1788	187	168	54%
Maryland	April 28, 1788	63	11	85%
S. Carolina	May 23, 1788	149	73	67%
New Hampshire	June 21, 1788	57	47	55%
Virginia	Jun. 25, 1788	89	79	52%
New York	Jul. 26, 1788	30	27	53%
North Carolina	Nov. 21, 1789	194	77	72%
Rhode Island	May 29, 1790	34	32	52%

2. Which statement most accurately reflects the data in the table?

   (A) The Great Compromise had little influence on states' votes.

   (B) The number of states required by Article VII to ratify the Constitution was reached by June 1788.

   (C) The Articles of Confederation had more support than the Constitution.

   (D) The highest Anti-Federalist sentiment was seen in New Jersey, Delaware, and Georgia.

3. The process depicted in the above chart reflects which governmental concept?

   (A) Direct democracy

   (B) Representative republic

   (C) Checks and balances

   (D) Judicial review

4. Which of the following is the best example of results from political negotiation and compromise at the Constitutional Convention?

   (A) The creation of the House and Senate

   (B) Establishing a federal court system

   (C) Protecting individual property rights

   (D) Determining which citizens could vote in elections

Questions 5 and 6 refer to the following passage.

Each State shall appoint, in such Manner as the Legislature thereof may direct, a Number of Electors, equal to the whole Number of Senators and Representatives to which the State may be entitled in the Congress: but no Senator or Representative, or Person holding an Office of Trust or Profit under the United States, shall be appointed an Elector . . . The Congress may determine the Time of choosing the Electors, and the Day on which they shall give their Votes; which Day shall be the same throughout the United States.

—Article II, Section 1 of the U.S. Constitution, 1787

5. The above passage defines which of the following constitutional structures or procedures?

   (A) Lawmaking requirements

   (B) The presidential selection process

   (C) The necessary and proper clause

   (D) Ratification requirements

6. The above procedure explained in Article II resulted from which of the following?

(A) The drafting of the Bill of Rights

(B) A belief that the popular vote should elect the president

(C) A compromise necessary for the adoption of the Constitution

(D) The successful war against Great Britain

FREE-RESPONSE QUESTIONS

Concept Application

1. "On January 25, 1787, forces led by Daniel Shays moved toward the Confederation arsenal in Springfield and were met by Massachusetts general William Shepard and his troops . . . One central fact about the rebellion was not lost on most leaders across the country: the Confederation's weakness had forced Massachusetts to fend for itself. Although Congress had authorized new troops that could be used there, it requisitioned nearly half of them from Massachusetts itself, and it could not pay for any of them . . . it was the high-water mark of violent social unrest during the post-war Confederation period."

—George William Van Cleves, *We Have Not a Government*, 2017

After reading the excerpt, respond to A, B, and C below:

(A) Explain how the Articles of Confederation made the above scenario possible.

(B) Describe how this scenario influenced the framers' decisions in creating the Constitution.

(C) Explain how an additional governing issue made Shays' Rebellion a decisive point in the creation of the U.S. Republic.

Quantitative Analysis

RESULTS OF EARLY PRESIDENTIAL ELECTIONS			
Election Year	Top Candidates	Party	Electoral College Votes
1792	George Washington	Federalist	132
	John Adams	Federalist	77
	George Clinton	Democratic-Republican	50
1796	John Adams	Federalist	71
	Thomas Jefferson	Democratic-Republican	68
	Thomas Pinckney	Federalist	59
	Aaron Burr	Anti-Federalist	30
1800	Thomas Jefferson	Democratic-Republican	73
	Aaron Burr	Democratic-Republican	73
	John Adams	Federalist	65
	C. C. Pinckney	Federalist	64
1804	Thomas Jefferson	Democratic-Republican	162
	C.C. Pinckney	Federalist	14

2. Use the information graphic above to answer the questions.

   (A) Identify a victorious presidential candidate.

   (B) Describe a trend in political party electoral success.

   (C) Draw a conclusion about that trend.

   (D) Explain how the data in the table demonstrates a difference between the Constitution and the Articles of Confederation.

CHAPTER 3

Federalism

Topics 1.7–1.9

Topic 1.7 Relationship Between the States and Federal Government

CON-2.A: Explain how societal needs affect the constitutional allocation of power between national and state governments.

- – Required Foundational Document:
  - • The Constitution of the United States

Topic 1.8 Constitutional Interpretations of Federalism

CON-2.B: Explain how the appropriate balance of power between national and state governments has been interpreted differently over time.

- – Required Foundational Document:
  - • The Constitution of the United States

- – Required Supreme Court Cases:
  - • *McCulloch v. Maryland* (1819)
  - • *United States v. Lopez* (1995)

Topic 1.9 Federalism in Action

CON-1.B: Explain how the distribution of powers among three federal branches and between national and state governments impacts policymaking.

Source: Flickr

August 11, 2010. Congresswoman Nancy Pelosi (D-CA) joins Transportation Secretary Ray LaHood, San Francisco Mayor Gavin Newsom, Senator Barbara Boxer (D-CA), and local leaders to break ground on the new Transbay Transit Center in San Francisco, a joint project of federal, state, and regional governments.

Relationship Between the States and Federal Government

"Some may feel that my decision is at odds with my philosophical viewpoint that state problems should involve state solutions . . . .In a case like this . . . I have no misgivings about a judicious use of Federal inducements to . . . save precious lives,"

—Ronald Reagan, on the National Minimum Drinking Age Act, 1984

Essential Question: How do the needs of society affect the allocation of power between national and state governments?

The framers of the U.S. Constitution had to balance the powers of Congress and the federal government at the national level with the powers held by the states. Where the power ultimately lies, however, has been a source of controversy since the U.S. Constitution was framed. The national legislature has stretched its powers in trying to address national needs, while states have tried to maintain their sovereignty. **Federalism**, the sharing of powers between the national government and state governments, has evolved, as has Congress's authority and modern function. This development has blurred the line between state and national jurisdictions, and modern leaders have tried to balance authority divided between the two tiers of government.

Federalism

In creating and empowering the new federal government, the framers debated where power should lie. The experience of having just defeated a tyrannical central government in Britain to secure liberty locally did not make centralizing power in the new United States very attractive. BIG IDEA The U.S. Constitution establishes a system of checks and balances among branches of government and allocates power between federal and state governments. This system is based on the rule of law and the balance between majority rule and minority rights.

Provisions Defining Federalism

The foundation for federalism can be found in various parts of the original Constitution and the Bill of Rights.

Constitutional Provisions Article VI, which includes the **supremacy clause**, places national law, treaties, and presidential action above state authority. National law, however, is limited by the enumerated list of Congress's powers in Article I, Section 8, while presidential authority is also limited by the Constitution. (See Topic 2.5.) So unless federal actions or policies violate the Constitution, states cannot disregard them.

Additional provisions define the relations among the states and national supremacy. Article IV explains **full faith and credit**, protections of **privileges and immunities**, and **extradition**. The article requires each state to give full faith and credit "to the public acts, records, and judicial proceedings of every other state." In other words, states must regard and honor the laws in other states. The privileges and immunities clause declares "citizens of each state shall be entitled to all privileges and immunities of citizens in the several states." States have created laws to protect their own residents or to give them priority over nonresidents, but the Supreme Court has struck down many of them based on this clause. States can, however, charge different college tuition prices for in-state and out-of-state students, largely because in-state students and their families have paid into the state's tax system that supports state colleges. The extradition clause obligates states to deliver captured fugitive criminals back to the state where they committed the original crime.

Skeptics and Anti-Federalists desired an expressed guarantee in the Constitution to assure the preservation of states' rights. It came in the form of the Tenth Amendment. "The powers not delegated to the United States . . . ," the amendment declares, "are reserved to the states."

CONSTITUTIONAL PROVISIONS THAT GUIDE FEDERALISM	
Article I, Section 8	Enumerated powers of Congress, including the necessary and proper clause
Article I, Section 9	Powers denied Congress; no regulating slave trade before 1808; states to be treated uniformly
Article I, Section 10	Powers denied to the states, such as treaties; impairing contracts
Article IV	Full faith and credit; privileges and immunities; extradition
Article VI	Supremacy of the national government
Ninth Amendment	Rights not listed reserved by the people
Tenth Amendment	Powers not delegated to the federal government reserved by the states

Exclusive Powers

Powers that are delegated only to the federal government are called **exclusive powers**. National needs require consistency across state lines, such as having uniform weights and measures and a national currency. To establish this consistency, Article I enables Congress to legislate on military and diplomatic affairs and international and interstate commerce. It also allows Congress to define such crimes as counterfeiting, mail fraud, immigration violations, and piracy. However, the framers also put limits on Congress with Article I, Section 9.

States already had prisons, state militias, and other services when the federal system was created. The framers left these concerns up to the states, along with the management of elections, marriage laws, and the maintenance of deeds and records. States have **police powers**, or powers to create and enforce laws on health, safety, and morals. These concerns encompass much of state budgets today. States fund and operate hospitals and clinics. Law enforcement is predominantly composed of state personnel. States can set their own laws on speed limits, seat belts, and smoking in public places.

Concurrent Powers

The Tenth Amendment distinguishes the two governing spheres. The reserved powers are not specifically listed, and thus any powers not mentioned remain with the states. Some powers are held by authorities at both levels, state and federal. These are called **concurrent powers**. The states and the nation can both levy and collect taxes, define crimes, run court systems, and improve lands.

Federalism: A Sharing of Powers

Federal
Declare War
Regulate Interstate commerce
Define Immigration and naturalization

Concurrent
Levy taxes
Enforce laws

States
Operate schools
Regulate health, safety, and morals
Incorporate cities and companies

Overlap and Uncertainty Marriage has been at the heart of a number of power struggles between the federal and state governments. For example, the federal Defense of Marriage Act (1996) defined marriage as between one man and one woman. States generally honored marriage licenses from other states, but the legalization of same-sex marriages in some states early in the 21st century caused other states to expressly refuse recognition of these marriages. Opposing states rewrote their marriage laws and added amendments to their state constitutions to define marriage as between a man and a woman only. This controversy put Article IV in direct conflict with the Tenth Amendment. The full faith and credit clause suggests that if Vermont sanctioned the marriage of two men, Missouri would have to honor it. Yet the reserved powers clause in the Tenth Amendment grants Missouri's right to define marriage within its borders. The Supreme Court, with the Fourteenth Amendment's equal protection clause also in play, settled this dispute in 2015 in *Obergefell v. Hodges*, ruling 5:4 that the right to same-sex marriage was guaranteed. (See Topic 1.8.)

Federalism leaves schools, elections, and most law enforcement up to the states. Why, then, do we have a national Department of Education, the Federal Elections Commission, and a Federal Bureau of Investigation? These questions will be answered in Topic 1.8 as you read about how the new nation began to walk the delicate line that divided state and federal power, how the Supreme Court has defined federalism, and how Congress became keenly interested in issues of education, political campaigns, and crime.

THINK AS A POLITICAL SCIENTIST: *ARTICULATE A DEFENSIBLE CLAIM*

Federalism is the sharing of powers between federal and state governments. Certain powers are delegated to each level of government and several are shared. For example, Colorado and Washington legalized marijuana for recreational use in 2012. Since then, more than 20 other states have challenged federal law by legalizing marijuana in some form. At the federal level, marijuana is illegal.

Practice: Read the excerpt below and make a claim about how the concept of federalism relates to the legalization of marijuana.

> As of July 2017, 28 states and the federal district have legalized medical marijuana, but medical marijuana use is still illegal nationally under the *Controlled Substances Act*, and marijuana is listed under the Schedule 1 list of drugs, along with heroin and LSD.
>
> The conflict between state laws that allow limited marijuana use and the federal law that bars it, in theory, falls somewhere in the domain of the Constitution's supremacy clause, which reads in part that "This Constitution, and the Laws of the United States which shall be made in Pursuance thereof . . . shall be the supreme Law of the Land."
>
> Some states-rights supporters argue that the Tenth Amendment, which grants rights to the states and the people not reserved to the federal government, allows for states to choose their own marijuana laws and how the laws are enforced by state and local law enforcement officers.

Source: constitutioncenter.org

Federal Grant Program

The overlap of federal and state authority in exclusive and concurrent powers is probably nowhere more obvious than in **federal grant** programs. In advancing the constitutional definition of federalism, Congress has dedicated itself to addressing national issues with federal dollars. Congress collects federal tax revenues and distributes these funds to the states to take care of particular national concerns. This process has different names, such as **revenue sharing** and **fiscal federalism**. For decades, the federal government has used incentives to prompt, and at times require, states and localities to address safety, crime, education, and civil rights. Congress has largely done this by directing federal funds to states that qualify for aid and withholding funds when they do not. These **grants-in-aid programs** have developed over a 200-year history and picked up steadily to meet the needs of society during the Progressive Era, with Franklin Roosevelt's New Deal, and then under Lyndon Johnson's Great Society program of the 1960s. This financial aid helps states take care of basic state needs. Grants come in different forms with different requirements, and they sometimes stretch the limits of constitutionality. Political realities in Washington, DC, and at the local level, explain why these grants have gone through so many variations.

Addressing National Issues

Though state officials are well schooled in the reserved powers clause of the Tenth Amendment and want to protect those powers, they also find it challenging to turn away federal money to handle state concerns. States do not necessarily want to cede their authority, but at the same time, they want the federal funds that are dangled before them to meet state needs. The federal government has decided many times to pay the bill, as long as the states follow federal guidelines while taking care of the issue. Grants with particular congressional guidelines or requirements are known as **categorical grants**. Categorical grants with **strings**, or conditions of aid, became the norm. In addition to the political benefits congressional members experience, grant recipients at the state and local levels enjoy categorical grants. Special interest groups could lobby Congress for funding their causes. State agencies, such as those that support state health care or road construction, depend on federal aid and appreciate these grants. Community groups and nonprofit agencies thrive on these as well.

Grants Through the Mid-1900s After Americans earned independence and attained the vast lands west of the Appalachian Mountains, high-ranking soldiers received land grants for their service in the Revolution. The federal government later granted large sums of money to states so they could maintain militias. In 1862, Congress passed the Morrill Land-Grant Act. It allowed Congress to parcel out large tracts of land to encourage states to build colleges. Congress started using grants heavily in 1916 to fund road construction as the automobile became central to American society and as roads became central to economic improvement.

The federal income tax caused the national treasury to grow exponentially. With these extra financial resources, Congress addressed concerns that were traditionally out of its jurisdiction. Additionally, larger numbers of people who had gained the right to vote pressed for more government reform and action. Women and other groups began voting and engaging in civic endeavors that resulted in the national government addressing more of society's concerns.

The economic crisis that followed, the Great Depression, caused the federal government to grow more, largely by implementing more grants. Traditionally, states, localities, and private charitable organizations provided relief for the poor. By 1935, most states had enacted laws to aid impoverished mothers and the aged. State funds did not always cover this effort, so President Franklin D. Roosevelt and Congress were pressured to address the issue.

"In Two Words, Yes And No"

Source: Herblock

Describe the characters, objects, and actions in this cartoon. How does the text help convey the message? What perspective about federalism is the cartoonist trying to convey? What is the implication of the cartoonist's perspective or argument?

Societal Concerns of the 1960s and 1970s The fight for civil rights and school desegregation, the desire for clean air and clean water, and the concern for crime gained national interest. Once again, federal dollars spoke loudly to local officials. The 1964 Civil Rights Act, for example, withheld federal dollars from schools that did not fully desegregate their students. Under President Johnson, the federal government increased the number of grants to address poverty and health care. Congress also began to redefine the grants process to give more decision-making power to local authorities. Some states felt grants had too many strings attached. In 1966, Congress introduced block grants. **Block grants**, which refers to federal money given to states for broadly defined reasons, differ from categorical grants in that they offer larger sums of money to the states without the strings of the categorical grants.

President Richard Nixon, a believer in clear boundaries between state and federal jurisdictions, wanted to return greater authority to local governments, using a mix of block grants, revenue sharing, and welfare reform. In 1971, Nixon proposed to meld one-third of all federal programs into six loosely defined megagrants, an initiative called "special revenue sharing." He didn't achieve this goal, but in 1972, general revenue sharing provided more than $6.1 billion annually in "no strings" grants to virtually all general-purpose governments. Congress passed two major block grants: the Comprehensive Employment and Training Act of 1973 (CETA) and the Community Development Block Grant program (CDBG) in 1974. By 1976, Congress had created three more large block grants. Fiscal conservatives, who also favored local control, liked Nixon's plan of mixing state and federal authority.

As soon as Nixon tried to steer federal money to states in larger, less restrictive ways, members of Congress realized the authority and benefits they would lose. Block grants took away Congress's role of oversight and, politically, denied individual representatives and senators the ability to claim credit. Congress was losing control, and individual members felt some responsibility to provide federal dollars to their districts in a more specific way. In response, Congress passed only five block grants between 1966 to 1980. Categorical grants with strings, or conditions of aid, became the norm again.

Grants in the 1980s and Beyond The federal government offered states one notable categorical grant in the early 1980s as a way to both satisfy the upkeep of highways and to ease the national drunk driving problem. Congress offered large sums of money to states on the condition that states increase their drinking age to 21. Studies showed that raising the legal drinking age would likely decrease the number of fatalities on the highways. Most states complied with the National Minimum Drinking Age Act of 1984 to secure these precious dollars. South Dakota, however, challenged the act.

In *South Dakota v. Dole*, the Supreme Court ruled that Congress did have the power to set conditions on the drinking age for states to receive federal dollars for highway repair and construction. Congressional restrictions on grants to the states are constitutional if they meet certain requirements. They must be for the general welfare of the public and cannot be ambiguous. Conditions must be related to the federal interest in particular national projects or programs, and they must not run afoul of other constitutional provisions. That is, Congress cannot use a conditional grant to induce states to engage in unconstitutional activities. South Dakota lost, and Congress continued creating and controlling strings.

Mandates With strings, states receive federal monies in exchange for following guidelines. Federal **mandates**, on the other hand, require states to comply with a federal directive, sometimes with the reward of funds and sometimes—in unfunded mandates—without. The legislative, executive, or judicial branches can issue mandates in various forms. Mandates often address civil rights, environmental concerns, and other societal needs. Federal statutes require state environmental agencies to meet national clean air and water requirements.

Significant intergovernmental regulations in the late 1980s and early 1990s include the Clean Air Act Amendments, the Americans with Disabilities Act, the Civil Rights Restoration Act, the Family and Medical Leave Act, and the National Voter Registration Act (also known as the motor-voter law).

Source: Executive Office of the President of the United States

President George H.W. Bush signs the Americans with Disabilities Act in 1990.

The Clean Air Act, originally passed in 1970, set requirements and timetables for dealing with urban smog, acid rain, and toxic pollutants. The Americans with Disabilities Act required public sector buildings and transportation systems be accessible for disabled individuals. Cities and states had to make their buildings wheelchair accessible and install wheelchair lifts. The mandate imposed, according to the Congressional Budget Office's best estimates, as much as $1 billion in additional costs on states and localities. The Clean Air Act Amendments imposed $250 million to $300 million annually, and the cost of the motor-voter law would reach $100 million over five years.

The federal courts have also issued mandates to ensure that state or local governing bodies act in certain ways. Judges have decreed that cities redefine their hiring practices to prevent discrimination. They have placed firm restrictions on federal housing projects. In the early 1970s, federal judges mandated that public schools arrange appropriate black-to-white enrollment ratios, essentially mandating busing for racial balance.

Devolution Ronald Reagan's philosophy of New Federalism is characterized by the return of power to states, or **devolution**. Reagan returned to the practice of giving block grants to states, allowing them more discretion in spending. Throughout his presidency, Reagan worked for consolidation of categorical grants into block grants, having limited success.

In the 1990s, Republicans continued to push Reagan's devolution policies. With bipartisan support and President Bill Clinton's signature, they managed to pass the Unfunded Mandates Reform Act and the **Personal Responsibility and Work Opportunity Reconciliation Act**. The first act denied Congress the ability to issue unfunded mandates, laws that were taking up some 30 percent of state budgets. The second act restructured the welfare system to return much authority and distribution of welfare dollars—Medicaid, for example—to the states. As Clinton declared in a 1996 address, "The era of big government is over."

REFLECT ON THE ESSENTIAL QUESTION

Essential Question: *How do the needs of society affect the allocation of power between national and state governments? On separate paper, complete a chart like the one below.*

Powers Allocated to the Federal Government	Example of Powers

Powers Allocated to State Governments	Example of Powers

KEY TERMS AND NAMES

block grants

categorical grants

concurrent powers

cooperative federalism

Defense of Marriage Act (1996)

devolution

exclusive powers

extradition

federalism

federal grants

fiscal federalism

full faith and credit

grant-in-aid programs

mandates

Personal Responsibility and Work
    Opportunity Reconciliation Act (1996)

police powers

privileges and immunities

revenue sharing

strings

supremacy clause

Constitutional Interpretations of Federalism

"At the beginning of its third century, the condition of American federalism is best characterized as ambiguous but promising."

—Daniel Elazar, *Opening the Third Century of American Federalism: Issues and Prospects*, 1990

Essential Question: How has a balance of power between national and state governments been interpreted over time?

The different needs of the 13 colonies guided the framers' decisions in creating the system of federalism that is at the heart of the Constitution. The role they intended for state governments was at the forefront of involvement in issues that had a daily impact on citizens. This struggle for power has led to national and state governments having varied amounts of control as the needs of the nation have changed.

As Daniel Elazar explains above, federalism has continued its evolution, from federal control to distribution of power among other levels of government, as "... a great advance for noncentralized government over the situation which had prevailed between 1965 and 1980, during which the trend was rather unambiguously centralizing."

Constitutional Definition of Federalism

The foundation for federalism is embedded in various parts of the original Constitution and the Bill of Rights.

Federal Power

Article I defines the basic setup and operation of Congress. It has ten sections and is the longest article—about half of the entire Constitution—revealing the framers' concern for representative lawmaking and their reverence for the legislative branch. Sections 8, 9, and 10 detail the powers and limitations of Congress and the powers of the states. The framers identified a limited list of **enumerated powers**, Section 8, which include the powers to tax, borrow money, raise an army, create a postal system, address piracy on the seas, define the immigration and naturalization process, and a few others. The **commerce clause** empowers the Congress to "regulate commerce with other nations, and among the several states."

The final clause in Section 8 is the **necessary and proper clause**, or **elastic clause**. This provision states, "The Congress shall have power . . . to make all laws which shall be necessary and proper for carrying into execution the foregoing powers." Since this power goes beyond the explicitly enumerated powers, the elastic clause is said to grant *implicit* powers. After a fierce debate, the framers included this to assure the Congress some flexibility in legislating.

Section 9 lists what Congress *cannot* do. For example, the federal legislature cannot tax exported goods. Congress cannot take away the right of *habeas corpus* (the right to be formally charged after an arrest), cannot pass bills of attainder (legislative acts declaring one guilty of a crime), and cannot create *ex post facto* laws (making an act illegal after one has committed it). Nor can Congress grant any title of nobility. Section 10 lists powers the states are denied. States cannot, for example, enter into treaties with other countries, coin money, or tax exports.

The States

The terms of the **Tenth Amendment** (1791) distinguish the two governing spheres. The delegated powers (or expressed powers) are those the Constitution delegates to the federal government, listed in Article I, Section 8, and the job descriptions for the president and the courts in Articles II and III, respectively. The reserved powers are not specifically listed, and thus any powers not mentioned remain with the states. Some concurrent powers are held by authorities at both levels, state and federal.

The **Fourteenth Amendment** (1868) was created after the Civil War with the intention to protect freed slaves. It promises U.S. citizenship to anyone born or naturalized in the United States. The Fourteenth Amendment requires states to guarantee privileges and immunities to its own citizens as well as those from other states. The amendment's equal protection clause prohibits state governments from denying persons within their jurisdiction equal protection of the laws.

> All persons born or naturalized in the United States, and subject to the jurisdiction thereof, are citizens of the United States and of the state wherein they reside. No state shall make or enforce any law which shall abridge the privileges or immunities of citizens of the United States; nor shall any state deprive any person of life, liberty, or property, without due process of law; nor deny to any person within its jurisdiction the equal protection of the laws.
>
> —Fourteenth Amendment, U.S. Constitution

The Supreme Court Shapes Federalism

"Has the government of the United States power to make laws on every subject?" delegate John Marshall asked at the Virginia ratifying convention in Richmond in 1788. Then he quickly asserted that the new federal judiciary "would declare . . . void" any law going against the Constitution. In 1801, outgoing president John Adams appointed Marshall as chief justice of the Supreme Court. Taking the seat as Jefferson became president, Marshall and Jefferson served as leading rivals in the Federalist states' rights debate as the nation entered the 19th century. In 1819, the Supreme Court made a landmark decision in ***McCulloch v. Maryland***, addressing the balance of power between the states and the federal government.

MUST-KNOW SUPREME COURT CASES: *MCCULLOCH V. MARYLAND* (1819)

The Constitutional Question Before the Court:
Does the federal government have implied powers and supremacy under the necessary and proper (elastic) clause and the supremacy clause?

Decision: Yes, for McCulloch, 6:0

Facts: The powers and supremacy of the federal government were the focus of a Supreme Court case when the U.S. bank controversy arose again. The state of Maryland, among others, questioned the legality of a congressionally created bank in Baltimore, where James McCulloch was the chief cashier. The Constitution does not explicitly mention that Congress has the power "to create a bank." So Maryland, recognizing the state's authority over everything within its borders, passed a law requiring all banks in Maryland not incorporated by the state to pay a $15,000 tax. The purpose of this law was to force the U.S. bank out of the state and to overcome

Source: thinkstock
Chief Justice John Marshall

the federal government's power. When McCulloch refused to pay the tax, the state brought the case to court. On appeal, the case of *McCulloch v. Maryland* (1819) landed in John Marshall's Supreme Court.

The dispute centered on two central questions. One, can Congress create a bank? And two, can a state levy a tax on federal institutions?

Reasoning: Article I, Section 8, was key to answering the first question. It contains no expressed power for Congress to create a bank, Maryland and strict constructionists had argued. But it did contain the phrases "coin money," "borrow money," "collect taxes," determine "laws on bankruptcies," and "punish counterfeiting." Banking was therefore very much the federal government's business, and supporters argued it was constitutional under the necessary and proper clause. John Marshall's Court agreed unanimously. Marshall himself wrote the opinion.

Unanimous Opinion: We admit, as all must admit, that the powers of the Government are limited, and that its limits are not to be transcended. But we think the sound construction of the Constitution must allow to the national legislature that discretion with respect to the means by which the powers it confers are to be carried into execution which will enable that body to perform the high duties assigned to it in the manner most beneficial to the people. Let the end be legitimate, let it be within the scope of the Constitution, and all means which are appropriate, which are plainly adapted to that end, which are not prohibited, but consist with the letter and spirit of the Constitution, are Constitutional. . . .

The word "necessary" is considered as controlling the [elastic clause], and as limiting the right to pass laws for the execution of the granted powers to such as are indispensable, and without which the power would be nugatory [worthless].

To answer the second question—can a state tax a federal institution—the Court declared, "The power to tax involves the power to destroy." It broadened what Congress could do, denoting its **implied powers** in the Constitution (those not specifically listed in the Constitution but deriving from the elastic clause), and it declared that constitutional federal law will override state law.

The sovereignty of a State extends to everything which exists by its own authority or is introduced by its permission, but does it extend to those means which are employed by Congress to carry into execution powers conferred on that body by the people of the United States? We think it demonstrable that it does not. Those powers are not given by the people of a single State. They are given by the people of the United States, to a Government whose laws, made in pursuance of the Constitution, are declared to be supreme. Consequently, the people of a single State cannot confer a sovereignty which will extend over them.

Since *McCulloch v. Maryland*: The federal government has used its powers implied in the necessary and proper clause to play a role in other matters, such as education, health, welfare, disaster relief, and economic planning. In *Gibbons v. Ogden* (1824), a dispute between New York and the federal government over navigation rights on the Hudson River, the Court looked to Article I, Section 8, Clause 3—the **commerce clause**—to certify Congress's authority over most commercial activity as well. That interpretation of the commerce clause, as well as the interpretation of the necessary and proper clause and other enumerated and implied powers in *McCulloch v. Maryland*, became the centerpiece of the debate over the balance of power between the national and state governments.

Political Science Disciplinary Practices: Analyze and Interpret Supreme Court Decisions

Apply: Write an essay in which you identify the two constitutional questions addressed in *McCulloch v. Maryland* and explain the reasoning for the answer to each question. Cite specific passages from the opinion and/or the Constitution to back up your explanation.

Finally, explain how the opinion relates to political processes and behavior. For example, what impact did it have on the development of the growing nation?

Dual Federalism and Selective Exclusiveness Since the national government did not engage in too much legislation regarding commerce at the time, the *Gibbons* decision eventually led to a system of **dual federalism**, in which the national government is supreme in its sphere—having the authority given it in Article I—and the states are equally supreme in their own sphere. Article I entitled Congress to legislate on commerce "among the states" while it did not forbid the states from regulating commerce within their borders. Chief Justice Marshall did qualify that states still had some rights to commerce, rejecting an exclusive national authority over internal, intrastate commercial activity. This became known as **selective exclusiveness**—a doctrine asserting that Congress may regulate only when the commodity requires a national uniform rule. For years, this system worked because commerce and trade were mainly local, with fewer goods crossing state lines than they do today. Congress's relative inaction in regulating commerce until the Industrial Revolution during the mid-1700s to the mid-1800s allowed dual federalism to prevail. As the nation's business, manufacturing, transportation, and communication capabilities advanced, Congress became more and more interested in legislating business matters. Organized labor, reformers, and progressive leaders focused the national agenda on regulating railroads, factories, and banks and on breaking up monopolies. On some occasions, the federal government crossed into the states' domain on the strength of the commerce clause—the most frequently contested congressional power—and on some occasions lost.

National Concerns, State Obligations

State and federal governments generally followed dual federalism into the early 20th century. However, this practice gave way in response to changing societal needs as Congress's increased use of the commerce clause empowered it to legislate on a variety of state concerns.

The Progressive movement (1890–1920) brought much federal legislation that created a power play over commerce authority. In the early 1900s, democracy became stronger through a variety of government reforms. The Sixteenth Amendment, for example, created the federal income tax and expanded Congress's reach of regulation.

As the nation grew and citizens became more mobile, the nation's problems, much like its goods, began to travel across state borders. The police powers originally left up to the states now became national in scope, and Congress created the Federal Bureau of Investigation (FBI). Reformers pressured Congress to act on issues when states refused or could not act. Since the Constitution nowhere gave Congress the direct power to legislate to improve safety, health, and morals, it began to rely on its regulatory power over commerce to reach national goals of decreasing crime, making the workplace safer, and ensuring equality among citizens. The commerce clause served as the primary vehicle for such legislation. For example, the Mann Act of 1910 forbade the transportation of women across state lines for immoral purposes to crack down on prostitution. The Automobile Theft Act of 1915 made it a federal offense to knowingly drive a stolen car across state lines. Since then, Congress has made racketeering, drug dealing, and bank robbery federal crimes (though they remain illegal at the state level as well). The federal executive can enforce these laws even if the criminal activity is entirely contained in one state.

The Supreme Court Stretches the Commerce Clause

The Supreme Court, however, disappointed reformers and issued a few setbacks. In the late 1800s and early 1900s, a conservative Court declared that corporations as well as individuals were protected by the Constitution, and it questioned many health and safety regulations through the era. For example, when Congress passed a law prohibiting a company from hiring and forcing children to work in factories, the Supreme Court blocked it. In *Hammer v. Dagenhart* (1918), the Court ruled that the evils of child labor were entirely in the sphere of manufacturing, not commerce, and child labor was thus outside congressional authority. This ruling established a line between manufacturing as the creation of goods and commerce as the exchange of goods. By the 1920s, however, the Court relied on Justice Oliver Wendell Holmes's words, which said the shipment of cattle from one state to another for slaughter and sale constituted "a typical, constantly recurring course" and thus made both production and commerce subject to national authority.

Numerous pieces of New Deal legislation caused a power play between the Supreme Court and Congress regarding the commerce clause. The Fair Labor Standards Act of 1938 barred commerce across state lines for firms failing to pay employees at least $0.25 per hour. The Court upheld the act and overturned the *Hammer* decision.

Source: Lewis Wickes Hine, Library of Congress

The Court's decision in *Hammer v. Dagenhart* (1918) put children who worked in manufacturing, sometimes against their will, beyond the jurisdiction of the federal government. That decision was later overturned.

THINK AS A POLITICAL SCIENTIST: *DESCRIBE THE REASONING OF A REQUIRED SUPREME COURT CASE*

In 1941, in *United States v. Darby*, the Supreme Court upheld the Fair Labor Standards Act of 1938 and with that decision also overturned *Hammer v. Dagenhart*. "We conclude," wrote Mr. Justice Stone in the unanimous opinion, "that the prohibition of the shipment interstate of goods produced under the forbidden substandard labor conditions is within the constitutional authority of Congress." One case to which the decision refers is *McCulloch v. Maryland* (pages 68–69).

Practice: Read another excerpt from the decision in *United States v. Darby* and answer the questions that follow.

> "There remains the question whether such restriction on the production of goods for commerce is a permissible exercise of the commerce power." Referring to the ruling in *McCulloch v. Maryland*, Stone explains, "The power of Congress over interstate commerce is not confined to the regulation of commerce among the states. It extends to those activities intrastate which so affect interstate commerce or the exercise of the power of Congress over it as to make regulation of them appropriate means to the attainment of a legitimate end, the exercise of the granted power of Congress to regulate interstate commerce."

1. Describe the reasoning in *McCulloch v. Maryland* to which the opinion refers.
2. Explain a similarity or difference in how the two decisions interpret the Commerce Clause.

Two centuries of Court interpretations, a drastic turn by the Court to broaden the scope of the commerce clause, changing societal needs, and prevailing attitudes of the last two generations have shaped American federalism into its current form. Congress has won more battles than the states in claiming authority on commerce-related legislation. But as you will see in the ***United States v. Lopez*** (1995) case, the Court does not always allow Congress to legislate under the guise of regulating commerce.

MUST-KNOW SUPREME COURT CASES: *UNITED STATES V. LOPEZ* (1995)

The Constitutional Question Before the Court: Does Congress have the authority under the commerce clause to outlaw guns near schools?

Decision: No, for Lopez, 5:4

Before *United States v. Lopez*: *Gibbons v. Ogden* (1824) broadened the authority of the federal government to control commerce.

Facts: Congress passed the Gun-Free School Zones Act in 1990 in hopes of preventing gun violence at or near schools. In 1992, senior Alfonso Lopez carried a .38 caliber handgun and bullets into a San Antonio high school. On an anonymous tip, school authorities confronted him, obtained the gun, and reported the infraction to the federal police. Lopez was indicted, tried, and sentenced in federal court for violating the statute. He challenged the ruling in the Supreme Court on the grounds that the federal government has no right to regulate specific behavior at a state-run school. The United States argued that the connections of guns and drug dealing put this area under federal jurisdiction and Congress's commerce power.

Reasoning: The Court sided with Lopez, refusing to let Congress invoke the commerce clause. "It is difficult to perceive any limitation on federal power," Chief Justice William Rehnquist wrote. "If we were to accept the Government's arguments, we are hard pressed to posit any activity by an individual that Congress is without power to regulate." Congress had stretched its commerce power too far. Most states have regulations on guns and where firearms can legally be carried. The states are where the Supreme Court said this authority should stay, ushering in a new phase of federalism that recognized the importance of state sovereignty and local control.

Chief Justice William Rehnquist, joined by justices O'Connor, Scalia, Kennedy, and Thomas, wrote the majority opinion arguing that a gun near school property does not have an impact on interstate commerce and is therefore not covered by the commerce clause.

Majority Opinion: The possession of a gun in a local school zone is in no sense an economic activity that might, through repetition elsewhere, substantially affect any sort of interstate commerce. Respondent was a local student at a local school; there is no indication that he had recently moved in interstate commerce, and there is no requirement that his possession of the firearm have any concrete tie to interstate commerce.

There were also two concurring and three dissenting opinions.

Concurring Opinions: Justice Anthony Kennedy, joined by Justice Sandra Day O'Connor, focused on the nature of commerce, the obligation of the government not to tip the balance of power, and the state's control over education. Justice Clarence Thomas's concurring opinion argued that recent cases have drifted too far from the Constitution in their interpretation of the commerce clause and that if something substantially affects interstate commerce, Congress could pass laws that regulated every aspect of human existence.

Dissenting Opinions: Justice John Paul Stevens's dissent argued that the possession of guns is the result of commercial activity and is therefore under the authority of the commerce clause. Justice David Souter's dissent argued that the majority opinion is a throwback to earlier times and goes against precedent. Justice Breyer's dissent, with which Justice Stevens, Justice Souter, and Justice Ruth Bader Ginsburg joined, argued in part that given the effect of education upon interstate commerce, gun-related violence in and around schools is a commercial as well as human problem, since a decline in the quality of education has an adverse effect on commerce.

Since _United States v. Lopez_: Congress revised the federal Gun-Free School Zones Act in 1994 so that it would tie more clearly to interstate commerce. That law withholds federal funding for schools that do not adopt a zero-tolerance law for guns in school zones.

Political Science Disciplinary Practices: Analyze and Interpret Supreme Court Decisions

The full opinion of the divided court in the case of _United States v. Lopez_ is available online. Refer to it as you work in small groups (or as your teacher directs) to understand the reasoning behind the various opinions. Different groups should study the reasoning behind the majority opinion, the concurring opinions, and the dissenting opinions and report a summary back to the class.

Apply: When studying your portion of the ruling, you may find the reading challenging. Take it slowly and make notes to yourself with any questions. Identify key passages in your portion of the ruling and use them as evidence to explain your interpretation. Discuss your understanding with your group until each member is clear on the main ideas. Then decide on a way to present your summary to the class and share the tasks in carrying that plan out.

After each group has made its presentation, discuss ways in which the concurring opinions and dissenting opinions are similar and different. Are there any points on which they all agree?

Related Case: How does the interpretation of the commerce clause in the majority opinion in *United States v. Lopez* compare to the interpretation of the commerce clause in *Gibbons v. Ogden*?

The commerce clause continued to be challenged. Congress passed the Violence Against Women Act in 1994 under the commerce clause on the basis that domestic violence had a significant cost for taxpayers in the form of health care, criminal justice expenses, and other costs. In 2000, in ruling on the case of *United States v. Morrison*, the Supreme Court stated the commerce clause was inappropriately used to legislate against domestic violence and struck down parts of the Violence Against Women Act. Chief Justice William Rehnquist stated, in the 5:4 majority opinion, that crimes of domestic violence were not economic in nature. He further explained that the Fourteenth Amendment didn't give Congress the authority to pass the law as a civil rights remedy, which is under the jurisdiction of the states.

REFLECT ON THE ESSENTIAL QUESTION

Essential Question: *How has a balance of power between national and state governments been interpreted over time? On separate paper, complete a chart like the one below.*

Examples of Interpretation Limiting Federal Power	Examples of Interpretation Limiting State Power

KEY TERMS AND NAMES

commerce clause

dual federalism

elastic clause

enumerated powers

Fourteenth Amendment (1868)

implied powers

McCulloch v. Maryland (1819)

necessary and proper clause

selective exclusiveness

Tenth Amendment (1791)

United States v. Lopez (1995)

Federalism in Action

*"Pollution doesn't respect state boundaries, and it is difficult if not
impossible to solve these problems on a state-by-state basis."*
—S. William Becker, National Association of Clean Air Agencies,
New York Times, 1989

Essential Question: How does the distribution of powers among three
federal branches and between national and state governments impact
policymaking?

Air pollution affects citizens across states. However, states have passed laws
and set up governing agencies to monitor their air and streams. Congress,
the national executive branch, and the federal courts have also had a role in
shaping environmental policy and regulating industry. This distribution of
power among the three national branches and between the federal and state
governments allows for multiple access points for stakeholders and institutions
to address environmental policy through federalism.

The Sharing of Powers

You may have heard people complain about how slow the national government
is to get anything done. In fact, the sharing of powers between and among the
three branches and the state governments does constrain national policymaking
and slow it down, an outcome many framers of the new Constitution sought in
order to protect the nation from popular but possibly rash policies.

Environmental Policymaking

Environmental policy provides a useful case in point for seeing how different
stakeholders compete. **BIG IDEA** Multiple actors and institutions interact to
produce and implement possible policies.

Executive Branch and Background on Environmental Policy The
executive branch provided the initial impetus for environmental policy.
President Teddy Roosevelt (1901–1909) is known as "the conservationist
president" because of his appreciation of and devotion to the natural beauty
and resources of the United States. During his presidency, 230 million acres of
land were set aside as public lands. One reason Roosevelt was able to achieve
so much environmental protection was that he believed the president was "the
steward of the people" who could claim broad powers to advance the good of

the American people. Congress was needed to establish national parks, but Roosevelt was able to hasten the protection of public lands by exercising his executive authority to establish national monuments. The Grand Canyon, now a national park, was originally established as a national monument by Teddy Roosevelt. National parks and forest preserves became mainstays on our American landscape.

Congress and Environmental Legislation It was not until the 1960s and 1970s that the environmental movement took off among the public, and Congress itself began to strongly regulate industry to assist this effort. As Congress imposed environmental standards, the business community opposed regulations. Over the ensuing decades, environmental policy in the United States became a competition between environmental activists and conservative free-market thinkers.

The National Environmental Policy Act (1970) requires any government agency, state or federal, to file an environmental impact statement with the federal government every time the agency plans a policy that might harm the environment, dams, roads, or existing construction. The 1970 amendments to the Air Pollution Control Act, commonly known as the **Clean Air Act**, call for improved air quality and decreased contaminants. The act ultimately requires the Department of Transportation to reduce automobile emissions. The **Clean Water Act** of 1972 regulates the discharges of pollutants into the waters of the United States and monitors quality standards for surface waters. The **Endangered Species Act** established a program that empowers the National Fish and Wildlife Service to protect endangered species.

After the catastrophic Love Canal toxic waste disaster in western New York in the mid-1970s, the federal government forced industry to pay for the insurance necessary to manage their dangerous by-products. In that disaster, a company had dumped toxic chemicals in the area that later became a residential development. Heavy rains washed some of the chemicals out of the ground into residential basements and yards. Adults and children developed serious liver, kidney, and other health problems. The company responsible for this major environmental catastrophe had already gone out of business. In response, Congress created the Superfund. Essentially, industry pays into the Superfund as insurance so taxpayers do not have to pay the bill for waste cleanup. Under the law, the guilty polluter pays for the cleanup, but when the guilty party is unknown or bankrupt, the collective fund will cover these costs, not the taxpayer.

Clashes Between Branches Over Environmental Policy Since 1970, the Environmental Protection Agency and the federal government have required states to set air quality standards, to reduce the damage done by automobiles, to measure city smog, and to set environmental guidelines. The EPA oversees the Superfund and toxic waste cleanup.

In 2012, the EPA established limits on how much mercury and other hazardous chemicals coal- and oil-fueled power plants could emit, asserting that although limiting these emissions would cost the plants nearly $10 billion, the cost should not be a factor since the risk of the emissions to human health justified the regulation. Exercising a countervailing force, however, the Supreme Court overturned that regulation in 2015, arguing that the EPA had unreasonably neglected to consider the cost burden to the power plants and customers and exerting a check and balance to the EPA.

Disagreements Over Climate Change The burning of fossil fuels and the resulting greenhouse gases have heightened attention to global warming, an increase in average global temperatures. Melting polar ice caps, unusual flooding in certain areas, animal habitat destruction, and a damaged ozone layer have caused the scientific community, including the Intergovernmental Panel on Climate Change, to conclude that the use of these damaging fuels should be limited and regulated. One international attempt to combat this problem came with the 1997 **Kyoto Protocol**, a multi-country agreement that committed the signing nations to reduced greenhouse gas emissions. Most industrialized nations joined the treaty, and U.S. President Bill Clinton agreed to it. However, the conservative-leaning U.S. Senate at the time did not achieve the two-thirds support necessary for ratification, so the United States did not sign the treaty.

During President Obama's tenure, the Senate remained conservative-leaning, constraining the power of the government to join another international climate agreement, the 2015 **Paris Agreement**. President Obama sought to go around this constraint by making acceptance of membership in the agreement a matter of executive order, without the approval of the Senate. In 2017, President Trump used the same bypass method to withdraw from the Paris Agreement, though some argued that the United States was never officially a member of the Paris Agreement since the Senate did not have a voice in deciding.

State Initiatives In response to Trump's decision, a number of states decided to adhere to the guidelines in the Paris Agreement anyway, demonstrating yet another check and balance in the federal system. In 2017, for example, California passed legislation to extend its program to reduce carbon emissions, known as cap and trade, from its original expiration date of 2020 to 2030. Using powers granted to states by the Tenth Amendment, California law states companies must buy permits to release greenhouse gas emissions.

Political Participation and Policymaking

Multiple access points for input into policy decisions are available at all levels of governments. A number of policy accomplishments owe their success to the active engagement and participation of citizens. (See Topic 4.8.)

Legalizing Marijuana

The movement to legalize marijuana is a good example of how policy reflects the attitudes of citizens who choose to participate at a given time and the balancing act between individual liberty and social order. A gradual but consistent change in public opinion over the past 20 years, especially by younger voters, has caused a fairly consistent state-by-state path of legalizing medical marijuana.

Order Over Liberty Marijuana, or cannabis, entered the United States in large amounts with Mexican immigrants who came across the border after the Mexican Revolution of 1910. As the substance moved further into the country, states, exercising their police powers, began outlawing marijuana.

Congressional Policy The federal government first acted with a 1932 policy, the Uniform State Narcotics Act, which strongly urged states to make marijuana and other drugs illegal. Meanwhile, a propaganda campaign that reached a peak with the release of the film *Reefer Madness* brought attention to the drug and alleged that cannabis caused users to become deranged. In 1937, the House of Representatives held hearings on the issue; only the American Medical Association spoke against criminalizing marijuana because there was no evidence it was anything more than a mild intoxicant. After only a half hour of floor debate, the House passed the 1937 Marijuana Tax Act in an effort to regulate the substance. By the end of the 1930s, most states and Congress had criminalized marijuana. Drug enforcement, other than interstate drug trafficking, was largely handled by state and local police.

Source: Wikimedia Commons

The film *Reefer Madness* placed the blame for all the lurid crimes in the story on cannabis.

The 1960s counterculture brought further attention to drug use and abuse. By 1970, the **Controlled Substances Act**, a comprehensive federal drug policy that was part of President Richard Nixon's war on drugs, was the first federal law with any teeth to enforce and heavily punish marijuana dealers and users. The law categorized heroin, cocaine, and other illegal substances in terms of potential harm and placed marijuana in the same category with no medical benefits. At the time, the Gallup organization found that only about 12 percent of respondents thought it should be legal.

Citizen Influence Balancing Liberty and Order Through the 1970s and 1980s, attitudes toward pot slowly shifted. Advocates for legalizing marijuana formed the special interest group National Organization for the Reform of Marijuana Laws (NORML) in 1970. Other advocacy groups formed as well.

Additional research and public education through advocacy brought growing acceptance of marijuana use. Some states began to decriminalize (keeping the drug illegal, but reducing punishments, in some cases down to a small fine for a small amount), as the trajectory toward acceptance and legalization grew. Some in the medical community recognized its palliative properties for patients with glaucoma, depression, and other conditions and helped strengthen a movement to legalize the plant for medical purposes.

California became the first state to legalize medicinal marijuana through a statewide vote, Proposition 215, in 1996—participatory democracy at work. Over the next two decades, additional states legalized marijuana by ballot measures. As citizens legalized, more state legislatures have taken up similar bills and approved them. In October 2013, one year after full legalization in Colorado and Washington state, Gallup reported for the first time that a majority of Americans supported legalizing pot.

Not every state that has sought to legalize pot has succeeded. Ohio placed an initiative on the ballot in 2015 that failed to pass by a vote of 65 to 35 percent. Analysts believe that the measure's attempt to legalize both medical and recreational pot at the same time may have brought its failure, since changes in government policy are usually incremental baby steps toward what might in time become sweeping policy change.

THINK AS A POLITICAL SCIENTIST: *SUPPORT AN ARGUMENT USING RELEVANT EVIDENCE*

An argument, or claim, is a statement that can be supported by facts or evidence. The more relevant evidence that can be presented, the stronger the argument is considered.

Practice: In a paragraph, support the following argument using evidence and examples from Topic 1.9.

Argument: The policymaking process built into the Constitution—drawing on checks and balances among the executive, legislative, and judicial branches of the federal government and the sharing of powers with the states—ensures that many stakeholders and institutions can influence public policy.

Presidential and Judicial Policymaking The 1970 Controlled Substances Act remains federal law. What happens, then, when a state legalizes marijuana while the drug remains illegal at the national level? The answer depends on whom you ask, which level and branch of government are being asked, and the political mood of the nation and states.

As the legalization movement was under way, but before it had crossed a tipping point, federal authorities in Republican President George W. Bush's administration began a crackdown on marijuana growing operations and medical marijuana dispensaries in California. Legalization advocates and patients sued the federal government, arguing that states had the authority under the Tenth Amendment and the police powers doctrine to determine the status of the drug's legality. However, on appeal, in *Gonzales v. Raich* (2005), the Supreme Court ruled that the Constitution's commerce clause entitles Congress to determine what may be bought and sold. Thus, federal marijuana crimes were upheld.

Though that precedent still stands, the Justice Department under Democratic President Barack Obama and Attorney General Eric Holder took a different approach. Through his eight years as president, eight states—those laboratories of democracy—legalized recreational marijuana. In 2014, the attorney general announced the Obama administration's revised approach to enforcing marijuana violations. In doing so, he did not rewrite the law. Holder did, however, declare that the Justice Department would not use federal resources to crack down on selling or using the drug in states where voters had democratically deemed marijuana legal. Ultimately, federal arrests for marijuana became nearly nonexistent.

Until recently, Democrats and Independents supported legalization more than Republicans. However, as Gallup reports, most Republicans now support legalizing marijuana. The policy debate on legalization and how federal law would be enforced surfaced in the 2016 primary and general elections for president with a variety of responses from candidates in both parties. After Donald Trump took office and Attorney General Jeff Sessions—an anti-drug conservative—was sworn in, pot users and medical marijuana proponents watched closely.

During the Trump administration, the Department of Justice under Attorney General Jeff Sessions declared that local U.S. attorneys—those presidentially appointed prosecutors who bring federal crime cases to court in their districts across the country—shall be the local determiners of how federal marijuana policy is handled. In fact, the Justice Department attorneys and the FBI deal with a variety of federal crimes on a daily basis and decide whether to prosecute and which crimes are higher on their priority list. This inconsistency from administration to administration may be confusing and destabilizing to some, but it is an inevitable element of administrative discretion.

Shared Policymaking in Education

Topic 1.5 covered the interactions of the federal and state governments in determining education policy. The chart below summarizes some of the interactions.

DIFFERENT GOVERNMENT ENTITIES SHAPE EDUCATIONAL POLICY		
Government Action	Description of Action	Deciding Body
Brown v. Board of Education (1954) (See Topic 3.11.)	The Supreme Court ruled that segregation in public education was unconstitutional.	Federal Supreme Court
Elementary and Secondary Education Act (1965)	Federal funding was offered to states if they met requirements in sections, or titles, of the act.	U.S. Congress in cooperation with state governments
No Child Left Behind (2002)	States were held more accountable for student achievement (standardized testing) under federal supervision.	U.S. Congress
Every Student Succeeds Act (2015)	The act kept student achievement standards but returned accountability largely back to the states.	U.S. Congress and state governments

Source: Florida Stop Common Core Coalition

In response to the Race to the Top initiative, many states adopted the Common Core State Standards. Members of the Florida Stop Common Core Coalition and Florida Parents R.I.S.E., like citizens in many other states, protested these standards, believing their adoption weakened local control of education and allowed the federal government to overreach. State decisions such as these provided an access point for citizens to make their voices heard.

REFLECT ON THE ESSENTIAL QUESTION

Essential Question: *How does the distribution of powers among three federal branches and between national and state governments impact policymaking? On separate paper, complete a chart like the one below.*

Constitutional Approach to Federalism	Federalism in Action

KEY TERMS, NAMES, AND EVENTS

Clean Air Act (1970)

Clean Water Act (1972)

Controlled Substances Act (1970)

Elementary and Secondary Education Act (1965)

Endangered Species Act (1973)

Every Student Succeeds Act (2015)

Kyoto Protocol (1997)

National Environmental Protection Act (1972)

No Child Left Behind Act (2002)

Paris Agreement (2015)

CHAPTER 3 Review:
Learning Objectives and Key Terms

TOPIC 1.7: Explain how societal needs affect the constitutional allocation of power between the national and state governments. (CON-2.A)

Exclusive and Concurrent Powers of National and State Governments (CON-2.A.1)	Distribution of Power to Meet Societal Needs (CON-2.A.2)
concurrent powers	block grants
Defense of Marriage Act (1996)	categorical grants
exclusive powers	cooperative federalism
extradition	devolution
federalism	federal grants
full faith and credit	fiscal federalism
police powers	grant-in-aid programs
privileges and immunities	mandates
supremacy clause	Personal Responsibility and Work Opportunity Reconciliation Act (1996)
	revenue sharing
	strings

TOPIC 1.8: Explain how the appropriate balance of power between national and state governments has been interpreted differently over time. (CON-2.B)

Balance of Power between National and State Governments (CON-2.B.1)	necessary and proper clause
commerce clause	selective exclusiveness
dual federalism	Tenth Amendment (1791)
elastic clause	
enumerated powers	**Judicial Interpretation of Balance of Power (CON-2.B.2)**
Fourteenth Amendment (1868)	*McCulloch v. Maryland* (1819)
implied powers	*United States v. Lopez* (1995)

TOPIC 1.9: Explain the principles of separation of power and "checks and balances" and their implication for the U.S. political system. (PMI-1.A, PMI-1.B)

Access Points to Influence Public Policy (CON-2.C.1)	Constraints on Policymaking Due to Sharing of Powers (CON-2.C.2)
Clean Air Act (1970)	Controlled Substances Act (1970)
Clean Water Act (1972)	Elementary and Secondary Education Act (1965)
Endangered Species Act (1973)	Every Student Succeeds Act (2015)
Kyoto Protocol (1997)	No Child Left Behind (2002)
Paris Agreement (2015)	

CHAPTER 3 Checkpoint: Federalism

Topics 1.7–1.9

MULTIPLE-CHOICE QUESTIONS

1. Which of the following statements accurately describes federalism?
   (A) It is a governing system that places a national authority above regional authority.
   (B) It ranks the sovereignty of the states over the power of the national government.
   (C) It is a balance of powers between state and local governments.
   (D) It is a sharing of powers between national and state governments.

2. In the *McCulloch v. Maryland* (1819) decision, which two provisions in the Constitution were upheld and strengthened?
   (A) Congress's power to regulate commerce and its power to levy taxes
   (B) The necessary and proper clause and the supremacy clause
   (C) The First and Tenth amendments
   (D) The president's power to nominate justices and negotiate treaties

Questions 3 and 4 refer to the following table.

FEDERAL GRANTS FROM THE TOP FIVE DEPARTMENTS, FY 2011	
Department of Health and Human Services	$332 Billion
Department of Transportation	$25.7 Billion
Department of Agriculture	$23.3 Billion
Department of Education	$17.3 Billion
Department of Housing and Urban Development	$6.7 Billion

Source: www.usaspending.gov

3. Which of the following statements is reflected in the table above?
   (A) Education and agricultural needs receive the most federal grant money.
   (B) Federalism prevents the national government from assisting with state responsibilities.
   (C) Grants appear to assist urban development, not agricultural interests.
   (D) Medical and social needs receive the most federal grant money.

4. Which governmental concept most likely results in lower funding for Education and Housing and Urban Development than for the other departments?

(A) Checks and balances prevent funding of these concerns.

(B) Federalism encourages states and localities to provide primary support for these services.

(C) Judicial review and court decisions have rendered government unable to provide these services.

(D) Separation of powers results in lower funding of these concerns.

Questions 5 and 6 refer to the following cartoon.

" WAIT A MINUTE! THIS PARKING METER HAS SLOTS FOR THE CITY, COUNTY, STATE AND FEDS."

5. Which of the following statements best describes the message expressed in the cartoon?

(A) Government overlap creates too many taxes and fees at multiple levels.

(B) Taxpayers are obligated to support multiple levels of government.

(C) Regulations for transportation and safety should be at the state level.

(D) Taxes and fees will be collected at convenient times.

6. Which of the following concepts would the cartoonist most likely support?

(A) Commercial development

(B) Devolution

(C) Categorical grants

(D) Mandates

Concept Application

1. "In this present crisis, government is not the solution to our problem; government is the problem. From time to time we've been tempted to believe that society has become too complex to be managed by self-rule, that government by an elite group is superior to government for, by, and of the people. Well, if no one among us is capable of governing himself, then who among us has the capacity to govern someone else? All of us together, in and out of government, must bear the burden. The solutions we seek must be equitable, with no one group singled out to pay a higher price."

    —President Ronald Reagan, First Inaugural Address,
    January 20, 1981

    After reading the excerpt, respond to A, B, and C:

    (A) Describe the political institution Reagan identifies as the problem.

    (B) In the context of the scenario, explain how the power of the institution described in part A can be affected by its interaction with the U.S. Supreme Court.

    (C) In the context of the excerpt, explain actions the public can take to influence the political institution described in part A.

Quantitative Analysis

DEPARTMENT OF TRANSPORTATION GRANT ACCOUNTS FISCAL YEAR 2016 (IN MILLIONS OF DOLLARS)	
Account	**Amount**
National Infrastructure Improvement	500
Grants-in-Aid to Airports	3,350
Federal Aid Highway Program	42,671
Motor Carrier Safety Grants	313
Highway Traffic Safety Grants	547
Grants to Amtrak & Rail Safety Grants	1,440
Formula Grants	9,348
Capital Investment Grants	2,177
Capital & Preventative Maintenance Grants	150
Assistance to Small Shipyards	5
Emergency Preparedness Grants	28
Total Grant Accounts	60,529
Total D.O.T. Funding	75,003

Source: U.S. Department of Transportation

2. Use the information graphic on the previous page to answer the following questions.

(A) Identify how much the Department of Transportation spends.

(B) Describe the difference between the largest and smallest grants.

(C) Draw a conclusion about this difference.

(D) Explain how Department of Transportation funding demonstrates the principle of federalism.

SCOTUS Comparison

3. In 1996, California legalized medical marijuana. However, that state law conflicted with the federal Controlled Substances Act, which made the possession of marijuana illegal. When federal agents from the Drug Enforcement Agency confiscated the drug from a medical marijuana user's home, a group of people prescribed medical marijuana sued the federal government. They argued that the Controlled Substances Act exceeded the government's authority since the use of medical marijuana was within the state of California, not between states.

The case reached the Supreme Court in 2004 as *Gonzales v. Raich*. The Court ruled 6:3 that the government did have authority to prohibit medical marijuana possession and use, even though it was legal in California. It reasoned that since marijuana sales are part of a national market, the federal government can control marijuana possession.

(A) Identify the constitutional clause that is common to both *Gonzales v. Raich* (2004) and *United States v. Lopez* (1995).

(B) Based on the constitutional clause identified in part A, explain why the facts of *Gonzales v. Raich* led to a different holding from the holding in *United States v. Lopez*.

(C) Describe an action that California users of medical marijuana might take to limit the impact of the ruling in *Gonzales v. Raich*.

Revolutionaries and American leaders established the United States government, which culminated in the creation of the Constitution. The same concerns that brought independence—a lack of representation, an autocratic centralized government, and violations of liberties—coupled with powerful political theory from Enlightenment philosophers shaped the design of the U.S. government. After a failed experiment under the Articles of Confederation, leaders created a new federal government that was national in character.

The union of states assumed unique and limited powers, the states assumed others, and some powers were concurrent. The "necessary and proper" clause, Congress's right to regulate interstate commerce, the full faith and credit clause, and the Tenth Amendment guide federalism. Starting with *McCulloch v. Maryland*, the Supreme Court has more often emboldened Congress's commerce power and authority; and the federal government, through grants and mandates, has created and funded national initiatives in spite of some overlap with states' reserved powers. In more recent years, however, Congress has slowed this trend and devolved some powers back on the states.

Since 1789, the Constitution, its alterations, and its government have endured. The written, transparent guidelines for government have allowed the United States to operate largely uninterrupted on the same basic plan. Never has the country missed an election. Leaders have been democratically pushed out of office without bloodshed. And our courts have settled intense, divisive matters of law to solve national crises.

MULTIPLE-CHOICE QUESTIONS

Questions 1 and 2 refer to the passage below.

Mr. Chairman, I come before the committee with no agenda. I have no platform. Judges are not politicians who can promise to do certain things in exchange for votes. I have no agenda, but I do have a commitment. If I am confirmed, I will confront every case with an open mind. I will fully and fairly analyze the legal arguments that are presented. I will be open to the considered views of my colleagues on the bench. And I will decide every case based on the record, according to the rule of law, without fear or favor, to the best of my ability. And I will remember that it's my job to call balls and strikes and not to pitch or bat.

—Federal Judge John Roberts, U.S. Supreme Court Chief
Justice confirmation hearing, 2005

1. What is this Supreme Court chief justice nominee's main point in his opening remarks?

(A) More legislative power should be in the hands of the judicial branch.

(B) Judicial review must be limited to keep from expanding the power of the judiciary.

(C) Federal judges must be impartial when contemplating shaping the law.

(D) Federal courts have leverage over the other branches of government.

2. Justice Robert's appearance before this committee illustrates the constitutional concept of

(A) Elastic powers

(B) Veto and two-thirds override

(C) Reserved powers

(D) Advice and consent

Questions 3 and 4 refer to the chart below.

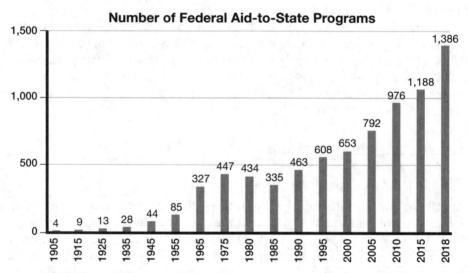

Number of Federal Aid-to-State Programs

Source: Cato Institute, 2019

3. Which of the following describes the information in the chart?

   (A) The programs that provided federal aid-to-state did not exist before 1905.

   (B) The number of federal aid-to-state programs has increased in most of the years shown.

   (C) The trend in the number of federal programs is a result of globalization.

   (D) The trend in the graph is a result of cutbacks in federal spending.

4. Which of the following is the most likely contributor to the trend in the chart?

   (A) The increase in policy areas the national government influences.

   (B) The increase in conservative beliefs, such as devolution in the 1970s.

   (C) The increase in grants were a result of the decision in *United States v. Lopez* (1995).

   (D) The increase in block grants resulting in fewer categorical grants.

5. Which of the following constitutional provisions most reflects federalism?

   (A) Equality clause

   (B) Supremacy clause

   (C) Article III

   (D) Tenth Amendment

6. Which of the following is an accurate comparison of Federalists and Anti-Federalists?

	Federalists	Anti-Federalists
(A)	Wanted to remain with Great Britain	Wanted states to have a greater degree of sovereignty
(B)	Wanted a stronger national government	More common among the merchant class
(C)	Patrick Henry was an outspoken leader	Favored the necessary and proper clause and supremacy clause
(D)	Argued for the ratification of the Constitution	Supported a bill of rights

Questions 7 and 8 refer to the map below.

**Seats in the House of Representatives
First Congress, 1789**

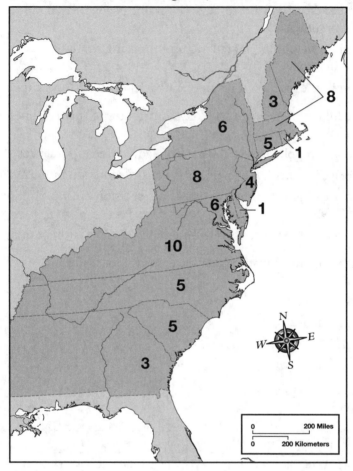

7. Which of the following statements best explains the information in
   the map?

   (A) States with the higher number of seats were controlled by
       Federalists.

   (B) Some states were so sparsely populated that they received no votes.

   (C) The population of enslaved people had little impact on these
       numbers.

   (D) The geographical size of the state does not determine the number of
       seats allotted to it.

8. Which of the following types of representative democracy is best reflected in the map?

(A) Pluralist democracy

(B) Elite democracy

(C) Participatory democracy

(D) Federal democracy

9. Which of the following is an accurate comparison of federal block grants and categorical grants?

	Block Grants	Categorical Grants
(A)	Let members of Congress control how to spend money in their districts	Give states control over how to spend federal money locally
(B)	Lead to loss of congressional oversight on spending grant money	Require states or localities to meet certain criteria
(C)	Are used primarily to combat terrorism at the local level	Are available to state governments but not city governments
(D)	Specify how the grant money is to be spent	Have declined in favor of block grants

10. More than half the members of Congress believe the legal driving age should be 18, because statistics show that drivers under 18 have many more accidents than those 18 and older. Which of the following is the most practical and lasting action Congress can take to address this issue?

(A) Urge the president to issue an executive order requiring drivers to be at least 18 years old.

(B) Mandate states to set the driving age at 18 and then withhold highway funds from any state that does not comply.

(C) Convince the Supreme Court that Congress, not the states, should regulate driving laws.

(D) Distribute educational materials on the issue to state legislatures.

Questions 11 and 12 refer to the infographic below.

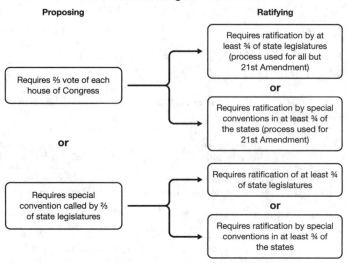

Article 5: Amending the Constitution

Proposing   Ratifying

Requires ⅔ vote of each house of Congress

Requires ratification by at least ¾ of state legislatures (process used for all but 21st Amendment)

or

Requires ratification by special conventions in at least ¾ of the states (process used for 21st Amendment)

or

Requires special convention called by ⅔ of state legislatures

Requires ratification of at least ¾ of state legislatures

or

Requires ratification by special conventions in at least ¾ of the states

11. Which of the following conclusions is best supported by the infographic above?

   (A) Once a proposed amendment passes the first round of approval, there are four ways it can be ratified.

   (B) Amendment proposals are more easily passed by Congress than by states.

   (C) Only a few amendments have been ratified by special conventions in at least three-fourths, or 34, of the states.

   (D) Nearly all proposed amendments have been ratified.

12. Which concern of the framers does the method illustrated in the infographic address?

   (A) Democracy and equality

   (B) Proportionality and fair representation

   (A) Popular sovereignty and adaptability

   (B) Due process and natural rights

FREE-RESPONSE QUESTIONS

Concept Application

The following is from President Lyndon Johnson's remarks at a signing ceremony.

1. "From our very beginnings as a nation, we have felt a fierce commitment to the ideal of education for everyone. It fixed itself into our democratic creed . . . For too long, political acrimony held up our progress. For too long, children suffered while jarring interests caused stalemate in the efforts to improve our schools. Since 1946 Congress tried repeatedly, and failed repeatedly, to enact measures for elementary and secondary education. Now, within the past three weeks, the House of Representatives, by a vote of 263 to 153, and the Senate, by a vote of 73 to 18, have passed the most sweeping educational bill ever to come before Congress. It represents a major new commitment of the federal government to quality and equality in the schooling that we offer our young people."

—President Lyndon B. Johnson, on the Elementary and Secondary Education Act, 1965

After reading the passage, respond to A, B, and C below:

(A) Describe an action states who oppose federal intervention in education can take in response to the scenario.

(B) In the context of the scenario, explain how the Tenth Amendment likely contributed to the delay spoken of by President Johnson.

(C) In the context of the scenario, explain how unfunded mandates complicate education policy.

Quantitative Analysis

TOTAL FEDERAL SPENDING ON STATE AND LOCAL GRANTS 1955–1985		
Year	Spending (in billions of constant dollars)	Percentage of Total Federal Spending
1955	24.4	4.7
1960	45.3	7.6
1965	65.9	9.2
1970	123.7	12.3
1975	186.8	15.0
1980	227.0	15.5
1985	189.6	11.2

Source: OMB Historical Tables, FY 2014

2. Use the table above to answer the following questions.

   (A) Identify the two years in which federal spending on state and local grants was highest.

   (B) Describe a trend in federal spending on state and local grants represented in the table.

   (C) Draw a conclusion about events or priorities that might explain this trend.

   (D) Explain how the figures shown in the chart demonstrate the principle of federalism.

SCOTUS Comparison

3. In 1831, the state of Georgia charged and convicted Samuel Worcester and other United States citizens for violating a state law that regulated and often prevented non-Native Americans from residing with the local Cherokee Indian tribe. Worcester and the others challenged their guilty conviction, arguing that the state of Georgia could not create and enforce such a law because it violated the Constitution, existing treaties between the United States and the Cherokee nation, and at least one congressional law that addressed relations between U.S. citizens and the Cherokee.

   In this case of *Worcester v. Georgia* (1832), the Supreme Court sided 5:1 with Worcester and fellow litigants, overturning the convictions. In his majority opinion, Chief Justice John Marshall wrote, "The Constitution, by declaring treaties already made, as well as those to be made, to be the supreme law of the land, has adopted and sanctioned the previous treaties with the Indian nations, and consequently admits their rank among the powers who are capable of making treaties." Marshall and the Court went on to say "treaty" and "nation" are words "selected in our diplomatic and legislative proceedings" that apply to Indians as to the other nations.

   (A) Identify a common constitutional principle used to make a ruling in both *McCulloch v. Maryland* (1819) and *Worcester v. Georgia (1831)*.

   (B) Explain how the facts of *McCulloch v. Maryland* and the facts of *Worcester v. Georgia* led to similar holdings in both cases.

   (C) Describe an action that the state of Georgia or its citizens could have taken if it disagreed with the Court's ruling and the outcome of this case.

WRITE AS A POLITICAL SCIENTIST: *WRITING THE ARGUMENT ESSAY*

The final task on the AP® exam is an argument essay that assesses your ability to use evidence and reasoning to support a claim—a statement asserted to be true. Few skills are more important in government and politics than developing and evaluating arguments. Every policy proposal or law has at its heart an argument to which multiple stakeholders have contributed their claims, evidence, and reasoning.

All of the skills within the disciplinary practice of argumentation will be assessed through the argumentation essay. The chart below identifies and explains these skills.

DISCIPLINARY PRACTICE OF ARGUMENTATION	
a. Articulate a defensible claim/thesis.	You will be presented options on a subject in the Argument Essay prompt, and you must clearly indicate the position you will defend in your thesis. A thesis or claim is a position you take on a subject of some controversy—that is, a position on which disagreement is likely. A defensible claim or thesis is one that you can use evidence and reasoning to prove or defend. Reasoning is the use of logic to make a defensible point. (See page 257–258 for more on defensible claims.)
b. Support the argument using relevant evidence.	The evidence, or proof, you will need to defend your thesis is evidence that is directly relevant to your position. It can come from texts, such as foundational documents or Supreme Court cases, or it can come from historical or current events, such as Shays' Rebellion or impeachment proceedings against a president. (See pages 390–391 for more on supporting an argument with relevant evidence.)
c. Use reasoning to organize and analyze evidence, explaining its significance to justify the claim or thesis.	Organize your evidence in logical order—for example, by comparing and contrasting, or explaining cause and effect. Explain clearly through reasoning how each piece of evidence directly supports your argument. (See pages 488–489 for more on using reasoning to show how your evidence supports your claim.)
d. Use refutation, concession, or rebuttal in responding to opposing or alternative perspectives.	Anticipate objections to your position. Address them by using refutation—showing conclusively how a claim and its supporting arguments are wrong; concession—admitting that parts of the opposing argument may have merit but overall your position still prevails; and rebuttal—casting doubt on an opposing view by presenting a counter argument or alternate perspective. (See pages 665–666 for more on responding to opposing or alternative perspectives.)

Application: As you complete the argument essay on the next page, refer back to this chart to remind yourself about each stage of developing your argument.

For current free response question samples, check the College Board's website.

Argument Essay

4. Develop an argument in favor of or against the addition of the Bill of Rights to the U.S. Constitution.

Use at least one piece of evidence from one of the following foundational documents:

- The Declaration of Independence
- *Brutus No. 1*

In your response, you should do the following:

- Respond to the prompt with a defensible claim or thesis that establishes a line of reasoning.
- Support your claim with at least TWO pieces of specific and relevant evidence.
  - One piece of evidence must come from one of the foundational documents listed above.
  - A second piece of evidence can come from any other foundational document not used as your first piece of evidence, or it may be from your knowledge of course concepts.
- Use reasoning to explain why your evidence supports your claim or thesis.
- Respond to an opposing or alternate perspective using refutation, concession, or rebuttal.

UNIT 2

Interactions Among Branches of Government

Four institutions carry out the responsibilities of the three branches. Congress is defined in Article I. The president and the executive branch's large bureaucracy derives from Article II. The courts are more vaguely described in Article III. Each branch has unique customs and rules, as well as unique ways to interact with other branches.

Congress is the most representative branch. Its 535 members, delegates, committees, and staffers determine policy in the areas of national defense, the economy, health care, trade, criminal law, and an array of government services. The House and Senate have developed unique leadership roles and legislative procedures to conduct their business.

The American presidency is an iconic, powerful institution that has gained influence over time and that is visible on a world stage. Presidents administer the law through a large bureaucracy of military, trade, financial, and law enforcement agencies. Chief executives meet with world leaders, design the national budget, and campaign for their party's candidates.

The judicial branch settles federal disputes (criminal and civil), ensures justice, and interprets the law. A loosely defined branch at the founding, the judiciary has become a complex three-level court system with courthouses across the country and a nine-member Supreme Court in Washington, DC that shapes much U.S. law.

ENDURING UNDERSTANDINGS: INTERACTIONS AMONG BRANCHES

CON-3: The republican ideal in the U.S. is manifested in the structure and operation of the legislative branch.

CON-4: The presidency has been enhanced beyond its expressed constitutional powers.

CON-5: The design of the judicial branch protects the court's independence as a branch of government, and the emergence and use of judicial review remains a powerful judicial practice.

PMI-2: The federal bureaucracy is a powerful institution implementing federal policies with sometimes questionable accountability.

Source: AP® United States Government and Politics Course and Exam Description

---

CHAPTER 4

Congress

Topics 2.1–2.3

Topic 2.1 Congress: The Senate and the House of Representatives

CON-3.A: Describe the different structures, powers, and functions of each house of Congress.

- Required Foundational Document:
  - The Constitution of the United States

Topic 2.2 Structures, Powers, and Functions of Congress

CON-3.B: Explain how the structure, powers, and functions of both houses of Congress affect the policy-making process.

Topic 2.3 Congressional Behavior

CON-3.C: Explain how congressional behavior is influenced by election processes, partisanship, and divided government.

- Required Supreme Court Cases:
  - *Baker v. Shaw* (1962)
  - *Shaw v. Reno* (1993)

Source: Getty Images
House of Representatives chamber, U.S. Capitol Building, Washington, DC

Congress: The Senate and the House of Representatives

"Congress has not unlimited powers to provide for the general welfare, but only those specifically enumerated."

—Thomas Jefferson, letter to Albert Gallatin, 1817

Essential Question: What are the structures, powers, and functions of each house of Congress?

The United States Congress is one of the world's most democratic governing bodies. Defined in Article I of the Constitution, Congress consists of the Senate and the House of Representatives. These governing bodies meet in Washington, DC, to craft legislation that sets out national policy. Congress creates statutes, or laws, that become part of the United States Code. Its 535 elected members and roughly 30,000 support staff operate under designated rules to carry out the legislative process. In January 2019, Speaker of the House Nancy Pelosi in the House of Representatives and Vice President Mike Pence in the Senate gaveled the 116th Congress to order for its new term.

Structure of Congress

After a war with Britain over adequate citizen representation and governance under the unworkable Articles of Confederation, creating a republican form of government that reflected citizen and elite views was of top concern for Americans at the Constitutional Convention. For that reason, the framers designed Congress as the most democratic and chief policymaking branch. The First United States Congress opened in 1789 in New York City.

Article I

The **bicameral**, or two-house, legislature resulted from a dispute at the Constitutional Convention between small and large states, each desiring different forms of representation. The Great Compromise (see Topic 1.5) dictated that the number of representatives in the House would be allotted based on the number of people living within each state. Article I's provision for a census every ten years assures states a proportional allotment of these members. Together, the members in the House represent the entire public. The Senate, in contrast, has two members from each state, granting states equal representation in that chamber. With this structure, the framers created a republic that represented both the citizenry at large and the states.

| DEMOGRAPHICS OF 116TH CONGRESS (2019-2020) ||
Classification	Total
Men	404
Women	131
African American	56
Latino	50
Asian or Pacific Islander	20
Native American	4
Caucasian	405
Born outside U.S.	28
Service in military	96
With law degrees	192

(Statistics largely self-reported. Totals include delegates from U.S. territories and account for four vacancies.)

The framers also designed each house to have a different character and separate responsibilities. Senators are somewhat insulated from public opinion by their longer terms (six years as opposed to two for members of the House), and they have more constitutional responsibilities than House members. Because they represent an entire state, each has a more diverse constituency compared with the House. In contrast, smaller congressional districts give House members a more intimate constituent-representative relationship (there are seven small-population states that elect one at-large representative and two senators, which results in each member of Congress from those states representing the entire state).

Originally, unlike House members, senators were elected by state legislators. This practice, which is a form of elite democracy, changed with the **Seventeenth Amendment**, ratified in 1913. This amendment broadened democracy by giving the people of the state the right to elect their senators.

The requirement that both chambers must approve legislation helps prevent the passage of rash laws. James Madison pointed out that "a second house of the legislature, distinct from and dividing the power with the first, must always be a beneficial check on the government. It doubles the people's security by requiring the concurrence of two distinct bodies." This system of checks and balances in Congress helps keep an appropriate balance between majority rule and minority rights.

Size and Term Length The more representative House of Representatives is designed to reflect the will of the people and to prevent the kinds of abuses that took place during the colonial period. Most representatives are responsible for a relatively small geographic area. With their two-year terms, House members must consider popular opinions, or unsatisfied voters will replace them. The entire House faces reelection at the same time.

DIFFERENCES BETWEEN HOUSE AND SENATE		
	House of Representatives	**Senate**
Qualifications	• At least 25 years old • Citizen for past 7 years • Resident of state they represent when elected	• At least 30 years old • Citizen for past 9 years • Resident of state they represent when elected
Unique Powers	• Originates revenue bills • Initiates impeachment • Breaks tie for president in Electoral College	• Provides "advice and consent" on treaties and presidential appointments • Handles trial of impeached officials
Members, Terms, and Constituencies	• 435 members • 2-year terms • Unlimited terms	• 100 members • 6-year terms • Unlimited terms
Structures and Processes	• Centralized and hierarchical • Rules Committee (majority party) controls agenda • Limited debate time • Powerful Speaker of the House • Focus on revenue and spending	• Less centralized • Committees do not have as much authority • Looser debate (filibuster allowed but limited by cloture vote) • Focus on foreign policy • Leaders less powerful except for the powerful majority leader

Since 1913, the House has been composed of 435 members, with the temporary exception of adding two more for the annexation of Alaska and Hawaii. Each congressional district has more than 700,000 inhabitants. The Reapportionment Act of 1929 mandates the periodic reapportionment and redistribution of U.S. congressional seats according to changes in the census figures. Each decade, the U.S. Census Bureau tabulates state populations and then awards the proportional number of seats to each state. Every state receives at least one seat. States gain, lose, or maintain the same number of seats based on the census figures. Because almost all states gain population over a ten-year period, even some growing states will lose seats if they grow at a proportionately slower rate.

The Senate, in contrast, always has 100 members. George Washington explained the character of the U.S. Senate with an analogy to cooling hot coffee. "We pour our coffee into a saucer to cool it, we pour legislation into the senatorial saucer to cool it." The framers wanted a cautious, experienced group to serve as yet another hurdle in the lawmaking process. Only one-third of the

Senate is up for reelection every two years, making it a continuous body. In *Federalist No. 64*, John Jay argued, "by leaving a considerable residue of the old ones [senators] in place, uniformity and order, as well as a constant succession of official information, will be preserved." Senators' six-year terms give them some ability to temper the popular ideas adopted by the House, since senators do not have to worry about being voted out of office so soon. The reelection rate for Senators is nearly 90 percent.

Collectively, these two bodies pass legislation. Bills can originate in either chamber, except for tax proposals, or revenue laws, which must originate in the House. To become law, identical bills must pass both houses by a simple majority vote and then be signed by the president.

Reapportioned House Of Representatives, 2012

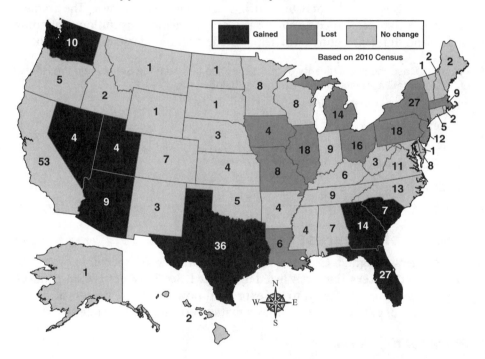

Caucuses In addition to formal policymaking committees (see Topic 2.2), Congress also contains groups of like-minded people organized into **caucuses**. These groups usually unite around a particular belief or concern. Each party has such a group in each house—the Democratic Caucus or the Republican Party Conference—which includes basically the entire party membership within each house. These groups gather to elect their respective leaders, to set legislative agendas, and to name their committee members. Many other smaller caucuses are organized around specific interests, some that cross party lines, such as agriculture, business, or women's issues. Members can belong to multiple caucuses. Caucuses can have closed-door meetings and can develop legislation, but they are not officially part of the lawmaking process.

Since legislators are members of both caucuses and official congressional committees, they can formulate ideas and legislative strategy in the caucuses, but they must introduce bills through the official, public committee system. (See Topic 2.2.)

With their longer terms, senators can build longer-lasting **coalitions** and working relationships. Although reelection rates tend to be high, House members with their shorter terms have more changeable coalition members.

THINK AS A POLITICAL SCIENTIST: *COMPARE POLITICAL INSTITUTIONS*

Political institutions are government organizations that make, enforce, or apply laws. Two of the most important political institutions are the House of Representatives and the Senate, which create our nation's laws. The framers designed each to serve specific purposes. Comparing these institutions by finding similar and different features will help provide a solid understanding of each.

Practice: Describe one similarity or one difference between the Senate and the House of Representatives related to the categories below:

1. Qualifications of the members
2. Length of term
3. Number of members
4. Role in lawmaking
5. Enumerated powers

Powers of Congress

The framers assigned Congress a limited number of specific powers, or **enumerated powers**. Expressly listed in Article I, Section 8 of the Constitution, they are sometimes referred to as "expressed powers." These powers allow for the creation of public policy—the laws that govern the United States.

Power of the Purse

The first congressional power enumerated is the power to raise revenue—to tax. Article I also provides that no money can be drawn from the treasury without the approval of Congress. Thus, Congress appropriates, or spends, those tax revenues through the public lawmaking process. Both chambers have committees for budgeting and appropriations. Congress also has the power to coin money.

The president proposes an annual budget while Congress members, who often differ on spending priorities, and their committees debate how much should be invested in certain areas. The budgeting process is complex and usually takes months to finalize.

Regulating Commerce

In recent years, Congress has used the commerce clause in Article I, Section 8, to assume authority over a wide policy area by connecting issues to every type of interstate and intrastate commerce. In an effort to protect the environment, for example, Congress has written regulations that apply to manufacturing and chemical plants to control the emissions these facilities might spew into our air. Congress can require gun manufacturers to package safety locks with the guns they sell. The commerce clause was the justification for the Patient Protection and Affordable Care Act (2010), or "Obamacare," which requires citizens to purchase health insurance and requires insurance companies to accept more clients.

However, there have been many legal challenges to wide-ranging congressional authority based on the commerce clause. The landmark case of *United States v. Lopez* (see Topic 1.8) is one of the few modern Supreme Court decisions that has restricted Congress's use of this clause to expand the power of the federal government.

Foreign and Military Affairs

Congress is a key player in U.S. foreign policy, and it oversees the military. It can raise armies and navies, legislate or enact conscription procedures, mandate a military draft, and, most important, declare war. Congress determines how much money is spent on military bases and, through an independent commission, has authority over base closings. It essentially determines the salary for military personnel.

Foreign and military policy are determined jointly by Congress and the president, but the Constitution grants Congress the ultimate authority to declare war. The framers wanted a system that would send the United States to war only when deemed necessary by the most democratic branch, rather than by a potentially tyrannical or power-hungry executive making a solo decision to invade another country. Yet the framers also wanted a strong military leader who was responsible to the people, so they named the president the Commander in Chief of the armed forces. Congress does not have the power to deploy troops or receive ambassadors, leaving chief influences on foreign policy to the executive branch.

FOREIGN AND MILITARY POWERS
Congress
• Has the exclusive power to declare war
• Funds the military, foreign endeavors, and foreign aid
• Has oversight of the State and Defense departments and relevant agencies
• Can institute a mandatory military draft to staff the Armed Forces
• Confirms presidential nominations for ambassadors and high-ranking military personnel—the Senate
• Ratifies treaties with other nations by a two-thirds vote—the Senate

The President
• Serves as Commander in Chief of the Armed Forces
• Appoints ambassadors and receives foreign ministers
• Negotiates treaties with other nations
• Issues executive orders that can impact foreign policy
• Makes executive agreements with other heads of state
• Commissions the military officers of the United States

The commander-in-chief power was expanded after the Gulf of Tonkin Resolution (see Topic 2.6) in 1964, which greatly enhanced a president's authority in conducting military affairs. After nearly a decade of an unpopular and ultimately failed Vietnam War, Congress passed the **War Powers Act** in 1973. This law reigns in executive power by requiring the president to inform Congress within 48 hours of committing U.S. forces to combat. Also, the law requires Congress to vote within 60 days, with a possible 30-day extension, to approve any military force and its funding. The War Powers Act strikes a balance between the framers' intended constitutional framework and the need for a strong executive to manage quick military action in the days of modern warfare. Congress can choose to waive the 60-day requirement, as it did at the request of President George W. Bush after the September 11 attacks. (See Topic 1.5.)

Implied Powers

At the end of the list of enumerated powers in Article I is the **necessary and proper** clause. It gives Congress the power "to make all Laws which shall be necessary and proper for carrying into Execution the foregoing Powers." Also called the *elastic clause*, it implies that the national legislature can make additional laws intended to take care of the items in the enumerated list.

The elastic clause first came into contention in the case of *McCulloch v. Maryland* in 1819 over whether or not Congress could establish a bank. (See Topic 1.8.) The Supreme Court ruled that items in the enumerated list implied that Congress could create a bank. Since then, the implied powers doctrine has given Congress authority to enact legislation addressing a wide range of issues—economic, social, and environmental.

If those who served in the first Congress could take part in the modern legislature, "they would probably feel right at home," says historian Raymond Smock. Other observers disagree and point to burgeoning federal government responsibilities. Using the elastic clause, Congress has expanded the size and role of the federal government. For example, it has created a Department of Education, defended marriage, and addressed various other modern issues outside the scope of Article I's enumerated powers.

Differing Powers for House and Senate

Certain powers are divided between the House and the Senate. In addition to priority on revenue bills, the House also has the privilege to select the president if no candidate wins the majority in the Electoral College. The House can impeach a president or other federal officers in the event that a majority of the House agree that one has committed "treason, bribery, or other high crimes and misdemeanors."

The Senate, representing the interests of the states, also has several exclusive powers and responsibilities. Its **advice and consent** power allows senators to recommend or reject major presidential appointees such as Cabinet secretaries and federal judges. Senators often recommend people for positions in the executive branch or as U.S. district judges to serve in their states. High-level presidential appointments must first clear a Senate confirmation hearing, at which the appropriate committee interviews the nominee. If the committee approves the nominee, then the entire Senate will take a vote. A simple majority is required for appointment. Historically, the upper house, as the Senate is called, has approved most appointees quickly, with notable exceptions. (See Topics 2.5 and 2.11.)

The Senate also has stronger powers related to foreign affairs. The Senate must approve by a two-thirds vote any treaty the president enters into with a foreign nation before it becomes official.

While the House can level impeachment charges, only the Senate can try and if found guilty, remove the official from office with a two-thirds vote.

Despite their different powers, both chambers have equal say in whether or not a bill becomes law, since both chambers must approve an identical bill before it is passed on to the president for signing.

REFLECT ON THE ESSENTIAL QUESTION

Essential Question: *What are the structures, powers, and functions of each house of Congress? On separate paper, complete a chart like the one below.*

Powers, Structure, and Function of the Senate	Powers, Structure, and Function of the House of Representatives

KEY TERMS AND NAMES

advice and consent	House of Representatives
bicameral	necessary and proper clause
caucuses	power of the purse
coalitions	Senate
enumerated powers	Seventeenth Amendment (1913)
implied powers	War Powers Act (1973)

Structures, Powers, and Functions of Congress

"Mr. Baker [Senate aide] proved especially adept at the math of the Senate. He would know precisely how many votes a piece of legislation could garner at any given moment, a valuable skill in the horse-trading world of Washington politics."

—Neil Genzlinger, Bobby Baker's obituary, *New York Times*, 2017

Essential Question: How do the structures, powers, and functions of Congress affect the policymaking process?

Congress's constitutional design shapes how it makes policy. Elected lawmakers work to improve the United States while representing people of unique views across the nation. The House and Senate differ overall, and within each are chamber-specific roles and rules that impact the law and policymaking process.

Congress is organized into leadership roles, committees, and procedures. Strong personalities and skilled politicians work their way into the leadership hierarchy, wielding great influence in running the nation's government. The way in which ideas become law, or more often, fail to become law, are essential to understanding the structures, powers, and functions of Congress.

Policymaking Structures and Processes

The design of Congress and the powers the framers bestowed on the two chambers within that institution have shaped how the legislative branch makes policy. Elected lawmakers work to improve the United States while representing people of unique views across the nation. Formal groups and informal factions operate differently in the House and Senate.

Congress is organized by house, political party, leadership, and committee. The parties create leadership positions to guide their own party members, to move legislation, and to carry out party goals. The party with the most members is the majority party and is in a strong position to set the agenda through its leaders and committee chairpersons. Standing committees are where the real work gets done, especially in the more structured House. Some of the powerful committees are institutions unto themselves, especially in the

House. Congress's formalized groups include both lawmaking committees and partisan or ideological groups.

Leadership

The only official congressional leaders named in the Constitution are the Speaker of the House, the President of the Senate, and the president *pro tempore* of the Senate. The document states that the House and Senate "shall choose their other Officers."

At the start of each congressional term in early January on odd years, the first order of business in each house is to elect leaders. The four *party caucuses*—that is, the entire party membership within each house—gather privately after elections, but days before Congress opens, to determine their choices for Speaker and the other leadership positions. The actual public vote for leadership positions takes place when Congress opens and is invariably a party-line vote. Once the leaders are elected, they oversee the organization *of* Congress, help form committees, and proceed with the legislative agenda.

House Leaders Atop the power pyramid in the House of Representatives is the **Speaker of the House**, which is the only House leadership position mentioned in the Constitution. As the de facto leader of the majority party in the House, the Speaker wields significant power. In 2007, Nancy Pelosi (D-CA) became the first female Speaker of the House and was reelected in 2019. Paul Ryan (R-WI) presided as Speaker over the Republican-controlled House before the Democrats regained the majority in the 2018 midterm elections.

The Speaker recognizes members for floor speeches and comments, organizes members for conference committees, and has great influence in most matters of lawmaking.

On the next rung down in the House are the majority and minority leaders. These floor leaders direct debate from among their party's members and guide the discussion from their side of the aisle. They are the first members recognized in debate. Party leaders have also become spokespersons for the party. They offer their party messages through news conferences and in interviews on cable networks and Sunday talk shows.

Below the floor leader is the deputy leader, or **whip**, who is in charge of party discipline. The whip keeps a rough tally of votes among his or her party members, which aids in determining the optimum time for a vote. Whips communicate leadership views to members and will strong-arm party members to vote with the party. Political favors or even party endorsements during a primary election can change the mind of representatives contemplating an independent or cross-party vote. The whip also assures that party members remain in good standing and act in an ethical and professional way. When scandals or missteps occur, the whip may insist a member step down from serving as a committee chair or leave Congress entirely.

Leadership in Congress

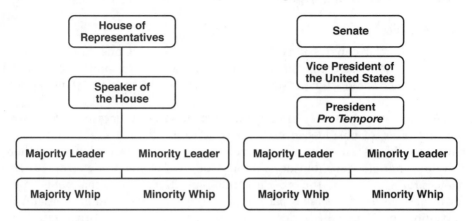

The Congressional leadership represented above results from a mix of constitutional, congressional, and party definitions. The Speaker is in charge in the House, while the majority leader has the most control and influence in the Senate.

Senate Leaders In the Senate, a similar structure exists. The Constitution names the vice president as the nonvoting **President of the Senate**, but vice presidents in the modern era are rarely present. In lieu of the vice president as the presiding officer, senators in the majority party will share presiding duties. In case of a tie vote, the Constitution enables the vice president to break it.

Article I also provides for the **president *pro tempore***, or temporary president. The "pro tem" is mostly a ceremonial position held by the most senior member of the majority party. The tasks involved with the role include presiding over the Senate in the absence of the vice president, signing legislation, and issuing the oath of office to new senators. The role of the president pro tem in presidential succession was addressed with the Twenty-fifth Amendment. Among several provisions, the Twenty-fifth Amendment states the president pro tem assumes the position of vice president if a vacancy in the office occurs.

The **Senate majority leader** wields much more power in the Senate than the vice president and pro tem. The majority leader is, in reality, the chief legislator, the first person the chair recognizes in debate and the leader who sets the legislative calendar and determines which bills reach the floor for debate and which ones do not. The majority leader also guides the party caucus on issues and party strategy. Senate leaders do not have final say in the decisions of individual party members; each makes his or her own independent choice, and the Senate's less formal rules for debate enable members to address their colleagues and the public more easily than in the House. Former Senate majority leaders have expressed frustration over the effort to guide party members. Senator Bob Dole (R-KS, 1974–1996), who served in a number of leadership positions in the Senate, once said the letter "P" was missing from his title, "Majority Pleader."

The Senate whips serve much the same purpose as their House counterparts. They keep a tally of party members' voting intentions and try to maintain party discipline. The conference chair also serves the same function in the Senate as in the House, overseeing party matters.

Committees

Committees are not mentioned in the Constitution, but they have been fixtures in Congress since it first met. Smaller groups can tackle tough issues and draft more precise laws than the entire House or Senate can. Committees allow lawmakers to put their expertise to use, and they make the process of moving a bill to a law manageable. The intricate committee system handles a vast amount of legislation. Committees dealing with finance, foreign relations, the judiciary, and other common topics have become permanent, public lawmaking groups. They conduct hearings and debate bills under consideration, playing key roles in the legislative process in both houses.

Standing Committees Permanent committees focused on a particular policy area are called standing committees. Members of Congress can specialize in a few topics and become experts in these areas. For example, the House Energy and Commerce Committee has wide authority on utilities and gasoline, as well as almost any business matter. The Committee on Transportation and Infrastructure oversees the creation and maintenance of U.S. highways, regulates airports, and delivers billions in grants.

Committee chairpersons are invariably senior members in the majority party experienced on that committee. The vice chair or "ranking member" is the senior committee member from the minority party. The majority party always holds the majority of seats on each committee and therefore controls the flow of legislation because a bill must first clear committee with a majority vote before it can move to the House or Senate floor for a vote.

As part of the Senate's advice and consent role, standing committees in this body hold confirmation hearings for presidential nominations. For example, a nominated secretary of defense must appear before the Armed Services Committee to answer individual senators' questions. After this hearing, a majority can recommend the nominee to the full Senate for approval.

Standing committees have a number of other vital roles. For example, the House Judiciary Committee drafts crime bills that define illegal behavior and outline appropriate punishments. It also handles impeachments. In 1974, the House Judiciary Committee voted 27 to 11 to recommend impeachment of President Richard Nixon. He resigned before the entire House took a vote. On December 13, 2019, this committee voted for articles of impeachment against President Donald Trump. The full House voted to impeach him five days later.

Members want to serve on the powerful House **Ways and Means Committee**, a committee exclusive to the House that determines tax policy. The Ways and Means Committee is the first to outline details when proposals are put forward to raise or lower income taxes. Other members want to serve on the Appropriations Committees, which are found in both houses. These two committees influence or control the "purse strings."

Lawmakers also seek committee appointments in fields in which they have expertise, or that have special interest for their state or district. For example, nearly 100 members of Congress have served in the Armed Forces; these members are well qualified to shape Congress's military policy. Some lawmakers have high-level business experience and will influence commerce regulations or international trade law. The Democrats and Republicans each have a committee for the purpose of assigning members to standing committees. The Democrats' Steering and Policy Committee and the Republicans' Committee on Committees recommend certain members for committee assignments, but ultimately each full house votes to approve committee membership.

COMMITTEE TYPES
Standing: Permanent committees that handle most of Congress's work
Joint: Members of both houses that address a long-term issue or program
Select or Special: Temporary committee that handles a particular issue or investigation
Conference: House and Senate members who reconcile similar bills

Congress has a few permanent **joint committees** that unite members from the House and Senate, such as one to manage the Library of Congress and the Joint Committee on Taxation. Members of these committees do mostly routine management and research.

Both houses form temporary or **select committees** periodically for some particular and typically short-lived purpose. A select or special committee is established "for a limited time period to perform a particular study or investigation," according to the U.S. Senate's online glossary. "These committees might be given or denied authority to report legislation to the Senate." Select committees can be exclusive to one house or can also have joint committee status.

Notable select committees have investigated major scandals and events, such as the 2012 terrorist attack on the U.S. Consulate in Benghazi, Libya. These groups also investigate issues to determine if further congressional action is necessary. Recently the House created a select committee on Energy Independence and Global Warming. A bill originally introduced in 1989, H.R. 40, was reintroduced in 2019 to establish a select committee to study the effects of slavery and possible reparations for decedents of the formerly enslaved.

When a bill passes both houses but in slightly differnet forms, a temporary **conference committee** is created to iron out differences on the bill. It is rare that legislation on a particular issue will be identical when approved by both the House and Senate. When two similar bills pass each house, usually a compromise can be reached. Members from both houses gather in a conference committee for a markup session, a process by which the bill is edited, or marked up. The final draft must pass both houses before going on to possibly receive the president's signature.

In addition to creating bills and confirming presidential appointments, committees also oversee how the executive agencies administer the laws Congress creates. Through its committees, Congress conducts congressional oversight to ensure that executive branch agencies, such as the FBI or the TSA, are carrying out the policy or program as defined by Congress. When corruption or incompetence is suspected, committees call agency directors to testify. Oversight hearings also may simply be fact-finding exchanges between lawmakers and Cabinet secretaries or agency directors about congressional funding, efficiency, or just general updates. (See Topic 2.14 for more on congressional oversight.)

Committees and Rules Unique to the House

Both the House and Senate follow parliamentary procedure outlined in Robert's Rules of Order, guidelines for conducting discussion and reaching decisions in a group. With so many members representing so many legislative districts, however, the House has rules that limit debate. A member may not speak for more than an hour and typically speaks for less. These legislators can offer only **germane** amendments to a bill, those directly related to the legislation under consideration. In the House, amendments to bills typically must first be approved by the committee overseeing the bill.

The presiding officer—the Speaker of the House or someone he or she appoints—controls chamber debate. House members address all their remarks to "Madam Speaker" or "Mister Speaker" and refer to their colleagues by the state they represent, as in "my distinguished colleague from Iowa." The control the presiding officer enjoys, time limits, and other structural practices help make the large House of Representatives function with some efficiency.

The House **Rules Committee** is very powerful. It can easily dispose of a bill or define the guidelines for debate because it acts as a traffic cop to the House floor. Nothing reaches the floor unless the Rules Committee allows it. This committee generally reflects the will and sentiment of House leadership and the majority caucus. It impacts every House bill because it assigns bills to the appropriate standing committees, schedules bills for debate, and decides when votes take place. The entire House must vote to make a law, but the Rules Committee wields great power in determining what issues or bills other members will vote on.

The **Committee of the Whole** is also unique to the House. It includes but does not require all representatives. However, the Committee of the Whole is more of a state of operation in which the House rules are relaxed than an actual committee. It was created to allow longer debate among fewer people and to allow members to vote as a group rather than in an individual roll call. Additionally, the otherwise nonvoting delegates from U.S. territories—Puerto Rico, Guam, and others—can vote when the House operates in the Committee of the Whole. Only 100 members must be present for the Committee of the Whole to act. When it has finished examining or shaping a bill, the Committee "rises and reports" the bill to the House. At that point the more formal rules of procedure and voting resume, and, if a quorum is present, the entire House will vote on final passage of the bill.

A modern device that functions as a step toward transparency and democracy in the House is the **discharge petition**. The discharge petition can bring a bill out of a reluctant committee. The petition's required number of signatures has changed over the years. It now stands at a simple majority to discharge a bill out of committee and onto the House floor. Thus, if 218 members sign, no chairperson or reluctant committee can prevent the majority's desire to publicly discuss the bill. This measure may or may not lead to the bill's passage, but it prevents a minority from stopping a majority on advancing the bill and is a way to circumvent leadership.

SELECTED CONGRESSIONAL COMMITTEES AND KEY POLICY FOCUS IN THE 116TH CONGRESS	
House of Representatives	**Senate**
Ways and Means Determines tax policy	**Finance** Oversees spending and budgeting
Rules Determines House proceedings	**Armed Services** Oversees the military
Armed Services Oversees the military	**Foreign Relations** Guides U.S. foreign policy
Judiciary Drafts crime bills; impeachments	**Judiciary** Confirms judges; oversees courts
Energy and Commerce Regulates energy and business	**Agriculture, Nutrition, and Forestry** Addresses farming, food, and nature

In 2019, there were 20 standing committees in the House and 16 in the Senate.

Rules and Procedures Unique to the Senate

The smaller Senate is much less centralized and hierarchical than the House with fewer restrictions on debate. Senators can speak longer. However, the presiding officer has little control over who speaks when, since he or she must recognize anyone who stands to speak, giving priority to the leaders of the parties. Like representatives, senators are not allowed to directly address anyone but the presiding officer. They refer to other senators in the third person ("the senior senator from Illinois," for example).

Senators can propose nongermane amendments. They can add amendments on any subject they want. Senators also have strategic ways to use their debate time. For example, they may try to stall or even kill a bill by speaking for an extremely long time, a tactic known as the **filibuster**, to block a nomination or to let the time run out on a deadline for voting on a bill. Filibusters are a Senate procedure (not a constitutional power) that any senator may invoke and use to wear down the opposition or extract a deal from the Senate leadership. In contrast, the only House members who are allowed to speak as long as they want are the Speaker of the House, the majority leader, and the minority leader. On February 6, 2018, House Minority Leader Nancy Pelosi spoke for eight hours straight in support of protections for people who were brought into the country illegally when they were children, the so-called "DREAMers." She could not take a seat or a bathroom break for the entire time or else she would have had to yield the floor.

The Senate also uses measures that require higher thresholds for action than the House and that slow it down or speed it up. These include **unanimous consent**—the approval of all senators—and the **hold**, a measure to stall a bill. Before the Senate takes action, the acting Senate president requests unanimous consent to suspend debate. If anyone objects, the motion is put on hold or at least stalled for discussion. For years, senators abused this privilege, since a few senators, even one, could stop popular legislation. Then and now, senators will place a hold on a motion or on a presidential appointment as a bargaining tool.

Such delays in the past have brought about changes in the rules. As the United States stepped closer to war in 1917, President Woodrow Wilson called for changes in Senate procedures so that a small minority of senators could not block U.S. action in arming merchant ships for military use. A filibuster had blocked his armed neutrality plan before the United States' entrance into World War I. President Wilson was enraged. He said the Senate "is the only legislative body in the world which cannot act when its majority is ready for action. A little group of willful men, have rendered the great government of the United States helpless."

A special session created Rule 22, or the **cloture rule**, which enabled and required a two-thirds supermajority to stop debate on a bill, thus, stopping a filibuster and allowing for a vote. In 1975, the Senate lowered the standard to three-fifths, or 60 of 100 senators. Once cloture is reached, each senator has the privilege of speaking for up to one hour on that bill or topic.

Foreign Policy Functions While both houses have a Foreign Affairs Committee, the Senate has more foreign relations duties. The framers gave the upper house the power to ratify or deny treaties with other countries. The Senate also confirms U.S. ambassadors. Because the Senate is smaller and originally served as agents of the states, the framers gave it more foreign policy power than the House. In *Federalist No. 75*, Hamilton pointed to its continuity. "Because of the fluctuating and . . . multitudinous composition of [the House, we can't] expect in it those qualities . . . essential to the proper execution of such a trust." The chair of the Senate Foreign Relations Committee works closely and often with the president and secretary of state to forge U.S. foreign policy.

The Legislative Process

Lawmaking procedures in each house have been developed to guide policymaking and legislative customs. Both bodies have defined additional leaders that guide floor debate, assure party discipline, and serve as liaisons to the opposing party, the president, and the media. The framers declared in Article I that each house would determine its own rules as further assurance of a bicameral system.

How a Bill Becomes a Law

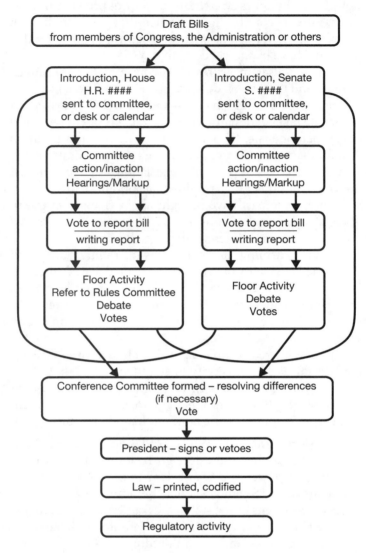

Draft Bills
from members of Congress, the Administration or others

Introduction, House
H.R. ####
sent to committee,
or desk or calendar

Introduction, Senate
S. ####
sent to committee,
or desk or calendar

Committee
action/inaction
Hearings/Markup

Committee
action/inaction
Hearings/Markup

Vote to report bill
writing report

Vote to report bill
writing report

Floor Activity
Refer to Rules Committee
Debate
Votes

Floor Activity
Debate
Votes

Conference Committee formed – resolving differences
(if necessary)
Vote

President – signs or vetoes

Law – printed, codified

Regulatory activity

Introducing and Amending Bills

Only House or Senate members can introduce a bill. Today, however, the actual authors of legislation are more often staffers with expertise, lobbyists, White House liaisons, or outside professionals. When a bill's **sponsor** (the member who introduces it and typically assumes authorship) presents it, the bill is officially numbered. Numbering starts at S.1 in the Senate or H.R.1 in the House at the beginning of each biennial Congress.

Several events take place in the process, creating opportunities for a bill to drastically change along the way. Additional ideas and programs can become attached to the original bill. The nongermane amendments, or **riders**, are often added to benefit a member's own agenda or programs or to enhance the political chances of the bill. Representative Morris ("Mo") Udall (D-AZ) once expressed frustration when he had to vote against his own bill, because it had evolved into legislation he opposed.

How each house, the president, and the public view a bill will determine its fate. The rough-and-tumble path for legislation often leads to its death. In a typical two-year period, thousands of bills are introduced and only a small portion are enacted into law. In the 115th Congress (January 2017–January 2019), representatives and senators introduced more than 13,000 bills and resolutions. About 9 percent, or 1,150, were enacted.

An **omnibus bill** includes multiple areas of law and/or addresses multiple programs. A long string of riders will earn it the nickname "Christmas Tree bill" because it often delivers gifts in the form of special projects a legislator can take home, and, like the ornaments and tinsel on a Christmas tree, the "decorations" so many legislators added to the bill give it an entirely different look.

Pork-Barrel Spending One product of these legislative add-ons is **pork barrel spending**—funds earmarked for specific purposes in a legislator's district. Federal dollars are spent all across the nation to fund construction projects, highway repair, new bridges, national museums and parks, university research grants, and other federal-to-state programs. Members of Congress try to "bring home the bacon," so to speak. Riders are sometimes inserted onto bills literally in the dark of night by a powerful leader or chair, sometimes within days or hours before a final vote to avoid debate on them.

Constituents who benefit from pork barrel spending obviously appreciate it. Yet, in recent years the competition for federal dollars has tarnished Congress's reputation. Citizens Against Government Waste reported an explosion of earmarks from 1994 to 2004. Congress passed more than five times as many earmarked projects, and such spending rose from $10 billion to $22.9 billion.

The most egregious example of pork barrel politics came when Senator Ted Stevens (R-AK) added a rider to a bill primarily meant to provide armor for U.S. troops in Iraq. The rider called for spending more than $400 million to connect a small community of about 50 residents and a regional airport to the Alaska mainland. Critics dubbed the construction project "The Bridge to Nowhere."

Assigning Bills to Committee

The Senate majority leader and the House Rules Committee assign bills to committees in their respective chambers. Sometimes multiple committees have overlapping jurisdiction. A military spending bill may be examined by both the Armed Services Committee and the Appropriations Committee. In that case, the bill may be given multiple referral status, allowing both committees to address it simultaneously. Or it might have sequential referral status, giving one committee priority to review it before others. Frequently, subcommittees with a narrower scope are involved.

Source: Department of Defense, Staff Sgt. Sean K. Harp

The secretary of defense and another ranking Pentagon official testify before a House Appropriations subcommittee.

In committee, a bill goes through three stages: hearings, markup, and reporting out. If the committee "orders the bill," then hearings, expert testimony, and thorough discussions follow. The chair will call for a published summary and analysis of the proposal with views from other participants, perhaps testimony from members of the executive branch or interest groups. Then the bill goes through markup, where committee members amend the bill until they are satisfied. Once the bill passes committee vote, it is "reported out" on the House or Senate floor for debate. The ratio of "yeas" to "nays" often speaks to the bill's chances there. Further amendments are likely added. From this point, many factors can lead to passage and many more can lead to the bill's failure.

The committee chair can also "pigeonhole" a bill—decide not to move it forward for debate until a later time, if at all.

Voting on Bills

Many lawmakers say one of their hardest jobs is voting. Determining exactly what most citizens want in their home state is nearly impossible. Legislators hold town hall meetings, examine public opinion polls, and read stacks of mail and emails to get an idea of their constituents' desires. Members also consider a variety of other factors in deciding how to vote.

"Very often [lawmakers] are not voting for or against an issue for the reasons that seem apparent," historian David McCullough once explained. "They're voting for some other reason. Because they have a grudge against someone . . . or because they're doing a friend a favor, or because they're willing to risk their political skin and vote their conscience."

Logrolling Another factor affecting lawmaking is **logrolling**, or trading votes to gain support for a bill. By agreeing to back someone else's bill, members can secure a vote in return for a bill of their own.

Generating a Budget

One of the most important votes congressional members take is on the question of how to pay government costs. The budgeting process is a complicated, multistep, and often year-long process that begins with a budget proposal from the executive branch and includes both houses of Congress, a handful of agencies, and interest groups.

In the 1970s, Congress created the Office of Management and Budget (OMB) and established the budgeting process with the Congressional Budget and Impoundment Control Act (1974). The OMB is the president's budgeting arm. Headed by a director who is essentially the president's accountant, the OMB considers the needs and wants of all the federal departments and agencies, the fiscal and economic philosophy of the president, federal revenues, and other factors to arrange the annual budget.

The 1974 act also defines the stages in *reconciling* the budget—passing changes to either revenue or spending by a simple majority in both houses with only limited time for debate—a process that can be used only once a year. It calls for Congress to set overall levels of revenues and expenditures, the size of the budget surplus or deficit, and spending priorities. Each chamber also has an appropriations committee that allots the money to federal projects. The Senate Finance Committee is a particularly strong entity in federal spending. Congress also created a congressional agency made of nonpartisan accountants called the Congressional Budget Office (CBO). This professional staff of experts examines and analyzes the budget proposal and serves as a check on the president's OMB.

Sources of Revenue For fiscal year 2019, the government expected to take in about $3.4 trillion. Every year, government revenue comes from five main sources:

- **Individual income taxes**—taxes paid by workers on the income they made during the calendar year. People pay different tax rates depending on their income level.
- **Corporate taxes**—taxes paid by businesses on the profits they made during the calendar year.
- **Social insurance taxes (sometimes called payroll taxes)**—taxes paid by both employees and employers to fund such programs as Social Security, Medicare, and unemployment insurance.
- **Tariffs and excise taxes**—taxes paid on certain imports or products. The tariff on imports is meant to raise their price so U.S.-made goods will be more affordable and competitive. Excise taxes are levied on specific products—luxury products, for example, or products

associated with health risks, such as cigarettes—as well as on certain activities, such as gambling.

- **Other sources**—taxes that include interest on government holdings or investments and estate taxes paid by people who inherit a large amount of money.

The table below shows the percentage of revenue from each category between 1950 and 2020.

CATEGORIES OF GOVERNMENT REVENUE					
Fiscal Year	Individual Income Tax	Corporate Income Tax	Social Insurance and Retirement (Payroll taxes)	Excise	Other
	% of total revenue	% of total revenue	% of total revenue	% of total revenue	% of total revenue
1950	39.9	26.5	11	19.1	3.4
1960	44	23.2	15.9	12.6	4.2
1970	46.9	17	23	9.2	5
1980	47.2	12.5	30.5	4.0	4.8
1990	45.2	9.1	36.8	3.4	5.4
2000	49.6	10.2	32.2	3.4	4.5
2010	41.5	8.9	40	3.1	6.5
2020 (est)	49.6	7.3	35.7	3.1	4.2

Source: U.S. Government Publishing Office, 2019 Budget

As you can see, the highest percentage of government revenue comes from individual income taxes. The budget for fiscal year 2019 called for spending $4.4 trillion. Each year spending falls into three categories: mandatory spending, discretionary spending, and interest on debt.

Mandatory Spending

Mandatory spending is payment required by law, or mandated, for certain programs. These programs include Social Security, Medicare, Medicaid, unemployment insurance, and other special funds for people in temporary need of help. Congress has passed laws determining the eligibility for these programs and the level of payments, so on the basis of those laws mandatory spending happens automatically. Of the $4.4 trillion, mandatory spending for 2019 was expected to be $2.7 trillion, more than 60 percent of the federal budget.

You may have noticed that the expected revenue for 2019 was $3.4 trillion, while the expected outlay was $4.4 trillion. The difference between spending and revenue, close to a trillion dollars in 2019, is the **deficit**. As in previous years, the government has to borrow money to pay that deficit, and each year's loans add to the already large national debt of $20 trillion.

The interest payments on the national debt are massive and must be a part of the annual budget. In 2020, the interest will be more than $400 billion, or about 10 percent of the federal budget, and must also be paid out of each year's revenue. Some consider interest on debt as mandatory spending, since the government must pay its creditors or risk default, which would result in a serious financial crisis.

Discretionary Spending

Discretionary spending is funding that congressional committees debate and decide how to divide up. This spending—about 38 percent of the 2019 budget—pays for everything else not required under mandatory spending. The chart below shows the percentage of government spending from 1950 to 2020 in various categories.

CATEGORIES OF GOVERNMENT SPENDING						
Fiscal Year	Defense (Military)	Human Resources*	Physical Resources**	Interest on Debt	Other Functions***	Undistributed Offsetting Receipts****
	% of total revenue	% of total revenue	% of total revenue	% of total revenue	% of total revenue	% of total revenue
1950	32.2	33.4	8.6	11.3	18.7	−4.3
1960	52.2	28.4	8.7	7.5	8.4	−5.2
1970	41.8	38.5	8.0	7.4	8.8	−4.4
1980	22.7	53	11.2	8.9	7.6	−3.4
1990	23.9	49.4	10.1	14.7	4.8	−2.9
2000	16.5	62.4	4.7	12.5	6.4	−2.4
2010	20.1	69	2.6	5.7	5.0	−2.4
2020 (est)	15.9	69.8	3.0	9.7	3.6	−2.0

Source: U.S. Government Publishing Office, 2019 Budget

* Includes Education, Health and Human Services, Housing and Urban Development, and mandatory spending on Social Security, Medicare, Income Security, and Veterans Benefits and Services

** Includes Energy, Natural Resources and Environment, Commerce and Housing Credit, Transportation, Community and Regional Development

*** Includes International Affairs; Science, Space, and Technology; Agriculture; Administration of Justice; General Government

**** Includes government earnings on oil and gas leases and collection of funds from government agencies for their employees' retirement and other benefits

As the chart on government spending shows, human resources spending is the largest category of discretionary spending. In 2020 it will account for more than half of discretionary spending. The rest of discretionary spending needs must be met by what remains.

Between 1950 and 2020, government spending in the Human Resources category, most of which is mandatory, has grown from about 30 percent of revenue to about 70 percent. That increase needs to be balanced with a decrease in discretionary spending or an increase in revenue or national debt. Conservatives tend to argue that people's tax burden is already significant and that instead of raising taxes or increasing debt, the government should pass laws that reduce the social programs that are responsible for most mandatory spending. Liberals tend to argue that rich people can bear a burden of higher taxes—historically the rich have paid taxes at a higher rate than they do today—and that the mandated social programs serve a vital function in an economy with a vastly unequal distribution of wealth. These principles, as well as pressures from a variety of interest groups (see Topic 5.6), are behind the annual push and pull of budget negotiations in Congress.

THINK AS A POLITICAL SCIENTIST: *DESCRIBE THE DATA PRESENTED*

Political scientists use their knowledge of political processes and institutions along with data available each year to understand changes in the patterns of government revenue and spending. They identify trends and then look for causes for these trends, reasons for the causes and/or effects, the significance of the causes and/or effects, and the implications of the changes over time. Being able to explain causes and effects is necessary for devising solutions to the many challenges facing government.

Practice: Review the tables on page 120 (Categories of Government Revenue) and page 121 (Categories of Government Spending) and complete the following tasks:

1. Study the table of revenue over time and identify one downward trend and one upward trend.

2. Study the table of government spending over time and identify the only spending category that has consistently risen.

3. Explain why the other categories of spending decreased.

4. Explain the significance of the changes over time in federal spending and their effect on possible directions the federal budget might take in the future.

REFLECT ON THE ESSENTIAL QUESTION

Essential Question: *How do the structures, powers, and functions of Congress affect the policy-making process? On separate paper, complete a chart like the one below.*

	Senate	House of Representatives
Committees and Policymaking		
Unique Rules and Procedures		

KEY TERMS AND NAMES

cloture rule
Committee of the Whole
conference committees
deficit
discharge petitions
discretionary spending
filibuster
germane
hold
joint committees
logrolling
mandatory spending
omnibus bill

pork-barrel spending
President of the Senate
president *pro tempore*
rider
Rules Committee
select committees
Senate majority leader
Speaker of the House
sponsor
unanimous consent
Ways and Means Committee
whip

Congressional Behavior

". . .in the contemporary Congress—the belief, especially in the House, that deliberation, fairness, bipartisanship, and debate are impediments to the larger goal of achieving political and policy success."

—Norm Ornstein and David Mann, *The Broken Branch*, 2006

Essential Question: How is congressional behavior influenced by election processes, partisanship, and divided government?

In December 2018, the longest government shutdown in the United States began. Among the causes of the shutdown were disagreements over financing a U.S.-Mexico border wall and funding government agencies. Democrats and Republicans each rejected proposals of the other and could not find common ground to move the budget talks along. Numerous government agencies were affected, and some had to partially stop providing their services; the most notable was the Transportation Security Administration (TSA). When New York's LaGuardia Airport had to shut down due to TSA short staffing, the population and the government took notice. After 35 days, the shutdown came to an end when President Trump signed a bipartisan spending bill.

Influences on Congress

Congress's effectiveness is determined by its ideological division, the changing nature of the job, the citizens lawmakers represent, and the way lawmakers represent them. Intensifying partisanship has caused **gridlock**—the "congestion" of opposing forces that prevents ideas from moving forward—within each house and between the Congress and the president. Also, the reshaping of House voting districts has created one-party rule in several districts, making winning legislative seats too easy for some members and practically impossible for others. Bitter election contests and longer campaign periods have put Republican and Democratic members at further odds. And legislators' differing approaches on voting have shaped the institution.

Partisanship and Polarization

The legislature has developed into a partisan and sometimes uncivil institution. A variety of factors has driven a wedge between liberal and conservative members (see Topic 4.7) and has placed them at points farther from the middle on each end of the ideological spectrum. From the 1950s into the 1970s, political scientists complained that on many issues it was difficult to tell the parties apart. As Republicans retired, more conservative Republicans replaced them. Southern Democrats, once a moderating force in Congress, have all but disappeared. Party-line voting is much more common than it once was, while straying from party positions has become dangerous for those interested in reelection.

Voting Models

Party leaders encourage members to follow the party-line vote, especially if political favors are expected. Other members are ideologically aligned with certain groups who back them at election time. Those following the lead of their party or some other group are operating in what is known as an organizational way.

However, different lawmakers use differing voting models, or approaches to how they vote. Those members trying to reflect the will of their constituency, especially in the House, follow the **delegate model**. At a town hall meeting in one member's district, an irritated and upset constituent shot down his representative's explanation for an unpopular vote. "We didn't send you to Washington to make intelligent decisions," the angry voter said, "we sent you to represent us." That representation can be *substantive*—that is, advocating on behalf of certain groups of constituents—or it can be *descriptive*, advocating not only for the views of constituents but also for the factors that make those constituents unique, such as geography, occupation, gender, and ethnicity.

Some members, especially in the Senate, vote according to the **trustee model**. Representatives believe they are entrusted by their constituency to use their best judgment, regardless of how constituents may view an issue. This approach sidesteps any concern over an uninformed constituency reacting from emotion rather than reason and knowledge.

The **politico model** of voting attempts to blend the delegate and trustee models. That is, lawmakers consider a variety of factors and decide their action or vote for whatever political calculations make the most sense to them at the time, especially when there seems to be little public concern. On matters generating strong public opinion, representatives using the politico model would take those opinions strongly into account.

Redistricting

Following the constitutionally required census every ten years, the reshaping of congressional districts based on shifts in population has influenced congressional behavior. State legislatures' redistricting processes are often competitive and contentious, and members of both parties vie to strengthen their party's chances of winning congressional elections. The redistricting process has increased partisanship and decreased accountabilities. The majority party in the state legislature often determines the new statewide congressional map, usually benefiting that party.

How district boundaries are drawn has an enormous impact on levels of democratic participation and the makeup of the House of Representatives, which in turn has an enormous impact on public policy. Until the 1960s, legislative districting was regarded as having too much political and partisan conflict for the Supreme Court to get involved, since the Court's reputation of neutrality is vital to its authority. However, a landmark decision in 1962 opened the door for the Supreme Court to play a role in making legislative districts as democratic as possible.

MUST-KNOW SUPREME COURT CASE: *BAKER V. CARR* (1962)

The Constitutional Question Before the Court: Can the Supreme Court render judgment on the constitutionality of legislative districts?

Decision: Yes, for Baker, 6:2

Before *Baker*: In 1946, the Court decided in *Colegrove v. Green* that if a state legislature wasn't dividing up congressional districts fairly, it was the people's duty to force the legislature's hand or to vote the legislators out of office. Political scientist Kenneth Colegrove of Northwestern University had brought suit against Illinois officials to stop the upcoming election because the congressional districts lacked "compactness of territory and approximate equality of population." The Supreme Court held that the districts were constitutional, since no law required districts to be compact and equal in population. Justice Frankfurter went further, stating the redistricting process was an issue that would take the Court into the "political thicket," a place it shouldn't go.

The Facts: A Tennessee law from 1901 laid out guidelines for redrawing state legislative boundaries, and the state constitution required redistricting every ten years based on census reports. However, the legislature had failed to redraw the state's 95 voting districts since the census of 1900 and instead had continued to apply the apportionment guidelines from the 1901 law. Over the years, the cities of Nashville, Memphis, Chattanooga, and Knoxville grew, while rural areas developed much more slowly. As a result, the rural areas kept much lower constituent-to-lawmaker ratios. This disparity strengthened some rural citizens' votes and diluted those of some urban voters. For example, one-third of the voters living in the rural areas were electing two-thirds of the state's legislators, so citizens in these districts had a stronger voice on Election Day than voters in the urban districts. In the most extreme cases, some voters had one-twentieth the voting power of other citizens. This practice resulted in minority rule, an outcome in conflict with democratic principles of majority rule and fair representation, since a minority of voters had the majority of voting power. Yet legislators were dissuaded from voting for new maps because they could lose power in the redistricting.

In 1959, Charles Baker and several other litigants sued the Tennessee secretary of state—typically a state's chief election official—because the populations in various state legislative districts varied greatly. The fact that one person's vote was not necessarily equal to another person's vote, Baker said, violated the equal protection clause of the Fourteenth Amendment.

Reasoning: Based on this political inequality, the petitioner wanted the question for the Court to be, "Do Tennessee's outdated and disproportionally populated legislative districts violate the equal protection clause of the Fourteenth Amendment?" But the

Court, having decided in *Colegrove*, had to first address the question of its jurisdiction. Was the issue a *political* question, one for the legislature and ultimately the people to decide? Or was it a *justiciable* question, a question capable of being answered with legal reasoning and, therefore, within the Court's jurisdiction?

The Court decided the matter was justiciable and ruled that the Court can intervene when states do not follow constitutional principles in defining political borders, since those practices undermine the democratic ideal of an equal voice for all voters. The Court also developed a set of six criteria for determining when a question is political and therefore outside of the realm of the Court. But it gave no judgment on the uneven districts and let the lower courts then determine if in fact an inequality existed.

Chief Justice Earl Warren served from 1953 to 1969, overseeing a number of dramatic landmark cases that protected civil liberties and promoted civil rights. Yet, he said after he retired that *Baker v. Carr* was the most important case during his tenure. It helped establish the **"one person-one vote" principle** that greatly expanded democratic participation and the voting rights of minorities.

The Court's Majority Opinion by Mr. Justice William Brennan:
. . . [W]e hold today only (a) that the court possessed jurisdiction of the subject matter; (b) that a justiciable cause of action is stated upon which appellants would be entitled to appropriate relief, and (c) because appellees raise the issue before this Court, that the appellants have standing to challenge the Tennessee apportionment statutes. Beyond noting that we have no cause at this stage to doubt the District Court will be able to fashion relief if violations of constitutional rights are found, it is improper now to consider what remedy would be most appropriate if appellants prevail at the trial . . .
. . . the 1901 statute constitutes arbitrary and capricious state action, offensive to the Fourteenth Amendment in its irrational disregard of the standard of apportionment prescribed by the State's Constitution or of any standard, effecting a gross disproportion of representation to voting population. The injury which appellants assert is that this classification disfavors the voters in the counties in which they reside, placing them in a position of constitutionally unjustifiable inequality vis-a-vis voters in irrationally favored counties. A citizen's right to a vote free of arbitrary impairment by state action has been judicially recognized as a right secured by the Constitution when such impairment resulted from dilution by a false tally, or by a refusal to count votes from arbitrarily selected precincts, or by a stuffing of the ballot box . . .
We conclude that the complaint's allegations of a denial of equal protection present a justiciable constitutional cause of action upon which appellants are entitled to a trial and a decision.

Since *Baker*: The effect of the Court's decision in *Baker v. Carr* was widespread, since not only Tennessee but all states had to redraw legislative boundaries as a result because each person's vote had to be weighted equally. In the 1964 case of *Reynolds v. Sims,* the Court reaffirmed its role in apportionment issues.

Political Science Disciplinary Practices: Analyze, Interpret, and Apply the Decision

The Supreme Court's decision in the *Baker* case overturned precedent established in the *Colegrove v. Green* decision.

Apply: Complete the following tasks.

1. Identify the constitutional principle at issue in this case.
2. Explain how the Court's reasoning in the majority opinion supported the opinion.
3. Explain differences between the opinion in *Colegrove v. Green* and the opinion in *Baker v. Carr*.

Gerrymandering

Too often, there are illogical district lines drawn to give the advantage to one party, a process called **gerrymandering**. Districts in which a party consistently wins by more than 55 percent of the vote are considered *safe seats*; those districts with closer elections are referred to as *marginal seats* or **swing districts**. Countless districts across the United States have been carved out to guarantee safe seats and one-party rule through a process known as *partisan gerrymandering*. Today, each party has more than 180 safe seats in Congress, meaning there are only about 75 marginal seats up for grabs. Certain victory for incumbents or for candidates of the majority party of districts with safe seats lowers the incentive to compromise and raises the incentive to stick with party doctrine. The large number of safe seats encourages a vast proportion of Congress members to take a far left or far right position. Partly because of that divide, at the end of a legislative session, fewer policies that address and appease the middle—the vast majority of the American people—will ever get beyond a committee hearing.

This gerrymandering of safe-seat congressional districts has sometimes made the primary election the determining race and made the general election in November a mere formality. "Getting primaried" has become the new term explaining how an ideologically more extreme challenger can expose an incumbent's record of compromise or tilt away from party positions in order to defeat him or her when the party faithful make that decision. Such challengers are often backed by special interests.

The result is a system of nominating the more conservative Republican or more liberal Democratic candidates who will ultimately win the primary and face off with their extreme counterparts in their respective legislative chambers. This system has shrunk the number of moderates in Congress. To counter this tactic, several states through citizen ballot initiatives and state laws have created independent commissions to remove the parties' dominance in the process of drawing the maps.

Racial Gerrymandering The intentional drawing of legislative districts on the basis of race has also been the subject of scrutiny for conflicting reasons. First, it has been used to dilute the votes of African Americans and therefore has been found to violate their Fifteenth Amendment voting rights. Second, in well-intentioned overcorrections of this problem, racial gerrymandering was found to violate other voters' rights to equal protection under the Fourteenth Amendment. This latter issue was the focus of another landmark redistricting decision from the Supreme Court, *Shaw v. Reno* (1993).

The Constitutional Question Before the Court: Does a congressional district, designed for the purpose of assuring a majority black population, violate the Fourteenth Amendment's equal protection clause?

The Answer: Yes, for Shaw, 5:4

Before *Shaw*: In the late 1950s, as greater numbers of African Americans registered and voted in Alabama, the case of *Gomillion v. Lightfoot* came to the Supreme Court. The city of Tuskegee contained a large black population and was on a path to constituting the majority of voters in the city. In response to this trend and fearing an African American-dominated government, the state legislature passed special legislation to alter the city's borders. What resulted was a 28-sided city border that placed black neighborhoods beyond the new city lines. Tuskegee Institute professor Charles Gomillion sued Tuskegee Mayor Phil Lightfoot. The Supreme Court decided the state, in its purposeful redesign of the city, had violated the litigants' Fifteenth Amendment right to vote.

Facts: After the 1990 census, and in compliance with the 1965 Voting Rights Act (see Topic 3.11), North Carolina submitted to the federal Justice Department its new map of congressional districts for review. Decades of racial gerrymandering in the era before the *Gomillion* decision had effectively disfranchised black voters and kept them from serving in the halls of government. To correct that problem, the Court had ruled that using race as a basis in creating legislative districts, including so-called majority-minority districts that contained more black than white residents, was permissible in the interest of fairness. In the North Carolina map submitted for review, only one district was a majority-minority district. Federal directives and goals encouraged U.S. Attorney General Janet Reno to send the map back to the state and insist it redraw the map with a second black-majority district. North Carolina complied and created some oddly shaped districts in the process.

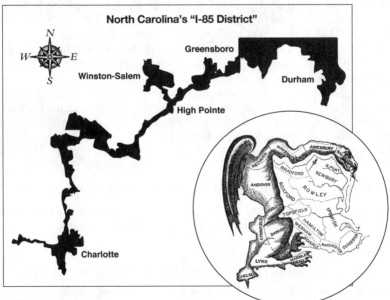

Source: Wikimedia Commons

This cartoon (inset) appeared in a Boston newspaper in 1812 in response to a redistricting in Massachusetts created to favor the party of then-Governor Elbridge Gerry. The oddly shaped district resembled a salamander but in "honor" of the governor was dubbed the "Gerry-mander."

Early court filings and editorials commenting on the illogical districts compared them to a Rorschach inkblot test and "a bug splattered on a windshield." North Carolina's serpent-like 12th district, measuring 160 miles in length, stretched and curved from inner-city neighborhood to inner-city neighborhood to accumulate a majority black population. At some points it was no wider than the Interstate it straddled. Dubbed the "I-85 District," this district and another resulted in two African American candidates—Mel Watt and Eva Clayton—winning seats in Congress. The map called into question the degree to which race can or should be used as a factor in drawing congressional districts. North Carolina's Republican Party and five white individual voters brought suit—Ruth Shaw among them—suggesting the effort came as a result of separating citizens into classes by race in order to form the districts.

Reasoning: In a close vote, the Court ruled for Shaw, not because race was used as a factor in drawing district boundaries but rather that *only* race as a factor could explain the highly irregular district shape and its lack of other characteristics, including geography, usually considered when drawing boundaries. Using race as the only factor in drawing lines opposed the "colorblind" ideal of United States law, separating citizens into different classes without the justification of a compelling state interest and violating the Fourteenth Amendment.

> **The Court's Majority Opinion by Justice Sandra Day O'Connor:**
> Our focus is on appellants' claim that the State engaged in unconstitutional racial gerrymandering. That argument strikes a powerful historical chord: It is unsettling how closely the North Carolina plan resembles the most egregious racial gerrymanders of the past . . .
> This Court never has held that race-conscious state decision making is impermissible in all circumstances. What appellants object to is redistricting legislation that is so extremely irregular on its face that it rationally can be viewed only as an effort to segregate the races for purposes of voting, without regard for traditional districting principles and without sufficiently compelling justification. For the reasons that follow, we conclude that appellants have stated a claim upon which relief can be granted under the Equal Protection Clause . . .
> Accordingly, we have held that the Fourteenth Amendment requires state legislation that expressly distinguishes among citizens because of their race to be narrowly tailored to further a compelling governmental interest . . .
> The message that such districting sends to elected representatives is equally pernicious. When a district obviously is created solely to effectuate the perceived common interests of one racial group, elected officials are more likely to believe that their primary obligation is to represent only the members of that group, rather than their constituency as a whole.

Political Science Disciplinary Practices: Analyze, Interpret, and Apply the Decision

The Court's decision in the *Shaw* case shows that using only race as a factor in creating districts was not aligned with the Fourteenth Amendment.

Apply: Complete the following tasks.

1. Identify two potentially conflicting constitutional principles at issue in this case.
2. Explain how the Court justified its reasoning in the majority opinion.
3. Describe a similarity and a difference between the opinion in *Shaw v. Reno* and the opinion in *Gomillion v. Lightfoot.*

Divided Government and Senate Showdowns

Government is divided when the president is from one party and the House and/or Senate is dominated by the other. It fuels partisan gridlock, especially with judicial nominations. As the Supreme Court has become the arbiter of law on affirmative action, abortion, marriage equality, and gun rights, the fight between the parties about who sits on the Court has intensified.

In 2016, after the death of Associate Justice Antonin Scalia, Democratic President Barack Obama nominated District of Columbia Circuit Judge Merrick Garland to replace him. However, the Republican-held Senate, in a rare though not unprecedented move, refused to consider his nomination during Obama's last year in office. At the time, President Obama was a so-called "**lame duck" president,** or executive who has not won reelection or who is closing in on the end of the second presidential term, highlighting the partisan divide in government. In 2017, President Trump nominated conservative judge Neil Gorsuch to the Scalia seat. Gorsuch was quickly confirmed by a Republican-dominated Senate.

In 2018, an even more contentious confirmation hearing took place over President Trump's nominated Supreme Court Justice Brett Kavanaugh. Democratic senators grilled Kavanaugh on a number of issues, but the most heated discussions revolved around the alleged sexual misconduct of Kavanaugh in the early 1980s. The Republican-held Senate eventually confirmed Kavanaugh.

In both chambers, real floor debate has been replaced by carefully orchestrated speeches, while combative media-hungry lawmakers face off in head-to-head confrontations on cable TV news. As historian Lewis Gould put it, "In this hectic atmosphere of perpetual campaigning, the older values of collegiality and comity, though rarer than senatorial memory had it, eroded to the point of virtual disappearance."

THINK AS A POLITICAL SCIENTIST: *DESCRIBE THE DECISIONS OF REQUIRED SUPREME COURT CASES*

All cases that reach the Supreme Court have previously been ruled on in lower courts. (See Topic 2.8.) The decisions of the Court can define laws and will become the "law of the land." The rulings of the Supreme Court often have a lasting and dramatic effect on many citizens.

Some of the Court's rulings are straightforward and easy to understand, while other rulings can be complicated and challenging to interpret. Occasionally, one Court ruling will relate to another to further clarify an issue. The Supreme Court ruled on several related cases dealing with unequal representation of voters in the 20th century.

Practice: Review the *Baker v. Carr* (1962) and *Shaw v. Reno* (1993) cases from this topic and answer the following questions:

1. What were the similarities between the rulings in the cases?

2. What were the differences between the rulings in the cases?

3. In your opinion, which case will have the larger impact on U. S. politics and policymaking in the 21st century? Explain your answer.

Congress's Public Image

When people asked humorist Will Rogers where he got his jokes, he replied, "Why I just watch Congress and report the facts." Critics from Mark Twain to comedian Jon Stewart have cast Congress in a bad light. The media have also contributed to its tarnished reputation. Members' conflicts of interest and an increased number of scandals have given the institution a black eye.

All of these factors help to create an image of an uncaring, "do nothing" Congress. The branch's overall approval rating, as measured by Gallup, hovered in the mid-30 percent range in the early 1970s. Over the past decade, it has generally fallen below 20 percent.

Yet most individual members of Congress enjoy about a 60 percent approval rating from their constituents. Veteran Congressman Lee Hamilton (D-IN, 1965–1999) once suggested this help-wanted ad to better define the job description: "Wanted: A person with wide-ranging knowledge of scores of complex policy issues. Must be willing to work long hours in Washington, then fly home to attend an unending string of community events. Applicant should expect that work and travel demands will strain family life, and that every facet of public and private life will be subject to intense scrutiny and criticism."

REFLECT ON THE ESSENTIAL QUESTION

Essential Question: *How is congressional behavior influenced by election processes, partisanship, and divided government? On separate paper, complete a chart like the one below.*

Factor that Influences Congressional Behavior	Impact of the Congressional Behavior

KEY TERMS AND NAMES

Baker v. Carr (1962)	politico model
delegate model	racial gerrymandering
gerrymandering	*Shaw v. Reno* (1993)
gridlock	swing district
"lame duck" president	trustee model
"one person-one vote" principle	

CHAPTER 4 Review:
Learning Objectives and Key Terms

TOPIC 2.1: Describe the different structures, powers, and functions of each house of Congress. (CON-3.A)

Structure of Congress (CON-3.A.1)	**Differences Between Houses of Congress** (CON-3.A.2 & 3)	**Powers of Congress** (CON-3.A.4)
bicameral	advice and consent	caucuses
House of Representatives	coalitions	enumerated powers
Senate	power of the purse	implied powers
Seventeenth Amendment (1913)		necessary and proper clause
		War Powers Act (1973)

TOPIC 2.2: Explain how the structures, powers, and functions of both houses of Congress affect the policy-making process. (CON-3.B)

Differing Policymaking Powers (CON-3.B.1 & 5)	**Chamber-Specific Procedures** (CON-3.B.2 & 3)	**Congressional Budget** (CON-3.B.4)
cloture rule	Committee of the Whole	deficit
filibuster	conference committee	discretionary spending
germane	discharge petition	mandatory spending
hold	joint committees	
logrolling	President of the Senate	
omnibus bill	president *pro tempore*	
pork-barrel spending	Rules Committee	
rider	select committee	
sponsor	Senate majority leader	
unanimous consent	Ways and Means Committee	
	whip	

TOPIC 2.3: Explain how congressional behavior is influenced by election processes, partisanship, and divided government. (CON-3.C)

Congressional Behavior (CON-3.C.1)

Baker v. Carr (1962)	politico model
delegate model	racial gerrymandering
gerrymandering	*Shaw v. Reno* (1993)
gridlock	swing district
"lame duck" president	trustee model
"one person-one vote" principle	

CHAPTER 4 Checkpoint:
Congress

Topics 2.1–2.3

Questions 1 and 2 refer to the passage below.

We have before us one of the most important duties of the U.S. Senate and of the U.S. Congress, and that is to decide whether or not we will be involved in war. I think it is inexcusable that the debate over whether we involve the country in war, in another country's civil war, that this would be debated as part of a spending bill, and not as part of an independent, free-standing bill. I think it is a sad day for the U.S. Senate. It goes against our history. It goes against the history of the country.

—Senator Rand Paul, Senate Floor Speech, 2014

1. Which of the following best explains Senator Paul's perspective?

   (A) The United States should not become involved in another country's civil war.

   (B) The president should not have war-making authority except in an emergency.

   (C) The military intervention the United States is considering needs a spending appropriation.

   (D) The U.S. Senate should decide on war-like action on its individual merits.

2. Which institutional power of Congress is Senator Paul most concerned about?

   (A) The power to tax and spend

   (B) The power to ratify treaties

   (C) The power to declare war

   (D) The power to regulate interstate commerce

3. When the Senate Judiciary Committee passes a proposed crime bill by a vote of 11 to 10, which is most likely to follow?

   (A) The Supreme Court will review the bill.

   (B) The full Senate will consider the bill.

   (C) The House of Representatives will consider the bill.

   (D) The president will sign the bill.

Questions 4 and 5 refer to the table below.

HOUSE AND SENATE MEMBERS' AVERAGE AGE, 2011–2018				
Congress	Representatives	Newly Elected Representatives	Senators	Newly Elected Senators
112th	56.7 years	48.2 years	62.2 years	52.1 years
113th	57.0 years	49.2 years	62.0 years	53.0 years
114th	57.0 years	52.3 years	61.0 years	50.7 years
115th	57.8 years	50.8 years	61.8 years	54.8 years

4. Which of the following statements accurately describes a trend in the data above?
   (A) Newly elected members in each chamber are older than the average age of members in that chamber.
   (B) Senators, on average, are younger than representatives.
   (C) The 115th Congress had the youngest newly elected senators compared with earlier Congresses.
   (D) Newly elected senators were on average older than newly elected House members.

5. Which of the following is an accurate conclusion based on the data in the table above?
   (A) Older people vote more frequently, and they want older people representing them.
   (B) Shorter terms allow representatives to be frequently replaced by younger members.
   (C) Serving in Congress often occurs following other successful careers.
   (D) The Constitution requires these lawmakers to be at least 35 years old.

6. Which of the following is an accurate comparison of the processes of the U.S. House of Representatives and the U.S. Senate?

	HOUSE	SENATE
(A)	Allows filibusters until a majority vote defeats the filibuster	Is a 101-member body, as the vice president can vote on all bills
(B)	Has committees chaired by members of the minority party	Is the first chamber to introduce tax bills
(C)	Has more procedural rules guiding its lawmaking process	Has authority over the ratification of treaties with other nations
(D)	Has the sole power to declare war	Has the sole power of impeachment

Concept Application

1. "Across the country, heroin and opioid abuse are growing at rapid rates, especially in New Hampshire. In schools, kids are learning to administer anti-overdose medication. That's how bad the problem is: Police and firefighters, even family and friends, must carry medication like Narcan and know how to use it at a moment's notice. We must protect them from liability laws that could interfere with emergency treatment. I'm grateful to the Judiciary Committee for helping to remove legal barriers."

    —Representative Frank Guinta (R-NH), sponsor
    of House bill (H.R. 5048), 2016

    After reading the scenario, respond to A, B, and C below:

    (A) Describe the power the House Judiciary Committee used to address the concerns outlined by Representative Frank Guinta.

    (B) In context of the scenario, explain how the legislative process was followed by the House of Representatives to deal with the problem.

    (C) In the context of the scenario, explain how the required interactions between the House of Representatives and the Senate would be required to move H.R. 5048 into law.

Quantitative Analysis

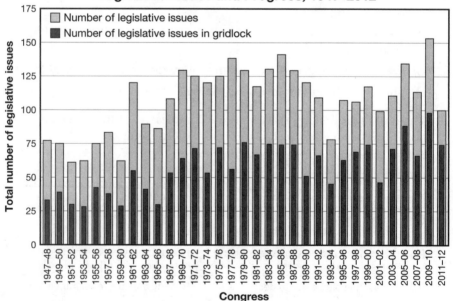

Source: Brookings

Numbers derived from mentions of legislative issues in *New York Times* editorials during Congressional sessions. Gridlock was determined by following progress on the issues.

2. Use the graph from the previous page to answer the questions.

(A) Describe the information the data conveys.

(B) Describe a trend illustrated in the graphic.

(C) Draw a conclusion about the causes of that trend.

(D) Explain how gridlock demonstrates a key characteristic of the U.S. government as envisioned by the framers.

SCOTUS Comparison

3. After the 2000 census, a federal judge drew legislative districts in Texas because Democrats and Republicans could not agree on a map. After gaining power in the elections of 2002, Republicans in the Texas legislature redrew the map in 2003. Plaintiffs sued, arguing that the plan was an unconstitutional partisan gerrymander and violated the equal protection clause and the Voting Rights Act of 1965 by diluting racial minority voting strength. They also believed the mid-decade redistricting was illegal. A three-judge panel ruled that the new map was not unconstitutional, and the case was appealed to the Supreme Court as *League of United Latin American Citizens v. Perry* (2006).

The Court ruled that only one of the new districts, District 23, was drawn in violation of Section 2 of the Voting Rights Act because under the previous redistricting it was a protected majority-minority district of Latinos, but Latinos became a minority of voting-age citizens in the newly drawn district. However, the Court also ruled that the legislature could redraw the map at any time as long as it was done at least every ten years. It also ruled that the map was not unconstitutional on the basis of partisan gerrymandering.

(A) Identify a difference between *League of United Latin American Citizens v. Perry* (2006) and *Shaw v. Reno* (1993).

(B) Explain how the facts in *Shaw v. Reno* (1993) led to a different holding than in *League of United Latin American Citizens v. Perry* (2006).

(C) Describe why these cases caused concern about the Supreme Court and the foundational principle of separation of powers.

CHAPTER 5

The Presidency

Topics 2.4–2.7

Topic 2.4 Roles and Powers of the President

CON-4.A: Explain how the president can implement a policy agenda.

- – Required Foundational Document:
    - • The Constitution of the United States

Topic 2.5 Checks on the Presidency

CON-4.B: Explain how the president's agenda can create tension and frequent confrontations with Congress.

Topic 2.6 Expansion of Presidential Power

CON-4.C: Explain how presidents have interpreted and justified their use of formal and informal powers.

- – Required Foundational Documents: *Federalist No. 70*
    - • The Constitution of the United States

Topic 2.7 Presidential Communication

CON-4.D: Explain how communication technology has changed the president's relationship with the national constituency and the other branches.

Source: Wikimedia Commons
The seal of the President of the United States

Roles and Powers of the President

"The executive branch shall construe [the law] in a manner consistent with the constitutional authority of the President . . .
as Commander in Chief . . . [to protect] the American people from further terrorist attacks."

—President George W. Bush, Signing Statement, 2005

Essential Question: How can a president implement a policy agenda?

The American presidency comes with ceremony, custom, and expectation. Presidential institutions, such as the White House, *Air Force One*, and the State of the Union address, are likely familiar to you. Signing ceremonies and photo opportunities with foreign dignitaries are common images. The Constitution lays out the president's job description in broad language. The president has both formal and informal powers and functions to accomplish a **policy agenda**, a set of issues that are significant to people involved in policymaking.

The American presidency, visible on a world scale, is an iconic and powerful institution that has become much more influential over time. Presidents administer the law through a large bureaucracy of law enforcement, military, trade, and financial agencies. Chief executives meet with world leaders, design the national budget, and campaign for their party's candidates.

Framers' Vision

The delegates in Philadelphia in 1787 voted to make the presidency an executive office for one person. Fears arose because skeptics saw this office as a potential "fetus of monarchy." One delegate tried to allay such fears, explaining "it will not be too strong to say that the station will probably be filled by men preeminent for their ability and virtue."

Article II

The Constitution requires the president to be a natural-born citizen, at least 35 years old, and a U.S. resident for at least 14 years before taking office. The president is the Commander in Chief and also has the power to issue pardons and reprieves, and to appoint ambassadors, judges, and other public ministers. The president can recommend legislative measures to Congress, veto or approve proposed bills (from Article I), and convene or adjourn the houses of Congress. The framers also created a system by which the Electoral College chooses the president every four years.

Presidential Powers, Functions, and Policy Agenda

The president has many powers and functions that enable him to carry out the policy agenda he laid out during the campaign. The president exercises the **formal powers** of the office, those defined in Article II, as well as the **informal powers,** those political powers interpreted to be inherent in the office, to achieve policy goals. Congress and the Supreme Court have bestowed additional duties and placed limits on the presidency.

Formal and Informal Powers

A president cannot introduce legislation on the House or Senate floor but in many ways still serves as the nation's chief lawmaker. Article II also gives the president the power to convene or adjourn Congress at times. As the head of state, the president becomes the nation's chief ambassador and the public face of the country. As Commander in Chief, the president manages the military. Running a federal bureaucracy that resembles a corporation with nearly three million employees, the president is a CEO. And finally, as the de facto head of the party, the president becomes the most identifiable and influential Republican or Democrat in the country.

> ### Article II: Qualifications, Duties, and Limits of the Presidency
> - Must receive a majority of Electoral College votes to win the office
> - Shall hold office for a four-year term
> - Must be natural-born citizen, 35 years old, and U.S resident 14 years
> - Shall be the Commander in Chief of the Army and Navy
> - May require opinions of advisers and department heads
> - May pardon convicted persons for federal offenses
> - Shall appoint ambassadors, judges, and make treaties with Senate approval
> - May recommend measures to Congress
> - May convene or adjourn Congress

Chief Legislator The Constitution provides that the president "may recommend [to Congress] such measures as he shall judge necessary and expedient." Presidents may recommend new laws in public appearances and in their State of the Union address or at other events, pushing Congress to pass their proposals. Congress often leaves this proactive approach to policy leadership to the president rather than taking it upon itself. Presidents have asked Congress to pass laws to clean up air and water, amend the Constitution, create a national health care system, and declare war. A president with a strong personality can serve as the point person and carry out a vision for the country more easily than any or all of the 535 members of Congress.

Powers of Persuasion The president uses a number of skills to win support for a policy agenda. The president will use bargaining and persuasion in an attempt to get Congress to agree with and pass the legislative agenda. President Trump's most notable bill to pass Congress in his first year was a major tax overhaul that reduced corporate taxes from 35 to 21 percent and changed federal income tax rates, lowering them, at least temporarily, for a vast majority of citizens. The Tax Cuts and Jobs Act passed only after Trump, a real estate developer, used his skills as a salesman to push for it. As *Politico* reported, "He has spent weeks wooing, prodding, cajoling and personally calling Republican lawmakers to pass sweeping tax legislation in time for Christmas." He closed on this tax bill as he would have closed a real estate deal decades ago, with a hard and convincing sell. Using his informal political powers, Trump personally called the wavering members of the Senate. The White House organized a speech and presentation, showcasing how the changes would impact some average families, personalizing the promises of the bill.

Veto The president has the final stamp of approval of congressional bills and also a chance to reject them with the executive **veto**. After a bill passes both the House and the Senate, the president has ten days (not including Sundays) to sign it into law. If vetoed, "He shall return it," the Constitution states, "with his objections to the House in which it shall have originated." This provision creates a dialogue between the two branches, enables Congress to consider the president's critique, and encourages consensus policies.

At times, a president will threaten a veto, exercising an informal power that may supersede the formal process. When disagreements between the president and his party or the majority of Congress over the details of a new law exist, the president may threaten to veto, conditionally, if the bill is not satisfactory. Congressional proponents of a bill will work cooperatively to pass it, reshaping it if necessary, to avoid the veto.

The use of the veto has fluctuated throughout presidential history. When there is a divided government—one party dominating Congress and another controlling the presidency—there is usually a corresponding increase in vetoes. The last three presidents, at times, each served with divided governments during their eight years as president. Democrat Bill Clinton had 37 vetoes; Republican George W. Bush and Democrat Barack Obama each had 12.

The president can opt to neither sign nor veto. Any bill not signed or vetoed becomes law after the ten-day period. However, if a president receives a bill in the final ten days of a congressional session and does nothing, this **pocket veto** allows the bill to die.

Congress can override a presidential veto if two-thirds of each house approves the bill. Reaching the two-thirds threshold is very challenging and fewer than 10 percent of a president's vetoes are overridden. (See Topic 1.6 for more on overriding vetoes.)

THINK AS A POLITICAL SCIENTIST: *DESCRIBE TRENDS IN DATA*

Data and statistics are valuable tools to political scientists. Studying trends in data over time helps political scientists understand how events and ideas affect individuals and institutions. This "big picture" view can help interpret the success of politicians and their actions. For example, U.S. presidents are granted the power of signing a bill into law or vetoing a bill. A president who uses the veto infrequently is often viewed as a successful executive because policy goals are accomplished easily. Conversely, a president who vetoes many bills can be regarded as less successful and might have difficulty implementing his policy goals. Does the number of vetoes used by a president show trends in individual success or success for the nation?

Practice: Study the table below, which shows trends in presidential vetoes at different times in the nation's history. Then, offer one reason why those trends might have varied so greatly.

NUMBERS AND TYPES OF VETOES OF SELECTED PRESIDENTS					
Congressional session	President	Years	Vetoes	Pocket vetoes	Divided government (chamber with the majority party opposite the president and number of years)
47th–48th	Chester Arthur (R)	1881–1885	4	1	House—2 years
49th–50th	Grover Cleveland (D)	1885–1889	304	2	House—4 years
51st–52nd	Benjamin Harrison (R)	1889–1893	19	1	House—2 years
71st–72nd	Herbert Hoover (R)	1929–1933	21	3	No
73rd–79th	Franklin Roosevelt (D)	1933–1945	372	9	No
83rd–86th	Dwight Eisenhower (R)	1953–1961	73	2	Both chambers— 6 years
87th–88th	John Kennedy (D)	1961–1963	12	0	No

Source: House of Representatives

Line-Item Veto Since the founding, presidents have argued for the right to a line-item veto. This measure would empower an executive to eliminate a line of spending from an appropriations bill or a budgeting measure, allowing the president to veto part, but not all, of the bill. Many state governors have the line-item veto power. In 1996, Congress granted this power to the president for appropriations, or new direct spending, and limited tax benefits. Unlike a Congress member, the president has no loyalties to a particular congressional district and can thus sometimes make politically difficult local spending cuts without concern for losing much regional or national support.

Under the new act, President Clinton cut proposed federal monies earmarked for New York City. The city sued, arguing that the Constitution gave Congress the power of the purse as an enumerated congressional power, and New York City believed this new law suddenly shifted that power to the president. The Court agreed that the only way to give the president this power would be through a constitutional amendment and struck down the act in *Clinton v. City of New York* (1998). Presidents and fiscal conservatives continue to call for a line-item veto to reduce spending. There is little doubt that such power would reduce at least some federal spending. However, few lawmakers (who can currently send pork barrel funds to their own districts) are willing to provide the president with the authority to take away that perk.

Commander in Chief

The framers named the president the **Commander in Chief** with much control over the military. The Constitution, however, left the decision of declaring war solely to the Congress. The question of what constitutes a war, though, is not always clear.

Senator Barry Goldwater proclaimed in the waning days of the Vietnam conflict, "We have only been in five declared wars out of over 150 that we have fought." His point was fair, although his estimate was debatable. The issue remains: Should all troop landings be considered wars that therefore require congressional declarations?

When a military operation is defensive, in response to a threat to or attack on the United States, the executive can act quickly. FDR ordered U.S. troops to Greenland in 1940 after the Nazis marched into Denmark but before any U.S. declaration of war. President Clinton bombed Iraq after discovering the failed assassination attempt on his predecessor, the elder President Bush. President Obama authorized the U.S. mission in 2011 to capture or kill Osama bin Laden, the al-Qaeda founder responsible for the September 11, 2001, attacks. A U.S. Navy Seal team was on the ground in Pakistan for only about 40 minutes. Some believe that actions such as these stretch the meaning of "defensive" too far. Yet how successful would this mission have been if Congress had to debate publicly and vote in advance on whether or not to invade the unwilling country that harbored bin Laden?

The Cold War era greatly expanded the president's authority as Commander in Chief. In the early 1960s, one senator conceded that the president must have some war powers because "the difference between safety and cataclysm can be a matter of hours or even minutes." The theory of a strong defense against "imminent" attack has obliterated the framers' distinction and has added an elastic theory of defensive war to the president's arsenal. Imminent-defense theorists argue the world was much larger in 1789, considering warfare, weaponry, and the United States' position in the world. Today, with so many U.S. interests abroad, an attack on American interests or an ally far from U.S. shores can directly and immediately impact national security.

Chief Diplomat

Through treaties, presidents can facilitate trade, provide for mutual defense, help set international environmental standards, or prevent weapons testing, as long as the Senate approves. President Woodrow Wilson wanted the United States to join the League of Nations after World War I, but the Senate refused to ratify Wilson's Treaty of Versailles.

An **executive agreement** resembles a treaty yet does not require the Senate's two-thirds vote. It is a simple contract between two heads of state: the president and a prime minister, king, or president of another nation. Like any agreement, such a contract is only as binding as each side's ability and willingness to fulfill the promise. To carry it out, a president will likely need cooperation from other people and institutions in the government. These compacts cannot violate prior treaties or congressional acts, and they are not binding on successive presidents.

Presidents have come to appreciate the power of the executive agreement. President Washington found conferring with the Senate during each step of a delicate negotiation extremely cumbersome and perhaps dangerous. It compromised confidentiality and created delays.

Executive agreements can ensure secrecy or speed or avoid ego clashes in the Senate. During the Cuban Missile Crisis in October 1962, President Kennedy discovered the Soviet Union's plan to install nuclear missiles in Cuba. Intelligence reports estimated these weapons would be operational within two weeks. After days of contemplation, negotiation, and a naval standoff in the Caribbean, the United States and the Soviet Union made a deal. The agreement stated that the Soviets would remove their offensive missiles from Cuba if the United States would later remove its own missiles from Turkey. Had Kennedy relied on two-thirds of the Senate to help him solve the crisis, a different outcome could very well have occurred. Time, strong words on the Senate floor, or an ultimate refusal could have drastically reversed this historic outcome.

Executive Powers and Policy—The Panama Canal

The policies of two presidents regarding the Panama Canal show two very different ways of using the powers of the executive branch to advance a policy agenda and interact with Congress.

Acquiring the Panama Canal Zone "Speak softly and carry a big stick." These words of President Theodore Roosevelt describe his foreign policy in relation to Latin America, where he wanted to assert U.S. power. However, the words might also describe his approach to Congress.

Shortly after becoming President, Roosevelt spoke to Congress about the importance of linking the Atlantic and Pacific Oceans to shorten trade routes with a canal through Panama. Using his powers of persuasion, Roosevelt convinced the Senate to pass a treaty to acquire the canal zone from Colombia, but the government of Columbia balked.

Panamanians had long wanted their independence from Colombia and struck a deal with the United States. If American forces supported Panamanian independence, the new government would sell the land to the United States to build a canal. Leaders of American business interests in the area offered bribes to Panamanian officials to let the rebellion prevail, and Roosevelt sent the *USS Nashville* to the region in a show of rebel support, an example of Roosevelt's so-called "gunboat diplomacy." Colombia agreed to grant independence to Panama. Soon after, the Canal Zone was sold to the United States.

Some in the United States saw Roosevelt's participation in the rebellion as an act of piracy or worse. But Roosevelt defended his actions and use of executive powers, saying years later, "If I had followed traditional, conservative methods, I should have submitted a dignified state paper of probably two hundred pages to Congress, and the debate would have been going on yet. But I took the Canal Zone, and let Congress debate, and while the debate goes on, the Canal does also!" The treaty was finally ratified in 1904; the canal opened in 1914.

Returning the Canal Zone to Panama The canal cut Panama into two sections, with the Canal Zone under the control of the United States. Over time, the continued involvement of the United States strained relations between the the two nations. Only after decades of conflict did the United States soften its "big stick" policy and support more democracy in the region.

Panama's desire to fly its flag over the Canal Zone had long been a source of tension. On January 9, 1964, violence erupted when the only Panamanian flag flying in the Canal Zone was torn. A number of protesting students overwhelmed Canal Zone police, and U.S. troops were brought in. Twenty Panamanians were killed. In Panama, that day has since become known as Martyrs Day. Panama broke off diplomatic relations with the United States and demanded a new treaty.

When Jimmy Carter became president (1977–1981), he articulated his approach to foreign policy with an emphasis on morality. "Our policy is based on a historical vision of America's role. . . . Our policy is rooted in our moral values, which never change. . . . Our policy is designed to serve [hu]mankind."

Returning the Canal Zone to Panamanian control was high on Carter's list of foreign policy objectives for several reasons. First, he saw the control of the Canal Zone as a holdover from an imperial past and wanted to remove any symbolic representation of imperialism, believing it affected U.S. relations with all Latin American countries. Also, he believed it was the moral responsibility of the United States to respect the complete self-governance of Panama.

Carter set in motion a carefully planned effort to win support in Congress for the return of the Canal Zone to Panama, relying on powers of persuasion and personal relationships to achieve his goals. Specifically, he and his legislative team provided extensive briefings and education to members of Congress and sent them to the region to gather information firsthand, and Carter got personally involved in discussions. His team was also meticulous about learning exactly which lawmakers' votes they could count on and which votes they needed to nurture. They developed an extensive public relations campaign to educate the American people on the issue and made visits to congressional districts where pressure from constituents might sway a member's vote.

Carter's patient diplomacy with Congress paid off. In 1978, new agreements that guaranteed the U.S. military protection of the canal to assure fair and full passage and also formally returned full sovereignty to Panama over the Canal Zone beginning on December 31, 1999, were ratified by a Senate vote of 68-32.

Chief Executive and Administrator

How the president and his appointees enforce or implement a new law will shape the administration's policy agenda. Using executive orders, signing statements, and running the machinery of the vast executive branch mark how a president carries out the powers and functions as the chief executive. The Supreme Court has defined some of the gray areas of presidential power. For example, the president can fire most Senate-approved subordinates without cause.

Executive Orders An **executive order** empowers the president to carry out the law or to administer the government. Unlike a criminal law or monetary appropriation, which requires Congress to act, a presidential directive falls within executive authority. For example, the president can define how the military and other departments operate.

Executive orders have the effect of law and address issues ranging from security clearances for government employees to smoking in the federal workplace. In 1942, for example, President Franklin Roosevelt (FDR) issued the infamous Executive Order 9066, which allowed persons identified by the secretary of war to be excluded from certain areas. This executive order resulted in the internment of Japanese Americans during World War II. In 1948, through an executive order, President Harry Truman directed the military to racially integrate. Recently, President Donald Trump issued an executive order outlining an immigration policy that limited travelers entering the United States from six countries with Muslim-majority populations. Executive orders cannot address matters under exclusive congressional jurisdiction, such as altering the tax code, creating new interstate commerce regulations, or redesigning the currency. Executive orders can also be challenged in court. The Supreme Court upheld both FDR's wartime internment and Trump's travel ban.

Signing Statements Though the president cannot change the wording of a bill, several presidents have offered **signing statements** when signing a bill into law. These statements explain their interpretation of a bill, their understanding of what is expected of them to carry it out, or just a commentary on the law. A signing statement allows a president to say, in effect, "Here's how I understand what I'm signing and here's how I plan to enforce it." Critics of the signing statement argue that it violates the basic lawmaking design and overly enhances a president's last-minute input on a bill.

Executive Privilege Starting with George Washington's precedent, presidents have asserted **executive privilege,** the right to withhold information or their decision-making process from another branch, especially Congress. They have particularly asserted that they need not make public any advice they received from their subordinates to protect confidentiality. Presidents have also claimed that such information is privileged, protected by the separation of powers.

President Richard Nixon tested executive privilege during the Watergate scandal when Nixon and others were accused of covering up criminal actions against political rivals. Nixon refused to turn over investigator-subpoenaed tapes, alleged to reveal the president's knowledge of the 1972 break-in at the Watergate Office Building to steal information about the Democratic Party. Nixon declared his secretly recorded conversations were protected from congressional inquiry by executive privilege. In *U.S. v. Nixon* (1974), the Supreme Court did acknowledge that executive privilege is constitutional and necessary at times. Yet the Court unanimously agreed the tapes amounted to evidence in a criminal investigation and therefore were *not* protected by executive privilege. Nixon turned over the recordings.

REFLECT ON THE ESSENTIAL QUESTION

Essential Question: *How can a president can implement policy agenda? On separate paper, complete a chart like the one below.*

Power Granted to the President	Example in Implementing Policy Agenda

KEY TERMS AND NAMES

bargaining and persuasion	informal powers
Commander in Chief	line-item veto
formal powers	pocket veto
executive agreement	policy agenda
executive order	signing statements
executive privilege	veto

Checks on the Presidency

"It is important, likewise, that the habits of thinking in a free Country should inspire caution in those entrusted with its administration, to confine themselves within their respective Constitutional spheres; avoiding in the exercise of the Powers of one department to encroach upon another."

—George Washington, Farewell Address, 1796

Essential Question: How could the president's agenda contribute to confrontations with Congress?

The president's formal powers enable him to appoint a team to execute the laws and to accomplish his policy agenda. Some of those administrators hold positions Congress created in 1789. Many more subordinate positions exist because Congress has since created them or has allotted funds for offices to support the president. A typical president will appoint thousands of executive branch officials during their tenure. Atop that list are the Cabinet officials, then agency directors, military leaders and commissioned officers, and the support staff that work directly for the president. Most of these employees serve at the pleasure of the president, and some are kept on when a new president is elected. Other positions are protected by statute or Supreme Court decisions.

The President's Team

The president is faced with countless decisions each day and many of those decisions have exceptionally important consequences to the fate of the nation. A large team is needed to assist the president in making these decisions. Article II, Section 2, of the Constitution gives the president the power to assemble that group and ". . . appoint ambassadors, other public ministers and consuls . . . and all other officers of the United States whose appointments are not herein otherwise provided for and which shall be established by law."

The Vice President

A political party's presidential nominee, in consultation with the party, selects a vice president before the election. Many assume the vice president is the second most powerful governmental officer in the United States, but in reality, the vice president is an assistant to the president with little influence and a largely undefined job description. Different presidents have given their vice presidents differing degrees of authority and assigned them different roles.

The Constitution names the vice president as the president of the Senate and declares that in case of presidential removal, death, resignation, or inability, the president's duties and powers "shall devolve on the vice president."

Shaping and Supporting Policy In recent years, the position has been especially influential on presidential policy. Many believed George W. Bush's vice president Dick Cheney, a hawkish former defense secretary, was overly influential. He promoted a tough stance on terrorists and also toward nations that harbor them. He pushed for the 2003 invasion of Iraq in search of "weapons of mass destruction" but none were found.

Vice President Joe Biden, serving under Obama, sustained his high influence for eight years. Obama assigned several policy goals to the affable former senator who had served in Washington since the early 1970s. Biden focused on concluding the mission in Iraq and gained budget deals with Republican congressional leaders. Biden was the point man on other foreign policy matters. The president gave "Uncle Joe" a presidential medal of freedom and called him "the best vice president America has ever had."

In 2020, after the global coronavirus pandemic upended life around the world and cost thousands of people their lives, President Trump appointed his vice president, Mike Pence, to coordinate the nation's response. Pence called upon the globally recognized expert on infectious disease Dr. Dorothy Birx to recommend policy based on scientific predictions of how the disease would spread.

The Cabinet and Bureaucracy

Article II alludes to a **Cabinet** when it mentions "the principal officers in each of the executive departments." Today, 15 Cabinet secretaries, such as the secretary of defense and secretary of transportation, advise the president, but they spend even more time running large governmental departments that take care of a wide range of national concerns. Presidents can add additional members to the Cabinet. President Trump has included the vice president, his chief of staff, and seven others beyond the 15 department heads in this formal group.

Secretaries When appointing Cabinet secretaries, modern presidents create some balance based on geography, gender, ethnicity, and even partisan ideology. Presidents have found showcasing minority appointments and stocking their team with a visible, diverse staff to be in the interest of accomplishing their agendas.

Franklin Roosevelt (1933–1945) appointed the first woman to the Cabinet, Secretary of Labor Francis Perkins, and Lyndon Johnson (1963–1969) appointed the first African American, Secretary of Housing and Urban Development Robert Weaver. This tokenism—or mainly symbolic appointment of a small number of underrepresented groups to give the impression of diversity—continued until President Jimmy Carter appointed substantial numbers of African Americans and women to his senior executive positions—16 percent women and 11 percent ethnic minorities. The Cabinet has since included Latinos, Asian Americans, and nontraditional appointees to Cabinet positions, and 53 percent of Obama's first-term Cabinet appointees were either women or minorities.

Source: Lyndon Baines Johnson Library and Museum

Robert Clifton Weaver, first Secretary of Housing and Urban Development and first African American Cabinet appointee who served from 1966–1968 under President Lyndon Johnson.

State Department The first department Congress created in 1789 was the Department of State, headed by Thomas Jefferson. Its role is to promote foreign policy of the United States across the globe. The State Department is the president's main diplomatic body. Deputy secretaries oversee U.S. relations in designated regions or continents. For each nation that the United States recognizes (nearly every nation in the world), the State Department operates an embassy in that country and employs an **ambassador,** a top diplomat appointed to represent the United States with that foreign nation. That country will likely have an embassy in Washington. About two-thirds of U.S. ambassadors come from careers in foreign affairs or are international experts. About one-third are political appointees—former senators, political friends, or well-known Americans to impress the host country.

Defense Department The Defense Department is headquartered at the Pentagon, just outside the nation's capital. Secretaries of defense are civilian officers who serve the president and have not served in the uniformed military service for at least seven years. The Constitution and U.S. tradition dictate that the military leadership and policymaking apparatus be distinct and separate from the uniformed divisions that carry out military missions. Ultimately, the people run the military through their elected and constitutional civil officers, in contrast to many dictatorships. Dictatorships, lacking constitutional protections, come into being when a strong military leader takes over the military first and the government second.

The Defense Department includes the Army, Navy, Air Force, and Marines—all of the nation's military branches under one command. The **Joint Chiefs of Staff**, a council of the top uniformed officials from each division, advises the president on military strategy. Defense comprises about one-fifth of the overall federal budget and the largest portion of the nation's discretionary spending.

Federal Agencies Federal agencies are subcabinet entities that carry out specific government functions. Many fall under larger departments. The Federal Bureau of Investigation (FBI)—a crime fighting organization—falls under the Justice Department. The Coast Guard falls under the Department of Homeland Security. Other agencies include the Food and Drug Administration (FDA), the Internal Revenue Service (IRS), the Central Intelligence Agency (CIA), and the Postal Service. Thousands of people in Washington and across the country staff these few hundred executive branch agencies. They carry out laws Congress has passed with funds Congress has allotted.

President's Immediate Staff

In 2008, 74 separate policy offices and 6,574 total employees worked for the president (most not working in the White House). Ideally, all of the offices and agencies play a part in implementing the president's policy goals.

The Executive Office of the President (EOP) operates within walking distance of the White House. It coordinates several independent agencies that carry out presidential duties and handle the budget, the economy, and staffing across the bureaucracy. Created in 1939 when FDR needed an expanded presidential staff, the EOP now includes the Office of Management and Budget, the Central Intelligence Agency, the Council of Economic Advisers, and other agencies.

White House Staff The president's immediate staff of specialists make up the White House Office. These staffers require no Senate approval and tend to come from the president's inner circle or campaign team. They generally operate in the West Wing of the building. Presidents sometimes come to rely on their White House staffs more than their Cabinet or agency heads because staff members serve the president directly. Unlike secretaries, they do not have loyalties to departments or agencies and do not compete for funding. The staff interacts and travels with the president daily and many staffers have worked with prior presidents. A staffer's individual relationship with and access to the president will determine his or her influence.

In the 1950s, President Eisenhower's **chief of staff** became his gatekeeper, responsible for the smooth operation of the White House and the swift and accurate flow of business, paper, and information. Though the chief of staff has no official policymaking power, a president seeks the chief of staff's opinion on many issues, giving the position a great deal of influence. Chiefs of staff tend to be tough, punctual, detail-oriented managers, and these qualities allow the president to concentrate on big-picture decisions.

The remainder of the president's inner circle includes the top communicator to the people, the White House press secretary; the president's chief legal counsel; and his national security adviser. The national security adviser coordinates information coming to the president from the CIA, the military, and the State Department to assess any security threat to the United States. This person heads the National Security Council that includes the president, secretaries of defense and state, top intelligence and uniformed military leaders, and a few others.

Selected Cabinet Level Departments and Agencies

Executive Office of the President	President Vice President	White House Office
Council on Economic Advisors Office of Management & Budget Central Intelligence Agency National Security Council Others	15 cabinet secretaries	White House Staff Chief of Staff Press Secretary Legal counsel

State	Treasury	Defense	Justice	Labor	Homeland Security
Regional offices, Ecomonic & Business Affairs Ambassadors United States Agency for International Development	IRS, Comptroller of Currency, Engraging & Printing, U.S. Mint Financial Crimes Enforcement Network	Joint Chiefs of Staff Army, Navy, Air Force, Marine Corp, National Guard, Defense Intelligence Agency	Solicitor General FBI, DEA, ATF, Civil rights Division, Bureau of Prisons, U.S. Attorneys, Marshals	Bureau of Labor Statistics Mine Safety & Health Disability Employment	FEMA, TSA, Customs & Border Protection Coast Guard Secret Service USCIS

Independent Agencies and Government Corporations	Independent Regulatory Agencies
NASA Post Office AMTRAK Corporation for Public Broadcasting Tennessee Valley Authority Others	FCC: FederalCommunications Commission FEC: Federal Elections Commission FDA: Food & Drug Administration EPA: Environmental Protection Agency SEC: Securities & Exchanges Ommission

Interactions with Other Branches

Since Congress writes most law, holds the federal purse, and confirms presidential appointments, presidents must stay in good graces with representatives and senators. The president's agenda is not always Congress's agenda, however, and tensions often arise between the branches. As chief legislator, the president directs the Office of Legislative Affairs to draft bills and assist the legislative process. (See Topic 2.2.) Sometimes the aides employ techniques to push public opinion in a lawmaker's home district in the direction of a desired presidential policy so that the lawmaker's constituency can apply pressure. As the president enforces or administers the law, the courts determine if laws are broken, misapplied, or unjust. For these reasons, a president regularly interacts with the legislative and judicial branches.

Checks on Presidential Powers

The framers took seriously the concerns of the Anti-Federalists and included specific roles and several provisions to limit the powers of the future strong, singular leader.

The Senate has the power to provide advice and consent on appointments, for example, and the presidential salary is set by Congress and cannot increase or decrease during the elected term. The framers also expressly made the president subject to impeachment. (See Topic 1.6.)

While some presidential powers, such as serving as Commander in Chief, appointing judges and ambassadors, and vetoing legislation, are explicit, presidents and scholars have argued about the gray areas of a president's job description. Most presidents have claimed **inherent powers**, those that may not be explicitly listed but are nonetheless within the jurisdiction of the executive. This debate has taken place during nearly every administration when an emergency has arisen or when the Constitution doesn't specifically address an emerging issue. Presidents have fought battles for expanded powers, winning some and losing others. The debate continues today.

The Senate and Presidential Appointees

In addition to the more visible Cabinet appointees, a president will appoint approximately 65,000 military leaders and about 2,000 civilian officials per two-year congressional term, most of whom are confirmed routinely, often approved *en bloc*, hundreds at a time. Occasionally, high-level appointees are subjected to Senate investigation and public hearing. Most are still approved, while a few will receive intense scrutiny and media attention, and some appointments will fail.

Because the founders did not anticipate that Congress would convene as frequently as it does in modern times, they provided for *recess appointments*. If the Senate is not in session when a vacancy arises, the president can appoint a replacement who will serve until the Senate reconvenes and votes on that official. This recess appointment is particularly necessary if the appointee is to handle urgent or sensitive work. This situation is rare, especially when the government is divided. Often a *pro forma*, or "in form only," session will be called to ensure the Senate technically remains in session. These sessions often last only a few minutes.

The Senate invariably accepts presidential Cabinet nominations. The upper house swiftly confirmed every Cabinet-level secretary until 1834, when it rejected Andrew Jackson's appointee, Roger Taney, as secretary of the treasury over Taney's opposition to a national bank. The makeup of the Senate changed with the next election and Jackson appointed Taney as chief justice of the Supreme Court, who was confirmed for the position by a slim margin. To date, the Senate has rejected, by vote, only nine department secretaries.

The Senate usually accepts Cabinet appointees based on the reasoning that since the president won a democratic election, he should therefore have the prerogative of shaping the administration. Presidents commonly choose senators to move over to the executive branch and serve in their Cabinet. In recent years, the president has selected one or more members of the opposite party. President Obama named three Republicans to serve as secretaries (though one declined the offer). Presidents and their transition teams do a considerable amount of vetting of potential nominees and connecting with senators to evaluate their chances before making official nominations. Though only nine nominations have been rejected by vote, 13 Cabinet appointees withdrew before the Senate voted. Additional names have been floated among senators, but they didn't receive the support to justify the official nomination.

Senate Standoffs The two most recent standoffs on Cabinet appointments came in 1989 and in 2017. President George H. W. Bush named former Senator John Tower as secretary of defense, and President Donald J. Trump nominated Betsy DeVos as secretary of education. Senator Tower had served in the Senate since Lyndon Johnson vacated the seat to become vice-president. Tower had the resume and experience to serve as defense secretary. He served in World War II and later as the chairman of the Senate Armed Services Committee. Upon his nomination, even Democratic Party leaders anticipated his nomination would sail through. However, allegations of heavy drinking and "womanizing" surfaced. Additionally, Tower owned stock in corporations with potential future defense contracts, an obvious conflict of interest. President Bush stuck by his former congressional colleague (Bush had represented Texas in the House). In the end, the Senate voted Tower down 53 to 47.

In 2017, President Trump nominated Betsy DeVos as education secretary. Like some conservatives, she held interest in privatizing education and, if confirmed, she would pursue that agenda goal. Despite DeVos advocating for private schools for many years before her nomination, she had never worked in public schooling in any capacity, including as a teacher, and along with her billionaire husband she had invested in for-profit charter schools and pushed for online education. The educational community was generally against her nomination, with some exceptions. At her public confirmation hearing, many senators expressed concern about her priorities, her experience, and her high-dollar donations to Republican candidates. As she fielded questions before the Senate committee, her competence in the field seemed shaky. Exchanges on school choice, guns in schools, students with disabilities, and private or online school accountability raised eyebrows on Capitol Hill and in news reports that followed. In the end, two Republican senators voted against her, leaving the Senate in a dead tie. Vice President Pence's tie-breaking vote made DeVos the secretary of education.

Ambassador Appointments The Senate is also likely to confirm ambassador appointments, although those positions are often awarded to people who helped fund the president's campaign rather than people well qualified for the job. On one of the "Nixon Tapes" from 1971, Nixon tells his chief of staff that "anybody who wants to be an ambassador must at least give $250,000." About 30 percent of ambassadors are political appointees. Some may have little or no experience to qualify them, though they are rarely rejected by the Senate.

Hotel magnate George Tsunis, appointed by President Obama as ambassador to Norway, was questioned critically by Senator John McCain (R-AZ) in 2014 and shown to have limited understanding of Norwegian political issues; he withdrew his nomination after a year when confirmation seemed unlikely. Trump's ambassador to the European Union, Gordon Sondland, donated $1,000,000 to Trump's inaugural fund.

THINK AS A POLITICAL SCIENTIST: *EXPLAIN HOW POLITICAL PROCESSES APPLY TO DIFFERENT SCENARIOS*

A political process enables the creation of public policy when public opinion and political institutions interact. For example, the Senate is the institution that ensures the worthiness of presidential appointments to various federal positions as a check on the executive branch. In addition to their individual opinions on nominees, senators have to consider the reaction of the public to those appointees. The approval or disapproval of presidential appointments can be an indicator of the opinion of the people of the United States on key issues at a point in the nation's history.

Practice: Read the summaries of Senate action on presidential nominees and answer the questions that follow.

Thurgood Marshall: Supreme Court, 1967. After having argued more than 30 cases before the Supreme Court as an attorney, he was approved by a vote of 69–11. He became the first African American to serve as a justice on the Court.

Sandra Day O'Connor: Supreme Court, 1981. Republican President Ronald Reagan nominated the conservative leaning O'Connor. Her confirmation hearing was the first televised and mostly dealt with the topic of abortion. O'Connor was unanimously approved and the first female to serve as a justice on the Court.

Robert Bork: Supreme Court, 1987. In one the most lopsided margins for a failed vote, 58–42, Bork was not approved by the Senate. Senators attacked Bork's belief that the Constitution had no right to privacy and subsequently was not guaranteed by federal actions. The American Civil Liberties Union (ACLU) and several women's groups expressed strong opposition to Bork's nomination.

John Tower: Secretary of Defense, 1989. President Bush's choice of Tower was met with strong congressional opposition, as he was believed to own stock in defense companies and therefore had a conflict of interest. There were also questions about his character as he was seen as a heavy drinker and womanizer. The Senate voted against Tower 53–47.

1. How would you characterize the approval of Thurgood Marshall, considering the state of race relations in the 1960s? (See Topic 3.10 for more on civil rights.)

2. How might the Supreme Court case of *Roe v. Wade* (1973) have influenced the nomination and approval of O'Connor? (See Topic 3.9 for more on *Roe v. Wade*.)

3. What can be inferred as a key issue of the 1980s from the failed appointments of Robert Bork and John Tower?

Removal The president can remove upper-level executive branch officials at will, except those that head independent regulatory agencies. (See Topic 2.13.) A president's power of removal has been the subject of debate since the writing of the Constitution. Alexander Hamilton argued that the Senate should, under its advice and consent power, have a role in the removal of appointed officials. James Madison, however, argued that to effectively administer the government the president must retain full control of subordinates. The Article II phrase that grants the president the power to "take care that the laws be faithfully executed" suggests the president has a hierarchical authority over secretaries, ambassadors, and other administrators. This issue brought Congress and the president to a major conflict in the aftermath of the Civil War. President Andrew Johnson dismissed Secretary of War Edwin Stanton, congressional Republicans argued, in violation of the Tenure of Office Act. This action led to Johnson's impeachment.

The question of removal resurfaced in 1926. The Supreme Court concluded that presidential appointees "serve at the pleasure of the president." The Court tightened this view a few years later when it looked at a case in which the president had fired a regulatory agency director. The Court ruled in that case that a president can dismiss the head of a regulatory bureau or commission but only upon showing cause, explaining the reason for the dismissal. The two decisions collectively define the president's authority: executive branch appointees serve at the pleasure of the president, except regulatory heads, whom the president can remove with explanation.

Judicial Interactions

Presidents interact with the judiciary in a few ways. As the head of the executive branch, presidents enforce judicial orders. For example, when the Supreme Court ruled in 1957 that Central High had to admit nine African American students into the school, President Eisenhower ordered the 101st Airborne Division into Little Rock, Arkansas, to ensure the school followed the court order. The branches also interact when courts check the executive if they find presidential action unconstitutional. For example, in 1952 the Supreme Court overturned President Truman's decision to nationalize steel industries during the Korean War. Truman had taken that step to mobilize resources for the Korean War and also to prevent a strike by steelworkers. The Court ruled, however, that the president lacked authority to seize private property.

In 2014, President Obama announced an executive order that would delay the deportation of millions of illegal immigrants. The order was met with strong opposition from Republicans. By the end of the year, 26 states, led by Texas, took legal action to stop Obama's plan. The case made it to the Supreme Court, and a 4-4 split affirmed a lower court injunction, ultimately blocking Obama's order. It was an eight-member Court due to the death of Justice Antonin Scalia.

Judicial Appointments A more frequent encounter of the two branches comes when presidents appoint federal judges. All federal judges serve for life terms, so only a fraction of the federal courts will have openings during a president's time in office. Yet presidents see this opportunity as a way to put like-minded men and women on federal benches across the country. Of course, like appointments in the executive branch, the Senate must approve these nominees.

While standoffs about Cabinet appointees are rare, judicial nominations are another story. Judges have greater influence of shaping the law and can serve for life, so there is more at stake. The president appoints scores of federal judges during each four-year term, because, in addition to the nine justices on the Supreme Court, nearly 1,000 federal judges serve the other federal courts. Throughout U.S. history, 30 Supreme Court nominees have been rejected by a Senate vote. Many other lower court nominees have also been rejected or delayed to the point of giving up on the job.

The interaction between the branches on these judicial nominees is complicated and sometimes contentious. Senate rules and traditions govern the process. Senators, especially those on the Judiciary Committee, expect to advise presidents on selecting these nominees and are sometimes slow to consent to the president's choices. They, too, realize the longevity of a federal judge's service. If the president appoints like-minded judges, senators on the opposite end of the ideological spectrum are unlikely to welcome the judges, since their future decisions could define controversial or unclear law.

A divided electorate has caused majority control of the Senate to shift from one party to the other, and the cloture motion has served a somewhat stabilizing function. (See Topic 2.2.) According to a 2013 decision, if a senator wants to block a judicial nomination with a filibuster, only a simple majority of senators would be required to prevent that.

REFLECT ON THE ESSENTIAL QUESTION

Essential Question: *How could the president's agenda cause confrontations with Congress? On separate paper, complete a chart like the one below.*

Areas of Conflict Between the President and Congress	Examples of Conflict Between the President and Congress

---

KEY TERMS AND NAMES

ambassadors	inherent powers
Cabinet	Joint Chiefs of Staff
chief of staff	

Expansion of Presidential Power

"The imperial presidency, created by wars abroad, has made a bold bid for power at home."

—Historian Arthur Schlesinger, *The Atlantic Monthly*, 1973

Essential Question: How have presidents interpreted and explained their use of formal and informal powers?

Since the creation of the office, United States citizens have come to expect more and more from the president. A constant push and pull on the office ultimately defines what a president can do. The framers set forth specific guidelines, yet presidents continue to challenge the constitutional framework. For example, not long after Donald J. Trump was sworn into office in January 2017, the debate about his powers intensified. As he tried to move his policy agenda forward, he met with resistance and tension from Congress, the courts, the media, and some protesting citizens. President Trump is not alone in facing resistance. Other presidents have also had conflicts as they increased the power of the office in their efforts to accomplish policy goals.

An Enhanced Presidency

The presidency is shaped by Article II, five constitutional amendments, federal law, Supreme Court decisions, customs, and precedents. This limited executive office was designed to carry out Congress's policies. The office, however, has become a powerful captain's ship of state, buoyed by support institutions and American expectation.

FOUNDATIONAL DOCUMENTS: *FEDERALIST NO. 70*

Critics of the proposed Constitution questioned Article II and the creation of the presidency. A single person in charge of the administration of government and the executive branch, the Anti-Federalists argued, would be dangerous. Twenty-five of the Federalists' essays address Article II, and 42 different passages across the collection of these essays make points about the chief executive, presidential powers, term, relationship to the other branches, and the method of elections. In *Federalist No. 70*, Alexander Hamilton, writing as Publius, foreshadows the "ingredients" of the presidency and mainly focuses on the value of the unity in a single executive to avoid conflicts and to ensure accountability.

[The framers] have declared in favour of a single executive, and a numerous legislature. They have with great propriety, considered energy as the most necessary qualification of the former, and have regarded this as most applicable to power in a single hand ... Wherever two or more persons are engaged in any common enterprise of pursuit, there is always danger of difference of opinion ... And what is still worse, they might split the community into the most violent and irreconcilable factions, adhering differently to the different individuals who composed the Magistracy ...

But the multiplication of the Executive adds to the difficulty of detection in either case. It often becomes impossible, amidst mutual accusations, to determine on whom the blame or the punishment of a pernicious measure, or series of pernicious measures, ought really to fall. It is shifted from one to another with so much dexterity, and under such plausible appearances, that the public opinion is left in suspense about the real author ...

When power, therefore, is placed in the hands of so small a number of men, as to admit of their interests and views being easily combined in a common enterprise, by an artful leader, it becomes more liable to abuse, and more dangerous when abused, than if it be lodged in the hands of one man; who, from the very circumstance of his being alone, will be more narrowly watched and more readily suspected, and who cannot unite so great a mass of influence as when he is associated with others.

Political Science Disciplinary Practices: Analyze and interpret *Federalist No. 70*

When Publius wrote the Federalist articles, the authors were trying to convince those in the Anti-Federalist camp to support ratification of the Constitution. For this reason, the arguments Hamilton presented reflected the concerns of the Anti-Federalists, those who feared the "fetus of monarchy" because of their recent experience with the British monarch. With this in mind, consider the perspective of each side of the debate.

Apply: Complete the activities below.

1. Describe the authors' central claim about a chief executive.

2. Explain how the authors' argument for that claim ensures a better government.

3. Explain how the implications of the authors' argument may affect the behavior of the chief executive.

Presidential Interpretation of Power

The presidential role has been shaped as unforeseen situations and events occurred during the nation's history. Several key presidents have had larger roles in defining the powers of the chief executive.

Washington's Example For first President George Washington, the Constitution provided a mere five-paragraph job description. He took on the role with modesty and accepted being addressed as "Mr. President" as a title, though some suggested more lofty labels.

Washington had some key accomplishments, primarily instilling public confidence in the nation's constitutional experiment. Though he surely would have won a third term, Washington chose to leave government after his second term to allow others to serve and to allay any fears of an overbearing executive. The presidents who followed Washington had moments of questionable initiative and international confrontation, but most of the early presidents faithfully carried out congressional acts, exercised the veto minimally, and followed Washington's precedent to serve no more than two terms. Thomas Jefferson purchased the Louisiana Territory without congressional approval. James Madison marshaled the Congress to a second war against Great Britain. James Monroe established the Monroe Doctrine, a foreign policy assuring U.S. dominance in the Western Hemisphere. For the most part, however, these powerful men let Congress fill its role as the main policymaking institution while the presidents executed Congress's laws.

The Imperial Presidency

Yielding to Congress, however, began to fade as stronger presidents came to office. The president's strength relative to that of Congress has grown steadily, with occasional setbacks, to create a kind of **imperial presidency**, a powerful executive position guided by a weaker Congress. *Webster's Dictionary* defines an imperial presidency as "a U.S. presidency that is characterized by greater powers than the Constitution allows." Historian Arthur Schlesinger Jr. popularized the term with his 1973 book of the same name. The book was published at the pinnacle of an overreaching Nixon presidency.

Enlightenment philosopher John Locke argued that legislative bodies are slow to respond in emergencies, so an executive should be occasionally allowed expanded powers. War, economic problems, and domestic crises have raised expectations for strong leadership.

BORN TO COMMAND.

OF VETO MEMORY.

HAD I BEEN CONSULTED.

KING ANDREW THE FIRST.

Source: Library of Congress

President Andrew Jackson's critics often questioned if he had stepped outside his authority. What symbols does the cartoonist use to signal this accusation? What is at Jackson's feet? What does he hold in his hand?

Personality and Popularity The dominating personality and popularity of the headstrong **Andrew Jackson** (1829–1837) brought about a noticeable shift in presidential power. Jackson was a successful military general who had led the southern expedition that forcibly relocated the Native Americans. As president, he blazed a path of executive dominance. He used the veto 12 times, more than any president had before. Jackson's opposition to a national bank, combined with his forceful demeanor, created a rift between the president and other branches, while his popularity among farmers and workers in an age of expanded suffrage and increased political participation enhanced his power even more.

During the presidencies of chief executives who served after Jackson and before Abraham Lincoln, the powers of the presidency contracted. None of these eight presidents served more than one term, and two died in office. Franklin Pierce and James Buchanan, who preceded Lincoln, are noted for their lack of presidential leadership and clear policy agenda and for allowing the nation to drift toward civil war. Historians rank Buchanan and Pierce near the bottom of the list of effective presidents.

National Crisis After Southern states seceded, **Abraham Lincoln** (1861–1865) once again expanded the presidency as he assumed sweeping presidential powers to save the Union and to limit slavery. Lincoln went as far as suspending *habeas corpus*, the protection against unlawful imprisonment, over fears that riots in Maryland might interrupt Union troop movement. Chief Justice Roger Taney issued an opinion that only Congress could suspend habeas corpus but had little power to enforce his views during the crisis of the Civil War. Historian Arthur Schlesinger wrote, "Lincoln ignored one constitutional provision after another. He assembled the militia, enlarged the Army and Navy beyond the congressional appropriation, suspended habeas corpus, arrested 'disloyal' people, asserted the right to proclaim martial law behind the lines, to arrest people without warrant, to seize property, and to suppress newspapers." Lincoln is generally excused for these constitutional violations because he stretched the powers of his office in the name of saving the United States and emancipating slaves.

On the World Stage In the late 1800s, the United States began to compete on an international stage with the industrial and imperial powers of Europe. For example, to protect U.S. "open door" trade interest in China, President William McKinley sent 5,000 American troops to end the Boxer Rebellion.

As the United States became a world military and industrial power, **Theodore Roosevelt** (1901–1909) and **Woodrow Wilson** (1913–1921) stretched presidential power in the name of advancing the nation and serving the people. Roosevelt's gallant Rough Rider background from the Spanish-American War and his brash, forward manner gained people's respect. His progressive actions for environmental conservation and standing against corporate giants contributed greatly to both his reputation and his legacy. He strengthened the Monroe Doctrine with his foreign policy motto that the United States would "speak softly and carry a big stick." During his tenure, he sent troops to Cuba and the Philippines, and he sent the U.S. Navy around the world. He also acquired property from Panama to build a canal. (See Topic 2.4.)

Roosevelt's so-called **stewardship theory** approach to governing presumed the president had a duty to act in national interests, unless the action was clearly prohibited by the Constitution. Like a good steward, Roosevelt insisted, the president should exercise as much authority as possible to take care of the American people, as Lincoln had done before him. "I have used every ounce of power there was in the office," he wrote.

Democrat Woodrow Wilson (1913–1919) became a strong leader with an international voice. When he delivered his State of the Union report to the Congress, the first in-person address since John Adams, Wilson created for himself a platform from which to present and gain popularity for his ideas. His involvement in international affairs became inevitable as the United States entered World War I. "We can never hide our president again as a mere domestic officer," he wrote. "We can never again see him the mere executive he was in the [past]. He must stand always at the front of our affairs, and the office will be as big and as influential as the man who occupies it."

The Turning Point In a discussion of presidents who expanded the reach of the office, there is perhaps no better example than Theodore Roosevelt's cousin, **Franklin Delano Roosevelt** (FDR) (1933–1945). He became president during the Great Depression (1929–1941), the most severe economic crisis in history. The large coalition that rallied behind him included people from nearly every walk of life who had been harmed by the Depression. His New Deal programs promised to bring the nation out of despair.

FDR arrived in Washington with revolutionary ideas that fundamentally changed not only the role of the presidency but also the role of the whole federal government. He recommended and Congress passed laws that required employers to pay a minimum wage, created the Social Security system, and started a series of public works programs to stimulate the economy. In trying to prevent a conservative Supreme Court from striking down his self-described liberal legislation, he moved to increase the number of seats on the Court with plans to place judges favorable to his proposals on the bench (See Topic 2.10.) This "court packing" plan failed, but it illustrates Roosevelt's imperial tendencies. He ran for and won an unprecedented third term, in 1940, as the United States moved closer to entering World War II.

The foreign policy dilemma that resulted in war with Germany and Japan only strengthened FDR's leadership and America's reliance on him. As Roosevelt mobilized the nation for an overseas war, he overpowered civil liberties in the name of national security by authorizing the creation of "military areas" that paved the way for relocating Japanese Americans to internment camps. At the time, FDR acted as a wartime Commander in Chief, not as an administrator concerned about constitutional rights. What would have seemed autocratic in peacetime was largely accepted as an appropriate security measure during wartime. This action by Roosevelt was upheld by the Supreme Court in *Korematsu v. United States* (1944). Americans rallied behind their Commander in Chief and accepted most of his measures, electing him to a fourth term, although he died 82 days into it.

THINK AS A POLITICAL SCIENTIST: *DESCRIBE THE AUTHOR'S CLAIM AND PERSPECTIVE*

The author of a speech has a main point, or several points, intended to make an impression on an audience. In an argument, the main point is called a claim. President Franklin Roosevelt is considered one of the great persuasive and inspirational speakers in U.S. history. His messages were clearly delivered and resonated with many people. He used his exceptional skill in his many radio speeches as the United States addressed its worst financial crisis, the Great Depression, and prepared for another crisis, World War II. President Roosevelt used executive powers to their fullest to get the nation moving toward recovery from the Depression. He also used his gift for argument and persuasion to mobilize the nation to face the challenges ahead.

Practice: The following excerpt is from Franklin Roosevelt's 1941 State of the Union Address. Read the excerpt and answer the questions that follow.

> ...These are the simple, basic things that must never be lost sight of in the turmoil and unbelievable complexity of our modern world.
>
> Many subjects connected with our social economy call for immediate improvement. As examples:
>
> We should bring more citizens under the coverage of old-age pensions and unemployment insurance.
>
> We should widen the opportunities for adequate medical care.
>
> We should plan a better system by which persons deserving or needing gainful employment may obtain it.
>
> I have called for personal sacrifice. I am assured of the willingness of almost all Americans to respond to that call.
>
> If the Congress maintains these principles, the voters, putting patriotism ahead of pocketbooks, will give you their applause.
>
> In the future days, which we seek to make secure, we look forward to a world founded upon four essential human freedoms.
>
> The first is freedom of speech and expression—everywhere in the world.
>
> The second is freedom of every person to worship God in his own way—everywhere in the world.
>
> The third is freedom from want—which, translated into world terms, means economic understandings which will secure to every nation a healthy peacetime life for its inhabitants—everywhere in the world.
>
> The fourth is freedom from fear—which, translated into world terms, means a world-wide reduction of armaments to such a point and in such a thorough fashion that no nation will be in a position to commit an act of physical aggression against any neighbor—anywhere in the world.

1. What is one claim Roosevelt makes in this speech?

2. What is FDR asking the American public to do?

3. Does Roosevelt's speech seem to be from the perspective, or point of view, of an "imperial president?" Explain your answer.

4. Is FDR acting within powers granted to the president in the Constitution?

The **Twenty-second Amendment**, however, ratified in 1951, prevents any president from serving more than two consecutive terms or a total of ten years. If a person becomes president by filling a vacancy, that person can still serve two consecutive terms—hence the ten-year limit.

Contemporary Expansion of Powers

In the post-World War II era, the presidency has grown even stronger. Cold War tensions, military engagements abroad, and greater expectations to protect Americans in the age of terrorism have further imperialized the American presidency.

War Powers Act President Johnson mobilized the U.S. Army into Southeast Asia in 1964. After reports of a naval skirmish off the coast of Vietnam in the Tonkin Gulf (which were later found to be untrue), Congress delegated power in times of war to the president with the Tonkin Gulf Resolution, allowing the president "to take all necessary measures to repel any armed attack against the forces of the United States to prevent further aggression." Congressional leaders rushed through the resolution in a stampede of misinformation and misunderstanding. This rapid reaction to aggressive Communists led to a long and unpopular war.

In 1973, Congress decided to fix this political mistake and passed the **War Powers Act**. The law maintains the president's need for urgent action and defense of the United States while preserving the war-declaring authority of Congress. The president can order the military into combat 48 hours before informing Congress. In turn, Congress can vote to approve or disapprove any presidential military action at any time, with the stipulation that the vote must take place within 60 days, or within 90 days if the Congress offers an extension.

The Commander in Chief's authority often shifts with each president. In the recent war on terrorism, President Obama developed his own policy for targeting top al-Qaeda enemies and operatives. In certain situations, taking into account knowledge of their whereabouts and calculations of potential innocent victims, Obama gave the order as Commander in Chief to kill these leading terrorists. Scores were eliminated by armed drones.

Source: Wikimedia Commons, Pete Souza

President Obama and his staff await an update on the status of the raid by U.S. Special Forces on the compound of terrorist leader Osama bin Laden.

In 2020 President Trump used his power as Commander in Chief to continue the war on terror with a drone strike that killed top Iranian general, Qassem Soleimani. The Trump administration claimed Soleimani was responsible for the deaths of hundreds of U.S. soldiers and was planning an "imminent" attack; therefore, the president's decision was in the interest of the security of the United States. The president did notify Congress within 48 hours of the strike in accordance with the War Powers Act. Yet some members of Congress decried the briefing as lacking in details about the killing and the plans to move forward, making it clear that any further military escalation with Iran would require congressional approval.

REFLECT ON THE ESSENTIAL QUESTION

Essential Question: *How have presidents interpreted and explained their use of formal and informal powers? On separate paper, complete a chart like the one below.*

Presidential Expansion of Power	Response to Expansion of Presidential Power

KEY TERMS AND NAMES

Federalist No. 70
imperial presidency
Jackson, Andrew
Lincoln, Abraham
Roosevelt, Franklin D.
Roosevelt, Theodore

stewardship theory
Twenty-second Amendment (1951)
Washington, George
War Powers Act (1973)
Wilson, Woodrow

Presidential Communication

"By the time he reached the presidency, Reagan had talked before so many audiences and cameras that they were both his friends."
—Presidential Aide David Gergen, *Eyewitness to Power*, 2000

Essential Question: How has communication technology changed the president's relationship with the American people and other branches?

The Constitution grants the president the power "to recommend" to Congress "such measures as he shall judge necessary and expedient," meaning he can try to influence the legislative actions of Congress, especially from the perspective of the manager who would carry out such policies. How a president attempts to persuade the legislative branch and shape policy has changed dramatically over the life of the Constitution. In addition, the way the president communicates to the people of the United States has changed significantly.

Communicator in Chief

In a democracy, the president's need to communicate with the citizenry and keep good relations with Americans is essential for success. Citizens must desire the president's proposed bills and foreign policy plans. If not, they will pressure their representative or senator to vote against them. The executive branch must publicize its reasons and benefits for proposed legislation. Another function the president assumes, then, is "communicator in chief." Meanwhile, a free press entitles citizen-journalists to tell their readers, listeners, and viewers about the government. Among the government entities they are most interested in is the executive branch and its head, the president.

Relationship with the Press

In the early 1900s, as national newspapers grew, Theodore Roosevelt developed a unique relationship with the press. He referred to the presidency as a **bully pulpit**—a prominent stage from where he could pitch ideas to the American people. With "bully," he meant "excellent," not aggressive or violent, persuasion. He could speak to the people using his powers of persuasion, and the people would in turn persuade Congress. He sometimes spoke with reporters while getting his morning shave. With his colorful remarks, unique ideas, and vibrant persona, Roosevelt always provided a good story. He and his Cabinet officials distributed speeches and photos to journalists to use in their reports, and he saved the richest pieces of information for his favorite journalists. The media's attention on the president enhanced the power of the bully pulpit. Though he did not mean "bully" in the modern sense, his actions often had that persuasive effect on Congress.

Later in the 1930s, in efforts to gain support for his New Deal legislation, Theodore Roosevelt's cousin, Franklin Delano Roosevelt (FDR) used his informal powers of persuasion to ensure that Congress enacted the measures. FDR used the popular radio medium to address Americans during his "fireside chats." He reassured a worried populace and articulated his solutions in a persuasive way. After each "chat," letters from listeners flooded Congress to support the president's ideas.

State of the Union Address The Constitution requires the president to report to Congress from time to time on the state of the Union. The president explains the economic, military, and social state of the nation, proposes new policies, and explains how government programs are being administered. George Washington and John Adams drafted their first reports and delivered these in person as speeches. Thomas Jefferson broke that pattern, declaring a speech looked too much like a British monarch opening Parliament, so he delivered his report on paper only, a practice that endured for a century after that.

In 1913, Woodrow Wilson revived the speech approach, thus redefining the report as an event. Since then all presidents have followed suit, taking advantage of the opportunity through the expanding media to reach millions of Americans who listen on the radio, watch on television, or stream online. In late January or early February, both houses of Congress convene and receive the president, Cabinet, and the address. Presidents realize they can command a large audience and a few news cycles to follow. Carefully crafted speeches include statistics and sound bites that will help propel presidents' initiatives.

Source: National Archives and Records Administration

In this cartoon, Theodore Roosevelt, a master of communication and manipulating the bully pulpit, notices that President Woodrow Wilson's in-person State of the Union Address upstaged his use of the bully pulpit.

THINK AS A POLITICAL SCIENTIST: *EXPLAIN HOW POLITICAL BEHAVIORS APPLY TO DIFFERENT SCENARIOS*

Political behavior refers to the broad category of involvement in the political process by individuals or groups. This behavior can involve such actions as voting, participating in interest groups, and working for social change. A president can have a significant effect on the public's political behavior. Evolving media throughout the nation's history have given the president many more opportunities to communicate with the public. The changing media have also given citizens much more access to the president.

Practice: Read the excerpts from three presidents' speeches during various economic crises the nation experienced. Identify the political behavior the president is trying to encourage in each excerpt. Also, explain one similarity and one difference among these messages to the people of the United States.

1. **James Madison, State of the Union, 1819—during the Panic of 1819:**

   "The great reduction in the price of the principal articles of domestic growth which has occurred during the present year, and the consequent fall in the price of labor, apparently so favorable to the success of domestic manufactures, have not shielded them against other causes adverse to their prosperity. . . . It is deemed of great importance to give encouragement to our domestic manufacturers. In what manner the evils which have been adverted to may be remedied, and how far it may be practicable in other respects to afford to them further encouragement, paying due regard to the other great interests of the nation, is submitted to the wisdom of Congress."

2. **Franklin Roosevelt, first Fireside Chat, 1933—during the Great Depression:**

   "After all, there is an element in the readjustment of our financial system more important than currency, more important than gold, and that is the confidence of the people themselves. Confidence and courage are the essentials of success in carrying out our plan. You people must have faith; you must not be stampeded by rumors or guesses. Let us unite in banishing fear. We have provided the machinery to restore our financial system; and it is up to you to support and make it work."

3. **Ronald Reagan, Address to the Nation on Federal Tax Reduction, 1981—during recession and high inflation of the early 1980s.**

   "It's been nearly 6 months since I first reported to you on the state of the nation's economy. I'm afraid my message that night was grim and disturbing. I remember telling you we were in the worst economic mess since the Great Depression. . . .all because government was too big and spent too much of our money. . . ."

   "Our struggle for nationhood, our unrelenting fight for freedom, our very existence. . . . no one can stop you from reaching higher or take from you the creativity that has made America the envy of mankind."

   "One road is timid and fearful; the other bold and hopeful. . . ."

   "It's been the power of millions of people like you who have determined that we will make America great again. You have made the difference up to now. You will make the difference again. Let us not stop now."

Communications Staff The expansion of the media has redefined the communications office's role. In the days before television, presidents from Coolidge to Eisenhower held press conferences before a mix of print journalists and radio broadcasters. In the 1930s, Franklin Roosevelt pioneered the radio message with his fireside chats, and John F. Kennedy did the first live televised press conferences in the early 1960s. The communication office works to control information coming out of the White House and try to shape the president's message that will ultimately define his policy agenda and its success or failure.

The White House press secretary is appointed by the president. The chief responsibility is to keep the White House press corps aware of important events in the president's schedule and knowledgeable about presidential actions.

Spin and Manipulation The press conference is in many ways a staged event. Press secretaries and presidents anticipate questions and rehearse in advance with planned answers. President George W. Bush's critics complained that his press relations were an affront to the media. Reporter and media expert Eric Alterman and others reported how the Bush administration was caught manipulating the news process. The president's administration distributed government-prepared "news reports" to local TV stations across the country to promote his programs, planted a fake reporter in the briefing room to throw softball questions at the president's press secretary, and paid large sums of public money to writers to promote their programs. The most notable example was a payment of $240,000 that went to conservative columnist and radio host Armstrong Williams to promote Bush's No Child Left Behind initiatives.

Modern Technology and a Social Media President

From advances in the printing press to the advent of Twitter, presidents have had to keep pace with technology. From Eisenhower to Clinton, the president could cut into the big three television networks with an announced speech. Now, with the exception of the State of the Union address, many public addresses are aired only by lesser-watched cable TV channels. The 24-hour news cycle is always hungry for headlines. The recent explosion of immediate electronic communication, social media use, push notifications, and the reliance on the Internet for information has transformed how the president communicates with the people to accomplish his policy agenda.

Obama Embraces New Media On his way to the White House, President Obama forecasted his media presence when he hired a 30-year-old "new media director," introduced a Twitter feed, and employed a videographer to upload segments on YouTube and, later, on WhiteHouse.gov. As president, Obama employed a 14-member staff on the new White House Office of Digital Strategy, a crew slightly larger than George W. Bush's press secretary's office. By his second term, President Obama had essentially created his own news service, digitally transmitting a stream of photo images, videos, blog posts, and interviews for social media sites for his fans and skeptics alike. Twitter, Facebook, Snapchat, Instagram, and Flickr quickly became standard platforms to broadcast his message.

The Obama team found this digital bully pulpit useful in a continuing effort to persuade the citizenry, who could then apply pressure on their representatives in Congress to accomplish the Obama agenda. During his two terms, the White House generated close to 300 infographics supplying people with quick and digestible data. The Obama team worked hard to successfully compress complex ideas and goals into Twitter bites. They found this strategy useful and easy to microtarget—that is, to target certain audiences with specific messages. In his quest for a health care law and amid the GOP's efforts to stop it, the White House established a "Reality Check" website which debunked his opponents' rumors about the drawbacks of the health care plan.

Image Control Presidents for some decades have employed a taxpayer-funded photographer. Congress has allotted the money for this purpose for the good of the office, to create a record, and to connect people with government. Obama's photographer, Pete Souza, and the new media team used photography as a way to legitimize his presidency, portray him as a man of the people, promote policy programs, and generally chronicle his presidency.

Source: Wikimedia Commons, Pete Souza

President Obama talks with Diego Diaz through the Make-a-Wish Foundation.

As photography has become affordable and common among media outlets, independent photojournalists want to show the presidency with their own original images and to tell the full story of the president, not the controlled story. Much like Teddy Roosevelt's efforts of shaping his image with expensive photography more than a century ago, Obama's publicly distributed photos were carefully curated to show the president in a particular light.

"Obama [took] unprecedented advantage of the digital revolution in photography," says expert Cara Finnegan in an Illinois News Bureau interview. By the end of his administration, his Flickr feed had more than 6,500 quality and well-chosen images. Meanwhile, the White House took steps to prevent independent journalistic photographs, hoping that a greater share of White House-released photos would dominate news websites. The press corps' response revealed a unique relationship between the president and the press. The president's press secretary, Jay Carney, found himself bombarded with complaints. "Our problem is access," said correspondent Ann Compton. "You can put out a million pictures a day from the White House photographer, but you bar photos [from *Air Force One*]." Correspondent Brianna Kieler declared, "Anyone here can tell you, that there's less access than under the Bush Administration." Journalists were chafed because the practice resembled media strategies of dictators in countries with no free press and only state-approved images. Obama's grand attempts to shape his image and get the citizenry to know him led the *New York Times* to call him "Obama the Omnipresent."

Tweeter in Chief Within his first year in office, President Trump became well known for the use of his Twitter feed to speak directly to the nation. Shortly before taking office, Trump tweeted, "I use Social Media not because I like to, but because it is the only way to fight a VERY dishonest and unfair 'press,' now often referred to as Fake News Media. Phony and non-existent 'sources' are being used more often than ever. Many stories & reports a pure fiction!"

Trump has all but severed the presidency's relationship with objective journalists and the mainstream media. Early in his tenure, Trump's first press secretary shared misleading information about crowd sizes and photos from Trump's inauguration. Daily press briefings were ended by the Trump administration in March 2019 after many contentious exchanges between the media and the president's press secretaries, and Trump has refused to appear at the White House Correspondents Association annual gala.

All presidents have a somewhat adversarial relationship with the press, but Trump disparages journalists and refers to any mainstream media outlet criticism as "fake news." He has broken established presidential communication norms repeatedly.

REFLECT ON THE ESSENTIAL QUESTION

Essential Question: *How has communication technology changed the president's relationship with the American people and other branches? On separate paper, complete a chart like the one below.*

Communication or Technology Change	Presidential Use of Communication or Technology

KEY TERMS AND NAMES

bully pulpit	State of the Union Address

CHAPTER 5 Review:
Learning Objectives and Key Terms

TOPIC 2.4: Explain how the president can implement a policy agenda. (CON-4.A)

Formal and Informal Powers to Accomplish Policy Agenda (CON-4.A.1 & 2)

bargaining and persuasion	informal powers
Commander in Chief	line-item veto
formal powers	pocket veto
executive agreement	policy agenda
executive order	signing statements
executive privilege	veto

TOPIC 2.5: Explain how the president's agenda can create tension and frequent confrontations with Congress. (CON-4.B)

Conflict with Senate Over Appointments (CON-4.B.1 & 2)	**Congressional Conflict Over Policy** (CON-4.B.3)
ambassador	inherent powers
Cabinet	
chief of staff	
Joint Chiefs of Staff	

TOPIC 2.6: Explain how presidents have interpreted and justified their use of formal and informal powers. (CON-4.C)

Defining the Role and Power of the President (CON-4.C.1, 2, & 3)

Federalist No. 70	stewardship theory
imperial presidency	Twenty-second Amendment (1951)
Jackson, Andrew	Washington, George
Lincoln, Abraham	War Powers Act (1973)
Roosevelt, Franklin D.	Wilson, Woodrow
Roosevelt, Theodore	

TOPIC 2.7: Explain how communication technology has changed the president's relationship with the national constituency and the other branches. (CON-4.D)

Modern Technology and Presidential Communication (CON-4.D.1)

bully pulpit	State of the Union Address

CHAPTER 5 Checkpoint:
The Presidency
Topics 2.4–2.7

MULTIPLE-CHOICE QUESTIONS

Questions 1 and 2 refer to the graph below.

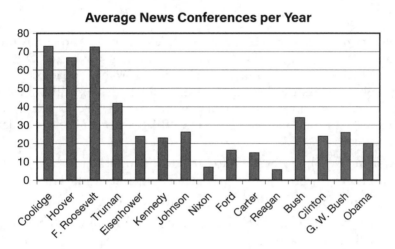

Average News Conferences per Year

Source: The American Presidency Project

1. Which of the following statements describes a trend in the data based on the chart?

   (A) Coolidge, Hoover, and Roosevelt were the first to take advantage of televised news conferences.

   (B) The average number of press conferences dropped in the 1970s and 1980s.

   (C) The most recent presidents have held the most frequent press conferences.

   (D) Presidents who gave more press conferences had higher approval ratings.

2. Which of the following statements do the data imply?

   (A) As more media platforms have become common, presidents have steadily increased their number of news conferences.

   (B) Recent presidents are communicating in various ways and thus need fewer press conferences.

   (C) Presidents who held fewer press conferences were elected to only one term.

   (D) Press conferences are a product of the television era.

3. Which of the following may the president do to control the implementation of a policy agenda?
   (A) The president can veto particular items or language in a bill he disagrees with while enacting the remainder of the bill.
   (B) The president can veto a congressional bill that has passed the House and Senate.
   (C) The president can refuse to spend money that Congress has appropriated.
   (D) The president can impeach selected members of Congress.

4. The president receives a bill in the middle of a congressional session that has recently passed the Democrat-controlled House and Democrat-controlled Senate. This omnibus bill deregulates the food and agriculture industries, something the president desires. Yet the bill also funds modern art museums in San Francisco and New York City, which the president thinks are unnecessary. Which action will the president likely take?
   (A) Exercise a line-item veto to exclude the funding for the art museums while passing the deregulation part of the bill.
   (B) Refuse to sign the bill, allowing it to die with a pocket veto.
   (C) Sign the bill to gain the deregulations understanding that Congress will fund the art museums.
   (D) Sign the bill and explain in a signing statement that the deregulations will be enforced but museum funds will not be appropriated.

5. Which of the following accurately describes the president's lawful use of the War Powers Act?
   (A) A president can declare war as long as it ends in 60 days.
   (B) A president can engage an enemy abroad but must wait for congressional approval and funding.
   (C) A president can use the military abroad in combat as long as Congress is informed within 48 hours.
   (D) A president cannot act as Commander in Chief without a congressional declaration of war.

6. Which of the following is an accurate comparison of the president's Cabinet and White House staff?

	CABINET	WHITE HOUSE STAFF
(A)	The Cabinet has more influence on the president's decision making than does the White House staff.	Presidents have continually relied less on their White House staff for input in guiding government.
(B)	Presidents can remove Cabinet officials but only with Senate approval.	The White House staffers require Senate approval before taking office.
(C)	The Cabinet includes department secretaries and others the president wishes to include.	The president engages with White House staff more frequently than with Cabinet secretaries.
(D)	The president can create new Cabinet-level positions and departments.	The White House staff includes the attorney general and the FBI director.

FREE-RESPONSE QUESTIONS

Concept Application

1. "This morning [Homeland Security] Secretary Napolitano announced new actions my administration will take to mend our Nation's immigration policy to make it more fair, more efficient, and more just, specifically for [young people. These] young people . . . study in our schools, they play in our neighborhoods, they're friends with our kids, they pledge allegiance to our flag. They are Americans in their heart, in their minds, in every single way but one: on paper. They were brought to this country by their parents . . . and often have no idea that they're undocumented . . . Over the next few months, eligible individuals who do not present a risk to national security or public safety will be able to request temporary relief from deportation proceedings and apply for work authorization."

—President Barack Obama, June 15, 2012

After reading the above passage, respond to A, B, and C:

(A) Describe the presidential power exhibited in the announced policy.

(B) In the context of the scenario, explain how the use of the power described in part A can be affected by interactions between the president and Congress.

(C) In the context of the scenario, explain how the interaction between the president and Congress can be affected by the media.

Quantitative Analysis

Makeup of Recent Presidential Cabinets

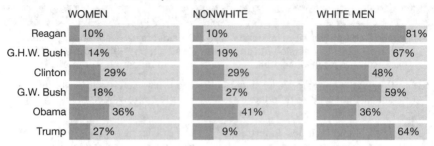

Notes

— The 22 Cabinet-level positions in the Obama administration (not counting the Vice President) are held constant across all five administrations, except for the Department of Homeland Security, which wasn't established until 2002. We have counted Tom Ridge, the first DHS secretary, as an initial pick for George W. Bush.

— Census Bureau classifications were used for race. Hispanics are counted as nonwhite.

2. Use the information graphic to answer the following questions.

   (A) Identify the demographic most represented in presidential cabinets.

   (B) Describe a difference in the demographic makeup of presidential cabinets, as illustrated in the information graphic.

   (C) Draw a conclusion about the difference you described.

   (D) Explain how the makeup of presidential cabinets as shown in the information graphic demonstrates the principle of presidential leadership of the executive branch.

CHAPTER 6

The Judiciary

Topics 2.8–2.11

Topic 2.8 The Judicial Branch

CON-5.A: Explain the principle of judicial review and how it checks the powers of the other institutions and state governments.

- Required Foundational Documents:
  - *Federalist No. 78*
  - The Constitution of the United States
- Required Supreme Court Case:
  - *Marbury v. Madison* (1803)

Topic 2.9 Legitimacy of the Judicial Branch

CON-5.B: Explain how the exercise of judicial review in conjunction with life tenure can lead to debate about the legitimacy of the Supreme Court's power.

Topic 2.10 The Court in Action

CON-5.B: Explain how the exercise of judicial review in conjunction with life tenure can lead to debate about the legitimacy of the Supreme Court's power.

Topic 2.11 Checks on the Judicial Branch

CON-5.B: Explain how the exercise of judicial review in conjunction with life tenure can lead to debate about the legitimacy of the Supreme Court's power.

CON-5.C: Explain how the other branches in the government can limit the Supreme Court's power.

Source: Wikimedia Commons
U.S. Supreme Court Building, Washington, DC

The Judicial Branch

"It is emphatically the province and duty of the judicial department to say what the law is."

—Chief Justice John Marshall, Opinion in
Marbury v. Madison, 1803

Essential Question: How does the principle of judicial review check the power of the other branches and state government?

Most people have some understanding of trials in which one party sues another and accused criminals are innocent until proven guilty. Courtroom drama has been popular since Perry Mason—a 1950s television defense attorney who lost only one case in a nine-year series. More recently, TV has stereotyped small claims courts with a feisty, tell-it-like-it-is judge, a beefy courtroom bailiff, and litigants who rudely yell at each other.

The true picture of the judiciary shows a revered institution shaped by Article III of the Constitution, the Bill of Rights, and federal and state laws. The courts handle everything from speeding tickets to death penalty cases. State courts handle most disputes, whether criminal or civil. Federal courts handle crimes against the United States, high-dollar lawsuits involving citizens of different states, and constitutional questions. Federal courts are designed to protect the judiciary's independence. The U.S. Supreme Court is the nation's highest tribunal, which, through judicial review and its rulings, shapes the law and how it is carried out.

Constitutional Authority of the Federal Courts

Today's three-level federal court system consists of the **U.S. District Courts** on the lowest tier, the **U.S. Circuit Courts of Appeals** on the middle tier, and the **U.S. Supreme Court** alone on the top. These three types of courts are known as "constitutional courts" because they are either directly or indirectly mentioned in the Constitution. All judges serving in these courts are appointed by presidents and confirmed by the Senate to hold life terms.

No national court system existed under the Articles of Confederation, so the framers decided to create a national judiciary while empowering Congress to expand and define it. Because states had existing courts, many delegates saw no reason to create an entirely new, costly judicial system to serve essentially the same purpose. Others disagreed and argued that a national judicial system with a top court for uniformity was necessary. "Thirteen independent [state] courts of final jurisdiction over the same cases, arising out of the same laws," *Federalist No. 80* argued, "will produce nothing but contradiction and confusion."

Article III

The only court directly mentioned in the Constitution is the Supreme Court, though Article III empowered Congress to create "inferior" courts. Article III established the terms for judges, the jurisdiction of the Supreme Court, the definition of treason, and a defendant's right to a jury trial.

Judge's Terms All federal judges "shall hold their offices during good behavior," the Constitution states. Although this term of office is now generally called a "life term," most U.S. judges retire or go on senior status at age 65, and a handful have been impeached and removed. This key provision empowers federal judges to make unpopular but necessary decisions. The life term assures that judges can operate independently from the other branches, since the executive and legislative branches have no power to remove justices over disagreements in ideology. The life term also allows for consistency over time in interpreting the law. Congress cannot diminish judges' salaries during their terms in office. This way, Congress cannot use its power of the purse to leverage power against this independent branch.

Jurisdiction The Supreme Court has **original jurisdiction**—the authority to hear a case for the first time—in cases affecting ambassadors and public ministers and those in which a state is a party. For the most part, however, the Supreme Court acts as an appeals court with **appellate jurisdiction**.

Treason Article III also defined *treason* as "levying war" or giving "aid or comfort" to the enemy. Treason is the only crime mentioned or defined in the Constitution. Because English kings had used the accusation of treason as a political tool in unfair trials to quiet dissent against the government, the founders wanted to ensure that the new government could not easily levy or prosecute that charge just to silence alternative voices. At least two witnesses must testify in open court to the treasonous act in order to convict the accused.

Right to Jury Trial Also mentioned in Article III is a criminal defendant's right to a jury trial. Many more rights of the accused were included later in the Bill of Rights, but the framers saw the right to a jury trial as a citizen check on government accusation and was thus included in the article.

FOUNDATIONAL DOCUMENTS: *FEDERALIST NO. 78*

Anti-Federalists were concerned about establishing an independent judiciary. In England, Parliament could vote to remove judges from office, and it could pass laws overriding judicial decisions. Brutus, the mouthpiece for the Anti-Federalists, expressed concern that there was no similar checking power on the

Supreme Court. "Men placed in this situation," he wrote in *Brutus No. 15*, "will generally soon feel themselves independent of heaven itself."

Alexander Hamilton and other Federalists did not share this concern. In *Federalist No. 78*, Hamilton affirmed that the independent judicial branch has the power of **judicial review** to examine acts of legislatures to see if they comport with the proposed Constitution. He also emphasized that as long as judges are acting properly, they shall remain on the bench. This "permanency" shall protect them from the other branches when they make unpopular but constitutional decisions. He believed an independent judiciary posed no threat.

However, the establishment of judicial review was not settled by Hamilton's writing. As you will read, the landmark decision in *Marbury v. Madison* (1803) established that principle. Nonetheless, it is still debated today.

[The judiciary] will always be the least dangerous to the political rights of the constitution; because it will be least in a capacity to annoy or injure them. . . .

[since it] has no influence over either the sword or the purse. . . .

[F]rom the natural feebleness of the judiciary, it is in continual jeopardy of being overpowered, awed, or influenced by its coordinate branches; and that as nothing can contribute so much to its firmness and independence as permanency in office . . . No legislative act contrary to the Constitution, can be valid. To deny this, would be to affirm, that the deputy is greater than his principal; that the servant is above his master; that the representatives of the people are superior to the people themselves. . . . A Constitution is, in fact, and must be regarded by the judges, as a fundamental law. It therefore belongs to them [the judges] to ascertain its meaning, as well as the meaning of any particular act proceeding from the legislative body. . . .

[T]he independence of the judges may be an essential safeguard against the effects of occasional ill humors in the society. These sometimes extend no farther than to the injury of the private rights of particular classes of citizens, by unjust and partial laws. That inflexible and uniform adherence to the rights of the Constitution, and of individuals, which we perceive to be indispensable in the courts of justice, can certainly not be expected from judges who hold their offices by a temporary commission.

Political Science Disciplinary Practices: Analyze and Interpret *Federalist No. 78*

When analyzing and interpreting sources, consider the following factors:

- Claims—What statements are asserted to be true?
- Perspective—How does the context (time, place, and circumstance) affect the author's viewpoints?
- Evidence—What facts or experiences does the author use to support claims?
- Reasoning—How does the author link the evidence to the claims?

Apply: Complete the following activities.

1. Describe Hamilton's claim about the power of the judiciary.
2. Describe Hamilton's perspective in terms of the context in which he argues his support of the Federalist plan of government.

3. Describe the evidence Hamilton offers to back up his claim on the relative power of the judiciary.

4. Describe Hamilton's reasoning for supporting life terms.

5. Explain how the implications of Hamilton's argument relate to checks and balances in government.

You can read the full text of *Federalist No. 78* online.

A Three-Level System

The first Congress essentially defined the three-tier federal court system with the Judiciary Act of 1789. Originally, one district court existed in each state. The law also defined the size of the Supreme Court with six justices, or judges. President Washington then appointed judges to fill these judgeships. In addition to the district courts, Congress created three regional circuit courts designated to take cases on appeal from the district courts. Supreme Court justices were assigned to oversee the U.S. appeals courts that includes clusters of states, a "circuit," and presided over periodic sessions. The justices would hold one court after another in a circular path, an act that became known as "riding circuit."

Federal Court System

U.S. Supreme Court
- The Created by Article III of the Constitution
- Nine justices
- Hears 80–100 cases from October through June
- Has original jurisidiction in unique cases
- Takes appeals from circuits and top state courts

↑

U.S. Circuit Court
- Created by Congress
- 11 regional courts
- 2 courts in Washington (D.C. and Federal)
- Nearly 200 total justices
- Takes appeals from district courts
- Justices sit in panel of three

↑

U.S. District Court
- Trial courts created by Congress
- 94 districts
- Nearly 700 total justices
- Hear federal criminal and civil matters

U.S. District Courts

There are 94 district courts in the United States—at least one in each state, and for many less-populated western states, the district lines are the same as the state lines. Districts may contain several U.S. courthouses served by several federal district judges. Nearly 700 district judges preside over trials concerning federal crimes, lawsuits, and disputes over constitutional issues. Annually, the district courts receive close to 300,000 case filings, most of a civil nature.

A Trial Court U.S. district courts are trial courts with original jurisdiction over federal cases. The litigants in a trial court are the plaintiff—the party initiating the action—and the defendant, the party answering the claim. In a criminal trial, the government is the plaintiff, usually referred to as the "prosecution." In civil trials, a citizen-plaintiff brings a lawsuit against another, the defendant, who allegedly injured the plaintiff. "Injury" could be physical injury—as one motorist may have recklessly caused to another—but more often it is a financial injury, alleging the defendant's fault, measured in dollars. At times, it is an accusation that the government has injured a citizen, or a company, by violating their liberty.

Federal Crimes The U.S. district courts try federal crimes, such as counterfeiting, mail fraud, or evading federal income taxes—crimes that violate the enumerated powers in the Constitution, Article I, Section 8. Most violent crimes, and indeed most crimes overall, are tried in state courts. However, Congress has outlawed some violent crime and interstate actions, such as drug trafficking, bank robbery, terrorism, and acts of violence on federal property. For example, in *United States v. Timothy McVeigh* (1998), the government argued that McVeigh was responsible for an explosion in an Oklahoma City federal building that killed 168 people. A federal court found him guilty and sentenced him to death.

U.S. Attorneys Each of the 94 districts has a U.S. attorney, appointed by the president and approved by the Senate, who represents the federal government in federal courts. These executive branch prosecutors work in the Department of Justice under the **attorney general**, assisted by the FBI and other federal law enforcement agencies. Nationally, they try nearly 80,000 federal crimes per year. Of those, immigration crimes and drug offenses take up much of the courts' criminal docket. Fraud is third.

Civil Cases Citizens can also bring civil disputes to U.S. court to settle a business or personal conflict. Some plaintiffs sue over torts, or civil wrongs that have damaged them. In a lawsuit, the plaintiff files a complaint, a brief explaining the damages and why the defendant should be held liable. The plaintiff must prove the defendant's liability or negligence with a "preponderance of evidence" for the court to award damages. Most civil disputes, even million-dollar lawsuits, are handled in state courts.

Disputes involving constitutional questions also land in this court. In these cases, a federal judge, not a jury, determines the outcome because these cases involve a deeper interpretation of the law. Sometimes a large group of plaintiffs accuse the same party caused damage to them and will file a class action suit. After a decision, courts may issue an *injunction*, or court order, to the losing party in a civil suit, making them act or refrain from acting to redress a wrong.

Federal Circuits and Districts

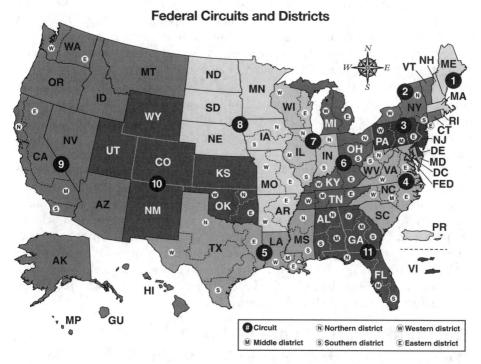

| # Circuit | N Northern district | W Western district |
| M Middle district | S Southern district | E Eastern district |

Suing the Government Sometimes a citizen or group sues the government. Technically, the United States operates under the doctrine of sovereign immunity—the government is protected from suit unless it permits such a claim. Over the years, Congress has made so many exceptions that it even established the U.S. Court of Claims to allow citizens to bring complaints against the United States. Individual citizens and groups also regularly bring constitutional arguments before the courts. One can sue government officials acting in a personal capacity. For example, the secretary of defense could be personally sued for causing a traffic accident that caused thousands of dollars in damage to another's car. But the secretary of defense or Congress cannot be sued for the loss of a loved one in a government-sanctioned military battle.

U.S. Circuit Courts of Appeals

Above the district courts are the U.S. Circuit Courts of Appeals. In 1891, with U.S. expansion and the increased caseload for the traveling Supreme Court justices riding circuit, Congress made the U.S. appeals courts permanent, full-time bodies. Appeals courts don't determine facts; instead, they shape the law. The losing party from a fact-based trial can appeal based on the concept of **certiorari**, Latin for "to make more certain." The appellant must offer some violation of established law, procedure, or precedent that led to the incorrect verdict in a trial court. Appeals courts look and operate differently than trial courts. Appeals courts have a panel of judges sitting at the bench but no witness stand and no jury box because such courts do not entertain new facts, but rather a narrow question or point of law.

The petitioner appeals the case, and the respondent defends the lower court's ruling. The public hearing lasts about an hour as each side makes oral arguments before the judges. Appeals courts don't declare guilt or innocence when dealing with criminal matters, and they don't generally reverse judgements in civil suits. They rule on procedural matters in which the lower courts or other parts of government may have erred, not followed precedent, or violated the Constitution. They periodically establish new principles with case law. After years of deciding legal principles, appeals courts have shaped the body of U.S. law.

The U.S. Courts of Appeals consist of 11 geographic circuits across the country. Appeals court rulings stand within their geographic circuits. In addition to the 11 circuits, two other appeals courts are worthy of note. The Circuit Court for the Federal Circuit hears appeals dealing with patents, contracts, and financial claims against the United States. The Circuit Court of Appeals for the District of Columbia, among other responsibilities, handles appeals from those fined or punished by executive branch regulatory agencies. The DC Circuit might be the second most important court in the nation and has become a feeder for Supreme Court justices.

The United States Supreme Court

Atop this hierarchy is the U.S. Supreme Court, with the chief justice and eight associate justices. The Supreme Court mostly hears cases on appeal from the circuit courts and from the state supreme courts. The nine members determine which appeals to accept, sit *en banc* (French for "on the bench," where all judges sit for the case) for attorneys' oral arguments, pose questions, and engage in a discussion with the litigants. They will consider their decision for weeks, sometimes months, vote whether or not to overturn the lower court's ruling, and issue their reasoning. The Court overturns about 70 percent of the cases it takes. Once the Supreme Court makes a ruling, it becomes the law of the land. Contrary to what many believe, the Supreme Court doesn't hear trials of serial murders or billion-dollar lawsuits. However, it decides on technicalities of constitutional law that have a national and sometimes historic impact. This power of judicial review, to check the other branches, was established in the 1803 case of *Marbury v. Madison*.

MUST-KNOW SUPREME COURT CASE: *MARBURY V. MADISON* (1803)

The Constitutional Question Before the Court: Can an appointed judge sue for his appointment, and does the Supreme Court have the authority to hear and implement this request?

Decision: Yes and no. Unanimous, 4:0

Facts: This controversy started as a dispute regarding the procedures of appointments during a presidential transition. Outgoing President John Adams had lost re-election to Thomas Jefferson and, in one of his final acts as president, appointed several members of his own Federalist Party to the newly created judgeships. The Senate had confirmed these "midnight judges," so-called because their appointment was made so late in the tenure of President Adams. Secretary of State John Marshall, who had just been named chief justice of the Supreme Court, had prepared the commissions, the official notices of appointment, and had most of them delivered. William Marbury was among 17 appointees who did not receive official notice. Marshall simply left these to be delivered by the next administration.

Once President Thomas Jefferson, a Democratic-Republican, took office, he instructed his new Secretary of State, James Madison, to hold the commissions. Jefferson did reappoint several of those appointees, but he refused others on partisan grounds. Marbury wanted the Supreme Court to issue a court order known as a writ of mandamus forcing Madison and the executive branch to deliver the appointment to him and, thus, his job.

Marbury brought the case to the Supreme Court because of language in the relatively new Judiciary Act of 1789 that defined the Supreme Court's jurisdiction in cases like his.

Reasoning: Marshall's Supreme Court took the case and determined that an appointed judge with a signed commission could sue if denied the job. (That is the yes vote.) However, the Court also ruled that the law entitling Marbury to the commission and the job, Section 13 of the Judiciary Act, ran contrary to Article III of the Constitution when it decided that the court had original rather than appellate jurisdiction in such cases. (That is the no vote.) Congress could not, the Marshall Court said, define the Court's authority outside the bounds of the Constitution.

The Court unanimously ruled that it had no jurisdiction in the matter, and in so ruling, cancelled Marbury's claim. It simultaneously instituted the practice of judicial review. The Court had asserted its powers and checked Congress.

> **The Court's Unanimous Opinion by Mr. Justice John Marshall:**
>
> If it had been intended to leave it in the discretion of the legislature to apportion the judicial power between the supreme and inferior courts according to the will of that body, it would certainly have been useless to have proceeded further than to have defined the judicial power, and the tribunals in which it should be vested . . . .
>
> The authority, therefore, given to the Supreme Court, by the act establishing the judicial courts of the United States [the Judiciary Act of 1789], to issue writs of mandamus to public officers, appears not to be warranted by the constitution . . . .
>
> The act to establish the judicial courts of the United States authorizes the Supreme Court "to issue writs of mandamus, in cases warranted by the principles and usages of law, to any courts appointed, or persons holding office, under the authority of the United States." The secretary of state, being a person, holding an office under the authority of the United States, is precisely within the letter of the description; and if this court is not authorized to issue a writ of mandamus to such an officer, it must be because the law is unconstitutional. . . .
>
> It is emphatically the province and duty of the judicial department to say what

the law is. Those who apply the rule to particular cases, must of necessity expound and interpret that rule. If two laws conflict with each other the courts must decide on the operation of each . . . .

So, if a law be in opposition to the Constitution; if both the law and the constitution apply to a particular case, so that the court must either decide that case conformably to the law, disregarding the constitution; or conformably to the constitution, disregarding the law; the court must determine which of these conflicting rules governs the case. This is of the very essence of judicial duty . . . .

Since *Marbury*: Marbury is a landmark case for its initiation of judicial review in American jurisprudence and in defining common law. Marshall had declared at the Virginian Ratifying Convention—a Federalist allaying fears of opponents to the proposed Constitution—that Congress would not have power to make law on any subject it wanted. A new federal judiciary, he said, "would declare void" any such congressional act repugnant to the Constitution. Marshall became the first judge to do just that.

Judicial review or striking down acts of Congress came as a rarity after Marbury. Not until the infamous Dred Scott case in 1857 did the Court again strike down a law, this time one that outlawed slavery north of the Missouri Compromise line. During the Industrial Era (1874–1920) and into the 20th century, the Court used its power of judicial review to strike down laws with greater frequency.

Political Science Disciplinary Practices: Analyze and Interpret Supreme Court Decisions

1. Describe the law that led to the *Marbury v. Madison* case.

2. Explain the Court's reasoning from the majority opinion.

3. Explain how the Court's ruling establishes the power of *judicial review*.

4. Explain how the ruling in *Marbury* relates to the U.S. Constitution.

5. Explain how the ruling in *Marbury* relates to *Federalist No. 78*.

 THINK AS A POLITICAL SCIENTIST: *EXPLAIN HOW A SUPREME COURT CASE RELATES TO A FOUNDATIONAL DOCUMENT*

As the foundation of the U.S. government, the Constitution defines the powers and roles of the branches. Yet, the Constitution has over the years needed to be refined with an amendment or an interpretation by the court system.

For example, Article III of the Constitution defines the judicial branch of the federal government but does not expressly confirm the power of judicial review—a power occasionally practiced by courts by this time. The Supreme Court's first exercise of judicial review came with *Marbury v. Madison* (1803).

Practice: Read the excerpts on the next page from Article III and Article VI of the Constitution and answer the questions that follow.

Article III

Section 1. *Federal Courts* The judicial power of the United States shall be vested in one Supreme Court, and in such inferior [lower] courts as the Congress may from time to time ordain and establish. The judges, both of the Supreme and inferior courts, shall hold their offices during good behavior, and shall, at stated times, receive for their services a compensation, which shall not be diminished during their continuance in office.

Section 2. *Jurisdiction of Federal Court* [1] The judicial power shall extend to all cases in law and equity arising under this Constitution, the laws of the United States, to controversies to which the United States shall be a party; to controversies between two or more states, between a state and citizens of another state, between citizens of different states, between citizens of the same state claiming lands under grants of different states, and between a state, or the citizens thereof, and foreign states, citizens, or subjects.

Article VI

Section 2. *Federal Supremacy* This Constitution, and the laws of the United States which shall be made in pursuance thereof, and all treaties made, or which shall be made, under the authority of the United States shall be the supreme law of the land; and the judges in every state shall be bound thereby, anything in the Constitution or laws of any state to the contrary notwithstanding.

1. What powers are given to federal courts in these sections?
2. How does the decision in *Marbury* build on the powers expressed in the articles above to establish the power of judicial review?

REFLECT ON THE ESSENTIAL QUESTION

Essential Question: *How does the principle of judicial review check the power of the other branches and state government? On separate paper, complete a chart like the one below.*

Checks on Other Branches and States	Judicial Review and *Marbury v. Madison*

KEY TERMS AND NAMES

appellate jurisdiction	*Marbury v. Madison* (1803)
Attorney General	original jurisdiction
certiorari	U.S. District Courts
Federalist No. 78	U.S. Circuit Courts of Appeals
judicial review	U.S. Supreme Court

Legitimacy of the Judicial Branch

"The Supreme Court, of course, has the responsibility of ensuring that our government never oversteps its proper bounds or violates the rights of individuals. But the Court must also recognize the limits on itself and respect the choices made by the American people."

—Justice Elena Kagan, Senate Confirmation Hearing, 2010

Essential Question: How has the Supreme Court's use of judicial review in conjunction with life tenure led to debates about the legitimacy of the court?

Supreme Court and lower court rulings can have considerable consequences for Americans. When those consequences are undesired, critics of courts express reasons to question its legitimacy. Life tenure, broad federal jurisdiction, a judge's ideology, and unfavorable decisions lead some to distrust the power of the courts.

Common Law and Precedent

Courts follow a judicial tradition begun centuries ago in England. Common law refers to the body of court decisions that make up part of the law. Court rulings often establish a **precedent**—a ruling that firmly establishes a legal principle. These precedents are generally followed later as subordinate courts must and other courts will consider following. The concept of *stare decisis*, or "let the decision stand," governs common law.

Lower courts must follow higher court rulings. Following precedent establishes continuity and consistency in law. Therefore, when a U.S. district court receives a case that parallels an already decided case from the circuit level, the district court is obliged to rule the same way, a practice called **binding precedent**. Even an independent-minded judge who disagrees with the higher court's precedent knows an appeal of a uniquely different decision, based in similar circumstances, will likely be overruled by the court above. That's why all courts in the land are bound by U.S. Supreme Court decisions.

Judges also rely on **persuasive precedent**. That is, they can consider past decisions made in other district courts or far away circuit courts as a guiding basis for a decision. Precedents can of course be overturned. No two cases are absolutely identical, which is precisely why judges make decisions on a case-by-case basis. Also, attitudes and interpretations differ and evolve over time in different courts.

Supreme Court Precedents Establish Policy

The Supreme Court's authority of binding precedent combined with its power of judicial review (see Topic 2.8) has given it a strong hand in establishing national policy. Early on, it addressed national supremacy and states' rights. Later, it defined the relationship between government and industry. Most recently, the Court's historic impact has shaped individual rights and liberties.

Source: Library of Congress

The Supreme Court is the only federal court named in Article III of the Constitution, yet it did not operate in its own building—shown here in a drawing before it was built—until 1935.

Defining Federalism The Supreme Court in its fledgling years was a nondescript institution held in low esteem. President Washington appointed Federalist John Jay as the first chief justice. At first, the Court operated in a second-floor room in a New York building and convened for only a two-hour session. Several early justices didn't stay on the Court long. Jay resigned in 1795 after only six years.

The Court's reputation and role would soon change. Once President John Adams appointed Federalist John Marshall as chief justice, the Court began to assert itself under a strong, influential leader. Marshall, a Federalist and Father of the Supreme Court, remained on the Court from 1801 until his death in 1835. He helped created a united court that spoke with one voice. Marshall insisted that this brotherhood of justices agree and unite in their rulings to shape national law. In virtually every important case during his time, that one voice was Judge Marshall's. "He left the Court," Chief Justice William Rehnquist wrote years later, "a genuinely coequal branch of a tripartite national government . . . the final arbiter of the meaning of the United States Constitution." He fortified the Union and federal powers with rulings that strengthened national supremacy and Congress's commerce power.

During Marshall's tenure, the *McCulloch v. Maryland* (1819) and *Gibbons v. Ogden* (1824) rulings empowered Congress to create a bank and strengthened its power to regulate interstate commerce. With the *Marbury v. Madison* (1803) decision, the Court struck down part of the Judiciary Act and thereby exercised judicial review.

Continuity and Change Over Time

The Supreme Court is known more for continuity than for change. Membership is small, and justices serve long tenures. The Court's customs are established through consensus and remain constant over generations. The contemporary group operates in many ways as earlier Supreme Courts did.

The combination of the *lifetime tenure* of justices and the Court's exercise of judicial review has given rise to debates over the legitimacy of the Supreme Court. Some people believe, as Anti-Federalist Brutus expressed more than 200 years ago, that with no power to hold them accountable, the justices on the Supreme Court are too separated from the real sources of power—the people and the legislature—to be legitimate arbiters of democratic law. Brutus believed the Supreme Court justices would "be placed in a situation altogether unprecedented in a free country—totally independent. No errors they may commit can be corrected by any power above them, if any such power there be, nor can they be removed from office for making ever so many erroneous adjudications."

Furthermore, the composition of the Court changes as seats become vacant, and the presidential appointments to fill them can lead to shifts in the ideology of the Court. These changes can result in the overturning of some precedents, calling into question the reliability and therefore legitimacy of Supreme Court decisions. Controversial and unpopular decisions can face a number of challenges.

CURRENT SUPREME COURT JUSTICES				
Current Justices	President	President's Party	Senate vote	Prior Job
Clarence Thomas	G.H.W. Bush	Republican	52–48	DC Circuit
Ruth Bader Ginsburg	Clinton	Democrat	96–3	DC Circuit
Stephen Breyer	Clinton	Democrat	87–9	First Circuit
John Roberts, Chief Justice	G.W. Bush	Republican	78–22	DC Circuit
Samuel Alito	G.W. Bush	Republican	58–42	Third Circuit
Sonia Sotomayor	Obama	Democrat	68–31	Second Circuit
Elena Kagan	Obama	Democrat	63–37	Solicitor General
Neil Gorsuch	Trump	Republican	54–45	Tenth Circuit
Brett Kavanaugh	Trump	Republican	50–48	DC Circuit

Overturning Precedent

Precedent plays an important role in judicial decision-making. Rulings by higher courts bind lower courts to the same ruling. However, in 1932 Justice Brandeis wrote in a dissenting opinion in *Burnet v. Coronado Oil &*

Gas Co., "*Stare decisis* is usually the wise policy, because in most matters it is more important that the applicable law be settled than it be settled right." This was especially true about rulings related to legislation, he argued, because errors in the Court's decision could be corrected by Congress. However, on matters related to the application of the Constitution, which the legislature has no power to change, Brandeis noted that the Court has often reconsidered and overturned its own previous ruling if an earlier one was made in error.

Consider the precedents set in two important cases: *Plessy v. Ferguson* (1896) that enabled states to provide separate schools for students based on race, and the later *Brown v. Board of Education* (1954) ruling that reversed the same principle. (See Topic 3.11 for more on both cases.) Of course, a half century had passed and race and education were viewed differently at those two points.

More telling examples of the Court's willingness to overturn precedent are seen in cases dealing with suffrage. The Court had ruled in 1935 in *Grovey v. Townsend* that the Democratic Party of Texas, as a private, voluntary organization, could determine its own membership rules. Even if those rules banned African Americans from voting in the primary, as the Constitution didn't apply to this non-government institution. In the 1944 case of *Smith v. Allwright,* Lonnie E. Smith brought suit with a similar argument about his Fifteenth Amendment voting rights. The Court ruled in his favor and furthered the discussion of *stare decisis* versus overturning a precedent. "In reaching this conclusion, we are not unmindful of the desirability of continuity of decision in constitutional questions. However, when convinced of former error, this Court has never felt constrained to follow precedent. . . . *Grovey v. Townsend* is overruled."

Why the dramatic shift in only nine years? By 1944, different justices occupied the seats on the Court, and, amid World War II, views changed on democracy, fairness, and equality.

THINK AS A POLITICAL SCIENTIST: *DESCRIBE POLITICAL PRINCIPLES IN DIFFERENT SCENARIOS*

Political principles are foundational concepts or ideas of government. Political scientists examine political principles in different scenarios to try to understand them as fully as possible. For example, one key principle of the judicial branch is to establish precedent, and the strength of the Supreme Court comes from this power. *Stare decisis,* or following precedent, is what binds lower courts to similar rulings. However, in different contexts, precedent may have different value. At times, a superior court can overturn precedent if it believes errors exist in previous decisions.

Practice: Read the scenarios on the next page and complete the tasks that follow.

Martin v. Hunter's Lessee (1816). Denny Martin, a British subject, had inherited land from his Loyalist uncle during the Revolutionary War. Virginia law stated property could be taken from Loyalists. The state seized the land, and Martin sued based on a federal treaty that had promised land returned to Loyalists after the war. Virginia's Supreme Court upheld the confiscation of land. Relying on the Constitution—Article III, Section 2, the supremacy clause—the Supreme Court reversed the decision and gave Martin's land back based on the idea federal treaties superseded state law.

Brown v. Board of Education (1954). A group of African American students (the Brown family was first alphabetically) sued because they had been denied access to certain public schools based on race. The case made it to the Supreme Court, where the Court ruled that "separate but equal" facilities are inherently unequal. The practice, established in the *Plessy v. Ferguson* (1896) case, violated the equal protection clause of the Fourteenth Amendment.

1. Explain the principle behind why the Supreme Court overturned Virginia's ruling in the *Martin* case.

2. Explain the precedent that was overturned in the *Brown* case.

The Supreme Court Today

When President George W. Bush replaced Chief Justice Rehnquist after his death with John Roberts (2005), the Court's membership had not changed for about 12 years. President Barack Obama appointed two women, Circuit Justice Sonia Sotomayor (2009), and U.S. Solicitor General Elena Kagan (2010). President Trump nominated Neil Gorsuch (2017) and Brett Kavanaugh (2018) as the Court's newest members.

Front row, left to right: Associate Justice Stephen G. Breyer, Associate Justice Clarence Thomas, Chief Justice John G. Roberts, Jr., Associate Justice Ruth Bader Ginsburg, Associate Justice Samuel A. Alito. Back row: Associate Justice Neil M. Gorsuch, Associate Justice Sonia Sotomayor, Associate Justice Elena Kagan, Associate Justice Brett M. Kavanaugh

Credit: Fred Schilling, Collection of the Supreme Court of the United States.

Ideology The Rehnquist Court and the current Roberts Court have been difficult to predict. The conservative and liberal wings had been balanced by the swing votes of Justices O'Connor and Kennedy. Swing votes are those often tie-breaking votes cast by justices whose opinions cannot always be easily predicted. For the past decade or so, most experts have been quick to characterize the Court as leaning conservative. However, the Court has limited states' use of the death penalty and upheld government's eminent domain authority for economic development. With Justice Kavanaugh as Kennedy's replacement, the direction of the Court is uncertain.

Chief Justice **John Roberts** has guided the Court with judicial minimalism. "Judges and justices are servants of the law, not the other way around. Judges are like umpires," he said during his confirmation hearing. "Umpires don't make rules; they apply them . . . nobody ever went to a ball game to see the umpire." Robert's operation takes fewer cases, while the conversations and conferences go longer. He has achieved more unanimity in decisions than some previous chief justices and has written more narrow opinions to address the questions before the Court.

Supreme Court Job Approval, by Political Party

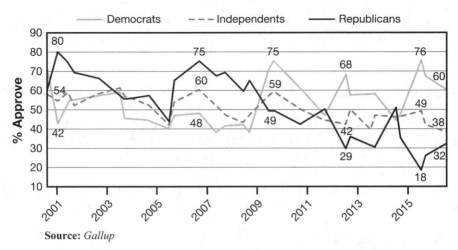

Source: *Gallup*

REFLECT ON THE ESSENTIAL QUESTION

Essential Question: *How has the Supreme Court's use of judicial review in conjunction with life tenure led to debates about the legitimacy of the court? On separate paper, complete a chart like the one below.*

Continuity or Change of the Supreme Court	Effect on Legitimacy of the Court

---

KEY TERMS AND NAMES

binding precedent
persuasive precedent
precedent

Roberts, John
stare decisis

2.10

The Court in Action

"John Marshall has made his decision, now let him enforce it."

—President Andrew Jackson, on the
Worcester v. Georgia decision, 1832

Essential Question: How have changes in the Supreme Court over time led to debates about the legitimacy of the court?

President Jackson didn't believe the Supreme Court had the final interpretation on matters of national interest, as the quote above attributed to Jackson suggests. This disagreement was not the only instance when the United States experienced a conflict between the branches of government. These conflicts can lead to questions about the legitimacy of the courts. Federal judges are appointed for life, directly unaccountable to any voter. The Supreme Court is often challenged when it renders unpopular decisions as well. Yet, it has created a lasting legacy with precedents it has set and law that it has shaped.

An Evolving Court

Since the Marshall Court, the Supreme Court's rulings have both caused and reflected changes in society because of the individual justices who have come and gone. Yet the Supreme Court has experienced more continuity than change. The Court's customs are established through consensus and remain over generations.

Early Courts to the New Deal

Chief Justice Roger Taney replaced John Marshall. The Court's operation changed somewhat with new leadership and new members. In 1837, Congress increased its membership to nine justices to ease the workload and created additional circuits. It also took up questions regarding slavery during the antebellum period. Taney and his fellow justices were determined to protect slavery as a state's right and upheld the congressional Fugitive Slave Act of 1850.

In 1857, as the North and the South grew further apart, the Court decided the Dred Scott case. The slave Dred Scott had traveled with his master into free territory and claimed, with the help of abolitionist lawyers, that having lived in free northern territory, he should have his freedom. Taney and the Court's majority shocked abolitionists with their decision and left one of the Court's worst legacies. The *Dred Scott v. Sandford* ruling held that Scott wasn't even a citizen and thus had no legal right to be a party in federal court, much less the country's top tribunal. The Court went further, stating that a slave owner's constitutional right to due process and property prevented government from depriving him of that property, regardless of where he traveled. Abolitionists and anti-slavery advocates in the territories immediately challenged the Court's legitimacy.

Corporations and the State

In the late 1800s, the Court examined concerns over business, trade, and workplace regulations as the nation had experienced vast economic expansion during the Industrial Revolution. Congress and state legislatures attempted to address the unfair and unsafe working conditions while facing strong resistance from business leaders who argued for more of a *laissez-faire,* or minimal government regulation, approach. When pressed by corporations to toss out worker protection laws, the Court had to decide two principles: what the Constitution permitted government to do and which government—state or federal—could do it.

The Court began to overturn various state health, safety, and civil rights laws, and in so doing, it shaped social policy. It threw out a congressional act that addressed monopolies. It also ruled Congress's income tax statute null and void. By the turn of the century, the Court had developed a conservative reputation as it questioned business regulation and progressive ideas. In *Lochner v. New York* (1905), the Court overturned a New York state law that prevented bakers from working more than 10 hours per day. The law was meant to counter the long hours required in an era before overtime pay.

During the Progressive Era, the Court made additional exceptions but quickly returned to a conservative, **strict constructionist** view of business regulation. A strict constructionist interprets the Constitution in its original context, while a **liberal constructionist** interprets the Constitution as a living document and takes into account changes and social conditions since ratification. The Court held that Congress could not use its commerce power to suppress child labor. The Court's conservative viewpoint turned further to the right, taking social policy with it, when former president William Howard Taft became chief justice. It ruled that minimum wage law for women also violated liberty of contract.

The New Deal and Roosevelt's Plan During the Depression, the Court transformed. Charles Evans Hughes replaced Taft as chief justice in 1929. Hughes managed a mixed group with four strong conservatives, nicknamed the "Four Horsemen," who overturned several New Deal programs. The Court struck down business regulations, invalidated the National Recovery Act (1933), and ruled against New York's minimum wage law.

After his 1936 landslide re-election, Franklin Roosevelt (FDR) responded to the rebuffs of the conservative Court by devising a plan to "pack the Court."

He proposed legislation to add one justice for every justice then over the age of 70, which would have allowed him to appoint up to six new members. FDR claimed this would relieve the Court's overloaded docket, but in reality he wanted to dilute the power of the conservative majority who had been unreceptive to his New Deal proposals. The sitting Court denied any need for more justices. Conservatives and liberals alike believed such a plan amounted to an attack on the Court's independence. Members of the Senate Judiciary Committee said, "The bill is an invasion of judicial power such as has never before been attempted in this country."

The Court changed ideologically, however, when one of the conservatives took an about-face in *West Coast Hotel v. Parrish* (1937), which sustained a Washington state minimum wage law. Justice Owen Roberts became "the switch in time that saved nine," meaning that there was no longer any need to try to pack the Court with additional justices. After the *West Coast Hotel* decision, the Court upheld every New Deal measure that had come before it. Roosevelt pressed ahead with more legislation, including a national minimum wage that has withstood constitutional scrutiny ever since. Winning four elections, he was able to appoint nine new justices to the Court who were friendly to his policies before his death in 1944.

A Court Dedicated to Individual Liberties

In the post-World War II years, the Court protected and extended individual liberties. It delivered mixed messages on civil liberties up to this point—holding states to First Amendment protections while allowing government infringements in times of national security threats. For example, it upheld FDR's executive order that placed Japanese Americans in internment camps after the Japanese attack in 1941. (See Topic 2.6 for more about the 1944 *Korematsu v. United States* case.) After that, however, the Court followed a fairly consistent effort to protect individual liberties and the rights of accused criminals. The trend crested in 1973 when the Court upheld a woman's right to an abortion in *Roe v. Wade*. (See Topic 3.9.)

The Warren Court The Court extended many liberties under Chief Justice Earl Warren after President Dwight Eisenhower appointed him in 1953. As attorney general for California during the war, Warren oversaw the internment of Japanese Americans, and in 1948 he was the Republican's vice-presidential nominee. But any expectations that Warren would act as a conservative judge were lost soon after he took the bench.

Warren's legacy did not please traditionalists because his Court overturned state policies created by democratically elected legislatures. The controversial or unpopular decisions led some people to challenge the Court's legitimacy. Several Warren Court decisions seemed to insult states' political cultures and threaten to drain state treasuries. Some argued that Earl Warren should be impeached. The Warren Court had made unpopular decisions, but it had not committed impeachable acts—such as taking bribes or failing to carry out the job—so only justices' retirements or deaths could change the Court's makeup.

Warren Court—Civil Rights and Civil Liberties	
Brown v. Board of Education (1954)	Overturned the 1896 *Plessy v. Ferguson* decision, stating the "separate but equal" standard violated the Fourteenth Amendment's equal protection clause. (See Topic 3.11.)
Mapp v. Ohio (1961)	Ruled that evidence illegally obtained would be inadmissible in court. (See Topic 3.8.)
Engle v. Vitale (1962)	Upheld the establishment clause of the First Amendment. Public school-sponsored prayer was unconstitutional. (See Topic 3.2.)
Gideon v. Wainwright (1963)	The court stated that all citizens must be provided a lawyer, even if they can't afford one. (See Topic 3.8.)
Miranda v. Arizona (1966)	An arrest suspect had to be formally informed of his or her rights—sometimes called Miranda rights. (See Topic 3.8.)
Tinker v. Des Moines Independent Community School District (1969)	Allowed for students to participate in non-disruptive symbolic speech in schools. (See Topic 3.3.)

Cases in bold are required Supreme Court cases for this course.

The Burger Court President Richard Nixon won the 1968 election, in part by painting Warren's Court as an affront to law enforcement and local control. When Warren retired, Nixon replaced him with U.S. appeals court justice Warren Burger. Burger by no means satisfied Nixon's quest to instill a conservative philosophy and largely failed in judicial leadership. While lacking Warren's leadership skills, Burger kept the Supreme Court on a somewhat similar path to the one Warren had begun.

In *Roe v. Wade*, Burger joined six others on the Court to outlaw or modify state anti-abortion laws as a violation of due process. With this ruling, a woman could now obtain an abortion, unconditionally, through the first trimester of pregnancy. He also penned a unanimous opinion to uphold lower-court-ordered school busing for racial enrollment balance.

The chief justice often couldn't round up enough agreement to get a five-justice majority. Thus, cases went undecided while the Court took on additional ones. The justices became overworked and took as many as 150 appeals in a year. Supreme Court historian and former clerk Edward Lazarus refers to Burger as "an intellectual lightweight" who had "alienated his colleagues and even his natural allies." By 1986, Burger had proven pretentious and chafing to his colleagues, and he had simply become tired. At the press conference announcing his retirement, a reporter asked him what he would miss most on the Court. Burger stalled, sighed, and said, "Nothing."

The Rehnquist Court At the same press conference, President Reagan elevated Associate Justice William Rehnquist to the chief position. Based on Rehnquist's strict constructionist views, President Nixon had nominated Rehnquist for the High Court. The Senate did not confirm him easily and accused him of racism, as he had recommended upholding the "separate but equal" doctrine when clerking for a justice in the early 1950s en route to the *Brown* ruling. This same controversy arose in 1986 as he accepted the chief justice position.

Initially, Rehnquist found himself in dissent and all alone on several cases, earning him the nickname "the Lone Ranger." When Rehnquist took over for Burger, however, additional strict constructionists soon joined him. He improved the conference procedures and decreased the Court's caseload. All the justices, liberals and conservatives alike, welcomed the changes. In the 1990s, the Rehnquist Court upheld states' rights to place limitations on access to abortions and limited Congress's commerce clause authority. In addition to efficiency, Rehnquist had ushered in another ideological shift.

Legislating after Unfavorable Decisions

Many people believe the Supreme Court's decision is final, but sometimes it is not. In many precedent-setting decisions, the High Court interprets language in the Constitution. That language can be subsequently changed through constitutional amendments.

The passage and ratification of the obscure Eleventh Amendment, which further defines court jurisdiction, was in response to the 1794 ruling in *Chisolm v. Georgia*. Anti-Federalists and states' rights advocates had warned that the new federal courts might overpower the state courts, and they saw the decision in *Chisolm v. Georgia* as such an encroachment. South Carolina residents seeking to recoup war debts from Georgia's government sued in federal court. Georgia denied the federal court's authority and refused to show up. The Supreme Court ruled in *Chisolm* that federal courts had jurisdiction over such cases and opened the door for additional pending suits against other states. In response, Congress members, especially those from the states involved in the lawsuits, proposed the Eleventh Amendment. It prohibits the federal courts from considering certain lawsuits against states and excuses state courts from hearing some suits against the state, if based on federal law. The Eleventh Amendment is the only amendment to alter the judicial branch's jurisdiction.

However, additional amendments that addressed the substance of law have been proposed and ratified as reactions to unfavorable Supreme Court decisions. For example, following the Civil War, the passage of the Fourteenth Amendment effectively overturned the Dred Scott decision by guaranteeing citizenship to those born in the United States and requiring states to afford their citizens "equal protection."

Later in the 1800s, Congress passed a national tax on individual incomes. Because the language in Article I, Section 8 is unclear on the types of taxes Congress can create and the manner in which these are to be applied, the Court struck down the law. However, later in the Progressive Era, enough support for such a tax enabled Congress to propose and the states to ratify the Sixteenth Amendment (1913) to assure this power to create the national income tax.

Amending the Constitution is the surest way to get around a Supreme Court decision, but it is a difficult task. In recent years, movements have surfaced to amend the document to stop abortions, to prevent same-sex marriage, and to enable legislatures to criminalize flag burning—all attempts to overturn unpopular Supreme Court decisions— and all failed. A more practical path is for Congress or state legislatures to pass laws that the Supreme Court has declared unconstitutional in a slightly different form.

Implementation Courts decide principles and order citizens or government entities to take action or refrain from action. The executive branch must then enforce this law. On a basic, local level, a state judge may issue a restraining order, but the police must do any necessary restraining.

When a court orders, decrees, or enjoins (issues an injunction to) a party, it can do so only from the courtroom. Putting a decision into effect is another matter. Judges alone cannot implement the verdicts and opinions made in their courts. Nine robed justices in Washington simply cannot put their own decisions into effect. They require at least one of several other potential governing authorities—the president, U.S. marshals, regulatory agencies, the military, or other government agencies—to carry out their decisions. Legislatures may have to rewrite or pass new laws or finance the enforcement endeavor. The implementing branch, charged with putting a court's decision into effect, doesn't always cooperate with or follow court orders.

When the Supreme Court makes decisions, it assesses potential enforcement and cooperation. When John Marshall's Court deemed that Georgia could not regulate Cherokee Indian lands in its state because such regulation was exclusive to the federal government, President Andrew Jackson strongly disagreed and allegedly said, "John Marshall has made his decision, now let him enforce it." In the late 1950s, after the Court ruled that a Little Rock high school had to integrate, the executive branch sent federal troops to escort the claimants into the formerly all-white school.

THINK AS A POLITICAL SCIENTIST: *COMPARE A REQUIRED SUPREME COURT CASE TO A NON-REQUIRED SUPREME COURT CASE*

Louisiana passed the Separate Car Act in 1890, which required all railroads to have "separate but equal" accommodations for passengers based on race. Homer Plessy, who was one-eighth African American, challenged the law. District Court Judge John Ferguson ruled the law to be constitutional. The Supreme Court upheld his ruling and established the policy of "separate but equal," which lasted for more than 50 years. The excerpt is from the majority opinion of Justice Henry Brown.

Practice: Review the *Marbury v. Madison* (1803) case in Topic 2.8. Then read the excerpt on the following page about the 1896 *Plessy v. Ferguson* case and complete the tasks that follow.

The constitutionality of this act [Separate Car Act] is attacked upon the ground that it conflicts both with the Thirteenth Amendment of the Constitution, abolishing slavery, and the Fourteenth Amendment, which prohibits certain restrictive legislation on the part of the States.

That it does not conflict with the Thirteenth Amendment. . . A statute which implies merely a legal distinction between the white and colored races — a distinction which is founded in the color of the two races and which must always exist so long as white men are distinguished from the other race by color — has no tendency to destroy the legal equality of the two races, or reestablish a state of involuntary servitude.

By the Fourteenth Amendment. . . The object of the amendment was undoubtedly to enforce the absolute equality of the two races before the law, but, in the nature of things, it could not have been intended to abolish distinctions based upon color, or to enforce social, as distinguished from political, equality, or a commingling of the two races upon terms unsatisfactory to either. Laws permitting, and even requiring, their separation in places where they are liable to be brought into contact do not necessarily imply the inferiority of either race to the other, and have been generally, if not universally, recognized as within the competency of the state legislatures in the exercise of their police power.

1. Describe the reasoning in the *Plessy* case that allowed "separate but equal."

2. Explain one important similarity and one difference in the circumstances that led to both cases.

3. Explain how the Supreme Court used judicial review in its decision in each case.

How Cases Reach the Supreme Court

The Supreme Court is guided by Article III, congressional acts, and its own rules. Congress is the authority on the Court's size and funding. The Court began creating rules in 1790 and now has 48 formal rules, as well as less formal customs and traditions that guide the Court's operation. The Court has both original and appellate jurisdiction. Only in rare situations does the Supreme Court exercise original jurisdiction and thus serve as a trial court, typically when one state sues another over a border dispute or to settle some type of interstate compact.

As the nation's highest appeals court, the Supreme Court takes cases from the 13 U.S. circuits and the 50 states. Two-thirds of appeals come through the federal system, directly from the U.S. circuit courts, because the Supreme Court has a more direct jurisdiction over cases originating in federal district courts than in state trial courts.

Like the circuit courts, the Supreme Court accepts appeals each year from among thousands filed. The petitioner files a **petition for certiorari**, a brief arguing why the lower court erred. The Supreme Court reviews this to determine if the claim is worthy and if it should grant the appeal. If an appeal is deemed worthy, the justices add the claim to their "discuss list." They consider past precedents and the real impact on the petitioner and respondent. The

Supreme Court does not consider hypothetical or theoretical damages; the claimant must show actual damage. Finally, the justices consider the wider national and societal impact if they take and rule on the case. Once four of the nine justices agree to accept the case, the appeal is granted. This **rule of four**, a standard less than a majority, reflects courts' commitments to claims by minorities.

Opinions and Caseload

Chief Justice John Marshall's legacy of unanimity has vanished. The Court comes to a unanimous decision only about 30 to 40 percent of the time. Therefore, it issues varying opinions on the law. Once the Court comes to a majority, the chief justice, or the most senior justice in the majority, either writes the Court's opinion or assigns it to another justice in the majority. Typically, those justices who write the **majority opinion**—reflecting the Court's ruling—have expertise on the topic or are obviously passionate about the issue. Like a statute for Congress or an executive order for the president, a court ruling is the judicial branch's contribution to the nation's law. The majority opinion sums up the case, the Court's decision, and its rationale.

Justices who differ from the majority can draft and issue differing opinions. Some may agree with the majority and join that vote but have reservations about the majority's legal reasoning. They might write a **concurring opinion**. Those who vote against the majority often write a **dissenting opinion**. A dissenting opinion has no force of law and no immediate legal bearing but allows a justice to explain his or her disagreements to send a message to the legal community or to influence later cases. On occasion, the Court will issue a decision without the full explanation, known as a *per curiam* opinion.

REFLECT ON THE ESSENTIAL QUESTION

Essential Question: *How has the Supreme Court's use of judicial review in conjunction with life tenure led to debates about the legitimacy of the court? On separate paper, complete a chart like the one below.*

Controversial or Unpopular Decision of the Court	Responses to the Decision

---

KEY TERMS AND NAMES

concurring opinion

dissenting opinion

liberal constructionist

majority opinion

petition for certiorari

rule of four

strict constructionist

Checks on the Judicial Branch

"These courts will eclipse the dignity, and take away from the respectability, of the state courts . . . and in the course of human events it is to be expected, that they will swallow up all the powers of the courts in the respective states."

—*Brutus No. 1,* to the People of New York, 1787

Essential Question: What issues lead to debates about the legitimacy of the Court, and how can other branches limit Supreme Court power?

The Constitution has granted the executive and legislative branches the ability to check the power of the Court. This idea directly relates to Enlightenment philosopher Montesquieu's beliefs on the need for separation of powers and the value of a system of checks and balances.

Judicial Activism vs. Judicial Restraint

Ever since the Supreme Court first exercised judicial review in *Marbury*, it has reserved the right to rule on government action in violation of constitutional principles, whether by the legislature or the executive. Judicial review has seemingly placed the Supreme Court, as Brutus predicted, above the other branches, making it the final arbiter on many controversies. On many topics, as *Brutus No. 1* warned, it has made the federal government supreme while defining what states, Congress, and the president can or cannot do. On other topics, it has restrained the federal government.

When judges strike down laws or reverses public policy, they are exercising **judicial activism**. (To remember this concept, think *judges acting* to create the law.) Activism can be liberal or conservative, depending on the nature of the law or executive action that is struck down. When the Court threw out the New York maximum-hours law in 1905 in *Lochner*, it acted conservatively because it rejected an established liberal statute. In *Roe v. Wade*, the Court acted liberally to remove a conservative anti-abortion policy in Texas. Courts at multiple levels in both the state and federal systems have struck down statutes as well as presidential, departmental, and agency decisions.

The Court's power to strike down parts of, or entire laws, has encouraged litigation and changes in policy. For example, gun owners and the National Rifle Association (NRA) supported an effort to overturn a ban on handguns in Washington, DC and got a victory in the *Heller* decision. (See Topics 3.5

and 3.7.) Several state attorneys general who opposed the Affordable Care Act sued to overturn it. In a 5:4 decision, in *National Federation of Independent Business v. Sebelius* (2012), the Court upheld the key element of the Affordable Care Act, the individual federal mandate that requires all citizens to purchase health insurance or pay a penalty. In striking down limits on when a corporation can advertise during a campaign season, it struck down parts of Congress's Bipartisan Campaign Reform Act (2002) in *Citizens United v. FEC* (2010). (See Topic 5.4.)

Critics of judicial activism tend to point out that, in a democracy, elected representative legislatures should create policy. These critics advocate for **judicial restraint**. Chief Justice Harlan Fiske Stone first used the term in his 1936 dissent when the majority outlawed a New Deal program. The Court should not, say these critics, decide a dispute in that manner unless there is a concrete injury to be relieved by the decision. Strict constructionist Antonin Scalia once claimed, "A 'living' Constitution judge [is] a happy fellow who comes home at night to his wife and says, 'The Constitution means exactly what I think it ought to mean!'" Justices should not declare a law unconstitutional, strict constructionists say today, when it merely violates their own idea of what the Constitution means in a contemporary context, but only when the law clearly and directly contradicts the document. To do otherwise is "legislating from the bench," say strict constructionists. This ongoing debate about judicial activism and restraint has coincided with discussions about the Court's role in shaping national policy.

Still other critics argue that judicial policymaking is ineffective as well as undemocratic. Wise judges have a firm understanding of the Constitution and citizens' rights, but they don't always study issues over time. Most judges don't have special expertise on matters of environmental protection, operating schools, or other administrative matters. They don't have the support systems of lawmakers, such as committee staffers and researchers, to fully engage an issue to find a solution. When courts rule, the outcome is not always practical or manageable for those meant to implement it. Additionally, many such court rulings are just unpopular, and with judges' life tenures, there's no recourse for the citizenry.

THINK AS A POLITICAL SCIENTIST: *DESCRIBE POLITICAL PRINCIPLES IN DIFFERENT SCENARIOS*

The principle of checks and balances prevents the concentration of too much power in a single branch of government. Critics of the judicial branch point to the concept of judicial activism as a way for that institution to gain too much power. Judicial activism is exercised when judges overlook legal precedents and follow their own political views in rulings. Conversely, when judges hesitate to inject their own preferences into legal rulings unless a law is clearly unconstitutional, they are exercising judicial restraint.

Practice: Read the cases below. Identify in each case whether the Court acted with *judicial restraint* or *judicial activism* and explain your reasoning.

1. *Korematsu v. United States* (1944). President Franklin Roosevelt signed Executive Order 9066 soon after the Japanese attack on Pearl Harbor, requiring Japanese Americans to relocate to internment camps for the security of the nation. Fred Korematsu refused to obey the order and was arrested. He sued, claiming his Fifth Amendment rights were violated. The Ninth Circuit Court affirmed his conviction.

   The Supreme Court found that the executive order did not show racial prejudice and was valid because of the necessity of protecting the nation from attack. Justice Frankfurter concurred, ". . . martial necessity arising from the danger of espionage and sabotage" justified the order.

2. *Obergefell v. Hodges* (2015). Numerous couples sued Ohio, Michigan, Kentucky, and Tennessee over the states' refusals to recognize same-sex marriages. The Sixth Circuit Court of Appeals reversed lower court rulings and upheld that the states' position doesn't violate the couples' Fourteenth Amendment rights.

   The Supreme Court ruled that the due process and the equal protection clauses guarantee the right to marry as a fundamental liberty and apply to same-sex couples. States may not deny same-sex couples the same right to marry as opposite-sex couples. Chief Justice John Roberts wrote in his dissent, "Five lawyers have closed the debate and enacted their own vision of marriage as a matter of constitutional law."

Interactions with Other Branches

Congress and the president interact with the judiciary in many ways. From the creation of various courts to the appointment of judges to implementation of a judicial decision, the judiciary often crosses paths with the other two branches. Despite the concern of some Anti-Federalists, the other branches of government do have ways to limit the power of the Supreme Court. **BIG IDEA** The U.S. Constitution establishes a system of checks and balances among branches of government and allocates power between federal and state governments. This system is based on the rule of law and the balance between majority rule and minority rights.

Presidential Appointments and Senate Confirmation

With hundreds of judgeships in the lower courts, presidents will have a chance to appoint judges to the federal bench over their four or eight years in office. When a vacancy occurs, or when Congress creates a new seat on an overloaded court, the president carefully selects a qualified judge because that person can shape law and will likely do so until late in his or her life.

Senate's Advice and Consent The Senate Judiciary Committee reviews the president's judicial appointments. Sometimes nominees appear before the committee to answer senators' questions about their experience or their views on the law. Less controversial district judges are confirmed without a hearing based largely on the recommendation of the senators from the nominee's state. The more controversial, polarizing Supreme Court nominees will receive greater attention during sometimes contentious and dramatic hearings.

The quick determination of an appointee's political philosophy has become known as a "litmus test." Much like quickly testing a solution for its pH in chemistry class, someone trying to determine a judicial nominee's ideology on the political spectrum will ask a pointed question on a controversial issue or look at one of the nominee's prior opinions from a lower court. Presidents, senators, or pundits can conduct such a "test." The very term has a built-in criticism, as a judge's complex judicial philosophy should not be determined as quickly as a black-and-white scientific measurement.

Senatorial Courtesy The Senate firmly reserves its right of advice and consent. "In practical terms," said George W. Bush administration attorney Rachel Brand, "the home state senators are almost as important as—and sometimes more important than—the president in determining who will be nominated to a particular lower-court judgeship." This practice of **senatorial courtesy** is especially routine with district judge appointments, as districts are entirely within a given state. When vacancies occur, senators typically recommend judges to the White House.

Senate procedure and tradition give individual senators veto power over nominees located within their respective states. For U.S. district court nominations, each of the two senators receives a blue slip—a blue piece of paper they return to the Judiciary Committee to allow the process to move forward. To derail the process, a senator can return the slip with a negative indication or never return it at all. The committee chair will usually not hold a hearing on the nominee's confirmation until both senators have consented. This custom has encouraged presidents to consult with the home-state senators early in the process.

All senators embrace this influence. They are the guardians and representatives for their states. The other 98 senators tend to follow the home state senators' lead, especially if they are in the same party, and vote accordingly. This custom is somewhat followed with appeals court judges as well.

Confirmation When a Supreme Court vacancy occurs, a president has a unique opportunity to shape American jurisprudence. Of the 162 nominations to the Supreme Court over U.S. history, 36 were not confirmed. Eleven were rejected by a vote of the full Senate. The others were either never acted on by the Judiciary Committee or withdrawn by the nominee or by the president. Few confirmations brought rancor or public spectacle until the Senate rejected two of President Nixon's nominees. Since then, the Court's influence on controversial topics, intense partisanship, the public nature of the contentious confirmation process, and contentious hearings have highlighted the divides between the parties.

BY THE NUMBERS RECENT PRESIDENTS' JUDICIAL APPOINTMENTS				
President	Supreme Court	Appeals Courts	District Courts	Total
Nixon (1969–1974)	4	45	182	231
Ford (1974–1977)	1	12	52	65
Carter (1977–1981)	0	56	206	262
Reagan (1981–1989)	3	78	292	373
G.H.W. Bush (1989–1993)	2	37	149	188
Clinton (1993–2001)	2	62	306	370
G.W. Bush (2001–2009)	2	61	261	324
Obama (2009–2017)	2	49	268	319
Trump (2017–2019)*	2	51	137	190

*President Trump's appointments are through the first two years of his presidency.

Source: U.S. Courts. Excludes Court of International Trade

What do the numbers show? Which presidents appointed more judges than others? On average, how many Supreme Court judges does a president appoint? How many lower court judges? Which president of recent years appointed the most? How do a president's judicial appointees impact law and government in the United States?

Interest Groups The increasingly publicized confirmation process has also involved interest groups. Confirmation hearings were not public until 1929. In recent years, they have become a spectacle and may include a long list of witnesses testifying about the nominee's qualifications. The most active and reputable interest group to testify about judicial nominees is the American Bar Association (ABA). Since the 1950s, this association of lawyers has been involved in the process. They rate nominees as "highly qualified," "qualified," and "not qualified." More recently, additional groups weigh in on the process, especially when they see their interests threatened or enhanced. Interest groups also target a senator's home state with ads urging voters to contact their senators in support of or in opposition to the nominee. Indeed, interest groups sometimes suggest or even draft questions for senators to assist them at the confirmation hearings.

Getting "Borked" The confirmation process began to focus on ideology during the Reagan administration. President Reagan nominated U.S. Appeals Court Judge Robert Bork for the Supreme Court in 1987. He was an advocate of original intent, or "originalism," seeking to uphold the Constitution as the framers intended. He made clear that he despised the rulings of the activist Warren Court. When asked about his nomination, then-Senator Joe Biden, chair of the Senate Judiciary Committee, warned the White House that choosing Bork would likely result in a confirmation fight. Senator Edward Kennedy drew a line in the sand at a Senate press conference. "Robert Bork's America," Kennedy said, "is a land in which women would be forced into back alley abortions, blacks would sit at segregated lunch counters, rogue police could break down citizens' doors in midnight raids, and schoolchildren could not be taught evolution." Kennedy's warning brought attention to Judge Bork's extreme views that threatened to turn back a generation of civil rights and civil liberties decisions.

Source: Wikimedia Commons
President Ronald Reagan meeting with Supreme Court nominee Robert Bork

After hearings with the committee, the full Senate, which had unanimously confirmed Bork as an appeals court judge in 1981, rejected him by a vote of 58 to 42. The term "to bork" entered the American political lexicon, defined more recently by the *New York Times*: "to destroy a judicial nominee through a concerted attack on his character, background, and philosophy."

Clarence Thomas In 1991, President Bush announced his replacement for retiring Justice Thurgood Marshall, the first African American on the Court. He nominated conservative U.S. Appeals Court judge Clarence Thomas, who, as an African American, reflected the left's desire for diversity and the right's desire for a strict constructionist.

Several concerns about Thomas' appointment arose. Thomas was known for very conservative views, causing liberals to take issue with his ideology. He had served as a district appeals judge for only about a year before his nomination, leading some to question Thomas' experience.

Then Anita Hill, a former employee of Thomas, came forward with accusations against him of sexual misconduct. The Judiciary Committee invited her to testify. In a highly televised carnival atmosphere, Hill testified for seven hours about the harassing comments Thomas had made and the pornographic films he discussed. Thomas denied all the allegations and called the hearing a "high-tech lynching." After a tie vote in an all-white male judiciary committee, the full Senate barely confirmed Thomas.

"The Nuclear Option" During George W. Bush's first term, Democrats did not allow a vote on 10 of the 52 appeals court nominees that had cleared the Judiciary Committee. Conservative nominees were delayed by Senate procedure. The Democrats, in the minority at the time, invoked the right to filibuster votes on judges. One Bush nominee waited four years.

Bush declared in his State of the Union message, "Every judicial nominee deserves an up or down vote." Senate Republicans threatened to change the rules to disallow the filibuster, which could be done with a simple majority vote. The threat to the filibuster became known as a drastic "nuclear option." The nuclear option was averted when a bipartisan group of senators dubbed the "Gang of 14" joined forces to create a compromise that kept the Senate rules the same while confirming most appointees.

Denying Garland In February 2016, Justice Antonin Scalia died. Republican presidential candidates in the primary race agreed on one thing: the next president should appoint Scalia's replacement. With Democratic President Obama in his final year on the job, Republican Senate Majority Leader Mitch McConnell announced that the Senate would not hold a vote on any nominee until the voters elected a new president. A month later, with ten months remaining until a new president would be sworn in, Obama nominated Judge Merrick Garland to replace Scalia. Garland was a judicial selection from the DC Circuit with a unanimous "well-qualified" rating from the ABA. Senator McConnell's decision was strategic if unusual, and he kept his promise to use "the nuclear option," to the dismay of many. Vacancies on the Supreme Court do occur, and the Court can operate temporarily with eight members, but to ensure the vacancy for more than ten months was unprecedented.

Constitutionally, nothing mandates a timeline on the Senate's confirmation process. In the end, Donald Trump won the presidency, Republicans retained control of the Senate, and Trump nominated Tenth Circuit Judge Neil Gorsuch within two weeks of his inauguration. The Senate confirmed Gorsuch by a vote of 54 to 45.

Executive and Legislative Influence on the Courts' Power

In addition to strategically choosing judicial nominees and selectively approving them, the president and Congress interact with lower courts and the Supreme Court in other ways. The other branches have the powers to bring matters and crimes to court, impeach and remove judges, use the power of the purse to affect the judiciary and judicial decisions, partially redefine courts' jurisdiction, and implement court rulings in their own way.

The Justice Department In addition to appointing the judiciary, the executive branch enters the federal courts to enforce criminal law and to weigh in on legal questions. The president's Department of Justice, headed by the attorney general, investigates federal crimes with the Federal Bureau of Investigation (FBI) or the Drug Enforcement Administration (DEA), and U.S. attorneys prosecute the accused criminals. These attorneys are also the legal authority for federal civil law on a more local basis. When a party sues the federal government, U.S. attorneys defend the United States. In appealed criminal cases, these attorneys present the oral arguments in the circuit courts.

Another high-ranking figure in the Department of Justice is the solicitor general, who works in the Washington, DC office. Appointed by the president and approved by the Senate, the solicitor general determines which cases to appeal to the U.S. Supreme Court and represents the United States in Supreme Court cases. When you see a Supreme Court case entitled the "*United States v. John Doe*," it means that the United States lost in one of the circuit courts and the solicitor general sought an appeal.

The solicitor general may also submit an *amicus curiae* brief (friend of the court brief) to the Supreme Court in cases in which the United States is not a party. An amicus brief argues for a particular ruling in the case. Several solicitors general have later been appointed to the High Court, notably Stanley Reed, Thurgood Marshall, and Elena Kagan.

Impeachment Federal judges who act criminally or perhaps unethically can be impeached and removed. In 1804, John Pickering, a Federalist, became the first judge to be impeached. Pickering refused to resign, so the House impeached him, and the Senate convicted him on the charges of drunkenness and unlawful rulings.

Almost immediately after Pickering's impeachment, Thomas Jefferson's party, the Democratic-Republicans, moved to impeach Supreme Court Justice Samuel Chase to weaken the Federalist presence on the Court. However, Jefferson wanted to avoid making the impeachment process a political tool to rid the third branch of opponents, so he withdrew his support, and Chase survived the Senate vote. Impeachment has served as Congress's check on the judges' life terms, and the House has impeached 15 federal judges.

Congressional Oversight and Influence Congress sets and pays judges' salaries. Congress budgets for the construction and maintenance of federal courthouses. It has passed an entire body of law that helps govern the judiciary. This includes regulations about courtroom procedures to judicial recusal— judges withdrawing from a case if they have a conflict of interest. Occasionally Congress creates new seats in the 94 district courts and on the 13 appeals courts. Congress has more than doubled the number of circuit and district judges over the last 50 years.

Defining Jurisdiction

Article III includes the power to consider all cases arising under the Constitution, federal law or treaty, and admiralty or maritime jurisdiction. It also addresses the types of cases that the judicial branch and specifically the "Supreme Court shall have . . . under such Regulations as the Congress shall make."

Since the initial Judiciary Act of 1789, Congress has periodically defined and reshaped the courts' jurisdiction. The most convenient and unquestioned power involves the legislature's power to define what types of cases are heard by which federal courts and which types of cases are left to the state courts. Article III also empowers Congress to define the types of parties that can go to the various courts, thereby defining **standing**, the requirements for bringing a case to court. Congress cannot create state courts, but it can endow them with concurrent power to hear certain cases concerning federal law.

Congress occasionally delves into "court-stripping," or jurisdiction stripping, when it wants to limit the judicial branch's power in hearing cases on particular topics. For example, in the 108th Congress of 2003–2005, in an effort to protect the Pledge of Allegiance, which was under fire for its "under God" phrase, the House voted to take away the courts' power to hear such cases. It also voted to deny funds in order to implement any such decisions. The same House voted to prevent federal courts from hearing cases regarding the Defense of Marriage Act. Conservative representatives were reacting to court filings, lower federal court decisions, and the coming strategy of using the courts to legalize same-sex marriage. The Senate failed to vote for the law, and thus courts have ruled on these matters.

REFLECT ON THE ESSENTIAL QUESTION

Essential Question: *What issues lead to debates about the legitimacy of the Court, and how can other branches limit Supreme Court power? On separate paper, complete a chart like the one below.*

Executive Checks on the Judicial Branch	Legislative Checks on the Judicial Branch

---

KEY TERMS AND NAMES

Bork, Robert	"nuclear option"
Garland, Merrick	senatorial courtesy
judicial activism	standing
judicial restraint	Thomas, Clarence

CHAPTER 6 Review:
Learning Objectives and Key Terms

TOPIC 2.8: Explain the principle of judicial review and how it checks the powers of the other institutions and state governments. (CON-5.A)

Judicial Power and Checks (CON-5.A.1)

appellate jurisdiction	*Marbury v. Madison* (1803)
Attorney General	original jurisdiction
certiorari	U.S. District Courts
Federalist No. 78	U.S. Circuit Courts of Appeals
judicial review	U.S. Supreme Court

TOPIC 2.9: Explain how the exercise of judicial review in conjunction with life tenure can lead to debate about the legitimacy of the Supreme Court's power. (CON-5.B)

Precedent and *Stare Decisis* (CON-5.B.1)	**Presidential Appointments and Ideological Changes** (CON-5.B.2)
binding precedent	Roberts, John
persuasive precedent	
stare decisis	
precedent	

TOPIC 2.10: Explain how the exercise of judicial review in conjunction with life tenure can lead to debate about the legitimacy of the Supreme Court's power. (CON-5.B)

Challenging the Court's Legitimacy and Power (CON-5.B.3)

concurring opinion	petition for certiorari
dissenting opinion	rule of four
liberal constructionist	strict constructionist
majority opinion	

TOPIC 2.11: Explain how the exercise of judicial review in conjunction with life tenure can lead to debate about the legitimacy of the Supreme Court's power. (CON-5.B)

TOPIC 2.11: Explain how the other branches in the government can limit the Supreme Court's power. (CON-5.C)

Judicial Activism vs. Judicial Restraint (CON-5.B.4)	**Limits on the Supreme Court's Power** (CON-5.C.1)
judicial activism	Bork, Robert
judicial restraint	"nuclear option"
	Garland, Merrick
	senatorial courtesy
	standing
	Thomas, Clarence

CHAPTER 6 Checkpoint:
The Judiciary

Topics 2.8–2.11

MULTIPLE-CHOICE QUESTIONS

1. Which of the following is an accurate comparison of judicial activism and judicial restraint?

	JUDICIAL ACTIVISM	JUDICIAL RESTRAINT
(A)	Can result in shaping federal, but not state, policies	Is practiced when an appeals court refuses to grant an appeal
(B)	Was established with the Judiciary Act of 1789	Was practiced in the Court's ruling in *Roe v. Wade*
(C)	Is a democratic way to assure popular polices in a representative government	Is practiced when courts limit the legislative or executive branches
(D)	Is practiced when courts overrule legislative acts or shape policy	Is exercised when courts hesitate from interfering with policies created by elected bodies

Questions 2 and 3 refer to the passage below.

If there are such things as political axioms, the propriety of the judicial power of a government being coextensive with its legislative, may be ranked among the number. The mere necessity of uniformity in the interpretation of the national laws, decides the question. Thirteen independent courts of final jurisdiction over the same causes, arising upon the same laws, is a hydra [a many-headed serpent in Greek mythology] in government, from which nothing but contradiction and confusion can proceed.

—Alexander Hamilton, *Federalist No. 80*, 1788

2. Which of the following statements best describes Hamilton's argument?

   (A) The thirteen states should retain their courts and have independence from national law.

   (B) The proposed federal courts and the Supreme Court will provide national consistency in law.

   (C) Because the national court system will have multiple judges, differing decisions will cause confusion.

   (D) The judicial branch should be the superior branch of government.

3. Those countering Hamilton's argument today might point to which of the following?

(A) The strength and impact of a judge's dissenting opinions

(B) The length of judges' terms during good behavior

(C) The differing views of federal judges and the resulting inconsistent rulings

(D) The Supreme Court's over-implementation of the rule of four

4. A U.S. district judge in Alabama has a dispute brought to his court in which an employee is suing her employer over improper termination on gender discrimination. The Ninth Circuit Court of Appeals, which includes several western states, and the U.S. District Court of Kansas have both previously ruled on very similar cases under the same law and sided with the employee. Which of the following is the likely action this federal judge will take?

(A) The judge must rule in the same way because of binding precedent.

(B) The judge will read the other two courts' opinions and consider them before making a ruling.

(C) The judge will ask the Justice Department for guidance.

(D) The judge will refuse to hear the case because the federal courts have no jurisdiction in this matter.

Questions 5 and 6 refer to the cartoon below.

Source: Jimmy Margulies, Politicalcartoons.com

5. Which of the following best illustrates the message of the cartoon?

(A) One judge shows judicial restraint; the other judge shows judicial activism.

(B) There are too many applicants for the Supreme Court.

(C) The Court is tied up in bureaucratic matters and cannot address judicial appointments.

(D) One president's judicial appointment was held and later replaced by the following president's appointment.

6. Which of the following constitutional principles allowed the events shown in the cartoon?

(A) The lawmaking process

(B) The Senate's advice and consent role

(C) The use of judicial review

(D) The original jurisdiction of U.S. District Courts

FREE-RESPONSE QUESTIONS

Concept Application

1. The Supreme Court closed out its 2011–12 term today in dramatic fashion, upholding the Affordable Care Act by a sharply divided vote [in *National Federation of Independent Business v. Sebelius*]. The Court's bottom line, reasoning and lineup of justices all came as a shock to many. . . . I don't think anyone predicted that the law would be upheld *without* the support of Justice Anthony Kennedy, almost always the Court's crucial swing vote. And while most of the legal debate focused on Congress's power under the Commerce Clause, the Court ultimately upheld the law as an exercise of the taxing power. . . . The most surprising thing of all, though, is that in the end, this ultraconservative Court decided the case, much as it did in many other cases this term, by siding with the liberals."

—David Cole, *The Nation*, June 28, 2012

After reading the scenario above, respond to A, B, and C below:

(A) Describe the process that led to an unexpected ruling by the Supreme Court on the challenge to the Affordable Care Act.

(B) In the context of this scenario, explain how the process described in part A can be affected by the executive branch.

(C) In the context of this scenario, explain how the ruling relates to enumerated powers.

Quantitative Analysis

Supreme Court Justices' Voting Relationships, 2017

Justice Agreement in full, in part, or in judgment

	AMK	CT	RBG	SGB	SAA	SMS	EK	NMG
JGR	87.5%	75%	81.25%	81.25%	75%	81.25%	85.71%	93.75%
	AMK	87.5%	68.75%	68.75%	87.5%	68.75%	71.43%	93.75%
		CT	68.75%	68.75%	100%	68.75%	71.43%	81.25%
			RBG	100%	68.75%	100%	100%	81.25%
				SGB	68.75%	100%	100%	75%
					SAA	68.75%	71.43%	81.25%
						SMS	100%	75%
							EK	78.57%
								NMG

Justices' Initials, Full Names, and President Who Appointed Them

JGR: Chief Justice John G. Roberts, appointed by Republican George W. Bush
AMK: Anthony Kennedy, appointed by Republican Ronald Reagan
CT: Clarence Thomas, appointed by Republican George H.W. Bush
RBG: Ruth Bader Ginsburg, appointed by Democrat Bill Clinton
SGB: Stephen G. Breyer, appointed by Democrat Bill Clinton
SAA: Samuel Anthony Alito Jr., appointed by Republican George W. Bush
SMS: Sonia Sotomayor, appointed by Democrat Barack Obama
EK: Elena Kagan, appointed by Democrat Barack Obama
NMG: Neil Gorsuch, appointed by Republican Donald Trump

Source: SCOTUSblog

2. Use the information in the graphic to answer the questions below.

(A) Describe what the data in the table shows about the voting of Supreme Court justices.

(B) Identify two justices who agree with the other's judgment one hundred percent of the time.

(C) Draw a conclusion about why the judges you identified in B agree so often.

(D) Explain how the design of the judicial branch protects the Supreme Court's independence.

SCOTUS Comparison

3. During the Watergate investigation in the early 1970s, the special prosecutor wanted information discussed on President Nixon's White House audio tapes as evidence in the investigation. When the lower court issued a subpoena for the tapes, the president refused to hand them over, claiming executive privilege (his right to keep his discussions confidential) because some were of delicate national security interests and not the business of the court. Only by guaranteeing confidentiality, he argued, could he preserve the candor of advisors. In *United States v. Nixon* (1974), the Supreme Court ruled in a unanimous decision that, in the fair administration of justice, a court could compel even the president with its power of subpoena during an investigation. Nixon had to comply by handing over the tapes as evidence in the investigation.

(A) Identify a similarity or difference between the rulings in *United States v. Nixon* (1974) and *Marbury v. Madison* (1803).

(B) Based on the similarity or difference identified in A, explain how *United States v. Nixon* relates to the interactions between branches.

(C) Describe an action the executive branch might take to limit the impact of *United States v. Nixon*.

Source: U.S. House of Representatives Photography Office

Barbara Jordan of Texas sat on the House Judiciary Committee as a freshman during the Watergate hearings.

CHAPTER 7

The Bureaucracy

Topics 2.12–2.15

Topic 2.12 The Bureaucracy

PMI-2.A: Explain how the bureaucracy carries out the responsibilities of the federal government.

Topic 2.13 Discretionary and Rule-Making Authority

PMI-2.B: Explain how the federal bureaucracy uses delegated discretionary authority for rule making and implementation.

Topic 2.14 Holding the Bureaucracy Accountable

PMI-2.C: Explain how Congress uses its oversight power in its relationship with the executive branch.

PMI-2.D: Explain how the president ensures that executive branch agencies and departments carry out their responsibilities in concert with the goals of the administration.

Topic 2.15 Policy and the Branches of Government

PMI-2.E: Explain the extent to which governmental branches can hold the bureaucracy accountable given the competing interests of Congress, the president, and the federal courts.

Source: Wikimedia Commons, Chuck Kennedy
President Barack Obama and his Cabinet

The Bureaucracy

*"Are you laboring under the impression that I read these
memoranda of yours? I can't even lift them."*

—attributed to President Franklin Delano Roosevelt
to an appointed bureaucrat

Essential Question: How does the bureaucracy carry out the
responsibilities of the federal government?

The federal government provides many services, such as maintaining
interstate highways, coordinating air traffic at airports and in flight,
protecting borders, enforcing laws, and delivering mail. Congress has
passed a law and created one or more executive branch departments or
agencies to carry out these responsibilities of government. The federal
bureaucracy is the vast, hierarchical organization of executive branch
employees—close to 3 million people ranging from members of the
president's Cabinet to accountants at the Internal Revenue Service—that
take care of the federal government's business.

As the nation has grown, so has the government and the bureaucracy.
Federal agencies interpret, administer, and enforce the laws that Congress
has passed. These responsibilities combined with administrative or
bureaucratic discretion have created a powerful institution.

Today's bureaucracy is a product of 200 years of increased public
expectation and increased federal responsibilities. Government
professionals assure the executive agenda and congressional mandates
are implemented and followed. The bureaucracy is involved in every
issue of the nation and provides countless services to U.S. citizens.

Structure of the Bureaucracy

The executive hierarchy is a vast structure of governing bodies headed
by professional bureaucrats. They include departments, agencies,
commissions, and a handful of private-public organizations known as
government corporations.

Cabinet Secretaries

To help manage the bureaucracy, presidents today appoint more than
2,000 upper-level management positions, deputy secretaries, and bureau
chiefs; many of these appointments require Senate confirmation. Most

of these people tend to be in the president's party and have experience in a relevant field of government or the private sector.

President John F. Kennedy named his brother, Robert, as the nation's attorney general. President Barack Obama brought with him the Chicago superintendent of schools to serve as his secretary of education. President Donald Trump named fellow New York financiers and Wall Street moguls to direct economic agencies.

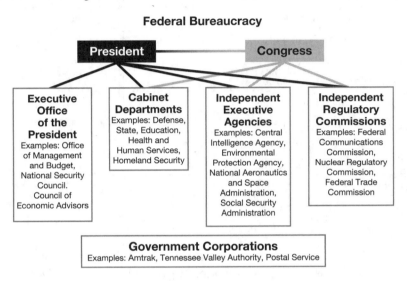

Federal Bureaucracy

Departments

The president oversees the executive branch through a structured system of 15 departments. Newer departments include Energy, Veterans Affairs, and Homeland Security. Departments have been renamed and divided into multiple departments. The largest department is by far the Department of Defense.

Each Cabinet secretary directs a department. Though different secretaries handle different areas of jurisdictions, and surely have different pressures and face different issues, they are all paid the same salary.

Agencies

The departments contain agencies that divide the departments' goals and workload. In addition to the term *agency*, these subunits may be referred to as divisions, bureaus, offices, services, administrations, and boards. The Department of Homeland Security houses the Immigration and Customs Enforcement (ICE), the Coast Guard, and the Transportation Security Administration (TSA). These agencies deal with protecting the country and its citizens. There are hundreds of agencies, many of which have headquarters in Washington, DC, as well as regional offices in large U.S. cities. The president appoints the head of each agency, typically referred to as the "director." Most directors serve under a president during a four- or eight-year term. Some serve longer terms as defined in the statute that creates the agency.

FEDERAL DEPARTMENTS	
Department	Originally Established
Department of State	1789
Department of Treasury	1789
Department of Defense	1789
Department of Interior	1849
Department of Agriculture	1862
Department of Justice	1870
Department of Commerce	1903
Department of Labor	1913
Department of Veterans Affairs	1930
Department of Health and Human Services	1953
Department of Housing and Urban Development	1965
Department of Transportation	1967
Department of Energy	1979
Department of Homeland Security	2002

The FBI is a law enforcement agency. Additional agencies fill the bureaucracy—embassies and ambassadors work within the State Department and tax collectors at the Internal Revenue Service work under the umbrella of the Treasury Department. Independent agencies, such as the National Aeronautics and Space Administration (NASA), are also in the executive branch bureaucracy, but they are not connected to a department. Congress has structured these in this way to avoid undue influence from a department. The much more complicated independent regulatory agencies can create policies with the enforcement of law for unique industries or jurisdictions. (See Topic 2.13.)

Commissions and Government Corporations

Cabinet agencies and executive agencies have one head. Independent commissions have a body (board) that consists of five to seven members. Members of these boards and commissions have staggered terms to ensure that a president cannot completely replace them with his own cronies. For example, if the Federal Reserve Board was composed of members appointed by one president, they could boost re-election chances by manipulating the interest rate and artificially stimulating the economy as an election nears. Such an action would make the agencies and commissions political rather than neutral.

Government corporations are a hybrid of a government agency and a private company. These started to appear in the 1930s, and they are usually created when the government wants to overlap with the private sector.

An argument, or claim, is a statement that can be supported by facts or evidence. The more evidence that can be presented, the stronger the argument. For example, a common claim made about the bureaucracy is that it is an inefficient and ineffective organization. The Transportation Safety Administration (TSA) especially, as a part of the bureaucracy, has experienced considerable criticism since its inception in 2001. The TSA safeguards air travel but has recently come under increased scrutiny for the problems that plague its security checkpoints at airports—weapons making it through screenings and long lines leading to missed flights, to name a few.

Practice: Read the excerpt about the TSA, written by Remington Tonar and Ellis Talton, business and leadership consultants and contributors to *Forbes*, a business publication. Then answer the questions that follow.

> In 2017, Homeland Security inspectors were able to transport facsimile firearms, explosives and knives through TSA checkpoints an appalling 70 percent of the time. This is not only unacceptable, but calls into question the effectiveness of the TSA. Many experts, in fact, have long criticized the TSA as "security theater," noting that body scanners are largely ineffective at detecting common explosive materials. Further, there's been very little evidence that measures such as the liquid ban are in any way essential or effective, and even the European Union has been trying to eliminate liquid restrictions for years. Numerous studies have found that the TSA has consistently mismanaged security investments and that private screeners perform as good or better than TSA screeners.
>
> With a nearly $8 billion annual budget, the TSA hardly seems like a good investment, especially when 10 percent of its workforce can call in sick without dramatically impacting efficiency or security (at least thus far). While we shouldn't put a price on human life, there's also an opportunity cost that needs to be considered. . . . There are more effective ways to deter, prevent and impede would-be hijackers and terrorists.

1. What is the author's main argument, or thesis, about how the TSA implements policy?

2. What evidence does the author provide to back up that argument?

3. What biases do the authors show related to the TSA or the bureaucracy in general?

Tasks Performed by the Bureaucracy

When Congress creates departments and agencies, it defines the organization's mission and empowers it to carry out the mission. The legislature gives the departments broad goals, as they administer several agencies and a large number of bureaucrats within those departments. Agencies have more specific goals, and independent regulatory agencies have even more specialized responsibilities in their administrative mission.

Writing and Enforcing Regulations

The legislation that creates and defines the departments and agencies often gives wide latitude as to how bureaucrats administer the law. Though all executive branch organizations have a degree of discretion in how they carry out the law, the independent regulatory agencies and commissions have greater leeway and power to shape and enforce national policies than the others.

Take, for example, the chief passage from the 1970 Clean Water Act that charged the Environmental Protection Agency (EPA) to enforce it, "The nation's waters should be free of pollutants in order to protect the health of our citizens and preserve natural habitats. Individuals or companies shall not pollute the nation's water. If they do, they will be fined or jailed in accordance with the law. The EPA shall set pollution standards and shall have the authority to make rules necessary to carry out this Act."

Few of the 535 legislators who helped pass this act are experts in the environmental sciences. So they delegated this authority to the EPA and keep in contact with the agency to assure that this mission is accomplished.

Enforcement and Fines

Like a court, the regulatory agencies, commission, and boards within the bureaucracy can impose fines or other punishments. This administrative adjudication targets industries or companies, not individual citizens. For example, the federal government collected civil penalties paid in connection with the 2010 Deepwater Horizon oil spill ranging from about $400 million in fiscal year 2013 to about $160 million in fiscal year 2016.

One key aspect of enforcement is **compliance monitoring**, making sure the firms and companies that are subject to industry regulations are following those standards and provisions. (See Topic 2.14 for more on compliance monitoring.)

Testifying Before Congress

Cabinet secretaries and agency directors are often experts in their field. For this reason, they frequently appear before congressional committees to provide expert testimony. For example, former FBI Director James Comey testified before the Senate Intelligence Committee in June 2017 about matters related to his bureau's investigation into Russian interference in the presidential election of 2016. In September 2017, Deputy Secretary of State John L. Sullivan testified before the House Committee on Foreign Affairs to discuss a redesign of the State Department. The Secretary of Veterans Affairs, the Honorable David J. Shulkin, M.D., testified before the Senate Veterans Affairs Committee in the same month to address the problem of suicide among veterans.

Iron Triangles and Issue Networks

Over time, congressional committees and agencies become well acquainted. Members of Congress and their staffs work with and rely upon the expert advice and information provided by the bureaucracy. In addition, lawmakers and leadership in the executive branch may have worked together in the past. At the same time, interest groups press their agendas with relevant federal agencies. Industry can also create political action committees (PACs) to impact policy and its success. These special interests meet with and make donations to members of Congress as elections near. (See Topic 5.6.) They also meet with bureaucrats during the rule-making process (see Topic 2.13) in an ongoing effort to shape rules that affect them.

The relationship among these three entities—an agency, a congressional committee, and an interest group—is called an **iron triangle** because the three-way interdependent relationships are so strong. The three points of the triangle join forces to create policy. Iron triangles establish tight relationships that are often collectively beneficial. Bureaucrats have an incentive to cooperate with congressional members who fund and oversee their agencies. Committee members have an incentive to pay attention to interest groups that can provide policy information and reward them with PAC donations. Interest groups and agencies generally are out to advance similar goals from the start. However, at times iron triangles are criticized for those goals when they are exclusively for the benefit of special interest and not for the common good.

Recently, scholars have observed the power and influence of **issue networks**. Issue networks include committee staffers (often the experts and real authors of legislation), academics, advocates, leaders of think tanks, interest groups, and/or the media. These experts and stakeholders—sometimes at odds with one another on matters unrelated to the issue they are addressing—collaborate to create specific policy on one issue. The policymaking web has grown because of so many overlapping issues, the proliferation of interest groups, and the influence of industry. **BIG IDEA** Multiple actors and institutions interact to produce and implement possible policies.

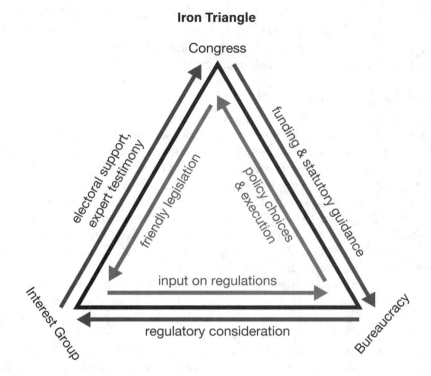

Iron Triangle

Congress

electoral support, expert testimony

friendly legislation

policy choices & execution

funding & statutory guidance

input on regulations

regulatory consideration

Interest Group

Bureaucracy

Follow the arrows in the above graphic so you can explain how the stages of the give-and-take process in an iron triangle relate to one other. How does the interest group benefit? How does the congressional committee benefit? How does the bureaucracy benefit?

From Patronage to Merit

For the bureaucracy to do its job well, federal employees need to be professional, specialized, and politically neutral. Reforms over the years have helped create an environment in which those goals can be achieved.

The Spoils System

In the early days of the nation, the bureaucracy became a place to reward loyal party leaders with federal jobs, a practice known as **patronage**. Jefferson filled every vacancy with members of his party. As presidents of different parties came and went, this "rotation system" continued regardless of merit or performance of appointees. On Andrew Jackson's Inauguration Day in 1829, job-hungry mobs pushed into the White House, aggressively seeking patronage jobs. Congressmen began recommending fellow party members, and senators—with advice and consent power— asserted their influence on the process.

Presidents appointed regional and local postmasters in the many branch offices across the nation expecting loyalty in return. This type of patronage system, which came to be known as the **spoils system**, made the U.S. Post Office one of the main agencies to run party machinery.

By the end of the Civil War, the spoils system, with ample opportunities for government corruption, was thoroughly entrenched in state and federal politics.

Civil Service Reform

The desire for the best government rather than a government of friends and family became a chief concern among certain groups and associations. Moral-based movements such as emancipation, temperance, and women's suffrage also encouraged taming or dismantling the spoils system. Reformers called for candidate appointments based on merit, skill, and experience.

In 1870, Congress passed a law that authorized the president to create rules and regulations for a civil service. Support for this reform gradually faded, however, until a murder of national consequence brought attention back to the issue. Soon after James Garfield was sworn in as president in 1881, an eccentric named Charles Guiteau began insisting Garfield appoint him to a political office. Garfield denied his requests. On July 2, only three months into the president's term, Guiteau shot Garfield twice as he was about to board a train. Garfield lay wounded for months before he finally died.

Garfield's assassination brought attention to the extreme cases of patronage and encouraged more comprehensive legislation. Congress passed the **Pendleton Civil Service Act** in 1883 to prevent the constant reward to loyal party members. The law ultimately created the **merit system**, which included competitive, written exams for many job applicants. The law also created a bipartisan **Civil Service Commission** to oversee the process and prevented officials from requiring federal employees to contribute to political campaigns.

Source: Wikimedia Commons. A. Berghaus and C. Upham, published in Frank Leslie's Illustrated Newspaper

An engraving of President Garfield's assassination by Charles Guiteau

The establishment of the civil service and an attempt by the U.S. government during the Industrial Era (1876–1900) to regulate the economy and care for the needy brought about the modern administrative state. The bureaucratic system became stocked with qualified experts dedicated to their federal jobs.

In 1887, the government created its first regulatory commission, the Interstate Commerce Commission, to enforce federal law regarding train travel and products traveling across state lines. The Pure Food and Drug Act (1906) brought attention to the meatpacking industry and other food industries, and thus, agencies were created to address these concerns. The Sixteenth Amendment (1913), which gave Congress the power to collect taxes on income, put more money into Treasury coffers, which helped the federal bureaucracy expand.

Improving the Effectiveness of the Bureaucracy

Efforts to make the bureaucracy a more professional and efficient institution of the government continued into the 20th century. President Carter promised, and delivered, reforms to the federal bureaucracy. The **Civil Service Reform Act** (1978) altered how a bureaucrat is dismissed, limited preferences for veterans in hopes of balancing the genders in federal employment and put upper-level appointments back into the president's hands. It also promoted merit and performance among bureaucrats while giving the president more power to move those not performing their jobs successfully.

The Civil Service Commission established by the Pendleton Act operated until the 1978 reforms replaced it with the **Office of Personnel Management (OPM)**. The OPM runs the merit system and coordinates the federal application process for jobs and hiring. The OPM's goals include promoting the ideals of public service, finding the best people for federal jobs, and preserving merit system principles. Many of the larger, more established agencies do their own hiring.

In 1993, President Clinton announced a six-month review of the federal government. The **National Performance Review (NPR)** became Clinton's key document in assessing the federal bureaucracy. The review was organized to identify problems and offer solutions and ideas for government savings. The group focused on diminishing the paperwork burden and placing more discretionary responsibility with the agencies. The report made almost 400 recommendations designed to cut inefficiency, put customers first, empower employees, and produce better and less-expensive government. One report, "From Red Tape to Results," characterized the federal government as an industrial-era structure operating in an information age. The bureaucracy had become so inundated with rules and procedures that it could not perform the way Congress had intended.

KEY TERMS AND NAMES

bureaucracy

Civil Service Commission

Civil Service Reform Act (1978)

compliance monitoring

iron triangle

issue networks

merit system

National Performance Review

Office of Personnel Management

patronage

Pendleton Civil Service Act (1883)

spoils system

"Get ready! The next wave of legislation is rolling in."

Source: Getty Images

After the Affordable Care Act was passed in 2010, the Center for Consumer Information and Insurance Oversight (CCIIO) was created to oversee and implement health insurance provisions. What does the cartoon suggest about such bureaucratic offices and their ability to do their jobs well?

Discretionary and Rule-Making Authority

"It is an inevitable defect, that bureaucrats will care more for routine than for results."

—A. Walter Bagehot, *The English Constitution*, 1867

Essential Question: How does the federal bureaucracy use delegated discretionary authority to make and implement rules?

There are 15 executive departments functioning in the United States and many more agencies and commissions working below those departments to implement policy. These departments and agencies administer laws that were created and shaped by Congress, the executive branch, and the courts. The process starts when Congress passes the initial law to create and define the mission and jurisdiction of the executive branch department, commission, or board. The president appoints and often directs the heads of these departments. He or she will issue executive orders and directives that shape how the agencies carries out their mission. Significant agency decisions and procedures can be contested in court. So every court opinion on an agency's power or the fairness of its procedures can have an impact on how the department or agency operates.

Delegated Discretionary Authority

The constitutional basis for bureaucratic departments or agencies stems from Congress's authority to create and empower them. Congress also guides and funds them. However, Congress leaves the specific regulations for implementing the policy up to the members of the bureaucracy. They allow **delegated discretionary authority**—the power to interpret legislation and create rules—to executive departments and agencies.

Congress has granted departments, agencies, bureaus, and commissions— staffed with experts in their field—varying degrees of discretion in developing their own rules and regulations required to implement sometimes vague legislation.

Sometimes the laws are so vague that it is not even clear that authority *has* been delegated to an agency. In some cases, the agency can simply claim broad authority. Interpreting the vagueness of the Clean Air Act, for example, the

Environmental Protection Agency has claimed vast authority over regulation of greenhouse gases. The Act provides no detail of EPA authority over these pollutants and contains no mention of greenhouse gases. Yet the EPA asserted its discretionary authority to develop regulations.

Rule-Making Process

Bureaucratic agencies continually survey their responsibilities and periodically create new rules and refine old ones. However, an outcry of support from the citizenry to handle an issue or address a societal danger could cause an agency to take action on devising new rules. New technologies also affect the way an agency must enforce a rule, and new technologies can bring about new rules entirely. For example, the Federal Elections Commission is in the process of addressing Facebook and other political advertising on the Internet much as it has addressed television advertising in the past. Occasionally, agencies with overlapping jurisdictions might suggest or request that a related organization craft rules to encourage efficiency or improve communication to better enforce their common area of law.

A Transparent and Public Process

If an agency determines new rules are needed, it would closely study the issue and the basics of the rule to some degree before seeking public response. Agency officials meet with experts, research the problem themselves, and may even engage industry officials, lobbyists, or citizens who might be subjects of the proposed regulations.

The Administrative Procedures Act The bureaucratic rule-making process has been formalized to make it fair and transparent. It is largely governed by the **Administrative Procedures Act** (APA), which Congress passed in 1946. The law guides agencies in developing their rules and procedures and assures that those citizens and industries affected by a policy can have input into shaping it, providing one of many access points for stakeholders to promote their interests.

Some congressional statutes require agencies to hold rule-making hearings. Others choose to hold public meetings to collect more information or to help inform the stakeholders or the affected groups of the proposed rule. Some agencies use webcasts and interactive Internet sessions to acquire more diverse input, a procedure many regard as democratic.

Congressional Responsibility in Rule Making

How responsible is Congress once the agency is operational and how much do they leave to the executive branch? To what extent does the process of handing off this responsibility undermine accountability to citizen-voters' desires on these issues? Scholars Justin Fox and Stuart Jordan have examined the degree to which politically elected Congress members choose to delegate authority to the bureaucracy. They found that for elected Congress members, three conditions must exist for a noticeable increase of this delegation of authority.

- Politicians must have access to much more information, and more technical information, than voters about the issue and bureaucratic actions.
- The bureaucrats must be policy experts, highly reliable and knowledgeable so they can support decisions presumed to be harmful to politicians' constituents.
- Politicians' electoral motives must be circumscribed to their policy motives. In other words, they care about fixing the problem more than they care about their personal approval rating.

Scholars differ, however, on how much Congress delegates discretionary authority to the bureaucracy and what effects this has. Politicians see pros and cons to the level of discretionary authority they might extend. Congress members may see a need to enact unpopular regulations, while they do not want the blame for the particulars of that regulation. For example, they might prefer bureaucrats to determine and administer fines to citizens for unpaid back taxes or closing a local factory for one too many safety violations. Being able to point to the bureaucracy for such a harsh policy might divert some resentment at election time.

Implementing the Law

Depending on its discretionary authority, any executive branch agency may have the power to make decisions and to take, or not take, a course of action. Congress has given the executive branch significant authority in three ways, by (1) creating agencies to pay subsidies to groups, such as farmers or Social Security recipients; (2) creating a system to distribute federal dollars going to the states, such as grant programs (see Topic 1.7); (3) and giving many federal offices the ability to devise and enforce regulations for various industries or issues. This quasi-legislative power enables departments and agencies to determine law. For example, the Federal Communications Commission can identify what is indecent for televised broadcasts and the EPA can define factory emission standards.

Due to the complexity of final rules or regulations, agencies are required to publish information about what is being implemented. This information will often consist of an introduction and official summary of the societal problem(s) and the regulatory goal that justifies the rule is required. The agency must identify its legal authority to create and enforce such a rule and publish the regulatory text in full. All new regulations must also list an effective date. Most finalized regulations must allow for a grace period, usually 30 days, sometimes as long as 180, before they can go into effect. A final printing of the law is placed in the U.S. **Code of Federal Regulations**. The *Federal Register* prints the record of how the regulation started, how it was developed, and how it landed in its final form. The Code more cleanly arranges the final regulation or law.

Independent Regulatory Agencies

Independent regulatory agencies and commissions have unique charges from Congress to enforce or regulate industry-specific law. These entities can create industry-specific regulations and issue fines and other punishments. Some are structured with a director and assistants, and some are headed by a board or commission led by a chairperson, such as the Federal Elections Commission. Members of these boards and commissions have staggered terms to ensure that a president cannot completely replace them with his own chosen appointees. Directors of such groups are appointed by a president but cannot be easily removed. In fact, a president can only remove these executives if the president shows cause.

The president might recommend or work with a regulatory agency in designing new rules but probably has less influence on them than other departments and agencies. He would certainly have less influence on the implementation and enforcement of such rules.

EXAMPLES OF DISCRETIONARY AUTHORITY IN SELECT DEPARTMENTS AND AGENCIES	
Homeland Security	Allowing certain exemptions for immigrants
Transportation	Determining which highway projects get special grants
Veterans Affairs	Deciding how to administer a health program for veterans
Education	Cancelling or lowering student debt
Environmental Protection Agency	Intervening in state environmental issues
Federal Election Commission	Administering and enforcing federal campaign finance laws
Securities and Exchange Commission	Determining if financial firms should be disqualified from raising money because of illegal conduct

Perhaps more familiar are the rules established by the Transportation Security Administration, the agency in the Department of Homeland Security that monitors passengers boarding airplanes. Who will be searched and how? These procedures change from time to time as the government finds new reasons to ban certain items from flights or to soften an overly strict list. The chief lawmaking body, Congress, with its complex lawmaking procedures and necessary debates, cannot keep up with the day-to-day changes in policies and procedures so it entrusts the TSA to monitor the airlines and empowers it to make rules to keep passengers safe.

The powers delegated to these regulatory agencies can change over time. The powers of the Federal Election Commission have been under fire recently. The authority of the FEC has been in question since the *Citizens United v. FEC* (2010) and *McCutcheon v. FEC* (2014) decisions opened up campaign contributions. Many argue that the agency still has the rule-making power to tighten up the regulations on campaign finance even after the Court's decisions, but weak leadership has stymied any efforts. Additionally, the 2019 resignation of another member of the Commission has left the agency short of the required four-person quorum. Until a new appointee is approved, the Federal Election Commission cannot perform some important functions, such as issuing fines for violations, conducting audits, or initiating investigations.

THINK AS A POLITICAL SCIENTIST: *DESCRIBE POLITICAL INSTITUTIONS IN CONTEXT*

The bureaucracy is an institution that is often considered the fourth branch of government. It has grown to become a very large and vital part of the government, yet the word "bureaucracy" doesn't appear in the Constitution. The ability for Congress to create bureaucratic agencies comes from Article I of the Constitution. Congress delegates the authority to these agencies to make and implement rules and policy.

Practice: Read the mission statements of these bureaucratic agencies found on their websites and answer the questions that follow.

Department of Transportation (1966): Ensure our nation has the safest, most efficient and modern transportation system in the world; that improves the quality of life for all American people and communities, from rural to urban, and increases the productivity and competitiveness of American workers and businesses.

Department of Veterans Affairs (1989): To fulfill President Lincoln's promise "To care for him who shall have borne the battle, and for his widow, and his orphan" by serving and honoring the men and women who are America's Veterans.

Environmental Protection Agency (1970): The mission of EPA is to protect human health and the environment.

Federal Election Commission (1974): The Federal Election Commission (FEC) is the independent regulatory agency charged with administering and enforcing the federal campaign finance law. The FEC has jurisdiction over the financing of campaigns for the U.S. House, Senate, Presidency and the Vice Presidency.

1. Based on the mission statements, explain which of the bureaucratic agencies would seem to wield the most rule-making authority.
2. According to the Administrative Procedures Act, the public has the opportunity to give input in creating bureaucratic regulations. What historical context might have prompted public interest in the creation of these regulations?

REFLECT ON THE ESSENTIAL QUESTION

Essential Question: *How does the federal bureaucracy use delegated discretionary authority to make and implement rules? On separate paper, complete a chart like the one below.*

Name of the Department, Agency, or Commission	Authority Delegated to the Body

KEY TERMS AND NAMES

Administrative Procedures Act (1946)

Code of Federal Regulations

Department of Education

delegated discretionary authority

Department of Homeland Security

Department of Transportation

Environmental Protection Agency

Federal Election Commission

Federal Register

independent regulatory agencies

notice-and-comment opportunity

Department of Veterans Affairs

Securities and Exchange Commission

Holding the Bureaucracy Accountable

"Government organizations are especially risk averse because they are caught up in a web of constraints so complex that any change is likely to rouse the ire of some important constituency."

—James Q. Wilson, *What Government Agencies Do and Why They Do It*, 1990

Essential Question: How is the bureaucracy held accountable by congressional oversight and by the president in carrying out goals of the administration?

Congress can legislate federal agencies into existence when they see a need. The legislative branch can also define the organization's role and sets the budget for federal departments. The president is tasked with appointing a leader and ensuring the organization executes its responsibilities. Bureaucratic agencies have to answer to both the executive and legislative branches, a requirement which should lead to an efficiently functioning federal bureaucracy. However, the oversight, or supervision, of two branches, especially during a time of divided government, can cause inefficiency in the bureaucracy. The bureaucracy can, at times, struggle to effectively handle their responsibilities. Nonetheless, despite the popular perception that the bureaucracy is an incompetent, oversized system, most federal functions are completed in an efficient manner through the bureaucracy.

Accountability for the Bureaucracy

Determining who is ultimately responsible for any bureaucratic decision is not always clear. Congress creates the big-picture laws and some of the regulations. The president shapes the departments and agencies when appointing Cabinet secretaries and agency directors who have discretionary authority. Challenges to department directives and agency rulings come in the courts, which may uphold or overrule the executive branch body while interest groups and industry try to influence regulations and their enforcement. With so many players interacting with these executive branch sub-units, it is difficult to tell to whom the bureaus, administrations, and offices are beholden.

Also, in trying to follow prescribed law, these executive branch bodies still face political constraints and challenges despite their discretionary latitude. Cabinet secretaries serve at the pleasure of the president but have to please many people, including, to some degree, their subordinates and staff in the field carrying out the law. These secretaries and their employees report to Congress and thus must please legislative members, especially when it comes to funding.

Congressional Oversight

The bureaucracy's discretion in rule-making authority raises many questions. Does it violate the separation of powers doctrine? How democratic is it for a handful of un-elected experts to create rules that entire industries must follow? Is due process followed when an agency fines an individual or company for violating a policy that no elected representative voted for and on which no American court ruled?

Committee Hearings

Congress has a responsibility to assure that the agencies and departments charged with carrying out the law are in fact doing so and doing so fairly. **Congressional oversight** is essentially a check and balance on the agencies themselves and competes with the president for influence over them. With some regularity, House and Senate committees hold oversight hearings to address agency action, inaction, or their relationship with the agency.

The list of standing House and Senate committees parallels a list of notable agencies. For example, the House Committee on Homeland Security has jurisdiction over the department with the same name. The Senate Committee on Agriculture, Nutrition, and Forestry oversees the National Parks Service, which is part of the Department of the Interior. Committees and subcommittees receive reports from directors and call the directors to testify. Cabinet secretaries, agency directors, and other ranking bureaucrats testify before the relevant committee. Sometimes these are routine and collegial encounters that allow for the agency or department to update Congress on how it is doing, what goals it has accomplished, or what plans it may have. At other times, the committee with oversight jurisdiction will call a hearing to get to the bottom of a thorny issue.

Nuclear Regulatory Commission (NRC) Chair Allison Macfarlane, far left, and (left to right) Commissioners Kristine Svinicki, William Magwood and William Ostendorf appear before the joint House Energy and Commerce subcommittees on July 24, 2012, to answer questions ranging from commission voting procedures to various aspects of safe disposal of nuclear waste.

Power of the Purse

In addition to general oversight, Congress determines how much funding these organizations receive, asks top-level bureaucrats how they can improve their goals, and sometimes tries to constrain agencies. With the **power of the purse**, Congress can determine the financial state of an agency and its success when it allocates money. The agency cannot spend public funds until a committee or subcommittee first passes **authorization of spending** measures. These measures state the maximum amount the agency can spend on certain programs. The distribution of money defined in such an authorization may be a one-time allotment of funds, or it could be a recurring annual allotment. The agency will not receive the actual funds until each house's appropriations committee and the full chamber also approve the spending. These **appropriations**—funds set aside for a certain purpose—are typically made annually as part of the federal budget.

THINK AS A POLITICAL SCIENTIST: *EXPLAIN TRENDS IN DATA TO DRAW CONCLUSIONS*

Bureaucratic agencies are accountable to the executive branch and legislative branch to carry out their responsibilities. Congress appropriates funds to all the bureaucratic agencies, and by so doing exercises oversight power. If agencies aren't functioning in acceptable ways, Congress can (and the president can propose) lower budgetary allowances. Additionally, Congress and the president can propose to increase an agency's budget in order to meet new or unexpected occurrences. For these reasons, the spending of bureaucratic agencies is carefully monitored. The graph on the next page shows the changing budget for the Environmental Protection Agency (EPA) over a 40-year period.

Practice: Use information in the graph to complete the tasks below.

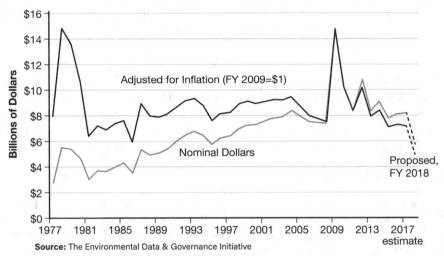

EPA's Budgetary Authority
FY 1977-FY 2016 and 2017 estimated; FY 2018 proposed

Adjusted for Inflation (FY 2009=$1)

Nominal Dollars

Proposed,
FY 2018

Source: The Environmental Data & Governance Initiative

1. What conclusions can you draw about environmental concerns from the spikes in the EPA's budget in the late 1970s and again around 2010?

2. Regarding the budget for the EPA in the 1980s, what conclusion can you draw from the trend of that decade?

The President and the Bureaucracy

Departments and agencies must compete with others for funding and for the president's ear. Similar departments and agencies have overlapping goals. They all contend that with more money they could better complete their missions.

At the same time, the president exerts authority and influence to make sure their executive ideology is delivered in policy. Through the regulatory review process, administered through the **Office of Information and Regulatory Affairs (OIRA)**, all regulations that have a significant effect on the economy, public health, and other major aspects of policy undergo close review. Any regulations that conflict with the president's agenda may be questioned, revised, and even eliminated. This office is part of the Office of Management and Budget, which prepares the president's annual budget proposal and reviews the budget and programs of the executive departments.

In 2017, during the Trump administration, the Federal Communications Commission rolled back the regulations covering oversight of Internet providers, often referred to as "net neutrality." This rollback lifted regulations from the Obama administration that required cable and telecommunications companies to treat all web traffic equally. The deregulation followed part of President Trump's ideology—as in other areas, he called for the government to reduce regulation on business so that businesses could grow and prosper in a freer marketplace.

Policy Goals and Streamlining The bureaucracy can be either an impediment or a vehicle for fulfilling presidential goals. When the bureaucracy works against or impedes the administration's ideas and goals, presidents are encouraged to shake up or restructure the system. Presidents have used both their formal powers, such as the power to appoint officials, and their informal powers, such as executive orders and persuasion, to make the bureaucracy work for their executive agenda.

Presidents have also tried to curb bureaucratic waste. President Ronald Reagan, who arrived in Washington in 1981, stated in his inaugural address, "Government is not the solution to our problem; government is the problem." To gain greater control over departments and agencies, he put people who agreed with the Reagan agenda into top positions. He sought officials who would show loyalty to the White House and reduce administrative personnel.

Policy Challenges

One key aspect of enforcement for government agencies is **compliance monitoring**, making sure the firms and companies that are subject to industry regulations are following those standards and provisions. The Environmental Protection Agency, for example, monitors for compliance in several ways. It assesses and documents compliance, requiring permits for certain activities. It collects measurable scientific evidence by taking water or air samples near a factory to measure the amount of pollutants or emissions coming from the factory. After an EPA decision or ruling, the agency checks whether those subject to the ruling are following it. Officials and regulators of the EPA also go back to the rule writers about the successes or failures of the rules and procedures to either assure fairness in future rules or to tighten them up.

REFLECT ON THE ESSENTIAL QUESTION

Essential Question: *How is the bureaucracy held accountable by congressional oversight and by the president in carrying out goals of the administration? On separate paper, complete a chart like the one below.*

Congressional Oversight of Executive Agencies	Presidential Oversight of Executive Agencies to Ensure Policy Goals

---

KEY TERMS AND NAMES

appropriations
authorization of spending
compliance monitoring
congressional oversight

Office of Information and Regulatory Affairs (OIRA)
power of the purse

Policy and the Branches of Government

"An efficient bureaucracy is the greatest threat to liberty."

—Eugene McCarthy, 1979

Essential Question: To what extent do the branches of government hold the bureaucracy accountable, given the competing interests of Congress, the president, and the federal courts?

"The only thing that saves us from the bureaucracy is inefficiency," Senator Eugene McCarthy (D-MN) continued his statement from above suggesting that if they operated more efficiently, bureaucratic agencies would end up wielding too much power. The branches have to rein in the bureaucracy to maintain accountability, while still attempting to fulfill their responsibilities.

Competing Interests

The federal bureaucracy is enormous, and its day-to-day functions involve thousands of people among hundreds of agencies. Keeping the "fourth branch" working properly and with accountability takes a concerted effort from the other branches.

Congress and the Final Say

Congress and regulatory agencies share a good deal of authority. This sharing has created an unclear area of jurisdiction. One procedure that has developed to sort out any overlap is *committee clearance*. Some congressional committees have secured the authority to review and approve certain agency actions in advance. Few executive branch leaders will ignore the actions the congressional committee requests, knowing the same committee determines its funding.

Congress established the **legislative veto** in the 1930s to control executive agencies. The legislative veto is a requirement that certain agency decisions must wait for a defined period of either 30 or 90 days. During the conflict in Vietnam, for example, Congress used the legislative veto to put some limits on the deployment of military activity. But the public interest groups that had fought to create regulatory agencies in the 1960s watched agencies' lawful decisions being stopped by one or the other house of Congress.

So when the opportunity arose for a case challenging the constitutionality of the legislative veto, Public Citizen, a group advocating for citizen protections and the separation of powers, used its litigation services to eventually bring it before the Supreme Court. The case centered on Jagdish Chadha, born in British-controlled Kenya, who immigrated to the United States in the 1960s to study. When his U.S. visa expired, neither Britain nor Kenya, which had gained independence from Britain in 1963, would accept him, so he applied for permanent residency in the United States. The Immigration and Naturalization Service (INS) approved his application. Two years later, the House rejected it through a legislative veto.

Chadha sued to retain his U.S. residency. Chadha's fight to remain in the United States became a power play between the president and Congress over the constitutionality of the legislative veto. In *INS v. Chadha* (1983), the Supreme Court sided with Chadha and against Congress's use of this procedure. The veto was intended only for the president, not the legislative branch. The Court stated that when the House rejected Chadha's application, it exercised a judicial function by expressing its opinion on the application of a law, something reserved for the courts. The Court ruled against Congress's use of the legislative veto as a violation of separation of powers.

CONGRESSIONAL ACTS AND THE BUREAUCRACY

- **Freedom of Information Act** (1966): Gives the public the right to request access to records or information
- **Sunshine Act** (1976): Requires most federal agencies to hold their meetings in publicly accessible places
- **Whistleblower Protection Act** (1989): Protects federal workers who report or disclose evidence of illegal or improper government action

Competition in the Executive Branch

The different beliefs or approaches of executive departments can create friction between them when the United States must state a position or make a decision. The Departments of State and Defense, for example, have had differences on foreign policy. The Department of State is the diplomatic wing of the government; the Department of Defense trains the military and prepares the country for armed conflict. These differing perspectives can make the development of coherent goals challenging.

Law enforcement agencies sometimes cooperate to find criminals, but they are also protective of their methods and desire recognition for their success in a way that breeds dissension across agencies. The lack of information sharing among the government's many intelligence organizations before the September 11, 2001, terrorist attacks likely increased the terrorists' chances of a successful and unexpected attack.

Sometimes upper-level bureaucrats get caught between their boss and the many people who work for them. The president's policy goals may not take into account some of the practical constraints of the bureaucracy and as a result may be too difficult to achieve. An appointed bureaucrat may therefore "go native" by siding with his or her own department or agency instead of with the president. Going native is a risky proposition, and many who have publicly disagreed with the president have been replaced.

Federal employees sometimes see corruption or inefficiency in their offices but are tempted to keep quiet. Exposing illegal or improper government activities can lead to reprisals from those in the organization or retaliation that can lead to their termination. However, citizens in a democracy want transparency in government and often encourage such exposure. That is why Congress passed the **Whistleblower Protection Act** in 1989, which prohibits a federal agency from retaliating or threatening an employee for disclosing acts that he or she believes were illegal or dishonest.

THINK AS A POLITICAL SCIENTIST: *EXPLAIN WHAT THE DATA IMPLIES ABOUT POLITICAL PROCESSES*

The size of the federal bureaucracy could allow for inefficiency or even corruption. To protect individuals who are willing to expose such problems and create a more transparent process, the government passed the Whistleblower Protection Act. To protect against problems in the Veterans Administration specifically, the Office of Accountability and Whistleblower Protection (OAWP) was formed. OAWP was created by executive order in 2017.

Practice: Analyze the graphic below and answer the questions that follow.

Complaints fielded by the VA Office of Accountability and Whistleblower Protection

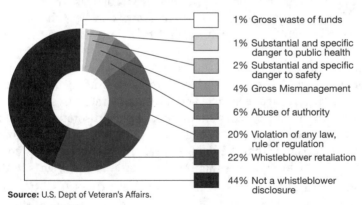

- 1% Gross waste of funds
- 1% Substantial and specific danger to public health
- 2% Substantial and specific danger to safety
- 4% Gross Mismanagement
- 6% Abuse of authority
- 20% Violation of any law, rule or regulation
- 22% Whistleblower retaliation
- 44% Not a whistleblower disclosure

Source: U.S. Dept of Veteran's Affairs.

1. What do the data imply about the complaints that the Office of Accountability and Whistleblower Protection receives?

2. What inferences can you make about either the Veterans Administration (VA) or the Office of Accountability and Whistleblower Protection based on the data in the graphic?

3. What additional information in the graphic would help make inferences in question 2?

The Courts and the Bureaucracy

Bureaucratic agencies interact with courts in a variety of ways. The implementation of some rules can result in a prosecution of an offender in a criminal trial. Agency fines and punishments can be appealed in federal court. And the U.S. Supreme Court has shaped how Congress can interact with agencies and has generally empowered the agencies with wider latitude to enact their missions—some would say at the expense of democratically developed policy and the rights of industry.

Courts and Accountability The courts are involved when citizens challenge federal bureaucratic decisions. Because agency actions are not always constitutional, fair, or practical, individuals have the right of due process and review of the law. This judicial review, writes one scholar, serves as a "check on lawlessness, a check on administrative agents making choices based on convenient personal or political preferences without substantial concern for matters of inconvenient principle."

U.S. Circuit Courts of Appeals Most judicial hearings challenging agency decisions and regulatory punishments are looking for a complicated interpretation of a law, its application, or its constitutionality. These are concerns for appeals courts.

For example, when Justin Timberlake accidentally exposed Janet Jackson's breast during the 2004 Super Bowl halftime show on a live CBS television broadcast, the Federal Communications Commission took action because of concerns that broadcast decency rules had been violated. The FCC punished Viacom, the CBS parent company, the standard fine for indecency of this type, $27,500, multiplied by the number of affiliates that broadcast the Super Bowl halftime show. It added up to $550,000. The network's lawyers challenged the ruling in the Third Circuit Court of Appeals. The federal court overruled the FCC and sided with CBS-Viacom.

The Supreme Court simply doesn't take many cases when appealed from the circuit courts, so the Courts of Appeals have largely become the final arbiter of agency decisions. These court decisions, and most of the rare cases the Supreme Court hears, tend to uphold the idea that unless agency discretion is blatantly unlawful or abusive, deference should go to the agency. The fundamental support for this approach is that the people's branch—Congress—has enabled the agency and that the bureaucrats making the decisions are experts in the in the field. And when federal courts examine these disputes, they focus more on the decision-making procedures than the substance of the rules or decisions.

Trends in Bureaucratic Authority Appeals courts are more likely to protect and uphold independent commission's decisions than general executive branch department and agency decisions. One study found that lower federal courts uphold the commission's decisions and punishments about 76 percent of the time. Another found the Supreme Court upheld challenges to these executive branch decisions 91 percent of the time.

When Congress bestows power on an entity it creates but has perhaps failed to explicitly define scenarios or rulings that the agency might make, the Court recommends erring on the side of the bureaucracy. The preeminent case that governs this approach is *Chevron v. National Resources Defense Council* (NRDC), decided in 1984. The case pitted Chevron Oil against an environmental protection group. But the real question was to what degree an agency can set industry standards when the law governing that power is incomplete or vague.

The Clean Air Act of 1970 required states to create permit programs for any new or modified plants that might affect air pollution. The EPA passed a regulation that grouped these plants into a geographic bubble-area for pollution measurement, creating the possibility that some plants would not need a permit if the modification would not affect their overall impact on the defined bubble. The NRDC challenged the EPA procedure in order to protect the air. The District of Columbia Circuit Court of Appeals set aside the EPA regulation, and Chevron appealed.

The Supreme Court overruled the DC Circuit Court and established the Chevron doctrine under which courts are supposed to defer to agencies when laws defining their responsibilities are vague or ambiguous. Under the *Chevron* concept, called the *Chevron deference*, agencies can not only determine what the law is, but they can also change that interpretation at any time.

REFLECT ON THE ESSENTIAL QUESTION

Essential Question: *To what extent do the branches of government hold the bureaucracy accountable, given the competing interests of Congress, the president, and the federal courts? On separate paper, complete a chart like the one below.*

Competing Interests of Congress and the Bureaucracy	Executive Branch Competition with the Bureaucracy	Judicial Checks of the Bureaucracy

KEY TERMS AND NAMES

Administrative Procedures Act (1946)   Whistleblower Protection Act (1989)

legislative veto

Chapter 7 Review:
Learning Objectives and Key Terms

TOPIC 2.12: Explain how the bureaucracy carries out the responsibilities of the federal government. (PMI-2.A)

Tasks Performed by the Bureaucracy (PMI-2.A.1)	Effectiveness of the Bureaucracy (PMI-2.A.2)
bureaucracy	Civil Service Commission
compliance monitoring	Civil Service Reform Act (1978)
iron triangle	merit system
issue networks	National Performance Review
	Office of Personnel Management
	patronage
	Pendleton Civil Service Act (1883)
	spoils system

TOPIC 2.13: Explain how the federal bureaucracy uses delegated discretionary authority for rule making and implementation. (PMI-2.B)

Discretionary and Rule-Making Authority (PMI-2.B.1)

Administrative Procedures Act (1946)	Federal Election Commission
Code of Federal Regulations	*Federal Register*
Department of Education	independent regulatory agencies
delegated discretionary authority	notice and comment opportunity
Department of Homeland Security	Department of Veterans Affairs
Department of Transportation	Environmental Protection Agency
Securities and Exchange Commission	

TOPIC 2.14: Explain how Congress uses its oversight power in its relationship with the executive branch. (PMI-2.C)

TOPIC 2.14: Explain how the president ensures that executive agencies and departments carry out their responsibilities in concert with the goals of the administration. (PMI-2.D)

Oversight of the Bureaucracy (PMI-2.C.1 & 2)	Bureaucracy and Policy Goals (PMI-2.D.1 & 2)
appropriations	Office of Information and Regulatory Affairs (OIRA)
authorization of spending	compliance monitoring
congressional oversight	
power of the purse	

TOPIC 2.15: Explain the extent to which governmental branches can hold the bureaucracy accountable, given the competing interests of Congress, the president, and the federal courts. (PMI-2.E)

Maintaining Bureaucratic Accountability (PMI-2.E.1)

Administrative Procedures Act (1946)	Whistleblower Protection Act (1989)
legislative veto	

CHAPTER 7 Checkpoint:
The Bureaucracy

Topics 2.12–2.15

MULTIPLE-CHOICE QUESTIONS

1. Which of the following is the best example of two points of an iron triangle at work?

   (A) A White House staffer talks to a journalist about a particular federal program.

   (B) An FBI director testifies before a House committee on federal arrests and prosecutions.

   (C) An academic researcher asks a magazine to publish her findings on pollution.

   (D) A senator meets with the president to discuss the failures of a new federal agency.

Questions 2 and 3 refer to the map below

**Total Fines Assessed for Hazardous Waste Violations
Environmental Protection Agency 2017**

Legend
- 0
- $1.000.00–$317,483.00
- $317,483.01–$1,088,409.00
- $1,088,409.01–$2,707,296.00
- $2,707,296.01–$6,154,400.00

Other States & Territories
- AK
- HI
- PR
- VI
- AS
- GU

Source: Environmental Protection Agency

2. What does the data in the map reveal?
    (A) Some states are exempt from monitoring and fines from the EPA.
    (B) The EPA fined more hazardous waste violators in the southeastern states than in any other states.
    (C) The EPA issued fines to every state.
    (D) Most states received fines totaling more than $1,088,409.01.

3. Which of the following is likely to result based on the information in the map?
    (A) The EPA director will likely ask Congress for more funding to pay these fines.
    (B) Congress members from the states without fines would insist on talking to the EPA about the issue more than other members.
    (C) Congressional delegations from states who were heavily fined might introduce legislation to rollback restrictions on hazardous waste disposal.
    (D) The power of the purse enables the EPA to fine these hazardous waste facilities.

4. Which of the following is an example of a constitutional check against the bureaucracy?
    (A) The president fires and replaces heads of departments or agencies.
    (B) Congress overrides a bureaucratic ruling with a two-thirds vote.
    (C) Congress votes to reduce a bureaucratic agency's budget.
    (D) The president overturns a regulatory agency ruling in a signing statement.

Questions 5 and 6 refer to the passage below.

[W]e find that the licensees of the CBS Network Stations . . . aired program material . . . during the halftime entertainment show of the National Football League's Super Bowl XXXVIII, that apparently violates the federal restrictions regarding the broadcast of indecent material. Based upon our review of the facts and circumstances of this case, Viacom Inc. ("Viacom"), as the licensee or ultimate parent of the licensees of the Viacom Stations, is apparently liable for a monetary forfeiture in the aggregate amount of Five Hundred Fifty Thousand Dollars ($550,000.00), which represents the statutory maximum of $27,500 for each Viacom Station that broadcast the material.

—Federal Communications Commission, Notice of

5. Which of the following statements best describe the actions of the Federal Communications Commission (FCC)?

(A) The FCC is overturning a fine because the First Amendment protects broadcasts.

(B) The FCC is fining Viacom because one of its companies violated broadcast regulations.

(C) The FCC is punishing Viacom and CBS, but an appeals court determined the amount of the fines.

(D) The FCC does not require television broadcasters to be responsible for what performers do on their broadcasts.

6. If Viacom disagrees with this notice, what is the most likely step it will take?

(A) Appeal the ruling to the appropriate Circuit Court of Appeals

(B) Contribute to congressional candidates who will vote against the ruling

(C) Convince its viewers to ask their Congress members to overrule the decision

(D) Pressure the president to fire the chair of the FCC

FREE-RESPONSE QUESTIONS

Concept Application

1. "Today our Nation must once again reorganize our Government to protect against an often-invisible enemy, an enemy that hides in the shadows and an enemy that can strike with many different types of weapons. . . Immediately after last fall's attack, I . . . [acted] to determine if the current structure allows us to meet the threats of today while preparing for the unknown threats of tomorrow. After careful study of the current structure, coupled with the experience gained since September 11 and new [understandings] have concluded that our Nation needs a more unified homeland security structure . . . I propose to create a new Department of Homeland Security by substantially transforming the current confusing patchwork of government activities into a single department whose primary mission is to secure our homeland."

—President George W. Bush, Message to Congress, 2002

After reading the scenario on the previous page, respond to A, B, and C below:

(A) Identify the informal power that the president is using in the excerpt.

(B) In the context of the scenario, explain how checks and balances could affect how Congress responds to the informal power exercised in part A.

(C) In the context of the scenario, describe how the creation of the Department of Homeland Security will enable the president to carry out the responsibilities of the federal government.

Quantitative Analysis

Federal Inspections and Evaluations EPA 2008–2018

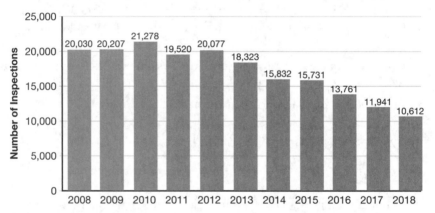

2. Use the information graphic above to answer the questions below

(A) Identify the year with the fewest total number of Environmental Protection Agency inspections and evaluations.

(B) Describe a trend in the number of annual EPA inspections and evaluations.

(C) Explain how the trend might reveal the EPA's approach to implementing policy.

(D) Explain how interactions between the president and Congress impacts this trend.

UNIT 2: Review

Our national institutions govern the United States through constitutional designs, historic customs, and practical relationships. Congress's bicameral setup provides an additional check within the legislature to assure the legitimacy and popularity of most legislation. The many committees in the House and Senate determine particulars of our national laws and handle the day-to-day business on Capitol Hill. Congress has become less a white man's institution and more a democratic and inclusive body with the Seventeenth Amendment, the one-person, one-vote rule, and legislative measures such as the discharge petition and the decreased threshold to break a filibuster.

The Executive Branch carries out Congress's laws. Presidents have become stronger with increased media attention, international face-offs, and their handling of domestic crises. The president is the chief executive of government and the chief of military and foreign policy as well as a manager of the nation's funds. Able and experienced advisors help the president develop policies and manage large departments and agencies. These sub-units range from the mammoth Department of Defense to the Federal Communications Commission.

The Judiciary adjudicates federal crimes and high-dollar civil disputes between citizens of different states. The Circuit Courts hear appeals and interpret law in their respective circuits. Special legislative courts hear cases dealing with specialized areas of law. The less visible, nine-judge Supreme Court hears about 80 cases a year to rule on constitutionality and national policy. Together these institutions govern the United States.

MULTIPLE-CHOICE QUESTIONS

1. Which of the following is the best explanation of congressional oversight?

    (A) Congress opens a legislative session on a legally scheduled day

    (B) Congress oversees the executive branch's implementation of policy

    (C) Congress oversees the management of a national election

    (D) Congress members monitor the well-being of their district

Questions 2 and 3 refer to the passage below.

The Secretary of Defense is in essence the deputy Commander in Chief. Just like the President, the Secretary of Defense must be prepared to carry out his military command responsibilities for 24 hours a day . . . I believe personally that [Secretary of Defense nominee] Senator [John] Tower has had a serious drinking problem . . . Standards must be set from the top down. If we want the sergeant at his post on the demilitarized zone in Korea, or the lieutenant standing alert with her SAC refueling tanker in the Midwest, to meet the high standards asked of those who wear our nation's uniform, we must make that clear here in the United States Senate.

—Senator Sam Nunn (D-GA), Senate Floor, 1989

2. Which of the following statements best reflects the author's primary claim?
   (A) The president's nominee is unfit for the office.
   (B) The United States lacks alertness in the armed forces.
   (C) The United States military needs to mobilize in several locations.
   (D) The actions of the president's party have caused his vote against the nominee.

3. What are the likely effects of the speaker's statement?
   (A) This Senator will choose the replacement for this appointee.
   (B) This Cabinet nominee will be confirmed by the Senate.
   (C) Senator Nunn will likely vote for the Secretary of Defense nominee.
   (D) Presidents will be more selective in appointing Cabinet positions.

4. Which of the following is an accurate comparison of executive orders and executive agreements?

	Executive Orders	Executive Agreement
(A)	Executive orders are not permitted by the U.S. Constitution.	Executive agreements may only be executed with other democracies.
(B)	A president can issue an executive order to overturn a prior president's executive order.	The Senate must approve executive agreements before they can go into effect.
(C)	Because of their lack of popularity, most presidents do not issue executive orders.	Executive agreements can be vetoed by Congress.
(D)	Executive orders must fall within the president's Article II powers.	Executive agreements can be reached more quickly than treaties.

5. A senator realizes that a Senate vote on an immigration bill is coming up. The senator examines public opinion polls on the issue and carefully reads her inbox for constituents' views on the bill and the issue. This senator is following which model of representation?

   (A) Trustee

   (B) Politico

   (C) Delegate

   (D) Partisan

6. Which of the following may Congress do in order to limit the president's power?

   (A) Refuse to spend money that the president has appropriated

   (B) Raise taxes on the president's supporters

   (C) Name new Cabinet secretaries that differ politically from the president

   (D) Override a presidential veto with a two-thirds vote

Questions 7 and 8 refer to the infographic below.

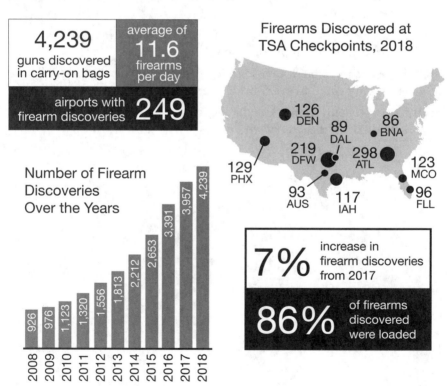

4,239 guns discovered in carry-on bags

average of **11.6** firearms per day

airports with firearm discoveries **249**

Firearms Discovered at TSA Checkpoints, 2018

126 DEN
89 DAL
86 BNA
219 DFW
298 ATL
123 MCO
129 PHX
93 AUS
117 IAH
96 FLL

Number of Firearm Discoveries Over the Years

Year	Value
2008	926
2009	976
2010	1,123
2011	1,320
2012	1,556
2013	1,813
2014	2,212
2015	2,653
2016	3,391
2017	3,957
2018	4,239

7% increase in firearm discoveries from 2017

86% of firearms discovered were loaded

Source: TSA.gov

7. Which of the following can you conclude from the data in the infographic?
   - (A) Guns in airports is only a problem in 10 major airports.
   - (B) Gun violence in airports is on the rise.
   - (C) The majority of guns found in airports are unloaded.
   - (D) Most guns discovered were fully functioning weapons.

8. What will likely result from the Transportation Security Administration's (TSA) released data?
   - (A) Constituents will pressure Congress to appropriate more funding to address this issue.
   - (B) The TSA director will petition the Congress to alter gun legislation.
   - (C) Courts will likely overturn convictions related to discovered firearms.
   - (D) The president will shift the TSA director toward different priorities.

9. Which of the following statements is most accurate about congressional reapportionment and redistricting?
   - (A) The federal government redraws districts every 10 years after a national census.
   - (B) States losing population will typically keep the same number of districts after a reapportionment.
   - (C) Districts must be drawn so that, within a state, every person's vote is roughly equal to every other person's vote.
   - (D) States with no significant change in overall population do not draw new district lines every ten years.

Questions 10 and 11 refer to the following passage.

The President will be elected to four years and is re-eligible as often as the people of the United States think him worthy of their confidence . . . we must conclude that the permanency of the President's four-year term is less dangerous than a three-year term for the top official in a single state. The President of the United States can be impeached, tried, and, on conviction of bribery, or other high crimes or misdemeanors, removed from office. Afterwards he would be liable to prosecution and punishment in the ordinary course of law.

—Alexander Hamilton, *Federalist No. 69*, 1788

10. Which of the following statements best explains one of the author's claims related to constitutional principles and procedures?

    (A) A dangerous president is limited by term limits.

    (B) People are protected from a dangerous president by elections.

    (C) Congress can imprison the president for crimes.

    (D) An impeached president will be removed from office.

11. Which of the following methods is the most certain way to override a Supreme Court decision?

    (A) Passing legislation the Court declared unconstitutional in a slightly different form

    (B) Appealing the decision to the Circuit Court of Appeals

    (C) Proposing and ratifying a constitutional amendment that counters the decision

    (D) Convincing the president to veto the decision in the case

12. A federal law enforcement agency in the Justice Department has been accused of inefficiency and not effectively enforcing the laws. Which action is most likely to follow?

    (A) The House Judiciary Committee will fire the agency director.

    (B) The agency director will ask the Ways and Means Committee for more funding.

    (C) The Senate or House Judiciary Committee will call for an oversight hearing.

    (D) The agency with jurisdiction will fine the director.

Concept Application

Chief Justice Hughes' letter was written as Congress considered the "court packing" bill.

1. "Everyone who has worked in a group knows the necessity of limiting size to obtain efficiency. And this is peculiarly true of a judicial body. It is too much to say that the Supreme Court could not do its work if two more members were added, but I think that the consensus of competent opinion is that it is now large enough . . . There would be more judges to hear, more judges to confer, more judges to discuss, more judges to be convinced and to decide."

   —Chief Justice Charles Evans Hughes, letter to Senate
   Judiciary Committee, 1937

   After reading the scenario above, respond to A, B, and C below:

   (A) Describe the proposed legislation by President Franklin Roosevelt that prompted the author's response.

   (B) In the context of this scenario, describe how judicial independence led to the proposed legislation in part A,

   (C) Explain how the proposed legislation may have altered U.S. policy.

Quantitative Analysis

President's Proposed Discretionary Spending (Fiscal Year 2015)

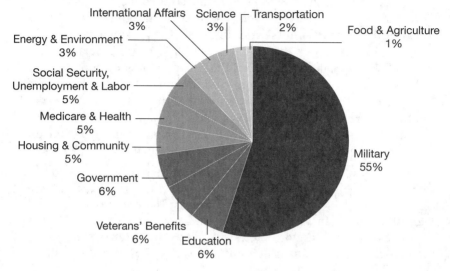

Source: nationalpriorities.org

2. Use the information graphic to answer the questions.

(A) Identify the largest and the smallest areas of federal spending.

(B) Describe a similarity or difference in federal discretionary spending.

(C) Draw a conclusion about that similarity or difference.

(D) Explain a constitutional process or principle that impacts the federal budget.

SCOTUS Comparison

3. In January 2017, President Donald Trump issued an executive order to prevent visitors from seven predominantly Muslim countries categorized as having a heightened terror risk from entering the United States for a 90-day period. The state of Hawaii challenged the constitutionality of Trump's order in court. The president revoked his order but in September 2017 issued a similar, revised proclamation. Hawaii filed suit again and argued that the president did not have authority under Article II or from congressional statute to ban travelers from the listed countries. It also argued that the order was overbroad, and that, in targeting Muslims, it violated the establishment clause. Hawaii won its claim in the lower courts. The president appealed and the Supreme Court took the case, *Trump v. Hawaii.*

The Supreme Court's first question was whether the courts had the authority to act on Hawaii's claim against the president's action. However, in its ruling, the Court looked past the initial question and found that President Trump's actions did not violate the president's constitutional or statutory authority, and the Court upheld the September 2017 proclamation limiting entry by the banned nationals.

(A) Identify the legal concern that is common to both *Trump v. Hawaii* (2017) and *Baker v. Carr* (1962).

(B) Based on the concern identified in part A, explain why the facts of *Baker v. Carr* led to a different holding than the holding in *Hawaii v. Trump.*

(C) Explain how a presidential administration could use the decision in *Hawaii v. Trump* to further shape United States foreign policy.

The claim or thesis statement of an argument essay must 1) respond to the question, 2) be defensible, and 3) establish a line of reasoning.

Response to the Question A strong thesis or claim directly responds to the question. The prompts for the argument essay on the AP* exam will be clearly based on a question. For example, the argument essay prompt might state, "Develop an argument that explains whether term limits for members of Congress would be beneficial or harmful." Phrasing the prompt as a question will help you focus your response so you can address the prompt directly. In this case, you might ask yourself, "Would term limits for members of Congress be beneficial or harmful?" Posing the prompt as a question will help you develop your position and write the claim or thesis that expresses that position.

Defensible Claim A thesis, or claim, is a nonfactual statement asserted to be true. It is a statement about which people can disagree because it requires an explanation or evaluation. A defensible claim in political science provides logical reasoning to support a position using sound evidence from foundational documents and other primary sources. For example, evidence to support a claim on term limits for members of Congress might include the Constitution, writings of the founders or later political scientists, or statistics and other facts about offices that do have term limits.

Line of Reasoning A thesis or claim also conveys a line of reasoning for the argument that you will use to explain the relationships among pieces of evidence. For example, you might decide that the best way to present your argument on term limits is to *define* and *analyze* the meaning of term limits—describe what the limits may be and explain how term limits demonstrate a political principle, process, or behavior. Another way you might present your argument is as *cause-and-effect*: limiting terms of Congress members (cause) would result in these outcomes (effects). You may also want to make your case by *comparing* the possibility of term limits on Congress to what is known about term limits on the presidency. Yet another way to present your case would be to lay out a *process*: for example, how would the process of using iron triangles and other relationships to forge legislation work if members of Congress had term limits? If you anticipate the line of reasoning your argument will use in your thesis statement or claim, you will help readers know what to expect and follow along as you reason your way through your argument. Using the word "because" as a transition will help move you from your claim to your reasoning. Here are some examples of thesis statements or claims that suggest a line of reasoning:

Definition claim: The very definition of term limits, as analyzed in the following paragraphs, suggests that they also impose restrictions on the democratic right to choose representatives, because citizens who have been satisfied with the representation of their district would be denied the opportunity to choose to continue that representation.

Cause-and-effect claim: Term limits on Congress members would cause serious problems in the process of negotiating competing claims and developing sound legislation, because they would remove experienced lawmakers who have policy expertise and replace them with less experienced legislators

Argument Essay

4. The power of the U.S. president has evolved since the New Deal of the 1930s. Develop an argument to explain whether this evolving power has made the presidency a dangerous office.

   Use at least one piece of evidence from one of the following foundational documents:

   - *Federalist No. 70*
   - *Brutus No. 1*
   - Article II of the Constitution

   In your response, you should do the following:

   - Respond to the prompt with a defensible claim or thesis that establishes a line of reasoning.
   - Support your claim or thesis with at least TWO pieces of accurate and relevant evidence:
       - ONE piece of evidence must come from one of the foundational documents listed above.
       - A second piece of evidence may come from any other foundational document not used as your first piece of evidence, or it may be from your knowledge of course concepts.
   - Use reasoning to explain why your evidence supports your claim or thesis.
   - Respond to an opposing or alternative perspective using refutation, concession, or rebuttal.

UNIT 3

Civil Liberties and Civil Rights

In a diverse America, people have used the institutions of government to seek individual liberties and equality. The Bill of Rights guarantees fundamental freedoms and prevents government from denying citizens free speech, free religion, privacy, a fair trial, and other essential liberties. The American Civil Liberties Union and other rights groups have fought to prevent government from squelching these freedoms. For both equal treatment and due process, advocates have emphasized the Fourteenth Amendment and turned to the courts as the most useful institution to secure these rights. The Supreme Court has ordered that states, too, must refrain from infringing on most of the same rights.

African Americans overcame the notorious legacy of slavery and persevered through a century of discrimination before experiencing legal equality and fair representation. Social organizations, such as the National Association for the Advancement of Colored People, have led the charge for racial equality, due process for black defendants, school desegregation, and voting rights for more than 100 years. By lobbying Congress, organizing public protests and voter registration drives, and pressing their cases in the courts, the NAACP and other civil rights groups dismantled laws that denied equality to African Americans in the South. Women, Asian Americans, Latinos, the LGBTQ community, people with disabilities, and other minorities have also taken a path toward equality via congressional laws, presidential directives, and court decisions.

ENDURING UNDERSTANDINGS: INTERACTIONS AMONG BRANCHES

LOR-2: Provisions of the U.S. Constitution's Bill of Rights are continually being interpreted to balance the power of government and the civil liberties of individuals.

LOR-3: Protections of the Bill of Rights have been selectively incorporated by way of the Fourteenth Amendment's due process clause to prevent state infringement of basic liberties.

PRD-1: The Fourteenth Amendment's equal protection clause as well as other constitutional provisions have often been used to support the advancement of equality.

PMI-3: Public policy promoting civil rights is influenced by citizen-state interactions and constitutional interpretation over time.

CON-6: The Court's interpretation of the U.S. Constitution is influenced by the composition of the Court and citizen-state interactions. At times, it has restricted minority rights and, at others, protected them.

Source: AP® United States Government and Politics Course and Exam Description

CHAPTER 8

The Bill of Rights and the First Amendment

Topics 3.1–3.4

Topic 3.1 The Bill of Rights

LOR-2.A: Explain how the U.S. Constitution protects individual liberties and rights.

LOR-2.B: Describe the rights protected in the Bill of Rights.

- Required Foundational Document:
  - The Constitution of the United States

Topic 3.2 First Amendment: Freedom of Religion

LOR-2.C: Explain the extent to which the Supreme Court's interpretation of the First and Second Amendments reflects a commitment to individual liberty.

- Required Supreme Court Cases:
  - *Engel v. Vitale* (1962)
  - *Wisconsin v. Yoder* (1972)

Topic 3.3 First Amendment: Freedom of Speech

LOR-2.C: Explain the extent to which the Supreme Court's interpretation of the First and Second Amendments reflects a commitment to individual liberty.

- Required Supreme Court Cases:
  - *Tinker v. Des Moines Independent Community School District* (1969)
  - *Schenck v. United States* (1919)

Topic 3.4 First Amendment: Freedom of the Press

LOR-2.C: Explain the extent to which the Supreme Court's interpretation of the First and Second Amendments reflects a commitment to individual liberty.

- Required Foundational Document:
  - The Constitution of the United States

- Required Supreme Court Case:
  - *New York Times Co. v. United States* (1971)

Source: Getty Images

First Amendment display in front of Independence Hall in Philadelphia

The Bill of Rights

"We will not, under any threat, or in the face of any danger, surrender the guarantees of liberty our forefathers framed for us in our Bill of Rights."
—President Franklin Roosevelt, radio address, December 15, 1941

Essential Question: How does the U.S. Constitution protect individual liberties and rights, and what rights are protected in the Bill of Rights?

Americans have held liberty in high regard, in part due to the violation of several fundamental liberties by British authorities. The original Constitution includes a few basic protections from government—Congress can pass no bill of attainder and no ex post facto law and cannot suspend *habeas corpus* rights in peacetime. Article III guarantees a defendant the right to trial by jury. However, the original Constitution lacked many fundamental protections, so critics and Anti-Federalists pushed for a bill of rights to protect **civil liberties**—those personal freedoms protected from arbitrary governmental interference or deprivations by constitutional guarantee.

Liberties and the Constitution

James Madison originally opposed adding a bill of rights to the proposed Constitution. Madison felt it was unnecessary, believing that the Constitution clearly diluted powers of the government into the three branches, greatly diminishing any chance government would run over citizen rights. The checks and limitations already in the Constitution, he argued, would remove the need for a specific listing of rights. Additionally, if such a new document listed all the rights that the government cannot take away, any rights not listed might be vulnerable to government overreach. An incomplete list would create danger to liberty in years to come.

James Madison's Role One of the main debates between the Federalists and the Anti-Federalists was over a bill of rights. Several delegates at the state-ratifying conventions voted against ratification on this point. Others voted conditionally or expressed a general acceptance of the Constitution in spite of this deficiency. As the debate continued after the ninth and requisite state ratified the original document, Madison's opinion began to change. When Congress opened in 1789, Madison served in the brand-new House of Representatives. Considering the complaints and suggestions of Anti-Federalists, including essays in the newspapers at the time and formal petitions from the states, he narrowed down dozens of points of law into twelve formal rights. Congress agreed and sent these rights to the states for ratification. One of the first major pieces of legislation enacted by the new republic was the ratification process. In the end, ten of Madison's amendments were added to the Constitution in 1791. The Father of the Constitution and original critic of this rights plan had become the Father of the Bill of Rights.

Protections in the Bill of Rights

The **Bill of Rights** was designed specifically to guarantee liberties and rights. These civil liberties include protections of citizens' thoughts, beliefs, opinions, and their right to express them. It protects property. Government cannot take away property without a just cause. A list of criminal justice rights embedded in the Bill of Rights guarantees a criminal defendant protection against government searches unless with probable cause; a right to cross-examine witnesses, to refuse to testify, and to be judged by a jury of peers; and protection against cruel and unusual punishment. (See Topics 3.7–3.9 for in-depth coverage of these rights.)

Madison and his new congressional colleagues included two disclaimers at the end of the list. The Ninth Amendment states there are rights that are protected and cannot be denied by the government, even those not explicitly listed in the Bill of Rights. The Tenth Amendment codifies an understanding from Philadelphia in 1787 and throughout the ratification debate on the proposed Constitution: All powers delegated to the federal government are expressly listed, and those that are not listed remain with the states.

Fear of a Central Government

Specifically, individuals were protected *from the federal government* and "misconstruction or abuse of its powers," according to the Preamble of the Bill of Rights. That list of protections did not originally apply to state governments. It did not prevent states from entangling church and government nor from taking private property for public use. Some states had laws on the books that required major officeholders to be members of a church. However, for the most part, state constitutions and common values across the country upheld the protections in the Bill of Rights. But in a landmark case, *Barron v. Baltimore* (1833), the Supreme Court said those protections didn't have to be guaranteed by the states. This precedent remained until the *selective incorporation doctrine* began to develop and was applied by the Supreme Court in the 20th century. (See Topic 3.7.)

Over the years, the Supreme Court has interpreted the provisions in the Bill of Rights in an effort to balance individual rights with public safety and order. Eight of the fifteen Supreme Court cases to know for the AP exam are tied to the Bill of Rights.

MUST-KNOW SUPREME COURT CASES AND RELEVANT AMENDMENTS		
Must-Know Supreme Court Cases	**Ruling**	**Amendment**
Schenck v. United States (1919)	Speech representing "a clear and present danger" is not protected. (See Topic 3.3.)	First
Engel v. Vitale (1962)	School-sponsored prayer violates the establishment clause. (See Topic 3.2.)	First
Tinker v. Des Moines Independent Community School District (1969)	Students in public schools are allowed to wear armbands as symbolic speech. (See Topic 3.3.)	First
New York Times Co. v. United States (1971)	The government cannot exercise prior restraint of the press (forbid publication ahead of time). (See Topic 3.4.)	First
Wisconsin v. Yoder (1972)	Requirements that Amish students attend school past the eighth grade violate the free exercise clause. (See Topic 3.2.)	First
McDonald v. Chicago (2010)	The right to keep and bear arms for self-defense in one's home applies to the states. (See Topic 3.7.)	Second
Gideon v. Wainwright (1963)	States must provide poor defendants with an attorney to guarantee a fair trial. (See Topic 3.8.)	Sixth
Roe v. Wade (1973)	The right of privacy extends to a woman's decision to have an abortion, though the state has a legitimate interest in protecting the unborn after a certain point and protecting a mother's health. (See Topic 3.9.)	The First, Third, Fourth, Fifth, and Ninth amendments have been interpreted as creating "zones of privacy."

A Culture of Civil Liberties

The freedoms Americans enjoy are about as comprehensive as those in any Western democracy. Anyone can practice or create nearly any kind of religion. Expressing opinions in public forums or in print is nearly always protected. Just outside the Capitol building, the White House, and the Supreme Court, protestors often gather to criticize law, presidential action, and alleged miscarriages of justice without fear of punishment or retribution. Nearly all people enjoy a great degree of privacy in their homes. Unless the police have "probable cause" to suspect criminal behavior, individuals can trust that government will not enter unannounced. When civil liberties violations have occurred, individuals and groups such as the American Civil Liberties Union (ACLU) have challenged them in court.

At the same time, however, civil liberties are limited when they impinge on the public interest, another cherished democratic ideal. **Public interest** is the welfare or well-being of the general public. For example, for the sake of public interest, the liberties of minors are limited. Their right to drive is restricted until they are teenagers (between 14 and 17 years old, depending on their state), both for their safety and the safety of the general public. And although people generally have the right to free speech, what they say cannot seriously threaten public safety or ruin a person's reputation with untruthful claims. In the culture of civil liberties in the United States, then, personal liberties have limits out of concern for the public interest.

Interpreting the Bill of Rights

The United States has experienced many changes in the more than two centuries it has existed. World wars, economic depressions, industrial revolutions, and social shifts have challenged the flexibility of the Constitution. Whether they are interpreting the Constitution, clarifying the meaning of the amendments, or determining the constitutionality of newly passed laws, the justices on the Supreme Court often dictate the direction of the nation. The Court has interpreted and reinterpreted liberties in an effort to protect them from encroachment by the federal government or local governments.

In addition to the Must-Know Cases in the table above, the Supreme Court has been involved in determining if the government—state or federal—crosses a line and violates a clause in the Bill of Rights. These Supreme Court decisions provide clarity on the law. Whether they permit the state to limit the Bill of Rights in the name of order or declare the government has gone too far and violated citizens' rights, these decisions further define civil liberty. Decisions over what exactly constitutes a "fair and impartial jury," a "speedy trial," or "excessive bail" have changed over time. These broad phrases enabled the Bill of Rights' ratification in 1791 but have kept the courts busy over the years. In the process of judicial review and defining these liberties, the courts will continue to clarify the balance between liberties and public order.

THINK AS A POLITICAL SCIENTIST: *DESCRIBE POLITICAL PRINCIPLES IN CONTEXT*

The protection of civil liberties is an important political principle of the United States. Free speech is among those civil liberties, but how far does the protection extend? In the *Schenck v. United States* (1919) case, free speech was limited when it presented a "clear and present danger." The Court saw this danger as Schenck had urged draftees during World War I to resist the draft. Justice Oliver Wendell Holmes used the following analogy to further explain, *"The most stringent protection of free speech would not protect a man in falsely shouting fire in a theatre and causing a panic . . ."* (See Topic 3.3 for more about *Schenck v. United States*.)

Practice: Read the scenario below and determine if the principle of free speech would be protected using the "fire in a theater" analogy:

After giving a speech at a rally, a white neo-Nazi leader is convicted under criminal syndicalism laws—laws to prevent illegal acts to achieve political reform. He spoke on private property to other neo-Nazi members and his speech alluded to action against the government if perceived threats against the Caucasian race continued due to government decisions. Does the First Amendment protect his speech?

(See *Brandenburg v. Ohio* for the Court's decision in a similar type of case.)

REFLECT ON THE ESSENTIAL QUESTION

Essential Question: *How does the U.S. Constitution protect individual liberties and rights, and what rights are protected in the Bill of Rights? On separate paper, complete the chart below.*

Rights Guaranteed in the Bill of Rights	Related Amendment

KEY TERMS AND NAMES

Bill of Rights (1791)   public interest
civil liberties

Source: Getty Images

While wearing a mask is inconvenient, many people wore one during the COVID-19 pandemic for the sake of the public interest. Others, however, believed required mask wearing infringed on their individual rights.

First Amendment: Freedom of Religion

"The Religion then of every man must be left to the conviction and conscience of every man; and it is the right of every man to exercise it as these may dictate. This right is in its nature an unalienable right."

—James Madison, *A Memorial and Remonstrance, on the Religious Rights of Man*, 1784–1785

Essential Question: To what extent does the Supreme Court's interpretation of freedom of religion reflect a commitment to individual liberty?

The Religious Freedom Restoration Act (RFRA) of 1993 states that "governments should not substantially burden religious exercise without compelling justification." This law was created out of anger at a Supreme Court ruling in the *Employment Division v. Smith* case in 1990. Both liberals and conservatives disapproved of the ruling because it weakened citizens' rights to religious practices that conflicted with government statutes. The Supreme Court struck down parts of the RFRA in 1997, stating it infringed on states' rights, and according to many, weakened Americans' right to religious freedom. Since the RFRA was passed, 31 states have passed similar legislation to protect religious liberty.

Today, the issue of free exercise of religion can collide with the state's power to assure fairness toward LGBTQ people. For example, can a state through its power to regulate commerce mandate a merchant to serve gay people if doing so conflicts with the merchant's religious beliefs about homosexuality?

The First Amendment: Church and State

The founders wanted to stamp out religious intolerance and outlaw a nationally sanctioned religion. The Supreme Court did not address congressional action on religion for most of the 1800s, and it did not examine state policies that affected religion for another generation after that. As the nation became more diverse and more secular over the years, the Supreme Court constructed what Thomas Jefferson had called a **"wall of separation"** between church and state. In this nation of varied religions and countless government institutions, however, church and state can sometimes encroach on each other. Like other interpretations of civil liberties, those addressing freedom of religion are intricate and sometimes confusing. Recently, the Court has addressed laws that regulate the teaching of evolution, the use of school vouchers, and the public display of religious symbols.

Freedom of Religion

Both James Madison and Thomas Jefferson led a fight to oppose a Virginia tax to fund an established state church in 1785. Madison argued that no law should support any true religion nor should any government tax anyone, believer or nonbeliever, to fund a church. During the ratification battle in 1787, Jefferson wrote Madison and expressed regret that the proposed Constitution lacked a Bill of Rights, especially an expressed freedom of religion. The First Amendment allayed these concerns because it reads in part, "Congress shall make no law respecting an *establishment* of religion or prohibiting the *free exercise* thereof." In 1802, President Jefferson popularized the phrase "separation of church and state" after assuring Baptists in Danbury, Connecticut, that the First Amendment builds a "wall of separation between church and state." Today some citizens want a stronger separation; others want none.

Members of the First Congress included the **establishment clause** in the First Amendment to prevent the federal government from establishing a national religion. More recently, the clause has come to mean that governing institutions—federal, state, and local—cannot sanction, recognize, favor, or disregard any religion. The **free exercise clause** in the First Amendment prevents governments from stopping religious practices. This clause is generally upheld, unless a religious act is illegal or threatens the interests of the community. Today, these clauses collectively mean people can practice any religion they want, provided it doesn't violate established law or harm others, and the state cannot endorse or advance one religion over another. The Supreme Court's interpretation and application of the establishment clause and free exercise clause show a commitment to individual liberties and an effort to balance the religious practice of majorities with the right to the free exercise of minority religious practices or no religious practices.

The Court Erects a Wall In the 1940s, New Jersey allowed public school boards to reimburse parents for transporting their children to school, even if the children attended parochial schools—those maintained by a church or religious organization. Some argued this constituted an establishment of religion, but in *Everson v. Board of Education* (1947), the Court upheld the law. State law is not meant to favor or handicap any religion. This law gave no money to parochial schools but instead provided funds evenly to parents who transported their children to the state's accredited schools, whether religious or public. Preventing payments to parochial students' parents would create an inequity for them. Much like fire stations, police, and utilities, school transportation is a nonreligious service available to all taxpayers.

Though nothing changed with *Everson*, the Court did signal that the religion clauses of the First Amendment applied to the states via the Fourteenth

Amendment in the selective incorporation process. (See Topic 3.7.) The Court also used Jefferson's phrase in its opinion and began erecting the modern wall of separation.

Prayer in Public Schools In their early development, public schools were largely Protestant institutions that began their day with a prayer. But the Court outlawed the practice in the early 1960s in its landmark case, ***Engel v. Vitale*** (1962). A year later, in *School District of Abington Township, Pennsylvania v. Schempp*, the Court outlawed a daily Bible reading in the Abington schools in Pennsylvania and thus in all public schools. In both cases, the school had projected or promoted religion, which constituted an establishment.

MUST-KNOW SUPREME COURT CASE: *ENGEL V. VITALE* (1962)

The Constitutional Question Before the Court: Does allowing a state-created, nondenominational prayer voluntarily recited in public schools violate the First Amendment's establishment clause?

Decision: Yes, for Engel et al., 6:1

Before *Engel*: Since the days of one-room schools, many public schools across the United States started the school day with a prayer. In the 1950s, the state of New York tried to standardize prayer in its public schools by coming up with a common, nondenominational prayer that would satisfy most religions. The State Board of Regents, the government body that oversees the schools, did so: "Almighty God, we acknowledge our dependence upon Thee, and we beg Thy blessings upon us, our parents, our teachers and our Country." Each school day, classes recited the Pledge of Allegiance followed by this prayer, which teachers were required to recite. Students were allowed to stand mute or, with written permission, to depart the room during the exercise.

Facts: In 1959, the parents of ten pupils organized and filed suit against the local school board because this official prayer was contrary to the beliefs, religions, or religious practices of both themselves and their children. Lead plaintiff Stephen Engel and the others argued the prayer—created by a state actor and recited at a state-funded institution where attendance was required by state law—violated the establishment clause. The respondent, William Vitale, was the chairman of the local Hyde Park, New York, school board.

Reasoning: The majority reasoned that since a public institution developed the prayer and since it was to be used in a public school setting with mandatory attendance, the Regents board had made religion its business, a violation of the establishment clause. Because of the Fourteenth Amendment and incorporation, states as well as the federal government are forbidden from officially backing any religious activity. They also noted that including the word "God" was denominational—not all religions believe in God. Further, they explained that even though participation was voluntary, students would likely feel reluctant not to take part in a teacher-led activity.

The Court's Majority Opinion by Mr. Justice Black: We think that, by using its public school system to encourage recitation of the Regents' prayer, the State of New York has adopted a practice wholly inconsistent with the Establishment Clause. . . .

The petitioners contend . . . the State's use of the Regents' prayer in its public school system breaches the constitutional wall of separation between Church and State. . . .

One of the greatest dangers to the freedom of the individual to worship in his own way lay in the Government's placing its official stamp of approval upon one particular kind of prayer or one particular form of religious services. . . .

It is true that New York's establishment of its Regents' prayer as an officially approved religious doctrine of that State does not amount to a total establishment of one particular religious sect to the exclusion of all others—that, indeed, the governmental endorsement of that prayer seems relatively insignificant when compared to the governmental encroachments upon religion which were commonplace 200 years ago. To those who may subscribe to the view that, because the Regents' official prayer is so brief and general there can be no danger to religious freedom in its governmental establishment, however, it may be appropriate to say in the words of James Madison, the author of the First Amendment:

"[I]t is proper to take alarm at the first experiment on our liberties. . . ."

Justice Douglas agreed with the majority but made the point that children may feel like a "captive" audience, even though they were technically free to leave the room.

Concurring Opinion by Mr. Justice Douglas: It is said that the element of coercion is inherent in the giving of this prayer.

. . . Few adults, let alone children, would leave our courtroom or the Senate or the House while those prayers are being given. Every such audience is in a sense a "captive" audience. . . . A religion is not established in the usual sense merely by letting those who choose to do so say the prayer that the public school teacher leads. Yet once government finances a religious exercise, it inserts a divisive influence into our communities.

Since *Engel*: The Court has since ruled against student-led prayer at official public school events. In the 1980s, Alabama created a policy to satisfy community wishes without violating the 1960s' precedents. The state provided that schools give a moment of silence at the beginning of the school day to facilitate prayer or meditation. In a 1985 ruling, however, the Court said this constituted an establishment of religion. The Court left open the possibility that an undefined, occasional moment of silence might pass constitutional muster.

Political Science Disciplinary Practices and Reasoning Processes: Explain Reasoning, Similarities, and Differences

Justice Black quoted James Madison, the author of the First Amendment, in the majority opinion: "[I]t is proper to take alarm at the first experiment on our liberties." Madison's words following that quote help explain why: "We hold this prudent jealousy to be the first duty of Citizens, and one of the noblest characteristics of the late

Revolution. The free men of America did not wait till usurped power had strengthened itself by exercise and entangled the question in precedents. They saw all the consequences in the principle, and they avoided the consequences by denying the principle."

Apply: Complete the following tasks.

1. Explain how Justice Black's point in the Court's majority opinion relates to Madison's admonition to be alarmed.

2. Explain how Justice Douglas elaborated on the majority opinion, especially the role of public money.

The Lemon Test In 1971, the Court created a measure of whether or not the state violated the establishment clause in *Lemon v. Kurtzman*. Rhode Island and Pennsylvania passed laws to pay teachers of secular subjects in religious schools with state funds. The states mandated such subjects as English and math and reasoned that it should assist the parochial schools in carrying out a state requirement. In trying to determine the constitutionality of this statute, the Court decided these laws created an "excessive entanglement" between the state and the church because teachers in these parochial schools may improperly involve faith in their teaching. In the unanimous opinion, Chief Justice Warren Burger further articulated Jefferson's "wall of separation" concept, and "far from being a 'wall,'" the policy made a "blurred, indistinct, and variable barrier." To guide lower court decisions and future controversies that might reach the High Court, the justices in the case of *Lemon v. Kurtzman* developed the Lemon test to determine excessive entanglement.

THE LEMON TEST
To avoid an excessive entanglement, a policy must:
• Have a secular purpose that neither endorses nor disapproves of religion
• Have an effect that neither advances nor prohibits religion
• Avoid creating a relationship between religion and government that entangles either in the internal affairs of the other

Education and the Free Exercise Clause In 1972, the Court ruled that a Wisconsin high school attendance law violated Amish parents' right to teach their own children under the free exercise clause. The Court found that the Amish's alternative mode of informal vocational training paralleled the state's objectives. Requiring these children to attend high school violated the basic tenets of the Amish faith because it forced their children into unwanted environments.

MUST-KNOW SUPREME COURT CASE: *WISCONSIN V. YODER* (1972)

The Constitutional Question Before the Court: Does a state's compulsory school law for children age 16 and younger violate the First Amendment's free exercise clause for parents whose religious beliefs and customs dictate they keep their children out of school after a certain age?

Decision: Yes, for Yoder, 7:0

Facts: A Wisconsin statute required parents of children age 16 and under to send their children to a formal school. Three parents in the New Glarus, Wisconsin, school system—Jonas Yoder, Wallace Miller, and Adin Yutzy—had teenagers which they did not send to school. Yoder and the others were charged, tried in a state criminal court, found guilty, and fined $5.00 each. The parents appealed the case to the state supreme court, arguing their religion prevented them from sending their children to public schools at their age. The state court agreed. State officials then appealed to the Supreme Court, hoping to preserve the law and its authority to regulate compulsory school attendance.

These same children had attended a public school through eighth grade. Their parents felt an elementary education suitable and necessary, but they refused to enroll their 14- and 15-year-olds in the public schools. Amish teens are meant to develop the skills for a trade, not continue learning subjects that do not have a practical application. Also, the parents did not want their children exposed to divergent values and practices at a public high school. The parents argued that the free exercise clause entitled them to this practice and this decision.

The state invoked the legal claim of *parens patriae*—parental authority—claiming it had a legal responsibility to oversee public safety and health and to educate children to age 16. Those who skipped this education would become burdens on society.

Reasoning: The Court found making the Amish attend schools would expose them to attitudes and values that ran counter to their beliefs. In fact, the Court also said that forcing the Amish teens to attend would interfere with their religious development and integration into Amish society. Further, the Court realized that stopping schooling a couple of years early and continuing informal vocational education did not make members of this community burdens on society.

The Court declared in this case that the free exercise clause overrode the state's efforts to promote health and safety through ensuring a full, formal education. In a rare instance, Justice William O. Douglas voted with the majority but wrote a partial dissenting opinion. Justices William Rehnquist and Lewis Powell did not participate.

> **The Court's Majority Opinion by Mr. Justice Burger**: Formal high school education beyond the eighth grade is contrary to Amish beliefs not only because it places Amish children in an environment hostile to Amish beliefs, with increasing emphasis on competition in class work and sports and with pressure to conform to the styles, manners, and ways of the peer group, but also because it takes them away from their community, physically and emotionally, during the crucial and formative adolescent period of life. During this period, the children must acquire Amish attitudes favoring manual work and self-reliance and the specific skills needed to perform the adult role of an Amish farmer or housewife. They must learn to enjoy physical labor. Once a child has learned basic reading, writing, and elementary mathematics, these traits, skills, and attitudes admittedly fall within

the category of those best learned through example and "doing," rather than in a classroom. And, at this time in life, the Amish child must also grow in his faith and his relationship to the Amish community if he is to be prepared to accept the heavy obligations imposed by adult baptism. In short, high school attendance with teachers who are not of the Amish faith—and may even be hostile to it—interposes a serious barrier to the integration of the Amish child into the Amish religious community. Dr. John Hostetler, one of the experts on Amish society, testified that the modern high school is not equipped, in curriculum or social environment, to impart the values promoted by Amish society.

Political Science Disciplinary Practices: Understanding Opposing Views

While the majority opinion becomes the lasting legacy of a Supreme Court case, knowing the arguments the opposing side made can help clarify the Court's decision.

Apply: Complete the following tasks.

1. Explain the First Amendment principle at issue in this case.

2. Identify the public policy or law the citizens challenged in this case.

3. Explain the Court's reasoning described in the majority opinion.

4. Analyze the Court's response to the state's two primary arguments by identifying the kind of evidence the Court relied on to address the state's arguments.

Source: Shutterstock

Amish families, such as this one in Pennsylvania, wear simple clothing, use horses and buggies rather than cars, and value manual labor. The Amish parents involved in *Wisconsin v. Yoder* believed that sending their children to high school would endanger their families' salvation.

The Supreme Court has ruled on many cases that deal with separating church and state. In its rulings, the Court has consistently "built a wall of separation" between the institutions, as the framers intended. In *Engel v. Vitale* (1962) and *Wisconsin v. Yoder* (1972), the Supreme Court ruled the First Amendment had been violated.

Practice: Review the majority decisions given in both cases and answer the questions that follow.

1. What were the similarities in the majority opinions given by Justice Black in *Engel v. Vitale* and Justice Burger in *Wisconsin v. Yoder*?

2. What were the differences in the majority opinions given by Justices Black and Burger in those two cases?

3. Which of the cases is likely to have a larger impact in future rulings on religious freedom? Explain your opinion.

Contemporary First Amendment Issues

Real and perceived excessive entanglements between church and state continue to make the news today. Can government funding go to private schools or universities at all? Does a display of religious symbols on public grounds constitute an establishment of religion? As with so many cases, it depends.

Public Funding of Religious Institutions Many establishment cases address whether or not state governments can contribute funds to religious institutions, especially Roman Catholic schools. Virtually every one has been struck down, except those secular endeavors that aid higher education in religious colleges, perhaps because state laws do not require education beyond the twelfth grade and older students are not as impressionable.

Vouchers Supporters of private parochial schools and parents who pay tuition argue that the government should issue vouchers to ease their costs. Parents of parochial students pay the same taxes as public school parents while their children don't receive the services of public schools. A Cleveland, Ohio, program offered as much as $2,250 in tuition reimbursements for low-income families and $1,875 for any families sending their children to private schools. The Court upheld the program largely because the policy did not make a distinction between religious or nonreligious private schools, even though 96 percent of private school students attended a religious-based school. This money did not go directly to the religious schools but rather to the parents for educating their children.

Religion in Public Schools Since the *Engel* and *Abington* decisions, any formal prayer in public schools and even a daily, routine moment of silence are considered violations of the establishment clause. The Court has even ruled against student-led prayer at official public school events. However, popular opinion has never endorsed these stances. In 2014, Gallup found that 61 percent of Americans supported allowing daily prayer, down from 70 percent in 1999.

Students can still operate extracurricular activities of a religious nature provided these take place outside the school day and without tax dollars. The free exercise clause guarantees students' rights to say private prayers, wear religious T-shirts, and discuss religion. Public teachers' actions are more restricted because they are employed by the state.

Religious Symbols in the Public Square Pawtucket, Rhode Island, annually adorned its shopping district with Christmas decor, including a Christmas tree, a Santa's house, and a nativity scene. Plaintiffs sued, arguing that the nativity scene created government establishment of Christianity. In *Lynch v. Donnelly* (1984), the Court upheld the city's right to include this emblem because it served a legitimate secular purpose of depicting the historical origins of the Christmas holiday. In another case in 1989, the Court found the display of a crèche (manger scene) on public property, when standing alone without other Christmas decor, a violation because it was seen as a Christian-centered display.

Ten Commandments In 2005, the Court ruled two different ways on the issue of displaying the Ten Commandments on government property. One case involved a large outdoor display at the Texas state capitol. Among 17 other monuments sat a six-foot-tall rendering of the Ten Commandments. The other case involved the Ten Commandments hanging in two Kentucky courthouses, accompanied by several historical American documents. The Court said the Texas display was acceptable because of the monument's religious and historical function. It was not in a location that anyone would be compelled to be in, such as a school or a courtroom. And it was a passive use of the religious text in that only occasional passersby would see it. The Kentucky courtroom case brought the opposite conclusion because an objective observer would perceive the displays as having a predominantly religious purpose in state courtrooms—places where some citizens must attend and places meant to be free from prejudice.

REFLECT ON THE ESSENTIAL QUESTION

Essential Question: *To what extent does the Supreme Court's interpretation of freedom of religion reflect a commitment to individual liberty? On separate paper, complete the chart below.*

Explanation of Free Exercise Clause Cases	Explanation of Establishment Clause Cases

---

KEY TERMS AND NAMES

Engel v. Vitale (1962)
establishment clause
free exercise clause

Lemon v. Kurtzman (1971)
wall of separation
Wisconsin v. Yoder (1972)

First Amendment: Freedom of Speech

"Free speech is not speech you agree with . . . It's speech that you find stupid, selfish, dangerous, uninformed or threatening . . . unpopular, contentious and sometimes ugly. It reflects a tolerance for differences. If everyone agreed on all things, we wouldn't need it."

—Robert J. Samuelson, *Washington Post*, 2014

Essential Question: To what extent does the Supreme Court's interpretation of freedom of speech reflect a commitment to individual liberty?

Freedom of speech is one of the cherished liberties in the First Amendment. Freedom of speech issues extend much further than just the words that come out of an individual's mouth. This right can inspire passionate arguments to protect and to limit speech depending on its content. The Supreme Court has ruled on this right many times. The Court's interpretations relate to topics like offensive or obscene speech, protest speech, symbolic speech, and the right not to "speak."

Defining Protected Speech

The Supreme Court has taken two generations of cases to define "free speech" and "free press," and free speech cases still occasionally appear on the Court's docket. When does one person's right to free expression violate others' right to peace, safety, or decency? Free speech is not absolute, but both federal and state governments have to show substantial or *compelling governmental interest*—a purpose important enough to justify the infringement of personal liberties—to curb it.

The creators of the First Amendment meant to prevent government censorship. Many revolutionary leaders came to despise the accusation of seditious libel—a charge that resulted in fines and/or jail time for anyone who criticized public officials or government policies. Expressing dissent in assemblies and in print during the colonial era led to independence and increased freedoms, therefore, members of the first Congress preserved this right as the very first of the amendments.

Time, Place, and Manner Regulations

In evaluating regulations of symbolic expression, the Court looks primarily at whether the regulation suppresses the content of the message or simply regulates the accompanying conduct. Is the government ultimately suppressing what was being said, or the time, place, or manner in which it was expressed?

Era of Protest The 1960s witnessed a revolution in free expression. As support for the Vietnam War waned, young men burned their draft cards to protest the military draft. Congress quickly passed a law to prevent the destruction of these government-issued documents.

David O'Brien burned his Selective Service registration card in front of a Boston courthouse and was convicted for that action under the Selective Service Act, which prohibited willful destruction of draft cards. He appealed to the Supreme Court, arguing that his protest was a symbolic act of speech that government could not infringe. The Court, however, upheld his conviction and sided with the government's right to prevent this behavior in order to protect Congress's authority to raise and support an army. O'Brien was disrupting the draft effort and publicly encouraging others to do the same. Others continued to burn draft cards, but after *United States v. O'Brien* (1968), this symbolic act was not protected.

In April 1968, Paul Robert Cohen wore a jacket bearing the words "F--k the Draft" while walking into a Los Angeles courthouse. Local authorities arrested and convicted him for "disturbing the peace . . . by offensive conduct." The Supreme Court later overturned the conviction in *Cohen v. California* (1971). The phrase on the jacket in no real way incited an illegal action. "One man's vulgarity is another's lyric," the majority opinion stated.

Compare the *Cohen* and *O'Brien* rulings. In both cases, someone expressed opposition to the Vietnam-era draft. O'Brien burned a government-issued draft card. The Court didn't protect the defendant's speech but rather upheld a law to assist Congress in its conscription powers. Cohen publicly expressed dislike for the draft with an ugly phrase printed on his jacket, but he did nothing to incite public protest and did not refuse to enlist, so the Court protected the speech.

Time, place, and manner regulations must be tested against a set of four criteria.

TIME, PLACE, AND MANNER TEST
1. The restriction must be *content-neutral*. That is, it must not suppress the content of the expression.
2. The restriction must serve a *significant government interest*. In the *United States v. O'Brien* (1968) case, the Court ruled that the burning of a draft card was disrupting the government's interest of raising an army.
3. The restriction must be *narrowly tailored*. That is, the law must be designed in the most specific, targeted way possible, avoiding spillover into other areas. For example, the law upheld in *O'Brien* was specifically about burning draft cards, not other items, such as flags, whose burning might express a similar message.
4. There must be adequate *alternative ways of expression*. The court can suppress expression on the basis of time, place, and manner if there are other times, places, and manners in which the idea can be expressed.

The question of "place" and "manner" became key aspects of a landmark case involving free speech in schools.

Symbolic Speech

People cannot invoke **symbolic speech** to defend an act that might otherwise be illegal. For example, a nude citizen cannot walk through the town square and claim a right to symbolically protest textile sweatshops after his arrest for indecent exposure. Symbolic speech per se is not an absolute defense in a free speech conflict. However, the Court has protected a number of symbolic acts or expressions.

The Court struck down both state and federal statutes meant to prevent desecrating or burning the U.S. flag in *Texas v. Johnson* (1989) and *United States v. Eichman* (1990), respectively. The Court found that these laws serve no purpose other than ensuring a government-imposed political idea—reverence for the flag.

MUST-KNOW SUPREME COURT CASE: *TINKER V. DES MOINES INDEPENDENT COMMUNITY SCHOOL DISTRICT* (1969)

The Constitutional Question Before the Court: Does a public school ban on students wearing armbands in symbolic, political protest violate a student's First Amendment freedom of speech?

Decision: Yes, for Tinker, 7:2

Facts: In December of 1965 in Des Moines, Iowa, Mary Beth Tinker, her brother John F. Tinker, their friend Christopher Eckhardt, and others developed a plan for an organized protest of U.S. involvement in the conflict in Vietnam. They planned to wear black armbands for a period of time as well as have two days of fasting. The school administrators learned of the organized protest and predicted it would become a distraction in the learning environment they had to maintain. They also believed it might be taken as disrespectful by some students and become, at minimum, a potential problem. School principals met and developed a policy to address their concerns. When the Tinkers and other students arrived at school wearing the armbands, principals instructed the students to remove them. The students, with support from their parents, refused. The school then suspended the students until they were willing to return without wearing the bands. The Tinkers and the others sued in U.S. district court on free speech grounds and eventually appealed to the Supreme Court.

Reasoning: Noting that the record or facts showed no disruption took place, the Court ruled in favor of the students who challenged the suspension, declaring that the students' right to political, symbolic speech based on the First Amendment overrode the school administrators' concerns for *potential* disorder. The decision protected this speech because the suspension failed the content-neutral criterion of the time, place, and manner test: It was intended to quiet the students' anti-war message to avoid possible disruptions.

The Court's Majority Opinion by Mr. Justice Abe Fortas: First Amendment rights, applied in light of the special characteristics of the school environment, are available to teachers and students. It can hardly be argued that either students or teachers shed their constitutional rights to freedom of speech or expression at the schoolhouse gate. This has been the unmistakable holding of this Court for almost 50 years . . . .

Our problem involves direct, primary First Amendment rights akin to "pure speech" . . . .

The school officials banned and sought to punish petitioners for a silent, passive expression of opinion, unaccompanied by any disorder or disturbance on the part of petitioners. There is here no evidence whatever of petitioners' interference, actual or nascent, with the schools' work or of collision with the rights of other students to be secure and to be let alone.

Accordingly, this case does not concern speech or action that intrudes upon the work of the schools or the rights of other students. . . .

Clearly, the prohibition of expression of one particular opinion, at least without evidence that it is necessary to avoid material and substantial interference with schoolwork or discipline, is not constitutionally permissible.

In our system, state-operated schools may not be enclaves of totalitarianism. School officials do not possess absolute authority over their students. Students in school, as well as out of school, are "persons" under our Constitution. In the absence of a specific showing of constitutionally valid reasons to regulate their speech, students are entitled to freedom of expression of their views.

Since *Tinker*: The Tinkers' war protest was a brand of political speech. A different brand of speech was at the center of another case involving a school suspension settled in 1986. High school student Matt Fraser gave a speech to a student assembly at his Bethel, Washington, school that showcased student government candidates. In introducing his friend, Fraser delivered a speech riddled with sexual innuendo that caused a roaring reaction and led the school to suspend him. Fraser challenged his suspension. The Court, after fully analyzing Fraser's sexually suggestive language, upheld the school's punishment (*Bethel School District v. Fraser*, 1986). The Court considered the *Tinker* precedent, but unlike the speech in *Tinker*, the speech in this case had no real political value and was designed to entertain an audience of high school students. Students still do not shed their rights at the schoolhouse gates, but neither are they entitled to lewd or offensive speech.

A similar case reached the Court in 2007 *(Morse v. Frederick)*. In Alaska, a student body gathered outside a school to witness and cheer on the Olympic torch as runners carried it by. In a quest for attention, one student flashed a homemade sign that read "BONG HITS 4 JESUS" as the torch passed the school. The student was suspended, and he lost his appeal challenging the suspension. The Court ruled that even though the event took place off of school grounds, it was school-sponsored and therefore a matter for school officials to decide, and the school was reasonable to see his sign as promoting illegal drug use.

Political Science Disciplinary Practices and Reasoning Processes: Explain Complex Similarities and Differences

Often, comparing Supreme Court cases can aid understanding of the constitutional principles in each. When you compare cases, you look for similarities and differences in the rulings and opinions.

Apply: Complete the following activities.

1. Explain the facts, majority decision, and reasoning in the *Tinker* case.

2. Explain the constitutional principle under consideration in this case.

3. Explain three points Justice Fortas made in the majority opinion.

4. Explain what the Supreme Court defined as the line between individual freedom and public order in *Tinker*.

5. Explain the similarities and differences of the outcome in *Tinker* with the outcomes of *Bethel School District v. Fraser* and *Morse v. Frederick*.

Source: Granger, NYC

Writing the majority opinion in the *Tinker* case, Justice Abe Fortas stated that schools could forbid conduct that would "materially and substantially interfere with the requirements of appropriate discipline" but not activities that merely create "the discomfort and unpleasantness that always accompany an unpopular viewpoint."

Obscenity

Some language and images are so offensive to the average citizen that governments have banned them. Though obscenity is difficult to define, two trends prevail regarding **obscene speech**: The First Amendment does not protect it, and no national standard fully defines it.

In the 19th century, some states and later the national government outlawed obscenity. Reacting to published birth control literature, postal inspector and moral crusader Anthony Comstock pushed for the first national anti-obscenity law in 1873, which banned the circulation and importation of obscene materials through the U.S. mail. Yet the legal debate since has generally been over state and local ordinances brought before the Supreme Court on a case-by-case basis. The Court has tried to square an individual's right to free speech or press and a community's right to ban obscene and offensive material.

A Transformational Time From the late 1950s until the early 1970s, the Supreme Court heard several appeals by those convicted for obscenity. In *Roth v. United States* (1957), Samuel Roth, a long-time publisher of questionable books, was prosecuted under the Comstock Act. He published and sent through the mail his *Good Times* magazine, which contained partially airbrushed nude photographs. On the same day, the Court heard a case examining a California obscenity law. The Court upheld the long-standing view that both state and federal obscenity laws were constitutionally permissible because obscenity is "utterly without redeeming social importance." In *Roth*, the Court defined speech as obscene and unprotected when "the average person, applying contemporary community standards," finds that it "appeals to the prurient interest" (lustful or lewd thoughts or wishes).

Defining Obscenity The new rule created a swamp of ambiguity that the Court tried to clear during the next 15 years. Before Roth finished his prison term, the law turned in his favor. The pornography industry grew apace during the sexual revolution of the 1960s and 1970s. States reacted, creating a battle between those declaring a constitutional right to create or consume risqué materials and local governments seeking bans. The Court struggled to determine this balance. In his frequently quoted phrase from a 1964 case regarding how to distinguish acceptable versus unacceptable pornographic images or expression, Justice Potter Stewart said, "I know it when I see it." Although the Court could not reach a solid definition of obscenity, from 1967 to 1971, it overturned 31 obscenity convictions.

THINK AS A POLITICAL SCIENTIST: *ARTICULATE A DEFENSIBLE CLAIM*

An argument, or claim, is a statement that can be supported by facts or evidence. Writing a clear and concise claim is essential to producing a good essay.

The Supreme Court has ruled in cases related to free speech many times in the 20th and 21st centuries. The Court has been willing to grant more freedom in some eras than at other times. As you have read, the Court has revised its definition of what is protected by the First Amendment over time.

Practice: Review the court cases in Topic 3.3. Write a claim in response to the following question based on the decisions in First Amendment cases in the last 100 years. Think of at least four cases that support your claim.

In the last 100 years, has the Supreme Court placed more limits on free speech or recognized more freedoms?

The conflict continued with **Miller v. California** (1973). After a mass mailing from Marvin Miller promoting adult materials, a number of recipients complained to the police. California authorities prosecuted Miller under the state's obscenity laws. On appeal, the justices reaffirmed that obscene material was not constitutionally protected, but they modified the *Roth* decision saying in effect that a local judge or jury should define obscenity by applying local community standards. Obscenity is not necessarily the same as pornography, and pornography may or may not be obscene. The Court has heard subsequent cases dealing with obscene speech, but the Miller Test—a set of three criteria that resulted from the *Miller* case—has served as the standard in obscenity cases.

THE MILLER TEST
- The average person applying contemporary community standards finds it appeals to the prurient interest.
- It depicts or describes, in a patently offensive way, sexual conduct specifically defined by state law.
- It lacks serious literary, artistic, political, or scientific value.

Balancing National Security and Individual Freedoms

The Supreme Court continually interprets provisions of the Bill of Rights to balance the power of government and the civil liberties of individuals, sometimes recognizing that individual freedoms are of primary importance and at other times finding that limitations to free speech can be justified, especially when needed to maintain social order. (For more on national security and other individual freedoms protected in the Bill of Rights, see Topic 3.1.)

Clear and Present Danger The first time the Court examined a federal conviction on a free speech claim was in *Schenck v. United States* (1919). This case helped establish that limitations on free speech may be warranted during wartime.

MUST-KNOW SUPREME COURT CASE: *SCHENCK V. UNITED STATES* (1919)

The Constitutional Question Before the Court: Does the government's prosecution and punishment for expressing opposition to the military draft during wartime violate the First Amendment's free speech clause?

Decision: No, for *United States*, 9:0

Facts: As the United States entered World War I against the Central Powers, the 1917 Sedition and Espionage Acts prevented publications that criticized the government, that advocated treason or insurrection, or that incited disloyal behavior in the military. A U.S. district court tried and convicted Charles Schenck, the secretary of the Socialist Party, when he printed 15,000 anti-draft leaflets intended for Philadelphia-area draftees. In an effort to dissuade people from complying with the draft, he argued in his pamphlet that a mandatory military draft, or conscription, amounted to involuntary servitude, which is denied by the Thirteenth Amendment. The government was very concerned at the time about the Socialist Party, German Americans, and those who questioned America's military draft and war effort. Schenck appealed the guilty verdict from the district court.

Reasoning: On hearing the case, the Supreme Court drew a distinction between speech that communicated honest opinion and speech that incited unlawful action and thereby represented a "clear and present danger." In a unanimous opinion delivered after the war's end, the Court upheld the government's right to convict citizens for certain speech. Schenck went to prison, as did defendants in five similar cases. The **clear and present danger** test became the balancing act between competing demands of free expression and a government needing to protect a free society.

The Court arrived at its opinion through recognizing that the context of an expression needs to be considered to determine its constitutionality. At other times, under other circumstances, the pamphlet or circular might have been allowed, but during wartime and because of the immediate actions the pamphlet could lead to, the harm from the circular overrode Schenck's right to publish and distribute it.

The Court's Majority Opinion by Mr. Justice Oliver Wendell Holmes: In impassioned language, [the pamphlet] intimated that conscription was despotism in its worst form, and a monstrous wrong against humanity in the interest of Wall Street's chosen few. . . . It described the arguments on the other side as coming from cunning politicians and a mercenary capitalist press, and even silent consent to the conscription law as helping to support an infamous conspiracy. . . Of course, the document would not have been sent unless it had been intended to have some effect, and we do not see what effect it could be expected to have upon persons subject to the draft except to influence them to obstruct the carrying of it out . . . .

We admit that, in many places and in ordinary times, the defendants, in saying all that was said in the circular, would have been within their constitutional rights, but the character of every act depends upon the circumstances in which it is done. The most stringent protection of free speech would not protect a man in falsely shouting fire in a theatre and causing a panic. It does not even protect a man from an injunction against uttering words that may have all the effect of force. The question in every case is whether the words used are used in such circumstances and are of such a nature as to create a clear and present danger that they will bring about the substantive evils that Congress has a right to prevent. It is a question of proximity and degree. When a nation is at war, many things that might be said in time of peace are such a hindrance to its effort that their utterance will not be endured so long as men fight, and that no Court could regard them as protected by any constitutional right.

Since *Schenck*: Justice Holmes famously reconsidered and redefined his views in a similar case that arrived in the Court soon after *Schenck*. In *Abrams* v. *United States (1919)*, an appeal by Russian immigrants convicted under the same law as Schenck had been, the Court decided once again—mainly for the same reason—to uphold convictions. Holmes, however, voted this time to overturn the conviction and wrote a dissenting opinion declaring the Court should uphold such convictions only if the speech "produces or is intended to produce clear and imminent danger that it will bring about . . . substantive evils." Decades later, the Court ruled in *Brandenburg v. Ohio (1969)*—an appeal of a convicted Klansman accused of inciting lawlessness at a rally— that such speech could be punished only if it is meant to incite or produce "imminent lawless action and is likely to . . . produce such action." The clear and present danger standard did not prevent all forms of speech nor was the claim always a justification for criminal charges.

Political Science Disciplinary Practices: Explain Reasoning, Similarities, and Differences

A number of Supreme Court cases have established a "test"—a set of criteria to determine whether speech is protected or not. Like other Supreme Court opinions, however, the tests are always being interpreted and reinterpreted over time.

Apply: Complete the following activities focusing on *Schenck v. United States*.

1. Explain the reasoning behind the Supreme Court's decision. Take into account the context in which the pamphlet was published.

2. Describe the "clear and present danger" the pamphlet was seen to create. What practical effect on the United States would that danger have had if it were realized?

3. Explain how later Court decisions reinterpreted or refined the "clear and present danger" test for protected or unprotected speech. In other words, how were the opinions in *Schenck* similar to and different from those in *Abrams* and *Brandenburg*?

REFLECT ON THE ESSENTIAL QUESTION

Essential Question: *To what extent does the Supreme Court's interpretation of freedom of speech reflect a commitment to individual liberty? On separate paper, complete the chart below.*

How the Court Has Addressed Symbolic Speech	How the Court Has Balanced Free Speech and Order

KEY TERMS AND NAMES

clear and present danger
Miller v. California (1973)
obscene speech
Schenck v. United States (1919)

symbolic speech
*Tinker v. Des Moines Independent
    Community School District* (1969)

First Amendment: Freedom of the Press

"Freedom of the press and constitutional liberty must
live or perish together."

—Salmon P. Chase, *Cincinnati Daily Gazette*, 1836

Essential Question: To what extent does the Supreme Court's interpretation of freedom of the press reflect a commitment to individual liberty?

The Internet and access to information have radically changed the nature of the press. Its reach gives it unrivaled power to connect people and also presents significant risks. False and potentially dangerous information can reach countless numbers of people in an instant. Minors are especially vulnerable to the threat of an unregulated Internet.

In most free speech cases, the Supreme Court rules to protect speech. It also has protected free press in many of its rulings. In the 21st century, does the Internet and those who create its content have the same protection as the traditional press under the First Amendment? Should the web be governed under the same protections as the traditional press, or are different rules needed to counter the significant risks?

Free Press in a Democracy

"Our liberty depends on the freedom of the press," Thomas Jefferson wrote, "and that cannot be limited without being lost." The absolute preservation of a free press, as Jefferson's posture signifies, assures a transparent and honest government. Free press can expose the actions of an evil state. In totalitarian counties today, you can see "state television," that is the news about the government brought to you exclusively by the government. When Western journalists and news crews visit these regimes, they are welcomed and monitored by "government minders," who keep the visitors' cameras and eyes off anything that might make the country look negative.

Centuries after Jefferson's quote, President Donald Trump referred to the press as "the enemy of the people" and repeatedly complained about "fake news." At a campaign rally in February 2016 he said, "I'm going to open up our libel laws so when they [the press] write purposely negative and horrible and false articles, we can sue them and win lots of money." Could he win those lawsuits? His past efforts, as well as the standards for freedom of the press, say no.

Press and Speech

The Court has not made much distinction between "speech" and "press" and ordinarily provides the same protective standards for both rights. "Speech" includes an array of expressions—actual words, the lack of words, pictures, and actions. An average citizen has as much right to free press as does a professional journalist. The First Amendment does not protect all speech, or all press, especially if communication invites danger.

Libel and "Breathing Space"

A charge of **libel** refers to false statements in print about someone that defames—or damages that person's reputation. Much negativity can be printed about someone of a critical, opinionated, or even speculative nature before it qualifies as libel. American courts have typically allowed for a high standard of defamation before rewarding a suing party.

The main decision that defined the First Amendment's protection of printed speech against the charge of libel was **New York Times Co. v. Sullivan** (1964). In 1960, a civil rights group, including Martin Luther King Jr., put an ad in the *New York Times* entitled "Heed their Rising Voices," which included some inaccuracies and false information about a Montgomery, Alabama, city commissioner, L. B. Sullivan. Sullivan sued for libel in an Alabama court and won $500,000 in damages. The *Times* appealed, arguing that the First Amendment protected against slight mistakes and these should differ from an intentional defamation. The Supreme Court sided with the newspaper. Uninhibited debate "may well include vehement, caustic, and sometimes unpleasantly sharp attacks on government and public officials," the Court noted. The fear of an easy libel suit would stifle robust debate and hard reporting. Even false statements, therefore, must be protected "if the freedoms of expression are to have the **'breathing space'** that they need . . . to survive."

The standard to prove libel is therefore high. The suing party must prove that they were damaged and that the offending party knowingly printed the falsehood and did so maliciously with intent to defame. Public officials are less protected than laypeople and cannot recover damages for defamatory falsehoods relating to their official conduct unless they can prove actual malice—that is, reckless disregard for the truth. The Court later broadened the category of "public figure" to include celebrities such as movie stars, top athletes, and business leaders.

New York Times Co. v. Sullivan and subsequent decisions have generally ruled that to win a libel suit in a civil court, the suing party must prove that the offending writer either knowingly lied or presented information with a reckless disregard for the truth, that the writer did so with **malicious intent** to defame, and that actual damages were sustained.

Prior Restraint

The government also has no exclusive privilege of **prior restraint**—the right to stop spoken or printed expression in advance. This position was first declared in *Near v. Minnesota* and later reaffirmed in **New York Times Co. v. United States** (1971). Governments cannot suppress a thought from entering the marketplace of ideas just because most people see the idea as repugnant or offensive. A government that can squelch ideas is one that violates the very essence of a free democracy. The Court, however, has never suggested that its reverence for free expression means that all expression should be tolerated at all times under all conditions. There are exceptions that allow state and federal governments to limit or punish additional forms of speech.

MUST-KNOW SUPREME COURT CASE: *NEW YORK TIMES CO. V. UNITED STATES* (1971)

The Constitutional Question Before the Court: Can the executive branch block the printing of reporter-obtained classified government information in an effort to protect national secrets without violating the First Amendment's free press clause?

Decision: No, for *New York Times*, 6:3

Before *New York Times Co. v. United States*: In the selective incorporation case of *Near v. Minnesota* (1931), the Supreme Court ruled that a state law preventing the printing of radical propaganda violated freedom of the press.

Facts: Daniel Ellsberg, a high-level Pentagon analyst, became disillusioned with the war in Vietnam and in June of 1971 released a massive report known as the Pentagon Papers to the *New York Times*. (The case also included the *Washington Post* since it, too, had been given the document.) The seven-thousand-page top-secret document—which unlike today's easily released digital content had to be photocopied—told the backstory of America's entry into the Vietnam conflict and revealed government deception. These papers questioned the government's credibility and, President Nixon claimed, hampered the president's ability to manage the war. Nixon's lawyers petitioned a U.S. district court to order the *Times* to refrain from printing in the name of national security. "I think it is time in this country," Nixon said of Ellsberg and the *Times*, "to quit making national heroes out of those who steal secrets and publish them in the newspaper." The lower court obliged and issued the injunction (order), and armed guards arrived at the newspaper's office to enforce the injunction.

The *Times* appealed, and the Supreme Court ruled in its favor. The ruling assured that the hasty cry of national security does not justify censorship in advance and that the government does not have the power of prior restraint of publications. Even Nixon's solicitor general, the man who argued his side in the Supreme Court, later said the decision "came out exactly as it should." This decision was "a declaration of independence," claimed *Times* reporter Hedrick Smith, "and it really changed the relationship between the government and the media ever since."

The Court ruled on the newspaper's right to print these documents, not on Ellsberg's right to leak them. In fact, Ellsberg was later indicted under the 1917 Espionage Act in his own trial.

Reasoning: In a rare instance, the Court in this case did not fully explain its ruling with a typical majority opinion. Instead, it issued a *per curiam* opinion, which is a judgment issued on behalf of a unanimous court or the court's majority without attribution to a specific justice. It relied heavily on the reasoning in previous cases. The judgment overruled the lower court's injunction and prevented the executive branch from stopping the printing.

> **Per Curiam Opinion**: "Any system of prior restraints of expression comes to this Court bearing a heavy presumption against its constitutional validity." *Bantam Books, Inc. v. Sullivan* . . . (1963); see also *Near v. Minnesota* (1931). The Government "thus carries a heavy burden of showing justification for the imposition of such a restraint." *Organization for a Better Austin v. Keefe* (1971). The District Court for the Southern District of New York, in the *New York Times* case, and the District Court for the District of Columbia and the Court of Appeals for the District of Columbia Circuit, in the *Washington Post* case, held that the Government had not met that burden. We agree.

Political Science Disciplinary Practices and Reasoning Processes: Explain Reasoning, Similarities, and Differences

In another concurring opinion, Justice William Brennan noted that the executive branch "is endowed with enormous power in the two related areas of national defense and international relations." Given this relatively unchecked power, he reasoned that in these areas "the only effective restraint upon executive policy and power . . . may lie in an enlightened citizenry—in an informed and critical public opinion which alone can here protect the values of democratic government. For this reason, it is perhaps here that a press that is alert, aware, and free most vitally serves the basic purpose of the First Amendment. For, without an informed and free press, there cannot be an enlightened people."

Apply: Complete the following activities.

1. Explain the reasoning behind Justice Brennan's views that an "enlightened citizenry" can protect the democratic values of our government.

2. Explain the role of the press in creating that citizenry.

3. Explain how the judgment in *New York Times Co. v. United States* balances claims for individual freedom with concerns for national security.

4. Read about the case *Near v. Minnesota* (1931) and the Court's decision at Oyez.org or supremecourt.gov, and then explain the similarities and differences between the opinions in *Near* and those in the *New York Times* case.

5. Explain the impact that this decision might have had on (1) the credibility of the government, (2) the outcome of the Vietnam War, and (3) the legal standing of whistleblowers today. Do research if necessary.

THINK AS A POLITICAL SCIENTIST: *EXPLAIN HOW THE VISUAL ELEMENT OF A CARTOON RELATES TO POLITICAL PRINCIPLES*

At one time, political cartoons were a way to express opinions even to people who could not read. Despite today's high literacy rate, cartoons have continued, often as a way to express political beliefs and principles. Interpreting a cartoonist's ideas or perspective can take critical thinking skills because cartoons are often created using irony, symbolism, or analogy.

Practice: View the political cartoon and answer the questions that follow.

1. What is the artist's view of the press?
2. How does the *New York Times Co. v. United States* ruling relate to the artist's view of the press?
3. How do either of the other Supreme Court cases from Topic 3.4 relate?

REFLECT ON THE ESSENTIAL QUESTION

Essential Question: *To what extent does the Supreme Court's interpretation of freedom of the press reflect a commitment to individual liberty? On separate paper, complete the chart below.*

Free Press Supreme Court Case	How the Ruling Affected Free Press

---

KEY TERMS AND NAMES

"breathing space"
libel
malicious intent
Near v. Minnesota (1931)

New York Times Co. v. United States (1971)
New York Times Co. v. Sullivan (1964)
prior restraint

CHAPTER 8 Review:
Learning Objectives and Key Terms

TOPIC 3.1: Explain how the U.S. Constitution protects individual liberties and rights. (LOR-2.A)

Describe the rights protected in the Bill of Rights. (LOR-2.B)

Protections in the Bill of Rights (LOR-2.A.1–3 AND LOR-2.B.1)

Bill of Rights (1791)

civil liberties

public interest

TOPIC 3.2: Explain the extent to which the Supreme Court's interpretation of the First and Second Amendments reflects a commitment to individual liberty. (LOR-2.C)

Interpretation and Application of Freedom of Religion (LOR-2.C.1)

Engel v. Vitale (1962)

establishment clause

free exercise clause

Lemon v. Kurtzman (1971)

wall of separation

Wisconsin v. Yoder (1972)

TOPIC 3.3: Explain the extent to which the Supreme Court's interpretation of the First and Second Amendments reflects a commitment to individual liberty. (LOR-2.C)

Balancing Freedom and Order in Free Speech (LOR-2.C.2 & 3)

clear and present danger

Miller v. California (1973)

obscene speech

Schenck v. United States (1919)

symbolic speech

*Tinker v. Des Moines Independent
Community School District* (1969)

TOPIC 3.4: Explain the extent to which the Supreme Court's interpretation of the First and Second Amendments reflects a commitment to individual liberty. (LOR-2.C)

Supreme Court Interpretations of Free Press (LOR-2.C.4)

"breathing space"

libel

malicious intent

Near v. Minnesota (1931)

New York Times Co. v. United States (1971)

New York Times Co. v. Sullivan (1964)

prior restraint

CHAPTER 8 Checkpoint:
The Bill of Rights and the First Amendment

Topics 3.1–3.4

MULTIPLE-CHOICE QUESTIONS

1. Which of the following is an accurate comparison of *Engle v. Vitale* and *Wisconsin v. Yoder*?

	Engel v. Vitale (1962)	Wisconsin v. Yoder (1972)
(A)	Involved the application of the establishment clause	Involved the protection of the free exercise clause
(B)	Involved the issue of school prayer	Involved reimbursement to parents of parochial school children
(C)	Involved the issue of prayer at city council meetings	Involved daily Bible readings in public schools
(D)	Found that state mandated prayer was unconstitutional	Found that religious symbols could not be displayed at state funded locations

2. What was the effect of the ruling in *Schenck v. United States?*
   (A) People can say or express anything as long as the nation is not at war.
   (B) During wartime, no person can criticize the U.S. government.
   (C) Printed materials are protected as free speech, even in times of war.
   (D) Speech that presents a clear and present danger can be punished.

3. Which of the following is protected by the First Amendment?
   (A) Political speech
   (B) Eminent domain
   (C) Obscenity
   (D) Gun ownership

4. With the variety of religious denominations and religions represented at a public high school, the administration has decided to ban students from wearing any religious symbols or garb that reflect a particular religious faith. Which of the following would be the best legal advice for school administrators?

(A) This is a constitutional policy because it reflects majoritarian religious practices.

(B) This is an unconstitutional policy because it violates the free exercise clause.

(C) This is a constitutional policy because religious practice is not allowed on public property.

(D) This is an unconstitutional policy because of the reserved powers clause.

Questions 5 and 6 refer to the cartoon below.

Bennett ©Clay Bennett Chattanooga Times Free Press

5. With which of the following statements would the cartoonist most likely agree?

(A) The government should be able to impose religion on its citizens.

(B) Elected officials cannot be religious.

(C) There is a constant struggle to define the separation of church and state.

(D) The government should provide more help to churches.

6. Which of the following Supreme Court cases is most related to the topic of the cartoon?

(A) *New York Times Co. v. United States* (1971)

(B) *Schenck v. United States* (1919)

(C) *Engel v. Vitale* (1962)

(D) *Tinker v. Des Moines* (1969)

Concept Application

1. RALEIGH – The American Civil Liberties Union of North Carolina Legal Foundation (ACLU-NCLF) today applauded a judge's ruling that declared North Carolina's ban on the public use of profanity to be an unconstitutional violation of freedom of speech. The statute at issue [makes] it a misdemeanor offense to use "indecent or profane language" in a "loud and boisterous manner" within earshot of two or more people on any public road or highway in North Carolina. . . . This 98-year-old law is a blatant violation of the First Amendment," said Jennifer Rudinger, Executive Director of the ACLU-NCLF. "We applaud the judge's ruling as an important victory for free speech. Our client, Samantha Elabanjo, never should have been charged with a crime just for saying 'damn' on a public street."

   —American Civil Liberties Union, Press Release, 2011

   After reading the scenario, respond to A, B, and C below:

   (A) Describe how the press release supports a commitment to individual liberty.

   (B) Explain how a state government action could alter the ruling described in the scenario.

   (C) In the context of this scenario, explain how the action described in B can result in different outcomes.

Quantitative Analysis

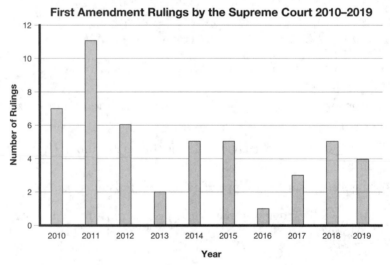

First Amendment Rulings by the Supreme Court 2010–2019

Source: Freedom Forum Institute

3. Use the information graphic on the previous page to answer the following questions.

   (A) Describe a trend regarding First Amendment cases and the U.S. Supreme Court.

   (B) Describe a similarity or difference in the number of First Amendment rulings the U.S. Supreme Court makes in different years.

   (C) Draw a conclusion about the cause of the similarity or difference described in part B.

   (D) Explain how U.S. Supreme Court rulings on the First Amendment may reflect a commitment to balancing liberty and order.

SCOTUS Comparison

4. On January 24, 2002, the Juneau [Alaska] School District sanctioned an outdoor event across the street from the high school—watching the Olympic torch as it passed by on its journey to Salt Lake City, where the winter games were going to be held. Just as the torch and camera crews passed by, student Joseph Frederick unfurled a 14-foot banner that said "BONG HITS 4 Jesus." Principal Deborah Morse confiscated the banner and suspended Frederick for ten days. Although he appealed his suspension, the Juneau School District upheld the suspension, arguing that the sign promoted illegal drug use and the school had a policy against displaying messages that promoted drug use. Frederick sued. A district court decided in favor of the principal. On appeal the Ninth Circuit Court decided that Frederick's constitutional rights were violated.

   The case reached the Supreme Court, which ruled 5:4 in *Morse v. Frederick* in 2007 that the school was within its rights to remove the banner and suspend Frederick. In the majority opinion, Justice Roberts argued that students' rights in schools do not extend to pro-drug messages, because an important objective of the school was to discourage drug use.

   (A) Identify the constitutional clause that is common to *Morse v. Frederick* (2007) and *Tinker v. Des Moines Independent School District* (1969).

   (B) Based on the similarity identified in part A, explain why the facts of *Tinker v. Des Moines Independent School District* led to a different holding than the holding in *Morse v. Frederick*.

   (C) Describe how the holding in *Morse v. Frederick* affected students' opportunities to hold gatherings on school grounds supporting alteration of marijuana law.

CHAPTER 9

Balancing Liberty and Safety

Topics 3.5–3.6

Topic 3.5 Second Amendment: Right to Bear Arms

LOR-2.C: Explain the extent to which the Supreme Court's interpretation of the First and Second Amendments reflects a commitment to individual liberty.

- – Required Foundational Document:
  - • The Constitution of the United States

Topic 3.6 Amendments: Balancing Individual Freedom with Public Order and Safety

LOR-2.D: Explain how the Supreme Court has attempted to balance claims of individual freedom with laws and enforcement procedures that promote public order and safety.

- – Required Foundational Document:
  - • The Constitution of the United States

Source: Wikimedia Commons

People march to advocate for gun rights in St. Paul, Minnesota.

Source: Wikimedia Commons

Students from schools in Brooklyn, New York, walk out of class to show support for stricter gun laws.

Second Amendment: Right to Bear Arms

"To disarm the people . . . was the best and most effectual way to enslave them."

—George Mason, Virginia Ratifying Convention, 1788

Essential Question: To what extent does the Supreme Court's interpretation of the Second Amendment reflect a commitment to individual liberty?

The founding fathers vigorously debated the necessity of a nation being able to defend itself from invading forces or from threats within. Today, a growing number of voices is calling for changes to local and national gun laws as gun violence increases. The debate about the meaning of the Second Amendment and the degree to which government may limit guns has become especially heated in the last few decades. Should an amendment created in 1791 still guide an industrialized and modernized nation's gun policy in the 21st century?

Founding Principles and Bearing Arms

At the 1787 Philadelphia Convention, the debate about weapons was generally related to a standing army. In light of the recent Shays' Rebellion, several attendees were inclined to enable Congress to maintain a regular armed force, a paid, professionally trained military. Others clung to the idea of states keeping regular militias that the federal government could call into service. The latter would require an extra step in times of need but would provide an additional check on a potential runaway central government if the army was going to be used for heinous purposes.

Constitutional Convention

The debates show us how far the Revolution and its aftermath had reversed traditional thinking. Previously, most statesmen of the day assumed that militias, locally controlled, would be less prone to corruption and abuse. By 1787, though, the men of the convention insisted an effective government required a national army, but, as historian Michael Waldman explains in *The Second Amendment: A Biography*, "there is no evidence—from James Madison's notes or those of any other participant—that the delegates in the Constitutional

Convention had the slightest inkling that private gun ownership was viewed at risk and required inclusion in a bill of rights. *It simply did not come up.*"

In the States

Several state constitutions had a bill of rights. Four of the thirteen states protected the right to bear arms as part of a militia force. Only one, Pennsylvania, protected the right to bear arms as individual self-defense.

Gun regulations were common. As historian Saul Cornell has described, various states and localities maintained laws that, among other things, designated the official location for gun and powder storage, barred firing guns within city limits, and prevented people deemed dangerous from gun ownership. In Maryland, Catholics were barred from having guns. Most states banned African Americans, free or slave, from joining militias or owning weapons. And Rhode Island created a gun registry in supporting the militia.

Much gun law came via common law court rulings. Gun ownership was common and protected. The legal argument for using a gun in self-defense was well established, but courts would eventually weigh the right to own a gun against actions and regulations meant to protect others.

A National Standard

As the ratification debate moved toward adding a bill of rights, George Mason and Virginia's other critics of the proposed Constitution drafted suggested amendments to send to the Congress. Their seventeenth suggestion read in part, "That the people have a right to keep and bear arms; that a well-regulated militia composed of the body of the people trained to arms is the proper, natural and safe defense of a free state." This, along with suggestions from multiple states, grew into the **Second Amendment**.

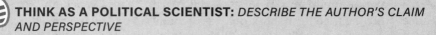

THINK AS A POLITICAL SCIENTIST: *DESCRIBE THE AUTHOR'S CLAIM AND PERSPECTIVE*

Looking at the context in which an article or document is written often helps you clarify an author's claim. The quotes from Michael Waldman above look at how colonial leaders viewed the right of citizens to bear arms soon after the American Revolution. Today, people see the right to bear arms from a different perspective. For example, gun violence has increased in American society. As a result, the arguments for and against citizens' rights to own firearms have heightened. One side emphasizes the right to own a gun to protect oneself and family. The other focuses on laws to restrict ownership of weapons to protect everyone from gun violence.

Practice: Read the excerpt below, and answer the questions that follow.

"On June 8, 1789, James Madison—who had won election to Congress only after agreeing to push for changes to the newly ratified Constitution—proposed 17 amendments on topics ranging from the size of congressional districts to legislative pay to the right to religious freedom. One addressed the "well-regulated militia" and the right "to keep and bear arms." We don't really know what he meant by it. At the time, Americans expected to be able to own guns, a legacy of English common law and rights. But the overwhelming use of the phrase "bear arms" in those days referred to military activities.

There is not a single word about an individual's right to a gun for self-defense or recreation in Madison's notes from the Constitutional Convention. Nor was it mentioned, with a few scattered exceptions, in the records of the ratification debates in the states. Nor did the U.S. House of Representatives discuss the topic as it marked up the Bill of Rights. In fact, the original version passed by the House included a conscientious objector provision. "A well regulated militia," it explained, "composed of the body of the people, being the best security of a free state, the right of the people to keep and bear arms shall not be infringed, but no one religiously scrupulous of bearing arms, shall be compelled to render military service in person."

—Michael Waldman, *Politico Magazine* "How the NRA Rewrote the Second Amendment", 2014

1. How does Waldman interpret Madison and other founders' arguments on owning guns?

2. What inferences can be made about the author's opinion of the Second Amendment?

3. What is the uncertainty that Waldman finds in the founders' opinion about the right of citizens to own guns?

The Second Amendment and Gun Policy

Supreme Court interpretations of the Second Amendment, like those of the First Amendment, represent a commitment to individual liberties. The amendment states, "A well-regulated militia, being necessary to the security of a free State, the right of the people to keep and bear arms, shall not be infringed." The precise meaning is difficult to ascertain in today's world, which is likely why the Second Amendment has been controversial. Was the amendment written to protect the state's right to maintain a militia or the citizen's unfettered right to own a firearm? Gun-control advocates might point out these state militias were "well regulated" and thus subject to state requirements such as training, occasional military exercises, and limitations on the type of gun possessed. The concern at the time was about the federal government imposing its will on or overthrowing a state government with a standing federal army. The original concern was not with the general citizenry's right to gun ownership. Today's gun advocates, however, supported by recent Supreme Court decisions, argue that the amendment guarantees the personal right to own and bear arms because each citizen's right to own a firearm guaranteed the state's ability to have a militia. Similarly, gun rights proponents argue that the "right of the people" clause means the same as it does with other parts of the Bill of Rights.

National and State Laws

Recall that the Bill of Rights was originally created to limit the federal government. States made their own gun-related laws for years and still do today. A handful of national gun laws exist based on the commerce clause. However, as you will read in the *McDonald* case, states must follow the Second Amendment because of selective incorporation. (See Topic 3.7.)

Gun laws, such as defining where people can carry, fall within the police powers of the state. (See Topic 1.7.) Not until 1934, in an era of bootleggers and gangsters, did Congress pass a national statute about possession of guns. The **National Firearms Act** required registration of certain weapons, imposed a tax on the sale and manufacture of certain guns, and restricted the sale and ownership of high-risk weapons such as sawed-off shotguns and automatic machine guns. The law was challenged not long after Congress passed the bill and it was upheld by the Supreme Court.

Increased urban crime, protest, and assassinations in the 1960s influenced the passage of the **Gun Control Act** of 1968. Along with other anti-crime bills that year, the act sought safer streets. It ended mail-order sales of all firearms and ammunition and banned the sale of guns to felons, fugitives, illegal drug users, people with mental illness, and those dishonorably discharged from the military. In reality, the law's effect was to punish those who owned a gun or used it illegally more than to prevent the purchase or possession of guns.

The Brady Bill The gun debate came to the forefront again after a mentally disturbed John Hinckley shot President Ronald Reagan in 1981. Reagan survived as did his press secretary James Brady, but Brady suffered a paralyzing head wound. His wife helped organize a coalition to prevent handgun violence. They pushed for legislation that became the **Brady Handgun Violence Prevention Act** in 1993. This law established a five-day waiting period for handgun purchases to allow for a background check. The wait also serves as a potential cooling-off period for anyone buying a gun from immediate impulse, anger, or revenge. The law expired in 1998, but a similar policy that established the National Instant Criminal Background Check System has gone into effect. The Brady Campaign to Prevent Gun Violence reported that the initial Brady law prevented the sale of guns to more than two million people.

The law, however, has several loopholes. Private gun collectors can avoid the background check when purchasing firearms at private gun shows, and some guns can be purchased via the Internet without a background check. Federal law and 28 states still allow juveniles to purchase long guns (rifles and shotguns) from unlicensed dealers, and the national check system has an insufficient database of non-felon criminals, domestic violence offenders, and mental health patients.

Meanwhile, states have increasingly passed laws favorable to the possession of a gun. The powerful National Rifle Association (NRA) and Republican-controlled legislatures have worked to pass a number of state laws to enable citizens to carry guns, some concealed, some openly. The NRA has also fought in the courts against laws restricting gun ownership.

The Road to Heller

In 2008 the Supreme Court issued its first Second Amendment decision in decades. The case arose out of a Washington, DC, security guard's desire to travel home with his revolver. Since 1976, a District of Columbia local ordinance barred individuals from keeping a loaded handgun at home without a trigger lock. Security guard Dick Heller and libertarian lawyers filed suit, claiming the ordinance violated his Second Amendment right.

In this case, **District of Columbia v. Heller** (2008), countless interest groups filed friend of the court briefs. Most members of Congress took positions on the issue. The U.S. solicitor general filed a brief that suggested the Court not reach too far in preventing regulation, as reasonable limits on guns should remain lawful.

Amid the oral arguments in the courtroom, little was said about current gun law across the country, the toll of gun violence, or any precedents. Justice Stephen Breyer did cite some statistics on annual deaths and injuries caused by pistols. "Would it be unreasonable for a city with a high crime rate to ban handguns?" he asked Heller's lawyer.

For the first time the Court ruled, in a five-to-four decision, that the Second Amendment recognizes an individual's right to own a gun unrelated to militia service. In the Court's opinion, Justice Antonin Scalia wrote of the amendment and its history, that it "conferred an individual right to keep and bear arms. Of course, the right was not unlimited, just as the First Amendment's right to speech is not" unlimited.

The *Heller* decision is unique in that it struck down an overreaching law put forth by the District of Columbia, the seat of the federal capital. This was not a state law, and thus it would not directly impact or alter similar bans and limitations in state law or local ordinances beyond DC. That would come with the *McDonald* decision. (See Topic 3.7.)

REFLECT ON THE ESSENTIAL QUESTION

Essential Question: *To what extent does the Supreme Court's interpretation of the Second Amendment reflect a commitment to individual liberty? On separate paper, complete the chart below.*

Government Action Related to the Second Amendment	Effect on Gun Rights

---

KEY TERMS AND NAMES

Brady Handgun Violence Prevention Act (1993)

District of Columbia v. Heller (2008)

Gun Control Act (1968)

National Firearms Act (1934)

Second Amendment (1791)

Amendments: Balancing Individual Freedom with Public Order and Safety

"When the people fear the government there is tyranny, when the government fears the people there is liberty."

—John Basil Barnhill, *Debate on Socialism*, 1914

Essential Question: How has the Supreme Court attempted to balance claims of individual freedom with laws and enforcement procedures that promote public order and safety?

While the First and Second Amendments focus on guaranteeing individual liberties in relation to speech, religion, assembly, and bearing arms, other amendments in the Bill of Rights protect minorities and vulnerable populations—those suspected or accused of crimes, the poor, and the indigent—through the due process clause of the Fifth and Fourteenth Amendments. Constitutional provisions also help guide conflicts between individual liberties and national security concerns. Those conflicts can range from the Second Amendment argument of the right of one person to own a gun versus another person's right to be safe from gun violence to the Fourth Amendment's protections against illegal searches and seizures versus the government promoting public safety. **BIG IDEA** Governmental laws and policies balancing order and liberty are based on the U.S. Constitution and have been interpreted differently over time.

Cruel and Unusual Punishments and Excessive Bail

The phrases decrying and preventing government from applying "cruel and unusual punishments" and requiring "excessive bail" had worked their way into the English Bill of Rights generations before the American Revolution. The colonists who formed the United States saw some of the punishments toward the early critics of the British monarchy during the pre-war period as cruel and unusual. Kings had imprisoned their foes on false charges and denied the possibility for bail. They had also mistreated or starved their foes to death. These actions were likely taken because a fair and public trial probably would not have rendered the guilty verdict the king wanted. In the new republic, the U.S. Bill of Rights would protect against these practices.

Eighth Amendment

The **Eighth Amendment** (1791) prevents cruel and unusual punishments and excessive bail. Capital punishment, or the death penalty, has been in use for most of U.S. history, and it was allowed at the time of ratification of the Constitution and the Bill of Rights. (The Fifth Amendment refers to individuals being "deprived of life.") There is nevertheless debate about whether the death penalty fits the definition, according to the framers, of cruel and unusual. A handful of U.S. states, as well as most Western and developed countries, have banned the practice.

States can use a variety of methods of execution; lethal injection is the most common. From 1930 through the 1960s, 87 percent of death penalty sentences were for murder, and 12 percent were for rape. The remaining 1 percent included treasonous charges and other offenses. In the United States, large majorities have long favored the death penalty for premeditated murders.

The Court put the death penalty on hold nationally with the decision in *Furman v. Georgia* in 1972. In a complex 5:4 decision, only two justices called the death penalty itself a violation of the Constitution. Justice Brennan wrote that most of society rejects the unnecessary severity of the death penalty, and there are other less severe punishments available. Justice Marshall called the death penalty excessive and served "no legislative purpose." Also, the Court's decision addressed the randomness of the application of the death penalty. Some justices pointed out the disproportionate application of the death penalty to the socially disadvantaged, the poor, and racial minorities.

With the decision of *Gregg v. Georgia* in 1976, the Court began reinstating the death penalty as states restructured their sentencing guidelines. No state can make the death penalty mandatory by law. Rather, a careful and deliberate look at the circumstances leading to the crime must be taken into account in the penalty phase—the second phase of trial following a guilty verdict. Character witnesses may testify in the defendant's favor to affect the issuance of the death penalty. In recent years, in cases of murder, the Court has outlawed the death penalty for mentally handicapped defendants and those defendants who were under 18 years of age at the time of the murder.

Guantanamo Bay and Interrogations

After the September 11, 2001, attack on the United States, in 2002 the U.S. military established a detention camp at its naval base in Guantanamo Bay, Cuba, to hold terror suspects captured in the global war on terror. Placing the camp at this base provided stronger security, minimal media contact, and less prisoner access to legal aid than if it had been within U.S. borders. Administration officials believed that the location of the camp and interrogations outside the United States allowed a loosening of constitutional restrictions. If the suspect never entered the U.S., would he be entitled to constitutional and Bill of Rights provisions?

Soon after the terrorist attacks on September 11, 2001, administration officials signaled that unconventional tactics would be necessary to prevent another devastating attack. In trying to determine the legal limits of an intense interrogation, President Bush's lawyers issued the now infamous "torture memo." In August of 2002, President George W. Bush's Office of Legal Counsel offered the legal definition of torture, calling it "severe physical pain or suffering." The memo claimed such pain "must be equivalent in intensity to the pain accompanying serious physical injury, such as organ failure, impairment of bodily function, or even death." One of the notorious techniques employed to gather information from reluctant detainees who fit this description was waterboarding—an ancient method that simulates drowning.

As these policies developed and became public, international peace organizations and civil libertarians in the United States questioned the disregard for both *habeas corpus* rights and the Eighth Amendment's prohibition of cruel and unusual punishment. The international community, too, was aghast and left wondering, "Do the protections of the Bill of Rights extend to suspected terrorists?"

President Obama reversed many of the Bush administration's positions regarding torture techniques on terrorism suspects. Many U.S. intelligence officials protested these changes, claiming a need for the flexibility of various techniques to acquire information vital to the nation's security from detainees.

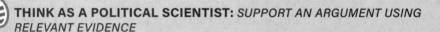

THINK AS A POLITICAL SCIENTIST: *SUPPORT AN ARGUMENT USING RELEVANT EVIDENCE*

Does the death penalty actually work as a deterrent to crime and make society safer? Strong arguments have been made on both sides of that question. Many times, evidence can support both sides of an argument, depending on how it is presented and interpreted. Both perspectives on the death penalty as a deterrent can use statistics like those below to strengthen their argument.

Practice: Using the information provided, answer the questions below.

MURDER RATES IN STATES WITH AND WITHOUT THE DEATH PENALTY								
Year	1990	1994	1998	2002	2006	2010	2014	2018
States with death penalty	9.5	9.24	6.54	5.74	6.1	4.97	4.75	5.34
States without death penalty	9.16	7.88	4.63	4.27	4.45	4.03	3.79	4.1

Source: deathpenaltyinfo.org

(Data for each year taken from the FBI's Uniform Crime Reports. Murder rates calculated by dividing the total number of murders by the total population in death penalty and non-death penalty states respectively and multiplying that by 100,000)

1. What are the trends in the data provided?
2. Statistics from which year(s) could show the effectiveness of the death penalty?
3. Statistics from which year(s) could show the ineffectiveness of the death penalty?
4. How could the visual representation of the death penalty data be improved?

Individual Rights and the Second Amendment

Attempts to shape gun policy continue at the federal level with little success. Most gun policy and efforts to balance order and freedom with respect to the Second Amendment are scattered among varying state laws and occasional lower court decisions.

Recent State Policy

About 33,000 American deaths result from handguns each year; roughly one-third are homicides, and two-thirds are suicides. In 2014, about 11,000 of the nearly 16,000 homicides in the United States involved a firearm. In addition to the thousands of single deaths, an uptick in mass shootings has brought attention to the issue of accessibility to weapons. With shootings at Virginia Tech (2007), Newtown (2012), Charleston (2015), Orlando (2016), San Bernardino (2017), Las Vegas (2017), and Parkland (2018), activists and experts on both sides of the gun debate push for new legislation at the state level in hopes of solving a crisis and preventing and protecting future would-be victims.

According to a count by the San Francisco-based Law Center to Prevent Gun Violence, more than 160 laws restricting gun use or ownership were passed in 42 states and the District of Columbia after the Newtown massacre. These included broadening the legal definition of assault weapons, banning sales of magazines that hold more than seven rounds of ammunition, and increasing the number of potentially dangerous people on the no-purchase list. By another expert's estimate, as G. M. Filisko reports in the *American Bar Association Journal*, about nine states have approved more restrictive laws, and about 30 have passed more pro-Second Amendment legislation. Pro-Second Amendment laws include widening open-carry and increasing the number of states that have reciprocity in respecting out-of-state permits. In 2009, only two states had permit-less carry. In 2017, North Dakota became the twelfth state to pass an open-carry law, sometimes called "constitutional carry" by its advocates.

After a mass shooting, the number of state firearms bills introduced increases. The types of laws passed depend on the party in power. Republican pro-Second Amendment civil liberties bills increased more permissive laws by 75 percent in states where Republicans dominate. In Democrat-controlled states researchers found no significant increase in new restrictive laws enacted.

Since the Las Vegas shooting in 2017, which resulted in a record number of deaths for a modern-day shooting, many people have focused on banning bump stocks, a device that essentially turns a semiautomatic rifle into an automatic one. New policies on both sides of the gun argument will continue to come and go with public concern over the issue, as legislatures design and pass them, and as courts determine whether they infringe on citizens' civil liberties.

Search and Seizure

Among the grievances that pushed the colonies toward revolution was the British practice of searching for smuggled goods. The British government issued **writs of assistance**, broad search warrants, that enabled British soldiers to search any vessel, warehouse, home, or wagon. Conflict between the overly aggressive soldiers and the already freedom-deprived colonists propelled the revolution.

Fourth Amendment

When many of the same revolutionaries worked to design the new government, they remembered this miserable chapter in relations between the colonies and Britain. James Madison and the First Congress added the **Fourth Amendment** to prevent a recurrence of such government overreach and violation of liberty, especially in the home. The amendment addresses searches and seizures of evidence and citizens. It specifically protects against *unreasonable* searches and seizures. It provides that warrants are necessary for government or law enforcement to enter a person's home. Courts can issue such warrants only when the information causing suspicion is delivered under oath and reaches the legal standard of a *probable cause*—a reasonable amount of suspicion that a crime has been committed. Probable cause is also needed to make an arrest—"seizing" a person—whether in the heat of the moment on the street or in an officer's planned knock on the door with warrant in hand.

> The right of the people to be secure [safe] in their persons, houses, papers, and effects [belongings] against unreasonable searches and seizures shall not be violated; and no [search] warrants shall issue but upon probable cause, supported by oath or affirmation, and particularly describing the place to be searched, and the persons or things to be seized.
>
> Fourth Amendment—U.S. Constitution

When law enforcement officers have probable cause to believe criminal activity has taken place or is planned, they are duty-bound to act to preserve order. As the likelihood of danger or harm increases, the threshold for limitations on government search and seizure diminishes. For this reason, there are exceptions to the warrant requirement. For example, officers who see crime in plain view do not need a warrant. Limitless searches can be conducted in airports and at border crossings. Public school principals need only *reasonable* cause or suspicion to conduct searches in schools. If people give consent, waiving their constitutional protection against unreasonable searches, then no warrant is required.

However, the Supreme Court has ruled that warrants are required for wiretapping a suspect's phone, bringing a drug-sniffing dog upon the porch of a home, and looking into a cell phone of a suspect or even an arrested defendant. The Supreme Court has ruled in other ways to shape search and seizure law that will be examined in Topic 3.7.

Cell Phones and Metadata

Major changes in the past two decades—the threat of terrorism and the availability of modern electronic communication—have altered the application of the Fourth Amendment. The concern over terrorism significantly spiked after al-Qaeda terrorists attacked the United States on September 11, 2001, killing more than 3,000 people. In a sweeping response to find these terrorists and prevent future attacks, the U.S. government capitalized on modern forms of investigation and electronic surveillance. (See Topics 1.5 and 3.8 on the USA PATRIOT Act.) Not long after the attack, President George W. Bush initiated a program by executive order that secretly allowed the executive branch to connect with third parties—such as Verizon and other telecommunications companies—to acquire and examine cell phone data. This third-party relationship excused the government from obtaining warrants as long as the third party was willing to give up the information. In some ways, this relationship was similar to the police asking third parties in other investigations (a suspect's boss, friend, business associate) about a suspect's activities. The degree to which phone companies need to keep phone records private is up to the customer and cellular provider. Some of the companies cooperated with the Bush administration in the name of catching terrorists, raising the legal question of whether such cooperation compromised citizens' right against unreasonable searches.

As governmental security organizations, especially the National Security Agency (NSA), increased their surveillance efforts, they instituted a program code-named PRISM. This program compels Internet service providers to give up information related to Internet activity and communications. Also, as revealed by NSA contractor and now U.S. fugitive Edward Snowden, a program that processed overwhelming amounts of data allowed the United States and its intelligence apparatus to collect telephone metadata. **Metadata** is all the cell phone communication information minus the actual conversation; that is, who is calling whom, when, and for how long. The constitutional acceptance for such collection parallels an earlier Court ruling that allowed police to monitor calls made, though not the content of the conversation, if disclosed by a third party. The government's motivation here is to determine who might be connected to terror suspects in the United States and abroad and to what degree.

REFLECT ON THE ESSENTIAL QUESTION

Essential Question: *How has the Supreme Court attempted to balance claims of individual freedom with laws and enforcement procedures that promote public order and safety? On separate paper, complete the chart below.*

Government Action to Promote Public Order and Safety	Effect on Individual Freedom

KEY TERMS AND NAMES

Eighth Amendment (1791)

Fourth Amendment (1791)

metadata

writs of assistance

CHAPTER 9 Review:
Learning Objectives and Key Terms

TOPIC 3.5: Explain the extent to which the Supreme Court's interpretation of the First and Second Amendments reflects a commitment to individual liberty. (LOR-2.C)

Supreme Court Interprets the Second Amendment (LOR-2.C.5)

Brady Handgun Violence Prevention Act (1993)   National Firearms Act (1934)

District of Columbia v. Heller (2008)   Second Amendment (1791)

Gun Control Act (1968)

TOPIC 3.6: Explain how the Supreme Court has attempted to balance claims of individual freedom with laws and enforcement procedures that promote public order and safety. (LOR-2.D)

Supreme Court Balances Freedom and Safety (LOR-2.D.1 & 2)

Eighth Amendment (1791)   metadata

Fourth Amendment (1791)   writs of assistance

CHAPTER 9 Checkpoint:
Balancing Liberty and Safety

Topics 3.5–3.6

MULTIPLE-CHOICE QUESTIONS

1. Which of the following interest groups works primarily to protect the rights enumerated in the Second Amendment?
   (A) American Civil Liberties Union
   (B) American Bar Association
   (C) National Rifle Association
   (D) National Council of State Legislatures

2. Which of the following statements best describes how the balance of liberties and safety has been interpreted over time?
   (A) The balance has been interpreted consistently over time.
   (B) The balance always leans more toward liberties than safety.
   (C) Different courts in different times have found different balances.
   (D) *Stare decisis* requires similar findings in similar cases.

Questions 3 and 4 refer to the chart below.

Cases Challenging Public School Discipline Reaching Appeals Courts

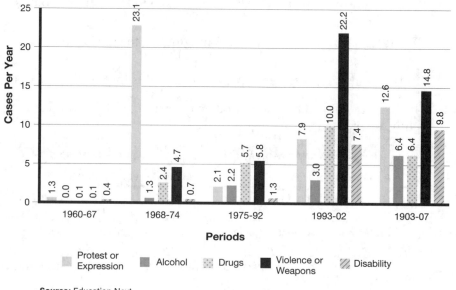

Source: Education Next

3. Which of the following is reflected in the data in the chart?
   (A) First Amendment-related challenges were the lead category in each period.
   (B) Appeals courts in the 1968–1974 period heard more First Amendment cases than more recent appeals courts.
   (C) Cases challenging punishment for student violence or weapons has steadily increased since 1968–1974.
   (D) The "War on Drugs" has virtually ended student drug-related cases.

4. Which of the following is an accurate conclusion based on your knowledge of U.S. government concepts and the data in the chart?
   (A) The Supreme Court's *Tinker v. Des Moines* (1969) ruling may have encouraged more student challenges based on First Amendment rights.
   (B) Virtually no challenges were made under the Fourth and Eighth Amendments.
   (C) As the courts became more conservative, they disposed of a greater number of cases.
   (D) Challenges based on disabilities were limited until the passage of the Americans with Disabilities Act in 1990.

5. Which of the following is an accurate statement related to the Supreme Court's ruling in *Heller v. District of Columbia* on the right to bear arms?
   (A) The case relied on the application of the Fourteenth Amendment
   (B) Gun-control activists have been outspoken in favor of the Court's ruling.
   (C) The Court overturned a broad handgun ban to assure minority rights.
   (D) The Court supported First Amendment rights in its ruling.

6. Which of the following is an accurate comparison of the Second and Eighth Amendments?

	Second Amendment	Eighth Amendment
(A)	Assures due process	Mandates equal protection
(B)	Guarantees the right to bear arms	Protects individuals from cruel and unusual punishment
(C)	Protected with *District of Columbia v. Heller* (2008)	Assured in *McDonald v. Chicago* (2010)
(D)	Upheld in schools with *Tinker v Des Moines* (1969)	Limited in *Wisconsin v. Yoder* (1972)

Concept Application

The following is from a broadcast news outlet.

1. The House [of Representatives] passed what advocates call the most significant gun control measure in more than two decades on Wednesday when it approved the first of two bills aimed at broadening the federal background check system for firearms purchases. The vote on the first bill, dubbed the Bipartisan Background Checks Act of 2019, passed largely along party lines, 240 to 190, with Democrats who control the House cheering as they carried the legislation across the finish line. A second bill, expected to be taken up Thursday, would extend the period federal authorities have to complete a background check before a gun sale can go through. Under current law, if a check isn't finalized in three business days, the transaction can automatically proceed.

   —Brakkton Booker, National Public Radio, 2019

   After reading the scenario, respond to A, B, and C below:

   (A) Describe how the bills would enhance government power.

   (B) Describe an action Congress can take regarding this legislation to better balance government power and civil liberties within the context of the scenario.

   (C) In the context of the scenario, if the policy proposals pass, explain how social movements might use constitutional provisions to advance their agenda.

Quantitative Analysis

Public's Shifting Concerns on Security and Civil Liberties (2004–2015)

2. Use the

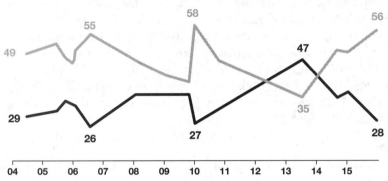

information graphic to answer the questions below.

(A) Identify the lowest percent of people believing that government has gone too far restricting civil liberties.

(B) Describe a trend in the data in the graph.

(C) Draw a conclusion about the reason for the trend described in part B.

(D) Explain how the information graphic demonstrates citizen concern for protecting the country and restricting liberties.

CHAPTER 10

Due Process

Topics 3.7–3.9

Topic 3.7 Selective Incorporation

LOR-3.A: Explain the implications of the doctrine of selective incorporation.

- – Required Foundational Document:
    - • The Constitution of the United States
- – Required Supreme Court Case:
    - • *McDonald v. Chicago* (2010)

Topic 3.8 Amendments: Due Process and the Rights of the Accused

LOR-3.B: Explain the extent to which states are limited by the due process clause from infringing upon individual rights.

- – Required Supreme Court Case:
    - • *Gideon v. Wainwright* (1963)

Topic 3.9 Amendments: Due Process and the Right to Privacy

LOR-3.B: Explain the extent to which states are limited by the due process clause from infringing upon individual rights.

- – Required Foundational Document:
    - • The Constitution of the United States
- – Required Supreme Court Case:
    - • *Roe v. Wade* (1973)

Source: Wikimedia Commons

A border patrol agent reads Miranda rights to a detainee.

Selective Incorporation

"For present purposes, we may and do assume that freedom of speech and of the press . . . are among the fundamental personal rights and 'liberties' protected by the due process clause of the Fourteenth Amendment from impairment by the States."

—Justice Edward Sanford, *Gitlow v. New York*, 1925

Essential Question: What are the implications of the doctrine of selective incorporation?

All levels of government adhere to most elements of the Bill of Rights, but that wasn't always the case. The Bill of Rights was ratified to protect the people from the *federal* government. The document begins with the First Amendment addressing what the government cannot do. "Congress shall make no law" that violates freedoms of religion, speech, press, and assembly. The document then goes on to address additional liberties Congress cannot take away. Most states had already developed bills of rights with similar provisions, but states did not originally have to follow the national Bill of Rights because it was understood that the federal Constitution referred only to federal laws, not state laws.

Incorporating the Bill of Rights

The Supreme Court has ruled in landmark cases that state laws must also adhere to certain Bill of Rights provisions through the Fourteenth Amendment's due process clause. The process of declaring only certain, or selected, provisions of the Bill of Rights applicable to the states rather than all of them at once is known as **selective incorporation**.

The concept of fundamental fairness that ensures legitimate government in a democracy is **due process**. It prevents arbitrary government decisions to avoid mistaken or abusive taking of life, liberty, or property (including money) from individuals without legal cause. (See Topic 3.8.)

The question of whether the Bill of Rights limited the federal government only, or also the states, was originally answered in the 1833 case *Barron v. Baltimore*. Justice John Marshall's Court made clear that states, if not restrained by their own constitutions or bills of rights, did not have to follow the federal Bill of Rights.

Fourteenth Amendment

Decades after the *Barron* case, the ratification of the **Fourteenth Amendment** (1868) in the aftermath of the Civil War strengthened due process. Before and during the Civil War, southern states placed many restriction on the basic liberties of African Americans and white citizens who tried to defend African American rights. After the war, Union leaders questioned if Southern states would comply with new laws that protected due process, especially for former slaves. Would an accused African American man receive a fair and impartial jury at his trial? Could an African American defendant refuse to testify in court, as a white person could? To ensure the states followed these commonly accepted principles in the federal Bill of Rights and in most state constitutions, Republicans in the House of Representatives drafted the most important and far-reaching of the Reconstruction Amendments, the Fourteenth. It declares that "all persons born or naturalized in the United States . . . are citizens" and that no state can "deprive any person of life, liberty, or property, without due process of law."

KEY SELECTIVE INCORPORATION SUPREME COURT CASES AND RELEVANT AMENDMENTS		
Selective Incorporation Case	**Ruling**	**Amendment**
Everson v. Board of Education (1947)	States that reimburse parents for transportation costs to get their children to parochial schools did not violate the Constitution.	First
McDonald v. Chicago (2010)	The Second Amendment must be protected by states based on the due process clause of the Fourteenth Amendment. (See pages 315–316.)	Second
Mapp v. Ohio (1961)	Evidence obtained in a manner that violated Fourth Amendment protections was inadmissible in state courts too. (See Topic 3.8.)	Fourth
Chicago, Burlington & Quincy Railway Co. v. Chicago (1897)	The requirement for just compensation, from the Fifth Amendment, applies when state government takes property.	Fifth
Gideon v. Wainwright (1963)	States must provide an attorney for defendants who can't afford one to guarantee a fair trial. (See Topic 3.8.)	Sixth
Timbs v. Indiana (2019)	State seizure of a convicted drug dealer's vehicle was a violation of the Eighth Amendment's prohibition of excessive fines.	Eighth

Required Supreme Court cases are **bold**

Early Incorporation

The first incorporation case used due process to evaluate issues of property seizure. In the 1880s, a Chicago rail line sued the city, which had constructed a street across its tracks. In an 1897 decision, the Court held that the newer due process clause compelled Chicago to award just compensation when taking private property for public use. This ruling incorporated the **just compensation clause** of the Fifth Amendment, requiring that the states adhere to it as well.

Incorporation and the First Amendment Later, the Supreme Court declared that the First Amendment prevents states from infringing on free thought and free expression. In a series of cases that addressed state laws designed to crush radical ideas and sensational journalism, the Court began to hold states to First Amendment standards. In the 1920s, Benjamin Gitlow, a New York Socialist, was arrested and prosecuted for violating the state's criminal anarchy law. The law prevented advocating a violent overthrow of the government. Gitlow was arrested for writing, publishing, and distributing thousands of copies of pamphlets called the *Left Wing Manifesto* that called for strikes and "class action . . . in any form."

In one of its first cases, the American Civil Liberties Union (ACLU) appealed his case and argued that the due process clause of the Fourteenth Amendment compelled states to follow the same free speech and free press ideas in the First Amendment as the federal government. In *Gitlow v. New York* (1925), however, the Court actually enhanced the state's power by upholding the state's criminal anarchy law and Gitlow's conviction because Gitlow's activities represented a threat to public safety. The court felt the substantive reason for the state's limitation of Gitlow's message was justified to preserve order. Nonetheless, the Court did address the question of whether or not the Bill of Rights *did or could* apply to the states. In the majority opinion, the Court said, "For present purposes, we may and do assume that freedom of speech and of the press . . .are among the fundamental personal rights and 'liberties' protected by the due process clause of the Fourteenth Amendment from impairment by the States." In other words, Gitlow's free speech was not protected because it was a threat to public safety, but the Court did put the states on notice.

The Court applied that warning in 1931. Minnesota had attempted to bring outrageous and obnoxious newspapers under control with a public nuisance law, informally dubbed the "Minnesota Gag Law." This statute permitted a judge to stop obscene, malicious, scandalous, and defamatory material. A hard-hitting paper published by the controversial J.M. Near printed anti-Catholic, anti-Semitic, anti-Black, and anti-labor stories. Both the ACLU and Chicago newspaper mogul Robert McCormick came to Near's aid, not for his beliefs, but on anti-censorship principles. The Court did too. In *Near v. Minnesota* it declared that the Minnesota statute "raises questions of grave importance. It is no longer open to doubt that the liberty of the press is within the liberty safeguarded by the due process clause of the Fourteenth Amendment." In this ruling, through the doctrine of selective incorporation, the Court imposed limitations on state regulation of civil rights and liberties.

It is appropriate that the Court emphasized the First Amendment freedoms early on in the incorporation process. The founding fathers generally believed that states, too, should not take away the freedoms in the First Amendment. In drafting the Bill of Rights in 1789, James Madison and others had originally stated, "No state shall infringe on the equal rights of conscience, nor the freedom of speech, or of the press." It was the only proposed amendment directly limiting states' authority.

In case after case, the Court has required states to guarantee free speech, freedom of religion, fair and impartial juries, and rights against self-incrimination. Though states have incorporated nearly all rights in the document, a few rights in the Bill of Rights remain denied exclusively to the federal government but not yet denied to the states.

MUST-KNOW SUPREME COURT CASE: *MCDONALD V. CHICAGO* (2010)

The Constitutional Question Before the Court: Does the Second Amendment apply to the states, by way of the Fourteenth Amendment, and thus prevent states or their political subdivisions from banning citizen ownership of handguns?

Decision: Yes, for McDonald, 5:4

Before *McDonald*: The Second Amendment prevents the federal government from forbidding people to keep and bear arms. In 2008, gun rights advocates and the National Rifle Association challenged a law in the District of Columbia, the seat of the federal government, which effectively banned all handguns, except those for law enforcement officers and other rare exceptions. In the case of **District of Columbia v. Heller**, the Court ruled that the Second Amendment applied and that the district's handgun ban violated this right. Because the Bill of Rights was intended to restrain Congress and the federal government, not the states, this ruling applied only to the federal government and did not incorporate the Second Amendment to state governments. Any existing state laws preventing handguns were not altered by this precedent—until Otis McDonald came to court.

Facts: Citizens in both Chicago and in the nearby suburb of Oak Park challenged policies in their cities that were similar to the ones struck down in Washington. Chicago required all gun owners to register guns, yet the city invariably refused to allow citizens to register handguns, creating an effective ban. The lead plaintiff, Otis McDonald, pointed to the dangers of his crime-ridden neighborhood and how the city's ban had rendered him without self-defense, and he argued that the Second Amendment should have prevented this vulnerability. His attorneys also attempted to take the *Heller* decision further, extending its holding to the state governments via the Fourteenth Amendment's due process clause.

Reasoning: In a close vote, the Court applied the Second Amendment to the states via the Fourteenth Amendment's due process clause, arguing that, based on *Heller*, the right to individual self-defense is at the heart of the Second Amendment. The majority also noted the historical context for the Fourteenth Amendment and asserted that the amendment sought to provide a constitutional foundation for the Civil Rights

Act of 1866. The selective incorporation doctrine has encouraged the Court to require state governments and their political subdivisions to follow most parts of the Bill of Rights. The ruling in *McDonald* highlighted yet another right that the states and their municipalities could not deny citizens.

Justice Samuel Alito wrote the Court's majority opinion; Justices Antonin Scalia and Clarence Thomas wrote concurring opinions.

Majority Opinion by Mr. Justice Alito: Self-defense is a basic right, recognized by many legal systems from ancient times to the present, and the *Heller* Court held that individual self-defense is "the central component" of the Second Amendment right. [T]he Court found that this right applies to handguns because they are "the most preferred firearm in the nation to 'keep' and use for protection of one's home and family. . . . It thus concluded that citizens must be permitted "to use [handguns] for the core lawful purpose of self-defense". . . . *Heller* also clarifies that this right is "deeply rooted in this Nation's history and traditions."

A survey of the contemporaneous history also demonstrates clearly that the Fourteenth Amendment's Framers and ratifiers counted the right to keep and bear arms among those fundamental rights necessary to the Nation's system of ordered liberty. . . .

After the Civil War, the Southern States engaged in systematic efforts to disarm and injure African Americans. These injustices prompted the 39th Congress to pass the Freedmen's Bureau Act of 1866 and the Civil Rights Act of 1866 to protect the right to keep and bear arms. Congress, however, ultimately deemed these legislative remedies insufficient, and approved the Fourteenth Amendment. Today, it is generally accepted that that Amendment was understood to provide a constitutional basis for protecting the rights set out in the Civil Rights Act. Evidence from the period immediately following the Amendment's ratification confirms that that right was considered fundamental.

Political Science Disciplinary Practices: Explain How the Court's Decision Relates to Political Principles

Justice Alito refers to the Fourteenth Amendment as the basis for the right to bear arms. Legislation passed by the 39th Congress (1865–1867) used the Fourteenth Amendment, ratified in 1868, to further extend the right to bear arms to African Americans. Examine how the Court's decision relates to the *Heller* decision and other principles by answering the questions below.

Apply: Complete the following tasks.

1. Explain the similarities and differences of the *Heller* and *McDonald* cases.

2. Identify the historic period to which Justice Alito referred in the majority opinion and explain the reasoning behind referring to this period.

3. Explain the impact of the *McDonald* ruling on the selective incorporation doctrine.

After *Heller* and *McDonald* The *Heller* and *McDonald* decisions partially govern gun policy in the United States, but the Court has done little to define gun rights and limits since. It declined to hear cases on assault weapons bans from Maryland and from a Chicago-area municipality. The Court has also declined to rule on a restrictive California limitation on who may carry concealed guns.

Congressional members are typically at loggerheads over gun policy. After each nationally notable mass shooting, the discussion about the Second Amendment becomes loud and intense, but little national law changes. Republicans tend to fiercely defend citizens' rights to own and carry guns, while Democrats tend to seek stronger restrictions on sale, ownership, and public possession. Presidential policy has shifted with changes in office. After a deranged young man shot and killed 20 schoolchildren and 6 adults in Newtown, Connecticut, President Barack Obama issued an executive order to keep guns out of the hands of mentally disabled Social Security recipients. President Donald Trump, a gun advocate, reversed the order in 2017.

Source: shutterstock

Otis McDonald outside the Supreme Court building. He was the lead plaintiff in the *McDonald v. Chicago* (2010) case in which the Court overturned a ban on handguns by the city of Chicago.

THINK AS A POLITICAL SCIENTIST: *EXPLAIN HOW A REQUIRED SUPREME COURT CASE RELATES TO A PRIMARY SOURCE*

A primary source, also called an original source, is a firsthand account of an event or situation. Primary sources tend to be reliable because they come from people who have a direct connection to a topic or event. An opinion from a

Supreme Court justice is a primary source—the original, firsthand explanation of a legal ruling. Supreme Court opinions, like other primary sources, are often called on again and again to determine interpretation of law.

For example, the Supreme Court ruling in *McDonald v. Chicago* was a victory for gun rights, but how would subsequent gun-related cases be interpreted by the Court? In *Voisine v. United States* (2016), the plaintiff had been convicted of causing reckless bodily injury to a romantic partner. Under Maine law it is a crime to own firearms after a misdemeanor conviction for domestic violence. Stephen Voisine claimed that reckless injury doesn't meet the federal standard for conviction and wanted charges dismissed. He lost in district and appellate courts. The Supreme Court also ruled against Voisine.

Practice: The excerpt is the majority opinion from Justice Kagan. Read the excerpt and answer the questions below.

"The federal ban on firearms possession applies to any person with a prior misdemeanor conviction for the 'use . . . of physical force' against a domestic relation. That language, naturally read, encompasses acts of force undertaken recklessly—i.e., with conscious disregard of a substantial risk of harm. And the state-law backdrop to that provision, which included misdemeanor assault statutes covering reckless conduct in a significant majority of jurisdictions, indicates that Congress meant just what it said. Each petitioner's possession of a gun, following a conviction under Maine law for abusing a domestic partner, therefore violates [Maine's gun laws]. We accordingly affirm the judgment of the Court of Appeals."

1. What similarities can you find between the decisions in the *McDonald* and *Voisine* cases?

2. How do the cases and the decisions differ?

REFLECT ON THE ESSENTIAL QUESTION

Essential Question: *What are the implications of the doctrine of selective incorporation? On separate paper, complete the chart below.*

Selective Incorporation Cases	Rulings' Effects on States' Rights

KEY TERMS AND NAMES

District of Columbia v. Heller (2008)	just compensation clause
due process	*McDonald v. Chicago* (2010)
Fourteenth Amendment (1868)	selective incorporation

Amendments: Due Process and the Rights of the Accused

"Ways someday may be developed by which the government . . . will be enabled to expose to a jury the most intimate occurrences in the home."
—Justice Louis Brandeis, *Olmstead v. United States*, 1928

Essential Question: To what extent are states limited by the due process clause from infringing upon individual rights?

The United States has struggled to fully interpret and define phrases in the Bill of Rights and has done so differently at different times. Justice Louis Brandeis's quote above—from his dissent in an early FBI wiretapping case— speaks to his concern for citizens' rights to privacy and protection from government intrusion into the home as basic wiretapping technology enabled the government to create a surveillance state. Brandeis could not have known how right he was in his prediction of the technological possibilities of invading citizen's dwellings, personal information, and everyday routines. The new technologies raise a familiar question: What is the proper balance between liberty and order? **BIG IDEA** Government laws and policies balancing order and liberty are based on the U.S. Constitution and have been interpreted differently over time.

Procedural Due Process

The right to due process dates back to England's Magna Carta (1215), when nobles limited the king's ability to ignore their liberties. Due process ensures fair procedures when the government burdens or deprives an individual. Due process also ensures accused persons a fair trial. The due process clause in the **Fifth Amendment** establishes that no person shall be "deprived of life, liberty, or property, without due process of law; nor shall private property be taken for public use, without just compensation."

There are two types of due process: procedural and substantive. **Procedural due process** addresses the manner in which the law is carried out. *Substantive due process* (see Topic 3.9) addresses the essence of a law—whether the point of the law violates a basic right to life, liberty, or property. Both types of due process apply to the federal and state governments through the Fifth and Fourteenth Amendments. These measures prevent government from unfairly depriving citizens of their freedoms or possessions without being heard or receiving fair treatment under the authority of law. The concept ensures that government is consistently fair and does not act arbitrarily on unstable whims. The government *can* take away life, liberty, and property, but only in a highly specific, prescribed manner. As one Supreme Court justice wrote in an early decision, "The fundamental requisite of due process of law is the opportunity to be heard." As the Court interpreted and defined due process in various cases, it also selectively required states to follow additional rights from the Bill of Rights, thus expanding the incorporation doctrine.

Procedural due process refers to the way in which a law is carried out. For example, did the local court give the defendant a fair trial? Did the zoning board accurately appraise the value of the citizen's house before seizing it under its legal powers? Were the suspended students given a chance to explain their side of the story? Such questions arise in cases that have defined the concept of due process nationally. Under the leadership of Chief Justice Earl Warren (1953–1969), the Court extended liberties and limited state authority in areas of **search and seizure**, the right to legal counsel, and the right against self-incrimination during police interrogations.

Fourth Amendment and the Exclusionary Rule

The **Fourth Amendment** prevents law enforcement from conducting unreasonable searches and seizures. (See Topic 3.6.) In 1914, in *Weeks v. United States*, the Court established the **exclusionary rule**, which states that evidence the government finds or takes in violation of the Fourth Amendment can be excluded from trial. This decision protected the citizenry from aggressive federal police by reducing the chances of conviction. The justice system rejects evidence that resembles the "fruit of the poisonous tree," as Justice Felix Frankfurter called evidence tainted by acquisition through illegal means.

In 1961, the Court incorporated the exclusionary rule to state law enforcement. Seven police officers broke into Dollree Mapp's Cleveland house in search of a fugitive suspect and gambling paraphernalia. The police found no person or evidence related to either suspect or paraphernalia, but they did find some obscene books and pictures. Mapp was convicted on obscenity charges and sent to prison. When her case arrived in the Supreme Court, the justices ruled the police had violated her rights and should never have discovered the illegal contraband. *Mapp v. Ohio* (1961) became the selective incorporation case for the Fourth Amendment. Since that ruling state laws must abide by the Fourth Amendment.

Chief Justice Burger's Court later refined the exclusionary rule to include the "inevitable discovery" and "good faith" exceptions. The inevitable discovery exception applies to evidence police find in an unlawful search but would have eventually found in a later, lawful search. The good faith exception addresses police searches under a court-issued warrant that is later proven unconstitutional or erroneous. In such instances, the police conducted the search under the good faith that they were following the law and thus have not abused or violated the Fourth Amendment. Evidence discovered under these exceptions will likely be admitted at trial.

Searches in Schools As the *Tinker* decision already stated, students' constitutional rights do not stop at the schoolhouse gate, though that decision addressed free speech. However, students in school have fewer protections against searches that may violate the public interest than do average citizens in public or in their home because, within the public school context, at times the public interest argument outweighs concerns for individual liberties.

This issue was decided in ***New Jersey v. TLO*** (1985). After a student informed a school administrator that another student, TLO (the Court used only initials to protect this minor's identity), had been smoking in the restroom, an assistant principal searched TLO's purse. He found cigarettes, as well as marijuana, rolling papers, plastic bags, a list of students who owed her money, and a large amount of cash. The administrator turned this evidence over to local authorities, who prosecuted the student. She appealed her conviction on exclusionary rule grounds. The Court ruled that although the Fourth Amendment does protect students from searches by school officials, in this case the search was reasonable. School officials are not required to have the same level of probable cause as police. Students are entitled to a "legitimate expectation of privacy," the Court said, but this must be weighed against the interests of teachers, administrators, and the school's responsibility and mission. The *New Jersey v. TLO* ruling gave administrators a greater degree of leeway than police in conducting searches, requiring that they have reasonable cause or suspicion, not full probable cause.

What if a student leaves a backpack behind on the bus? Can school officials search it, knowing or not knowing who the owner is? That was recently answered in Ohio after a bus driver discovered a backpack left behind on his bus. He handed it over to the school security officer, who reached not too deeply into the bag to find a paper with the rightful owner's name on it. He then recalled a rumor that this student was a gang member. Then, with the principal, he emptied the bag and found bullets. The bus driver and security officer then summoned the student and searched a second bag and found a gun. The state charged the student with possession of the gun. Were these discovered items found lawfully or in violation of the Fourth Amendment? On appeal, the Ohio Supreme Court found both the initial and secondary searches were reasonable. The school's public duty to act on unattended bags, and the student's relinquishing his expectation of privacy by leaving the bag behind, enhanced the school's ability to search. If the bag were just unattended while the owner went to the bathroom, of course, a high expectation of privacy would have remained. The Ohio court gave the administrators wide latitude on searching that bag, even if the administrators had no belief of imminent threat. Once the bullets were discovered, searching the second bag was within the school officials' scope.

What is the current national legal standard for a school official to conduct a search of a student's locker, backpack, or person?

Erring on the Side of Warrants In other recent Fourth Amendment rulings the U.S. Supreme Court has extended protections regarding cell phones, GPS locators, and narcotics-sniffing dogs at a person's front door. In one case, the Court ruled that attaching a GPS tracker to monitor a suspected drug dealer's movements and daily interactions was unconstitutional. When the challenge arrived at the Supreme Court, the government argued that a motorist moving about on the public streets does not have an expectation of privacy and their monitoring his movements did not even amount to a search. The Court, however, asserted that the government invades a reasonable expectation of privacy when it violates a subjective expectation of privacy. All motorists realize they might be seen, but few assume all their movements are monitored for 24-hour cycles. So this was indeed a search—an unreasonable search that might have been reasonable had the police secured a warrant ahead of time.

A final example from Florida, in which an officer walked a drug-sniffing dog up onto a citizen's front porch, arrived before the Court. The dog communicated to the officer that marijuana was inside the home. The officer secured a warrant, came into the home, and found 25 pounds of marijuana. Appealing the conviction, the suspect and his lawyer claimed that the search had taken place on the porch long before a warrant was obtained. Law enforcement cannot search willy-nilly along citizens' front porches in hopes of having their dogs smell incriminating evidence that the police can then pursue. The Court was divided on this case, but for now, police cannot take drug dogs onto a resident's porch without obtaining a warrant.

Contemporary Procedural Due Process Rights

In recent years in the United States, institutions of government have shaped the interpretations of procedural due process rights in light of modern invention and a complicated war.

Searches and the Electronic World

Has the federal government gone too far in its recent endeavors to catch terrorists or to conduct searches in the era of modern communication? The government contends that many of the new techniques, including the third-party mining of **metadata**—the who, when, and for-how-long details of a communication, but not the actual conversation—are in compliance with the Fourth Amendment. Metadata, according to David Cole of *The Nation*, "can reveal whether a person called a rape-crisis center, a suicide or drug-treatment hotline, a bookie, or a particular political organization." Should the government be privy to such information without probable cause or securing a particular warrant?

As David Gray sums up in his 2017 book *The Fourth Amendment in an Age of Surveillance*, investigative journalists report that "every major domestic telecommunications company provided telephonic metadata to the NSA" and that the NSA has gathered and stored metadata associated with a substantial proportion of calls made since 2006. The 2015 **USA FREEDOM Act** has altered the governments access to phone data. The new law does not completely eliminate the collection and storage of this metadata by cell phone operators, but it does prevent the government easy access to it. The new law requires the Executive Branch to acquire a warrant to examine the metadata.

September 11 and Executive Reaction

The USA PATRIOT Act (see Topic 1.5) was a response to the terrorist attacks on September 11, 2001, and the law raised civil liberties questions when government surveillance efforts intensified. Additional issues related to the "war on terror" also drew attention to civil liberties.

When President Bush declared a "war on terror," questions arose. For example, does the 1949 Geneva Convention, the international treaty that governs the basic rules of war, apply? Al-Qaeda is not a nation-state and is not a signatory (signer) of the Geneva Convention or any international treaty. In that case, does the United States have to honor Geneva provisions when acting against al-Qaeda? And does the Constitution apply to U.S. action beyond U.S. soil (especially when acting against enemies)? The Bush administration categorized those captured on the terror battlefield—meaning basically anywhere—as "enemy combatants" and treated their legal condition differently from either an arrested criminal or a conventional prisoner of war.

In the Courts

These legal complications and competing views on how to apply international law and the Bill of Rights in a war against an enemy with no flag have caused detainees and their advocates to challenge the government in court. A lower court has declared part of the USA PATRIOT Act unconstitutional. The Supreme Court has addressed *habeas corpus* rights.

The right of *habeas corpus* guarantees that the government cannot arbitrarily imprison or detain someone without formal charges. Could detainees at Guantanamo Bay question their detention? The president said no, but the Court said yes. *Rasul v. Bush* (2004) stated that because the United States exercises complete authority over the base in Cuba, it must follow the Constitution. Fred Korematsu, a Japanese American assigned to a World War II internment camp who lost his own *habeas corpus* claim in 1944, submitted an *amicus curiae* brief in support of Rasul. "It is during our most challenging and uncertain moments that our nation's commitment to due process is most severely tested," Justice Sandra Day O'Connor wrote, "and it is in those times that we must preserve our commitment at home to the principles for which we fight abroad."

In another case, *Hamdi v. Rumsfeld* (2004), the Court overruled the executive branch's unchecked discretion in determining the status of detainees. After this, the United States could not detain a U.S. citizen without a minimal hearing to determine the suspect's charge. In a separate case, *Hamdan v. Rumsfeld* (2006), the Court found that Bush's declaration that these detainees should be tried in military tribunals violated the United States Code of Military Justice. The commissions themselves, wrote Associate Justice John Paul Stevens, violated part of the Geneva Convention that governed non-international armed conflicts before a "regularly constituted court . . . affording judicial guarantees . . . by civilized peoples." As summed up in *Hamdi*, "We have long since made clear that a state of war is not a blank check for the president when it comes to the rights of the nation's citizens."

The Rights of the Accused

Procedural due process also guarantees that the accused are treated fairly and according to the law. The Fifth, Sixth, and Eighth Amendments have been mostly incorporated so they apply to the states as well.

Self-Incrimination

"You have the right to remain silent. . . ." goes the famed Miranda warning. This statement also reminds arrested suspects that "anything you say can and will be used against you." The warning resulted from an overturned conviction of a rapist who confessed to his crime under some pressure and without being informed that he did not have to talk. In **Miranda v. Arizona** (1966), Ernesto Miranda, an indigent man who never completed ninth grade, was arrested for the kidnapping and rape of a girl in Arizona. The police questioned Miranda for two hours until they finally emerged from the interrogation room with a signed confession. The confession was a crucial piece of evidence at Miranda's trial.

Through the 1950s, the Court handled a heavy appellate caseload addressing the problem of police-coerced confessions. Many losing defendants claimed during appeal that they had confessed only under duress, while police typically insisted the confessions were voluntary. The Fifth Amendment states, "nor shall [anyone] be compelled in any criminal case to be a witness against himself." Since a number of related cases about police procedures were reaching the Court, the justices took Miranda's case and created a new standard.

In *Miranda*, the Court declared the Fifth Amendment right applies once a suspect is in custody of the state. It declared that custodial interrogation carries with it a badge of intimidation. If such pressures from the state are going to occur, the police must inform the suspect of his or her rights. Civil libertarians hailed the Miranda ruling, while conservatives and law enforcement saw it as tying the hands of the police. Miranda received a new trial that did not use his confession. Additional proof, it turned out, was enough to convict this rapist. He went to prison while changing the national and state due process law.

THINK AS A POLITICAL SCIENTIST: *USE REASONING TO ANALYZE EVIDENCE AND JUSTIFY A CLAIM*

Technological advances have complicated the definition and interpretation of the Fourth Amendment. These advances have forced the Supreme Court to consider when and how technology can be used as evidence. Further complicating the matter are questions about the constitutionality of technologies used by the government to protect public safety.

In *Riley v. California* (2014), David Riley was pulled over for driving with expired registration tags, and officers discovered he was driving on a suspended license as well. Before the car was impounded, it was searched and two guns were found. Riley was arrested for illegal possession of firearms and his cell phone was taken. His phone was analyzed, without a warrant, and authorities discovered images and videos showing gang affiliation. This affiliation led to further investigation and police determined the guns found in Riley's car were used in a gang-related shooting. Because the analysis of the cell phone that led investigators to the gang connection was obtained without a warrant, Riley wanted the evidence thrown out. Based on the information the police had, did they have the authority and right to search for evidence on his phone?

Practice: From Topic 3.8, review the Fourth Amendment, *Miranda v. Arizona*, and the USA FREEDOM Act. Using evidence from those laws and the *Miranda* ruling, develop a claim about how the Court would rule on the case above. Use reasoning to explain how the evidence supports and justifies the claim you develop.

Public Safety Exception

A number of subsequent cases have allowed statements into court that were obtained before a suspect was warned of his or her rights. Courts have said that if the officer was acting in the name of public safety, a delayed reading or failure to read the warning would not necessarily exclude confessions or statements at court. This approach is known as the **public safety exception**, which puts the protection of people before procedural protections for suspects.

In the first public safety exception case, *New York v. Quarles* (1984), police chased Benjamin Quarles, who had been identified as assaulting a woman and carrying a gun, into a grocery store. After a search, the police found an empty gun holster. The police asked Quarles where the gun was, and Quarles indicated it was in an empty milk carton. In the original case, the suspect's attorneys tried to have Quarles's statement on the location of the gun and the gun itself suppressed from evidence because he had not been warned of his rights against self-incrimination, or "Mirandized." When the case reached the Supreme Court, however, the Court reasoned that although the suspect was surrounded by police, he was not otherwise coerced to answer the question, and the question was necessary to protect the public from the danger of a loaded gun.

Later cases upheld the public safety exception. If the questioning is for the purpose of neutralizing a dangerous situation, and a suspect responds voluntarily, the statement can be used as evidence even though it was made before the Miranda rights were read.

Right to Counsel

"If you cannot afford an attorney, one will be appointed for you," the Miranda warning continues. This wasn't always the case. Though the **Sixth Amendment's** right to counsel has been in place since the ratification of the Bill of Rights, it was first merely the right to have a lawyer present at trial, and, as with the rest of the Bill of Rights, it originally applied only to defendants in federal court. In a series of cases starting in the 1930s, the Supreme Court developed its view of right to counsel in state criminal cases. The first established that when the death penalty was possible, the absence of counsel amounted to a denial of fundamental fairness. In 1942, the Court ruled in *Betts v. Brady* that refusal to appoint defense counsel in noncapital cases did not violate the amendment, but that the state did have to provide counsel when defendants had special circumstances, like incompetency or illiteracy. These precedents were shaped further with *Gideon v. Wainwright* (1963).

MUST-KNOW SUPREME COURT DECISIONS: *GIDEON V. WAINWRIGHT* (1963)

The Constitutional Question Before the Court: Does a state's prosecution of a criminal defendant without counsel constitute a violation of the Sixth Amendment's right to counsel?

Decision: Yes, for Gideon, 9:0

Facts: Clarence Earl Gideon, a drifter who had served jail time in four previous instances, was arrested for breaking and entering a Florida pool hall and stealing some packaged drinks and coins from a cigarette machine. He came to his trial expecting the local court to appoint him a lawyer because he had been provided one in other states in previous trials.

Source: State of Florida

Clarence Earl Gideon

The Supreme Court had already ruled that states must provide counsel in the case of an indigent defendant facing the death penalty, or in a case in which the defendant has special circumstances, such as illiteracy or psychological incapacity. At the time of Gideon's trial, 45 states appointed attorneys to all indigent defendants. Florida, however, did not.

Gideon was convicted and sent away to Florida's state prison in Raiford. From prison, Gideon filed an *in forma pauperis* brief with the Supreme Court, a procedure "in the form of a pauper" available to those who believe they were wrongly convicted and do not have the means to appeal through the typical channels. The Court receives thousands of these each year, and every now and then it deems one worthy. The Court appointed an attorney for Gideon to argue this case. His attorney argued that the Fourteenth Amendment's due process clause required states to follow the Sixth Amendment provision. Since this decision in *Gideon v. Wainwright*, all states must pay for a public defender when a defendant cannot afford one.

The Court voted 9:0 for Gideon and ruled that Florida had to provide defense attorneys to all indigent defendants regardless of the severity of the crime.

Reasoning: The Court reasoned that a basic principle of the American system of government is that every defendant should have an equal chance at a fair trial and that without an attorney, a defendant does not have that equal chance. In the majority opinion, Justice Black quoted from a number of previous cases that supported the appointment of an attorney for indigent persons and argued that the 1942 case of *Betts v. Brady* went against the Court's own precedents. Further, the Court reasoned that there was no logical basis to the distinction between a capital offense, which would allow the appointment of an attorney for an indigent person, and a noncapital offense, which until the Gideon decision would not have allowed free legal representation to indigent persons.

The Court's Majority Opinion by Mr. Justice Hugo Black: In returning to these old precedents, we . . . restore constitutional principles established to achieve a fair system of justice. Not only these precedents, but also reason and reflection, require us to recognize that, in our adversary system of criminal justice, any person hauled into court, who is too poor to hire a lawyer, cannot be assured a fair trial unless counsel is provided for him. This seems to us to be an obvious truth. Governments, both state and federal, quite properly spend vast sums of money to establish machinery to try defendants accused of crime. Lawyers to prosecute are everywhere deemed essential to protect the public's interest in an orderly society. Similarly, there are few defendants charged with crime, few indeed, who fail to hire the best lawyers they can get to prepare and present their defenses. That government hires lawyers to prosecute and defendants who have the money hire lawyers to defend are the strongest indications of the widespread belief that lawyers in criminal courts are necessities, not luxuries. The right of one charged with crime to counsel may not be deemed fundamental and essential to fair trials in some countries, but it is in ours. from the very beginning, our state and national constitutions and laws have laid great emphasis on procedural and substantive safeguards designed to assure fair trials before impartial tribunals in which every defendant stands equal before the law. This noble ideal cannot be realized if the poor man charged with crime has to face his accusers without a lawyer to assist him.

Political Science Disciplinary Practices: Explain how the Court's Decision Relates to Political Principles

Justice Clark states in his concurring opinion that "there cannot constitutionally be a difference in the quality of the process based merely upon a supposed difference in the sanction involved." With this statement he affirms that if the principle of due process applies in one instance it should apply in other instances comparable in important ways. Examine how the Court's decision relates to other principles through the activity below.

Apply: Complete the following tasks.

1. Explain the principles on which Justice Black's opinion relies.

2. Explain the relationship between the Sixth and Fourteenth Amendments as they apply to selective incorporation.

3. Explain how the decision in this case balances the principles of individual liberties and state powers.

REFLECT ON THE ESSENTIAL QUESTION

Essential Question: *To what extent are states limited by the due process clause from infringing upon individual rights? On separate paper, complete the chart below.*

Due Process Cases and Laws	How the Case/Law Protects or Infringes Upon Individual Rights

KEY TERMS AND NAMES

exclusionary rule
Fifth Amendment (1791)
Fourth Amendment (1791)
Gideon v. Wainwright (1963)
Mapp v. Ohio (1961)
metadata
Miranda v. Arizona (1966)

New Jersey v. TLO (1985)
procedural due process
public safety exception
search and seizure
Sixth Amendment (1791)
USA FREEDOM Act (2015)

Amendments: Due Process and the Right to Privacy

"The explosive growth in the collection and sale of consumer information enabled by new technology poses unprecedented risks for Americans' privacy. The government has failed to respond to these new threats."

—Senator Ron Wyden (D-OR), on Consumer Data
Protection Act, 2018

Essential Question: To what extent are states limited by the due process clause from infringing upon individuals' rights to privacy?

The framers didn't explicitly state that citizens have a "right to privacy" in the Constitution. This idea of a "right to be left alone" or a right to privacy can be pulled from the wording of several amendments. The First Amendment deals with the privacy of one's thoughts or associations with others. The Third protects the privacy of one's home from the government's no-longer-used practice of mandating that private citizens house soldiers in peacetime. The Fourth protects against illegal searches, keeping a home or other area (purses, lockers) private. The Fifth entitles an accused defendant to refrain from testifying and thus to keep information private. Also, the Ninth Amendment is a cautionary limit to the power of the federal government in general, which states that the people have rights not specifically listed, such as privacy.

Substantive Due Process

Substantive due process places substantive limits on what liberties the government can take away or deprive a citizen of. If the substance of the law— the very point of the law—violates some basic right, even one not listed in the Constitution, then a court can declare it unconstitutional. State government policies that might violate substantive due process rights must meet some valid state or public interest to promote the police powers of regulating health, welfare, or morals. The right to substantive due process protects people from policies for which no legitimate state interest exists or the state interest fails to override the citizens' rights.

Substantive Due Process Denied

These policies became a thorny issue as labor unions and corporations debated the Constitution and while legislatures tried to promote the health and safety of citizens. The 1873 *Slaughterhouse Cases* forced a decision on the privileges or immunities clause of the recently ratified Fourteenth Amendment. The *Slaughterhouse Cases* were a group of cases relating to the state of Louisiana's consolidation of slaughterhouses into one government-run operation outside of New Orleans, causing butchers in other locations to close up shop and thereby infringing on their right to pursue lawful employment. The majority opinion ruled that the Fourteenth Amendment's privileges or immunities clause protected only those rights related to national citizenship and did not apply to the states, even though the state law in this case limited the butchers' basic right to pursue lawful employment. In a dissenting opinion, Justice Joseph Bradley asserted that "the right of any citizen to follow whatever lawful employment he chooses to adopt . . . is one of his most valuable rights and one which the legislature of a State cannot invade," so a law that violates such a fundamental, inalienable right cannot be constitutional. The Court majority, however, interpreted the law on a procedural basis rather than addressing the substance of the right involved. In later years, when the Court addressed business regulation in the industrial period, it developed the substantive due process doctrine in relation to state and federal regulations in the workplace.

Right to Privacy

In the 1960s, a new class of substantive due process suits came to the Court that sought to protect individual rights, especially those of privacy and lifestyle. In **Griswold v. Connecticut** (1965), the Court ruled an old anti-birth control state statute in violation of the Constitution. The overturned law had barred married couples from even receiving birth control literature. The Court for the first time emphasized an inherent **right to privacy** that, although not expressly mentioned in the Bill of Rights, could be found in the penumbras (shadows) of the First, Third, Fourth, and Ninth Amendments. The Court further bolstered the right to privacy in the **Roe v. Wade** (1973) decision. Primarily addressing the question of whether Texas or other states could prevent a woman from aborting her fetus, the decision rested on a substantive due process right against such a law. Whether a pregnant woman was to have or abort her baby was a private decision between her and her doctor and outside the reach of the government. These two cases together revived the substantive due process doctrine first laid down a century earlier.

MUST-KNOW SUPREME COURT CASE: *ROE V. WADE* (1973)

The Constitutional Question Before the Court: Does Texas's anti-abortion statute violate the due process clause of the Fourteenth Amendment and a woman's constitutional right to an abortion?

Decision: Yes, for Roe, 7:2

Facts: In 1971, when Texas resident Norma McCorvey, a single circus worker, became pregnant for the third time at age 21, she sought an abortion. States had developed anti-abortion laws since the early 1900s, and this case reached the Court as the national debate about morality, responsibility, freedom, and women's rights had peaked. At the time, only four states allowed abortions as in this case, and Texas was not one of them (Texas did allow abortions in cases when the mother's life was at stake).

With Attorney Sarah Weddington of the American Civil Liberties Union (ACLU), McCorvey filed suit against local District Attorney Henry Wade. To protect her identity the Court dubbed the plaintiff "Jane Roe" and the case became known as *Roe v. Wade*.

Reasoning: The legal principle on which the case rests was new and somewhat revolutionary. Weddington and her team argued that Texas had violated Roe's "right to privacy" and that it was not the government's decision to determine a pregnant woman's medical decision. Though there is no expressed right to privacy in the Constitution, the Court had decided in *Griswold v. Connecticut* in 1965 that the right to privacy was present in the penumbras of the Bill of Rights. Meanwhile, the state stood by its legal authority to regulate health, morals, and welfare under the police powers doctrine, while much of the public argued the procedure violated a moral code. Roe relied largely on the Fourteenth Amendment's due process clause, arguing that the state violated her broadly understood liberty by denying the abortion. However, the majority opinion recognized that the "potentiality of human life" represented by the unborn child is also of interest to the state.

> **The Court's Majority Opinion by Mr. Justice Harry Blackmun, with which Justices Douglas, Brennan, Stewart, Marshall, Powell, and Chief Justice Burger joined:** State criminal abortion laws, like those involved here . . . violate the Due Process Clause of the Fourteenth Amendment, which protects against state action the right to privacy, including a woman's qualified right to terminate her pregnancy. Though the State cannot override that right, it has legitimate interests in protecting both the pregnant woman's health and the potentiality of human life, each of which interests grows and reaches a "compelling" point at various stages of the woman's approach to term . . . .
>
> (a) For the stage prior to approximately the end of the first trimester, the abortion decision and its effectuation must be left to the medical judgment of the pregnant woman's attending physician.
>
> (b) For the stage subsequent to approximately the end of the first trimester, the State, in promoting its interest in the health of the mother, may, if it chooses, regulate the abortion procedure in ways that are reasonably related to maternal health.
>
> (c) For the stage subsequent to viability the State, in promoting its interest in the potentiality of human life, may, if it chooses, regulate, and even proscribe, abortion except where necessary, in appropriate medical judgment, for the preservation of the life or health of the mother.

Justice Stewart wrote a concurring opinion that stressed the foundational role of substantive due process and the Fourteenth Amendment in arriving at the majority opinion, arguing that the liberty to which the Fourteenth Amendment refers must be understood broadly.

In dissenting opinions, Justice Rehnquist raised a technical question about the legal standing of the case, questioning whether Roe, who already gave birth to her baby (and had given the baby up for adoption), could file a complaint on behalf of others who might find themselves in her position. He wrote that plaintiffs "may not seek vindications for the rights of others." Justice White addressed substantial disagreement with the interpretation of the majority.

Since *Roe*: The Court has addressed a series of cases on abortion since *Roe* and the abortion issue inevitably comes up at election time and during Supreme Court nominees' confirmation hearings. In *Planned Parenthood v. Casey*, the Court outlawed a Pennsylvania law designed to discourage women from getting an abortion or expose abortion patients via public records. It also did not uphold the "informed consent" portion of the law that required the aborting woman (mother), married or unmarried, to inform and secure consent from the father. However, the *Casey* decision did uphold such state requirements as a waiting period, providing information on abortion alternatives, and requiring parental (or judge's) consent for pregnant teens.

Political Science Disciplinary Practices: Explain the Court's Reasoning

The *Roe* case against the Texas law forbidding abortion came to the Supreme Court on appeal after a decision by the United States District Court for the Northern District of Texas. That decision struck down the Texas law on the basis of the Ninth Amendment, relying in part on the decision in *Griswold*. The Supreme Court, however, based its decision on the due process clause of the Fourteenth Amendment, reinforcing substantive due process.

Apply: Complete the following tasks.

1. Analyze the wording in the due process clause of the Fourteenth Amendment that supports the privacy right of a woman to decide whether or not to carry her unborn child to term. (See Topic 3.7 for the Fourteenth Amendment.) Explain your answer.

2. Explain how the Court distinguished different legal standards throughout a woman's pregnancy.

3. Explain the competing interests the Court had to consider and how it balanced those interests.

4. Explain the issues related to federalism in this decision.

5. Explain the similarities and differences in the *Roe* and *Planned Parenthood* rulings.

Roe and Later Abortion Rulings Before 1973, abortion on demand was legal in only four states. The *Roe* decision made it unconstitutional for a state to ban abortion for a woman during the first trimester, the first three months of her pregnancy. An array of other state regulations developed in response. States passed statutes to prevent abortion at state-funded hospitals and clinics. They adjusted their laws to prevent late-term abortions. In 1976, Congress passed the **Hyde Amendment** (named for Illinois Congressman Henry Hyde) to prevent federal funding that might contribute to an abortion.

THINK AS A POLITICAL SCIENTIST: *DESCRIBE THE REASONING OF A REQUIRED SUPREME COURT CASE*

When more than half of the justices of the Supreme Court agree on a ruling, it constitutes a majority decision. The most senior justice voting in the majority (always the chief justice if he or she is in the majority) will pick who writes the majority opinion, or explanation of the ruling. The excerpt below is from *Roe v. Wade*. Justice Blackmun justified the decision of the Court in his majority opinion.

Practice: Read the passage and answer the questions below.

". . . The Constitution does not explicitly mention any right of privacy. . . .[T]he Court has recognized that a right of personal privacy, or a guarantee of certain areas or zones of privacy, does exist under the Constitution. . . . This right of privacy, whether it be founded in the 14th Amendment's concept of personal liberty and restrictions upon state action, as we feel it is, or, as the District Court determined, in the Ninth Amendment's reservation of rights to the people, is broad enough to encompass a woman's decision whether or not to terminate her pregnancy. The detriment that the State would impose upon the pregnant woman by denying this choice altogether is apparent. Specific and direct harm medically diagnosable even in early pregnancy may be involved. Maternity, or additional offspring, may force upon the woman a distressful life and future. Psychological harm may be imminent. Mental and physical health may be taxed by childcare. There is also the distress, for all concerned, associated with the unwanted child, and there is the problem of bringing a child into a family already unable, psychologically and otherwise, to care for it. In other cases, as in this one, the additional difficulties and continuing stigma of unwed motherhood may be involved. All these are factors the woman and her responsible physician necessarily will consider in consultation."

1. How does Justice Blackmun use the Ninth Amendment to explain the ruling?
2. What additional reasoning does Justice Blackmun use to support the ruling of the case?

REFLECT ON THE ESSENTIAL QUESTION

Essential Question: *To what extent are states limited by the due process clause from infringing upon individuals' rights to privacy? On separate paper, complete the chart below.*

Right to Privacy Cases and Laws	How the Case/Law Protects or Infringes Upon Privacy Rights

KEY TERMS AND NAMES

Griswold v. Connecticut (1965)
Hyde Amendment (1976)
right to privacy

Roe v. Wade (1973)
substantive due process

CHAPTER 10 Review:
Learning Objectives and Key Terms

TOPIC 3.7: Explain the implications of the doctrine of selective incorporation. (LOR-3.A)

Selective Incorporation and States' Rights (LOR-3.A.1)

District of Columbia v. Heller (2008)	just compensation clause
due process	*McDonald v. Chicago* (2010)
Fourteenth Amendment (1868)	selective incorporation

TOPIC 3.8: Explain the extent to which states are limited by the due process clause from infringing upon individual rights. (LOR-3.B)

Restricting Indivdual Liberty (LOR-3.B.1)

New Jersey v. TLO (1985)

public safety exception

USA FREEDOM Act (2015)

Protecting Due Process (LOR-3.B.2–4)

exclusionary rule

Fifth Amendment (1791)

Fourth Amendment (1791)

Gideon v. Wainwright (1963)

Mapp v. Ohio (1961)

metadata

Miranda v. Arizona (1966)

procedural due process

search and seizure

Sixth Amendment (1791)

TOPIC 3.9: Explain the extent to which states are limited by the due process clause from infringing upon individual rights. (LOR-3.B)

Right to Privacy (LOR-2.B.5)

Griswold v. Connecticut (1965)	*Roe v. Wade* (1973)
Hyde Amendment (1976)	substantive due process
right to privacy	

CHAPTER 10 Checkpoint:
Due Process

Topics 3.7–3.9

MULTIPLE-CHOICE QUESTIONS

1. Which statement best describes the Supreme Court's interpretation of the Fourteenth Amendment?

   (C) The Fourteenth Amendment has restricted the application of judicial review.

   (D) The Fourteenth Amendment prevents states from taxing agencies of the federal government.

   (E) The Fourteenth Amendment's due process clause makes most rights contained in the Bill of Rights applicable to the states.

   (F) The Fourteenth Amendment's equal protection clause assures equality with regard to race, not gender.

2. Which of the following is an accurate comparison of substantive and procedural due process?

	Substantive Due Process	Procedural Due Process
(A)	Deals with "the how" of the law, or steps in carrying out the law	Must be followed by the states, not the federal government
(B)	Is followed when the ideas or points of the law are fundamentally fair and just	Focuses on the manner in which government acts toward its citizens
(C)	Applicable because of the Fifth Amendment, not the Fourteenth Amendment	Was violated in the *Roe v. Wade* case according to the Supreme Court
(D)	Must be followed by the federal government, not state governments	Is followed when state governors follow the legislative process in governing

3. Which of the following is an accurate description of the implication of the *McDonald v. Chicago* (2010) ruling and selective incorporation?

   (A) The ruling was based upon the Second Amendment only.

   (B) The case overturned a gun-restriction policy in the District of Columbia.

   (C) The case was first heard by the Supreme Court through an original jurisdiction case.

   (D) The ruling prevented infringement of basic liberties.

4. Which of the following is an accurate summary of the selective incorporation doctrine?

(A) Government policies can involve religion as long as these are decided selectively.

(B) States must protect most rights in the Bill of Rights based on the Fourteenth Amendment's due process clause.

(C) The Supreme Court is cautious about which civil liberties cases it accepts.

(D) The framers of the Constitution were selective about which rights they included.

Questions 5 and 6 refer to the graphic below.

MIRANDA WARNING

1. **YOU HAVE THE RIGHT TO REMAIN SILENT.**
2. ANYTHING YOU SAY CAN AND WILL BE USED AGAINST YOU IN A COURT OF LAW
3. YOU HAVE THE RIGHT TO TALK TO A LAWYER AND HAVE HIM PRESENT WITH YOU WHILE YOU ARE BEING QUESTIONED
4. IF YOU CANNOT AFFORD TO HIRE A LAWYER, ON EWILL BE APPOINTED TO REPRESENT YOU BEFORE ANY QUESTIONING IF YOU WISH.
5. YOU CAN DECIDE AT ANY TIME TO EXERCISE THESE RIGHTS AND NOT ANSWER ANY QUESTIONS OR MAKE ANY STATEMENTS.

WAIVER

DO YOU UNDERSTAND EACH OF THESE RIGHTS I HAVE EXPLAINED TO YOU? HAVING THESE RIGHTS IN MIND, DO YOU WISH TO TALK TO US NOW?

5. Which of the following best describes the information in the infographic?

(A) It is required reading before the police can conduct a lawful search.

(B) It requires law enforcement to protect civil liberties.

(C) It must be read to a defendant at the beginning of a trial.

(D) It results from the state's police powers.

6. The above information fulfills the application of an accused person's due process rights as protected by the

(A) First and Second Amendments

(B) Fourth and Tenth Amendments

(C) Fifth and Sixth Amendments

(D) Fourth and Fifth Amendments

Concept Application

1. "The defendants were convicted of conspiring to violate the National Prohibition Act. Before any of the persons now charged had been arrested or indicted, the telephones by means of which they habitually communicated with one another and with others had been [wire] tapped by federal officers. . . . [T]he defendants objected to the admission of the evidence obtained by wiretapping on the ground that the Government's wiretapping constituted an unreasonable search and seizure . . . Discovery and invention have made it possible for the Government, by means far more effective than stretching upon the rack, to obtain disclosure in court of what is whispered in the closet. . . . Whenever a telephone line is tapped, the privacy of the persons at both ends of the line is invaded and all conversations between them upon any subject, and, although proper, confidential and privileged, may be overheard. Moreover, the tapping of one man's telephone line involves the tapping of the telephone of every other person whom he may call or who may call him. As a means of espionage, writs of assistance and general warrants are but puny instruments of tyranny and oppression when compared with wiretapping."

   —Justice Louis Brandeis, Dissenting Opinion,
   Olmstead v. United States, 1928

   After reading the scenario, respond to A, B, and C below:

   (A) Describe Justice Brandeis's point of view on the government and its infringing on individual liberty.

   (B) In the context of this scenario, explain how Justice Brandeis's point of view described in Part A has subsequently enhanced Fourth Amendment protections.

   (C) In the context of the scenario, explain how either the executive branch or legislative branch of government could take action to address the justice's concern.

Quantitative Analysis

Appeals Courts' Pro-Student Rulings on Challenges to Discipline

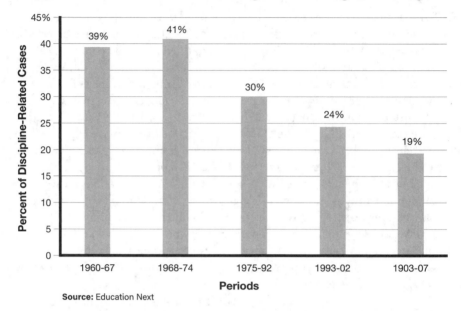

Source: Education Next

2. Use the information graphic above to answer the following questions.

   (A) Identify the percent of pro-student rulings by appeals courts from 1975–1992.

   (B) Describe a trend in the appeals courts' pro-student rulings.

   (C) Draw a conclusion about what led to the trend described in part B.

   (D) Explain how the data in the chart could result from judicial interpretation of students' constitutional rights.

SCOTUS Comparison

3. In *Planned Parenthood v. Casey* (1992), the Supreme Court ruled on a case that challenged a Pennsylvania law that placed certain requirements on women seeking an abortion. These were: (1) a doctor had to provide information on the procedure to the woman at least 24 hours before the procedure; (2) in most cases, a married woman had to notify her husband of the planned procedure; (3) minors had to obtain informed consent from a parent or guardian or let the court assume a parental role; (4) if a doctor determined the pregnancy was a medical emergency endangering the mother, an abortion could be performed; (5) facilities providing abortions were held to reporting and record-keeping standards. A divided Court upheld the essential ruling in *Roe v. Wade* but said that the state could not interfere with a woman's right to an abortion until the fetus reached viability—the condition that would allow it to survive outside the womb—which could happen as early as 22 weeks. The ruling also set an "undue burden" test for state abortion laws—those that presented an undue burden on the mother seeking an abortion were unconstitutional. The only one of the five provisions explained above that failed that test was the notification of the husband.

(A) Identify the constitutional right that is common to both *Planned Parenthood v. Casey* (1992) and *Roe v. Wade* (1973).

(B) Based on the constitutional right identified in part A, explain why the facts of the case in *Planned Parenthood v. Casey* led to a different holding than that in *Roe v. Wade*.

(C) Describe an action interest groups could take to limit the impact of the ruling in *Planned Parenthood v. Casey*.

CHAPTER 11

Civil Rights

Topics 3.10–3.13

Topic 3.10 Social Movements and Equal Protection

PRD-1.A: Explain how constitutional provisions have supported and motivated social movements.

- Required Foundational Documents:
  - The Constitution of the United States
  - "Letter from a Birmingham Jail"

Topic 3.11 Government Response to Social Movements

PMI-3.A: Explain how the government has responded to social movements.

- Required Foundational Document:
  - The Constitution of the United States
- Required Supreme Court Case:
  - *Brown v. Board of Education* (1954)

Topic 3.12 Balancing Minority and Majority Rights

CON-6.A: Explain how the Court has at times allowed the restriction of the civil rights of minority groups and at other times has protected those rights.

- Required Supreme Court Case:
  - *Brown v. Board of Education* (1954)

Topic 3.13 Affirmative Action

CON-6.A: Explain how the Court has at times allowed the restriction of the civil rights of minority groups and at other times has protected those rights.

Source: Wikimedia Commons

President Lyndon Johnson meets with civil rights leaders Martin Luther King Jr. of the Southern Christian Leadership Conference (left), Whitney Young of the Urban League (second from the right), and James Farmer from the Congress of Racial Equality (far right) in 1964.

Social Movements and Equal Protection

"It ought to be possible . . . for American students of any color to attend any public institution they select without having to be backed up by troops. . . . for American consumers of any color to receive equal service in places of public accommodation, [and] to register and to vote in a free election without interference or fear of reprisal."

—President John F. Kennedy, White House Address, 1963

Essential Question: How have constitutional provisions supported and motivated social movements?

The United States places a high priority on freedom and equality and **civil rights**, protections from discrimination based on such characteristics as race, color, national origin, religion, and sex. These principles are evident in the founding documents, later constitutional amendments, and laws such as the 1964 Civil Rights Act. They are guaranteed to all citizens under the due process and **equal protection clauses** in the Constitution and according to acts of Congress. Civil rights organizations representing African Americans and women have pushed for government to deliver on the promises in these documents. In recent years, other groups—Latinos, people with disabilities, and LGBTQ individuals—have petitioned the government for fundamental fairness and equality. A pro-life movement emerged to fight for the rights of the unborn, and a pro-choice movement fought for the right of women to control decisions about their bodies. All three branches have responded in varying degrees to these movements and have addressed civil rights issues. Even so, racism, sexism, and other forms of bigotry have not disappeared. Today, a complex body of law shaped by constitutional provisions, Supreme Court decisions, federal statutes, executive directives, and citizen-state interactions defines civil rights in America.

Equality in Black and White

In the United States, federal and state governments generally ignored civil rights policy before the Civil War. The framers of the Constitution left the legal question of slavery up to the states, allowing the South to strengthen its plantation system and relegate enslaved and free African Americans to subservience. The North had a sparse black population and little regard for fairness toward African Americans. Abolitionists, religious leaders, and progressives sought to outlaw slavery and advocated for African Americans in the mid-1800s.

The NAACP Pushes Ahead

The Fourteenth Amendment's equal protection clause spurred citizens to take action. One organization, the **National Association for the Advancement of Colored People (NAACP)** stood apart from the others in promoting equal rights for African Americans. State-sponsored discrimination and a violent race riot in Springfield, Illinois, led civil rights leaders to create the NAACP in 1909. On Abraham Lincoln's birthday, a handful of academics, philanthropists, and journalists sent out a call for a national conference. Harvard graduate and Atlanta University professor Dr. W.E.B. DuBois was among those elected as the association's first leaders. By 1919, the organization had more than 90,000 members.

Before World War I, the NAACP and its leaders pressed President Woodrow Wilson to overturn segregation in federal agencies and departments. The citizen group had also hired two men as full-time lobbyists in Washington, one for the House and one for the Senate. The association joined in filing a case to challenge a law that limited voter rights based on the then-legal status of voters' grandparents. (See Topic 3.11 for more on this "grandfather clause.") The Supreme Court ruled the practice a violation of the Fifteenth Amendment. Two years later, the Court again sided with the NAACP when it ruled government-imposed residential segregation a constitutional violation.

Legal Defense Fund

The NAACP has regularly argued cases in the Supreme Court. It added a legal team that was led by Charles Hamilton Houston, a Howard University law professor, and his assistant, Baltimore native Thurgood Marshall. They defended mostly innocent black citizens across the South in front of racist judges and juries. They successfully convinced the Supreme Court to outlaw the white primary—a primary in which only white citizens could vote. In southern states, the white primary had essentially extinguished the post-Civil War Republican Party, the party of Lincoln, allowing southern Democrats to stay in power and pass discriminatory laws.

The NAACP began a legal strategy to chip away at state school segregation, filing lawsuits to integrate first college and graduate schools and then K–12 schools. Early success came in 1938, when Lloyd Gaines integrated the University of Missouri's Law School. The state had offered to pay his out-of-state tuition at a neighboring law school, but the Fourteenth Amendment specifically requires states to treat the races equally and failing to provide a "separate but equal" law school, the Court claimed, violated the Constitution. In 1950, the NAACP won decisions against schools in Oklahoma and Texas to provide integrated graduate and law schools.

Motivating the Movement

Additional groups joined the NAACP in the effort to make the United States a place of equality. The Congress on Racial Equality, the Urban League, and the Southern Christian Leadership Conference, led by **Dr. Martin Luther King Jr.**, took up the cause of racial equality. The civil rights movement had a pivotal year in 1963, with both glorious and horrific consequences. On one hand, King assisted the grassroots protests in Birmingham and more than 200,000 people gathered in the nation's capital for the March on Washington. On the other hand, Mississippi NAACP leader Medgar Evers was shot and killed. In Birmingham, brutal police Chief Bull Connor turned fire hoses and police dogs on peaceful African American protesters.

Amid the face-offs and protests of the movement, in one of the darker but telling moments of the movement, authorities arrested Dr. Martin Luther King for leading a protest despite a court order forbidding civil rights demonstrations. From his cell in the Birmingham jail, he wrote his discourse on race relations at the time.

FOUNDATIONAL DOCUMENTS: *"LETTER FROM A BIRMINGHAM JAIL"*

Motivated by the Fourteenth Amendment's **equal protection clause**, on April 12, 1963—Good Friday, the Friday before Easter—the Alabama Christian Movement for Human Rights and the Southern Christian Leadership Conference sponsored a parade down the streets of Birmingham, Alabama, to protest the continued segregation of the city's businesses, public spaces, and other institutions. Three key leaders headed the march of about 50 participants: the Reverends Fred Shuttlesworth, Ralph Abernathy, and Dr. Martin Luther King Jr. Because the city feared disruption from the march, the protesters had been denied a parade permit, and, on those grounds, Dr. King and Ralph Abernathy were arrested and put in jail.

On the day of the march, "A Call for Unity," written by eight white clergymen from Birmingham and published in a Birmingham newspaper, called on the protesters to abandon their plans, arguing that the proper way to obtain equal rights was to be patient and let those in a position to negotiate do their job. While serving 11 days in solitary confinement in a Birmingham jail, Dr. King composed a response to the clergymens' request and, in so doing, laid out the foundations for the nonviolent resistance to segregation that guided the civil rights movement.

Fred Shuttlesworth (left), Ralph Abernathy (middle), and Martin Luther King Jr. lead the Good Friday March.

In any nonviolent campaign there are four basic steps: 1) Collection of the facts to determine whether injustices are alive. 2) Negotiation. 3) Self-purification and 4) Direct Action. We have gone through all of these steps in Birmingham. Birmingham is probably the most thoroughly segregated city in the United States. Its ugly record of police brutality is known in every section of this country. Its unjust treatment of Negroes in the courts is a notorious reality. There have been more unsolved bombings of Negro homes and churches in Birmingham than any city in the nation. These are the hard, brutal and unbelievable facts. On the basis of these conditions Negro leaders sought to negotiate with the city fathers. But the political leaders consistently refused to engage in good faith negotiation . . . we had no alternative except that of preparing for direct action, whereby we would present our very bodies as a means of laying our case before the conscience of the local and the national community. We were not unmindful of the difficulties involved. So we decided to go through a process of self-purification. We started having workshops on nonviolence and repeatedly asked ourselves the questions, "Are you able to accept blows without retaliating?" "Are you able to endure the ordeals of jail?"

Dr. King also expressed disappointment in the white clergy, in whom he had hoped and expected to find allies. Yet he tried to understand their call for patience.

We know through painful experience that freedom is never voluntarily given by the oppressor; it must be demanded by the oppressed. For years now I have heard the word "Wait!" . . . I guess it is easy for those who have never felt the stinging darts of segregation to say, "Wait." But when you have seen vicious mobs lynch your mothers and fathers at will and drown your sisters and brothers at whim; when you have seen hate filled policemen curse, kick, brutalize and even kill your black brothers and sisters with impunity; when you see the vast majority of your twenty million Negro brothers smothering in an air tight cage of poverty in the midst of an affluent society; . . . when you are forever fighting a degenerating sense of "nobodiness;" then you will understand why we find it difficult to wait. There comes a time when the cup of endurance runs over, and men are no longer willing to be plunged into an abyss of injustice where they experience the bleakness of corroding despair. I hope, Sirs, you can understand our legitimate and unavoidable impatience.

Political Science Disciplinary Practices: Explain How Argument Influences Behaviors

Dr. King's "Letter from a Birmingham Jail" is an argument—or more precisely, a counterargument. King addresses each of the points the white clergy make in "A Call for Unity" to make a clear case for the need for nonviolent direct action. Think about the implications of that argument on the political behaviors of African Americans and whites.

Apply: Complete the following activities.

1. Explain how the four basic steps of a nonviolent campaign were carried out in Birmingham before the Good Friday demonstration.

2. Explain the implications of Dr. King's argument on breaking or upholding the law.

3. Compare the lawbreaking of the protestors marching without a permit to the lawbreaking King refers to by mobs.

4. Explain how the civil rights movement was motivated by constitutional provisions.

Then read the full "Letter from a Birmingham Jail" online.

Women's Rights Movement

Obtaining the franchise, the right to vote, was key to altering public policy toward women, and Susan B. Anthony led the way. In 1872, in direct violation of New York law, she walked into a polling place and cast a vote. An all-male jury later convicted her. She later authored the passage that would eventually make it into the Constitution as the Nineteenth Amendment (1920).

Women and Industry

Industrialization of the late 1800s brought more women into the workplace. They often worked for less pay than men in urban factories. In 1908, noted attorney Louis Brandeis defended an Oregon law preventing women from working long hours. Brandeis argued that women were less suited physically for longer hours and needed to be healthy to bear children. The Court upheld a state's right to make laws that treated women differently. This consideration protected the health and safety of women, but the double standard gave lawmakers justification to treat women differently.

Suffragists pressed on. By 1914, 11 states allowed women to vote. In the 1916 election, both major political parties endorsed the concept of women's suffrage in their platforms and Jeanette Rankin of Montana became the first woman elected to Congress. The following year, however, World War I completely consumed Congress and the nation and the issue of women's suffrage drifted into the background.

After the war ended, suffragist leader Alice Paul continued to press President Woodrow Wilson, eventually persuading him to support women's suffrage. President Wilson pardoned a group of arrested suffragists and spoke in favor of the amendment, influencing Congress's vote. The measure passed both houses in 1919 and was ratified as the **Nineteenth Amendment** in 1920.

From Suffrage to Action

What impact did the amendment have on voter turnout for women? An in-depth study of a Chicago election from the early 1920s found that 65 percent of potential women voters stayed home, many responding that it wasn't a woman's place to engage in politics or that the act would offend their husbands. Initially, men outvoted women by roughly 30 percent, but that statistic has changed and now turnout at the polls is higher for women than men.

Voting laws were not the states' only unfair practice. The Supreme Court had ruled in 1948 that states could prevent women from tending bar unless the establishment was owned by a close male relative and states were allowed to seat all-male juries. However, women made advancements in the workplace in the 1960s. In 1963, Congress passed the **Equal Pay Act** that required employers to pay men and women the same wage for the same job. However, even after the Equal Pay Act, it was still legal to deny women job opportunities. That is, equal pay applied only when women were hired to do the same jobs that men were hired to do. The 1964 Civil Rights Act protected women from discrimination in employment.

In addition, Betty Friedan, the author of *The Feminine Mystique*, encouraged women to speak their minds, to apply for male-dominated jobs, and to organize for equality in the public sphere. Friedan went on to cofound the **National Organization for Women (NOW)** in 1966.

Women and Equality

In the 1970s, Congress passed legislation to give equal opportunities to women in schools and on college campuses. Pro-equality groups pressured the Court to apply the **strict scrutiny** standard—the analysis by courts to guarantee legislation is narrowly tailored to avoid violation of laws—to policies that treated genders differently. The application of strict scrutiny can be seen most clearly in **Title IX** of the Education Amendments of 1972, which guaranteed that women have the same educational opportunities as men in programs receiving federal government funding. (See Topic 3.12.)

However, the women's movement fell short of some of its goals. The Court never declared that legal gender classification deserves the same level of strict scrutiny as classifications based on race. Additionally, the movement was unable to amend the Constitution to declare absolute equality of the sexes. The proposed **Equal Rights Amendment (ERA)** stated "Equality of rights under the law shall not be denied on account of sex" and gave Congress power to enforce this. The amendment passed both houses of Congress with the necessary two-thirds vote in 1972. Thirty of the thirty-eight states necessary to ratify the amendment approved the ERA within one year. At its peak, 35 states had ratified the proposal, but when the chance for full ratification expired in 1982, the ERA failed. Nonetheless, the 1970s was a successful decade for women gaining legal rights and elevating their political and legal status.

Roe v. Wade *and the Pro-Life Response*

The *Roe v. Wade* decision (see Topic 3.9), prevented government from outlawing abortion. Though seen as a victory among feminists, most of the population in the 1970s did not approve of the decision. The *Roe* decision likely harmed the credibility of the ERA's allies, such as the National Organization for Women (NOW), a group that advocated for women's rights. Many women's groups and other civil rights groups, such as the American Civil Liberties Union (ACLU), believed state restrictions on abortion denied a pregnant woman and her doctor the right to make a highly personal and private medical choice. The Court in *Roe v. Wade* agreed and decided that a state cannot deny a pregnant woman the right to an abortion during the first trimester of the pregnancy. In a 7:2 decision, the *Roe* opinion erased or modified statutes in most states, effectively legalizing abortion.

However, the battle over abortion has continued. States can still regulate abortion by requiring brief waiting periods and other restrictions. Anti-abortion or pro-life groups continue to press for legal rights for the unborn, many believing that life begins at conception and, for that reason, even a zygote—a fertilized egg—is entitled to legal protection. This argument for a legal recognition of fetal personhood is atop the pro-life movement's agenda.

THINK AS A POLITICAL SCIENTIST: *EXPLAIN HOW THE IMPLICATIONS OF AN AUTHOR'S ARGUMENT AFFECT POLICIES*

After a president nominates a judge to fill a vacancy in the Supreme Court, the Senate Judiciary Committee holds a hearing to question the nominee and decide if the full Senate will vote on the nominee. The responses given by the nominee to Senators' questions during the hearing are vital to receiving a majority vote before a formal appointment.

When Ruth Bader Ginsburg was nominated by President Bill Clinton for a Supreme Court position in 1993, one of the key areas she was questioned on during the confirmation hearing was abortion. Ginsburg's abortion views, specifically her thoughts on *Roe v. Wade* from a lecture she had given at New York University the previous year, came up in questioning. Below is an excerpt from that lecture.

Practice: The following excerpt was in *Time* magazine from Ruth Bader Ginsburg's lecture regarding the ruling in *Roe v. Wade* and its lasting effects. Read the excerpt, and then answer the questions that follow.

The seven to two judgment in *Roe v. Wade* declared "violative [in violation] of the Due Process Clause of the Fourteenth Amendment" a Texas criminal abortion statute that intolerably shackled a woman's autonomy; the Texas law "except[ed] from criminality only a life-saving procedure on behalf of the [pregnant woman]." Suppose the Court had stopped there, rightly declaring unconstitutional the most extreme brand of law in the nation, and had not gone on, as the Court did in *Roe*, to fashion a regime blanketing the subject, a set of rules that displaced virtually every state law then in force. Would there have been the twenty-year controversy we have witnessed, reflected most recently in the Supreme Court's splintered decision in *Planned Parenthood v. Casey*? A less encompassing *Roe,* one that merely struck down the extreme Texas law and went no further on that day, I believe . . . might have served to reduce rather than to fuel controversy.

1. What is the main argument Ginsburg makes in the excerpt?

2. According to Ginsburg, how were policy or other Supreme Court rulings affected by the *Roe* decision?

3. According to Ginsburg, how might policy or other Supreme Court rulings have been affected had the *Roe* decision been different?

LGBTQ Rights and Equality

Like African Americans and women, those who identify as LGBTQ have been discriminated against and have sought and earned legal equality and rights to intimacy, military service, and marriage.

State and federal governments had long set policies that limited the freedoms and liberties of LGBTQ people. President Eisenhower signed an executive order banning any type of "sexual perversion," as it was defined in the order, in any sector of the federal government. Congress enacted an oath of allegiance for immigrants to assure that they were neither communist nor gay. State and local authorities closed gay bars. Meanwhile, the military intensified its exclusion of homosexuals.

The first known public gay rights protest outside the White House took place in 1965. In 1973, psychiatrists removed homosexuality as a mental disorder from their chief diagnostic manual. Throughout the 1970s and 1980s, in part to seek legal protections and gain a political voice, homosexuals "came out" and began publicly proclaiming their sexual identity. A quest for legal marriage followed.

Debates regarding these issues are complex, with a wide array of overlapping constitutional principles. The states' police powers, privacy, and equal protection are all involved. Federalism and geographic mobility create additional complexities. To what degree should the federal government intervene in governing marriage, a reserved power of the states? When gays and lesbians moved from one state to another, differing state laws concerning marriage, adoption, and inheritance brought legal standoffs as the Constitution's full-faith-and-credit clause (Article IV) and the states' reserved powers principle (Tenth Amendment) clashed.

Seeking Legal Intimacy

Traditionalists responded to the growing visibility of gays by passing laws that criminalized homosexual behavior. Though so-called anti-sodomy laws had been around for more than a century, in the 1970s, states passed laws that specifically criminalized same-sex relations and behaviors. In *Lawrence v. Texas* (2003), the court struck down a state law that declared "a person commits an offense if he engages in deviate sexual intercourse with another individual of the same sex." Lawrence's attorneys argued that the equal protection clause voided this law because the statute specifically singled out gays and lesbians. The Court agreed.

Military

Up to the late 20th century, the U.S. military discharged or excluded homosexuals from service. In the 1992 presidential campaign, Democratic candidate Bi ll Clinton promised to end the ban on gays in the military. Clinton won the election but soon discovered that neither commanders nor the rank and file welcomed reversing the ban. In a controversy that mired the first few months of his presidency, Clinton compromised as the Congress passed the **"don't ask, don't tell"** policy in 1994. This rule prevented the military from asking about the private sexual status of its personnel but also prevented gays and lesbians from acknowledging or revealing it. In short, "don't ask, don't tell" was meant to cause both sides to ignore the issue and focus on defending the country.

The debate continued for 17 years. Surveys conducted among military personnel and leadership began to show a favorable response to allowing gays to serve openly. In December 2010, with President Obama's support, the House and Senate voted to remove the "don't ask, don't tell" policy so all service members could openly serve their country.

Marriage

Not long after Hawaii's state supreme court became the first statewide governing institution to legalize same-sex marriage in 1993, lawmakers elsewhere reacted to prevent such a policy change in their backyards. Utah was the first state to pass a law prohibiting the recognition of same-sex marriage. In a presidential election year at a time when public opinion was still decidedly against gay marriages, national lawmakers jumped to define and defend marriage in the halls of Congress. The 1996 **Defense of Marriage Act (DOMA)** defined marriage at the national level and declared that states did not have to accept same-sex marriages recognized in other states. The law also barred federal recognition of same-sex marriage for purposes of Social Security, federal income tax filings, and federal employee benefits. This was a Republican-sponsored bill that earned nearly every Republican vote. Democrats, however, were divided on it. Civil rights pioneer and Congressman John Lewis declared, "I have known racism. I have known bigotry. This bill stinks of the same fear, hatred, and intolerance." The sole Republican vote against the law came from openly gay member Steve Gunderson who asked on the House floor, "Why shouldn't my partner of 13 years be entitled to the same health insurance and survivor's benefits that individuals around here, my colleagues with second and third wives, are able to give them?" The bill passed in the House 342 to 67 and in the Senate 85 to 14. By 2000, 30 states had enacted laws refusing to recognize same-sex marriages in their states or those coming from elsewhere.

If members of the LGBTQ community could legally marry, not only could they publicly enjoy the personal expressions and relationships that go with marriage, they could also begin to enjoy the practical and tangible benefits granted to heterosexual couples: financing a home together, inheriting a deceased partner's estate, and qualifying for spousal employee benefits. In order for these benefits to accrue, states would have to change their marriage statutes.

Initial Legalization The first notable litigation occurred in 1971 when Minnesota's highest court heard a challenge to the state's refusal to issue a marriage license to a same-sex couple. The Supreme Court upheld the decision to not recognize the marriage largely on the definition of marriage in the state's laws and in a dictionary.

These may seem like simple sources for courts to consult, but the issue is very basic: Should the state legally recognize same-sex partnerships and, if so, should the state refer to it as "marriage"? In the past two decades, the United States has battled over these two questions, as advocates sought for legal equality and as public opinion on these questions shifted dramatically.

Vermont was an early state to legally recognize same-sex relationships and did so via the Vermont Supreme Court. The legislature then passed Vermont's "civil unions" law, which declared that same-sex couples have "all the same benefits, protections and responsibilities under law . . . as are granted to spouses in a civil marriage" but stopped short of calling the new legal union a "marriage." Massachusetts' high court also declared its traditional marriage statute out of line, which encouraged the state to legalize same-sex marriage there. What followed was a decade-long battle between conservative opposition and LGBTQ advocates, first in the courts and then at the ballot box, creating a patchwork of marriage law across the United States. By 2011, more than half of the public consistently favored legalizing same-sex marriage, and support for it has generally grown since.

Two Supreme Court rulings secured same-sex marriage nationally. The first was filed by New York state resident Edith Windsor, legally married in Canada to a woman named Thea Spyer. Spyer died in 2009. Under New York state law, Windsor's same-sex marriage was recognized, but it was not recognized under federal law, which governed federal inheritance taxes. Windsor thus owed taxes in excess of $350,000. A widow from a traditional marriage in the same situation would have saved that amount. The Court saw the injustice and ruled that DOMA created "a disadvantage, a separate status, and so a stigma" on same-sex marriage that was legally recognized by New York.

After separate rulings in similar cases at the sixth and ninth circuit courts of appeals, the Supreme Court decided to hear ***Obergefell v. Hodges*** (2015). In that case, the Court considered two questions: Does the Fourteenth Amendment require a state to issue a marriage license to two people of the same sex?" and "Does the Fourteenth Amendment require a state to recognize a marriage between two people of the same sex when their marriage was lawfully licensed and performed out-of-state?" If the answer to the first question is "yes," then the second question becomes moot. On June 26, 2015, the Court ruled 5:4 that states preventing same-sex marriage violated the Constitution. Justice Anthony Kennedy wrote the opinion, his fourth pro-gay rights opinion in nearly 20 years.

Issues Since *Obergefell* Within a year of the same-sex marriage ruling, the percent of cohabiting married same-sex couples rose from about 38 to 49, according to *Congressional Quarterly*. Now the Court has ruled that states cannot deny gays the right to marry, but not all Americans have accepted the ruling. Some public officials refused to carry out their duties to issue marriage licenses, claiming that doing so violated their personal or religious views of marriage. In 2016, about 200 state-level anti-LGBT bills were introduced (only four became law). Though the *Obergefell* decision was recent and was determined by a close vote of the Court, public opinion is moving in such a direction that the ruling is on its way to becoming settled law. Yet controversies around other public policies—such as hiring or firing people because they are transgender, refusing to rent housing to same-sex couples, or refusing business services, such as catering, for same-sex weddings—affect the LGBT community and have brought debates and changes in the law.

Workplace Discrimination

When the 1964 Civil Rights Act prevented employers from refusing employment or firing employees for reasons of race, color, sex, nationality, or religion, it did not include homosexuality or gender identity as reasons. No federal statute has come to pass that would protect LGBT groups. Twenty-two states and the District of Columbia barred such discriminatory practices and afforded a method for victims of such discrimination to take action against the employer. Conservatives argued that these policies created a special class for the LGBT community and were thus unequal and unconstitutional. (The map on the next page shows the states' employment protections in 2018.) However, a 2020 landmark Supreme Court decision in ***Bostock v. Clayton County*** held that workplace discrimination was illegal throughout the nation under Title VII of the 1964 Civil Rights Act.

Source: Getty Images

In 1990, the Boy Scouts dismissed a Scoutmaster because he was gay. The Scoutmaster won a civil suit at the state level, but the Supreme Court ruled against him, stating the Boy Scouts could create and enforce its own policies in regard to membership under the First Amendment protection of "expressive association." Since then, Boy Scouts of America has changed its position on allowing gays, but some believe *Bostock* does not change the doctrine of expressive association.

LGBT Employment Protections before *Bostock*, 2018

Employment Protections for LGBT Population

- Employment non-discrimination law covers sexual orientation and gender identity
- Employment non-discrimination law covers sexual orientation, though federal law offers some protection
- No employment non-discrimination law covering sexual orientation or gender identity, though federal law offers some protections

Until June 15, 2020, about half the states allowed employment discrimination againts LGBT persons. On that date, the Supreme Court ruled in *Bostock v. Clayton County, Georgia*, that workplace discrimination was illegal under Title VII of the Civil Rights Act of 1964, a landmark ruling for workplace fairness.

Sexual harassment is another expression of workplace discrimination. In the 1986 case *Meritor Savings Bank v. Vinson,* the Supreme Court ruled that sexual harassment creates unlawful discrimination against women by fostering a hostile work environment and is a violation of Title VI of the 1964 Civil Rights Act. Sexual harassment became a major issue in 2017 when a number of women came forward to accuse men in prominent positions in government, entertainment, and the media of sexual harassment. In a number of the high-profile cases, the accused men lost their jobs and the victims received financial compensation. In a show of solidarity and to demonstrate how widespread the problem of sexual harassment is, the #MeToo movement went viral. Anyone who had experienced sexual harassment or assault was asked to write #MeToo on a social media platform. Millions of women took part. A 2016 report by the Equal Employment Opportunity Commission found that between 25 and 85 percent of women experience sexual harassment at work but most are afraid to report it for fear of losing their jobs.

Refusal to Serve and Religious Freedom

The 1964 Civil Rights Act did not include LGBT persons when it defined the persons to whom merchants could not refuse service, the so-called public accommodations section of the law. So, depending on the state, businesses might have the legal right to refuse products and services to same-sex couples planning a wedding. In reaction to *Obergefell*, a movement sprang up to enshrine in state constitutions wording that would protect merchants or employees for this refusal, particularly if it is based on the merchant's religious views. How can the First Amendment promise freedom of religion if the state can mandate participation in some event or ceremony that violates the individual's religious beliefs? About 45 of these bills were introduced in 22 states in the first half of 2017. Debate and litigation continue in an effort to resolve the clash between religious liberty and equal protection.

Transgender Issues

How schools and other government institutions handle where transgender citizens go to the restroom or what locker room they use is another area of conflict. Several "bathroom bills" have surfaced at statehouses across the country. The issue has also been addressed at school board meetings and in federal courts. President Obama's Department of Education issued a directive based on an interpretation of language from Title IX to guarantee transgendered students the right to use whatever bathroom matched their gender identity. President Donald Trump's administration rescinded that interpretation. The reversal won't change policy everywhere, but it returns to the states and localities the prerogative to shape policy on student bathroom use, at least for now as courts are also examining and ruling on the issue.

REFLECT ON THE ESSENTIAL QUESTION

Essential Question: *How have Constitutional provisions supported and motivated social movements? On separate paper, complete the chart below.*

Social Movements		

KEY TERMS AND NAMES

Bostock v. Clayton County	*Lawrence v. Texas* (2003)
Defense of Marriage Act (1996)	"Letter from a Birmingham Jail"
"don't ask, don't tell" (1994)	National Women's Organization
Equal Pay Act (1963)	Nineteenth Amendment (1920)
equal protection clause	*Obergefell v. Hodges* (2015)
Equal Rights Amendment (1972)	strict scrutiny
King Jr., Martin Luther	Title IX (1972)

Government Responses to Social Movements

"It's really just a variation on Title VI of the Civil Rights Act of 1964. Instead of 'race, color or national origin,' we substituted 'sex.'"
—Congressional Staffer Bunny Sandler, regarding Title IX, 1972

Essential Question: How has the government responded to social movements?

Social movements have challenged the status quo and traditions of society throughout the nation's history. The inevitable resulting conflicts have often required the government to step in with legislation or a Supreme Court ruling to settle the matter. The desegregation of public K–12 schools, prevention of discrimination in employment, commercial service, college programs, and voting required the government to step in with legislation or a Supreme Court ruling to settle the matter.

Reconstruction and Its Legacy

During the Civil War, a Republican-dominated Congress outlawed slavery in the capital city and President Abraham Lincoln issued the Emancipation Proclamation. After the Confederacy surrendered and after Lincoln's assassination, Radical Republicans in the Congress took the lead. Three constitutional amendments were ratified to free the slaves (Thirteenth Amendment), to declare African Americans citizens assuring due process (Fourteenth Amendment), and to give African Americans voting rights (Fifteenth Amendment).

Defining Equality and Discrimination

The **Fourteenth Amendment** (1868) became the foundation for policy and social movements for equality. The Fourteenth Amendment had a host of provisions to protect freed slaves. It promised U.S. citizenship to anyone born or naturalized in the United States. The Fourteenth Amendment required states to guarantee privileges and immunities to its own citizens as well as those from other states. The due process clause (see Topic 3.8) ensured all citizens would be afforded due process in court as criminal defendants or in other areas of law.

The amendment's **equal protection clause** prohibited state governments from denying persons within their jurisdiction equal protection of the laws.

Section 1 of the Fourteenth Amendment is the section used most often in legal cases. It reads:

> All persons born or naturalized in the United States, and subject to the jurisdiction thereof, are citizens of the United States and of the state wherein they reside. No state shall make or enforce any law which shall abridge the privileges or immunities of citizens of the United States; nor shall any state deprive any person of life, liberty, or property, without due process of law; nor deny to any person within its jurisdiction the equal protection of the laws.
>
> —Fourteenth Amendment, U.S. Constitution

Like the other Reconstruction amendments, the Fourteenth Amendment was obviously directed at protecting freed slaves, making them citizens, and ensuring equal treatment from the states. But since neither slaves nor African Americans are specifically mentioned in the amendment, several other groups—women, ethnic minorities, LGBTQ people—have benefitted from it in their search for equality. Criminal defendants have made claims against states to establish new legal standards. Because of the Fourteenth Amendment, children born to U.S. citizens as well as children born in the United States to immigrant parents—documented or undocumented—are recognized as U.S. citizens.

Federal Actions During Reconstruction	
Thirteenth Amendment	Outlawed slavery across the United States, trumping the Tenth Amendment's reserved powers to the states.
Fourteenth Amendment	Guaranteed U.S. citizenship to anyone born or naturalized in the United States. The equal protection clause protected individuals' rights when in other jurisdictions [states].
Fifteenth Amendment	Prohibited states from denying the vote to anyone "on account of race, color, or previous condition of servitude."
Civil Rights Act of 1875	Made it illegal for privately owned places of public accommodation—trains, hotels, and taverns—to make distinctions between black and white patrons. Also, it outlawed discrimination in jury selection, public schools, churches, cemeteries, and transportation.
Civil Rights Cases (1883)	The conservative Court overruled the Civil Rights Act of 1875 and enabled discrimination in commercial affairs.
Plessy v. Ferguson (1896)	The Supreme Court ruled that the equal protection clause was not violated by segregated public places, claiming **"separate but equal"** facilities satisfied the Fourteenth Amendment. Segregation and Jim Crow continued for two more generations.

Circumventing the Franchise

The **Fifteenth Amendment** was passed to guarantee no citizen would be denied the right to vote on account of race. However, many former Confederates and slave owners wanted to return African Americans to second-class status by taking away that right to vote. The South began requiring property or literacy qualifications to vote. Several states elevated the **literacy test**—a test of reading skills required before one could vote—into their state constitutions. A **poll tax**—a simple fee required of voters—became one of the most effective ways to turn black voters away. The **grandfather clause**, which allowed states to recognize a registering voter as it would have recognized his grandfather, prevented thousands of blacks from voting while it allowed illiterate and poor whites to be exempt from the literacy test and poll tax. The **white primary**—a primary in which only white men could vote—also became a popular method for states to keep African Americans out of the political process. These state-level loopholes did not violate the absolute letter of the Constitution because they never prevented blacks from voting "on account of race, color, or previous condition of servitude," as the Fifteenth Amendment prohibits.

Disenfranchisement, economic reprisals, and discrimination against African Americans followed. States created a body of law that segregated the races in the public sphere. These **Jim Crow laws**—named after a disrespected character in a minstrel show in which whites performed in "blackface"—separated blacks and whites on trains, in theaters, in public restrooms, and in public schools.

The Courts Assert Equality

By mid-20th century, the Supreme Court had started to deliver decisions in favor of civil rights groups and their goal of integration. The NAACP (see Topic 3.10) had already filed several suits in U.S. district courts to overturn *Plessy v. Ferguson* (1896), which had provided the justification for K–12 segregation. The group filed suits across the South and found a greater number of willing plaintiffs and fewer white reprisals in the border South. With assistance from sociologists Kenneth and Mamie Clark, two academics from New York, the NAACP improved its strategy. In addition to arguing that segregation was morally wrong, they argued that separate schools were psychologically damaging to black children. In experiments run by the Clarks, when black children were shown two dolls identical except for their skin color and asked to choose the "nice doll," they chose the white doll. When asked to choose the doll that "looks bad," they chose the dark-skinned doll. With these results, the Clarks argued that the segregation system caused feelings of inferiority in the black child. Armed with this scientific data, attorneys sought strong, reliable plaintiffs who could withstand the racist intimidation and reprisals that followed the filing of a lawsuit.

MUST-KNOW SUPREME COURT CASE: *BROWN V. BOARD OF EDUCATION OF TOPEKA, KANSAS* (1954)

The Constitutional Question Before the Court: Do state school segregation laws violate the equal protection clause of the Fourteenth Amendment?

The Decision: Yes, 9:0 for Brown

Before *Brown*: In 1896, the case of *Plessy v. Ferguson* reached the Supreme Court. In this effort, civil rights activists and progressive attorneys argued that Louisiana's state law segregating train passengers by race violated the Fourteenth Amendment's equal protection clause. In a 7:1 decision, the Court ruled that as long as states provided separate but equal facilities, they were in compliance with the Constitution.

Facts: Topeka, Kansas, student Linda Brown's parents and several other African American parents similarly situated filed suit against the local school board in hopes of overturning the state's segregation law. In fact, the NAACP had filed similar cases in three other states and against the segregated schools of the District of Columbia. The Supreme Court took all these cases at once, and they were together called *Brown v. Board of Education*.

Reasoning: The petitioners, led by Thurgood Marshall, put forth arguments found in social science research that the racially segregated system did damage to the black child's psyche and instilled feelings of inferiority. The inevitably unequal schools—unequal financially, unequal in convenience of location—created significant differences between them. Marshall and the NAACP argued that even in the rare cases where black and white facilities and education were the same tangibly, the separation itself was inherently unequal. In fact, part of this strategy resulted in southern governments and school boards increasing funding late in the game so black and white educational systems would appear equal during the coming court battles. Black leaders felt true integration was the only way to ever truly reach equality.

Chief Justice Earl Warren and all eight associate justices agreed and ruled in favor of striking down segregation and overturning *Plessy* to satisfy the equal protection clause of the Fourteenth Amendment. *Brown's* unanimous ruling came in part as a result of former politician and current Chief Justice Earl Warren pacing the halls and shaping his majority opinion as he tried to bring the questionable or reluctant justices over to the majority.

> **Majority Opinion by Mr. Justice Warren**: Here, unlike *Sweatt v. Painter* [a case in which the Court ordered the University of Texas Law School to admit a black applicant because the planned "law school for Negroes" would have been grossly inferior], there are findings below that the Negro and white schools involved have been equalized, or are being equalized, with respect to buildings, curricula, qualifications and salaries of teachers, and other "tangible" factors. Our decision, therefore, cannot turn on merely a comparison of these tangible factors in the Negro and white schools involved in each of the cases. We must look instead to the effect of segregation itself on public education.
>
> In approaching this problem, we cannot turn the clock back to 1868, when the Amendment was adopted, or even to 1896, when *Plessy v. Ferguson* was written. We must consider public education in the light of its full development and its present place in American life throughout the Nation. Only in this way can it be determined if segregation in public schools deprives these plaintiffs of the equal protection of the laws. . . .

> We conclude that, in the field of public education, the doctrine of "separate but equal" has no place. Separate educational facilities are inherently unequal. Therefore, we hold that the plaintiffs and others similarly situated for whom the actions have been brought are, by reason of the segregation complained of, deprived of the equal protection of the laws guaranteed by the Fourteenth Amendment. This disposition makes unnecessary any discussion whether such segregation also violates the Due Process Clause of the Fourteenth Amendment.

Since *Brown*: The *Brown* decision of May 17, 1954, decided the principle of segregation but did not determine a timeline for when this drastic societal change would happen or how it would happen. So the Court invited litigants to return and present arguments. In *Brown II*, the Court determined that segregated school systems should desegregate "with all deliberate speed" and that the lower federal courts would serve as venues to determine if that standard was met. That is, black parents could take local districts to U.S. district courts to press for integration.

It took a decade before any substantial integration occurred in the Deep South and a generation before black-to-white enrollments were proportional to the populations of their respective school districts.

Political Science Disciplinary Practices: Analyze and Interpret Supreme Court Decisions

As you read above, Chief Justice Warren wanted to make certain this ruling was unanimous. He also wanted to make sure that the wording in the ruling was in plain language so that everyone reading it could understand the rationale. The opinion is also relatively brief. You may read the entire opinion, which you can do online at Oyez or other sites.

Apply: Complete the following activities.

1. Explain why the Court based its decision on factors other than "the tangible factors in the Negro and white schools."

2. Identify the constitutional clause at issue, and describe the type of evidence on which the NAACP relied to make its case.

3. Explain the reasoning of the Court's unanimous opinion.

4. Describe the differences between the opinion in *Brown* and the opinion in *Plessy*.

Source: Granger, NYC

The great-grandson of a slave, Thurgood Marshall was a leader in shaping civil rights law well before he became the first African American justice on the Supreme Court in 1967.

Legislating Toward Equality

As the events of the early 1960s unfolded, President John F. Kennedy (JFK) became a strong ally for civil rights leaders. His brother Robert Kennedy, the nation's attorney general, dealt closely with violent, ugly confrontations between southern civil rights leaders and brutal state authorities. Robert persuaded President Kennedy to act on civil rights. President Kennedy began hosting black leaders at the White House and embraced victims of the violence. By mid-1963, Kennedy buckled down to battle for a comprehensive civil rights bill.

President Kennedy addressed Congress on June 11, 1963, informing the nation of the legal remedies of his proposal. "They involve," he stated, "every American's right to vote, to go to school, to get a job, and to be served in a public place without arbitrary discrimination." Kennedy's bill became the center of controversy over the next year and became the most sweeping piece of civil rights legislation to date. The proposal barred unequal voter registration requirements and prevented discrimination in public accommodations. It empowered the attorney general to file suits against discriminating institutions, such as schools, and to withhold federal funds from noncompliant programs. Finally, it outlawed discriminatory employment practices.

THINK AS A POLITICAL SCIENTIST: *EXPLAIN HOW A REQUIRED SUPREME COURT CASE RELATES TO A PRIMARY SOURCE*

Laws can lay the groundwork for later more comprehensive legislation. For example, the Civil Rights Act of 1875 was passed after five years of contentious debate. The law guaranteed equal protection in public accommodations for African Americans. Yet in 1883, the Supreme Court limited the effects of the law by ruling that it applied to government institutions but its application to private individuals and businesses was unconstitutional. Many years later, the *Brown v. Board of Education* case continued efforts for equality.

Practice: Read the excerpt below from the Civil Rights Act of 1875, and answer the questions that follow.

Section 1. Be it enacted, That all persons within the jurisdiction of the United States shall be entitled to the full and equal enjoyment of the accommodations, advantages, facilities, and privileges of inns, public conveyances on land or water, theaters, and other places of public amusement; subject only to the conditions and limitations established by law, and applicable alike to citizens of every race and color, regardless of any previous condition of servitude.

Section 2. That any persons who shall violate the foregoing section by denying to any citizen, except for reasons by law applicable to citizens of every race and color, and regardless of any previous condition of servitude, the full enjoyment of any of the accommodations, advantages, facilities, or privileges in said section enumerated, or by aiding or inciting such denial, shall, for every such offense, forfeit and pay the sum of five hundred dollars to the person aggrieved thereby. . . .

1. What is a similarity between the Civil Rights Act of 1875 and the decision in *Brown v. Board of Education*?
2. What events or conditions necessitated the *Brown* decision after the passage of the Civil Rights Act of 1875?

The Turning Tide of Public Opinion

By the early 1960s, nationwide popular opinion favored action for civil rights. In one poll, 72 percent of the nation believed in residential integration and a full 75 percent believed in school integration. Kennedy's popularity, however, was dropping; his 66 percent approval rating had sunken below 50 percent. The main controversy in his plan was the bill's public accommodations provision. Many Americans—even those opposed to segregation in the public sphere—still believed in a white shop owner's legal right to refuse service to a black patron. But Kennedy held fast to what became known as **Title II** of the law and sent the bill to Capitol Hill on June 19, 1963.

By mid-1963, the national media had vividly presented the civil rights struggle to otherwise unaffected people. Shocking images of racial violence published in the *New York Times* and national periodicals such as *Time* and *Life* were eye-opening. Television news broadcasts that showed violence at Little Rock, standoffs at southern colleges, slain civil rights workers, and Bull Connor's aggressive Birmingham police persuaded some northerners to support the movement. Suddenly the harsh, unfair conditions of the South were very real to the nation. In a White House meeting with black labor leader A. Phillip Randolph and Martin Luther King Jr., President Kennedy reportedly joked when someone criticized Connor: "I don't think you should be totally harsh on Bull Connor. After all, Bull Connor has done more for civil rights than anyone in this room."

President Johnson and the 1964 Civil Rights Act

On November 22, 1963, Kennedy was slain by a gunman in Dallas. Within an hour, Vice President Lyndon Baines Johnson (LBJ) of Texas was sworn in as the 36th president. Onlookers and black leaders wondered how the presidential agenda might change. Johnson had supported the 1957 Civil Rights Act but only after he moderated it. Civil rights leaders hadn't forgotten Johnson's southern roots or the fact that he and Kennedy had not seen eye to eye.

Fortunately, President Johnson took up the fight. "No memorial oration or eulogy could more eloquently honor President Kennedy's memory," Johnson stated to the nation, "than the earliest passage of the civil rights bill for which he fought so long." Days later, on Thanksgiving, Johnson promoted the bill again: "For God made all of us, not some of us, in His image. All of us, not just some of us, are His children."

Johnson was a much better shepherd for this bill than Kennedy. Johnson, having been a leader in Congress, was skilled at both negotiation and compromise. He had a better chance to gain support for legislation as the folksy, towering Texan than Kennedy had as the elite, overly polished Ivy League patriarch. Johnson was notorious for "the treatment," an up close and personal technique of muscling lawmakers into seeing things his way. Johnson beckoned lawmakers to the White House for close face-to-face persuasion that some termed "nostril examinations."

President Johnson (left) was known for getting "up close and personal" to push his agenda. He is shown here with Senator Richard Russell (D-GA).

With LBJ's support, the bill had a favorable outlook. On February 10, after the House had debated for less than two weeks and with a handful of amendments, the House passed the bill 290 to 130. The fight in the Senate was much more difficult. A total of 42 senators added their names as sponsors of the bill. Northern Democrats, Republicans, and the Senate leadership formed a coalition behind the bill that made passage of this law possible. After a 14-hour filibuster by West Virginia's Robert C. Byrd, a cloture vote was finally taken. (For more on cloture and filibusters, see Topic 2.2.) The final vote came on June 19 when the civil rights bill passed by 73 to 27, with 21 Democrats and six Republicans in dissent.

The ink from Johnson's signature was hardly dry when a Georgia motel owner refused service to African Americans and challenged the law. He claimed it exceeded Congress's authority and violated his constitutional right to operate his private property as he saw fit. In debating the bill, Congress had asserted that its power over interstate commerce granted it the right to legislate in this area. Most of this motel's customers had come across state lines. By a vote of 9:0, the Court in *Heart of Atlanta Motel v. United States* (1964) agreed with Congress.

KEY PROVISIONS OF THE CIVIL RIGHTS ACT OF 1964
• Required equal application of voter registration rules (Title I)
• Banned discrimination in public accommodations and public facilities (Titles II and III)
• Empowered the Attorney General to initiate suits against noncompliant, still segregated schools (Title IV)
• Cut off federal funding for discriminating government agencies (Title VI)
• Outlawed discrimination in hiring based on race, color, religion, sex, or national origin (Title VII)

Impact of the Civil Rights Act of 1964

In April 2014, President Barack Obama gave a speech at a ceremony in Austin, Texas, in honor of the 50th anniversary of President Lyndon Johnson's signing of the Civil Rights Act of 1964. Obama reminded listeners that LBJ himself had grown up in poverty, that he had seen the struggles of Latino students in the schools where he taught, and that he pulled those experiences and his prodigious skills as a politician together to pass this landmark law. "Because of the laws President Johnson signed," Obama said, "new doors of opportunity and education swung open . . . Not just for blacks and whites, but also for women and Latinos and Asians and Native Americans and gay Americans and Americans with a disability. . . . And that's why I'm standing here today."

The **Civil Rights Act of 1964** established the Equal Employment Opportunity Commission, which investigates allegations of discrimination in hiring and firing. The law helped set the stage for passage of an immigration reform bill in 1965, which did away with national origin quotas and increased the diversity of the U.S. population. Senator Hubert Humphrey said before the bill's passage: "We have removed all elements of second-class citizenship from our laws by the Civil Rights Act. We must in 1965 remove all elements in our immigration law which suggest there are second-class people." Instruction in schools in students' first language, even if it is not English, relates back to the Civil Rights Act of 1964, which prohibits discrimination on the basis of national origin. The Americans with Disabilities Act, passed in 1990, was modeled on the 1964 law and forbade discrimination in public accommodation on the basis of disability. Cases in the news today—from transgender use of bathrooms to wedding cakes for a same-sex couple—relate back to the bedrock provisions of the Civil Rights Act of 1964.

Impact on Women's Rights

Successes for African Americans' rights in the 1960s led the way for women to make gains in the following decade. **Title IX** of the Education Amendments of 1972, which amended the 1964 Civil Rights Act, guaranteed that women have the same educational opportunities as men in programs receiving federal government funding. Two congresswomen, Patsy Mink (D-HI) and Edith Green (D-OR), introduced the bill, which passed with relative ease.

The law states, "No person in the United States shall, on the basis of sex, be excluded from participation in, be denied the benefits of, or be subjected to discrimination under any education program or activity receiving federal financial assistance." This means colleges must offer comparable opportunities to women. Schools don't have to allow females to join football and wrestling teams—though some have—nor must schools have precisely the same number of student athletes from each gender. However, any school receiving federal dollars must be cognizant of the pursuits of women in the classroom and on the field and maintain gender equity.

To be compliant with Title IX, colleges must make opportunities available for male and female college students in substantially proportionate numbers based on their respective full-time undergraduate enrollment. Additionally, schools must try to expand opportunities and accommodate the interests of the underrepresented sex.

The controversy over equality, especially in college sports, has created a conundrum for many who work in the field of athletics. Fair budgeting and maintaining programs for men and women that satisfy the law has at times been difficult. Some critics of Title IX claim female interest in sports simply does not equal that of young men and, therefore, a school should not be required to create a balance. In 2005, the Office of Civil Rights began allowing colleges to conduct surveys to assess student interest among the sexes. Title IX advocates, however, compare procedures like these to the burden of the freedom-of-choice option in the early days of racial integration. Federal lawsuits have resulted in courts forcing Louisiana State University to create women's soccer and softball teams and requiring Brown University to maintain school-funded varsity programs for girls.

In 1972, about 30,000 women competed in college varsity-level athletics. Today, more than five times that many do. When the U.S. women's soccer team won the World Cup championship in 1999, President Clinton referred to them as the "Daughters of Title IX."

Voting Rights Act of 1965 and the Franchise

The 1964 Civil Rights Act addressed discrimination in voting registration but lacked the necessary provisions to fully guarantee African Americans the vote. Before World War II, about 150,000 black voters were registered throughout the South, about 3 percent of the region's black voting-age population. In 1964, African American registration in the southern states varied from 6 to 66 percent but averaged 36 percent.

BY THE NUMBERS REGISTERED AFRICAN AMERICAN VOTERS BEFORE AND AFTER THE 1965 VOTING RIGHTS ACT		
	1964	1971
Alabama	18%	54%
Arkansas	42%	81%
Georgia	28%	64%
Mississippi	6%	60%
North Carolina	44%	43%

What do the numbers show? What impact did the 1965 Voting Rights Act have on black voter registration? Which states had the lowest voter registration before the law? Which states experienced the greatest increases in registration? Is there a regional trend regarding registration among these southern states?

Twenty-fourth Amendment In 1962, Congress passed a proposal for the **Twenty-fourth Amendment**, which outlaws the poll tax in any federal, primary, or general election. At the time, only five states still charged such a tax. By January 1964, the required number of states had ratified the amendment. It did not address any taxes for voting at the state or local levels, but the Supreme Court ruled those unconstitutional in the 1966 *Harper v. Virginia Board of Elections* case.

Citizen Protest in Selma Many loopholes to the Fifteenth Amendment had been dismantled, yet intimidation and literacy tests still limited the number of registered African American voters. Dr. King had focused attention on Selma, Alabama, a town where African Americans made up about 50 percent of the population but only 1 percent of registered voters. Roughly 9,700 whites voted in the town compared to only 325 blacks. To protest this inequity, King organized a march from Selma to Alabama's capital, Montgomery. Alabama state troopers violently blocked the mostly black marchers at the Edmund Pettus Bridge as they tried to cross the Alabama River. Mounted police beat these activists and fired tear gas into the crowd. Two northerners died in the incident.

Again, the media offered vivid images that brought great attention to the issue of civil rights. President Johnson had handily won the 1964 presidential election, and the Democratic Party again dominated Congress. In a televised speech before Congress, Johnson introduced his voting rights bill, ending with a line that defined the movement: "We shall overcome."

The **Voting Rights Act** was signed into law on August 6, 1965, 100 years after the Civil War. It passed with greater ease than the 1964 Civil Rights Act. The law empowered Congress and the federal government to oversee state elections in southern states. It addressed states that used a "test or device" to determine voter qualifications or any state or voting district with less than 50 percent of its voting-age population actually registered to vote. The law effectively ended the literacy test.

The law also required these states to ask for *preclearance* from the U.S. Justice Department before they could enact new registration policies. If southern states attempted to invent new, creative loopholes to diminish black suffrage, the federal government could stop them.

REFLECT ON THE ESSENTIAL QUESTION

Essential Question: *How has the government responded to social movements? On separate paper, complete the chart below.*

Government Response to Social Movements	Effects of the Government's Action

KEY TERMS AND NAMES

Brown v. Board of Education (1954)
Civil Rights Act of 1875
Civil Rights Act of 1964
Civil Rights Cases (1883)
equal protection clause
Fifteenth Amendment (1870)
Fourteenth Amendment (1868)
grandfather clause
Jim Crow laws
literacy test
Plessy v. Ferguson (1896)

poll taxes
"separate but equal"
Thirteenth Amendment (1865)
Title II (Civil Rights Act of 1964)
Title IX (Educational Amendments Act of 1972)
Voting Rights Act of 1965
Twenty-fourth Amendment (1964)
white primary
white flight

Source: Getty Images

The recent concern over civil rights violations led to protests headed by Black Lives Matter. In 2020, as many as 26 million people participated in protests and civil disobedience. This movement was ignited by the killing of African Americans by police, making Black Lives Matter one of the largest social movements in U.S. history.

Balancing Minority and Majority Rights

. . . the will of the majority is in all cases to prevail, that will to be rightful must be reasonable; that the minority possess their equal rights, which equal law must protect and to violate would be oppression."

—Thomas Jefferson, First Inaugural Address, 1801

Essential Question: How has the Supreme Court allowed the restriction of the civil rights of minorities and at other times protected those rights?

A constitutional democracy, such as the United States, is founded on the concept of majority rule. Without protections of minority rights, tyranny and oppression can develop. The framers saw the need for upholding the will of the people while still preventing possible abuses of power. When tension between those with power and those without power arises, the court system is often left to determine whose rights will be protected.

Desegregation

During and after Reconstruction, policymakers continued to draw lines between the races. They separated white and black citizens on public carriers, in public restrooms, in theaters, and in public schools. Jim Crow laws (see Topic 3.11) had become the accepted practice in many southern states to guarantee segregation.

"Separate but Equal"

Institutionalized separation was tested in *Plessy v. Ferguson* (1896). Challenging Louisiana's separate coach law, Homer Adolph Plessy, a man with one-eighth African blood and thus subject to the statute, sat in the white section of a train. He was arrested and convicted and then appealed his conviction to the Supreme Court. His lawyers argued that separation of the races violated the Fourteenth Amendment's **equal protection clause**. The Supreme Court saw it differently, however, and sided with the state's right to segregate the races in public places, claiming **"separate but equal"** facilities satisfied the amendment. One lone dissenter, Justice John Marshall Harlan, decried the decision (as he had in the *Civil Rights Cases*) as a basic violation of the rights of freed African Americans. Harlan's dissent was only a minority opinion. Segregation and Jim Crow continued for two more generations.

Fulfilling the Spirit of Brown

The *Brown v. Board of Education* decision overturned the separate but equal doctrine and started desegregating schools in the 1950s and early 1960s. Soon, interest groups and civil rights activists questioned the effectiveness of the *Brown* decision on schools across the nation. The ruling met with varying degrees of compliance from state to state and from school district to school district. Activists and civil rights lawyers took additional cases to the Supreme Court to ensure both the letter and the spirit of the *Brown* ruling. From 1958 until the mid-1970s, a series of lawsuits—most filed by the NAACP and most resulting in unanimous pro-integration decisions—brought greater levels of integration in the South and in cities in the North.

The *Brown* ruling and the *Brown II* clarification spelled out the Court's interpretation of practical integration, but a variety of reactions followed. The so-called "Little Rock Nine"—African American students who would be the first to integrate their local high school—faced violent confrontations as they entered school on their first day at Central High School in 1957. School officials and the state government asked for a delay until tempers could settle and until a safer atmosphere would allow for smoother integration. The NAACP countered in court and appealed this case to the high bench. In *Cooper v. Aaron* (1958), the Court ruled potential violence was not a legal justification to delay compliance with *Brown*.

In other southern localities, school administrators tried to weaken the impact of the desegregation order by creating measures such as **freedom-of-choice plans** that placed the transfer burden on black students seeking a move to more modern white schools. Intimidation too often prevented otherwise willing students to ask for a transfer. In short, "all deliberate speed" had resulted in a deliberate delay. In 1964, only about one-fifth of the school districts in the previously segregated southern states taught whites and blacks in the same buildings. In the Deep South, only 2 percent of the black student population had entered white schools. And in many of those instances, there were only one or two token black students who had to stand up to an unwelcoming school board and face intimidation from bigoted whites. Rarely did a white student request a transfer to a historically black school. Clearly, the intention of the *Brown* ruling had been thwarted.

Balancing Enrollments

By the late 1960s, the Court ruled the freedom-of-choice plans, by themselves, an unsatisfactory remedy for integration. The Supreme Court addressed a federal district judge's solution to integrate a North Carolina school district in *Swann v. Charlotte-Mecklenburg* (1971). The judge had set a mathematical ratio as a goal to achieve higher levels of integration. The district's overall white-to-black population ratio was roughly 71 to 29 percent. The district judge ordered the school district to assign students to schools across the district to roughly reflect the same proportion of black-to-white student enrollment in each building. The Supreme Court later approved his decision and thus sanctioned mathematical ratios to achieve school integration in another unanimous decision.

The *Swann* opinion ended a generation of litigation necessary to achieve integration, but it did not end the controversy. A popular movement against busing for racial balance sprang up as protesters questioned the placement of students at distant schools based on race. Though the constitutionality of busing grew out of a southern case, cases from Indianapolis, Dayton, Buffalo, Detroit, and Denver brought much protest. Those protests included efforts to sabotage buses as well as seek legal means to stop similar rulings. The antibusing movement grew strong enough to encourage the U.S. House of Representatives to propose a constitutional amendment to outlaw busing for racial balance, though the Senate never passed it. White parents in scores of cities transferred their children from public schools subject to similar rulings or relocated their families to adjacent suburban districts to avoid rulings. This situation, known as **white flight**, became commonplace as inner cities became blacker and the surrounding suburbs became whiter.

Source: A. Y. Owen, Getty Images

President Dwight Eisenhower dispatched the 101st Airborne Division to Arkansas to escort African American students into Little Rock's Central High School, executing a court order to desegregate.

BY THE NUMBERS DESEGREGATED DISTRICTS 1964	
Percent of African Americans Attending Schools with Whites	
South Alabama	0.03
Arkansas	0.81
Florida	2.65
Georgia	0.37
Louisiana	1.12
Mississippi	0.02
North Carolina	1.41
South Carolina	0.10
Tennessee	5.33
Texas	7.26
Virginia	5.07
Border Delaware	57.8
DC	86.0
Kentucky	62.5
Maryland	51.7
Missouri	44.1
Oklahoma	31.7
West Virginia	88.1

What do the numbers show? What percentage of African American students attended with whites? How effective was the *Brown* ruling in integrating previously segregated schools? What states reached the highest integration levels? Describe the factors that kept the percentage of African Americans in traditionally white schools low.

In an attempt to mandate racial integration across adjacent districts, the NAACP tried to convince the Supreme Court to approve a multidistrict integration order from the Detroit area that otherwise followed the *Swann* model. The Court stopped short of approving this plan (by a close vote of 5:4) in its 1974 ruling in the Detroit case of *Milliken v. Bradley*, noting that if the district boundaries were not drawn for the purpose of racial segregation, therefore, interdistrict busing is not justified by the *Brown* decision. In his dissent, former NAACP attorney and then current justice on the Supreme Court, Thurgood Marshall wrote, "School district lines, however innocently drawn, will surely be perceived as fences to separate the races when . . . white parents withdraw their children from the Detroit city schools and move to the suburbs in order to continue them in all-white schools."

It took many years and numerous Supreme Court cases to get public schools to fully comply with integration required by the *Brown* decision. In one such case, *Cooper v. Aaron* (1958), the school board and superintendent of the Eastern District of Arkansas asked that integration plans be stalled for two and a half years to guarantee the safety of students. The district court granted the request, but the U.S. Court of Appeals reversed the decision. The Supreme Court then held that the supremacy clause required the state to abide by the *Brown* ruling, and Justice Frankfurter wrote a concurring opinion to the per curiam decision.

Practice: Read the opinion from Justice Frankfurter and answer the question below.

By working together, by sharing in a common effort, men of different minds and tempers, even if they do not reach agreement, acquire understanding and thereby tolerance of their differences. This process was under way in Little Rock. The detailed plan formulated by the Little Rock School Board, in the light of local circumstances, had been approved by the United States District Court in Arkansas as satisfying the requirements of this Court's decree in *Brown v. Board of Education*. . . . the right of colored children to the equal protection of the laws guaranteed by the Constitution, Amend. 14, had peacefully and promisingly begun. The condition in Little Rock before this process was forcibly impeded by those in control of the government of Arkansas was thus described by the District Court, and these findings of fact have not been controverted:

Up to this time, no crowds had gathered about Central High School and no acts of violence or threats of violence in connection with the carrying out of the plan had occurred. Nevertheless, out of an abundance of caution, the school authorities had frequently conferred with the Mayor and Chief of Police of Little Rock about taking appropriate steps by the Little Rock police to prevent any possible disturbances or acts of violence. . . .

On the few tragic occasions in the history of the Nation, North and South, when law was forcibly resisted or systematically evaded, it has signaled the breakdown of constitutional processes of government on which ultimately rest the liberties of all. Violent resistance to law cannot be made a legal reason for its suspension without loosening the fabric of our society. What could this mean but to acknowledge that disorder under the aegis [authority] of a State has moral superiority over the law of the Constitution? For those in authority thus to defy the law of the land is profoundly subversive not only of our constitutional system, but of the presuppositions of a democratic society. The State "must . . . yield to an authority that is paramount to the State."

1. What are Justice Frankfurter's reasons for the Court decision?
2. How do these reasons support the decision in *Brown v. Board of Education*?

Electoral Balance

The Voting Rights Act of 1965 (see Topic 3.11) was the single greatest improvement for African Americans' access to the ballot box. By 1967, black voter registration in six southern states had increased from about 30 to more than 50 percent. African Americans soon held office in greater numbers. Within five years of the law's passage, several states saw marked increases in their numbers of registered voters. The original law expired in 1971, but Congress has renewed the Voting Rights Act several times, most recently in 2006.

Section 2 of the Voting Rights Act of 1965 further requires that voting districts not be drawn in such a way as to "improperly dilute minorities' voting power." The Supreme Court in *Thornburg v. Gingles* (1982) determined that recently drawn districts in North Carolina "discriminated against blacks by diluting the power of their collective vote," and the Court established criteria for determining whether vote dilution has occurred. The Court also ruled that **majority-minority districts**—voting districts in which a minority race or group of minorities make up the majority—can be created to redress situations in which African Americans were not allowed to participate fully in elections, a right secured by the Voting Rights Act.

Over time, as the makeup of the Court changed, the Court has revised its position. The Court ruled in 1993 in *Shaw v. Reno* that if redistricting is done on the basis of race, the actions must be held to strict scrutiny in order to meet the requirement of the equal protection clause, yet race must also be considered

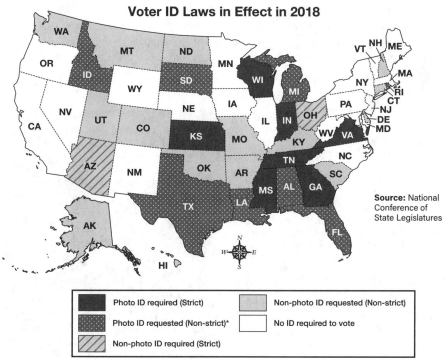

Voter ID Laws in Effect in 2018

Source: National Conference of State Legislatures

- Photo ID required (Strict)
- Photo ID requested (Non-strict)*
- Non-photo ID required (Strict)
- Non-photo ID requested (Non-strict)
- No ID required to vote

*Other forms of ID accepted

to satisfy the requirements of the Voting Rights Act, bringing into question the "colorblind" nature of the Constitution. Justice Blackmun, in his dissent to *Shaw v. Reno,* noted that "[i]t is particularly ironic that the case in which today's majority chooses to abandon settled law . . . is a challenge by white voters to the plan under which North Carolina has sent black representatives to Congress for the first time since Reconstruction."

The Court once again interpreted the law, upholding the rights of the majority, in its 2017 ruling in *Cooper v. Harris,* by determining that districts in North Carolina were unconstitutionally drawn because they relied on race as the dominant factor.

REFLECT ON THE ESSENTIAL QUESTION

Essential Questions: *How has the Supreme Court allowed the restriction of the civil rights of minorities and at other times protected those rights? On separate paper, complete the chart below.*

Restrictions of Minority Rights	Protections of Minority Rights

---

KEY TERMS AND NAMES

Brown v. Board of Education (1954)
equal protection clause
freedom-of-choice plans
majority-minority districts

Plessy v. Ferguson (1896)
"separate but equal"
Swann v. Charlotte-Mecklenburg (1970)

Source: Wikimedia Commons

Associate Justice John Marshall Harlan (shown here in 1899) wrote the sole dissent in *Plessy v. Ferguson:*

"In the eye of the law, there is in this country no superior, dominant, ruling class of citizens. There is no caste here.

"Our constitution is colorblind, and neither knows nor tolerates classes among citizens. In respect of civil rights, all citizens are equal before the law. The humblest is the peer of the most powerful. . . .The arbitrary separation of citizens on the basis of race, while they are on a public highway, is a badge of servitude wholly inconsistent with the civil freedom and the equality before the law established by the Constitution. It cannot be justified upon any legal grounds."

3.13

Affirmative Action

"The only way you get to the goal of colorblindness is to be color conscious along the way."

—Judge Harry Edwards, PBS: *That Delicate Balance*, 1982

Essential Question: How has affirmative action shaped the Supreme Court's restriction or protection of the civil rights of minorities?

Affirmative action is the label placed on institutional efforts to diversify by race, gender, or otherwise. Companies and government entities have practiced affirmative action in recruitment, in awarding government contracts, and in college admissions over the years. The federal government somewhat supports the practice but does not require states to enforce this policy. Since 1996, eight states have banned race-based affirmative action in college admissions of state schools through voter referenda.

Seeking Diversity

Presidents Kennedy and Johnson helped define the key terms as they developed policy in the hope of creating an equal environment for the races. Both men knew that merely overturning "separate but equal" would not bring true equality. Kennedy issued an executive order to create the Committee on Equal Employment Opportunity and mandated that federal projects "take affirmative action" to ensure that hiring was free of racial bias. Johnson went a step further in his own executive order requiring federal contractors to "take affirmative action" in hiring prospective minority contractors and employees. President Johnson also said in a speech at Howard University, "You do not take a man who for years has been hobbled by chains, liberate him, bring him to the starting line of a race, saying, 'you are free to compete with all the others,' and still justly believe you have been completely fair."

Civil rights organizations, progressives, and various institutions agree with Kennedy's ideas and Johnson's statements. The federal government, states, colleges, and private companies have echoed these sentiments in their hiring and admissions practices. Yet, affirmative action has been mired in controversy since the term was coined.

Blindness of Competing State Interests

Two current schools of thought generally divide into a pro- or anti-affirmative action line, though neither willingly accepts those labels. One group believes that our government institutions and society should follow *Brown* and later decisions and be blind to issues of race and gender. Another group, influenced by feminists and civil rights organizations, asks government and the private sector to develop policies that will create parity by elevating those individuals and groups who have been discriminated against in the past. The debate on affirmative action includes Supreme Court justices who insist that the Constitution is colorblind and other justices who maintain that it forbids racial classifications only when they are designed to harm minorities, not help them.

These two groups have divergent views on college admissions and hiring practices. Colleges and companies have set aside spots for applicants with efforts to accept or hire roughly the same percent of minorities who exist in a locality or in the nation. Institutions that use such numeric standards refer to these as "targets," while those opposed call them "quotas."

THINK AS A POLITICAL SCIENTIST: *EXPLAIN HOW POLITICAL PRINCIPLES AND POLICIES APPLY TO DIFFERENT SCENARIOS*

The principle of equal protection has been interpreted and refined many times in the nation's history. For more than 50 years, the government has looked to the Supreme Court for rulings on affirmative action cases. The Supreme Court has decided on affirmative action cases in different ways for different reasons. In fact, on the same day—June 23, 2003—the Court handed down different decisions on two affirmative action cases, both involving racial factors in admissions at the University of Michigan. In one case, *Gratz v. Bollinger*, the Court ruled in favor of the petitioner, concluding that the undergraduate admissions practices violated the equal protection clause of the Fourteenth Amendment and Title VI of the Civil Rights Act of 1964. In the other case, *Grutter v. Bollinger*, the Court ruled that the admissions practices of the University of Michigan Law School did not violate the equal protection clause of the Fourteenth Amendment or Title VI of the Civil Rights Act of 1964.

Practice: Read the synopses of both *Gratz v. Bollinger* and *Grutter v. Bollinger* at oyez. org or a similar site. Then study the decisions and reasoning in each case as expressed in the majority opinions. Explain why the different scenarios behind the cases led to different legal conclusions on the principle of equal protection.

Supreme Court and Affirmative Action

The issue of affirmative action came to a head in the decision in ***Regents of the University of California v. Bakke*** (1978). This case addressed the UC Davis medical school and its admission policy. The school took in 100 applicants annually and had reserved 16 spots for minorities and women. Allan Bakke, a white applicant, was denied admission and sued to contest the policy. He and his lawyers discovered that his test scores and application in objective measurements were better than some of the minorities and women who were admitted ahead of him. He argued that the university violated the equal protection clause and denied his admission because of his race.

A 2003 protest in Washington, DC, as the Supreme Court was preparing to hear arguments in two University of Michigan cases that challenged affirmative action policies in college admissions. Nearly 75,000 attended the rally to defend the gains made by the affirmative action policy.

Reverse Discrimination

In this reverse-discrimination case, the Court sided with Bakke in a narrow 5:4 ruling, leaving the public and policymakers wondering what was constitutional and what was not. As far as mandatory quotas are concerned, this case made them unconstitutional. Yet the Court, through its nine different opinions (all justices gave an interpretation), made it clear that the concept of affirmative action was permitted, provided the assisted group had suffered past discrimination and the state has a compelling governmental interest in assisting this group. Clearly, recruitment of particular groups could continue, but government institutions could not be bound by hard and fast numeric quotas.

Since Bakke

The ruling was a victory for those who believed in equality of opportunity, but it by no means ended the debate. Since *Bakke*, the Court has upheld a law that set aside 10 percent of federal construction contracts for minority-owned firms. It overturned a similar locally sponsored set-aside policy. Then it upheld a federal policy that guaranteed a preference to minorities applying for broadcast licenses.

Legal scholars and government students alike are confused by this body of law. Quotas have a hard time passing the strict scrutiny test that is applied to them. To give preference, a pattern of discriminatory practices must be proven.

The Court heard two more cases regarding admissions policies from the University of Michigan. The Michigan application process worked on a complex numeric point system that instantly awarded 20 extra points for ethnic minorities including African Americans, Hispanics, and Native Americans. By contrast, an excellent essay was awarded only one point. Though the school did not use a quota system per se, the point breakdown resembled something close to what *Bakke* banned. The Court reaffirmed its 1978 stance and made it plain by rejecting the University of Michigan's use of fixed quotas for individual undergraduate applicants, though it upheld the practice for admission to the university's law school. In 2016, the Supreme Court ruled race-based admissions at the University of Texas were permissible only under a standard of strict judicial scrutiny. A federal judge ruled in 2019 that Harvard's race-based admissions process of capping the number of Asian American students was not discriminatory.

REFLECT ON THE ESSENTIAL QUESTION

Essential Question: *How has affirmative action shaped the Supreme Court's restriction or protection of the civil rights of minorities? On separate paper, complete the chart below.*

Affirmative Action Being Protected by the Supreme Court	Affirmative Action Being Restricted by the Supreme Court

KEY TERMS AND NAMES

affirmative action
Regents of the University of California v. Bakke (1978)

CHAPTER 11 Review:
Learning Objectives and Key Terms

TOPIC 3.10: Explain how constitutional provisions have supported and motivated social movements. (PRD-1.A)

Constitutional and Legislative Protections (PRD-1.A.1)

Defense of Marriage Act (1996)
"don't ask, don't tell" (1994)
Equal Pay Act (1963)
equal protection clause
Equal Rights Amendment (1972)
Lawrence v. Texas (2003)
Nineteenth Amendment (1920)
Obergefell v. Hodges (2015)
strict scrutiny
Title IX (1972)

Civil Rights Movement (PRD-1.A.2)

King Jr., Martin Luther
"Letter from a Birmingham Jail"
National Women's Organization

TOPIC 3.11: Explain how the government has responded to social movements. (PMI-3.A)

Government Responses to Social Movements (PMI-3.A.1)

Brown v. Board of Education (1954)
Civil Rights of 1875
Civil Rights Act of 1964
Civil Rights Cases (1883)
equal protection clause
Fifteenth Amendment (1870)
Fourteenth Amendment (1868)
grandfather clause
Jim Crow laws
literacy test
Plessy v. Ferguson (1896)

poll taxes
"separate but equal"
Thirteenth Amendment (1865)
Title II (Civil Rights Act of 1964)
Title IX (Educational Amendments Act of 1972)
Voting Rights Act of 1965
Twenty-fourth Amendment (1964)
white primary
white flight

TOPIC 3.12: Explain how the Court has at times allowed the restriction of the civil rights of minority groups and at other times has protected those rights. (CON-6.A)

Protecting Rights (CON-6.A.1)

Brown v. Board of Education (1954)
Fourteenth Amendment (1868)
majority-minority districts
Swann v. Charlotte-Mecklenburg (1970)

Restricting Rights (CON-6.A.1)

freedom-of-choice plans
Plessy v. Ferguson (1896)
"separate but equal"

TOPIC 3.13: Explain how the Court has at times allowed the restriction of the civil rights of minority groups and at other times has protected those rights. (CON-6.A)

Debate Over Affirmative Action (CON-6.A.2)

affirmative action

Regents of the University of California v. Bakke (1978)

CHAPTER 11 CHECKPOINT:
Civil Rights

Topics 3.10–3.13

MULTIPLE-CHOICE QUESTIONS

Questions 1 and 2 refer to the cartoon below.

Source: Mike Keefe, InToon.com

1. Which of the following best describes the message of the political cartoon?
   (A) The policy of affirmative action should not be allowed in the United States.
   (B) The Supreme Court has limited the way colleges can recruit minorities.
   (C) The college admissions process should be blind to the applicant's color.
   (D) The Supreme Court refuses to consider the constitutionality of affirmative action policies.

2. Which of the following constitutional principles coincides with the topic in this cartoon?
   (A) Due process
   (B) Equal protection
   (C) Citizenship
   (D) Free expression

3. Which statement accurately describes the NAACP's strategy to desegregate schools?

   (A) The chief focus was on the Constitution's Bill of Rights to secure equal education.

   (B) The organization primarily filed cases for plaintiffs in the Deep South states.

   (C) The NAACP battled for equal education at college and graduate schools before the K–12 level.

   (D) The NAACP's intent was to lobby Congress and state legislatures to desegregate schools.

4. The 1972 congressional act commonly referred to as "Title IX" does which of the following?

   (A) Guarantees equal funding and opportunities for men and women in school programs

   (B) Guarantees entrance into restaurants and theaters and other public accommodations to people of all races

   (C) Guarantees equal access to all sports teams in college

   (D) Guarantees the same number of women as men be admitted to public universities

Questions 5 and 6 refer to the passage below.

[A]ll government contracting agencies shall include in every government contract hereafter entered into the following provisions: "In connection with the performance of work under this contract, the contractor agrees as follows:

"(1) The contractor will not discriminate against any employee or applicant for employment because of race, creed, color, or national origin. The contractor will take affirmative action to ensure that applicants are employed, and that employees are treated during employment, without regard to their race, creed, color, or national origin . . . [in] employment, upgrading, demotion or transfer; recruitment or recruitment advertising; layoff or termination; rates of pay or other forms of compensation; and selection for training, including apprenticeship . . .

"(2) The contractor will, in all solicitations or advertisements for employees . . . state that all qualified applicants will receive consideration for employment without regard to race, creed, color, or national origin."

—President John F. Kennedy, Executive Order 10925, 1961

5. Based on the text passage, with which of the following statements would the author most likely agree?

(A) The government should be blind to company hiring and firing practices.

(B) Business firms should act affirmatively to hire and promote African American workers.

(C) Contractors hired by the government should employ equal numbers of black and white employees.

(D) The federal government promotes equal opportunity.

6. Which of the following federal statutes contains similar ideas and principles as the above executive order?

(A) Civil Rights Act of 1957

(B) Civil Rights Act of 1964

(C) Voting Rights Act of 1965

(D) Equal Housing Act of 1968

FREE-RESPONSE QUESTIONS

Concept Application

1. A Senate Judiciary subcommittee gave unanimous approval today to a proposed constitutional amendment that would allow both Congress and the states to ban or regulate abortion. . . . [an earlier] piece of anti-abortion legislation . . . would define life as beginning at conception, thus giving a fetus constitutional rights and making abortion illegal. The proposed amendment considered today, sponsored by Senator Orrin G. Hatch, Republican of Utah, the subcommittee chairman, declares "a right to abortion is not secured by this Constitution" and that Congress and the states "shall have the concurrent power to restrict and prohibit abortions." The amendment would permit a state law to have precedence if it was more restrictive than legislation approved by Congress.

—*New York Times*/Associated Press on the Hatch Amendment, 1981

After reading the scenario, respond to A, B, and C below:

(A) Describe the objective of the proposed amendment.

(B) In the context of this scenario, explain how ratification of this proposed amendment could alter U.S. policy.

(C) In the context of the scenario, explain other steps Senator Hatch or backers of the amendment could take to achieve similar ends if this proposal fails.

Quantitative Analysis

White Citizens' Views Toward Integration
1942–1963
(Percent Favorable)

	EDUCATION			TRANSPORTATION			RESIDENTIAL		
	"White students and Negro students should go to the same schools."			There should not be "separate sections for Negroes on streetcars and buses."			No difference if "a Negro with the same income and education . . . moved into your block."		
	Total	South	North	Total	South	North	Total	South	North
1942	30	2	40	44	4	57	35	12	42
1956	49	15	61	60	27	73	51	38	58
1963	62	31	73	79	52	89	64	51	70

Source: Thernstrom and Thernstrom, *America in Black and White*, 1997

Numbers indicate the percent of respondents answering "yes" or agreeing with the statement.

2. Use the information graphic above to answer the following questions.

   (A) Identify a trend in white public opinion toward integration.

   (B) Describe a similarity or difference in white attitude toward integration as illustrated in the graphic.

   (C) Draw a conclusion about the similarity or difference identified in B.

   (D) Explain how the data in the graphic relates to the advancement of equality in political institutions.

SCOTUS Comparison

3. In the mid-1970s, California resident Allan Bakke, a white, 35-year old man, applied to the University of California-Davis medical school. The school's affirmative action policy set aside 16 of the 100 spots exclusively for qualified minority applicants. The medical school denied Bakke's admission while it accepted minorities with lower grade point averages (GPAs) and test scores. Bakke alleged the state university violated both the 1964 Civil Rights Act and the Constitution in rejecting his application based on his race while accepting applicants of a minority status with lower GPAs and test scores.

In the decision of *Regents of the University of California v. Bakke* (1978), the U.S. Supreme Court held in a unique 5:4 ruling, that the university had violated the 1964 statute, but that using race as a criterion in higher education admissions was constitutionally permissible. The Court did not declare the practice of affirmative action unconstitutional but did declare that overly strict racial guidelines violate the Constitution.

(A) Identify the constitutional clause relevant to both *Regents of the University of California v. Bakke* (1978) and *Brown v. Board of Education* (1954).

(B) Explain how the rulings differed in the *Bakke* and *Brown* cases.

(C) Describe an action that students who oppose the *Bakke* ruling can take to limit its impact.

UNIT 3: Review

Noted groups and individuals have pushed for the civil liberties promised in the Bill of Rights. Though at times states have infringed on free speech, free religion, and rights of the accused, the Supreme Court has generally restored these liberties. This process has occurred on a case-by-case basis via the selective incorporation doctrine. The Court has prevented government censorship, protected people from aggressive police and overzealous school administrators, set standards to allow localities to define public obscenity, and prevented excessive entanglements of church and state.

Women, African Americans, and other ethnic and political minorities have pushed for fairness and equality because they were overlooked at the U.S. founding and by state and federal governments during the decades that followed. The Bill of Rights, later amendments, and subsequent laws were meant to afford these groups and individuals real justice and freedoms. Brave, principled leaders and organized groups had to press the government to fully deliver these freedoms.

The Supreme Court's evolving interpretation of the Fourteenth Amendment's equal protection clause eventually required states to treat citizens equally. From *Brown v. Board of Education* to the current debate about affirmative action, civil rights have been on the front burner of public policy. Women's rights came partially with the ratification of the Nineteenth Amendment in 1920 but more fully after Congress mandated equal pay and a fair footing in college. Homosexuals have successfully sought to serve openly in the military and have won the right to marry.

MULTIPLE-CHOICE QUESTIONS

1. Under what circumstance can police conduct searches?
   (A) If they have a court-issued warrant
   (B) If they have slight suspicion of wrongdoing
   (C) If they have been asked to do so by a crime victim
   (D) If they have been tipped off by an anonymous source

Questions 2 and 3 refer to the passage below.

It is now clear that the challenged laws burden the liberty of same-sex couples, and it must be further acknowledged that they abridge central precepts of equality. Here the marriage laws enforced by the respondents are in essence unequal: same-sex couples are denied all the benefits afforded to opposite-sex couples and are barred from exercising a fundamental right. Especially against a long history of disapproval of their relationships, this denial to same-sex couples of the right to marry works a grave and continuing harm. The imposition of this disability on gays and lesbians serves to disrespect and subordinate them.

—Justice Anthony Kennedy, Majority Opinion in
Obergefell v. Hodges (2015)

2. Which statement best summarizes Justice Kennedy's opinion?
   (A) Some level of burden on the liberty of same-sex couples is acceptable.
   (B) The framers of the Constitution did not support legal marriage of gays and lesbians.
   (C) Same-sex couples are unfairly harmed by state-level decision making.
   (D) Gay couples have the right to all tangible benefits under civil unions but not in marriage.

3. Which of the following constitutional provisions would the author cite to support the opinion?
   (A) The equal protection clause of the Fourteenth Amendment
   (B) The establishment clause of the First Amendment
   (C) The reserved powers clause of the Tenth Amendment
   (D) The due process clause of the Fifth Amendment

4. What action was taken several years after the *Brown v. Board of Education* ruling to more fully integrate schools?
   (A) States spent more money to make all-black schools equal to all-white schools.
   (B) Congress amended the Constitution to require racial balance in public schools.
   (C) Interest groups convinced Congress to fund traditionally all-black schools at a level equal to mostly-white schools.
   (D) Federal courts mandated enrollment ratios that required busing students to distant schools.

5. What must a suing party prove to win a libel lawsuit?

(A) A factual mistake was made in reporting.

(B) The offending party acted maliciously and caused damages.

(C) An unfair criticism of public officials was made.

(D) His or her reputation was tarnished.

Questions 6 and 7 refer to the graphic below.

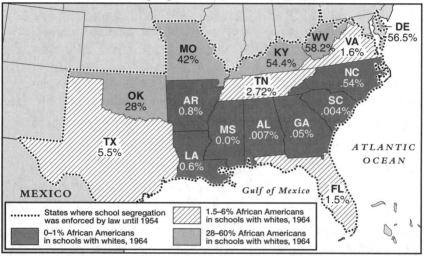

Source: Mary Beth Norton et al., A People and a Nation, Vol. II, 1986 (adapted)

6. Which of the following statements best reflects the data in the map?

(A) More than half of Tennessee's African American student population attended desegregated schools in 1964.

(B) The most racially segregated state in 1964 was South Carolina.

(C) No school had desegregated more than 50 percent of its schools.

(A) West Virginia had desegregated the highest percentage of African American students.

7. Based on your knowledge and the map, which of the following is true regarding school desegregation?

(A) The *Brown v. Board of Education* (1954) ruling resulted in immediate and widespread desegregation.

(B) Federal judges in the states with the least desegregation slowed the integration process.

(C) Once the equal protection clause was added to the Constitution, the rate of desegregation increased.

(D) Disagreement with the *Brown v. Board of Education* decision slowed the rate of desegregation.

8. Which of the following is an accurate comparison of the two court cases?

	Brown v. Board Of Education	Roe v. Wade
(A)	Required all-black schools to have facilities and faculties of the same quality as all-white schools	Brought vocal opposition to abortion and encouraged legislatures to reshape abortion policy
(B)	Required students to be bused	Made abortion illegal in all states
(C)	Concluded that "separate but equal" schools are impossible	Assured a pregnant woman's right to have an abortion in the first trimester
(D)	Upheld the separation of races in public accommodations	Upheld states' police powers to regulate safety, health, and morals

9. An employee wrongly terminated from her job because of race or gender should contact which government institution or office for help?

(A) Equal Employment Opportunity Commission

(B) Local police

(C) Federal Bureau of Investigation

(D) Secretary of State

10. What is the key difference between the due process clause in the Fifth Amendment and the due process clause in the Fourteenth Amendment?

(A) The Fifth Amendment prevents government from depriving persons of liberty, while the Fourteenth Amendment prevents a deprivation of life.

(B) The Fifth Amendment sets limits on the private sector, while the Fourteenth Amendment restrains governmental institutions.

(C) The Fifth Amendment protects citizens against the federal government, while the Fourteenth Amendment protects citizens against the states.

(D) The Fifth Amendment protects citizens against criminal charges, while the Fourteenth Amendment protects citizens against civil lawsuits.

Questions 11 and 12 refer to the table below.

Public Opinion on Burning the U.S. Flag

Poll Question: *"Do you favor or oppose a constitutional amendment that would allow Congress and state governments to make it illegal to burn the American flag?"*

Year	Favor	Oppose	No Opinion
1990	68	27	5
1995	62	36	2
1999	63	35	2

Source: Gallup

11. Which of the following can you conclude from the data in the table?

    (A) Most Americans place free speech rights above punishment for burning the U.S. flag.

    (B) Most Americans see flag burning as protected speech.

    (C) Most Americans would never burn the flag and therefore have no concern about the issue.

    (D) Most Americans support limits on certain types of symbolic speech.

12. Based on your knowledge and the above data, which of the following is an accurate statement regarding flag burning and free speech?

    (A) Because of these opinions, the number of public flag burnings greatly changed.

    (B) A constitutional amendment allowing legislatures to criminalize flag burning was eventually ratified.

    (C) Despite failed attempts to amend the Constitution around this issue, flag burning remains protected speech.

    (D) Most of the public does not have a position on the legality of flag burning, making the law uncertain.

Concept Application

The following is an excerpt from the *Federalist Papers*.

1. The most considerable of the remaining objections is that the plan of the [Constitutional] Convention contains no bill of rights. . . . the constitutions of several of the States are in a similar predicament . . . The Constitution proposed by the convention contains, as well as the constitution of this State, a number of such provisions. . . . "The privilege of the writ of habeas corpus shall not be suspended, . . . "No bill of attainder or ex-post-facto law shall be passed." . . . "The trial of all crimes, except in cases of impeachment, shall be by jury . . . Section 3, of the same article "Treason against the United States shall consist only in levying war against them, or in adhering to their enemies, giving them aid and comfort. No person shall be convicted of treason, unless on the testimony of two witnesses to the same overt act, or on confession in open court." . . .

    —Alexander Hamilton, *Federalist No. 84*, 1788

After reading the scenario, respond to A, B, and C below:

(A) Describe the objection to the Constitution in the scenario.

(B) In the context of the scenario, explain how Hamilton defends the proposed Constitution's commitment to protecting liberty.

(C) Explain how the outcome of this debate balanced the power of government while protecting individual's civil liberties.

Quantitative Analysis

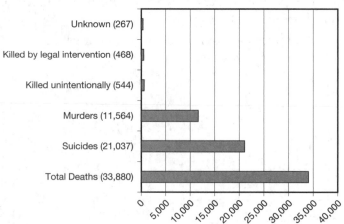

Average Number of U.S. Deaths Per Year from Gun Violence (2011–2015)

2. Use the information in the graph on the previous page to answer the questions below.
   (A) Based on the data in the graph, identify the most common type of death from guns.
   (B) Describe a similarity or difference in the data presented in the chart.
   (C) Draw a conclusion about how a gun-control interest group might use this information to promote its cause.
   (D) Explain how those protecting Second Amendment liberties might respond to this information.

SCOTUS Comparison

3. In 2012, Charlie Craig and David Mullins, a gay couple preparing for their marriage, entered Masterpiece Cake Shop in Lakewood, Colorado, to purchase a wedding cake. The baker and owner Jack Phillips refused to provide Craig and Mullins their desired wedding cake, based on his religious beliefs and his disapproval of gay marriage. Craig and Mullins filed a complaint with Colorado's Civil Rights Division, claiming Phillips violated the Colorado Anti-Discrimination Act (CADA), a state law preventing discrimination in public accommodations. The state government found probable cause against Phillips, but he appealed to the Supreme Court on the grounds Colorado's law and enforcement violated his First Amendment right.

   The Supreme Court examined the issue in *Masterpiece Cake Shop, Ltd. v. Colorado Civil Rights Commission* and ultimately found for Phillips. Though the Court did not rule broadly on whether or not the First Amendment enables a merchant or public accommodation to refuse service to gays, the Court looked specifically at and spoke specifically to the state's disregard for Phillips' religious claim with "elements of a clear and impermissible hostility."

   (A) Identify the constitutional provision that is common in both *Masterpiece Cake Shop, Ltd. v. Colorado Civil Rights Commission* (2018) and *Wisconsin v. Yoder* (1972).
   (B) Based on the constitutional provision identified in part A, explain how the facts of *Wisconsin v. Yoder* (1972) led to a similar holding as from the Court's holding in *Masterpiece Cake Shop, Ltd. v. Colorado Civil Rights Commission (2018)*.
   (C) Describe an action that Colorado residents who disagree with the decision in *Masterpiece Cake Shop, Ltd. v. Colorado Civil Rights Commission* (2018) might take in response.

Throughout this course you have examined foundational documents and Supreme Court cases, analyzing their evidence and the reasoning they use to back up their arguments. Use what you have learned from reading and analyzing others' arguments to write your own.

After you have developed a claim or thesis statement that takes a defensible position and lays out a line of reasoning (see page 257), gather the evidence you need to support it. The task requires that you use at least one piece of evidence from one of several foundational documents the prompt identifies. In addition, you must use a second piece of evidence from any other foundational document not used as your first piece of evidence, or your second piece of evidence could come from your knowledge of course concepts.

Suppose, for example, that you are given the following prompt for an argument essay: "Develop an argument that explains whether the federal government went too far in restricting civil liberties after the September 11 terrorist attacks." After reading the prompt, identify the Big Idea or core principle it relates to and focus your essay on that concept rather than the particulars of the attacks. You are told that at least one piece of evidence must come from one of the following foundational documents:

The Constitution

The Declaration of Independence

First piece of evidence:

- Chances are good you might go straight to the Fourth Amendment for evidence related to what the government can and cannot do in relation to searches. It says that people have the right to be secure in their homes, safe from government searches without probable cause and a warrant.

- You might also, however, recognize that the USA PATRIOT Act relates to First Amendment protections, since some searches may be made on the basis of a person's speech.

- The Fifth Amendment also provides possible evidence to use in your argument, since it guarantees everyone due process of law. Searches under the USA PATRIOT Act sometimes do not follow standard processes of law.

- Remembering that the initiative to combat terror through surveillance was an executive order by President Bush, you may also look to Article II of the Constitution for evidence related to your subject.

Any of the sections of the Constitution listed above could provide your first piece of evidence in an argument about civil liberties after September 11.

- You would also think about what evidence you might find in the Declaration of Independence, the second identified foundational document. Evidence from that might include the long list of grievances the colonists had against the British government, some of which described government intrusions and harassments.

Second piece of evidence:

- While you are considering the evidence from one of the required foundational documents, you might also be thinking of evidence from other sources you could gather to use in your argument. This evidence might include information you remember about the USA PATRIOT Act, objections over access to cell phone meta-data, and the political science concepts of public safety and order and their tension with liberty.

Application: As you complete the argument essay below, take time to think through all the possible pieces of evidence you can use to support your claim. Be sure that at least one piece is from one of the required foundational documents, and be sure to list at least two pieces of evidence, the second (and any additional ones) from a different source from the first.

For current free response question samples, check the College Board's website.

Argument Essay

4. The 1964 Civil Rights Act prevents merchants, public accommodations, and employers from denying service and practicing discrimination in employment based on defined criteria. Develop an argument explaining whether Congress should alter or maintain this law.

   Use at least one piece of evidence from one of the following foundational documents:

   - Bill of Rights
   - Commerce Clause
   - "Letter from a Birmingham Jail"

   In your response, you should do the following:

   - Respond to the prompt with a defensible claim or thesis that establishes a line of reasoning.
   - Support your claim or thesis with at least TWO pieces of specific and relevant evidence:
     - One piece of evidence must come from one of the foundational documents listed above.
     - A second piece of evidence can come from any other foundational document not used as your first piece of evidence, or it may be from your knowledge of course concepts.
   - Use reasoning to explain why your evidence supports your claim or thesis.
   - Respond to an opposing or alternative perspective using refutation, concession, or rebuttal.

UNIT 4

American Political Ideologies and Beliefs

What the public thinks and how that thinking is conveyed to government officials are factors in shaping public policies. Professionals try to measure public opinion for a variety of reasons, using a method that makes the results as accurate as possible. Analysts and citizens alike should consider the legitimacy of a poll as much as its general finding, because if its method is faulty, its findings will be as well.

Public opinion changes, but the factors that help determine public opinion remain fairly constant. Voters' backgrounds, professions, and a range of demographic traits have an impact on their political opinions. The family has the largest impact, since it is an early source of political information and understanding.

Public opinion and diverse political ideologies have an influence on policy debates and choices. Liberal, conservative, and other political ideologies compete to shape policy in such areas as monetary and fiscal policy, social equality and opportunity, and civil liberties. **BIG IDEA** Using various types of analyses, political scientists measure how U.S. political behavior, attitudes, ideologies, and institutions are shaped by a number of factors over time.

ENDURING UNDERSTANDINGS: AMERICAN POLITICAL IDEOLOGIES AND BELIEFS

MPA-1: Citizen beliefs about government are shaped by the intersection of demographics, political culture, and dynamic social change.

MPA-2: Public opinion is measured through scientific polling, and the results of public opinion polls influence public policies and institutions.

PMI-4: Widely held political ideologies shape policy debates and choices in American policies.

Source: AP® United States Government and Politics Course and Exam Description

---

CHAPTER 12

Citizens' Beliefs and Political Ideology

Topics 4.1–4.4

Topic 4.1 American Attitudes About Government and Politics

MPA-1.A: Explain the relationship between core beliefs of U.S. citizens and attitudes about the role of government.

Topic 4.2 Political Socialization

MPA-1.B: Explain how cultural factors influence political attitudes and socialization.

Topic 4.3 Changes in Ideology

MPA-1.B: Explain how cultural factors influence political attitudes and socialization.

Topic 4.4 Influence of Political Events on Ideology

MPA-1.B: Explain how cultural factors influence political attitudes and socialization.

Source: Getty Images

Family is a key influence in shaping political attitudes.

American Attitudes About Government and Politics

"An idea is something you have; an ideology is something that has you."
—Morris Berman, *Coming to Our Senses*, 2015

> **Essential Question**: What is the relationship between the core beliefs of U.S. citizens and their attitudes about the role of government?

Citizen beliefs include a range of opinions that help guide political actions and shape public policy. Some views amount to a clear consensus. A consensual political culture demonstrates that some values are shared among most of the population and that beliefs overlap. For example, nearly everyone agrees children should be educated and that the government should punish violent criminals. However, people might disagree on aspects related to those issues. For example, exactly what topics should children learn? What is the appropriate punishment for premeditated murder? Political culture can also be conflictual when groups with opposing beliefs clash over key issues. Those key issues range from gay rights to U.S. foreign intervention.

Policymakers try to answer these questions in a society of diverse and constantly shifting views. The framers built processes into the Constitution so that different interpretations of the core values Americans share can be debated and shaped into policy that represents the divergent views of Americans. The most effective way to reach consensus on these issues is for citizens to debate their ideas in a civil and respectful way.

Core Values and Attitudes

Citizens' attitudes toward government and toward one another are influenced by the way they interpret core American values. American citizens, coming from a range of backgrounds and experiences, have widely different views of how government ought to govern. Even when citizens generally agree on a core value, they often disagree on how public officials should address it, how to define the terms of the debate, and how government should fund it. For example, most citizens believe that government should provide an economic safety net for citizens, some kind of welfare system that will help those who have lost their jobs, fallen to ill health, or found themselves without shelter.

Yet citizens differ greatly on what defines "poor," at what point the government should help people, and what type of assistance government should give.

Similarly, nearly all Americans oppose murder and all want to correctly identify the killer before punishment is administered. However, we differ noticeably on how government might prosecute the accused and what punishment a guilty defendant will receive.

You'll notice an "either or," or maybe even a linear spectrum, to the ideological views outlined above. (See Topic 4.7 for more about political ideologies.) Some citizens believe in having a strict threshold to qualify for welfare and longer prison sentences for convicted criminals. People at this end of the spectrum are usually known as **conservative**.

Conservatives typically believe in law and order and would choose to lean toward order even at the expense of some liberties. Conservatives believe in traditions and institutions. They favor a small government that provides fewer services over a large government that provides many. They tend to favor harsh punishments for lawbreakers. Often, change comes slowly for a conservative.

Although conservatives may favor government support for people who are very poor, other groups of citizens may want government to provide welfare to people at a higher, though still impoverished, income level. These same people may desire leniency from the government on punishments for lawbreakers. People at this other end of the spectrum are usually known as **liberal**.

Liberals are more likely to experiment with policy. They believe in law and order as well but are concerned about protecting the rights of the accused. They are also accepting of higher taxes in exchange for more government services. **BIG IDEA** Governmental laws and policies balancing order and liberty are based on the U.S. Constitution and have been interpreted differently over time.

Political Ideology

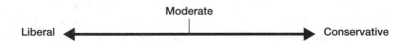

Relying on a linear scale to discuss citizens' views oversimplifies the array of viewpoints that stretch across multiple dimensions, but the simple scale can be useful for discussion. No matter where on the scale people's views might lie, people of the United States have embraced common views that form the country's **political culture**—the set of attitudes that shape political behavior. The cornerstones of political culture are individualism, equal opportunity, free enterprise, the rule of law, and limited government.

Individualism

From the days of self-reliant colonists and rugged settlers in the West to today's competitive entrepreneurs, **individualism**—a belief in the fundamental worth and importance of the individual—has been a value of American social and political life. It is rooted in the Enlightenment philosophy that helped shape American government in which "inalienable rights" of individuals precede government—they are not bestowed by government. Individual liberties are enshrined in and protected by the Bill of Rights. Individualism is the value that encourages people to pursue their own best interest.

Different interpretations of individualism create a spectrum of views between *self-centered individualism*, which places the individual's interest above the group's interest and wants little interference from the government, to *enlightened self-interest*, which sacrifices some individual freedom for the greater good and expects the government to help promote the public good. American individualism and self-reliance seek the freedom to fulfill one's own promise while enjoying the benefits and protections of living in society.

Individualism, however, can be in tension with other social values Americans share, such as respect for the common good and protection of the public interest. Alexis de Tocqueville, the Frenchman who toured America in the 1830s making observations and later cataloguing them in his book, *Democracy in America*, warned about the dangers of individualism. He wrote that individualism "disposes each citizen to isolate himself from the mass of his fellows and withdraw into the circle of family and friends." If everyone sought only his or her best interest, society as a whole would become fractured.

Equality of Opportunity

Thomas Jefferson included the line "all men are created equal" in the Declaration of Independence. The purpose of the line was not to suggest that every person was an absolute equal to every other in ability or character or any other subjective measure. Rather, the purpose of the line was to emphasize the equal rights of people to pursue life, liberty, and happiness. Yet, not until the ratification of the Fourteenth Amendment in 1868 was there a national constitutional demand for state governments to guarantee the equal protection of citizens. In the Progressive Era (1890–1920), as government began to protect citizens from the harmful effects of industrialization and unfair business practices, President Theodore Roosevelt spoke of practical equality for all and declared, "[E]very man will have a fair chance to make of himself all that in him lies; to reach the highest point to which his capacities . . . can carry him." He also pointed out the practical result that would enhance our nation, "[E]quality of opportunity means that the commonwealth will get from every citizen the highest service of which he is capable."

The equal protection clause of the Fourteenth Amendment guarantees that people in similar conditions in every state will be treated equally under the law.

Unequal treatment was not limited to the states. The federal government also had discriminatory practices. Over time, the federal government has provided remedies to redress these as well as state laws that resulted in unequal treatment. Title VII of the Civil Rights Act of 1964, for example, prohibits employment discrimination based on race, sex, national origin, color, and religion. In 1965,

Congress created an agency to combat discrimination in the hiring or firing of employees, the Equal Employment Opportunity Commission (EEOC). The EEOC investigates complaints of discrimination in job termination or refusal to hire based on race, sex, and other Title VII criteria.

Citizens argue the practical side of equality of opportunity by pointing to the efforts of an individual that lead to success. Others will agree that the occasional rags-to-riches story is impressive but not always possible without some level of government support for advancement. Still others claim that it is appropriate for the government to step in and, by law and policy, influence the natural forces of society and the market. Despite these different viewpoints, nearly all agree that equality of opportunity is a shared value.

Free Enterprise

Most Europeans came to North America for economic reasons: jobs, opportunity, or distance from a government that might inhibit economic success. In 1776, the same year the colonists declared independence, Scottish economist and philosopher Adam Smith wrote *The Wealth of Nations*, an examination of government's role in the economy. Smith claimed that the state (meaning government in general) should be primarily concerned with protecting its people from invasion and with maintaining law and order and should intervene in the natural flow of human economic interaction only to protect the people. Businesses and merchants would succeed or fail based on their decisions and decisions of the consumer. Government should take a *laissez-faire* ("let it be") approach. An "invisible hand," guided by the interactions of producers and consumers, would regulate the economy over time. This approach is called **free enterprise** and those who adhere to this approach are known as free-market advocates.

Smith would no doubt take issue with today's government-required overtime pay and limits on factory emissions. Times have changed. Today, even most strict free-market advocates believe in a minimum wage and some controls to keep clean the air we breathe.

Conservatives tend to want government to stay out of the way and want fewer burdensome regulations on businesses. For these reasons, small businesses owners and corporate leaders tend to vote with the Republican Party. Republican President Donald Trump issued a number of executive orders rolling back regulation on business, and in 2017, the Republican-dominated Congress passed a tax bill that greatly reduced corporate taxes. In contrast, liberals tend to see government regulation as necessary to assure fairness and safety, and labor union leaders and hourly workers tend to side with the Democratic Party. The Republican-backed tax law of 2017 passed without support from any member of the Democratic Party.

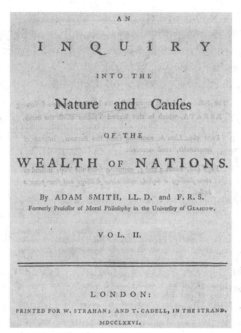

Adam Smith's study of the influence of government on the economy

Rule of Law

Every four years, the newly elected (or reelected) president is required to make the following promise before taking office: "I do solemnly swear (or affirm) that I will faithfully execute the Office of President of the United States, and will to the best of my ability, preserve, protect and defend the Constitution of the United States." In fact, it is the Constitution itself that spells out this requirement in Article II, Section 1, Clause 8. This oath assures that even the president, the highest office holder in the land, must obey and protect the laws of the nation. **Rule of law**—the principle of a government that establishes laws that apply equally to all members of society and prevents the rule and whims of leaders who see themselves as above the law—was a cornerstone of Enlightenment political thought. John Adams cited Enlightenment philosophers when pointing to the British injustices leading to the Revolution: "They [the philosophers] define a republic to be a government of laws, and not of men."

The rule of law assures stability and certainty. In many foreign governments today, whatever dictator happens to be in charge will make most decisions in the government, regardless of prior policy, including when and even if there will be elections. In contrast, the U.S. Constitution dictates a presidential election every four years under the rule of law, and the United States has never missed an election, nor has it had a serious problem with the transfer of power.

At times, however, government officials disregard the rule of law for personal gain, corruption, or power. Fortunately, there are systems in place to address or reverse such disregard. Public records of government spending, regular auditing of the public purse, independent law enforcement, a free press, whistleblower protections, and public opinion all preserve the rule of law.

Sometimes the law is not followed for the sake of leniency. A traffic cop might let a young motorist go without a speeding ticket because the infraction was small. A president might provide a new interpretation for how the government treats immigrants. Our laws are written in language that has evolving meaning. Separation of powers allows each branch of government some discretion in enforcing or interpreting laws.

Limited Government

American individuality and the story of the nation's creation after a battle with an over-reaching government have ingrained in citizens a desire for **limited government**—one kept under control by law and by checks and balances and the separation of powers. The Constitution is filled with as many devices and designs to prevent government action as to empower it. The Bill of Rights is a list of rights, but also a list of what government cannot do. Citizens of all political viewpoints agree that none should suffer from the heavy hand of government.

Both parties have embraced the idea of a limited government. For nearly a century, the Democrats represented the party of limited government with a largely conservative approach to government. After a transformation through the Progressive Era (1890–1920) and the New Deal (1932–1937), the Democrats fully embraced liberal government action for the greater good with President Lyndon Johnson's Great Society (1964–1965). Republicans were once the party that used the federal government to free enslaved people, to build railroads, and to create state colleges transformed during various eras in the nation's history also. Republicans came to desire less government involvement in business, strong lines defining federalism, and a blindness to assure equality in hiring and college admissions.

Limited government is key to civil liberties, another arena in which public opinion is divided. Limited government is at issue when people grapple with such questions as "When can government come into your home? When can it regulate affairs related to church and morality?" among others.

THINK AS A POLITICAL SCIENTIST: *DESCRIBE POLITICAL PRINCIPLES IN DIFFERENT SCENARIOS*

People's attitudes about the role of government shift over time and in different situations or scenarios. Events and laws can influence the values on which people base their attitudes. For example, the many and far-reaching reforms during the Depression altered how many people viewed the role of government. Some favored the larger, more active federal government while others felt their liberties threatened by stronger government.

Five core values define political culture and attitudes: individualism, equality of opportunity, free enterprise, rule of law, and limited government.

Practice: For each of the following laws, decisions, or Constitutional clauses, explain which core value likely motivated it and how it may have influenced attitudes toward that core value subsequently.

1. Title IX (Topics 3.10 & 3.11)
2. The USA PATRIOT Act (Topic 1.5)
3. The Fourteenth Amendment—due process clause (Topics 1.8, 3.7 & 3.11)
4. *Brown* v. *Board of Education* (Topics 3.11 & 3.12)
5. The commerce clause—Article I, Section 8 (Topic 1.8)

REFLECT ON THE ESSENTIAL QUESTION

Essential Question: *What is the relationship between the core beliefs of U.S. citizens and attitudes about the role of government? On separate paper, complete the table below.*

	Liberal Beliefs	Conservative Beliefs
Individualism		
Equality of opportunity		
Free enterprise		
Rule of law		
Limited government		

KEY TERMS AND NAMES

conservative	limited government
equality of opportunity	liberal
free enterprise	political culture
individualism	rule of law
laissez-faire	

Political Socialization

*"Democracy does not guarantee equality of conditions,
it only guarantees equality of opportunity."*

—Irving Kristol, *Two Cheers for Capitalism,* 1978

Essential Question: How do cultural factors influence political attitudes and socialization?

What factors caused you, or anyone, to think about politics and policy in particular ways? Attending college, getting married, purchasing a home, and having children can have an enormous impact on one's thinking. Even career politicians whose political positions are well known can switch views in response to an evolving world, changing life experiences, and competing for voter support in an election. Every constituent and political participant is affected by many influences that shape their political development.

Cultural Factors, Political Socialization, and Attitudes

If you try to pinpoint yourself with an X on the ideological spectrum shown on page 446, where would you fall? Would you be on the continuum at all, or would you identify with one of the other ideologies you read about? How did you arrive at that point on the continuum? The process by which you develop political beliefs, **political socialization,** begins as soon as you are old enough to start forming opinions on public matters, and it never really ends.

Family

Family has long been regarded as the biggest influence on political socialization. As children begin to inquire about world events or local issues, parents share opinions that will likely influence their children. At the dinner table, families discuss "kitchen table politics," considering events currently happening and what impact they might have on the family.

The children's magazine *Weekly Reader* conducted an unscientific poll on presidential elections from 1956 through 2008. Critics might dismiss such a poll of young, nonvoters as a joke. Yet, responding children generally answered as one or both of their parents would have, and thus the nationwide sample became reflective of the parent population at large. Only one time in its history did the *Weekly Reader* presidential poll fail to accurately predict the outcome.

Children can also differ from their parents in political opinions as do the parents between themselves. Younger people have less consistent views than older people. People aged 18–24 are frequently aligned with their parents. A 2005 Gallup study found that 71% of teens had a political ideology similar to their parents.

Yet, new research has discovered a higher percentage of children don't follow their parents' political party affiliation. "Children" include people aged 18 to 82, so the research looks at lifelong parental influence on political beliefs. The body of work from *The British Journal of Political Science* and *American Sociological Review* made several findings. In homes where politics is intensely discussed, values may immediately transfer from parent to child. However, those discussions also model for the child how to discuss politics into adulthood, which exposes them to varied views and information that can cause ideological shifts. Increased access to information and resources has reduced relative parental influence. And, roughly one-third of children misperceived their parent's affiliation or values anyway, which calls parental political influence into question. These studies are worth further examination, and associated trends may continue, but for now, family is still likely the most significant influence in political socialization.

School and College

Both teachers and peer groups can have a large impact on student beliefs. In school, topics come up in classes that may allow a teacher to influence students politically, intentionally or not. There is no solid evidence that the K–12 experience makes one more conservative or liberal.

College campuses are places where professional scholars and students can discuss new ideas and explore revolutionary theories. College classrooms have more flexible rules than high school classrooms. College deans and professors encourage a free flow of ideas in classroom discussion. Nonetheless, business, economics, and engineering majors tend to be Republicans while students majoring in English and humanities tend to be Democrats.

Fewer high school graduates attended college from the 1950s to the early 1980s than today's high school graduates. In fact, in 1968 only about 13 percent of Americans had a four-year college degree. In 2012, more than 33 percent of Americans aged 24–29 had attended college and earned a degree. Because such large numbers of people attend college and because so many post-college forces influence one's beliefs, how the undergraduate experiences tilts voters is difficult to determine precisely.

Graduate school, however, is a different story. When researchers examine voters with advanced degrees—people with master's and doctoral degrees—they find they more frequently vote Democratic and hold more liberal attitudes. The highest percentage of people with advanced degrees (46.1%) consider themselves moderate, according to a 2007 study by academics Neil Gross and Solon Simmons.

Peers

Political scientists and sociologists have long looked at the relationships of peers and how they might influence an individual's political beliefs and voting. Social conformity is no doubt a factor in influencing individuals' thinking, as people want acceptance by others in the group. Elizabeth Suhay of Lafayette College posits an explanation regarding political conformity in that "self-conscious emotions encourage individuals to adopt the norms of groups with which they closely identify."

Betsy Sinclair, author of *The Social Citizen*, finds that peer pressure works to activate civic action or participation at the polls. A nonvoter living with a voter will feel pressure to cast a ballot. She also finds that group campaign fundraisers—potential donors gathered to meet and hear a candidate—turn out higher amounts of donations because there's a sense of social obligation to contribute.

Media

As forms of media have spread to so many aspects of daily life, the media have a significant influence on political socialization. In fact, young people spend so much time in front of a screen—on their computers, phones, and other digital devices—that they spend less time with their family members, and for this reason the influence of the family on political socialization may be weakening somewhat. Young people are exposed to a great deal of political information and opinion through their exposure to media. Engaging with that content helps young people form their political identity. They follow politicians they admire and join groups that plan citizen events. As in face-to-face experiences, peer influence is strong in social media, and through online discussions with friends and family, young people develop their viewpoints.

Media are also influential in political socialization because of the way they depict politics and politicians through both news coverage and fictional television shows that are politically oriented. Even nonpolitical figures in the media—fictional characters with a strong sense of individualism, for example, or real-life people whose acts of bravery or self-sacrifice (or cowardice and greed, on the other side of the coin)—both reflect and help shape political and social views. (For more on the media as a linkage institution, see Topic 5.12.)

Social Environments

A person's social environments beyond family and schools also influence political socialization. Two types of environments are especially important: religious institutions and civic institutions.

Religious Institutions Churches and other places of worship influence individuals' political thought. The National Election Study estimates that 33 percent of Americans attend church on a weekly or near-weekly basis. Churches are more ideological and convey a more coherent philosophy than does a typical school. There are so many different churches, religions, and sects in this nation that there is no way to say how religion in general influences the average voter's ideology. However, people who attend church are more likely to vote or participate in politics in other ways than those who don't attend church. Specific religious affiliations, though, can be directly tied to a political stance. Fundamentalists and Evangelical Christians have a strong political presence in the South and somewhat in the Midwest. Fundamentalists believe in a literal interpretation of the Holy Bible. Evangelicals promote the Christian faith. Both tend to take conservative positions and vote Republican. Catholics have traditionally voted with the Democratic Party, though their vote is less attached to Democratic candidates today than in earlier years because the demographics of Catholics have become so diverse. Jews make up a small part of the national electorate and tend to vote for Democrats.

Civic Institutions   If you are a Girl Scout, Boy Scout, an athlete on a neighborhood team, or a volunteer at a hospital, you are part of a civic institution. Civic institutions make up civil society—the nongovernmental, non-business, and voluntary sector of social life. Some civic institutions with extreme political views bring only like-minded people together, while other civic institutions bring together people from a variety of backgrounds and viewpoints and help them learn how to work around their differences. Both types influence political socialization: one reinforces already held beliefs while the other socializes a person to accept diversity.

Geography

Geographic location plays a key role in the way people think about certain issues. For example, for a century after the Civil War, the most identifiable Democratic region was the South. The party went through a long-term metamorphosis that shifted its strongest support away from southern states. A close look at Electoral College results from a recent election will give you some indication where the two parties, and thus the two ideologies, are strong or weak. The candidate with the most votes in each state received the electoral votes for that state.

In the Northeast, liberal Democrats dominate and more liberal policies prevail. For example, higher tax rates fund more services, such as public transportation. Vermont and Massachusetts were among the first states to legalize civil unions and same-sex marriage. New York has followed. Democrats dominate the congressional delegations from New England, New York, and New Jersey. California and other western states also lean Democratic with liberal philosophies, having a strong concern for the environment and acceptance of diverse lifestyles.

The South is more influenced by conservative Christian values than are the Northeast and West. Southern states contain higher percentages of gun ownership than in other regions and are less friendly to organized labor. The South is more religious than other parts of the country. Church attendance is higher, and voters are decidedly more Protestant. Roughly 76 percent of the South is Protestant versus 49 percent for the remainder of the nation.

Southerners also have a high concern for issues related to farming and agriculture.

Republicans have enjoyed southern majorities in the last several national elections, but there are still many southern voters who remain Democrat, reflecting generations of party loyalty and the growth of southern cities. The working-class southerner may side with the Democratic Party on economic issues such as worker pay and employee benefits, but these same working-class voters want tighter immigration enforcement, and they tend to vote with traditional values in mind.

THINK AS A POLITICAL SCIENTIST: *DESCRIBE THE DATA PRESENTED*

Political socialization can be used to understand the distribution of votes (popular and electoral) for presidential candidates. For example, in the 2016 Presidential Election, considered to be one of the most significant elections in the nation's history, the country was clearly divided by the candidates and the platforms of the major parties by geography.

Practice: Study the map and answer the questions that follow.

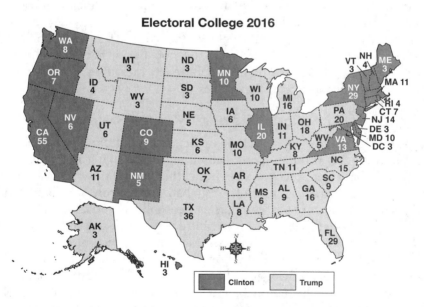

Electoral College 2016

1. How do the factors of political socialization explain the results on the map?

2. Explain the implications of this information by looking for patterns and trends. For example, are there any meaningful clusters of states?

3. Based on what you know about the main regions of the United States (West, Midwest, South, Northeast), do you see any patterns? If so, how might you explain them?

Globalization

The process of an ever-expanding and increasingly interactive world economy is known as **globalization**. The impact of globalization, though, goes beyond the economy. The political culture of the United States has both influenced and been influenced by the values of other countries as a result of globalization.

U.S. Influence on Other Countries

The United States is the dominant economic power affecting globalization, with U.S. businesses and products spread throughout the world. For example, American film, television, commercials, streaming content, music, and video games are popular throughout the world. These products reflect American values, such as individualism and equality of opportunity, and consumers in foreign countries, even those with political cultures very different from that of the United States, can be influenced by these values. That influence may heighten tension between the American values and local values. For example, in countries where women do not have social or legal equality, American movies and television shows portraying women as equals clash with local values. In some places, that clash has led to the weakening of certain cultural values and the adoption of more Western values. In other cases, however, that clash has led to a strengthening of local cultures that do not want to see their cultural ideals become subsumed into a dominant world culture.

In general, however, U.S. influence in the world is seen as "democratizing"—promoting the principles of democracy. The more people in other countries are exposed to the United States' political culture, the more they may wish to have a democratic political culture themselves.

Influence of Other Countries on the United States

Although most of the globalization influence flows from the United States to other countries, through globalization and encouraging immigration, the United States also is exposed to values from other parts of the world. The nation's diversity has increased as a result of globalization. Professionals and other workers from all parts of the world bring their political and cultural ideas with them, and as they engage with American society, they exert influence. People from Asian countries, for example, tend to put the needs of the community above individual needs. For this reason, these cultures are called collectivistic, while the culture of the United States is called individualistic. Collectivistic values have had an influence on American culture, especially in the workplace, where collaboration, a collectivistic ideal, has been shown to lead to better results than those of individuals working in isolation.

Global Identification

Globalization has also created a political culture in which people think beyond national borders for their identity. For example, the European Union (EU) is a group of sovereign European nations that function as an economic and political unit, somewhat like the early confederation of states under the Articles of Confederation. Many people within the EU, while not abandoning their national identity, also feel a political and cultural kinship with other members of the Union.

The global reach of news coverage can also foster a sense of global citizenship. In 2019–2020, news coverage of forest fires in Australia engendered global support—volunteers and donations of money—from a sense of shared humanity. A number of international, non-governmental organizations, such as Doctors Without Borders, provide services wherever they are needed, many on a volunteer basis.

Pressures on the world's resources, especially global warming, remind people that they share their fate with other people around the world and can promote a sense of global citizenship.

REFLECT ON THE ESSENTIAL QUESTION

Essential Question: *How do cultural factors influence political attitudes and socialization? On separate paper, complete the table below.*

	Influence on Political Attitude and Socialization
Family	
School	
Peers	
Media	
Social environments	
Location	

KEY TERMS AND NAMES

globalization   political socialization

Changes in Ideology

"Principles that have served their day expire and new principles are born."
—Justice Benjamin Cardozo, *The Nature of
the Judicial Process*, 1921

Essential Question: How do generational and life cycle events influence political attitudes and socialization?

At various points in the nation's history the population may see similar events very differently. As you read in Topic 4.2, family, schools, peers, media, social environments, and location are key to an individual's development of political attitudes. Other key factors include the generation in which a person was born and the person's stage of life. For example, someone born in the 1930s who grew up during World War II is likely to have different views about America's involvement in foreign wars than someone born in the 1950s who grew up during the Vietnam War. In a similar way, senior citizens wondering if they can afford to retire have different priorities from parents of young children who want better schools in their community.

Generational Effects

Many polls show the differing voting patterns for people in different generations. In the past few presidential elections, Democrats have won a majority of the younger vote. The 2016 CNN exit poll shows Democrat Hillary Clinton won voters under 45 years old, and Republican President Trump won those 45 and older. Clinton's share of younger voters was larger than Trump's share of older voters. Clinton won 56 percent of voters age 18 to 24, while Trump took only 34 percent of that age group. For those 65 years of age and over, Trump won 52–45 percent.

Yet when we examine generations as voting blocs, we examine millions of people who come from all parts of the United States, each influenced not only by their age but also by additional demographic characteristics. (See Topic 4.1.) In fact, there is more variation in political attitudes within a given generation or age bloc than between generations. As you have read, notable events can have different effects on liberal- or conservative-leaning citizens. Citizens in different generations can learn different lessons from the same events.

The impressionable-age hypothesis posits that people forge most of their political attitudes during the critical period between ages 14 and 24. Political and perhaps personal events occurring when a person is 18 are about three times as likely to influence partisan voting preferences as similar events occurring when a voter is 40 years old.

Political scientists, psychologists, and pollsters typically place Americans into four generational categories to measure attitudes and compare where they might stand on a political continuum. They include from youngest to oldest: **Millennials, Generation X, Baby Boomers**, and the **Silent Generation**. Different authorities define the cutoffs at slightly different years. The Silent Generation, those born before 1945, are senior citizens born during the Great Depression or as late as the aftermath of World War II. Baby Boomers (those born between 1946–1964) lived during an era of economic prosperity after World War II and through the turbulent 1960s. Generation X includes those Americans born after the Baby Boomers (between about 1962–1982), and Millennials came of voting age at or after the new millennium. Generation Z, those people born between 1995 and 2010, tend to share similar outlooks as Millennials but are still being defined. A look at two of the age groups on this timeline will show the role of generational effects on political socialization.

Millennials

This under-40 population tends to be more accepting of interracial and same-sex marriage, legalization of marijuana, and second chances in the criminal justice system than their elders. They are also more ethnically and racially diverse than previous generations. About 12 percent of Millennials are first-generation Americans. They tend to be tech-centered, generally supportive of government action to solve problems, and highly educated. They have a high level of social connectedness and great opportunities for news consumption. By any measure, they are more liberal than previous generations. Gallup researcher Jeffrey Jones says that Millennials will remain more liberal and the United States will become more liberal as this group ages.

On Foreign Policy As Millennials began reading their news online, they encountered a world characterized by a complex distribution of power, a network of state and non-state actors shaping the foreign policy process and international relations. Millennials' frequent interactions with people not exactly like them and at great distances have led them to be more willing to promote cooperation over the use of force in foreign policy compared with other generations. Although they are hopeful about the future of the country, only about 70 percent of Millennials regard themselves as patriotic, a lower percentage than older Americans.

Economic Views Millennials tend to follow a similar "stay out" mindset in regard to social questions and some economic questions, yet their lines separating government from the economy are not easy to draw. They are business friendly but not opposed to regulation. They want citizens to earn their way, but they want to protect the consumer, the environment, and society at large. Their coming of age in a post-Earth Day world has created a desire to protect the environment through recycling and other measures. They often acknowledge government waste and are troubled by it, but they believe in a higher degree of regulation than do typical conservatives. Nearly four out of five Millennials believe Americans should adopt a sustainable lifestyle by conserving energy and consuming fewer goods.

Millennials are more conservative on free trade and a meritocracy, with 48 percent saying that government programs for the poor undermine initiative and responsibility and 29 percent disagreeing with that statement.

THINK AS A POLITICAL SCIENTIST: *DESCRIBE TRENDS IN DATA*

Statistics are a valuable tool to political scientists. Studying statistics over decades or generations helps political scientists understand how groups change over time and reveals differences in political attitudes and beliefs between generations. As you read, some issues can demonstrate the expanse of the divide between age groups more than others. For example, attitudes about the amount of services provided by the federal government shows how people of varying ages disagree on a key issue.

Practice: Study the data below and answer the questions that follow.

Generational Divides in Size and Scope of Government

Percentage who would prefer a bigger government providing more services

	1980	1989	1996	1999	2007	2011	2014	2017
	%	%	%	%	%	%	%	%
Total	32	48	30	43	43	41	42	48
Millennial	–	–	–	–	68	56	54	57
GenX	–	–	53	54	51	45	46	50
Boomer	45	52	24	41	33	35	35	43
Silent	25	35	19	34	30	25	27	30

Source: PEW RESEARCH CENTER, 2017

1. Describe a trend about Boomers in the decade between 2007 and 2017.

2. Compare the trend for the Boomers in that decade with the trend for Millennials.

3. Describe the trend of the total population of U.S. adults from 1980 to 2017.

4. Describe a difference in the trends of total U.S. adults and the Silent Generation between the years 2007 to 2017. Draw one possible conclusion about the reason for that difference.

Voting Though Millennials' views show subtle differences, their voting habits on Election Day do not. The Pew Research Center found in a 2016 study that 55 percent of 18- to 35-year-olds identified as Democrats or leaning Democrat, and 27 percent called themselves "liberal Democrats." More than two out of three young Americans has a progressive tilt on energy, climate change, government efforts to assist people and the economy, and fighting inequality.

Silent Generation

On the opposite end of the age spectrum, senior citizens are defined as those over 65 years old. The Silent Generation and Baby Boomers overlap in this age group, but the following information focuses on the older generation. Unique times and political events shaped this generation's thinking.

On Foreign Policy Members of the Silent Generation are the last group to remember the era before the 1960s counterculture movement and before the Vietnam War. Most of this generation grew up hating communism, and many of them supported America's nine-year involvement in Southeast Asia until the U.S. departure from the region in the mid-1970s. American prosperity, patriotism, and a Judeo-Christian moral code were foremost in shaping their views during their impressionable years.

On Social Issues The same generation gave religious values high priority and opposed the cultural changes that came during the 1960s and 1970s. Racial integration led to more interracial marriage and societal acceptance of racial equality, but that acceptance came more slowly to those who grew up in segregated societies.

The women's movement changed the traditional roles of the family and eventually legalized abortion. Casual drug use and a counterculture movement caused many who had come of age in the 1950s and early 1960s to question the order of things, yet many of those who started voting in the 1970s stood with the old guard, influenced by their parents' choices. They held conservative beliefs and questioned changing American values.

As Molly Ball of *The Atlantic* explained in 2016, this cohort "has fought through the culture wars, has watched God and prayer leave the public square, and has watched immigration infiltrate U.S. society and culture." The same group today wants government to be tougher on criminal defendants and terror suspects than do younger groups, they more often oppose gay marriage, and they are bewildered with states' decisions to legalize marijuana. A 2016 PRRI-Brookings survey showed that a majority of those over 65 believe America's "culture and way of life" have changed for the worse.

Voting Seniors are the most reliable voters. The retired and elderly show up consistently to vote in the highest percentages. This group often has lifelong investment in their communities and concerns over many key issues, not just Social Security and Medicare, as is sometimes portrayed.

According to a 2015 study by the U.S. Census Bureau, in the 2014 midterm elections, 59 percent of those over 65 voted. National averages in most midterm elections average around 38 percent. In fact, this senior midterm measure beats most voting blocs even in presidential election years. The 55–64 year-old group turned out in large numbers in the 2016 presidential election, about 66 percent, but still somewhat lower than their elders whose turnout was about 71 percent.

Lifecycle Effects

Just as each generation experiences dynamic social changes, people experience change as they move through the life cycle. **Lifecycle effects** include the variety of physical, social, and psychological changes that people go through as they age. These can affect political socialization in several ways. For one, they can shift focus to issues that are important at different age levels. For example, many college-age students are concerned about the accumulation of student debt and the challenges in finding a job that provides both a good income and health insurance benefits. In part because of these concerns, many Millennials and the following generation were drawn to the candidacy of U.S. Senator Bernie Sanders (I-VT) in the Democratic presidential primaries in 2016 and 2020 because he called for free education at public colleges, more corporate regulations, and an expansion of Medicare—the health insurance program for seniors managed by the government—to include everyone, paid for in part by a tax increase for the wealthiest citizens.

When people in this group move into the next stage of life, which often involves marriage and family, their priorities might shift to other issues related to a stable economy and to schools their children might attend. At this point, a second lifecycle effect also becomes apparent. The demands of adult responsibility and raising children may limit the amount of active political participation people in this stage of the lifecycle can manage. They may be less able to volunteer in election efforts or to participate in demonstrations.

Source: Getty Images

The Silent Generation and Baby Boomers are often more politically active than younger citizens. Older generations would have a keen interest in this news conference where Florida lawmakers share information about a 2003 bill that would aid seniors in obtaining prescription drugs.

Just as young adults focus on the issues that matter at their life stage, seniors are worried about things that matter most as they age. The American Association of Retired Persons (AARP), the powerful interest group that directly represents more than 40 million seniors, lists among its major issues on its website: Social Security, health issues, Medicare, retirement, and consumer protection. Retirees who have paid into the Social Security system start collecting their benefits, and trips to the doctor become necessary and more expensive. According to a 2016 AARP study, 81 percent of seniors think prescription drug prices are too expensive and 87 percent say they support a tax credit to help families afford caregivers.

By the time they become seniors, people have had a full life to forge their political attitudes and to practice political habits—consuming news, interacting with government on a local level, and developing the habit of voting. They have likely already registered to vote and are familiar with voting routines, and they usually don't have to schedule voting around work.

REFLECT ON THE ESSENTIAL QUESTION

Essential Question: *How do generational and life cycle events influence political attitudes and socialization? On separate paper, complete the chart below.*

Influences on Millennials' Political Attitudes	Influences on the Silent Generation's Political Attitudes

KEY TERMS AND NAMES

Baby Boomers	lifecycle effects
Generation X	Millennials
generational effects	Silent Generation

Influence of Political Events on Ideology

"September 11 is one of our worst days but it brought out the best in us. It unified us as a country and showed our charitable instincts and reminded us of what we stood for and stand for."

—Senator Lamar Alexander, (R-TN)

Essential Question: How do significant events influence political attitudes and socialization?

Political beliefs can be shaped by major national political events, such as war, a charismatic president completing his agenda, or a landmark Supreme Court ruling that alters society. Events closer to home can also have lasting political impact. Watching a friend or loved one benefit or be harmed by affirmative action, serving in a war zone, or experiencing the effects of very high taxes or business regulation costs can shape one's views of national policy.

Influence of Major Political Events

Each generation has its own political and economic events that bring about dynamic social change. Living through these events has an influence on political attitudes and socialization.

The Older Generation

Those who endured the economic hardships of the **Great Depression** (1929–1933) lived in an era in which many people had a favorable attitude toward government involvement in social life. President Franklin D. Roosevelt's New Deal put people back to work by creating government jobs related to infrastructure (roads, canals, railroads) and even the arts. Social Security provided support for seniors and lifted many members of that age group out of poverty. Through the political socialization process, these events influenced ideology—in this case advancing trust in the government and support for the role of government in providing a social safety net.

As the Depression waned, the United States became involved in World War II. The war brought the nation together against fascism, creating a sense of united purpose and a belief in the reliability of the government. Women's entrance into the workforce to help industrial output of needed war materials redefined the role of women in society and helped shape political attitudes about gender.

After World War II, the Russians (Soviets at the time) replaced the Axis powers as the new enemy, and the United States stood up to totalitarianism and the Soviet annexation of or influence on vulnerable nations. The Vietnam War was one of the final major efforts that placed large numbers of American GIs on the battlefield to defeat communism. As the mission in Vietnam proved to be a failure and as a rising number of Americans disagreed with U.S. involvement, many of those over 35 years old, especially blue-collar workers and those in rural communities, differed from the Baby Boomers. Unlike the Boomers, these Americans trusted and supported their government on the way into Vietnam and refrained from criticizing their government as failure became imminent. They were more forgiving of their government in the aftermath of the conflict.

Source: Library of Congress

Vietnam War protestors at the White House. The division over the war shaped the ideology of many who are now the older generation.

The Baby Boomers

"Where were you when you heard that President Kennedy had been shot?" is a question most people of school age or older in 1963 can answer without a second thought. Such an event has a lasting impact on a person's absorption of political culture. Kennedy's assassination was one of an unfortunate number of assassinations during the 1960s: presidential candidate and brother Robert Kennedy and civil rights leaders Medgar Evers, Malcolm X, and Martin Luther King Jr. These assassinations were in the same decade known for protests—of racial segregation and discrimination, of the United States' involvement in the conflict in Vietnam, and the draft of young men to defend the interests of the country in Vietnam. Mass protests were a feature of the political culture of the time and influenced the political socialization of both participants and observers as an active democracy engaged members of society over life and death matters. Challenging the government became a political norm, and people tended to feel they had the power to bring about social changes through their actions.

From 1992 to 2006, Boomers were primarily a Democratic voting group. They took the place of the Silent Generation—the massive **New Deal Coalition** of Americans who voted for Franklin Roosevelt and Democrats who followed him—after the elders died. However, as Boomers aged, they joined other seniors in flocking to the Republican Party from the Democratic Party, a consistent trend that began in 2006 and held true on election night in 2016.

The shift of this generation is due in part to the shift in policy positions by each of the major parties. The Democratic Party, though redefined as "liberal" economically in the New Deal era, still held somewhat conservative views and dominated in the South into the 1970s and 1980s. As the party took on more liberal social views, supporting the right to abortion, same-sex marriage, and affirmative action, followers of Roosevelt and their children have shifted to the Republican Party.

The Younger Generation

The two seminal events in Millennials' formative years were the September 11, 2001 attacks orchestrated by al-Qaeda (see Topic 1.5) and the military conflicts in Afghanistan and Iraq that followed. Two schools of thought prevail on how Millennials view the September 11 attacks. One is that the attack on U.S. soil calls for aggressive homeland security and counterterrorism measures. Events that threaten national security have led Millennials to patriotism and trust in government, although in smaller percentages than older groups. Another point of view is that the event should serve as a wake-up call that the United States should be less involved in the Middle East. Some studies report that 53 percent of Millennials believe the United States ultimately provoked the attacks.

The U.S. and North Atlantic Treaty Organization (NATO) military attacks on Afghanistan following September 11 and the 2003 **Iraq invasion** and subsequent occupation have also helped shape Millennials' views. The war in Afghanistan eventually surpassed Vietnam as America's longest military conflict, and the chief premise for invading Iraq, a search for weapons of mass destruction, proved groundless. This younger generation will likely compare future conflicts to the war in Iraq, predisposing this cohort to be more reluctant to intervene or use military force than older generations. A 2014 study by the Chicago Council on Global Affairs found that almost 50 percent of Millennials say the United States should stay out of world affairs, the largest percentage by a generational group since the Council began the survey in 1974.

Many in this generation became politically aware around the time of the **Great Recession** (2007–2012). Studies show that growing up in an economic recession can greatly shape attitudes toward government redistribution of wealth—welfare and Social Security. Nearly 70 percent of Millennials accept the idea of government intervention in a failing economy, 10 percent more than the next older cohort. Pessimistic views formed during a sudden economic downturn tend to be long-lasting. Such experiences could increase the chances these citizens vote for a Democratic presidential candidate by 15 percent.

In the 2016 presidential election, Millennials favored the Democratic Party by 43 percent, while only 26 percent of that group favored the Republican Party. About 10 percent of Millennials voted for someone other than Donald Trump or Hillary Clinton, while those 40 and older voted for minor candidates only about 4 percent of the time.

THINK AS A POLITICAL SCIENTIST: *EXPLAIN HOW THE AUTHOR'S ARGUMENT AND PERSPECTIVE RELATE TO POLITICAL PRINCIPLES AND BEHAVIORS*

Much of what has been written or spoken about political life in the United States can be tied to the core values of individualism, equal opportunity, free enterprise, the rule of law, and/or limited government. Significant events can have an effect on how a generation interprets those values. For example, the COVID-19 pandemic will likely influence people's ideas about the proper role of government in public health and safety.

Practice: Read the excerpt about Social Security by Senator Bernie Sanders (I-VT) from 2019 and answer the questions that follow.

Social Security is the most successful government program in our nation's history. Before Social Security was signed into law, nearly half of seniors lived in poverty. Today, while much too high, the poverty rate for seniors is down to 9.2 percent. Through good times and bad, Social Security has paid every nickel owed to every eligible American – on time and without delay. That is an extraordinary accomplishment.

Despite what you may have heard from those who want to cut back on Social Security, let's be clear: Social Security is not "going broke." Social Security has a $2.9 trillion surplus and can pay every benefit owed to every eligible American for the next 16 years.

Although Social Security's finances are strong, Congress must strengthen and expand it for generations to come. How do we do that? Simple.

At a time of massive income and wealth inequality, the wealthiest Americans in this country must pay their fair share into the system. Today, a billionaire pays the same amount of money into Social Security as someone who makes $132,900 a year because the Social Security payroll tax is capped.

[My] Social Security plan would lift this cap and apply the payroll tax on all income over $250,000.

1. What is Sanders's main point in the excerpt?

2. Sanders refers to "good times and bad" through which Social Security came through. Based on what you read in this section, what are some of the significant events to which he refers?

3. Explain how Sanders's position on Social Security relates to the principles of equal opportunity and limited government.

REFLECT ON THE ESSENTIAL QUESTION

Essential Question: *How do significant events influence political attitude and socialization? On separate paper, complete the table below.*

Generations	Events	Impact on Political Attitudes
Millennials and Generation X		
Silent Generation and Baby Boomers		

KEY TERMS AND NAMES

Great Depression (1929–1933)
New Deal Coalition

Iraq invasion (2003)
Great Recession (2007–2012)

CHAPTER 12 Review:
Learning Objectives and Key Terms

TOPIC 4.1: Explain the relationship between core beliefs of U.S. citizens and attitudes about the role of government. (MPA-1.A)

Effect of Core Values on Citizens' Attitudes (MPA-1.A.1)

conservative	limited government
equality of opportunity	liberal
free enterprise	political culture
individualism	rule of law
laissez-faire	

TOPIC 4.2: Explain how cultural factors influence political attitudes and socialization. (MPA-1.B)

Factors Influencing Political Attitudes (MPA-1.B.1 & 2)

globalization	political socialization

TOPIC 4.3: Explain how cultural factors influence political attitudes and socialization. (MPA-1.B)

Generational and Life Cycle Effects on Attitudes (MPA-1.B.3)

Baby Boomers	lifecycle effects
Generation X	Millennials
generational effects	Silent Generation

TOPIC 4.4: Explain how cultural factors influence political attitudes and socialization. (MPA-1.B)

Influence of Cultural Factors on Socialization (MPA-1.B.4)

Great Depression (1929–1933)	New Deal Coalition
Iraq invasion (2003)	Great Recession (2007–2012)

CHAPTER 12 Checkpoint:
Citizens' Beliefs and Political Ideology

Topics 4.1–4.4

MULTIPLE-CHOICE QUESTIONS

Question 1 refers to the information below.

TWO CITIZEN PROFILES	
William	**Sarah**
Hometown: Huntsville, Alabama	Hometown: Boston, Massachusetts
Age: 57	Age: 27
Level of Education: B.A. in Business	Level of Education: M.A. in English
Socio-economic Level: Upper	Socio-economic Level: Middle

1. Based on the information in the infographic, which political beliefs are these citizens most likely to have?
   (A) Sarah's views would be pro-life on abortion and William would be pro-choice.
   (B) William would support legalization of marijuana while Sarah would oppose legalizing marijuana.
   (C) Sarah and William both would hold liberal views on free speech.
   (D) William would want fewer regulations on commerce, while Sarah would be more supportive of welfare programs.

2. Millennials' political socialization was affected by the September 11 attacks by al-Qaeda terrorists, showing most clearly which effect on the formation of political views?
   (A) The generational effect
   (B) The lifecycle effect
   (C) The effect of social media
   (D) The effect of globalization

3. Which of the following is an accurate comparison of Millennials and members of the Silent Generation?

	MILLENNIALS	SILENT GENERATION
(A)	Favor tough punishments for criminals	Favor lenient punishments for criminals
(B)	Generally oppose same-sex marriage	Generally support same-sex marriage
(C)	Tend to believe the United States should stay out of foreign countries	Tend to see the United States as a world guardian of democracy
(D)	Tend to be Republicans	Tend to be Democrats

Questions 4 and 5 refer to the excerpt below.

The social condition of the Americans is eminently democratic; this was its character at the foundation of the Colonies, and is still more strongly marked at the present day. I have stated in the preceding chapter that great equality existed among the emigrants who settled on the shores of New England. The germ of aristocracy was never planted in that part of the Union. . . . [in the middle states] some great English proprietors had settled, who had imported with them aristocratic principles . . . it was impossible ever to establish a powerful aristocracy in America; these reasons existed with less force to the southwest of the Hudson. In the South, one man, aided by slaves, could cultivate a great extent of country: it was therefore common to see rich landed proprietors. But their influence was not altogether aristocratic as that term is understood in Europe, since they possessed no privileges; and the cultivation of their estates being carried on by slaves, they had no tenants depending on them, and consequently no patronage.

—Alexis de Tocqueville, *Democracy in America*, 1835

4. Based on the text, which of the following prevented the emergence of an American aristocracy?

(A) High levels of taxation of inherited wealth

(B) The reliance of wealthy landowners on slave labor rather than tenant labor

(C) The existence of relatively cheap land in the United States

(D) Laws that prohibited an aristocracy from emerging

5. Which of the following core beliefs about American government is emphasized most by the author?

(A) Equality of opportunity

(B) Free enterprise

(C) Rule of law

(D) Limited government

6. Which of the following statements accurately describes the relationship between family and political opinions?

   (A) Children are rarely surveyed, so it is difficult to determine the relationship.

   (B) Children's political opinions are heavily influenced by their parents, but not as much as they used to be.

   (C) Children who discuss politics at a younger age with parents have fewer political discussions with parents over time.

   (D) Children are keenly aware of their parents' political opinions and invariably follow them.

FREE-RESPONSE QUESTIONS

Concept Application

The following is a passage from a notable article in the *Journal of Democracy*.

1. "The vibrancy of American civil society has notably declined over the past several decades. . . . it was the Americans' propensity for civic association that most impressed [the French observer Alexis de Tocqueville] as the key to their unprecedented ability to make democracy work . . . The norms and networks of civic engagement also powerfully affect the performance of representative government. . . . Americans ha[ve] forsaken their parents' habitual readiness to engage in the simplest act of citizenship [voting] . . . . It is not just the voting booth that has been increasingly deserted . . . . more Americans are bowling today than ever before, but bowling in organized leagues has plummeted in the last decade or so. . . . [it is] the social interaction and even occasionally civic conversations over beer and pizza that solo bowlers forgo. Whether or not bowling beats balloting in the eyes of most Americans, bowling teams illustrate yet another vanishing form of social capital [social relationships that enable society to function] . . . . High on America's agenda should be the question of how to reverse these trends in social connectedness, thus restoring civic engagement and civic trust."

   —Professor Robert Putnam, "Bowling Alone: America's Declining Social Capital," 1995

   After reading the excerpt above, respond to A, B, and C below:

   (A) Describe changes in political participation based on the excerpt.

   (B) In the context of this scenario, explain why social capital has declined in the 20th and 21st centuries.

   (C) In the context of the scenario, explain how social capital and other cultural factors influence political attitudes and socialization.

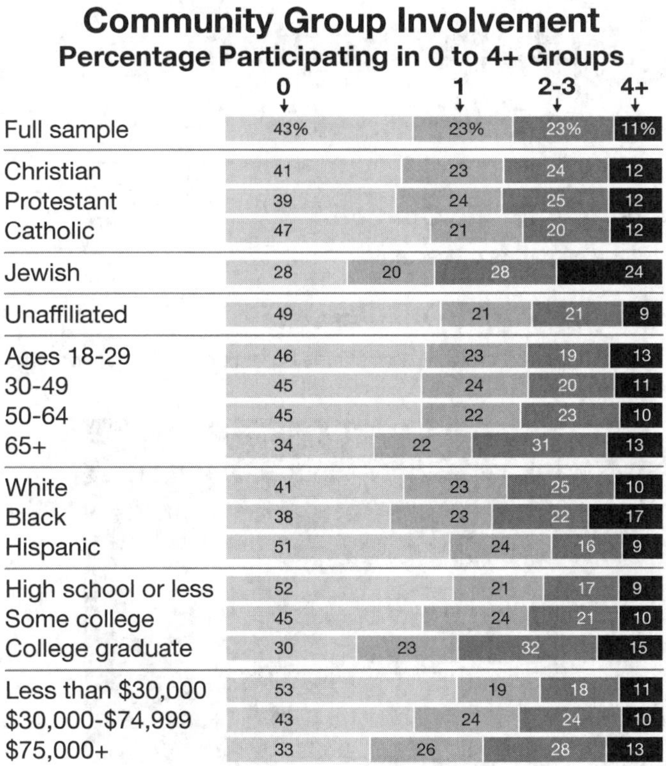

Quantitative Analysis

Community Group Involvement
Percentage Participating in 0 to 4+ Groups

	0	1	2-3	4+
Full sample	43%	23%	23%	11%
Christian	41	23	24	12
Protestant	39	24	25	12
Catholic	47	21	20	12
Jewish	28	20	28	24
Unaffiliated	49	21	21	9
Ages 18-29	46	23	19	13
30-49	45	24	20	11
50-64	45	22	23	10
65+	34	22	31	13
White	41	23	25	10
Black	38	23	22	17
Hispanic	51	24	16	9
High school or less	52	21	17	9
Some college	45	24	21	10
College graduate	30	23	32	15
Less than $30,000	53	19	18	11
$30,000-$74,999	43	24	24	10
$75,000+	33	26	28	13

Source: Pew Research Center, 2019

2. Use the graph above to answer the following questions.

(A) Identify the religious group with the highest percentage participating in four or more community groups.

(B) Describe a difference in community group participation across income levels.

(C) Draw a conclusion about why the difference from part B exists.

(D) Explain how the data in the chart could influence citizens' political ideology.

CHAPTER 13

Public Opinion

Topics 4.5–4.6

Topic 4.5 Measuring Public Opinion

MPA-2.A: Describe the elements of a scientific poll.

Topic 4.6 Evaluating Public Opinion Data

MPA-2.B: Explain the quality and credibility of claims based on public opinion data.

Source: Wikimedia Commons

President Harry Truman holds up an early edition of the *Chicago Tribune*, which incorrectly reported in November 1948 that he lost the presidential election to Thomas Dewey, based in part on incorrect public opinion measures.

Measuring Public Opinion

"You don't want to outthink the polls on Election Day. Sometimes the polls are right, sometimes they're wrong."

—Pollster Nate Silver, Talk to NASA Researchers, 2019

Essential Question: What are the elements of a scientific poll and how do these elements impact elections and policy?

Mining the views of Americans has become a keen interest of political scientists and a major industry in this age of data. Candidates running for office want to know their chances of winning and which groups support them. Once elected, members of Congress want to know how their constituents regard proposed bills and how they view different types of government spending. These elected officials and their staff members monitor public opinion by reading constituents' letters and emails, holding town hall meetings, and reviewing surveys that are conducted in their states or districts. News organizations rely on, and even sponsor, polls to see where the public stands on important issues and political candidates.

Measures

Done scientifically, polling is the most reliable way to assess public opinion. It entails posing well-developed, objective questions to a small, random group of people to find out what a larger group thinks. Public opinion polling now follows a sophisticated methodology.

Scientific polling began in the mid-1930s, and since the Gallup Poll correctly predicted the re-election of President Franklin Delano Roosevelt in 1936, measuring Americans' views has become increasingly sophisticated and popular. Many universities have established polling centers and major television networks and large newspapers have created their own polling departments.

Types of Polls

Pollsters use different kinds of **public opinion polls** to gauge attitudes on issues or support for candidates in an election in a cross-section of the population. **Benchmark polls** are often the first type of poll used by a political campaign, often before a potential candidate has declared his or her intentions. Benchmark polls are used to measure support for a candidate and to gather information about the issues that people care about. **Tracking polls** ask people questions to measure how prospective voters feel about an issue and how they may vote on election day. Tracking polls used during the course of an election allow a campaign to "track" issues and how a candidate is faring with voters. This kind of information helps candidates make decisions for shaping the campaign, particularly in the final weeks and days of the election. **Entrance polls** and **exit polls** are conducted outside polling places on election day to publicly predict the outcome of the election after the polls close. Polling services and the news media use these polls in national and statewide elections to help them offer predictions as well as to gain insight into the thoughts and behaviors of voters or to identify and analyze how different demographics actually voted.

Presidential Approval

Polls regularly ask about presidential approval. **Approval ratings** are gauged by pollsters asking whether the respondent approves, yes or no, of the president's job performance. Presidents usually begin their term with a fairly high approval as the people, Congress, and the news media get to know them during the so-called "honeymoon period." Presidential "honeymoons" generally last a few months and are characterized by some degree of bipartisanship in Congress and generally positive coverage by the news media. Approval ratings usually reflect this time of good feeling and predictably these ratings will begin to decline as a president begins staking out positions on issues.

According to Gallup, presidents after Harry Truman average 45 to 49 percent approval over their term of office. Some of the highest presidential approval ratings have come when the nation prospered economically or when the country found itself in an international crisis and rallied around the president. The two highest recorded presidential approval ratings came after al-Qaeda attacked the United States in September 2001, when President George W. Bush scored 90 percent approval, and when his father, President George H. W. Bush, received 89 percent approval after leading a military coalition to oust Iraqi dictator Saddam Hussein from Kuwait in 1991.

However, approval ratings change, sometimes dramatically. The approval rating of President George H.W. Bush dipped to 29 percent amid high unemployment and racial discord just one year after record highs. The approval of his son, George W. Bush also dropped significantly to below 30 percent, following what many believed was an ineffective response to Hurricane Katrina and skyrocketing gas prices by the end of his second term.

Of the 12 chief executives following President Truman, six averaged an approval rating of about 47 percent and six averaged about 60 percent. According to *RealClearPolitics*, President Donald Trump's job approval average at the end of his first full year was 39 percent and rising to his highest rating of 49 percent in January 2020.

Source: Wikimedia Commons, Eric Draper

President George W. Bush addresses the media at Barksdale Air Force Base in Louisiana after the September 11 attacks. Bush takes a strong stance against terrorism. "Make no mistake: The United States will hunt down and punish those responsible for these cowardly acts." His approval rating reached record highs soon after.

Poll respondents are also often asked: "Is the nation on the right track or wrong track?" That question is commonly asked to determine Americans' satisfaction with perceived success of the nation. A positive "right-track" response generally means incumbent presidents will fare well in their re-election campaigns, while a high "wrong-track" response will make incumbents uncomfortable at election time. The generic party ballot simply asks respondents if they will vote for Republicans or Democrats during an upcoming election without mentioning candidates' names. Analyzing responses to these questions together serves as a relative measure of citizen support for each party.

Focus Groups

A small group of citizens—10 to 40 people—who are gathered to hold conversations about issues or candidates form a **focus group**. Though less scientific than many types of polls, focus groups allow for deeper insight into a topic. Pollsters can ask follow-up questions and examine body language and intensity that would be missed in a simple automated questionnaire over the phone. For example, Republican presidential candidate Mitt Romney began wearing jeans more often when campaigning in the 2012 election after focus groups responded more positively to him in jeans than in formal clothes.

Methodology

Reliable pollsters take great pains to ensure their measurements are legitimate. They do so by constructing questionnaires with properly worded and appropriately ordered questions and selecting a representative sample from which to analyze the data and draw the appropriate conclusions.

Questions

Pollsters phrase survey questions to avoid skewing the results. The wording should be objective and not emotionally charged. Poll results on such emotional issues as abortion, same-sex marriage, and affirmative action can be distorted depending on the wording. On foreign aid, imagine how the following two questions would bring noticeably different results: "Should the United States provide foreign aid to other nations?" and "Should the U.S. give foreign aid to other nations if such a decision would lead to higher taxes in this country?"

Question order can also affect the results. In a 2002 poll on President George W. Bush's performance, for example, researchers asked the same questions but in a different sequence to two different groups. When people were asked first about the performance of the president and then the direction of the country, the president fared better. If respondents were asked about the state of the country first, which many said was bad, then the president's approval dropped 6 percent.

How a question is framed also affects responses. *Framing* a question means posing it in a way that emphasizes a certain perspective. For example, researchers found that respondents had widely varying views on whether abortion should be legal depending on how the question was framed. Only 28 percent of Americans believe abortion should be legal under all circumstances, while many more supported abortion when the question was framed with a certain condition emphasized, as the chart below shows.

BY THE NUMBERS WHEN SHOULD ABORTION BE LEGAL?	
When a woman's life is endangered	84%
When a woman's physical health is endangered	81%
When the pregnancy was caused by rape or incest	78%
When the woman's mental health is endangered	64%
When there is evidence the baby may be physically or mentally impaired	53%
When the woman or family cannot afford to raise the child	34%

Source: R. Michael Alvarez and John Brehm, Hard Choices, Easy Answers, 2002. © Princeton University Press

What do the numbers show? How does wording the question differently affect opinions? How do people differ on the legality of abortion? What factors in the question make the policy more or less favorable?

Sampling Techniques

Which people are polled is just as important as the question's nature and wording. Proper **sampling techniques** assure an accurate poll with a random and fair representation of the population. The pollster takes a **representative**

sample, a group of people meant to represent the large group in question, known as the **universe**. A nationally representative sample often has about 1,500 respondents, while a sample to determine public opinion within a single state would be much smaller.

Pollsters must obtain a **random sample**. That is, every single member of the universe must have an equal chance of selection into the sample. A reporter or marketer standing on a street corner asking questions to passersby may determine some indication of public opinion, but this system is not random, because the person collecting the data may have biased who was included in the sample by approaching only those people who look "safe" or who otherwise look like they might be more willing to participate in the study. Since the 1980s, pollsters have used telephones as the primary contact for surveys, though there are concerns with this method. For example, roughly 30 percent of the populace has an unlisted number either by choice or because of mobility. To make telephone polling more reliable and efficient, pollsters use **random-digit dialing**. A computer randomly calls possible numbers in a given area until enough people respond to establish a representative sample.

Though technology has advanced, reaching voters has become more challenging. Landline use is dropping. About 95 percent of American adults own a cell phone, and a majority of homes have wireless-only phone service. More than 70 percent of all adults aged 25 to 34 years old use cell phones only and do not have landlines.

Pollsters are trying to combat this phenomenon in a few ways. One is mixing their broadly dialed, automated random phone surveys with more actual human interviewers. Federal law prohibits pre-recorded interactive surveys to cell phones. The Pew Research Center requires that 75 percent of their samples are cell phone participants.

Once the pollster has enough respondents, he or she checks to see if the demographics in the sample are reflective of those of the universe. If disproportionately more women than men answer the phone and take the poll, the pollster will remove some female respondents from the sample in order to make it proportional. If a congressional district contains roughly 25 percent African Americans, the sample needs to mirror that. Manipulating the sample to compensate for this is known as **weighting** or **stratification**—making sure demographic groups are properly represented in a sample.

THINK AS A POLITICAL SCIENTIST: *EXPLAIN TRENDS IN DATA TO DRAW CONCLUSIONS*

Scientific polling gives political campaigns large amounts of data to consider. At the individual level, data helps a candidate make many strategic decisions about their campaign. On a national scale, data can give the major parties an idea who is the popular candidate at the moment and who is gaining or losing popularity.

Practice: Study the information below from December 2019 and answer the questions that follow.

Polling Data from December 2019

POLL	DATE	BIDEN	SANDERS	WARREN	BUTTIGIEG	BLOOMBERG	KLOBUCHAR	SPREAD
RCP Average	12/5–12/24	28.1	18.8	15.2	8.4	4.9	3.5	Biden +9.3
Economist/YouGov	12/22–12/24	30	17	19	7	4	5	Biden +11
Morning Consult	12/20–12/22	31	21	15	9	6	3	Biden +10
Emerson	12/15–12/17	32	25	12	8	3	2	Biden +7
NBC News/Wall St. Jrnl	12/14–12/17	28	21	18	9	4	5	Biden +7
CNN	12/12–12/15	26	20	16	8	5	3	Biden +6

Source: realclearpolitic.com

1. What additional information might make this table more useful?
2. What might explain the different results among the various polls?
3. What conclusions might be drawn from this information?

Sampling Error

Even the most cautious survey with appropriate sampling techniques cannot guarantee absolute precision. The only way to know what everyone thinks is to ask everyone and assure they are entirely honest, both of which are impossible. Every poll has a **sampling error**, the difference between poll results, also called **margin of error**. The sample size and the margin of error have an inverse relationship. That is, as the sample gets larger, the margin of error decreases. The way to determine this sampling error is to measure the results in two or more polls. For example, the same basic poll with two similar samples revealed that 55 percent of the first sample opposed a particular congressional bill, while 58 percent of the second sample opposed the law. This poll has a sampling error of 3 percent. A margin of error of plus-or-minus 4 percent or less is usually considered satisfactory.

Non-Attitudes The simplest yet most perplexing problem in public opinion polling is the presence of non-attitudes. Many people do not have strong opinions on the issues of the day, or they are uninformed or simply concerned about their privacy and do not want to share their views. Just over half of eligible voters actually cast votes in presidential elections. Matters of extreme importance to journalists and policymakers may be unimportant to average citizens, so while poll results measure the views of average citizens on these matters, they don't show the relative importance of the matters to citizens. In a similar way, matters important to citizens may not be of interest to journalists, so polls may not reflect what is really on the minds of voters.

Another phenomenon affecting poll results is the high frequency of uninformed citizens responding. Political scientist Herb Asher explains a poll asking about the repeal of the Public Affairs Act. In reality, no such act or repeal effort existed, but fully 43 percent of those questioned had an opinion of the nonexistent law. Pollsters often ask screening questions to establish a respondent's knowledge or to ensure they are registered voters, such as "Do you plan to vote in the November election?" Such a question, however, does not eliminate the problem entirely. In fact, more than 90 percent of people answering phone surveys claim they will vote while far fewer do. Discerning pollsters may even ask if the respondent knows the day of the upcoming election as a way to increase the chances that the respondent is a bona fide voter.

Human Bias How the interviewer contacts and interacts with the respondent and the respondent's views can also impact a poll. The difference between mailed questionnaires and telephone interviews is stark. People are more honest with the anonymity of a paper questionnaire than a live telephone call. Some studies show women and men answer differently to male or female callers. A woman's right to choose an abortion was supported by 84 percent of women when interviewed by females, while only 64 percent gave a pro-choice response to a male caller. Race, or perceived race, can matter as well. Asher claims that African Americans are more critical of the political and criminal justice system to black interviewers while more supportive to white interviewers. White respondents are less likely to reveal attitudes of racial hostility when interviewed by African Americans than by whites.

Still other problems exist because not everyone conducting a poll represents an objective journalist or an academic. Fundraising under the guise of polling has cheapened polling's reputation. Political parties and candidates use phone and mail surveys to assess where their followers stand and then ask for a donation.

Also, **push polling** is a controversial and deceptive way to influence potential voters. Push polls are done via the telephone and rather than a series of neutral questions meant to determine public opinion on a candidate, the caller, or more commonly a tape-recorded voice, offers positive points about the candidate or negative points about the opponent. These attempts to "push" certain views on people aren't actually polls but a form of political campaigning.

Internet polling can be problematic because there is no way to assure a random sample. When directed toward an Internet poll, only those strongly motivated will participate. Some online polls allow respondents to complete the questions as many times as they like. Internet users also tend to be younger, better educated, more affluent, white, and suburban than those offline more often and do not represent a genuine cross section of society.

REFLECT ON THE ESSENTIAL QUESTION

Essential Question: *What are the elements of a scientific poll and how do these elements impact elections and policy? On separate paper, complete the chart below.*

Elements of a Scientific Poll	Possible Effects on Decision-Making

KEY TERMS AND NAMES

approval rating
benchmark polls
entrance polls
exit polls
focus group
public opinion polls
push polling

random-digit dialing
random sample
representative sample (universe)
sampling error (margin of error)
sampling techniques
tracking polls
weighting (stratification)

Evaluating Public Opinion Data

"The experts get more wrong every time."

—President Harry Truman, on polling to
Clark Clifford, 1948

Essential Question: How can you determine the quality and credibility
of claims based on public opinion data?

What the public thinks and how that thinking is conveyed to government officials are factors in shaping public policies. Professionals try to measure public opinion for a variety of reasons, using methods that make the results as accurate as possible. Analysts and citizens alike should consider the legitimacy of a poll as much as its general findings, because if its method is faulty, its findings will be as well.

Claims, Credibility, and Public Opinion Data

As participants in democracy either at or approaching voting age, you will be surrounded by public opinion polls and claims based on them. Knowing how to evaluate the quality and credibility of those claims will help you make informed decisions.

Public Opinion and Political Influence

Polls lend themselves to "horse race" news coverage in which elections are reported as if the most important aspect is which candidate is in the lead. Critics of "horse race" journalism argue voters need more substance, such as how a candidate views major issues that affect social policy or government spending.

This kind of media coverage can translate into significant political influence as well. National polling influences whose voice will be heard at the televised debate and whose would be silenced. For example, early in the Republican primary season in 2016, the first debate among the party's candidates was being planned with 17 candidates vying for the nomination. How could a reasonable debate be carried out with so many people on stage? The host of the debate, Fox News, made a decision to limit the number of participants to 10. Fox would choose from the 17 candidates those who registered in the top spots from an average of five national polls as the debate grew near. If anyone in the top ten failed to earn at least a 5 percent ranking in the polls, that person would be eliminated from the debate. In such debates, candidates with higher poll numbers are stationed toward the middle of the stage allowing them to appear on the screen more frequently and say more.

National polling also exerts influence on elections through the **bandwagon effect**—a shift of support to a candidate or position holding the lead in public opinion polls and therefore believed to be endorsed by many people. The more popular a candidate or position, the more likely increasing numbers of people will "hop on the bandwagon" and add their support. People like to back a winning candidate. For this reason, most media outlets do not report the findings from their statewide Election Day exit polls until polls have closed in that state. If people who have not yet voted learn that Candidate A is way ahead in votes, they may not bother going to the polls, because they support either Candidate A (that candidate will win anyway) or a rival who was behind (that candidate has no chance of winning).

The bandwagon effect is also partly responsible for the direct link between a candidate's rank in national polls and the ability to raise campaign funds. The higher the national ratings, the more campaign contributions a candidate can elicit. The larger a candidate's war chest—the funds used to pay for a campaign—the more ads a candidate can buy and the larger the staff a candidate can maintain. Both greatly influence the outcome of an election.

Influence on Policy Debate

Scientific polling also exerts an influence on government policy and decision-making, although its effects are less clear than on elections. The three branches of the government tend to respond to public opinion polling in somewhat different ways, if at all.

The legislative branch is sometimes responsive to public opinion polls, especially the House of Representatives where lawmakers face reelection every two years. Many try to represent their constituencies and to keep them satisfied with their performance to encourage fundraising and subsequent votes, so knowing constituent views pays off. Senators, with longer terms, do not seem as sensitive to pressure from public opinion.

The executive branch has sometimes been influenced by public opinion and at other times has tried to use the power of the "bully pulpit" to shift public opinion. (See Topic 2.7.) A president usually enjoys high approval ratings in the first year of office and tries to use that popularity as a "mandate" to advance his or her agenda as quickly as possible.

The judicial branch may be influenced by the general mood of the nation. Different studies have drawn varying conclusions about why. However, many have concluded that when the opinions of the nation shift toward liberal, the Court will hand down more liberal rulings. This was apparent with the growing liberal attitudes of the 1960s and the often-liberal decisions handed down by the Warren Court. (See Topic 2.10.) Conversely, when the nation moved toward conservative ideology near the end of the 20th century, the Rehnquist Court's rulings often mirrored those beliefs.

However, federal judges are appointed for life and are not at the mercy of the ballot box, keeping the judicial branch somewhat removed from the sway of public opinion.

Reliability and Veracity of Public Opinion Data

One way to gauge the accuracy of a pre-election poll is to measure "candidate error"—the percentage point difference in the poll's estimate and the candidate's actual share of the vote after the election. Candidate error has gradually declined as polling techniques have become more sophisticated. But in the last few years, what has been a consistently improving science and practice, with the occasional setback, has had some less-than-accurate predictions.

For example, Gallup predicted Mitt Romney as the winner of the 2012 presidential election with 50 percent of the vote and President Obama at 49 percent. In reality, Obama won nationally by nearly four points. This failure led to Gallup's eventual decision to no longer predict presidential election outcomes through the so-called horse-race polls, but to stick instead to its vast polling of issues and views in other areas of public policy. Gallup wasn't the only firm that had an erroneous prediction outside the margin of error in 2012.

In the waning days of the 2016 presidential election, national polls projected that Hillary Clinton would defeat Donald Trump. Election forecasters, those who aggregate polls and other data to make bold predictions, put Clinton's chances of winning at 70 to 99 percent. The final round of polling by most major firms had Clinton winning by anywhere from 1 to 7 percentage points in the national vote.

However, the election was ultimately decided by 51 state elections (counting the electoral votes from Washington, DC). On the day prior to the election, 26 states had polling results with Trump ahead. His strongest support was in Oklahoma and West Virginia where 60 percent of respondents claimed a vote for Trump. 23 states had Clinton ahead. Maryland and Hawaii showed the strongest support for Clinton with 63 percent and 58 percent respectively. Once the vote was counted, Clinton won the popular vote by 2 percentage points but lost the Electoral College vote.

Several factors may explain why polls may be inaccurate and unreliable. One factor relates to the psychology of the respondents. Another factor relates to undecided voters and when they finally make up their minds.

Social-Desirability Bias

The psychology behind the errors in recent polls is at least in part explained by **social desirability bias**—the tendency for respondents and declared voters to tell pollsters what they think the pollsters want to hear. Social desirability bias affects the predictions of voter turnout. Respondents may give the interviewer the impression that they will indeed vote, because they do not want to be seen as shirking a responsibility, but often on Election Day they do not vote. In a recent estimate, when asked their likelihood of voting on a scale of 1 to 9, U. S. citizens tended to say 8 or 9, yet only about 60 percent of eligible voters cast ballots.

Social desirability bias can fool pollsters on matters beyond inflated turnout. Voters do not want to be perceived negatively, so they may give the interviewers a socially acceptable response, or what they perceive as the acceptable response, and yet act or vote in a different way. This phenomenon was noticeable in the 1982 California governor's race. The election included a popular candidate, Los Angeles Mayor Tom Bradley, who would have been the state's first African American governor. Bradley led by a clear margin in the polls throughout the campaign but lost on Election Day. Most experts attributed the discrepancy to interviewees' falsely claiming they supported Bradley only later to vote for a white candidate. These poll participants did not want to appear bigoted or against the African American candidate. In what has become known as the **Bradley effect**, recent African American candidates have also underperformed against their consistently inflated poll predictions.

Pundits in 2017 encouraged speculation as public opinion polls shifted in the special U.S. Senate election in Alabama. In some polls, Republican candidate Roy Moore, the favorite for weeks, was suddenly losing to Democrat Doug Jones after Moore was alleged to have committed sexual assault or aggressions toward several women when they were teenagers. Skeptics of the new polls pointed out that voters might not willingly admit on the phone that they were going to vote for this accused candidate. In fact, one famous political pundit, Nate Silver, pointed out that in polls using robocalls, or automated pre-recorded polls, Moore was ahead, and in polls using live interviews, Jones was ahead. Jones won in a close contest.

Undecideds Breaking Late

According to exit polling and research after the election, a likely explanation for Trump's surprise win was that a larger than usual share of undecided voters "broke"—made their final decision late—for Trump. Nate Cohn of *The New York Times* explains how likely voters who said they were voting for a third-party candidate mostly did so. But 26 percent of those voters turned to Trump and only 11 percent switched to Clinton. Pollsters theorize that a disproportionate number of so-called "shy Trump voters" simply declined to participate in any polling opportunities. Perhaps the same anti-establishment, anti-media attitude that drew these voters to the outsider candidate also turned them away from pollsters, a phenomenon known as **non-response bias.**

THINK AS A POLITICAL SCIENTIST: *EXPLAIN WHAT THE DATA IMPLIES ABOUT POLITICAL PROCESSES AND BEHAVIORS*

Pre-election polls are not an exact science. Polls have been wrong in the last two presidential elections. Were the problems with the methodology of the polls? Was there human error or respondent bias to blame for the inaccuracies? Whatever the cause, ample data pointed to a Clinton victory in 2016.

Practice: Study the information below from October and November of the election year 2016, and answer the questions that follow.

CLINTON-TRUMP 2016 HEAD-TO-HEAD PRESIDENTIAL POLLS (OCT.-NOV. 2016)					
Poll	**Clinton**	**Trump**	**Unsure or Other**	**Margin of Error**	**Sample Size**
Economist/YouGov Nov. 4–7, 2016	49%	45%	6%	NA	3,669
Fox News Nov. 3–6, 2016	48%	44%	8%	+/-2.5	1,295
CBS News Nov. 2–6, 2016	47%	43%	10%	+/-3	1,426
NBC News/SurveyMonkey Oct. 31–Nov. 6, 2016	51%	44%	5%	+/-1	30,145

Source: Ballotpedia.org

1. What additional information might make this table more useful?
2. What might explain the different results among the various polls?
3. What might explain the incorrect polling results leading up to the 2016 election?

Opinions in Social Media

The willingness of people to take part in polls is declining. About 37 percent of randomly called citizens would participate in a telephone poll in 1997. Today, pollsters get about a 10 percent response rate with live callers, and about 1 percent participation with robocalls. However, as Kristin Soltis Anderson, author of *The Selfie Vote*, points out, "The good news is, at the same time people are less likely to pick up the phone and tell you what they think, we are more able to capture the opinions and behaviors that people give off passively." Pollsters can take the public's pulse from available platforms widely used by a large swath of the general public. Examining what is said on social media and in the Google toolbar can tell us a lot about public opinion.

Though blogs and the Twitter-verse constitute a massive sample, the people active on social media may have very different views from those who are not active on social media, so the sample is not representative. A 2015 study found that people who discuss politics on Twitter tend to be overwhelmingly male, urban, and extreme in their ideological views. Another problem that makes this endeavor less than reliable is that researchers use computer programs to gauge the Internet's dialogue but cannot easily discern sarcasm and unique language. And overly vocal people can go onto the Internet repeatedly and be tabulated multiple times, dominating the conversation disproportionately.

Biased Pollsters and Data vs. Fact

Reputable pollsters seek ways to avoid bias in sampling techniques and the wording of their questions. However, many polls are funded by political parties and special interest groups who want the poll results to tip a certain way. Interest groups will use those results to move their agendas forward, claiming that the data generated by their polls represent fact. "The numbers don't lie," they might say. Parties may use information to convince the public that their candidate is popular and doing well among all voters or various blocs of voters.

Unless you know about the organization doing the polling, the methods it used, the wording of the questions, and the context of the poll, you will not be able to evaluate a poll's veracity, or truthfulness. You have already read about how push polls (see Topic 4.5) slant their questions to produce certain outcomes. Political Action Committees (PACs), special interest groups, and partisan organizations all have a vested interest in getting a response from a poll that supports their cause. To help journalists evaluate the reliability and veracity of polls, the National Council on Public Polls (NCPP) provides 20 questions journalists should ask and answer before reporting on a poll. You can find that list on the NCPP website. The checklist below provides some of the key questions to ask about any poll.

QUESTIONS FOR EVALUATING CLAIMS BASED ON PUBLIC OPINION POLLS	
1. Who conducted the poll, and who paid for it?	If it was done by a reputable polling organization, it is probably accurate; if it was done (or paid for) by special interests, you need to consider possible bias.
2. What methodology did the pollsters use?	Reliable polls are often released with a report that explains how the results were obtained: the sampling methods, whether or not the results are weighted, and the margin of error.
3. What were the exact questions, and in what order were they presented?	As you read, the wording and ordering of questions can have a significant impact on the poll results.
4. How were the results obtained?	People tend to be more honest in mailed polls than when interacting with an interviewer because of social desirability bias.
5. In what context was the poll taken?	The date information is collected can be a factor in poll results. For example, if a statewide poll was taken in the days following a barrage of media ads for a certain candidate, the poll results may inflate the candidate's actual popularity.
6. Whose opinion might be missing from the poll?	Good polls need to make an accommodation for people who refused to participate in the poll in order to provide a fair sample.
7. How do the poll results compare with other poll results?	If the results of a poll match up with other polls taken under the same circumstances and at the same time, chances are good the poll is reliable.

KEY TERMS AND NAMES

bandwagon effect   non-response bias
Bradley Effect   social desirability bias

CHAPTER 13 Review:
Learning Objectives and Key Terms

TOPIC 4.5: Describe the elements of a scientific poll. (MPA-2.A)

Effects of Scientific Polling on Elections and Policy (MPA-2.A.1)

approval rating	random-digit dialing
benchmark polls	random sample
entrance polls	representative sample (universe)
exit polls	sampling error (margin of error)
focus group	tracking polls
push polling	weighting (stratification)

TOPIC 4.6: Explain the quality and credibility of claims based on public opinion data. (MPA-2.B)

Relationship Between Polling and Elections and Policy (MPA-2.B.1)

bandwagon effect	non-response bias
Bradley effect	social desirability bias

CHAPTER 13 Checkpoint:
Public Opinion

Topics 4.5–4.6

MULTIPLE-CHOICE QUESTIONS

Questions 1 and 2 refer to the cartoon below.

CartoonStock.com

1. Which of the following statements best reflects the cartoonist's point of view?

   (A) Citizens accept poll results from reliable news organizations.

   (B) Polling during campaigns is overdone, and the media does not give careful consideration to the polls they present.

   (C) Opinion polls are used often, but they have a low margin of error.

   (D) Polling and the reporting of polls can improperly influence an election.

2. Which of the following might encourage the media to limit their reporting of polling during a campaign season?

   (A) The static nature of public opinion

   (B) The bandwagon effect

   (C) Sampling error

   (D) Equality of opportunity

3. Which of the following is necessary for a public opinion poll to be valid?

   (A) The poll must use objective, open-ended questions.

   (B) The poll must include equal numbers of people from different demographic groups.

   (C) The poll must be conducted by a responsible news organization.

   (D) The poll must have a low margin of error.

Questions 4 and 5 refer to the passage below.

So-called "Push polls" are not polls at all. They are a form of political telemarketing whose intent is not to measure public opinion but to manipulate—"push"—voters away from one candidate and toward the opposing candidate. Such polls defame selected candidates by spreading false or misleading information about them. The intent is to disseminate campaign propaganda under the guise of conducting a legitimate public opinion poll.

> —American Association for Public Opinion Research,
> "Condemned Survey Practices," 2017

4. Based on the text, with which of the following statements would the authors most likely agree?

   (A) As long as all sides use push polling equally, the effect should be minimal.

   (B) Despite its problems, push polling gives pollsters a fair sense of public opinion.

   (C) Telemarketing disguised as research has decreased response rates and discredited public opinion polling.

   (D) The government should provide campaign funding and regulate campaign practices.

5. Which of the following questions is most likely to appear on a push poll?

   (A) Do you approve of increasing the military budget?

   (B) Do you approve of raising property taxes slightly to help fund schools?

   (C) Do you approve of rolling back environmental regulations to encourage business investment?

   (D) Do you approve of the waste of money on failing social service agencies under the current governor?

6. A Republican candidate for U.S. Senate has hired a pollster who conducts a poll among likely voters across the state and collects a sample of over 2,500 respondents. He conducted his poll carefully, but his sample has 65% women and 35% men. What technique in measuring public opinion must the pollster use to make the poll accurately reflect public opinion?

(A) Randomization

(B) Enhance the questions

(C) Stratification

(D) Ask additional respondents

FREE-RESPONSE QUESTIONS

Concept Application

1. "Consider the motives of the media reporting on the polls. Conservative and liberal media outlets are more likely to report on polls more favorable to their candidates or portray outlier polls as the true state of the race. And even nonpartisan media outlets know that 'New Poll Shows Race Hasn't Changed' isn't a great headline. Additionally, a media company that sponsors a poll is probably going to want to hype up their own findings."

—Harry Enten, fivethirtyeight.com, September 2, 2016

After reading the excerpt above, respond to A, B, and C below:

(A) Describe a reason media outlets engage in the behaviors described in the excerpt.

(B) In the context of the scenario, explain how polling has increased partisanship.

(C) In the context of the scenario, explain how the interaction between polling and voters can impact government.

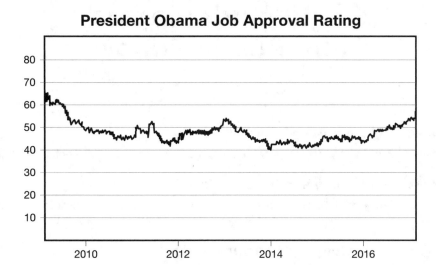

President Obama Job Approval Rating

2. Use the line graph above to answer the following questions.

(A) Identify the point in the Obama presidency when his job approval was the highest.

(B) Describe a trend in the graph regarding President Obama's approval rating.

(C) Draw a conclusion about what might explain the trend from part B.

(D) Explain the impact public opinion can have on a presidency.

CHAPTER 14

Political Ideologies and Public Policy

Topics 4.7–4.10

Topic 4.7 Ideologies of Political Parties

PMI-4.A: Explain how ideologies of the two major parties shape policy debate.

Topic 4.8 Ideology and Policy Making

PMI-4.B: Explain how U.S. political culture (e.g., values, attitudes, and beliefs) influences the formation, goals, and implementation of public policy over time.

Topic 4.9 Ideology and Economic Policy

PMI-4.C: Describe different political ideologies in the role of government in regulating the marketplace.

PMI-4.D: Explain how political ideologies vary on the government's role in regulating the marketplace.

Topic 4.10 Ideology and Social Policy

PMI-4.E: Explain how political ideologies vary on the role of the government in addressing social issues.

PMI-4.F: Explain how different political ideologies impact policy on social issues.

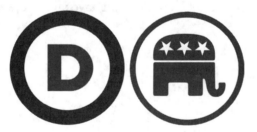

Source: Wikimedia Commons
The symbols for the Democratic Party (left) and the Republican Party (right)

4.7

Ideologies of Political Parties

"A political ideology is a very handy thing to have. It's a real time-saver, because it tells you what you think about things you know nothing about."
—Hendrik Hertzberg, *Politics: Observations and Arguments*, 2004

Essential Question: How have ideologies of the two major parties shaped policy debate?

The modern Republican Party holds a conservative party doctrine. Republicans for decades have preached against wasteful spending and for a strong national defense, limited regulation of businesses, and maintaining cultural traditions. Democrats, on the other hand, uphold a more liberal doctrine advocating for civil rights, women's rights, and rights of the accused. Democrats also desire more government services to solve public problems and greater regulations to protect the environment.

These general ideological positions of the two major parties tend to determine the terms of debate on public policy issues. Additional minor parties are players in this political game and have a degree of influence in policymaking.

Political Ideologies

People take positions on public issues and develop a political viewpoint on how government should act in line with their ideology. An **ideology** is a comprehensive and mutually consistent set of ideas. When there are two or more sides to an issue, voters tend to fall into different camps, either a conservative or a liberal ideology. However, this diverse nation has a variety of ideologies that overlap one another. (You will read more about political ideologies in Topic 5.3.)

Regardless of ideology, most Americans agree that the government should regulate dangerous industries, educate children at public expense, and protect free speech, at least to a degree. Everyone wants a strong economy and national security. These are **valence issues**—concerns or policies that are viewed in the same way by people with a variety of ideologies. When political candidates debate valence issues, "the dialogue can be like a debate between the nearly identical Tweedledee and Tweedledum," says congressional elections expert Paul Herrnson.

In contrast to valence issues, **wedge issues** sharply divide the public. Wedge issues are used by political groups in strategic ways to gather support for an issue, especially among those who have yet to develop strong opinions. Wedge politics leaves little room for acceptance of competing ideas, each ideology considers their opinion right and the other side wrong. These could include the issues of abortion or the 2003 invasion and later occupation of Iraq.

The more divisive issues tend to hold a high **saliency**, or intense importance, to an individual or a group. For senior citizens, for example, questions about reform of the Social Security system hold high saliency. For people eighteen to twenty years old, the relative lack of job opportunities may have high saliency, since their unemployment rate is higher than that of older age groups.

The Liberal-Conservative Spectrum

Political scientists use the terms *liberal* and *conservative*, as well as the corresponding "left" and "right," to label each end of an ideological spectrum. Most Americans are **moderate,** meaning somewhere in between, and never fall fully into one camp or the other. Many others may think conservatively on some issues and have liberal beliefs on others.

Even labeling the two parties as liberal or conservative is an oversimplification. Some self-described conservatives want nothing to do with the Republican Party, and many Democrats dislike being labelled as liberal.

Political Ideology

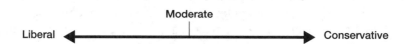

The meanings of the terms *liberal* and *conservative* have changed through history. In the early United States, a "liberal" government was one that did little. Thomas Jefferson believed in a high degree of liberty, declaring that a government that governs best is one that governs least. With this statement, Jefferson described the government's liberal approach toward the people, allowing citizen freedom, a free flow of ideas, free markets, fewer laws, and fewer restrictions. This understanding of the word continued into the late nineteenth century.

In the Progressive Era (1890–1920), the federal government expanded its activity, going outside the confines of traditional government. Then, in the 1930s, Democratic President Franklin Delano Roosevelt (FDR) proposed a "liberal" plan for emergency legislation amidst the Great Depression. His New Deal agenda was new and revolutionary. The government took on new responsibilities in ways it never had. The government acted in a liberal way, less constrained by tradition or limitations that guided earlier governments. Since the 1930s, the term **liberal** has usually meant being open to allowing the government to act flexibly and expand beyond established constraints.

The term **conservative** describes those who believe in following tradition and having reverence for authority. Modern-day conservatives often invoke Jefferson and argue that government should do less and thus allow people more freedom. In the early 1960s, Arizona Senator Barry Goldwater embraced the conservative label and published a book, *The Conscience of a Conservative*, en route to his 1964 Republican presidential nomination. He and much of his party believed that Roosevelt's New Deal policies had unwisely altered the role of government. Goldwater and his party wanted less economic regulation and more responsibility on the citizenry. Many conservatives today call themselves "fiscal conservatives" because they want to see less taxation and less government spending overall.

Since FDR's presidency and Goldwater's nomination, these political terms have further evolved, and now it is difficult to know exactly what they mean. Roosevelt would likely not support some of the more liberal goals of the Democratic Party today, and Goldwater, in retirement, supported Democratic President Bill Clinton's initiatives to open the military for LGBTQ volunteers and recruits. Additionally, an array of cultural and social issues that came to the forefront in the 1960s and 1970s changed the dynamic between those who consider themselves conservative and those who consider themselves liberal, thus changing the meaning of the terms.

Traditional Christian voters, family values groups, and others who oppose abortion and same-sex marriage and support prayer in school have adopted the conservative label and have aligned themselves with the Republican Party. However, policies that restrict abortion, censor controversial material in books or magazines, or seek to more tightly define marriage actually require more, not less, law and regulation. For supporters of these policies, then, the conservative label is not necessarily accurate. People who believe in more regulation on industry, stronger gun control, and the value of diversity are generally seen as liberal. But when government acts to establish these goals, Jefferson might say, it is not necessarily acting liberally in relation to the rights of the people.

Off the Line

If you have trouble finding the precise line between liberal and conservative, you are not alone. Cleavages, or gaps, in public opinion make understanding where the public stands on issues even more difficult. Few people, even regular party members, agree with every conservative or every liberal idea. Many people simply do not fall on the linear continuum but rather align themselves with one of several other notable political philosophies: **libertarian, populist**, or **progressive**.

Voters who generally oppose government intervention or regulation are **libertarian**. As their name suggests, they have a high regard for civil liberties, those rights outlined in the Bill of Rights. They oppose censorship, want lower taxes, and dislike government-imposed morality. Though a small Libertarian Party operates today (in 2016, Libertarian candidate Gary Johnson won 3.2 percent of the national vote) more citizens claim the libertarian (small "l") label than formally belong to the party. Libertarian-minded citizens can be found in both the Republican and Democratic parties. In short, libertarians are conservative on economic issues, such as government spending or raising the minimum wage, while they tend to be liberal on moral or social issues. Most libertarians are pro-choice on abortion and support the equal treatment of LGBTQ people. As Nick Gillespie and Matt Welch of the libertarian *Reason* magazine write in their book, *Declaration of Independents*, "We believe that you should be able to think what you want, live where you want, trade for what you want, eat what you want, smoke what you want, and wed whom you want."

Populists have a very different profile. Generally, a **populist** will attend a Protestant church and follow fundamental Christian ideas: love thy neighbor, contribute to charity, and follow a strict moral code. More populists can be found in the South and Midwest than along each coast. They tend to come from working-class families. They favor workplace safety protections and farm subsidies, as these are necessary expenses for the welfare of the citizenry. Yet they also would curb obscene or unpatriotic speech and would be less sympathetic to the accused criminal defendant.

Donald Trump was the populists' candidate in 2016. No serious observer would call Trump a populist, but there is little doubt populist voters helped swing the election in Trump's favor. Men without a college degree who work in the Rustbelt factories of Youngstown, Detroit, and Pittsburg, who normally vote Democratic, came out and voted for Trump. The blue-collar worker and those with steadfast religious views rallied around a strong voice and promises to protect police, veterans, and American jobs.

The **Progressive** Movement emerged in cities from the roots of the Republican Party. It peaked in the United States in the early 1900s when reformers challenged government corruption that ran counter to the values of equality, individualism, democracy, and advancement. At that time, the Republican Party split into its two wings: conservative and progressive. Progressives criticized traditional political establishments that concentrated too much power in one place, such as government and business. Modern progressives are aligned with labor unions. They believe in workers' rights over corporate rights, and they believe the wealthier classes should pay a much larger percentage of taxes than they currently do.

With some variation, 35 to 45 percent of Americans consider themselves moderate. Yet there are more conservatives than liberals in the U.S. In 1992, Gallup measured the difference between self-described conservatives at 36 percent and liberals at 17 percent, with 43 percent calling themselves moderate. In 2019, the annual poll found self-described conservatives remained at 35 percent, but self-described liberals have risen steadily to 26 percent (35 percent said claimed to be moderate). Views have changed, and so have the perceptions of these labels.

A 2020 Gallup survey on party affiliation found that 27 percent claimed to be Democrats, 30 percent called themselves Republicans, and 42 percent considered themselves independent. Many people's views fall between these ideologies and between the two major political parties.

Party Platforms

The best way to determine a party's primary ideology is to read its platform, or list of principles and plans it hopes to enact. Platforms are approved at the party's national convention every four years and committee members argue over the wording of the document. The arguments have revealed strong intraparty differences or fractures.

In addition to basic principles, the party platforms drafted in 2016 include the legacies of each party's noted historical heroes, some specific proposals, and accusations against the opposite party. Below and on the next page are some selected quotes from the Democratic and Republican platforms on a wide range of issues.

Democratic Party Platform 2016

- **On health care for the poor:** "We will keep fighting until the [Affordable Care Act's] Medicaid expansion has been adopted in every state."
- **On equal rights for women:** "We are committed to ensuring full equality for women. Democrats will fight to end gender discrimination in the areas of education, employment, health care, or any other sphere."
- **On equality and sexual orientation:** "Democrats will fight for the continued development of sex discrimination law to cover LGBT people."
- **On immigration:** "Democrats believe we need to urgently fix our broken immigration system—which tears families apart and keeps workers in the shadows—and create a path for citizenship for law-abiding families."
- **On climate change:** "Democrats share a deep commitment to tackling climate challenge . . . We believe America must be running entirely on clean energy by mid-century."
- **On abortion:** "Democrats are committed to protecting and advancing reproductive health, rights, and justice. . . . every woman should have access to quality reproductive health care services, including safe and legal abortion . . ."

These statements reveal why each party has a unique following of voters. The Democrats have claimed that they are an inclusive party that works for minority rights. Republicans, on the other hand, rely on conservative voters who support limited gun regulation, anti-abortion legislation, and increased national security. The electoral map of recent years shows these same geographic trends. The Democratic Party generally carries the more liberal northeastern states and those on the West Coast, while Republicans carry most of the South and rural West and Midwest. In recent decades, Democrats have increased their votes among women, African Americans, and the fastest-growing minority in the United States, Hispanics.

Republican Party Platform 2016

- **On poverty and welfare:** "We propose . . . work requirements in a growing economy, where opportunity takes the place of a hand-out, where true self-esteem can grow from the satisfaction of a job well done."

- **On the death penalty:** "With the murder rate soaring in our great cities, we condemn the Supreme Court's erosion of the right of the people to enact capital punishment in their states."

- **On marriage:** "[Family] is the foundation of civil society, and the cornerstone of the family is natural marriage, the union of one man and one woman."

- **On immigration:** "Our highest priority . . . must be to secure our borders and all ports of entry and to enforce our immigration laws."

- **On gun control:** "We salute the Republican Congress for defending the right to keep and bear arms by preventing the President from installing a new liberal majority on the Supreme Court."

- **On abortion:** "We oppose the use of public funds to promote or perform abortion. . . . We will not fund or subsidize healthcare that includes abortion coverage."

Democrats and Republicans also tend to disagree on economic matters and issues related to law and order. Democrats, for example, tend to support increasing government services for the poor, including health care, and they tend to support regulations on business to promote environmental quality and equal rights. Republicans tend to oppose higher levels of government spending and the expansion of entitlements—programs such as Social Security and Medicare—while supporting a strong national defense. They also tend to support limited regulation of business. On law and order, Democrats tend to prefer rehabilitation for prisoners over severe punishments and often oppose the death penalty. Republicans tend to favor full prison sentences with few opportunities for parole and, as their platform states, they support the right of courts to impose the death penalty in certain cases.

THINK AS A POLITICAL SCIENTIST: *EXPLAIN HOW POLITICAL PRINCIPLES APPLY TO DIFFERENT SCENARIOS*

As you have read in this topic, beliefs of conservatives and liberals (and other political ideologies) have evolved over time as new issues capture the attention of the nation. These changing issues can occasionally make it difficult to identify the views of ideological groups. Even during these times of change there will still be divisive topics, or wedge issues, that highlight the differences between ideologies.

Practice: Read the question and ideological summaries below. Determine which of the three answers shows *conservative*, which shows *liberal*, and which shows *libertarian* views. Then, explain why you identified a particular ideology with each statement.

1. **Should the federal government have a mandated minimum wage?**

   A) No. Wages should be set based on market competition. This will allow employers to hire the best workers at fair wages.

   B) Yes. Employers could exploit workers with subsistence level wages. This is protection for workers and a guarantee of a living wage.

   C) No. Employers and employees have a right to strike their own deals. Minimum wages violate the invisible hand of the market and historically have caused unemployment to rise.

2. **How should the federal government deal with the budget deficit?**

   A) Reduce taxes and federal spending to stimulate the economy. Limit government spending to specifically listed tasks and pay toward the national debt with saving.

   B) Borrow money in the short term to maintain the defense budget without raising taxes. In the long term, offer supply-side economic stimulation.

   C) Keep federal social programs by raising taxes on the wealthy.

REFLECT ON THE ESSENTIAL QUESTION

Essential Question: *How have ideologies of the two major parties shaped policy debate?* *On separate paper, complete the table below.*

Key Issues	Liberal Ideology	Conservative Ideology

KEY TERMS AND NAMES

conservative	populist
ideology	progressive
liberal	saliency
libertarian	valence issues
moderate	wedge issues

Ideology and Policy Making

"No matter where you stand politically—even if you're unsure of what your political ideology is—it is important to take part in the process of shaping our government."

—Governor Brad Henry (D-OK), 2010

Essential Question: How does U.S. political culture influence the formation, goals, and implementation of public policy over time?

Widely held political ideologies shape policy debates and choices, including the government's domestic, economic, and foreign policies. Policy is created and shaped by the federal government, even in small ways, such as when a member of Congress inserts language into a bill, when the president discusses relations with another head of state, when the U.S. Postal Service changes its delivery schedule, or when a court sets a precedent. The impetus for those policies, however, stems from Americans' values, attitudes, and beliefs. These drive the formation, goals, and implementation of public policy over time.

Influences on Public Policy

Americans have a range of values, attitudes, and beliefs. These influence the development, goals, and implementation of public policy over time. Policies in place at any given time represent the success of the parties whose ideologies they represent and the political attitudes and beliefs of citizens who choose to participate in politics. Following are some of the key theories or pathways to policy. These differing pathways reflect some of the different types of democracy you read about in Topic 1.2, since the United States has elements of each of them.

Majoritarian Policy Making

Democratic government, a foundational principle in America, is meant to represent the people's views through elected representatives. This principle is reflected through **majoritarian** policy making, which emerges from the interaction of people with government in order to put into place and carry out the will of the majority. Popular ideas will work their way into the body politic via state and national legislatures. A president seeking a second term may go with public opinion when there is an outcry for a new law or a different way of enforcing an existing law. State referenda and initiatives, too, are a common way for large grassroots efforts to alter current policy when state assemblies refuse to make laws that reflect the public will. These are examples of participatory democracy.

This democratic system sounds fair and patriotic. But the framers also put into place a republic of states and a system to ensure that the tyranny of the majority did not run roughshod over the rights of the minority. Additionally, the framers warned, factions—often minority interests—will press government to address their needs, and at times government will comply.

Interest Group Policy Making

Interest groups have a strong influence and interact with all three branches in the policy making process. They fund candidates who support their agendas, experts sympathetic to their concerns provide testimony at hearings, and they push for specific areas of policy to satisfy their members and their philosophy.

Interest groups represent a pluralist approach to policymaking. The interests of the diverse population of the United States, ethnically and ideologically, compete to create public policy that addresses as many group concerns as compromise allows.

Balancing Liberty and Order

No matter the approach to public policymaking, two underlying principles guide debate. One is the core belief in individual liberties. The other is the shared belief that one important role of government is to promote stability and social order. Policy debates are often an effort to find the right balance between these fundamental values. **BIG IDEA** Governmental laws and policies balancing order and liberty are based on the Constitution and have been interpreted differently over time.

Formation of Policy

In creating policy, public officials follow a general routine. Legislators and bureaucrats develop and reshape an **agenda**—a list of potential policy ideas, bills, or plans to improve society. These could be new methods of law enforcement, alterations of the tax system, or a long-term plan to improve relations with a foreign nation. With each new policy idea comes a cost-benefit analysis, a full look into the efforts and sacrifice that come with a new policy compared to the benefits the new policy would bring. For example, building an overhead skywalk at every intersection would reduce pedestrian injuries and deaths, but the costs—the actual price, the disruption caused by their construction, the unsightliness, and pedestrian confusion from such a network of skywalks— might outweigh the benefits.

Sequence

Ideally, governments at all levels recognize an issue, study it, and try to solve it. First an issue gains attention. The attention may come from a widespread citizen push to ban smoking in public places, for example, or it may come from a defense contractor's proposed design for new fighter jets. Once the issue becomes of public concern, Congress may exercise its investigatory power to better understand the issue. If interest in an issue reaches this stage, the relevant committee(s) will hear experts testify. Ideally, all sides of the issue and particular concerns about solving the problem will be heard.

Source: DigitalVision
State referenda give voters direct power over policy.

Then, government formulates the policy on paper, whether it is a new bill or a new way for police to enforce existing law. As the topic is discussed in theory and the language of a bill or an executive directive is developed and refined, the government will work toward adopting the policy. Changes in law usually come incrementally, with the most passable ideas coming before any major overhauls.

Implementation and Administration

The government must also figure out a way to finance the enforcement of new laws. Each new policy requires the executive branch to enforce it, which means either creating an additional agency to oversee the law or giving more responsibilities to an existing one. Then, the government will evaluate the new policy sometime after its implementation. This evaluation could be achieved through required agency reports or with congressional oversight.

Challenges to new policies quickly come from those who oppose the law. Opponents often file suit to overturn the law in the courts. Many times, a state legislature will pass a controversial bill with a marginal vote only to see the citizenry rise up and repeal it through a referendum. In Ohio, for example, the state legislature had passed a bill (Senate Bill 5) limiting collective bargaining for 400,000 state employees, preventing them from striking and limiting their ability to conduct collective bargaining for better pay and benefits. The bill was signed into law on March 31, 2011. Opponents of the law collected more than one million signatures to put the law on the ballot as a referendum. The voters repealed the law in November 2011. Policies, especially the wedge issues, will swing back and forth in relatively short periods of time.

Diverse ideologies of the citizens of the United States are reflected in political cartoons that show different sides to issues.

Practice: View the cartoon and answer the questions that follow.

"Let's switch. I'll make the policy, you implement it, and he'll explain it."

Source: Cartoonstock

1. What is the main point the artist makes?
2. How does the main point reflect the challenges of policymaking?
3. Does the artist show any bias in the cartoon toward policymaking?

REFLECT ON THE ESSENTIAL QUESTION

Essential Question: *How does U.S. political culture influence the formation, goals, and implementation of public policy over time? On separate paper, complete the chart below.*

Majoritarian Influence on Policy Making	Interest Group Influence on Policy Making

KEY TERMS AND NAMES

agenda	majoritarian

Ideology and Economic Policy

"Balancing the Budget is like going to heaven. Everybody wants to do it, but nobody wants to do what you have to do to get there."
—Senator Phil Graham, ABC This Week, 1990

Essential Question: What are the differing political ideologies on the government's role in regulating the marketplace, and what impact do those ideologies have?

The philosophy of the president and the collective attitude of Congress can drastically impact the federal budget, taxes paid into the federal purse, the value of the dollar, and trade relationships with foreign nations. Except for partisan identification, there are no greater determiners on Election Day than a voter's view of the economy and the economic scorecard for politicians in power. Incumbent presidents who sought reelection during a bad economy invariably lost their bid for a second term. The classic example is Herbert Hoover, who in 1932 sought reelection during the worst economy in history and suffered a landslide loss to Franklin Roosevelt. Presidents Ford in 1976, Carter in 1980, and Bush Sr. in 1992 all lost their quests for a second term during poor economic times. In 1992, with the Cold War over and the economy in bad shape, Bill Clinton's campaign manager, James Carville, reminded his candidate, "It's the economy, stupid." People who are adversely affected by the economy will vote against members of the incumbent party.

Political Ideologies and the Marketplace

Governing economic and budgetary issues is challenging, especially considering the general desires of the citizenry. Most people have three desires for government finances: lower taxes, no national debt, and enhanced government services. Having all three is impossible. So how do politicians satisfy these wants? "Don't tax me, don't tax thee, tax that fellow behind the tree," Senator Russell Long (D-LA) allegedly said. Long came from a family of adept Louisiana politicians who knew that the answer was to raise taxes on "other people." For example, governments create excise taxes on particular products or services, such as cigarettes or gambling (often called "sin taxes"), hitting only a few people, many of whom won't stop making such purchases even when taxes lead to higher prices.

A key difference between political ideologies is a set of beliefs about the extent to which the government should be involved in the economy. Liberal ideologies favor considerable government involvement in the economy as a way to keep it healthy and protect the public good. For example, during the economic decline of the Great Recession (2007–2013), President Obama and Democrats in power supported a high level of government spending to stimulate the economy with the Recovery Act of 2009. The law received practically no Republican support in Congress. Republicans criticized the bill for its emphasis on government spending rather than tax cuts, which is what the previous president, George W. Bush, had supported in the Economic Stimulus Act of 2008. Republicans argued the tax cuts put more money into the hands of citizens, giving them more control over how to spend it. Libertarian opposition was even stronger, since libertarians saw the law as an inappropriate expansion of government power.

Varying views on the role of government involvement and regulation of the economy are based on different economic theories. Liberals subscribe to the theory of English economist John Maynard Keynes (1883–1946) to support their views. Conservatives rely on "supply-side" theories developed by economists during the presidency of Republican Ronald Reagan (1981–1989). Libertarians have been influenced by economists such as Alan Greenspan, who was Chairman of the Board of the Federal Reserve System from 1987–2006, and Milton Friedman, winner of the Nobel Prize in Economics in 1976.

Keynesian Economics

Keynesian economics addresses **fiscal policy**, that part of economic policy that is concerned with government spending and taxation. Keynes offered a theory regarding the aggregate demand (the grand total spent by people) in an economy. He theorized that if left to its own devices, the market will not necessarily operate at full capacity. Not all persons will be employed, and the value of the dollar may drop. Much depends on how much people spend or save. Saving is wise for individuals, but when too many people save too much, companies will manufacture fewer products and unemployment will rise. When people spend too much, conversely, their spending will cause a sustained increase in prices and shortages of goods.

Keynes believed that the government should create the right level of demand. When demand is too low, the government should put more money into the economy by reducing taxes and/or increasing government spending, even if doing so requires borrowing money. This approach led to the 2009 American Recovery and Reinvestment Act. If demand is too high, the government should take money out of the economy by taxing more (taking wealth out of citizens' pockets) and/or spending less.

Keynesian economics also recognizes a *multiplier effect*, a mechanism by which an increase in spending results in an economic growth greater than the amount of spending. That is, output increases by a multiple of the original change in spending that caused it. For example, with a multiplier of 1.5, a

$10 billion increase in government spending could cause the total output of goods and services to rise by $15 billion. In concrete terms, consider what happens if the government begins public construction projects. Not only are unemployed construction contractors put to work, but bricklayers, electricians, and plumbers are too. With an income once again, these workers can afford to buy products and services from other retail businesses, whose income and demand for more employees increases.

Keynesian economics represents one end of the spectrum on the role of government regulation of the marketplace, calling for significant government involvement. Liberal ideologies tend to favor this level of government involvement. Democrat Franklin Roosevelt based his New Deal concept largely on the Keynesian model. The federal government built an array of public works during the Great Depression (1929–1939). Agencies such as the Works Progress Administration (WPA), the Public Works Administration (PWA), and the Civilian Conservation Corp (CCC) built new schools, dams, roads, libraries, and other capital investments. The government had to borrow money, which was then pumped into the economy providing jobs. Recently, the Recovery Act of 2009 helped create new jobs by investing in education, infrastructure, health, and renewable energy resources.

Source: Wikimedia Commons, WPA derivative work

A poster to promote one of the many jobs created by the Works Progress Administration. FDR used the WPA to stimulate the economy through increased employment opportunities during the Depression.

Supply-Side Theory

At the other end of the economic ideological spectrum are supply-side theorists. They, too, address fiscal policy, but in a different way. Harvard economist Arthur Laffer, a key advisor to Republican President Ronald Reagan, came to define **supply-side economics**. Supply-sider theorists—fiscal conservatives— believe that the government should leave as much of the money supply as possible with the people, letting the laws of economics, such as supply and demand, govern the marketplace. This approach, known as *laissez-faire* (French for "let it be") or free-market theory, means taxing less and leaving that money in citizens' pockets. According to this theory, such a stance serves two purposes: 1) people will have more money to spend and will spend it, and 2) this spending will increase purchasing, jobs, and manufacturing. Under this concept, the government will still earn large revenues via the taxes collected from this spending. The more people spend, the more the state collects in sales taxes. The federal government will take in greater amounts of income tax because more people will be employed and salaries will increase. Government will also take in greater quantities of revenues in corporate taxes from company profits. Supply-siders try to determine the right level of tax to strengthen firms and increase overall government revenues.

Keeping taxes low also provides incentives for people to work more and earn more, knowing they will be able to save more money. They will also invest in other ways. If they are not spending money at the store, they may put more money into the economy with larger investments, such as purchasing stocks or bonds. These activities boost the economy and show consumer confidence.

Conservative ideologies favor this supply-side theory with its limits on government regulations and reduced taxation. The Republican Congress in late 2017 passed the Tax Cuts and Jobs Act, promoted by President Trump, which overhauled the tax code, temporarily lowering taxes for individuals and permanently lowering taxes for corporations. Proponents of the bill, which passed in the Senate with no votes from Democrats, argued that the lower taxes for corporations will induce them to pass some of the savings on to workers in the form of higher wages and to hire more workers, both of which would help the economy grow.

Libertarians favor even fewer government regulations. Libertarians believe the government should do no more than protect property rights and voluntary trade. Beyond that, they want to let the free market work according to its own principles.

Fiscal Policy

In addition to conflicting views on the extent of government involvement in the economy, liberals and conservatives have differing views on the tax laws that produce revenue and policies that guide government spending.

Taxing

Article I of the Constitution gives Congress the power to lay and collect taxes, but when the framers empowered Congress to lay and collect taxes, they only vaguely defined how Congress would assess and collect those taxes. For the first several decades, customs duties on imports supplied most of the government revenues. During this time, however, the federal government provided many fewer services than it does in modern times.

Congress passed the first temporary income tax to support the Union cause during the Civil War. Later, Congress instituted the first-ever peacetime income tax to support the growing federal government. In *Pollock v. Farmers' Loan and Trust* (1892), the Supreme Court ruled income taxes unconstitutional because Article I did not specifically grant Congress the power to directly tax individuals' incomes. This was a classic late-1800s ruling that exemplified the Court's judicial activism and adherence to *laissez-faire* or free-market thought. It was also the ruling that brought the **Sixteenth Amendment** (1913), which trumped the Court and allows Congress to tax people's incomes. Soon after, Congress began defining the income tax system and later created the **Internal Revenue Service (IRS)** to oversee the collection process. Today, the largest share of federal revenue comes from income taxes on individuals.

Congress regularly alters the tax code for a variety of reasons. Our national income tax is a **progressive tax**, meaning one's tax rate increases, or progresses, as one's income increases. During World War II, the highest tax bracket required a small number of Americans, only those making the equivalent of $2.5 million a year in today's dollars, to pay 94 percent of their income in tax. Since President Kennedy encouraged a major drop in the tax rate in 1962, the top tax bracket has gradually diminished. In the 1970s, the richest taxpayers paid around 70 percent. While conservative Ronald Reagan was in office in the 1980s, it fell to below 30 percent, and in the most recent decades, it has hovered between 35 and 40 percent. The Trump administration's Tax Cuts and Jobs Act of 2017 lowered the highest individual tax bracket to 37 percent.

Source: Wikimedia Commons

(From left to right) Senate Majority Leader Mitch McConnell, Speaker of the House Paul Ryan, President Donald Trump, and Vice President Mike Pence celebrate the signing of the Republican-sponsored Tax Cuts and Jobs Act of 2017.

Congress has used taxing power not only as a revenue source but also as a way to draft social policy, by encouraging certain behaviors and discouraging others. When liberals have been in charge of drafting tax laws, Congress has created incentives to encourage people to purchase energy-efficient cars, appliances, solar panels, doors, and windows for their homes in order to protect the environment. The 2017 tax reform eliminated some of those incentives while providing incentives for families who hold what many call traditional values. These incentives include increased child tax credits to encourage having children, with married couples receiving the greatest benefits.

Paying nearly 40 percent of what one earns to the national government seems high, but only the richest Americans do so. Today, only people earning hundreds of thousands of dollars per year are paying at this high rate. In fact, more than 18 million people in the United States need not even file a tax return, and well over 30 million others still end up paying no federal income tax at all. Middle-class Americans—families earning under $165,000 per year—pay roughly between 12 and 22 percent of their incomes to the federal government. Public opinion supports a mildly progressive tax code, and that has been the standard since the Progressive Era (1890–1920). Some conservatives on the far right, however, argue for a **flat tax**, one that taxes citizens at the same rate. Libertarians go even further, arguing that the government should not coerce people to do anything, including paying taxes.

Spending

The budget process has become very partisan as Republicans and Democrats differ on spending priorities. Republicans tend toward fiscal conservatism; Democrats tend to spend federal dollars more liberally on social programs to help the disadvantaged or to support the arts.

The president initiates the annual budget, the plan for how revenue will be spent. (See Topic 2.2 for more on the budget process.) Members of Congress from the party opposite the president commonly claim the president's budget plan is "dead on arrival." The reality is that typically both parties vote to spend more than the federal government takes in, increasing the national debt, while they argue about philosophical differences on parts of the budget that make up a fraction of the total. For example, some argue against spending money on NASA and other scientific endeavors. For the 2017 budget, all funds going to science, space exploration, and technology totaled $19.6 billion, a huge sum, but less than 1 percent of the overall budget. The National Endowment for the Arts, always a target for criticism from fiscal conservatives, was eliminated completely from President Trump's 2018 budget proposal, as was the National Endowment for the Humanities, even though these endowments represented a mere 0.009 percent of the budget. In the final budget, however, their funding was extended. Welfare programs, a somewhat controversial slice of the federal pie, typically amount to between one and two percent.

Balancing the budget—spending no more than the revenue brings in—is a nearly impossible task. Democrat Bill Clinton (1993–2001) has been the only president in recent time to balance the budget, which he accomplished with no Republican support by raising taxes on the wealthy. Neither party has been able to sustain a balanced budget with all of the demands on government spending, though Democrats have done a slightly better job.

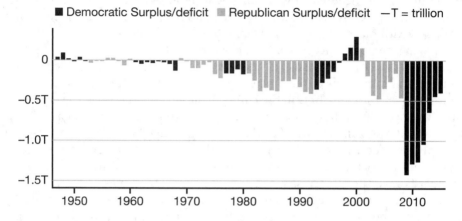

Federal Surplus and Deficit

■ Democratic Surplus/deficit   ■ Republican Surplus/deficit   —T = trillion

The sudden increase in the federal deficit in 2008 reflects the government stimulus programs to get the economy back on track after the "Great Recession."

Monetary Policy

The basic forces of supply and demand that determine prices on every product or service from lemonade to cars also determine the actual value of the U.S. dollar. Of course, a dollar is worth 100 cents, but what will it buy? Diamonds and gold are worth a lot because they are in short supply. Paper clips are cheap for the opposite reason. These same principles affect the value of money itself. **Monetary policy** is how the government manages the supply and demand of its currency and thus the value of the dollar. How much a dollar is worth depends on how many printed dollars are available and how much people in both in the United States and around the world want those dollars.

When there are too many dollars in circulation, **inflation**—rising prices and devaluation of the dollar—occurs. If a government closely monitors how much currency makes its way into circulation, the value of a dollar will remain relatively high. Conservatives tend to prefer monetary policy adjustments to regulate the economy over fiscal policies, which they tend to regard as wasteful government spending and unnecessary interference.

The Federal Reserve System

To manage the money supply, Congress created the Federal Reserve System in 1913. It consists of the **Federal Reserve Board** and 12 Federal Reserve Banks. The Federal Reserve Board, or "The Fed," is the board of seven "governors" appointed by the president and approved by the Senate for staggered 14-year terms. One governor serves as the chairman for a four-year term. This agency sets monetary policy by buying and selling securities or bonds, regulating money reserves required at commercial banks, and setting interest rates.

The 12 Federal Reserve Banks serve as the channel for money traveling from the government printing press to the commercial banks in your hometown. The U.S. government loans these printed dollars to the commercial banks and charges interest.

The Fed also sets the **discount rate**, the interest rate at which the government loans actual dollars to commercial banks. Since 1990, this rate has fluctuated from 4 to 6 percent; recently it has dropped below 1 percent. Raising or lowering the discount rate has a direct impact on commercial banking activity and the economy in general. Commercial banks will borrow larger sums when the rate is lower and drop their interest rates accordingly in order to loan more money to its customer-borrowers. When banks can offer lower interest rates to consumers, people purchase more cars and houses. When more homes or cars are purchased, employment rises as more car sales associates, realtors, and housing contractors are needed; and demand is generated for lumber, bricks, rubber, and gasoline.

Sometimes an economy can grow too fast or too much causing inflation. The Fed can raise the discount rate, slowing the flow of dollars and ultimately placing more national money into the reserve, resulting in a drop in prices of consumer goods.

THINK AS A POLITICAL SCIENTIST: *EXPLAIN LIMITATIONS OF THE DATA PROVIDED*

The Fed can affect the overall health of the economy by manipulating the discount rate. Looking at the discount rate over time can give indications of the nation's economic success.

Practice: Study the graphic and answer the questions that follow.

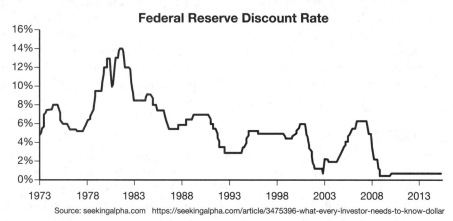

Source: seekingalpha.com https://seekingalpha.com/article/3475396-what-every-investor-needs-to-know-dollar

1. What inferences can be made from the data?

2. What additional information about the government's economic activity over this period might make this graphic more valuable in understanding the discount rate?

The Fed also regulates how much cash commercial banks must keep in their vaults. This amount is known as the **reserve requirement**. While these banks give you an incentive to keep your money with them by offering small interest rates on savings or checking accounts, they charge higher rates to those borrowing from them. The Fed sets reserve requirements, the amount of money that the bank must keep on hand as a proportion of how much money the bank rightfully possesses (though much of it is loaned out to borrowers). This reserve requirement has a direct effect on how much the bank can loan out. If the reserve requirement declines from $16 on hand for every $100 it loans out to $12 on hand per $100, the bank will be encouraged to loan out more. If the reserve requirement rises, the interest rates will also rise.

The Fed also determines the rates for government **bonds,** or securities—government IOUs—and when to sell or purchase these. In addition to taxes, the federal government takes in revenue when individual citizens or even foreign governments purchase U.S. bonds or other Treasury notes on a promise that the United States will pay them back later with interest. The Fed both sells bonds to and purchases them from commercial banks. When it buys them back with interest, it is giving the banks more money with which to operate and to loan to customers.

THE FEDERAL RESERVE AND THE ECONOMY

- The Fed sets the terms for U.S. bonds and treasury bills.
- The Fed can raise or lower the discount rate.
- The Fed can alter banks' reserve requirement.

As you can see, decisions at the Fed can have monumental impact on the value of the dollar and the state of the economy. That is why the Federal Reserve Board is an independent agency in the executive branch. Presidents can shape the Fed with appointments, but once confirmed, these federal governors and the chairman act in the best interest of the nation, not at the whims of the president or of a political party. The president cannot easily remove the governors. Their lengthy 14-year terms allow for continuity. The chairman's four-year term staggers the president's term to prevent making the president's appointment to the position an election issue.

Differing Views on Monetary Policy

Supporters of monetary policy as the best stabilizing factor in an economy—mainly conservatives—look to the work of Milton Friedman and Alan Greenspan (Fed chairman from 1987–2006) as their theoretical base. Both disagree with the Keynesian analysis of the economy and have supported an "easy-money" policy of lowering interest rates to stimulate banks to loan more money, which in turn stimulates consumption and economic growth. This policy also guards against inflation. Critics of this approach, including many liberals, point to studies that show it has not had the desired effects and may have even been part of the cause of the Great Recession. During this recession housing prices fell dramatically, stranding homeowners who borrowed with easy money and then found themselves with mortgage amounts exceeding the value of their homes. Many were forced to abandon their homes and the equity they had invested.

Political Ideologies on Trade

The process of an ever-expanding and increasingly interactive world economy is known as **globalization**. Nations have increased their trading over the past two generations. Today, most products you find in your local department store were produced overseas. The U.S. government, mostly through Congress, can decide to increase or decrease trade with foreign nations. A government wants to encourage its firms to export to larger world markets so that wealth from other nations enters the U.S. economy. A nation that exports more than it imports has a favorable **trade balance**. One that purchases more goods from other nations than it sends out has a trade deficit. The size of this surplus or deficit is but one measure of U.S. economic success. On the other hand, Congress imposes import duties on products coming into the country to protect U.S. manufacturers.

According to the U.S. Constitution, Article I, Section 9, to encourage American production, Congress cannot tax exports. The framers did, however, expect Congress to tax imported goods, charging fees to foreign manufacturers in order to give American manufacturing an advantage. Import taxes require foreign firms to raise prices on their goods once they arrive in the United States. The idea was to create a favorable trade balance, hoping Americans would produce and export more than they imported.

Since trade has an impact on the economy, trade agreements generate ideological differences of opinion. For example, the 1994 **North American Free Trade Agreement (NAFTA)** lifted trade barriers among the three largest North American countries: the United States, Canada, and Mexico. This agreement effectively removed import taxes among these powers. The debate about this agreement created a battle between generally conservative corporations and generally liberal labor unions. The business community, manufacturing firms, and economic conservatives generally favor free trade. To *laissez-faire* economists, lifting barriers and government interference will create a free flow of goods and services on a global scale. These same proponents of globalization argue that the process has decreased poverty and enhanced quality of life in foreign nations as well as opening new markets for U.S. goods and services.

Many laborers, however, feared that American firms would outsource their labor requirements, which they have done. The auto industry suffered a major blow over the past decade and the automakers in Detroit closed plants and laid off workers. The free traders responded that the Mexican economy has grown, and Mexico has bought more goods and services from the United States.

REFLECT ON THE ESSENTIAL QUESTION

Essential Question: *What are the differing political ideologies in the government's role in regulating the marketplace, and what impact do those ideologies have? On separate paper, complete the table below.*

	Conservative Ideology	Liberal Ideology
Regulating the Marketplace		
Fiscal Policy		
Monetary Policy		
Trade		

KEY TERMS AND NAMES

bonds
discount rate
Federal Reserve Board
fiscal policy
flat rate
inflation
Internal Revenue Service (IRS)
monetary policy

multiplier effect
North American Free Trade Agreement (NAFTA) (1994)
progressive tax
reserve requirement
Sixteenth Amendment (1913)
supply side economics
trade balance

4.10

Ideology and Social Policy

"Many of what are called social problems are differences between the theories of intellectuals and the realities of the world—differences which many intellectuals interpret to mean that it is the real world that is wrong and needs changing."

—Thomas Sowell, *Intellectuals and Society*, 2010

Essential Questions: How do different political ideologies influence the role of government in addressing social issues?

Many people believe the goals of the Constitution are best served when the government plays a key role in providing **social welfare**—support for disadvantaged people to meet their basic needs. The nation's social welfare policy has tried to provide that support, especially the New Deal programs of the 1930s and the Great Society programs of the 1960s. More recently, Congress passed and President Obama signed into law a national health care law, although it has been under attack by a Republican-dominated Congress and the Trump administration.

Social Issues and Ideology

Just as political ideologies vary on the issue of government involvement in the economy, so do they vary on the extent to which the government should address social issues. The Preamble to the Constitution declares that the government will "promote the general welfare" of its citizens. Yet opinions vary widely on the best way to accomplish that goal.

A Social Safety Net

In the liberal view of social policy, the government should provide a safety net for people in need and pay for it with higher taxes. This safety net takes the form of **entitlements**—government services Congress has promised by law to citizens—that are major contributors to both annual deficits and the overall debt. (See Topics 2.2 and 2.14.) Congress frequently defines criteria that will award cash to individuals, groups, and state or local governments. Congress must cover this **mandatory spending**, paying those who are legally "entitled" to these funds. Entitlements include Social Security, Medicare, Medicaid, block grants, financial aid, food stamps, money owed on bonds, and the government's many contractual obligations.

Social Security The largest entitlement program is Social Security. Congress passed the **Social Security Act** amid the Great Depression (1929–1939) to create a federal safety net for the elderly and those out of work. This program greatly expanded the role of government, creating what some call the welfare state. The economic disaster had bankrupted local charities and state treasuries, forcing the national government to act. The law created an insurance program that required the employed to pay a small contribution via a payroll tax into an insurance fund designed to assist the unemployed and to help financially strapped retirees.

Officially called Old Age, Survivors, and Disability Insurance (OASDI), Social Security requires most employed citizens to pay 12.4 percent (the employer pays 6.2 percent and the employee pays 6.2 percent) into a trust fund that is kept separate from the general treasury as an independent agency to protect it. The Social Security Administration handles the fund and distributes the checks. It is a large agency composed of almost 60,000 employees and more than 1,400 offices nationwide. This mandatory government-run retirement plan constitutes more than 20 percent of the budget.

Compared to the 1930s, however, Americans are living much longer, extending the time they will collect Social Security benefits. Some predict the Social Security trust fund—an account set aside and protected to help maintain the system—will become exhausted in 2042. At that time, the annual revenue for the program is projected to drop by 25 percent.

Politicians began realizing the potential hazards within this program years ago. Political daredevils have discussed privatizing the program or raising the retirement age. However, people who have paid into the system for most of their lives become upset when they hear politicians' plans to tamper with Social Security or to suddenly change the rules. These factors have made Social Security the "third rail" of politics. Nobody wants to touch the third rail of a train track because it carries the electrical charge, and no politician wants to touch Social Security because of the shockwave in constituent disapproval that might hurt a candidate politically.

Medicare and Medicaid Combined, Medicare and Medicaid make up nearly 20 percent of the federal budget. **Medicare** is a government-run health insurance program for citizens over 65 years old. **Medicaid** is a health care program for the impoverished who cannot afford necessary medical expenses.

President Franklin Roosevelt's plan to pay for the elderly's medical care was tabled until Congress passed the Medicare law in 1965 during the Democratic administration of President Lyndon Johnson. It is administered by an agency in the Department of Health and Human Services and is funded by a payroll tax of 1.45 percent paid by both employer and employee. For those earning more than $200,000 per year, the rate has recently increased to 3.8 percent. The law, which has since been amended, is broken into four parts that cover hospitalization, physicians' services, a public-private partnership known as Medicare Advantage that allows companies to provide Medicare benefits, and a prescription drug benefit. For those over age 65 who qualify, Medicare can cover up to 80 percent of their health care costs. Many retires carry a supplemental private insurance as well. Medical expenses in the golden years can get expensive.

Medicaid provides health insurance coverage for the poorest Americans. To be eligible for Medicaid services, the applicant must meet minimum-income thresholds, have a disability, or be pregnant. Medicare and Medicaid are largely administered by the states while the federal government pays the bill.

Liberals supported other measures in President Johnson's Great Society initiative, including programs in a War on Poverty that provided additional aid for the poor, subsidized housing, and job retraining programs, with the total increasing from nearly $10 billion in 1960 to about $30 billion in 1968. The percentage of people living in poverty fell dramatically, especially among African Americans.

Source: LBJ Presidential Library

President Lyndon Johnson toured poverty-stricken areas of the country in 1964 as part of his War on Poverty to offer hope for better times.

Conservative Opposition Conservatives and libertarians, however, had long opposed these expensive government programs. As early as 1964, Ronald Reagan clearly articulated the conservative view in a speech in supporting the candidacy of Republican presidential candidate Barry Goldwater. Reagan said, "the Founding Fathers knew a government can't control the economy without controlling people. And they knew when a government sets out to do that, it must use force and coercion to achieve its purpose."

When Reagan became president in 1981, he built on efforts he made while governor of California to cut back on government social spending. "Reaganomics," as the economic programs of Reagan have come to be called, stressed lowering taxes and supporting free market activity. With lower taxes, welfare programs, such as the food stamp program and construction of public housing, were cut back.

Health Care American citizens purchase health insurance coverage either through their employer or on their own. Health insurance eases the cost of doctor visits, prescription medicines, operations, and other medical costs. Many politicians and several presidents have favored the idea of a government-based health care system for decades. Some health insurance regulations have existed for years, sometimes differing from state to state. Recently, with the continual increases in insurance prices and the diminishing level of coverage, more people have bought into the idea of expanding government regulation of health insurance and making the service more affordable.

This idea finally became law with the passage of the **Patient Protection and Affordable Care Act** in 2010. Sometimes referred to as "Obamacare" because of President Obama's initiative for the law, the comprehensive Affordable Care Act (ACA) became a divisive issue in party politics, with opponents concerned about the overreach of government. Conservative legislators, many of them backed by wealthy campaign donors with libertarian leanings, objected to the government's involvement in health care and fought the bill fiercely. Conservatives tend to believe that private companies can do a better job providing social services, including health care, than the government. They push for privatization of Medicare and Medicaid as a way to reduce mandatory spending and to energize the private sector. In their view, privatizing health care would increase competition among providers, which in turn will lead to generally lower health care costs. Popularity of this law and program has increased gradually since its passage. A range of polls on whether Americans favor or oppose the ACA as of late 2019 show a noticeable favorability, ranging from 2- to 9-point differential.

Labor

As an economic issue, conservatives tend to view labor as an element of the free market that should not be regulated by the government. Wages, according to this view, should be determined by supply and demand. Liberals, in contrast, view labor as a unique element in the marketplace because of the complexities of human behavior. For example, workers with higher wages tend to be more motivated to do a good job and remain with an employer longer than workers with lower wages, factors not considered in the supply-and-demand model.

Conservatives tend to view organized labor as a negative influence. In some states at some places of business, whether they want to join a union or not, workers are required to pay union dues. Many people believe that such requirements are an infringement of their individual liberties, especially since labor unions actively campaign for candidates and not all workers support the candidates the unions endorse. Liberals have a much more positive view of organized labor as a force that has lifted workers into a position of some power through collective bargaining, which has resulted in the 40-hour work week, employer-provided health care, and many other benefits.

Corporations and workers struggled as the labor union movement developed from the late 1800s into the Great Depression. During periods of liberal or progressive domination of the federal government, Congress passed various laws that prevented collusion by corporations, price fixing, trusts, and yellow dog contracts (forcing newly hired employees into a promise not to join a labor union). As part of the New Deal program, Congress passed the Wagner Act (1935) which created a federal executive branch commission that regulates labor organizations and rules on alleged unfair labor practices. A second law established minimum wage, defined the 40-hour work week, and required companies to pay employees overtime pay.

After World War II, Republicans gained control of Congress in the 1946 mid-term elections and passed the Taft-Hartley Act (1947), generally favored by business and partly counteracting the labor movement. It enabled states to outlaw the closed shop—a company policy or labor contract that requires all employees to join the local union. States could now pass "right to work" laws and, by 2020, 28 states have.

During the conservative presidency of Ronald Reagan, however, organized labor received a blow that has been hard to overcome. Reagan spoke out against the August 1981 strike by air traffic controllers. He declared the strike illegal because the controllers were public employees, and he fired them. Their union was later decertified. Reagan was in general a supporter of workers' rights to collective bargaining, but his firm stand against the air traffic controllers, according to labor expert Joseph A. McCartin, "shaped the world of the modern workplace," which has seen dramatically fewer participants in labor walkouts.

President Ronald Reagan (C), with his Transportation Secretary Andrew L. Lewis (R) and Attorney General William French Smith

Ideological Differences on Government and Privacy

Other social issues besides government spending and labor also divide liberals and conservatives. These concern matters related to personal choice and individual freedoms. Liberals tend to think that the government should not regulate private, personal matters, while many modern social conservatives believe the government needs to protect core values even if doing so intrudes on some individual freedoms.

Privacy and Intimacy

Many of the issues that divide liberals and conservatives on privacy relate to intimate decisions. With the 1965 ruling in *Griswold v. Connecticut* (see Topic 3.9), the Court established a precedent for a right to privacy on intimate matters. That decision found that a Connecticut state law forbidding married persons from using contraception and forbidding people such as health care professionals from helping or advising someone else to use contraception was unconstitutional. The decision enshrined a right to privacy in the Bill of Rights that led to later decisions that prevented states from outlawing abortion and same-sex marriage.

Conservatives tend to believe that if the states pass laws in these areas of personal privacy, the federal government does not have authority to overrule them since the right to privacy is not explicit in the Constitution. A number of recent cases highlight the difference between liberal and conservative views on privacy. For example, does the federal government through the Supreme Court have a right to overrule a state law that requires transgender people to use public bathrooms that match their birth sex rather than their gender identity? Conservatives argue that the state law should stand. Some students argue that being forced to use a school bathroom with people of the opposite physical sex violates their right to privacy. Conservatives have pushed for the so-called bathroom bills, sometimes with dubious constitutionality that could violate rights to privacy.

THINK AS A POLITICAL SCIENTIST: *EXPLAIN HOW AN AUTHOR'S ARGUMENTS AFFECT POLITICAL POLICIES*

The Supreme Court has ruled on only a handful of cases about abortion since *Roe v. Wade* (1973). One of those cases was *Planned Parenthood v. Casey* (1992), in which the Court ruled on a Pennsylvania law that set provisions in place before a woman could have an abortion. The provisions included 24-hour waiting period, parental consent for a minor seeking an abortion, and notification of her husband, if the woman was married. Justices O'Connor, Kennedy, and Souter authored the 5–4 opinion.

Practice: Read the excerpt on the next page from the opinion in *Planned Parenthood v. Casey* (1992) and complete the tasks that follow.

The Court's duty in the present case is clear. In 1973, it confronted the already-divisive issue of governmental power to limit personal choice to undergo abortion, for which it provided a new resolution based on the due process guaranteed by the Fourteenth Amendment. Whether or not a new social consensus is developing on that issue, its divisiveness is no less today than in 1973, and pressure to overrule the decision, like pressure to retain it, has grown only more intense. A decision to overrule *Roe*'s essential holding under the existing circumstances would address error, if error there was, at the cost of both profound and unnecessary damage to the Court's legitimacy, and to the nation's commitment to the rule of law. It is therefore imperative to adhere to the essence of *Roe*'s original decision, and we do so today.

From what we have said so far it follows that it is a constitutional liberty of the woman to have some freedom to terminate her pregnancy. We conclude that the basic decision in *Roe* was based on a constitutional analysis which we cannot now repudiate. The woman's liberty is not so unlimited, however, that from the outset the State cannot show its concern for the life of the unborn, and at a later point in fetal development the state's interest in life has sufficient force so that the right of the woman to terminate the pregnancy can be restricted. . . .

Yet it must be remembered that *Roe v. Wade* speaks with clarity in establishing not only the woman's liberty but also the state's "important and legitimate interest in potential life." That portion of the decision in *Roe* has been given too little acknowledgement and implementation by the Court in its subsequent cases.

1. Explain how the ruling supports and does not support the original abortion ruling in *Roe v. Wade* (1973).

2. Explain which political ideology is supported by the Court in this decision.

Informational Privacy

Liberals and conservatives often disagree on issues of informational privacy as well. Though both perspectives value the privacy of an individual's personal data, they sometimes disagree on where the balance between individual liberty and national security lies. Conservatives tend to be more supportive of government surveillance efforts, especially when the nation may be under threat. Liberals tend to favor stricter limits on government surveillance.

However, over the years, as technology has made sweeping data collection simple, liberals and conservatives have joined in opposing the National Security Agency's collection of bulk data. Both ideologies support the requirement that requests for information need to be approved by the court authorized under the Foreign Intelligence Surveillance Act (FISA), but both liberals and conservatives worry about the easy access the government may have to personal information. (For a full discussion of informational privacy and the Fourth Amendment, see Topic 3.6.)

Education and Religion

On some matters related to education and religion, conservatives want less government intrusion than liberals. For example, many parents choose to send their children to private schools, which are often associated with a religious denomination. However, they still must pay local taxes that support the public schools. A number of states provide vouchers—diversions of public funds—to these families to defray the costs of these private schools.

Conservatives argue that the freedom to choose the educational environment and curriculum of their children is fundamental. They also argue that private schools create competition for public schools which provides an incentive for public schools to improve to keep their students.

This free market approach to education is very different from the free public education value cherished by liberals, who worry that funds diverted from public schools will weaken an already challenged system. Conservatives are likewise more opposed to government interference in the practice of their religious beliefs, even when that practice may clash with federal nondiscrimination law. For example, some businesses that provide services for weddings, such as caterers and bakeries, have refused to work with same-sex couples on the grounds that doing so violates their religious beliefs. They do not deny service to same-sex couples on non-wedding related items—only those that support same-sex marriage. The Supreme Court narrowly ruled in *Masterpiece Cake Shop v. Colorado Rights Commission* (2017) on First Amendment grounds that the state could not compel a merchant to serve homosexual customers preparing for a same-sex wedding.

Source: Getty Images

Although the Supreme Court ruled in favor of the merchant in *Masterpiece Cake Shop v. Colorado Rights Commission*, it also asserted that gay persons and same-sex couples are afforded equal protections under the law.

VIEWS OF THE COLLEGE EDUCATED ON SELECTED SOCIAL ISSUES		
Issue	Democrats	Republicans
Prefer government-run health care	72%	8%
Government should make sure all have health care	84%	22%
Taxed too little or the right amount	71%	30%
Poor people pay too much in taxes	57%	27%
Abortion is morally acceptable	82%	41%
Homosexuality is morally acceptable	86%	49%

Source: Gallup, 2016–2017

Public policy at any time is a reflection of the success of liberal or conservative perspectives in political parties. When Republicans are in power, conservative policies on marketplace regulation, social services, and privacy are often voted or adjudicated into law. When Democrats are in power, they tend to promote liberal social, economic, and privacy policies.

REFLECT ON THE ESSENTIAL QUESTION

Essential Questions: *How do different political ideologies impact the role of government in addressing social issues? On separate paper, complete the table below.*

	Liberal Beliefs	Conservative Beliefs
Safety Net		
Labor		
Privacy		
Education		

KEY TERMS AND NAMES

entitlements
mandatory spending
Medicaid
Medicare

Patient Protection and Affordable Care
   Act (2010)
Social Security Act (1935)
social welfare

CHAPTER 14 Review:
Learning Objectives and Key Terms

TOPIC 4.7: Explain how ideologies of the two major parties shape policy debate. (PMI-4.A)

Ideology and Political Parties (PMI-4.A.1)

conservative	populist
ideology	progressive
liberal	saliency
libertarian	valence issues
moderate	wedge issues

TOPIC 4.8: Explain how U.S. political culture influences the formation, goals, and implementation of public policy over time. (PMI-4.B)

Ideology Reflected in Public Policy (PMI-4.B.1 & 2)

agenda	majoritarian

TOPIC 4.9: Describe different political ideologies in the role of government in regulating the marketplace. (PMI-4.C)

Explain how political ideologies vary on the government's role in regulating the marketplace. (PMI-4.D)

Ideological Differences and Regulating the Marketplace (PMI-4.C.1)

globalization	trade balance
progressive tax	North American Free Trade Agreement (1994)
supply side economics	

Ideology and Economic Policy (PMI-4.D.1)

bonds	Internal Revenue Service
discount rate	monetary policy
Federal Reserve Board	multiplier effect
fiscal policy	reserve requirement
flat rate	Sixteenth Amendment (1913)
inflation	

TOPIC 4.10: Explain how political ideologies vary on the role of government in addressing social issues. (PMI-4.E)

Explain how political ideologies impact policy on social issues. (PMI-4.F)

Ideological Differences and Social Issues (PMI-4.E.1)

entitlements	social welfare
mandatory spending	

Ideology and Social Policy (PMI-4.F.1)

Medicaid	Patient Protection and Affordable Care Act (2010)
Medicare	Social Security Act (1935)

CHAPTER 14 Checkpoint:
Political Ideologies and Public Policy

Topics 4.7–4.10

MULTIPLE-CHOICE QUESTIONS

1. Which argument do supporters of supply-side economics make?

   (A) The more revenue the government takes in and spends the better off the economy will be.

   (B) Leaving more money in the citizens' pockets will stimulate the economy and generate government revenues through other taxes.

   (C) The federal government should follow the ideas of John Maynard Keynes.

   (D) The government should increase the supply of currency into circulation to bring down inflation.

Questions 2 and 3 refer to the passage below.

"Today, I have signed into law H.R. 3734, the Personal Responsibility and Work Opportunity Reconciliation Act of 1996. While far from perfect, this legislation provides an historic opportunity to end welfare as we know it and transform our broken welfare system by promoting the fundamental values of work, responsibility, and family. This Act . . . requires work of welfare recipients, limits the time they can stay on welfare, and provides child care and health care to help them make the move from welfare to work . . . I am especially pleased that the Congress has preserved the guarantee of health care for the poor, the elderly, and the disabled . . . The current welfare system is fundamentally broken, and this may be our last best chance to set it straight."

—President Bill Clinton, Signing Statement, 1996

2. Which of the following perspectives is reflected in this passage?

   (A) There is a consensus belief that people should work, but the government should provide a social safety net.

   (B) Leaders of different parties have starkly different views of economics and work ethic.

   (C) This imperfect plan could be better so we should strive to perfect it later.

   (D) Only those citizens who work should be supported.

3. Which of the following statements is most consistent with the passage?
   (A) The government should strive to end welfare programs.
   (B) If citizens were more focused on work and family this law would not be necessary.
   (C) This law is the best possible way to tackle the welfare problem.
   (D) This proposal will limit those taking advantage of welfare, while it will still protect those who need it.

4. Which of the following is an accurate comparison of Democrat and Republican ideologies?

	Democrat	Republican
(A)	Supported by business elites	Supported by minority voters
(B)	Supports the expansion of welfare programs	Supports government-funded health care for all
(C)	Desires an increase in the minimum wage	Favors fewer regulations on businesses
(D)	Follows a libertarian approach on the marketplace	Wants more environmental controls

Questions 5 and 6 refer to the cartoon below.

5. With which of the following statements would the cartoonist agree?

(A) The government is working hard to fix problems in Social Security.

(B) To provide tax cuts, politicians are willing to make Social Security less stable.

(C) Tax cuts are going to boost the economy and save Social Security.

(D) Nothing can be done to save Social Security.

6. Which of the following ideologies most likely aligns with the cartoonist's perspective?

(A) Libertarian

(B) Conservative

(C) Liberal

(D) Independent

FREE-RESPONSE QUESTIONS

Concept Application

1. "[The College for All Act] would provide $47 billion per year to states to eliminate undergraduate tuition and fees at public colleges and universities.

   Today, total tuition at public colleges and universities amounts to about $70 billion per year. Under the College for All Act, the federal government would cover 67% of this cost, while the states would be responsible for the remaining 33% of the cost. . . .

   States would be able to use funding to increase academic opportunities for students, hire new faculty, and provide professional development opportunities for professors. . . .

   [This program would be] fully paid for by imposing a Robin Hood tax on Wall Street. . . . It has been estimated that this provision could raise hundreds of billions a year which could be used not only to make tuition free at public colleges and universities in this country, it could also be used to create millions of jobs and rebuild the middle class of this country."

   —Senator Bernie Sanders, Summary of College for All Act, April 2017

   After reading the above, respond to A, B, and C below:

   (A) Describe the political ideology behind Senator Sanders's proposed law.

   (B) In the context of the scenario, explain how the proposed law would affect federal fiscal policy.

   (C) Explain how ideologies vary on the government's role in providing college education.

Quantitative Analysis

Projected Government Spending on Entitlements
Percent of Gross Domestic Product (total economic output)

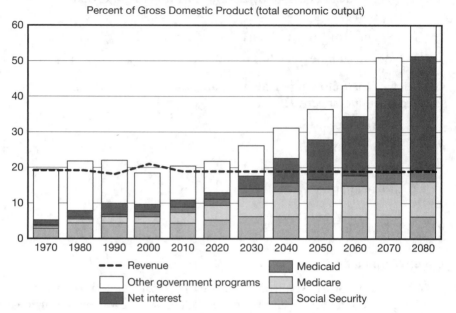

Source: Government Accounting Office

2. Use the information in the graphic above to answer the questions below.

(A) Describe the information conveyed in the graph.

(B) Describe a trend conveyed in the graph.

(C) Draw a conclusion about the causes of the trend in part B.

(D) Explain how liberals and conservatives would disagree on the data showing how the government assures individual liberty and promotes stability.

UNIT 4: Review

Those in government need to understand public opinion to create democratic laws. Opinion polls are useful to the news media, politicians, and academics. Polling has its limits as well as its benefits. A poll is only valid if it has properly worded questions and a representative sample. In measuring public opinion, pollsters find that Americans fall into many political categories. People following liberal or conservative ideology tend to align with the Democrats or Republicans, respectively. The largest segment of the United States, however, is moderate and made up of independent voters and nonvoters. Countless other ideologies also exist. These are formed by many factors in the political socialization process, such as the influence of family, schooling, religion, and geographic region.

The values, attitudes, and beliefs of Americans influence the development, goals, and implementation of public policy over time. Policies in place at any given time represent the success of the parties whose ideologies they represent and the political attitudes and beliefs of citizens who choose to participate in politics at a given time.

MULTIPLE-CHOICE QUESTIONS

1. Which term best describes a person who believes in minimal government regulations on businesses and has a strong regard for personal freedoms?

   (A) Liberal
   (B) Conservative
   (C) Progressive
   (D) Libertarian

2. Which of the following is an accurate comparison of the family and attending college contribute to the development of one's political beliefs?

	Family	**College**
A	With so many households with both Republicans and Democrats, family has no noticeable impact on political thought.	Those who attend college move into a higher income bracket, and therefore vote Republican.
B	As teens become adult voters, they tend to disagree with parents, and veer toward a different ideology.	The liberal orientation of college faculty have a strong impact on students' political thought.
C	About 25 percent of children adopt the political philosophies of their parents.	Those who do not adopt their parent's partisan beliefs become political independents more than joining the other major party.
D	Family is the single most influential influence on political thought.	The longer one attends college, the more liberal their views will become

Questions 3 and 4 refer to the passage.

"It's getting hard to escape the conclusion that traditional ways of measuring public opinion no longer seem capable of accurately predicting outcomes the way they more or less once did. One reason for this is that prospective voters are much harder to reach than they used to be . . . landlines, as you may have noticed, have become far less prevalent . . . as more and more Americans-especially young ones-choose to live in cell-only households. Meanwhile, Federal Communications Commission regulations make it far more expensive to survey people via mobile phones. On top of that, more people are screening their calls, refusing to answer attempts from unknown numbers."

—Steven Slade, "Why Polls Don't Work,"
Reason Magazine, 2016

3. Which of the following statements best summarize Slade's argument?

(A) Most voters are not educated enough on the issues to have solid opinions.

(B) Lifestyles and communications customs have called the validity of public opinion polling into question.

(C) As more people turn to cell phones, they become less interested in politics and policy.

(D) Polling as a measure of public opinion should not be trusted.

4. Based on the passage, which statement would the author most likely agree with?

   (A) As long as caution is taken, the polls should remain accurate.

   (B) Public opinion cannot be measured accurately in the age of cell phones.

   (C) Measuring citizen views on policy issues is worthy while predicting elections is not.

   (D) For polling reliability, some innovations to measuring public opinion are necessary.

5. The practice of designing a poll in order to influence one's attitude is known as

   (A) Logrolling

   (B) Push polling

   (C) Exit polling

   (D) Stratification

Trump Approval Rating in Ohio

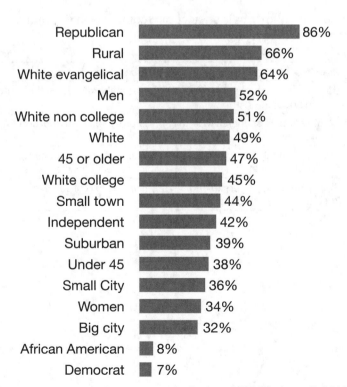

Republican	86%
Rural	66%
White evangelical	64%
Men	52%
White non college	51%
White	49%
45 or older	47%
White college	45%
Small town	44%
Independent	42%
Suburban	39%
Under 45	38%
Small City	36%
Women	34%
Big city	32%
African American	8%
Democrat	7%

Source: NBC/Marist poll, 2018
Sample: 909 Ohio Residents

6. Which of the following does the graph on the previous page conclude?
   (A) Partisan affiliation has little impact on citizen views of the president.
   (B) Though there is a gender gap in citizen voting, there is no apparent gender gap in Trump's presidential approval.
   (C) Older voters approve of this president more than younger voters do.
   (D) There is no relationship between approval and population density.

7. Based on this poll and bar graph, which of the following is true?
   (A) Because this poll was conducted by the news media, it probably has a liberal bias.
   (B) The sample is too small to consider this poll representative of the universe.
   (C) The approval rating among independents is more indicative of the overall approval rating of the president than any other group in this survey.
   (D) The gap between Republican and Democrat views of the president will likely narrow.

8. Which of the following is an accurate comparison of populist and libertarian ideology?

	Populist	Libertarian
(A)	Believes in a strong separation of church and state	Has a liberal view of the welfare state
(B)	Would support an increase in the national minimum wage	Is pro-choice on abortion
(C)	More commonly found in the South and rural Midwest	Wants higher penalties and punishments for recreational marijuana use
(D)	Sides with NFL players taking a knee during the National Anthem	Is accepting of same-sex marriage

9. A voter receives a phone call from a pollster days before the election. One of the candidates for the relevant election is African American, and the incumbent is white. Recently, the local news media broadcast a news story on how local black candidates are rare, how this particular candidate's viability reveals progress in race relations, but still no black candidate has ever won local office. The independent voter answering the pollster's call has every intention of voting for the opposing, white candidate, but considers the recent news report, and misleads the pollster that he will vote for the black candidate. This answer is an example of which phenomenon?

(A) Racial prejudice

(B) Social desirability bias

(C) The life-cycle effect

(D) Stratification

Questions 10 and 11 refer to the graphic below.

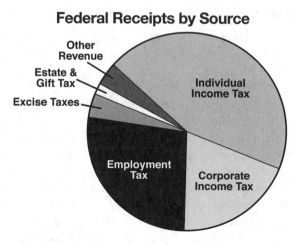

Federal Receipts by Source

Source: OMB Historical tables, FY 2011

10. The pie graph above represents a key element of which of the following?

(A) Fiscal policy

(B) Monetary policy

(C) Keynesian economic theory

(D) Supply-side theory

11. To reduce the deficit, Democrats would most likely recommend increasing which source of revenue?

   (A) Individual Income Tax

   (B) Corporate Income Tax

   (C) Employment Tax

   (D) Excise Taxes

12. Which group has the highest percentage of its members voting for Democratic candidates in recent elections?

   (A) White southerners

   (B) Blue collar workers

   (C) Elderly voters

   (D) African Americans

FREE-RESPONSE QUESTIONS

Concept Application

1. "Before they make their final decision [in an upcoming bill, Republican lawmakers] should bear in mind the estate tax is as economically inefficient as it is socially indefensible . . . The federal estate tax (often called the "death tax" by its detractors) has existed in its modern form since 1916. Essentially, it's a tax on the right to transfer property at one's death and applies to the market value of everything owned at that time including cash, stocks, bonds, buildings, trusts, vehicles, and even books . . . While it may seem like a reasonable means of raising revenue at the expense of folks who no longer need their money, it isn't. The estate tax typically totals less than 1 percent of annual federal tax revenue, largely because many Americans, through clever estate planning, are able to sidestep its grasp. . . . some Americans who lack the foresight or means to evade the tax are beleaguered by unproductive and exorbitant compliance costs . . . the collective compliance burden is roughly equal to the amount of revenue raised . . . [and] the tax tend[s] to curb people's income as they enter their golden years . . . Ultimately, the estate tax compels Americans to waste their money on evasive estate planning and compliance costs, discourages them from pursuing profits in old age, and stymies America's unique cultural dynamic."

   —Michael Shindler, *Washington Examiner* "Trump is Right, Kill the Death Tax," 2017

After reading the excerpt on the previous page, respond to A, B, and C below:

(A) Describe the author's ideology regarding this policy.

(B) In the context of this scenario, explain how ideological divisions could prevent the author's goals from being accomplished.

(C) Explain why the author might argue that taxpayers' rights are violated with the estate tax policy.

Quantitative Analysis

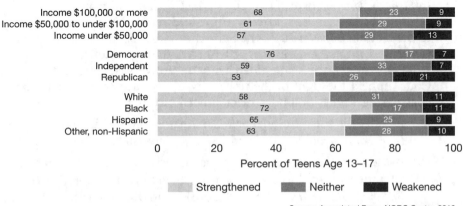

Teen's Opinions on Diversity and Democracy

Source: Associated Press-NORC Center, 2016

2. Use the information graphic above to answer the following questions.

(A) Identify the demographic group that is most prone to believe that diversity strengthens democracy.

(B) Describe a similarity or difference of teenagers' views on how diversity impacts democracy.

(C) Draw a conclusion regarding what may explain the similarity or difference from part B.

(D) Explain how the data in the chart might affect policy debates with regard to equality of opportunity.

SCOTUS Comparison

3. In 2013, the Supreme Court ruled on a case involving a white student, Abigail Fisher, who was denied undergraduate admission to the University of Texas. The University of Texas accepts all in-state students who graduate in the upper 10 percent of their class, but for the remainder of the admissions, the university considers race as one factor among many in an effort to reflect the diversity of the population. Fisher was not in the upper 10 percent of her class, and when she was denied admission, she sued the school on the grounds that her constitutional rights were violated because the university used race to consider applicants. The district and circuit courts affirmed the university's policy, so she appealed to the Supreme Court.

   In *Fisher v. University of Texas* (2013), the Court found that the circuit court had not exercised strict scrutiny and remanded the case back to the circuit court. In 2015, the Supreme Court heard the case again (*Fisher v. University of Texas II, 2016*) after the lower court, applying strict scrutiny, once again sided with the university. This time the Court upheld the right of the university to use race as one factor in considering admission under strict judicial scrutiny.

   (A) Identify the constitutional provision that is common to both *Brown v. Board of Education* (1954) and *Fisher v. University of Texas II* (2016).

   (B) Based on the constitutional provision identified in part A, explain why the facts of the case in *Brown v. Board of Education* (1954) and *Fisher v. University of Texas II* (2016) led to different rulings by the Supreme Court.

   (C) Explain how the ruling in *Fisher v. University of Texas II* relates to the principle of equality of opportunity.

WRITE AS A POLITICAL SCIENTIST: *USE REASONING TO ORGANIZE AND ANALYZE EVIDENCE*

You have developed a claim or thesis statement that takes a defensible position and lays out a line of reasoning (see page 257) and you have gathered the evidence you need to support it (see page 390). Your argument essay is starting to take shape. However, you now need to stitch your ideas together by using reasoning to show how your evidence supports your claim.

Suppose, for example, that you are given the following prompt for an argument essay: "Develop an argument that explains whether or not the federal government's involvement in education promotes democracy." In response, you have developed this arguable and defensible claim:

CLAIM: "Although states have decisive power over the education of their children, federal involvement in education promotes democracy because administration of educational policy by a single national government can assure equality."

From the sources you were given to choose from, you have selected evidence from the First Amendment and the Title IX to back up your claim. The specific evidence you identify in these sources may be something like the following:

EVIDENCE:

- The First Amendment protects religious freedom and prohibits the government from establishing religion.
- Title IX guarantees that women get the same educational opportunities as men in federally funded institutions (This example uses a second piece of evidence that is not taken from a foundational document).

Those pieces of evidence, on their own, cannot justify the claim you made. You need to provide your **reasoning**—your explanation of why the evidence you chose supports your claim. You may develop your reasoning along the following lines.

REASONING:

- "The First Amendment's guarantee of freedom of religion has been incorporated through such cases as *Everson v. Board of Education* (1947) and *Wisconsin v. Yoder* (1972) and promotes democracy by both forbidding public-school authorized prayer (to keep religion out of public schools) and allowing parents to make educational choices for their children, including not sending them to high school or choosing to send them to religious school (keeping public education laws out of certain religious spheres). Using the powers reserved for the states in the Tenth Amendment, states can choose to provide vouchers for families who send their children to religious schools to offset the taxes they are required to pay for public schools."
- "Title IX, as a part of the Education Amendments of 1972, made colleges and universities accountable in providing equal opportunities for both genders in the classroom and on the field. The Fourteenth Amendment's "equal protection under the law" provided the basis for Title IX by applying the equal protection principle, originally intended for former slaves in post-Civil War America, to women in the 20th century. Without federal laws like this, some states were noncompliant in enforcing equality in education."

Reasoning plays at least one other important role in shaping your essay. You use reasoning to decide how best to organize your essay.

ORGANIZATIONAL REASONING:

- After reviewing your evidence and the reasoning you offered to explain how the evidence supports your claim, you may decide that the strongest evidence is from Title IX and place that first in your essay.
- You may decide that the evidence from the First Amendment might be a transition to address those arguing a different position, such as that the federal government overreaches states' rights when it is involved in education. Addressing alternate or opposing views will strengthen your position.

Application: As you complete the argument essay on the next page, be sure to weave together your evidence and use reasoning to explain how your evidence supports your claim. Think about the best way to organize your essay as well.

For current free response question samples, check the College Board's website.

Argument Essay

4. The media commonly measure and present public opinion. Develop an argument that explains whether public opinion polling has a positive or negative effect on American democracy.

   Use at least one piece of evidence from one of the following foundational documents:

   - *Federalist No. 10*
   - Declaration of Independence
   - The U.S. Constitution

   In your response, you should do the following:

   - Respond to the prompt with a defensible claim or thesis that establishes a line of reasoning.
   - Support your claim or thesis with at least TWO pieces of specific and relevant evidence:
     - One piece of evidence must come from one of the foundational documents listed above.
     - A second piece of evidence can come from any other foundational document not used as your first piece of evidence, or it may be from your knowledge of course concepts.
   - Use reasoning to explain why your evidence supports your claim or thesis.
   - Respond to an opposing or alternative perspective using refutation, concession, or rebuttal.

UNIT 5

Political Participation

On the edge of U.S. government, organized groups interact with government to shape policy. These so-called **linkage institutions**—political parties, interest groups, and the media—connect people with the government, keeping people informed and trying to shape public opinion and policy. Since the 1820s, two political parties, Democrats and Republicans, have dominated, battling back and forth for control of the government. On national, state, and local levels, parties recruit candidates, campaign, and play watchdog when the other party is in power. Elections themselves also serve as a way to link citizens—who have constitutionally protected rights to vote—and the government.

Elections are held for offices from president to sheriff. Presidential candidates spend massive amounts of money as they travel a hard road to the White House through a series of primary elections, a national convention, and televised debates. Congressional and state candidates also compete in distinct yet smaller campaigns en route to state-level office.

Interest groups adopt formal goals and raise money for their causes. Some are larger and more powerful than others and thus have more influence. They engage in several activities throughout the United States to influence policymaking.

The media are also a major force in U.S. politics. The press shapes public opinion, voter perceptions, campaign strategies, and the agenda. For this reason, candidates and members of government have a symbiotic and conflict-prone relationship with the media.

ENDURING UNDERSTANDINGS: POLITICAL PARTICIPATION

MPA-3: Factors associated with political ideology, efficacy, structural barriers, and demographics influence the nature and degree of political participation.

PMI-5: Political parties, interest groups, and social movements provide opportunities for participation and influence how people relate to government and policymakers.

PRD-2: The impact of federal policies on campaigning and electoral rules continues to be contested by both sides of the political spectrum.

PRD-3: The various forms of media provide citizens with political information and influence the ways in which they participate politically.

Source: AP® United States Government and Politics Course and Exam Description

---

CHAPTER 15

Voting Rights and Voter Behavior

Topics 5.1–5.2

Topic 5.1 Voting Rights and Models of Voting Behavior

MPA-3.A: Describe the voting rights protections in the Constitution and in legislation.

MPA-3.B: Describe different models of voting behavior.

Topic 5.2 Voter Turnout

MPA-3.C: Explain the roles that individual choice and state laws play in voter turnout in elections.

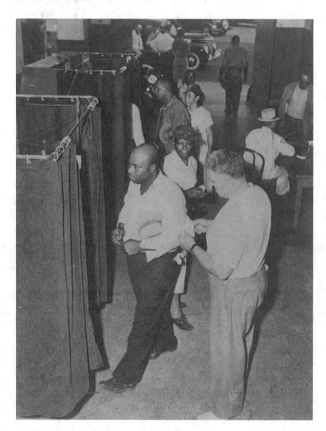

Source: Library of Congress

Voters enter voting booths in a 1945 local election. The 1944 *Smith v. Allright* decision (see Topic 5.1) found the practice of "white primaries" unconstitutional, opening the door for black voters to participate in primary elections.

Voting Rights and Models of Voting Behavior

"A voter without a ballot is like a soldier without a bullet."
—Dwight Eisenhower, in *The New York Times*, 1957

Essential Question: How does the Constitution and legislation protect voting rights, and how do models relate to voting behavior?

The framers decided state governments were best to define citizen qualifications for voting and for managing elections. In early U.S. history, only property-owning men could vote. In the quote above, President Eisenhower referred to the power that the right to vote meant, yet state legal barriers and intimidation kept most African Americans from voting in the South. Today, constitutional amendments and legislation assure almost all adult citizens the right to vote. These citizens use a variety of criteria to make their voting choices.

Redefining "We the People"

The most common form of political participation is voting. Every four years, a large percentage of Americans, known as the **electorate**, "go to the polls" to cast a vote for the American president and other offices. Elections also occur between those four years at the local, state, and federal levels. **BIG IDEA** Popular sovereignty, individualism, and republicanism are important considerations of U.S. laws and policy making and assume citizens will engage and participate. Over the nation's history, voter eligibility expanded, redefining "We, the People" to include the working class, African Americans, women, residents of Washington, DC, and young adults.

An Expanding Electorate

States extended the **franchise,** or right to vote, to white working-class men much earlier than most countries did, but for decades, only property-owning white males had been able to vote. Only a handful of these political elites decided the first presidential election. The Constitution originally called for state legislatures to appoint electors who then later elected the president in an electoral college. On a designated day, every state's electors met in their capitals to cast votes for president. There was no popular vote for George Washington, but every one of the 69 electors cast their first ballots for Washington. By the 1800 presidential election, five of 16 states expanded participation by using popular elections to name the electors, and by 1823 all states allowed for popular selection of electors.

State governments typically did not grant **suffrage**, or qualifications for voting, equally. The Constitution forbade religious tests for federal office but did not prevent such tests in determining who could vote. In addition to early religious tests, states' imposed property requirements and poll taxes. They also barred women, African Americans, and immigrants from the political process. Courageous activists worked for more than 100 years to persuade states to alter voting practices, create equitable voting laws, and ratify amendments to extend suffrage. Until they were enfranchised, citizens participated in politics in the only channels available to them—through protest and expression of opinion in other ways.

Voter participation continued to grow in the 1830s. President Andrew Jackson, a popular leader and advocate for expanding suffrage to all white men, was influential in increasing citizen participation. Jackson didn't come from wealth or privilege and embodied the common man. He bravely rose through military ranks and through Congress to become the seventh president of the United States. He called for the end of the property requirement to vote. During and after Jackson's presidency (1829–1837), universal male suffrage became a reality, greatly increasing voter turnout. In 1824, four candidates had tallied a collective 350,671 votes. Four years later the popular vote total reached 1,155,350. By 1830, almost all states had removed the property requirement. North Carolina was the last state to abandon property requirements in 1856.

Suffrage Amendments

By the 1860s, America had yet to give the franchise to African Americans, women, and other minorities. That situation changed with the passage of three constitutional amendments: the Fifteenth, Nineteenth, and Twenty-sixth. Two other amendments, the Twenty-third and Twenty-fourth, extended suffrage further, allowing residents of the nation's capital to vote for the president and outlawing poll taxes, respectively.

SUFFRAGE AMENDMENTS
• **Fifteenth Amendment (1870):** Citizens shall not be denied the right to vote by the states or the United States "on account of race, color, or previous condition of servitude."
• **Nineteenth Amendment (1920):** Citizens shall not be denied the right to vote by the states or the United States "on account of sex."
• **Twenty-third Amendment (1961):** For presidential and vice presidential elections, "the District constituting the seat of government" shall appoint a number of electors "in no event more than the least populous State."
• **Twenty-fourth Amendment (1964):** Citizens shall not be denied the right to vote by the states or the United States "by reason of failure to pay any poll tax or other tax."
• **Twenty-sixth Amendment (1971):** Citizens "eighteen years of age or older" shall not be denied the right to vote by the states or the United States "on account of age."

All suffrage amendments state in Section 2, "The Congress shall have the power to enforce this article by appropriate legislation." This enforcement clause has allowed Congress to assure that the spirit of the amendments is carried out.

African American Suffrage As suffrage expanded in its first phase, legislatures and groups of people discussed the potential for free African Americans to vote. In the 1830s, six northern states permitted African Americans to vote. After the North defeated the South in the Civil War in 1865, Congress passed the Reconstruction Amendments, the Thirteenth, Fourteenth, and Fifteenth. The Thirteenth Amendment freed the enslaved, and the Fourteenth Amendment granted citizenship and guaranteed legal protection. The **Fifteenth Amendment** gave African American males the right to vote and was the first constitutional mandate affecting state voting requirements.

The Fifteenth Amendment, like the other amendments, passed through a northern-dominated Congress without southern support and was initially enforced during Reconstruction when African Americans voted in large numbers. The Union Army's continued presence in the former Confederacy ensured that African Americans could vote, and several were elected to public office. In 1876, Rutherford B. Hayes won a disputed presidential election and soon after withdrew Union troops from the South. A decade later, as the era of Jim Crow began, southern legislatures segregated their citizens and established loopholes to circumvent the Fifteenth Amendment. White citizens, including members of the Ku Klux Klan, intimidated and abused African Americans to turn them away from the polls.

Structural Barriers Several southern states denied African Americans suffrage with property or literacy requirements. Several states elevated the **literacy test** into their state constitutions. The **poll tax**—a simple fee required to vote—became one of the most effective ways to discourage the potential black voter. And the **grandfather clause**, which allowed states to recognize a registering voter as it would have recognized his grandfather, prevented scores of African Americans from voting, while it allowed illiterate and poor whites to circumvent the literacy test and poll tax requirements.

These state-level loopholes suppressed the black vote but never explicitly violated the letter of the Constitution because they never prevented someone from voting, "on account of race, color, or previous condition of servitude." The impact can be demonstrated by change in registered black voters in Louisiana. Historian C. Vann Woodward reveals that in 1896, the state had 130,334 registered black voters, who outnumbered registered white voters in 26 parishes (counties). By 1900, white voters dominated every parish, and by 1904, only 1,342 African Americans were on the poll books and registered to vote. The **white primary**, too, became a popular method for southern states to keep African Americans from voting. State Democratic Party organizations set rules for their primaries, defining their membership as white men's clubs. By 1915, thirteen southern states had established the white primary. A generation of intimidation, lynching, and a host of public policies to prevent African Americans from voting resulted in a steady decline in turnout that began as soon as the Union pulled out of the South. Black voting reached an all-time low in the 1920s.

Progress Through Law The framers had also endorsed the elite model of democracy (see Topic 1.2) by calling for the election of senators by state legislatures. However, with the ratification of the **Seventeenth Amendment** in 1913, popular elections for senators became the law of the land. With this change, the two federal senators from each state began to pay more attention to how citizen-voters in their state regarded them.

THE WAY WE BECOME SENATOR NOWADAYS.

Source: Getty Images

A cartoon from *Puck* magazine commented on Senate elections before the Seventeenth Amendment.

The growing quest for equality and the post-World War II Civil Rights Movement brought the greatest increases in African American turnout in a century. Some inroads to making the Fifteenth Amendment a reality had been made earlier. In 1915, in *Guinn v. United States*, the Supreme Court ruled the grandfather clause unconstitutional. In 1944, the Court declared the white primary a violation of the Constitution's equal protection clause in *Smith v. Allwright*. One estimate of southern black registration before and after the white primary shows a statewide increase from 151,000 to 595,000 registered voters. Southern black voter turnout increased from 4.5 percent in 1940 to 12.5 percent in 1947. The Democratic Party included a pro-civil rights plank in its 1948 platform that called for equal treatment regardless of race, creed, or color. The Civil Rights Movement of the 1950s and 1960s caused greater increases in voter participation following key congressional acts, additional Supreme Court rulings, and one more constitutional amendment.

Women's Suffrage The push for women's suffrage began in the mid-1800s. Wyoming, Idaho, and Utah were among the first states to admit women to the polls. In the late 1800s, women entered the workplace and, later, in World War I, served the nation on the home front. Women's suffrage became a national reality with ratification of the **Nineteenth Amendment** in 1920.

Activists had worked hard and courageously to secure the amendment's passage. Susan B. Anthony became a leading suffragist. She spoke at political conventions and helped organize different associations. In 1872, in direct violation of New York law, she walked into a polling place and cast a vote. She was tried and convicted by an all-male jury.

Source: Library of Congress

In July 1919, Missouri Governor Frederick Gardner signed the resolution signaling Missouri's ratification of the Nineteenth Amendment.

Suffragists continued the fight. By 1914, eleven states allowed women to vote. In the 1916 election, both major political parties endorsed the concept of women's suffrage in their platforms, and Montana elected the first woman to Congress, Jeanette Rankin. Women's groups picketed the White House to persuade President Woodrow Wilson to get behind the cause. He finally supported the amendment, and it was ratified in 1920. Females became more and more accustomed to voting and became active participants in politics.

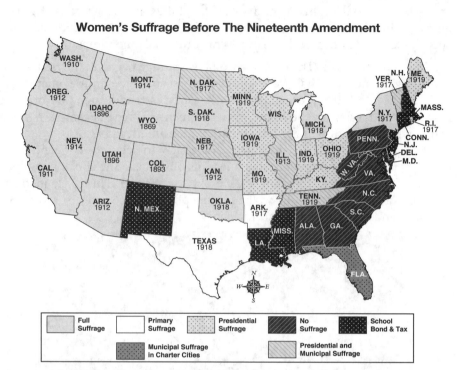

Women's Suffrage Before The Nineteenth Amendment

WASH. 1910
OREG. 1912
MONT. 1914
N. DAK. 1917
MINN. 1919
IDAHO 1896
S. DAK. 1918
WIS.
WYO. 1869
MICH. 1918
NEV. 1914
NEB. 1917
IOWA 1919
OHIO 1919
PENN.
UTAH 1896
COL. 1893
ILL. 1913
IND. 1919
CAL. 1911
KAN. 1912
MO. 1919
KY.
W. VA.
VA.
ARIZ. 1912
N. MEX.
OKLA. 1918
ARK. 1917
TENN. 1919
N.C.
S.C.
TEXAS 1918
MISS.
ALA.
GA.
LA.
FLA.
N.H.
VER. 1917
ME. 1919
N.Y. 1917
MASS.
R.I. 1917
CONN.
N.J.
DEL.
M.D.

	Full Suffrage		Primary Suffrage		Presidential Suffrage		No Suffrage		School Bond & Tax
	Municipal Suffrage in Charter Cities				Presidential and Municipal Suffrage				

Rounding Out the Electorate

By the late 1950s, American values on democracy and defining who could vote were only partially set. Real political participation for suppressed African Americans, newly involved women, and younger people had yet to emerge. Additionally, the seat of the nation's capital had exploded in population but still lacked state status and votes in the presidential contest. Some powerful legislation and three more amendments would round out the U.S. electorate.

The **1957 Civil Rights Act**, the first such bill since Reconstruction, addressed discrimination in voter registration and established the U.S. Office of Civil Rights, an enforcement agency in the Justice Department. Before World War II, about 3 percent of the South's black voting-age populace was registered. In 1964, statewide averages varied from 6 to 66 percent, averaging 36 percent.

The expansive **1964 Civil Rights Act** also addressed voting. (See Topic 3.11.) That same year, Congress proposed and the states ratified the **Twenty-fourth Amendment**, which outlawed poll taxes in federal elections. By the time the amendment was introduced in Congress in 1962, only four states still charged such a tax. The Supreme Court later ruled taxes on any election, such as state and local elections, unconstitutional because they violated the equal protection clause of the Fourteenth Amendment.

The 1965 **Voting Rights Act** was the most effective bill to bring the black populace into the political process. This act outlawed literacy tests and put states with low voter turnout under the watchful eye of the Justice Department. The law gave the department jurisdiction over states that had any type of voting test and less than 50 percent turnout in the 1964 election. These states would be subject to federal election examiners and the **preclearance** provision of the act's Section Five. The preclearance provision put these states under federal supervision if they attempted to invent new, legal loopholes to diminish black suffrage, such as moving polling places or gerrymandering. By 1967, black voter registration in six southern states increased from about 30 to more than 50 percent. African Americans soon held office in greater numbers. The original law expired in 1971, but Congress has renewed the Voting Rights Act several times since.

Recently, the preclearance provision landed in the Supreme Court. Shelby County, Alabama, challenged the 1965 point of law, and the Court declared in a 5:4 decision that this section of the law imposes burdens that are no longer responsive to current conditions. In *Shelby County v. Holder* (2013), the Supreme Court struck down the Voting Rights Act (and the Reauthorization Act in 2006) because of the burdens placed on states. Chief Justice John Roberts wrote in the majority opinion, "And voter registration and turnout numbers in the covered States have risen dramatically in the years since [the 2006 Voting Rights Act Reauthorization]. Racial disparity in those numbers was compelling evidence justifying the preclearance remedy and the coverage formula. There is no longer such a disparity."

Justice Ruth Bader Ginsburg made a comparison of the Court's decision in her dissent, stating that "throwing out preclearance when it has worked and is continuing to work to stop discriminatory changes is like throwing away your umbrella in a rainstorm because you are not getting wet."

The District of Columbia The Electoral College system awards each state the same number of electors that it has senators and representatives. Washington, DC, is not a state and had no electors until passage of the **Twenty-third Amendment** (1961). The founding fathers were concerned about the potential political influence of those living in and near the nation's capital. Delegates at the constitutional convention feared the advantages a state might gain if it also housed the capital city. The Constitution therefore empowers Congress to "exercise exclusive Legislation in all Cases whatsoever, over such District...[to] become the Seat of the Government of the United States." After short terms in New York City and Philadelphia, the national capital moved to Washington, DC, on a parcel of land (the Constitution mandated that it not exceed 10 square miles) ceded by Virginia and Maryland. The town's permanent population remained small for decades, but as the role of government and the size of the town grew, the permanent population of citizens desired representation.

The Twenty-third Amendment provides that the District shall appoint electors, but never more than those of the smallest state so that the District never has stronger influence than the smallest state. The Constitution, however, does not give this District "state" status, and therefore it has no voting representatives in the House or the Senate and no presidential electors. Delegates from Washington, DC, cannot introduce or vote on legislation but can vote at the committee level. (According to the U.S. Census the nation's least populous state, Wyoming, has 544,270 residents represented by three total members to Congress and three electoral votes. The District of Columbia has 599,657 residents with no voting representation in Congress.) In 1964, the first national election in which its residents could exercise their right to vote, the District voted for Democrat Lyndon Johnson, and it has voted for the Democratic candidate every year since.

Young Adults Most states used to require voters to be 21 years old, while four states allowed 18-year-olds to vote. In the post-World War II years, however, a move to enfranchise 18-year-olds gained momentum. The president and Congress had sent scores of 18-, 19-, and 20-year-old draftees to Vietnam, most of whom had no right to vote for president or Congress. In 1970, Congress passed amendments to the 1965 Voting Rights Act that lowered the national voting age to 18 for presidential and congressional elections. States challenged the new law in the Supreme Court based on reserved powers. The Court narrowly ruled that Congress did have the authority to set a voting age on *federal* elections but not for state and local offices. This ruling prompted Congress to propose and the states to ratify the **Twenty-sixth Amendment,** which prevents states from denying citizens 18 and over the right to vote, in July 1971.

The rapid ratification of the measure with strong majorities in each state put younger citizens on the road to voting. President Nixon proclaimed that some 11 million young men and women who "have participated in the life of our nation through their work, their studies, and their sacrifices for its defense now are to be fully included in the electoral process of our country."

Voting Models

The decision-making process voters use when choosing a candidate can be influenced by several models. All of these models affect voting behavior with various levels of influence.

Rational-Choice Voting

A voter who has examined an issue or candidate, evaluated campaign promises or platform points, and consciously decided to vote in the way that seems to most benefit the voter is following the **rational-choice voting** model. What matters most to one rational-choice voter might mean much less to another voter. One voter might approach the voting booth with his or her own individual interests atop her priority list—who will help me obtain medical care, for example—while another could act out of concern for a larger group, posing such questions as, "What is best for America?" or "What is best for our schools?"

Either way, rational-choice voters have consciously decided what choice would most directly affect them or represents their values, and they vote accordingly. A retiring citizen about to collect Social Security votes for the candidate promising to protect the Social Security system. A young voter might have a genuine interest in securing retirees' quality of life, and though this issue has little direct implication on this voter's life, he or she may rationally choose to vote with that issue as a priority based on values of security for elders.

Analysts point out that sometimes people vote against their self-interest to support larger issues. For example, Donald Trump gained much support from the non-college educated, wage-earning voters. Critics point out that the president's policies of lowering the marginal tax rate and deregulating businesses will possibly harm these voters. If those voters made their choice based on concerns about immigration and protection for the Second Amendment rather than their economic interests, they still made their own rational choice.

Retrospective Voting

Citizens who apply the **retrospective voting** model look backward to consider candidates' track records. If the race for local office includes an incumbent, the voter will assess the official seeking reelection and his or her accomplishments while in office before deciding. If the race is for an open seat, the voter will likely consider the incumbent party's recent track record, or maybe the challenging candidates' accomplishments or shortcomings in previous offices. If Republicans are in control of Congress and the White House, and a bad economy ensues on their watch, a retrospective independent voter will likely cast his vote for the Democrats.

Prospective Voting

In contrast, using **prospective voting**, citizens anticipate the future. They consider how candidates or proposed ballot initiatives might affect their lives or the operation of government. For example, casinos and gambling companies have recently backed efforts to alter gambling laws and to legalize casinos in several states. Prospective voters, looking ahead, see the prospect of new jobs and increased tax revenues and decide on that basis to support legalizing gaming.

In the 2020 democratic primary, amidst a crowded field of contenders, the choice came down to Senator Bernie Sanders (I-VT) and former Vice President Joe Biden. As he did in his run in 2016, Sanders campaigned on working toward "Medicare for all," free tuition at public colleges, and a $15 minimum wage. Joe Biden campaigned on building on the work of the Obama administration, including expanding affordable health care, and making change incrementally rather than in the dramatic way envisioned by the Sanders campaign. Both gained millions of backers who were trying to choose the candidate with a vision for the future they supported. When the tide clearly shifted to Biden, Sanders dropped out of the race to unite the party.

Party-Line Voting

Citizens who affiliate with a political party or hold a strong party loyalty will likely vote with that party at most opportunities. In some states, voters register with a party; in others there is no legal state-level affiliation. All partisans have various levels of loyalty or strength of relationship with their party, but when one "self-identifies" with a party, acknowledging membership or openly referring to himself or herself as a Democrat or Republican, then chances are good he or she will vote for that party. This **party identification**, rather than party registration, is the easiest way to predict a voter's habits. According to the 2016 CNN exit poll, 89 percent of Democrats voted for Clinton; 90 percent of Republicans voted for Trump.

THINK AS A POLITICAL SCIENTIST: *DESCRIBE POLITICAL INSTITUTIONS AND BEHAVIORS IN DIFFERENT SCENARIOS*

Voting is the most important way citizens can participate in government. Voting gives people a voice that may influence the decisions of their government. Over time, suffrage has been granted to more and more people. Political scientists seek to understand how groups exercise this right and what influences their choices. For example, the experiences and perspectives of one generation will have very different effects on their voting patterns compared to those of another generation.

Practice: Read the scenarios below and determine:

A) What protections exist for the individual's voting rights?

B) Which model might best explain the individual's voting behavior?

1. A 19-year-old male considers his choice in the 1972 presidential election. He feels the incumbent, Richard Nixon, has the best foreign policy plans to limit the expansion of Communist influence around the globe.

2. A 35-year-old female considers her vote in the 1932 presidential election. She wants a president who will more actively involve the government in economic reforms that will benefit those in lower socioeconomic classes.

Other Factors: Candidates and Issues

Party loyalists are occasionally drawn to a candidate from the other team. A voter may consider the track record of the incumbent while simultaneously considering the promises of the challenger, using both retrospective and prospective thinking. Another impact on the voter's selection is the personality, integrity, or competence of a candidate. In fact, in candidate-centered campaigns (see Topic 5.4) rather than in those focusing on party loyalty, the campaign will often forgo the party label or refrain from printing "Democrat" or "Republican" on their yard signs or including such information in their commercials. Instead, the emphasis might be on the candidate's military service or successes at managing a business before entering a campaign.

The candidate's character may also be a factor in how a voter decides to cast a ballot. In 2017, for example, Alabama held a special election to fill a Senate seat left vacant when President Donald Trump appointed Jeff Sessions as attorney general. The Republican candidate, Judge Roy Moore, received an endorsement from President Trump, and the state of Alabama had voted solidly for Trump in the 2016 election and solidly Republican for 20 years. However, Moore's defiance of court orders and allegations of sexual abuse turned public opinion against him. Even the other Republican senator from Alabama, Richard Shelby, said he would not vote for Moore. Democrat Doug Jones, with an exemplary character and a strong record—including securing convictions against Ku Klux Klan members responsible for the 1963 church bombing in Birmingham that killed four children—won a close victory. The African American vote played a decisive role.

The most important political issues of the day also have an influence on how citizens choose to cast their votes. For "pocketbook" voters, the economy is often at the top of the list. If the nation is in an economic downturn, the incumbent is usually held responsible for it, so votes tend to go for the challenger. If a challenger from a party other than a voter's preference has a good idea for improving the economy, the candidate's position on that issue can sway the vote.

REFLECT ON THE ESSENTIAL QUESTION

Essential Question: *How does the Constitution and legislation protect voting rights, and how do models relate to voting behavior? On separate paper, complete the chart below.*

Government Actions to Protect Voting Rights	Voter Behavior Models

KEY TERMS AND NAMES

Civil Rights Act of 1964

electorate

Fifteenth Amendment (1870)

franchise

grandfather clause

literacy test

Nineteenth Amendment

party identification

party-line voting model

poll tax

preclearance

prospective voting model

rational-choice voting model

retrospective voting model

Seventeenth Amendment (1913)

suffrage

Twenty-fourth Amendment (1964)

Twenty-sixth Amendment (1971)

Twenty-third Amendment (1961)

Voting Rights Act of 1965

white primary

Voter Turnout

"There's no such thing as a vote that doesn't matter."

—President Barack Obama, speech at the Congressional
Black Caucus Foundation, 2016

Essential Question: What roles do individual choice and state laws play in voter turnout?

In November 2016, about 138 million people turned out to vote for the next president. That's just over 60 percent of Americans who are old enough to vote. A citizens' upbringing, political ideology, efficacy, awareness, and cultural background will influence their level of civic participation. State laws and local administration of an election, too, will affect how many people register and vote. The offices on the ballot have an impact on voter turnout. Fewer citizens show up to vote in congressional midterm, county, municipal, and school board elections than in presidential elections. Those who identify with a political party—in other words, those who call or consider themselves Democrats or Republicans—invariably vote for candidates from that party. Other major factors that influence voter turnout and behavior are the candidate, contemporary political issues, and the voter's religion, ethnicity, and gender.

Influences on Voter Turnout

The number of voters who actually cast votes as a percentage of the **voting-age population**—everyone at or over the age of 18—is **voter turnout**. During the late 19th century, voter turnout was the highest in American history, though with restrictions on race, sex, and age, those eligible to vote were a minority of the population. Some estimates show that up to 90 percent of the legal electorate voted. However, manipulation of the ballot box and fraudulent practices such as voting more than once surely skewed those estimates.

State and Local Administration of Elections

Most states require a voter to register in advance of an election and to be at least 18 years old, a citizen of the United States, a resident of the state where voting will take place, and a non-felon. States can require **voter registration**—enrollment in the electoral roll—30 days in advance of the election so county boards of elections can create and maintain the voter rolls, or poll books.

States' election laws authorize a state department, bureaucratic agency, and/or a secretary of state to oversee elections statewide. Certain customs and procedures are consistent statewide, such as voter registration guidelines, the times voting locations are open, procedures for candidates to file candidacy, and the criteria for candidates to get their names on the ballot. County or local governments conduct and oversee local elections even when the election is for federal offices.

Typically, a county-level elections board governs the election and vote-counting process and serves as a referee when controversies arise. For purposes of voting, counties, cities, and towns are subdivided into **wards**, which are broken into **precincts**. A precinct is a small geographic area of about 500–1,000 voters who all vote at an assigned **polling place**, often a school or community center. Its size is determined by the supervisor of elections. States can allow 17-year-olds to vote, and many do so in the primary elections if the voter will be 18 by the date of the general election in November. A state elections official oversees the process statewide, while the county-level boards of elections tabulate and report the election returns. Typically, winning candidates are known late on election night or by the following day, but election authorities do not certify the election for days or weeks while they verify the count and wait for absentee ballots to come in.

WHO GOVERNS ELECTIONS?	
State	**Federal**
Sets times and locations for elections (based on federal, state, and local criteria), sets most dates	Sets date for federal, general elections
Chooses format of acceptable ballots and how to file for candidacy	Has judicial jurisdiction on election policy
Creates rules and procedures for voter registration	Addresses suffrage in constitutional amendments
Draws congressional district lines	Enforces relevant civil rights legislation
Certifies election results days or weeks after election day	Administers and enforces campaign finance rules

Government Policies and Voter Participation

Although states have the authority to administer elections, the federal government has passed election laws that the states must follow. For example, Congress passed the **National Voter Registration Act (NVRA)** in 1993 to increase citizen participation and to alleviate the burden of having to make a special effort to register to vote. Also known as the **motor-voter law,** it addresses national standards and enforcement of voter registration, mail-in registration, and government agency-based registration. The law requires states to offer citizens a chance to register at state-run agencies, such as the bureaus of motor vehicles (hence the "motor-voter law" nickname). The NVRA increases the number of eligible citizens who register to vote, expands the number of locations where voters can register, and protects the integrity of elections by ensuring accurate voter rolls.

A recent U.S. Census Bureau report shows that 21 percent of voters registered at a county registration office; another 21 percent did so at a motor vehicle agency. More than 13 percent mailed in their registration, and 6 percent reported registering at the polls on election day (15 states allow that) at a school, hospital, campus, or registration booth.

Federal Response to the 2000 Election

The 2000 presidential election between Texas Governor George W. Bush and Vice President Al Gore was one of the closest and most controversial elections in U.S. history. The controversial Florida recount ended with a Supreme Court ruling that stopped it because the Court said the Florida procedures violated the equal protection clause. George W. Bush became president.

Congress responded by passing the national **Help America Vote Act (HAVA)** in 2002. HAVA imposes a number of requirements on states, mostly to create national standards for voting and election management. All states had to upgrade their voting systems to an electronic format. The law required states to replace punch card and lever systems and provided funds for the changeover. HAVA also addresses voting for people with disabilities. States and counties must make polling places accessible for blind people and those with physical handicaps to "ensure full participation in the electoral process." Largely due to the confusion among Florida's voters in 2000, the law requires states to use a voting system that allows the voter to glance at his or her choices before confirming the vote. Through this provision, voters have an opportunity to change their vote if they make a mistake.

To prevent voter fraud, registering voters must provide a driver's license or the last four digits of a Social Security number that they must verify at the polling place on election day. The law also makes sure that military personnel serving overseas have access to absentee ballots, registration forms, and election information.

Since the 2000 election, 75 percent of the nation has changed the way it votes. Elections are now more accurate. There is less chance that voters will make mistakes and more safeguards in place if they do. Access has been expanded, and millions now vote by mail.

Voter Registration

Election schemes during the age of organized corruption in politics at the end of the 19th century brought the need for voter registration. Registration enables governments to prepare for an election, verify voter qualifications, and assign a voter to only one polling place to prevent repeat voting.

Citizens can register to vote in a few ways. At a local board of elections, any adult resident can walk in during business hours with ID and Social Security number and register. The laws discussed earlier require states to offer opportunities by mail as well. In most cases, voters can find a printable form online, complete it, and mail it in. Because of the motor-voter law, registration forms are also available at public libraries and where motorists obtain a drivers' license.

Source: Voice of America

Students at Washington University in St. Louis register people to vote in the 2016 election.

Nearly 40 states allow citizens to register online. One of the first studies examining online registration showed a per-registrant cost to the state dropping from 83 cents to 3 cents. These savings do not take into account the expensive implementation costs, but those costs will diminish over time.

A criminal record can affect one's voting right. All but two states prevent felons from voting while in prison. Most states, however, reinstate felons' voting rights after parole. Twelve states deny felons who committed severe crimes the right to ever vote again.

Types of Ballots

Not only registration but also voting has been upgraded in an effort to increase accuracy and voter participation.

Election Day Ballots The ballot used today, known as the **Australian ballot** since a version of it was first used in Australia in 1872, helps make elections fair. Some form of the Australian ballot is used in all U.S. states. The ballot must 1) be printed and distributed at public expense, 2) show all

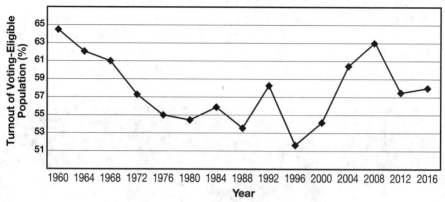

Voter Turnout In Presidential Elections, 1960–2016

qualifying candidates' names, 3) be available only at the polling places, and 4) be completed in private.

Sometimes registration records can be incomplete or incorrect. Citizens' names may be purged from voting rolls after years of inactivity. Voters move residences from one precinct to another and forget to change their registration. When discrepancies like these occur at the polling place, states offer **provisional ballots**. These are set aside until election officials verify that voting occurred at the correct polling place based on the voter's registration address. When these controversies of residency or registration come up, citizens may feel questioned or partially disfranchised. But modern procedures afford a greater chance of a fair and accurate election.

Absentee Ballots Voters can also vote by **absentee ballot**. If a voter cannot make it to the polls, he or she can mail a completed ballot instead. In years past, voters needed an excuse, such as illness or travel, to vote absentee. An increasing number of states have embraced no-excuse absentee and early voting. A majority of states allow any qualified voter to cast a ballot in person during a designated period before the election. Early voting is not only convenient to the voter—it also makes for easier management and vote counting on election day. Voting lines decrease, and fewer poll workers are needed. In the 2012 election, fully one-third of Americans had already voted when election day arrived. Today, few states require in-person election day voting.

These convenience-voting changes usually bring noticeable increases in participation, followed by a leveling of voter turnout. As ProPublica reported in 2016, the research on how convenience voting has increased turnout is mixed. Some research shows that early voting has increased turnout by 2 to 4 percent. One report shows that early in-person voting actually *decreased* voter turnout. More consistent findings are that African American turnout has increased with early, in-person voting, and that same-day voting and registration has increased turnout somewhat overall. Oregon's automatic registration process may have been the key factor in a 4-point increase in participation and one of the top voter turnout states in the United States.

Online Voting Scholars, technology specialists, and fiscal conservatives have put forth good points in favor of using the Internet to conduct elections online or at least as an alternative to traveling to a voting booth. Voting online would be easier for some, could lower the administration cost of elections, and could propel younger tech-savvy voters into an influential and formidable force. However, it could make obvious a "digital divide" that still partially exists in the U.S., and it could open the door to hacking and other manipulation.

Voter ID Laws

State laws requiring voters to present some form of identification at the voting booth have passed in 35 states, generally advanced by Republican majorities. Some states accept multiple forms of ID, including a utility bill or a paycheck stub. Others require government-issued photo identification. Some allow citizens to cast provisional ballots if they don't have their IDs with them. If they return with the necessary ID, their provisional ballots can be cast.

These requirements have brought criticism and constitutional challenges. Some conservatives say the IDs are necessary to decrease the chances of voter fraud and to further guarantee accuracy in elections. Liberals and progressives, in contrast, believe Republicans are trying to set up barriers to those voters less likely to have an ID, most of whom tend to vote Democratic.

In the courts, legal challenges to photo-ID policies emphasize the way these laws disproportionately impact people of different classes. In 2008, the Supreme Court upheld an Indiana voter ID statute that requires a photo ID, but since then, federal appeals courts have struck down similar laws from other states.

What is the practical impact of these measures? Are these voter ID requirements suppressing the vote? The Brennan Center for Justice reports that about 25 percent of eligible African American voters and 16 percent of Hispanics do not have IDs, compared to 9 percent of white voters. Participation among these groups has generally grown in recent years, and such laws could interfere with that growth. At the same time, voter ID laws seemed to serve as a rallying cry against voter suppression and actually help increase turnout of the groups claimed to be suppressed.

Long Lines at the Polls Most voters wait an average of 14 minutes to cast their votes. However, 5 percent of voters—which amounts to several million people—have to wait much longer, up to two hours. Minority voters are six times as likely as whites to wait more than an hour to vote. Since their historic turnout rates have been lower than those of whites, there may be fewer voting machines and poll workers in their precincts, and those deficits slow down the voting process. For hourly workers, long wait times result in lower wages for the day. However, these long waits in line have a significant consequence beyond lost wages. One study estimates that for every hour spent in line, a voter is 1 percent less likely to vote in the next election. Long lines, then, are a voter-suppression mechanism.

Voting and Nonvoting

From 1928 to 1968, the November voter turnout in presidential elections hovered generally over 60 percent. In 1972, an election year that embraced a new voting bloc of young voters, turnout actually dipped down to 57 percent. The anti-government feelings about the unpopular Vietnam War and later Nixon's Watergate scandal resulted in a number of people disengaging from politics during the next two decades. Party loyalty in elections became weaker and weaker. The connection between money and elections further disturbed Americans and required Congress to regulate the flow of dollars through campaigns. From 1972 to 2000, presidential election turnout hovered just above 50 percent of the voting-age population.

According to the U.S. Elections Project, in 2016, 59.3 percent of the **voting-eligible population** voted, that is, citizens who could legally vote if they wished. However, 54.7 percent of the *voting-age* population voted, which includes in the denominator released felons and others who may be old enough but not legally eligible. Of course, as a percentage of *registered* voters, voter turnout is much higher. In that measure, only the number of actual registered voters—those who are legal and have taken the extra step of registration—are in the denominator. Voter turnout among registered voters reached about 70 percent in 2016.

Type of Election Turnout varies based on the type of election. More voters cast ballots during the presidential contest than any other. Congressional **midterm elections**, those federal elections that occur midway through a president's term, have a lower turnout. Turnout in the 2018 midterm congressional elections was close to 50 percent of the voting eligible population. Turnout for county-level and municipal races is even less, ranging from 15 to 35 percent.

Some people don't vote because logistical factors interfere—they are sick on election day or they can't arrange childcare. Also, certain people are excluded by law from voting in some states, including felons and people ruled to be mentally incompetent. Others may not have the kind of ID their states require. (See Topic 3.11.)

Political Efficacy However, many people who have the right to vote choose not to exercise it. This **voter apathy**, a lack of concern for the election outcome, has different causes. Some citizens feel no **political efficacy**, or sense that their vote makes a difference. Voters who have supported losing candidates or did not experience the change promised during a campaign feel a lack of efficacy, and they may see little reason to vote in the next election.

Also, many people are generally satisfied with the government and don't feel the need to participate. Since the United States has a high number of elections, not all citizens vote in every election, reducing turnout. Nonvoters get involved in other ways by volunteering in their communities, for example.

Country	Turnout (by %)
Denmark	83.2
Australia	82.7
Italy	79.1
France	76.8
Israel	71.2
Portugal	69.2
Japan	66.6
United Kingdom	58.3
United States	**58.2**
Switzerland	39.8

Source: The International Institute for Democracy and Electoral Assistance

What do the numbers show? Which countries lead in voter turnout? Which countries have the lowest turnout? What are the reasons why turnout would be high or low?

Factors Influencing Voter Choice

Gender, age, education level, race and ethnicity, and religious beliefs appear to correlate to rates of voting. Older, better-educated, wealthier voters show up to vote in higher numbers. Activists, people who attend church, military veterans, and members of civic organizations also turn out to vote in higher numbers. Some groups tend to vote in noticeable patterns. These groups are known as **voting blocs**. BIG IDEA Using various types of analyses, political scientists measure how U.S. political behavior, attitudes, ideologies, and institutions are shaped by a number of factors over time.

Gender

One of the easiest ways to divide and analyze voters is along gender lines. The **gender gap** is the difference in political views between men and women and how these views are expressed at the voting booth. Women tend to oppose harsh punishments and the death penalty more than men; they favor government spending on welfare; and they are less war-prone. These leanings have resulted in more women voting with the Democratic Party rather than the Republican Party. Men tend to believe in harsher punishments against accused criminals and are more fiscally conservative; they have a tendency to vote Republican. In 2016, 53 percent of men voted for Trump, and 41 percent voted for Clinton. For women, 54 percent voted for Clinton, and 42 percent voted for Trump.

Since the 1980 election, women have turned out to vote in slightly higher numbers than men. Married and unmarried women tend to have different voting patterns. In 2000, unmarried females strongly voted with Democrats. Single women tend to place importance on health care, employment, education, job security, and retirement benefits. In contrast, in the 2002 midterms, 56 percent of married women voted for Republicans, compared to 39 percent of unmarried women. Married women tend to be "moral traditionalists" with concerns for traditional marriage and family. In the 2016 presidential election, 56 percent of married women voters chose Trump, compared to 42 percent for Clinton. Unmarried female voters, in contrast, chose Clinton by a 62 to 35 percent margin.

Age

Since ratification of the Twenty-sixth Amendment in 1971, the nation's youngest voters have had the lowest turnout. Reasons include their undeveloped views of candidates, lack of strong views on political issues, and mobility. Working a full-time job, owning a home, paying a substantial amount of one's income to taxes—activities of older people—are all things that make people notice the details of public policy.

Yet young voter turnout and interest in politics have risen. Authors Dan Balz and Haynes Johnson found in the 2008 election that citizens in the larger bloc of 18- to 30-year-olds turned out in the highest numbers in a generation. This group is dominated by self-described liberals, 38 percent, while only 23 percent considered themselves conservative. A U.S. Census report on the 2016 election shows the 18- to 29-year-old bloc turned out at 46 percent.

In contrast, senior citizens vote in reliably high numbers. This generational disparity in turnout results from older citizens having more experience and understanding of the political process, regular voting habits, and likely more at stake—property, investments, and Social Security and Medicare. Senior citizens turned out at nearly 71 percent in the 2016 election, with 52 percent voting for Trump and 45 percent for Clinton.

Race and Ethnicity

Minorities are increasing as a percentage of the U.S. population, and along with the increase in numbers comes an increase in political clout. However, with the exception of the 2012 presidential election, in which African American voters proportionally outnumbered white voters, turnout among minorities has stalled or declined.

African Americans The disenfranchising and intimidation of potential African American voters in the South for generations created a consistently low voter turnout among African Americans. Because the Republican Party freed enslaved people and enfranchised African Americans after the Civil War, blacks largely sided with the Republican Party during their first generation at the voting booth. By 1932, however, these voters began a relationship with the Democratic Party that only became stronger under Democratic presidents Truman, Johnson, and Obama. (See Topic 5.4.)

African Americans tend to have a less favorable view of the criminal justice system than whites. A recent University of Cincinnati poll shows that African Americans favor abolishing the death penalty by 51 percent, compared with 23 percent of white respondents. They also want less attention and money focused on international affairs and foreign policy and more on Americans in need. Upon the 2012 presidential election, the PEW Research Center estimated that 95 percent of voting-eligible African Americans voted for Democrat Barack Obama. For the first time ever, black voter turnout in 2012 surpassed that of whites; 66.2 percent of African Americans voted, compared to 64.1 percent of white voters. African American turnout in the 2016 presidential election dropped to 59.6 percent.

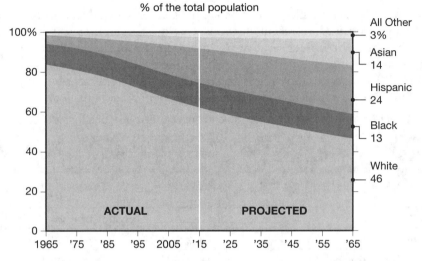

Demographic Trends, 1965–2065

% of the total population

Hispanics Hispanics are the fastest growing minority in the United States, now numbering well over 43 million. Hispanics live in large numbers in the southwestern and western states, the Sunbelt states, New York, and Florida. Hispanic turnout rose from 2.5 million nationally in 1980 to more than 11 million in 2012. Hispanics turn out in lower percentages than whites and blacks. Hispanic participation peaked at 50 percent in 2008; in 2016 their participation was 47.6 percent.

The Latino voting population has sided with Democrats on urban, minority, and labor issues, although Cuban Americans have a history of favoring Republicans. Also, conflict over immigration laws has created a wedge between Hispanic voters and conservative lawmakers. Heightened rhetoric and a Republican desire for strict citizenship requirements have driven Hispanics closer to Democrats.

Asian Americans Asian Americans come mostly from China, the Philippines, India, Japan, Korea, and Vietnam. They make up only about 3 percent of the U.S. voting population, though that figure is higher in the West Coast states. They have concerns like other minorities for civil liberties and equal protection, but for years Asian Americans have voted conservatively, probably because the Republican Party has been stronger against the repressive regimes in the nations some have departed. Also, Republican leaders have pushed for fewer regulations on business, which satisfies the Asian business community, and because conservative values often align with ethical beliefs in

Asian cultures. Yet in 2012, exit polls reveal that roughly 73 percent of Asians voted for Obama, and Indian Americans, many of them in the United States for less than 10 years, voted overwhelmingly for Hillary Clinton in 2016.

THINK AS A POLITICAL SCIENTIST: *EXPLAIN PATTERNS AND TRENDS IN DATA*

A number of factors affect voter behavior: gender, age, education level, race, and religious beliefs. In recent elections, race has had an increasing impact on the outcome. The influence of minority groups on presidential elections has grown as the United States experiences an increase in non-white population. Political scientists can look at the participation of different races in presidential elections to better understand influence of race on voter behavior.

Practice: Use the information in the table to answer the questions that follow.

Year and race and Hispanic origin	Total votes cast	Net change from previous presidential election
VOTER TURNOUT 1996 TO 2012 **BY RACE AND HISPANIC ORIGIN** (NUMBERS IN THOUSANDS)		
2012		**(change from 2008 election)**
Total	**132,948**	**1,804**
White, non-Hispanics	98,041	−2,001
Blacks	17,813	1,680
Asians	3,904	547
Hispanics	11,188	1,443
2000		**(change from 1996 election)**
Total	**110,826**	**5,809**
White, non-Hispanics	89,469	2,865
Blacks	12,917	1,531
Asians	2,045	304
Hispanics	5,934	1,006

Source: U.S. Census Bureau, Current Population Survey, November Select Years.

1. Which group has seen the largest increase in voter turnout in the 21st century?
2. Which group has seen the largest decrease in voter turnout in the 21st century?
3. What factors can account for the changes in voter turnout?
4. What conclusions can be made from the data presented?

Religious Affiliation

Religions share certain beliefs among their members and often tend to vote as blocs. By far the largest religious group is made up of Protestant and other Christian denominations. A majority of this group has consistently voted for Republican candidates.

Evangelicals White, born-again Evangelical Protestants have become the largest religious group. They tend to hold conservative beliefs. They have become ardent supporters of the Republican Party and have joined Republicans to create the "religious right." Televangelists and leaders of conservative family-oriented groups have large followings and thus great political influence. Most members of this group do not believe in human evolution and don't want their sons or daughters to be taught this science in public schools. They are frustrated by the removal of prayer from school and the public square. They are a strong political force in the South and Midwest. Evangelicals supported Donald Trump in the 2016 presidential election by 80 percent and have become one of the president's most reliable groups within his base.

Catholics Catholics make up almost as large a group as evangelicals. Catholic voters have historically voted with the Democratic Party but today cast votes for both parties because they constitute such a large swath of the electorate. Catholic faith and custom are defined largely by papal decrees (the Pope's orders) from Rome, which have established some strict rules and beliefs.

The historical alliance between Catholics and Democrats began in 1856 when the party denounced the anti-immigrant, anti-Catholic American (or "Know Nothing") party and instead called for a "spirit of tolerance" in their platform. The relationship continued into the 20th century, as Catholics played a large role in the politics of the urban North. According to Gallup, Catholic votes for Democrats in presidential elections peaked when John Kennedy, himself a Catholic, won in 1960 with roughly 78 percent of those voters.

Today, the Catholic vote seems to lean Democratic nationwide but is no longer a monolith; it straddles the ideological spectrum. Roughly 25 percent of the country, Catholics overlap so many other demographics—rich and poor, young and old, white and Latino, northeast urban and Midwest suburbs—that they defy categorization. The Papacy denounces birth control and abortion, for example, thereby aligning with Republican ideals; yet the church opposes the death penalty and promotes charity, positions embraced by more Democrats than Republicans.

A recent finding of the National Election Study shows that 36 percent of Catholics identify themselves as conservative, while 35 percent say they are moderate, and 29 percent claim to be liberal.

Jews Jewish voters participate in large numbers and vote mainly with the Democrats. They comprise a small fraction of the electorate, about 2 percent, but their participation in elections averages about 10 percent higher than the general population. Some estimates show that roughly 90 percent of Jewish people vote. Jewish-American political history parallels American Catholic history—with ethnic, often immigrant, minorities occupying larger, northern urban centers. Subject to discrimination, Jews have developed strong concerns about the power of the state and infringements on civil liberties. Jewish voters place a high priority on privacy, on ensuring basic rights for the accused, and supporting charities. These factors have caused the Jewish vote to swing in a liberal direction.

The first measurable Jewish vote went to Woodrow Wilson with 55 percent in 1916. In the 1920s, many Jews who identified as Socialists joined the Democratic Party because they feared the "Communist" label. When the United States entered World War II and later defeated the Jews' worst enemy—Adolf Hitler and Nazi Germany—FDR gained full backing from American Jewish voters. His successor, Harry Truman, sealed a generation of Jewish support for Democrats with his embrace of establishing a Jewish state in the Middle East in what became Israel. From 1952 to 1968, Jewish support for Democratic presidential candidates ran 20 to 30 percent higher than that of the general population. According to exit polls, about 71 percent of Jews voted for Hillary Clinton over Republican Donald Trump in 2016.

Business, Labor, and Unions

Entrepreneurs, leaders in the business community, CEOs of companies, shareholders, and much of the upper class tend to embrace a conservative political philosophy and capitalist principles. Small business owners also want less regulation and interference by the state in the business world. They want lower taxes and an ability to make more profits. This voting profile usually results in voting Republican.

In contrast, the wage earner, the craftsman, and the factory line worker tend to view politics through the lens of the workplace and often in line with their labor union. Since their rise in the late 1800s and early 1900s, labor unions such as the American Federation of Labor have supported government-mandated fair wage laws, child labor laws, safety regulations in the workplace, and fairness on the job. Aligned with Socialists in their earlier years, the labor unions struck a tight relationship with FDR's party during the implementation of New Deal policies. Unions have lost much of their influence today, and membership is down from the prior generation. The decline is explained in part by laws in 28 states that prohibit making union membership mandatory in places of business that have voted to unionize. In the 2016 election, estimates show that the Democratic presidential candidate still carried the union vote, by perhaps 16 percentage points, but by 2 points less than four years ago and a noticeable drop from the prior generation.

VOTER TURNOUT AMONG BLOCS	
Voting Bloc	**Turnout (by%)**
Males	59.3
Females	63.3
Whites	65.3
African Americans	59.6
Hispanic	47.6
Asians	49
18 to 29	46.1
65 and older	70.9
No high school diploma	33

Source: U.S. Census, United States Elections Project, 2016

REFLECT ON THE ESSENTIAL QUESTION

Essential Question: *What roles do individual choice and state laws play in voter turnout? On separate paper, complete the chart below.*

Characteristics that Influence Voter Choice	State Laws that Influence Voter Turnout

KEY TERMS AND NAMES

absentee ballot

Australian Ballot

gender gap

Help America Vote Act (2002)

midterm election

motor-voter law

National Voter Registration Act (1993)

political efficacy

polling place

precincts

provisional ballot

voter apathy

voter registration

voter turnout

voting-age population

voting blocs

voting-eligible population

wards

CHAPTER 15 Review:
Learning Objectives and Key Terms

TOPIC 5.1: Describe the voting rights protections in the Constitution and in legislation. (MPA-3.A)

Describe different models of voting behavior. (MPA-3.B)

Legal Protections for Voting Rights (MPA-3.A.1)	**Voting Behavior Models** (MPA-3.B.1)
Civil Rights Act of 1964	electorate
Fifteenth Amendment (1870)	party identification
franchise	party-line voting model
grandfather clause	prospective voting model
literacy test	rational-choice voting model
Nineteenth Amendment	retrospective voting model
poll tax	
preclearance	
Seventeenth Amendment (1913)	
suffrage	
Twenty-fourth Amendment (1964)	
Twenty-sixth Amendment (1971)	
Twenty-third Amendment (1961)	
Voting Rights Act of 1965	
white primary	

TOPIC 5.2: Explain the roles that individual choice and state laws play in voter turnout in elections. (MPA-3.C)

Structural Barriers for Voters (MPA-3.C.1)	**Factors Influencing Voter Choice** (MPA-3.C.2 & 3)
absentee ballot	gender gap
Australian Ballot	political efficacy
Help America Vote Act (2002)	voter apathy
midterm elections	voting blocs
motor-voter law	voting-age population
National Voter Registration Act (1993)	voting-eligible population
precincts	
polling place	
provisional ballot	
voter registration	
wards	
voter turnout	

CHAPTER 15 Checkpoint:
Voting Rights and Voter Behavior
Topics 5.1–5.2

MULTIPLE-CHOICE QUESTIONS

Questions 1 and 2 refer to the following table.

TOP REASONS FOR NOT VOTING	
Too busy	17.5%
Illness/disability	14.9%
Not interested	13.4%
Didn't like candidates/issues	12.9%
Out of town	8.8%
Registration problems	6.0%

Source: U.S. Census, 2010

1. Which of the following is the most accurate conclusion based on the data in the table?
   - (A) Voter registration problems have become the chief deterrent to full participation in U.S. elections.
   - (B) The top reason for not voting is lack of time.
   - (C) Lack of political efficacy is the chief reason people do not vote.
   - (D) Voter identification laws have reduced voter turnout.

2. How have most states responded to the reasons offered for non-voting?
   - (A) States have required more accurate media coverage of candidates and issues.
   - (B) States have switched to online voting.
   - (C) States have moved election day to Saturdays and Sundays.
   - (D) States have provided for early voting and no-excuse voting by mail.

Questions 3 and 4 refer to the Supreme Court opinion below.

"A photo identification requirement imposes some burdens on voters that other methods of identification do not share. For example, a voter may lose his photo identification, may have his wallet stolen on the way to the polls, or may not resemble the photo in the identification because he recently grew a beard. Burdens of that sort arising from life's vagaries, however, are neither so serious nor so frequent as to raise any question about the constitutionality of SEA 483 [the Indiana law requiring photo IDs]; the availability of the right to cast a provisional ballot provides an adequate remedy for problems of that character."

—Justice John Paul Stevens, majority opinion, *Crawford v. Marion County Elections Board,* 2008

3. Which of the following statements best summarizes the Supreme Court's opinion?

   (A) Election day burdens on citizens are acceptable if there are comparable burdens placed on the government to guarantee fair elections.

   (B) As long as a citizen can cast a temporary vote to be checked later, the citizen need not prove his or her identity on election day.

   (C) A state's goal to conduct an accurate and legitimate election does not justify a state law to show photo ID to cast a vote.

   (D) The burdens of providing photo-ID are so frequent that they make the provision unconstitutional.

4. Which of the following constitutional principles did the Supreme Court follow in letting states implement the policy referred to in the opinion?

   (A) Federalism

   (B) Suffrage amendments

   (C) Necessary and proper clause

   (D) Commerce clause

5. Which of the following constitutional amendments did Congress seek to enforce when it passed the Voting Rights Act of 1965?

   (A) Fifteenth Amendment

   (B) Twenty-third Amendment

   (C) Twenty-sixth Amendment

   (D) Twenty-seventh Amendment

6. A wage-earner who identifies as a political independent has heard a Senate candidate promise to push for an increase in the national minimum wage while her opponent does not support that. The citizen votes for this candidate primarily for this reason so his own pay might increase. Which of the following models best explains this citizen's voting behavior?

(A) Rational-choice voting

(B) Retrospective voting

(C) Prospective voting

(D) Party-line voting

FREE-RESPONSE QUESTIONS

Concept Application

The following passage refers to the 2018 midterm elections.

1. "A lot of naysayers doubted that efforts to inspire college students to vote could make much of a difference. We heard harsh judgements of the young: "They aren't interested; they don't plan ahead; they don't follow through; they'd rather protest than vote."

Recent results of national studies show these naysayers are wrong. According to the U.S. Elections Project, turnout rose in all age groups in 2018, with an overall jump of about 14 percentage points from 36.7 percent (in 2014) to 50.3 percent. Although the absolute rate of voting by college students remained lower than that of older groups, college students increased their turnout even more. The National Study of Learning, Voting, and Engagement reported an increase in voting for college students nationally of 20 percent."

—Professor Edie Goldenberg, *Bridge Magazine*, 2019

After reading the scenario, respond to A, B, and C below:

(A) Describe voter turnout as described in the scenario.

(B) In the context of the scenario, explain how voter turnout in part A may have resulted from government voting policy.

(C) Explain how the intersection between state and federal government may impact voter turnout.

Quantitative Analysis

Number of Registered African American Voters 1964 and 1975

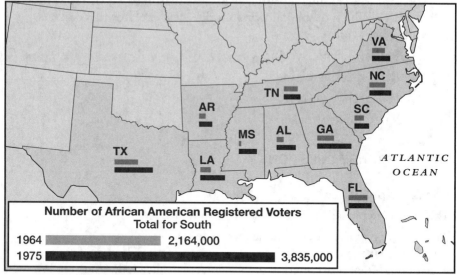

Source: *America's History*, Seventh Edition.

2. Use the information in the map to respond to the questions.

   (A) Identify the state with the greatest relative change in African American voter registration from 1964 to 1975.

   (B) Describe a trend in African American voter registration from 1964 to 1975.

   (C) Explain how that trend affects black voter participation.

   (D) Explain how federal policy may have brought about the data depicted in the map.

CHAPTER 16

Political Parties

Topics 5.3–5.5

Topic 5.3 Political Parties

PMI-5.A: Describe linkage institutions.

PMI-5.B: Explain the function and impact of political parties on the electorate and the government.

Topic 5.4 How and Why Political Parties Change and Adapt

PMI-5.C: Explain how and why political parties change and adapt.

Topic 5.5 Third-Party Politics

PMI-5.D: Explain how structural barriers impact third-party and independent candidate success.

Source: Wikimedia Commons, Pete Souza

Democratic President Barack Obama and Republican President-elect Donald Trump meet in the Oval Office two days after Election Day 2016.

Political Parties

"I don't like bipartisans. Whenever a fellow tells me he's bipartisan, I know he's going to vote against me."

—Harry S. Truman, campaign endorsement speech, 1961

Essential Question: What role do linkage institutions play in political parties, and what effect do political parties have on the electorate and government?

Political parties are organized groups of people with similar political ideologies and goals. They work to elect candidates to public office who will represent those ideologies and accomplish those goals. Political parties developed in the aftermath of the American Revolution because of diverging opinions about the structure and power of the new government. In his farewell address, George Washington criticized political parties as being driven by self-interest rather than by a desire to enhance the well-being of the new nation. Other founders agreed that political parties could be a damaging force to the nation.

However, when like-minded people desire certain policy changes in a democratic society, existing political parties take action or new parties form. Organized parties provide important opportunities and link people to government.

Linking People to Government

Political parties are one of several entities that serve as **linkage institutions**—channels that connect people with the government—keeping people informed and trying to shape public opinion and policy. Other linkage institutions are interest groups (see Topics 5.6–5.7), elections (see Topics 5.8–5.9), and the media. (See Topics 5.12–5.13.)

Political parties connect with and persuade voters, and sometimes the persuasion goes the other way as well: Enough voters can change a party's overall views. Parties engage in varied activities to mobilize their members, to gain new ones, and to get them to vote on election day. The parties are organized into a somewhat hierarchical institution that have written bylaws, a platform on the issues, goals, and a funding system.

Impact on Voters and Policy

Political parties can exert a great influence on voters. They can both shape and reflect voters' political ideologies. They play a large role in deciding which candidates will run for office, and they exercise significant control over the drawing of legislative districts, a process that can tilt the likelihood of election victory to the party in power, especially in gerrymandered districts. (See Topic 2.3.)

Republican or Democratic Party "members" could be lifelong party loyalists, just common voters who tend to side with the party on election day, or somewhere in between. Parties have no restrictions on who can become members. People who refer to themselves as Republicans or Democrats, or who regularly vote that way, are considered party members. More active and dedicated members volunteer for the party, make donations, or run for office.

Parties also engage voters in the routines of public life. For example, more active, local party members may hold monthly meetings, make calls to get voters to the polls, volunteer at the polling places on election day, and gather at a neighborhood restaurant to watch the election results come in. Through these activities, the party is connecting with the electorate and members are connecting with other members, building social and political bonds. These activities link the voters to government and provide access to participation.

Mobilization and Education of Voters

Political parties always look to add rank-and-file members, because winning elections is essential to implementing party policy. Local activists register and mobilize voters as they recruit more members—not just the party regulars but those who are on the fence about which side to take. They contact citizens via mail, phone, email, text message, social media, or at the door. Volunteers operate phone banks and make personal phone calls to citizens. Parties also use **robocalls**—prerecorded phone messages delivered automatically to large numbers of people to remind people to vote for their candidates and to discourage voting for opposing candidates.

Political parties also hold voter registration drives. As elections draw near, small armies of volunteers canvass neighborhoods, walking door to door spreading the party philosophy, handing out printed literature and convincing citizens to vote for their causes and candidates. What is sometimes termed a "shoe-leather campaign" can gain more votes than a less personalized email blast. On election day, volunteers will even drive people to the polls.

At the national, state, and local levels, parties educate their membership on key issues and candidates. Parties also inform members of government activity, both good and bad. They may tout accomplishments of local officeholders they support and criticize those in the opposing party in an effort to stop unwanted policies.

Parties provide extensive training to candidates in how to run an effective campaign. They also train volunteers in the process of building party membership, getting out the vote, and interacting with elected officials. This education effort goes both ways. To make sure their officeholders make decisions that reflect the voters' desires, parties conduct opinion surveys on the issues and share results with officeholders and candidates to educate them on party members' positions.

Creation of Party Platforms

A party expresses its primary ideology in its **platform**—a written list of beliefs and political goals. In drafting a platform, national party leaders try to take into account the views of millions of voters.

The modern **Republican Party** supports a conservative doctrine. Republicans for decades have advocated for a strong national defense, a reduction of government spending, and limited regulations on businesses. The **Democratic Party**, on the other hand, support aggressive efforts for minority rights and stronger protections for the environment. Democrats also desire more government services for the citizenry and programs to solve public problems. These views are reflected in each party's platform.

Gathering of party leaders established a tradition and necessary function— the **national convention**. Democrats and Republicans arrive at their respective conventions with drafts of their platforms constructed weeks earlier. Each party has an official platform committee appointed by its leadership. As multiple presidential candidates within each party compete for the nomination, party leaders address the different factions' concerns. Once the party has a nominee, the runners-up maintain strong input on the platform. In 2016, for example, second-place Democratic candidate Bernie Sanders of Vermont was allowed to name five of the 15 members of the platform-writing committee; the winning presidential nominee, Hillary Clinton, got to name six members; and the party chair appointed the others. Because of Sanders's influence, the final platform included a desire for a $15 minimum wage. Giving a runner-up this much influence on the document is both principled and practical. Sanders received votes from party members in the primary election. The party wants them represented and needs those members to vote in the general election.

Political parties define their principles, which are shaped by the more ideological and active members, while remaining practical and looking ahead to the next election. They must strategize how to attract voters. After the Republicans lost their second consecutive presidential election in 2012, the party took a step back to evaluate its performance and assess how it could gain members and thus voters. Their so-called "autopsy report" suggested that the GOP needed to do more to reach out to Hispanics and younger citizens. Instead, however, during the 2016 election, the party platform and Republican winner Donald Trump took a strong position against illegal immigration—an issue affecting large numbers of Hispanics—and voiced the party's continued opposition to gay marriage—an issue that younger citizens tend to support. These policies appealed to a traditional, mostly white voter base. Trump also promoted protectionist trade policies, expanded oil and gas drilling, and an

America-first program, attracting a significant number of blue-collar voters who traditionally voted with the Democrats. Trump didn't win the popular vote, but despite not following the recommendations of the autopsy report, he did win the majority of Electoral College votes, in part thanks to conservative voters who wanted a change in leadership.

As official statements of position, platforms matter to party leaders. However, most citizens do not follow the platform fight at the convention or read the final draft once it is available on the Internet. Nuances in platform language do not affect too many voters, but they could signal the beginning of an evolution in the party that may take a few election cycles to appear.

Candidate Recruitment

Parties are always looking for talented candidates to run for office, especially those with their own financial resources or a strong, established following. For instance, after World War II, both parties at the national level, sought to recruit General Dwight Eisenhower to run for president. Because he was a career soldier, mostly apolitical, and widely popular for his role in the victory over the Axis powers, a "Draft Eisenhower" movement started among some Democrats for the 1948 election. The Republicans succeeded in making him their candidate in 1952. Party officials have recruited other presidential candidates, but typically there's no shortage of experienced and well-funded contenders who have their eye on the presidency.

The party apparatus will look aggressively for candidates to run for the state legislature or for the U.S. Congress, especially in "safe" districts, those where a party consistently wins by more than 55 percent. Both major parties have recruiting programs that operate from Washington, DC. These recruiters mark swing districts and swing states (see Topic 5.8) on maps and keep an eye on rising talent in those areas. Ideally, they find energetic, telegenic, and scandal-free candidates with good resumes and a talent for fundraising, especially in the move toward candidate-centered elections. (See Topic 5.4.) National officials from Washington will sometimes call or visit these prospects and convince them to run.

For the down-ballot races, a local county-level party chair might talk a friend into running for city commissioner or school board member. Party leaders look for charismatic people who have a good grasp of the issues and who can articulate the party's positions. They also want candidates who can connect with voters. First-time candidates might include lifelong party volunteers, community leaders known around town, or people energized about a particular political issue.

Campaign Management

As election season draws near, political parties get busy. Regular, everyday activities continue, but an increase in engaging voters, holding campaign events, raising money, and trying to win elections consumes the party for a months-long battle to take office and ultimately shape policy according to their ideology.

Most campaigns have a two-stage process: The parties' rank-and-file voters nominate their candidates in a primary election, then these nominees compete against each other in the general election in November. The party and its leaders will act more like a referee in the process of candidate nomination than a coach. Factions of members will coalesce around their favorite candidates. Sometimes these divisions are split along ideological beliefs—a primary contest might pit a liberal or conservative candidate against a more moderate one—or they could be based on differences in personality or region.

Democrats and Republicans sponsor intraparty debates or forums featuring the declared candidates. Debates enable voters to get a sense of each candidate's principles and issue positions.

During the general election campaign, the party typically unites around its slate of nominees for different offices and works to get them elected. Parties seek success by hosting political rallies or fundraisers; canvassing for votes; distributing literature and campaign items, such as bumper stickers, signs, and buttons; making "get-out-the-vote" phone calls; and of course, running television advertising, text message campaigns, and social media outreach.

Fundraising and Media Strategy

Among the parties' most important functions are raising and spending money in order to win elections. Popular candidates or those moving from one level of government up to the next may already have established a **war chest** of funds to spend. Winning an election involves travel, hotel accommodations, a small staff, yard signs, and bumper stickers. Televised and online advertising accounts for the largest part of a campaign bill.

Campaign finance laws at the national and state levels limit how much donors can contribute. National and state party organizations must register with the Federal Election Commission (FEC) and are limited in how much they donate to candidates' war chests. Party organizations can give a federal candidate up to $5,000 per election. However, they can spend much more on their own, non-coordinated efforts to help candidates. For example, the Democratic Party can pump $5,000 into a candidate's account and the candidate can spend that money for any political or electoral purpose. Yet, the party can also buy limitless TV ads in the candidate's district to promote the candidate or to criticize the opponent, as long as the candidate is not involved. (See Topic 5.11 for more on campaign finance.)

For the 2016 federal elections, the Democratic National Committee (including its auxiliary committees) received a little more than $755 million and spent all but $20 million of it. The Republican National Committee received more than $652 million and had nearly $44 million remaining after the election.

One reason fundraising is such an important function of political parties is that the cost of buying TV, radio, and other media ads is very high, but an effective media strategy is fundamental to winning votes. Over the past 50 years, people received the bulk of their news from television. Even today, the average adult over 35 years of age watches about 3.5 hours of TV per day. About three-quarters of all voters say television is where they obtain most of their information about elections. For this reason, political parties try to develop the most effective media strategy possible, taking full advantage of the power of television. According to Borrell Associates, the total spending on television advertisements for the 2016 presidential election by party organizations and other sources totaled nearly $4.4 billion.

Although television is still central to media strategy, the trend in how people get their news is shifting. As of 2017, about two-thirds of Americans got at least part of their news from social media. Examples of **social media** include Facebook, Instagram, Snapchat, and Twitter (all social networks), YouTube (video posting), WordPress and Tumblr (blog sites), or Quora and Digg (discussion groups). These social media outlets share certain traits that make them powerful tools for parties and candidates to spread a message and build a brand, especially their ability to mine data that can be used to target potential voters and donors. (See Topic 5.10.)

Source: The Granger Collection

Television shines a spotlight on image and appearance. More than 33 million TV viewers watched Hillary Clinton deliver a speech at the Democratic National Convention in July, 2016.

National Party Structure

Both the **Democratic National Committee (DNC)** and the **Republican National Committee (RNC)** comprise a hierarchy of hundreds of employees and a complex network dedicated to furthering party goals. Each committee includes public leaders and other elite activists. The RNC and DNC meet formally every four years at their national conventions and on occasion between presidential elections to sharpen policy initiatives and to increase their influence.

The **national chairperson** is the chief strategist and spokesperson. Though a leading official such as the current president or an outspoken congressional leader tends to be the public face of the party, the party chair runs the party machinery.

The position is nongovernmental, though some chairs have simultaneously served in Congress or as state governors. Some famous past party chairpersons include Republican George H. W. Bush (before serving as president) and former Vermont governor and Democrat Howard Dean (after his failed campaign for the presidential nomination). In 2017, Republicans chose as their new chair Ronna Romney McDaniel of Michigan, a former state-level leader (and niece of 2012 Republican presidential nominee Mitt Romney), and the Democrats elected Tom Perez, former U.S. secretary of labor.

Both the RNC and the DNC have subcommittees that draft the party platform and manage recruitment, communications, and mobilization. Employees conduct surveys to ensure the party's philosophy aligns with that of its members and vice versa. Staffers meet with interest groups that have similar goals. They also regularly meet with their congressional leaders to further their policy agenda.

Both parties also have non-lawmaking committees in each house of Congress. Their purpose is to strategize how to win seats in the House and Senate. These four groups, known as Congressional Campaign Committees (or Hill Committees), are composed of members of Congress and have permanent offices and support staff. They recruit candidates and try to reelect incumbents. They conduct polls, help candidates with fundraising activities, contribute to campaigns, create political ads, and purchase television time. Candidates running for election spend great amounts of time and energy seeking the parties' help and endorsement. During the 2016 federal election effort, the four groups each raised and spent between $130 million and $220 million in trying to elect or reelect their members to Congress.

CONGRESSIONAL CAMPAIGN COMMITTEES IN CONGRESS
National Republican Senatorial Committee (NRSC)
National Republican Congressional Committee (NRCC)
Democratic Senatorial Campaign Committee (DSCC)
Democratic Congressional Campaign Committee (DCCC)

Parties' Impact on Government

In addition to their impact on voters, political parties have a significant influence on the way government works at all levels. On the national level, Republicans and Democrats construct policy, pass legislation, and maintain power. Holding the presidency allows the party in power to appoint judges who will rule on the constitutionality of laws. Holding congressional office allows members to send funding for projects to their home states. The majority party in the House and Senate controls the flow of legislation in each house and the committee chairmanships. Party control over state legislatures and governorships is also sought to shape state law and legislative district maps.

THINK AS A POLITICAL SCIENTIST: *DESCRIBE POLITICAL INSTITUTIONS AND BEHAVIORS*

Linkage institutions provide people a chance to connect with the government and their elected representatives. Political parties, as linkage institutions, give citizens an opportunity to interact with and influence public policymaking. Political parties serve many functions:

1. mobilize and educate voters
2. create platforms that define their ideas and goals
3. recruit candidates
4. manage campaigns
5. provide committee and party leadership systems in the legislature

Practice: Describe, with examples, how political parties attempt to accomplish each of the functions above.

REFLECT ON THE ESSENTIAL QUESTION

Essential Question: *What role do linkage institutions play in political parties, and what effect do political parties have on the electorate and government? On separate paper, complete the chart below.*

How Political Parties Connect Citizens to Government	Impact of Political Parties on Government and Policy

KEY TERMS AND NAMES

Democratic National Committee (DNC)	Republican National Committee (RNC)
Democratic Party	Republican Party
linkage institutions	robocalls
national chairperson	social media
national convention	war chest
platform	

How and Why Political Parties Change and Adapt

"To those who say that this civil-rights program is an infringement on states' rights, I say this: The time has arrived in America for the Democratic Party to get out of the shadow of states' rights and to walk forthrightly into the bright sunshine of human rights."

—Senator Hubert Humphrey, Convention Speech, 1948

Essential Question: Why and how do political parties change and adapt?

Political parties developed in the decades following the founding. Before long, a two-party system emerged, formalized by national conventions, nomination systems, ideological principles, and a leadership structure. These organized parties provide citizens opportunities to participate with government and relate to policymakers.

During nearly two centuries, these national organizations have changed their views on policy and adapted their campaign methods and nomination systems. Through a few generations, the parties have become more democratic (small 'd') and participatory, causing party leaders to lose some control over their nominations. Candidate-centered campaigns have become more common. In the era of television, candidates' wealth and direct connections with voters have also weakened the party leaders' control over candidates.

Politics is a game of addition, and both parties welcome new voters into their respective "big tent." Parties modify their policies and messaging to bring in various demographic coalitions. As coalitions form and support parties, and when they break up to join other factions, they go through a political realignment. They modestly ebb and flow with ideology and with geographic dominance. Campaign finance and communication techniques, too, have shaped the way political parties operate.

Changing Political Parties

Political parties as we think of them today didn't exist in the early history of the United States. The debate over ratification of the Constitution put the voting populace into two camps, Federalists and Anti-Federalists, and political factions emerged during the first years of the New Republic. (See Topic 1.3.) Into the 1800s, however, parties formed as like-minded men elected to Congress gathered in congressional caucuses and rallied behind their desired presidential candidate. The two camps—small government conservatives who favor states' rights versus nationalists who support a strong federal government—essentially continued to oppose each other on public issues. This new alignment defined politics of the day. The Federalists maintained their label and sent members to Congress until about 1820. The Democratic-Republicans, headed first by Thomas Jefferson, came to dominate politics in the Era of Good Feelings in the first half of the 1800s as the power of the Federalists faded.

This dichotomy continued into the 1830s, but as the nation expanded westward, its political party system grew and strengthened. A formal, structured organization formed around the strong personality of President Andrew Jackson. Soon this coalition held national conventions and drew up a party platform. The Democratic Party, or "The Democracy," as it was often called, held a conservative, states-rights view and dominated politics until the Civil War. The alternative party favored a loose interpretation of the Constitution and national government spending to expand and enhance the country. Operating under a variety of names at first, this side formalized into the Whigs.

As the country fell into disunion in the 1850s, the Whig Party died and a new party was born. In two separate gatherings in 1854 in Wisconsin and Michigan, former Whigs, abolitionists, and disaffected northern Democrats gathered to conceive the Republican Party. The new group embraced "republican" ideals and national improvements, and many members opposed slavery. This developing political party at first branded itself the Free-Soil Party and competed in the 1856 presidential election. By the next election, they fully embraced the "Republican Party" label.

Candidate-Centered Campaigns

Historically, voters identified with political parties more than with individual candidates. Even the mechanical voting booth—by which a person could pull one lever and vote for a single party's entire slate of candidates—encouraged this party identification. In the 1960s, this trend began to shift, for two main reasons. First, the more widespread use of television allowed candidates to build a following based on their own personalities rather than on party affiliation. Second, during the 1960s, society seriously questioned all public institutions, including political parties, as the Vietnam War dragged on, race riots burned cities across the nation, and the press revealed that President Nixon lied about both personal and public issues.

One result was the rise of the candidate-centered campaign. Increasingly—especially with social media and Internet technologies—candidates speak directly to the people, weakening the power of the parties. Candidates who build their own campaigns are less beholden to party elites and can wield more personal power once they are in office. For this reason, parties are forced to work closely with charismatic candidates on both platform development and campaigning for down-ticket candidates—lesser known candidates in the lower profile elections further down the ballot.

Appealing to Coalitions

Each party has its core demographic groups and continually attempts to broaden its appeal to gain more voters. A demographic group—such as Hispanics, African Americans, Millennials, women, blue-collar workers, or LGBTQ persons—voting as a bloc can determine the outcome of an election. A party's image during televised events such as nominating conventions can convey how inclusive it is—or isn't—of various demographic groups.

For example, the 1968 Democratic National Convention in Chicago revealed deep divisions within the party and brought major changes in how the Democratic Party nominated its presidential candidate. Old-line conservative party regulars, who favored Vice President Hubert Humphrey as the presidential candidate, faced off against the anti-Vietnam War wing, who favored Senator Eugene McCarthy. Dominated by party elites and older members, the convention nominated Humphrey, who had not run in a single primary or caucus, while young antiwar protesters battled in the streets with the Chicago police. The televised spectacle sent the ugly message that the old, white, and still conservative delegates inside the arena made party decisions, while the younger members—who were eligible for the draft in the unpopular Vietnam conflict but ineligible in many states to vote for a candidate responsible for sending them to war—were relegated to expressing themselves in the streets. The media focused on the party's imperfect and undemocratic nominating procedure.

The Democratic Party responded by creating the **McGovern-Fraser Commission** to examine, consider, and ultimately rewrite convention rules. Headed by Senator George McGovern, the commission brought significant changes that ensured minorities, women, and younger voters' representation at future conventions and as delegates voting to nominate their candidate.

However, a decade later, after having won only one presidential contest, largely as a reaction to Nixon's Watergate scandal, the Democrats radically modified the system's emphasis on the party's rank-and-file when they voted to give more independence to the party's elites. The party created **superdelegates**, high-ranking delegates not beholden to any state primary vote. Superdelegates include Democratic members of Congress, governors, mayors of large cities, and other party regulars who comprise roughly 20 percent of the Democratic delegates.

Before the Democratic Convention in 2016, however, a DNC Unity Reform Commission met to reform the superdelegates' roles in elections in the interest of making elections more democratic. Reforms included reducing the percentage of uncommitted delegates—those free to vote for whomever they chose—to one-third, requiring the remaining two-thirds of the superdelegates to cast their votes according to the popular vote in their states.

The Republican Party faced its own challenges in appealing to a wider swath of voters. Even today, its convention delegates are overwhelmingly white, in contrast to the Democrats' now inclusive and diverse participants. The House chamber also reflects these differences between the parties during the president's State of the Union televised speeches. The Republican side of the aisle tends to be older, white, and male. The Democratic side of the aisle includes more women and people of color.

Another vital way parties appeal to their demographic coalitions is through their policy views. Will party members, if elected to office, try to overturn abortion laws, thereby appealing to social conservatives, including many older white people? Will these persons provide immigration protection to Deferred Action on Childhood Arrivals (DACA) recipients and thereby appeal to Hispanics and other immigrant populations? What about making good on a promise to maintain broad rights to gun ownership, thereby appealing to mainly conservative white males? Different demographic coalitions have different views on these issues, and party members will shape their policy positions in part to attract the demographic groups they believe they need to win elections while still working for their ideological principles.

Changes Influence Party Structure

Parties have also adjusted to developments that affect their structure. At times throughout history, shifts in voter alignments transferred power to the opposition party and redefined the mission of each party. Campaign finance laws have brought about structural changes as well, altering the relationships among donors, parties, candidates, and interest groups. And in order to remain relevant, parties must continually adjust to changing communication technology and voter-data management systems to spread and control their message and appeal to voters.

Critical Elections and Realignments

Such **party realignment** is simply a "change in underlying electoral forces due to changes in party identification," according to the *Oxford Concise Dictionary of Politics*. Party realignments are marked by **critical elections**, those contests that reveal sharp, lasting changes in loyalties to political parties. Realignments may or may not result in a shift in party dominance and may or may not redefine the mission of each party. There are at least two causes of realignments: (1) a party is so badly defeated it fades into obscurity as a new party emerges, or (2) large blocs of voters shift allegiance from one party to another as a result of a social, economic, or political crisis.

Although political scientists and historians classify realignments differently, most agree the United States has seen five national realignments, some occasional shifts by unique groups, and some regional realignment in the post-WW II era.

The First Alignment The **Democratic-Republicans**, or **Jeffersonians**, enjoyed two decades of dominance starting in 1800 with the decline of the

Federalists. From 1824 to 1832, the Democratic Party coalesced around Andrew Jackson and followed many principles of the Democratic-Republicans. In 1828, Jackson won the presidency with support from small Western farmers. By this time, suffrage had expanded because property qualifications had been dropped in most states, and many more citizens voted. This shift toward greater democracy for the common man and away from the aristocracy that had previously held the power was called **Jacksonian Democracy**. Opponents formed the **Whig Party** and advocated for a strong central government that would promote westward expansion, investment in infrastructure, and support these investments with a strong national bank. Both northerners and southerners joined the Whig Party. In time, the slavery issue would fracture the Whig Party.

Several party innovations developed to influence their structure. The Democrats started building state and local party organizations to help support the national party efforts. They also cultivated the custom of political patronage. That is, if victorious, they would reward those members who helped the campaign with government jobs. The Whigs and Democrats also developed more modern campaigns by holding nominating conventions.

New Alliances for the Republicans: The Second Realignment The 1850s marked a controversial time of intense division on the issue of slavery. The 1860 election marked a national realignment with the new "Republicans" nominee, Abraham Lincoln, winning the presidency. Though the Republican Party was technically a third party at the time—the last third party to win the White House—it quickly began to dominate national politics. The immediate secession by so many southern Democrats from the House and Senate intensified the Republicans' dominance in Washington during the Civil War years.

Today, the Republicans are often referred to as the **"Grand Old Party"** or **GOP**. From 1860 to 1932, Republicans dominated national politics with their pro-growth, pro-business agenda. As African Americans began to vote, they sided invariably with the party that freed them, the Republican Party. Democrats continued to be strong in the South. The Democrats also took in large numbers of immigrants, Catholics, and factory workers in their northern cities.

Expanding Economy and the Realignment of 1896 The next realignment point came during the era of big business and expansion, with Republicans still dominant. The critical 1896 election realigned voters along economic lines. The economic depressions of the 1880s and 1890s (or panics, as they were often called) hit the South and the Midwest hard. The Democratic Party joined with third parties such as the Greenbacks and Populists to seek a fair deal for the working class and represent voters in the South and West. Democrats also supported Protestant reformers who favored prohibition of alcohol.

For the 1896 presidential election, congressman and orator William Jennings Bryan captured the Democratic nomination. The Populist Party also endorsed him. However, anti-Bryan Democrats realigned themselves with the Republican Party, which nominated William McKinley. The Republicans were still aligned with big business, industry, capitalists, urban interests, and immigrant groups. These groups feared the anti-liquor stance of so many in the evolving Democratic Party, which increasingly focused on class conflict and workers' rights. As Democratic legislatures began to regulate industry to protect laborers, conservative Republican judges declared such regulations unconstitutional. These differences began the division that continues today between Republican free-market capitalists and Democrats who favor regulation.

Democrats, the Depression, and the Fourth Realignment In the 1930s during the Great Depression, America went from being mostly Republican to being solidly Democratic thanks to Franklin Delano Roosevelt's **New Deal coalition**, which was made up of Democratic state and local party organizations, labor unions and blue-collar workers, minorities, farmers, white southerners, people living in poverty, immigrants, and intellectuals.

Source: Clifford Berryman, Library of Congress

The 1928 presidential election pitted Democrat Al Smith against Republican Herbert Hoover. When interpreting a political cartoon, first notice the symbols and read the labels. What symbols does the cartoonist provide to indicate the party that nominated each candidate? What are the tools of persuasion in campaigning?

The 1932 presidential election marked the first time that more African Americans voted Democrat than Republican, a loyalty that grew stronger and remains today. This massive coalition sent Roosevelt to the White House four times. His leadership during the economic crisis and through most of World War II allowed the Democrats to dominate Congress for another generation. The New Deal implemented social safety nets and positioned the federal government as a force in solving social problems. It reined in business, promoted union protections and civil liberties, and increased participation by involving women and minorities.

Shifts Since the 1960s Although a mix of politicians from both parties favors equality among the races, the post-World War II fight for equality for African Americans was dominated by the liberal northern wing of the Democratic Party. President Lyndon Johnson accurately predicted the Democratic Party would lose the South for a generation when he signed the Civil Rights Act in the summer of 1964. (See Topic 3.11.)

In November 1964, a regional realignment became apparent after the presidential election between President Johnson and Arizona Republican

Barry Goldwater. Johnson handily won nationally, while Goldwater won the Deep South states, a region that had served as the "Solid South" for Democrats for most presidential elections over the previous century. Most scholars mark 1968 as the breakup of the New Deal coalition and the beginning of an era of **divided government**—a situation in which one party controls Congress and the other controls the White House.

Today, southern white voters have all but left the New Deal coalition and joined the Republican Party. Additionally, decisions that resulted in busing public school children for racial balance and those that legalized abortion convinced conservative voters to move to the GOP. Yet, many of the voting blocs that backed FDR in the 1930s continued to stick together at election time for the Democrats: laborers, Jews, African Americans, urbanites, and academics.

Source: Library of Congress

African American and white children ride a bus from the suburbs to the inner city of Charlotte, North Carolina as part of a school integration plan.

Since 1968, the major parties have continued on similar ideological paths, especially on economic issues. However, a growing number of citizens became independents or turned away from politics altogether, resulting in a **party dealignment.** The unpopular Vietnam War and Richard Nixon's Watergate scandal brought mistrust of government and a mistrust of the parties. Voter turnout dropped over the following three decades. Party loyalty decreased, a fact made obvious by an increased number of independent voters. These voters split their tickets—or voted for candidates from both parties—which resulted in divided government, common at the federal level.

| BY THE NUMBERS |||||
| PRESIDENT, RUNNER-UP, AND MAJORITY PARTY IN CONGRESS |||||
Year	President	Runner-up	House	Senate
1968	Nixon (R)	Humphrey (D)	DEM	DEM
1970			DEM	DEM
1980	Reagan (R)	Carter (D)	DEM	REP
1982			DEM	REP
1992	Clinton, W. J. (D)	Bush (R)	DEM	DEM
1994			REP	REP
2004	Bush, G. W. (R)	Kerry (D)	REP	REP
2006			DEM	DEM
2016	Trump (R)	Clinton, H. (D)	REP	REP
2018			DEM	REP

What do the numbers show? Since 1968, how many times did Democrats hold the majority? How many time did Republicans dominate? In what years do you see a president governing with a Congress dominated by the opposing party? In which years was Congress split? In what elections do you see a change in party power? What caused these changes?

The Democratic Party has gone from supporting states' rights and raw capitalism to believing in big government and national regulations, while the Republican Party has gone from being the progressive anti-slavery party to one that is fiscally conservative and denounces affirmative action. (See Topic 3.13.) These drastic transitions did not happen overnight but through a series of changing voter habits and adjusted party alignments over more than a century.

PARTY SYSTEMS AND REALIGNMENT PERIODS		
1789–1800	**Federalists** won ratification of the Constitution and the presidency for the first three terms.	**Anti-Federalists** opposed strong national government and favored states' rights and civil liberties.
1800–1824	**Federalists** maintained beliefs in a loose interpretation of the Constitution to strengthen the nation.	**Democratic-Republicans** (Jeffersonians) put less emphasis on a strong Union and more on states' rights.
1824–1860	**Democrats** (Jacksonians) encouraged greater participation in politics and gained a Southern and Western following.	**Whigs** were a loose band of eastern capitalists, bankers, and merchants who wanted internal improvements and stronger national government.

(continued)

PARTY SYSTEMS AND REALIGNMENT PERIODS		
1860–1896	**Democrats** became the second-place party, aligned with the South and the wage earner and sent only Grover Cleveland to the White House.	**Republicans** freed the slaves, reconstructed the Union, and aligned with industrial interests.
1896–1932	**Democrats** join with Populists to represent the Southern and Midwestern farmers, workers, and Protestant reformers.	**Republicans** continue to dominate after a realignment based on economic factors.
1932–Present (including dealignment starting in 1968)	The Great Depression created the **New Deal coalition** around FDR's programs. **Democrats** dominated politics until the mid-1990s.	**Republicans** have taken on a *laissez-faire* approach to economic regulation and a brand of conservatism that reflects limited government.

Campaign Finance Laws

Starting in the late 19th century with industrialization, business became increasingly interested in the laws governing their practices. Throughout most of the 1900s, businesses contributed growing amounts of money to political campaigns to get their desired laws passed. Since the early 1970s, national law and landmark Supreme Court cases have governed campaign finance rules. These laws are intended to regulate the sources, recipients, and amounts of contributions to political campaigns. (You will read more about campaign finance laws in Topic 5.11.)

Changes in Communication and Data-Management Technology

Political parties rely heavily on polling and on mining databases to gain insights into voter preferences, so they must quickly adapt to changes in technology. President Obama's campaigns, especially for his reelection in 2012, devoted many resources to using available technology and media to their fullest to understand and target voters.

Parties use this information to craft, control, and clarify their messages. Voter data can reveal where people eat and shop, the people they're connected to, and which media sources they use to access news and information. Increasingly, political organizations are able to target with pinpoint accuracy who gets which message thanks to data-management technology. Data-management technology is a field that uses skills, software, and equipment to organize information and then store it and keep it secure.

These digital resources are so valuable in learning about voters that they have been abused. Before the 2016 election, a British political data firm called Cambridge Analytica managed to obtain 50 million Facebook user profiles from another company's personality quiz app. The data firm was an offshoot of the SCL Group, a company owned largely by the Mercer family, which includes conservative billionaire Republican Party supporters. Cambridge Analytica then created detailed "psychographic" profiles used to target voters during the campaign. Facebook suspended Cambridge Analytica and found itself in the crosshairs over its oversight and corporate policies and the role it played in presidential politics.

Managing Political Messages and Outreach

Demographics explain "who" the voters are—race, gender, age, neighborhood, church or political affiliation, and similar traits. Psychographic segmentation uses data about personality, lifestyle, and social class to categorize groups of voters. Psychographics, in contrast to demographics, explains "why" they vote the way they do. What are their values, hobbies, habits, and likes? This valuable information helps candidates and parties tailor their messages and conduct political outreach.

Part of a message's appeal is based on the candidate's appearance and choice of venues for delivery. A Western state candidate might appear wearing a cowboy hat and boots, riding on horseback along a river. An urban candidate could roll up her sleeves and visit a public works project that rehabilitates neighborhoods. Language is carefully crafted in messages to remind voters of key ideas and values espoused by the party.

Another key element of messaging and outreach is timing. In the early stages of a campaign, more abstract messages resonate. That's when the candidate will remind voters about core values and ideals. For instance, during the 2008 presidential primaries, Democrat Barack Obama spoke enthusiastically of hope and change, while his rivals focused on the concrete details of managing the Iraq War and closing a "doughnut hole" in Medicaid that made drug costs out of reach for some. Closer to election day, voters become receptive to messages that are more concrete. Candidates can specify the programs they plan to implement and how those changes will improve the lives of Americans.

Perhaps the greatest challenge for parties is to spark interest in unaligned or apathetic voters. In recent elections, Barack Obama succeeded in doing this and won elections in 2008 and 2012 with his brand and message of hope and change. In 2016, Donald Trump won the election by promising a very different brand of change—draining the Washington swamp of corrupt insiders.

THINK AS A POLITICAL SCIENTIST: *EXPLAIN HOW THE AUTHOR'S ARGUMENT RELATES TO POLITICAL PROCESSES AND BEHAVIORS*

Political campaigns evolve continuously to give candidates the best possibility to win elections. Recently, technological advances in campaigning have been the focus of both of the major parties. For example, the Obama campaign invested heavily in "data-mining" technologies for reelection in 2012. President Obama's plan became known as Project Narwhal. Mitt Romney, the Republican candidate, countered with Project ORCA to understand voters' interests.

Practice: Read the excerpt about Project Narwhal and answer the questions that follow.

> On Jan. 22, a young woman in a socially conservative corner of southwestern Ohio received a blast email from Stephanie Cutter, a deputy campaign manager for Barack Obama. Years earlier, the young woman had registered for updates on Obama's website, completing a form that asked for her email address and ZIP code. For a while, the emails she received from Obama and his Organizing for America apparatus were appeals to give money and sign petitions, and she responded to one that required that she provide her name. The emails kept on coming, rarely with anything an Obama supporter could disagree with, and certainly not the type of hard-edged political message that could scare one away.
>
> ... This year, however, as part of a project code-named Narwhal, Obama's team is working to link once completely separate repositories of information so that every fact gathered about a voter is available to every arm of the campaign. Such information-sharing would allow the person who crafts a provocative email about contraception to send it only to women with whom canvassers have personally discussed reproductive views or whom data-mining targeters have pinpointed as likely to be friendly to Obama's views on the issue.
>
> —Sasha Issenberg, Slate.com, *Obama's White Whale*, 2012

1. Describe the authors' claim about the new method used by political parties.

2. In the context of changing political tactics, explain why the new methods have been so successful.

3. Explain how voter behavior will continue to be affected by improving campaign strategies.

REFLECT ON THE ESSENTIAL QUESTION

Essential Question: *Why and how do political parties change and adapt? On separate paper, complete the chart below.*

Factors that Influence Change in Political Parties	Changes Within Political Parties

---

KEY TERMS AND NAMES

critical elections	McGovern-Fraser Commission
Democratic-Republicans	New Deal Coalition
Democrats	party dealignment
divided government	party realignment
Grand Old Party (GOP)	superdelegates
Jacksonian Democracy	Whig Party
Jeffersonians	

Third-Party Politics

"Throughout American history, independent parties outside the two-party power establishment have been responsible for introducing urgently-needed changes, whether the parties themselves won electoral success (like the anti-slavery Republican Party in the mid-1800s) or not."

—Green Party, Platform, 2016

Essential Question: How do structural barriers impact third-party and independent candidate's success?

Political parties can afford people with similar beliefs the opportunity to participate in government. These parties are often influenced by special interest groups and social movements, and their goal is always to capture the largest share of the votes possible so that they can wield power. The United States has traditionally had a two-party system that discourages third-party and independent candidates, especially at the national level.

At times in the nation's history, third parties have surfaced and had an impact in politics. Often these parties come and go and enjoy only a limited amount of success in winning elections. Structural barriers within the electoral system and barriers outside of it prevent these organizations from gaining the traction necessary to fully succeed. Yet they can influence policy and play a significant role, especially because voters are so evenly split among their loyalties to the two major parties.

Third-Party and Independent Candidates

Though a two-party system has generally dominated the American political scene, competitive **minor parties**, often called **third parties**, have surfaced and played a distinct role. Technically, the Jacksonian Democrats and Lincoln's Republicans began as minor parties. Since Lincoln's victory in 1860, no minor party has won the White House, but several third-party movements have met with some levels of success. These lesser-known groups have sent members to Congress, helped add amendments to the Constitution, and forced the larger parties to take note of them and their ideas. Despite these victories, structural barriers in our political system have limited the impact and influence—and therefore the success—of third-party and independent candidates.

Why Third Parties Form

Because the two major parties compete to win the majority of voters, and majorities always occupy the center of our political spectrum, the more ideological citizens may believe neither major party hears or implements their desired agenda, so they create their own party. For instance, in the early 1900s as a response to conservative robber barons, uncontrolled industrial growth, and massive wealth inequality, the Socialist Party formed and introduced a leftist agenda whose ideas were eventually incorporated into American politics. During the 1970s, following a long period of Democratic dominance, the Libertarian party formed. Its supporters wanted a more traditional liberalism: *laissez-faire* (unregulated) capitalism, abolition of the welfare state, non-intervention in foreign affairs, and individual rights—such as the right to opt out of paying into Social Security and receiving its benefits. Socialists and Libertarians are **ideological parties** because they subscribe to a consistent ideology across multiple issues.

Sometimes third parties form as **splinter parties** when large factions of members break off from a major party. In 1912, when former President Teddy Roosevelt wanted to return to the White House and sought the Republican nomination, the party instead renominated their incumbent, William Howard Taft. When Roosevelt lost the vote at the Chicago convention, he immediately declared he would run for president anyway. To one inquiring reporter he responded that he felt as strong as a Bull Moose. The new Progressive Party formed around him, nicknamed the Bull Moose Party. Another example came in 1968 when segregationist George Wallace splintered off from the liberal-leaning Democratic Party and formed the American Independent Party. White southerners followed him, splitting the Democratic vote, and that—along with opposition to the Vietnam conflict and Humphrey's non-democratic nomination—led to the election of Republican Richard Nixon.

In both cases, these third parties failed to win the presidency, but their impact spoiled the outcome for the parties they departed. When a strong personality or a politician with a following appears to consider splintering off and taking his supporters along, the party will treat them and their ideas differently, hoping they stay in the tent. And if the splintering happens and the party loses the election, it will consider the group's desires and add them to their agenda or platform to prevent a loss next time.

Some parties form as **economic-protest parties**. In the late 19th century, the Greenback Party opposed monopolies. During that same period, farmers created the Populist Party to fight against railroads, big banks, corporations, and the politicians those interests controlled. Other third parties rise and fall as **single-issue parties**. The Prohibition Party, for example, was founded in 1869 as part of the temperance movement to ban alcohol. The Green Party arose in the 1970s to advocate for environmental awareness, social justice, and nonviolence. Some of these parties still exist in America today. Protest parties are formed within a specific context—a social condition that demands reform.

MINOR PARTY CANDIDATES AND INDEPENDENT POLITICAL LEADERS	
Recent Minor Party Presidential Candidates	**Becoming Independent**
• **H. Ross Perot**—Texas millionaire ran with United We Stand America, 1992 and 1996 • **Ralph Nader**—Consumer advocate ran with the Green Party, 1996 and 2000 • **Gary Johnson**—Former governor of New Mexico ran as Libertarian, 2012 and 2016 • **Jill Stein**—Physician and activist ran as Green Party candidate, 2012 and 2016	• **Jim Jeffords**—Vermont Republican Senator, 2001 • **Joe Lieberman**—Connecticut Democratic Senator, 2006

Modern Third Parties

Since 1968, there have been additional minor party candidates seeking the presidency, but no such candidate has won a plurality in any one state, and therefore none has ever earned even one electoral vote. Texas oil tycoon H. Ross Perot burst onto the political scene in 1992 to run for president as an independent. Funded largely from his own wealth, Perot created United We Stand America (later renamed the Reform Party) and campaigned in every state. He won nearly 20 percent of the national popular vote. But with no strong following concentrated in any one state, he failed to earn any electoral votes.

Perennial candidate Ralph Nader was the Green Party candidate in the 2000 election. The votes he drew from Democrat Al Gore likely helped propel Republican George W. Bush into the presidency in a very close election. After Nader allegedly spoiled it for the Democrats, the party did what it could to keep him off the swing states' ballots in 2004.

THINK AS A POLITICAL SCIENTIST: *DESCRIBE WHAT THE DATA IMPLY ABOUT POLITICAL BEHAVIORS*

At different points in the nation's history, third parties have played a significant role in the outcome of presidential elections. On several occasions, a candidate from a third—and even fourth—political party has received a significant number of electoral votes, influencing who wins the presidency. Political scientists study the effects that third parties have on voting behavior and how they can affect elections.

Practice: Read the popular vote election summaries and answer the questions that follow.

1860 Election—A time of social and political division in America was reflected in the presidential election. Republican Abraham Lincoln won the election with only 39.7 percent of the popular vote. The Democrats were divided between Northern Democrat Stephen A. Douglas and Southern Democrat John C. Breckinridge. Together they accrued 47.6 percent of the vote, significantly more than Lincoln. John Bell of the Constitution Union Party got 12.6 percent.

1912 Election—After leaving politics, former President Theodore Roosevelt was displeased with the direction of the Republican Party and current president, William Taft. Failing to win the Republican nomination in 1912, Roosevelt started the progressive "Bull Moose Party." Roosevelt won 27.4 percent of the vote and Taft received 23.7 percent. The Socialist Party had a successful race that year, as Socialist nominee Eugene V. Debs secured 6 percent. This division opened the door for Democrat Woodrow Wilson to win the election with almost 43 percent of the vote.

1992 Election—Democrat Bill Clinton won this election with 43.3 percent of the popular vote. The incumbent, George H.W. Bush, received 37.1 percent of the vote. The Reform Party appealed to voters from both major parties, but ideologically it aligned closer to Republicans. Its candidate, Ross Perot, took nearly 20 percent of the popular vote.

1. What is one inference you can draw about the impact of third-party candidates from the results of these presidential elections?

2. Why are third-party candidates not as successful, as those in the examples above, in most presidential elections?

3. Despite institutional barriers to winning a presidential election, how do third parties influence elections?

Barriers to Third-Party Success

No minor party has won the presidency since 1860, and no third party has risen to second place in the meantime. Minor parties have a difficult time competing with the highly organized and well-funded Republicans and Democrats. The minor parties that come and go cannot effectively participate in the political process in the United States, at national, state, and local levels, because the institutional reasons for the dominance of the two major parties are many and complex. They include single-member districts, money and resources, the ability of the major parties to incorporate third-party agendas and winner-take-all voting.

Single-Member Districts

The United States generally has what are called single-member districts for elective office. In **single-member districts**, the candidate who wins the most votes, or a plurality in a field of candidates, wins that office. Many European nations use proportional representation. In that approach, multiple parties compete for office, and voters cast ballots for the party they favor. After the election those offices are filled proportionally. For example, a party that wins 20 percent of the votes cast in the election is then awarded 20 percent of the seats in that parliament or governing body. This method encourages and rewards third parties, even if minimally. In nearly all elections in the United States, contests are within a local, defined geographic district. If three or more candidates seek an office, the candidate winning the most votes—even if it is with a minority of the total votes—wins the office outright. There is no rewarding second, much less third, place.

Money

Minor party candidates also have a steeper hill to climb in terms of financing, ballot access, and exposure. The Republican and Democratic parties have organized operations to raise money to convince donors of their candidates' ability to win—and by so doing attract even more donors. Full-time employees at the DNC and RNC constantly seek funding between elections. Even more important, according to campaign finance law, the nominee's party needs to have won a certain percentage of the vote in the previous election in order to qualify for government funding in the current election. Political candidates from minor parties have a difficult time competing financially unless they're self-financed, as was Ross Perot.

Independents also have a difficult time with **ballot access**. Every state has a prescribed method for candidates to earn a spot on the ballot. It usually involves a fee and obtaining a minimum number of signatures. The Democratic and Republican candidates have the advantage of a strong, existing party network. They can simply dispatch party regulars and volunteers throughout a state's counties to collect signatures for the ballot petition. The statewide director can set goals for signatures that each county chairman is meant to obtain. Green Party, Libertarian, or independent candidates must first secure assistance or collect those signatures themselves or with only a meager party organization. Since a ballot petition often requires thousands of registered voters, this task alone is daunting and discouraging to potential third-party candidates.

The media tend not to cover minor party candidates. Independents are rarely invited to public debates or televised forums at the local and national levels. Buying exposure and support through advertising costs millions of dollars. So, for third parties it is hard to get noticed.

Incorporation of Third-Party Agendas

Throughout U.S. history, there have been 52 independent political parties, yet none of them has gained traction. No one other than a Democrat or a Republican has been elected since 1860. Does that mean third parties play no role other than annoyance and spoiler for the major parties? Definitely not.

In order to attract the third-party candidate's voters, the most closely aligned major party will often incorporate items from that party's agenda into its platform. Although this practice serves to discourage third-party candidates from running, it can also result in positive social change. For instance, Socialists promoted women's suffrage and child labor laws in the early 1900s, now taken for granted by both parties. Populists eventually got Americans a 40-hour work week. Ross Perot planted the idea of a balanced federal budget in the national consciousness. Ralph Nader fought for consumer protections and a clean environment. Minor parties play an important role as the conscience of the nation.

Since the first political contests before the Republic was created, most citizens have fallen into two camps with very different points of view about how government should be run. Parties provide an identity that simplifies the task of parsing important issues for members. Yet, this simplification can also be divisive. More and more Americans are looking for ways to stop being "red" or "blue" (the colors typically used on election maps, with states that voted Republican colored red and states that voted Democratic colored blue). Most Americans want practical compromises to solve big problems. This is the challenge for the two-party system: for each to hold on to its base voters while appealing to the middle.

Winner-Take-All Voting

Perhaps the largest barrier is the winner-take-all system of the Electoral College. The Electoral College determines the presidential candidate, but the popular vote within each state determines how the electors cast their ballots.

All states, with the exception of Maine and Nebraska, award all their electoral votes to the candidate who wins the plurality of the popular vote, a process called the **winner-take-all voting** system. The biggest problem for third-party and independent candidates is that they very rarely win a state's popular vote and thus can't accumulate the required 270 electoral votes to win, nor do they even appear to have potential as no third-party candidate has won electoral votes since 1968. This challenge discourages independent voters from considering third-party candidates because they feel they are throwing their votes away.

With winner-takes-all voting, **swing states**—those that could go either way in an election—tend to get most of the attention. Swing states, sometimes called battleground states, shift party resources to certain regions, and third-party and independent candidates always have trouble matching that level of investment.

REFLECT ON THE ESSENTIAL QUESTION

Essential Question: *How do structural barriers impact third-party and independent candidate's success? On separate paper, complete the chart below.*

Barriers to Candidate's or Party's Success	Explanation of Limits

---

KEY TERMS AND NAMES

ballot access
economic-protest parties
ideological parties
single-issue parties
single-member districts

splinter parties
swing states
third parties (minor parties)
two-party system
winner-take-all voting

CHAPTER 16 Review:
Learning Objectives and Key Terms

TOPIC 5.3: Describe linkage institutions. (PMI-5.A)

Explain the function and impact of political parties on the electorate and the government. (PMI-5.B)

Linkage Institutions (PMI-5.A.1) Democratic Party linkage institutions Republican Party	**Function and Impact of Political Parties** (PMI-5.B.1) Democratic National Committee (DNC) national chairperson national convention platform Republican National Committee (RNC) robocalls social media war chest

TOPIC 5.4: Explain how and why political parties change and adapt. (PMI-5.C)

How Parties Adapt to Appeal to Groups (PMI-5.C.1, 2, & 4) McGovern-Fraser Commission superdelegates	**Influences on Party Structure** (PMI-5.C.3) critical elections Democrats Democratic-Republicans Jacksonian Democracy Jeffersonians divided government Grand Old Party (GOP) New Deal Coalition party dealignment party realignment Whig Party

TOPIC 5.5: Explain how structural barriers impact third-party and independent candidate success. (PMI-5.D)

Voting Barriers to Third-party Candidates (PMI-5.D.1) economic-protest parties single-issue parties splinter parties third parties (minor parties) two-party system winner-take-all voting	**Incorporation of Third-Party Platforms as Barriers** (PMI-5.D.2) ballot access ideological parties swing states single-member districts

CHAPTER 16 Checkpoint:
Political Parties

Topics 5.3–5.5

MULTIPLE-CHOICE QUESTIONS

Questions 1 and 2 refer to the passage below.

"In this campaign, I've met so many people who motivate me to keep fighting for change. And, with your help, I will carry all of your voices and stories with me to the White House. I will be a president for Democrats, Republicans, and Independents. For the struggling and the successful. For those who vote for me and those who don't. For all Americans."

—Hillary Clinton, Acceptance Speech, Democratic
National Convention, 2016

1. Why was this passage most likely included in the candidate's message?
   (A) To cast a positive light on her opponent
   (B) To gain voters outside the Democratic Party
   (C) To show how much effort it takes to win the White House
   (D) To promise her voters that she would implement Democratic policies

2. What guidelines of messaging best align with this passage?
   (A) Since the nominating process is over, she can start to be specific about which groups to mention.
   (B) Since the general election is next, she needs to keep her message general and not ideological.
   (C) Since the nominating process is over, she has concerns about keeping the support of fellow party members.
   (D) Since the general election is months away, she needs to start addressing specific solutions to specific problems.

Questions 3 and 4 refer to the following table.

EXIT POLL, 2016 PRESIDENTIAL ELECTION			
Voters	**Clinton-Democrat**	**Trump-Republican**	**Other**
Men	41%	52%	7%
Women	54%	41%	5%
Ages 18 to 29	55%	36%	9%
Ages 30 to 44	51%	41%	8%
Ages 45 to 64	44%	52%	4%
Ages 65 and older	45%	52%	3%

Source: CNN.com

3. Which of the following statements is reflected in the data in the table?

(A) The youngest voting bloc favored Trump over Clinton.

(B) Trump likely won because of the southern and rural vote.

(C) The relative support for the two majority party candidates reveals a gender gap.

(D) The largest bloc voting for third-party candidates was 45- to 64-year-olds.

4. Based on the information in the table, what conclusion can you draw?

(A) There are very few Democrats over 65 years old.

(B) A minor party candidate will likely win the presidency in the near future.

(C) Young voters tend to vote more for the Democrat than for the Republican.

(D) Younger men voted for Trump more than older women did.

5. Which of the following best illustrates a critical election?

(A) An intense election with many controversial issues

(B) An election that is so close it requires a recount

(C) An election that reveals a lasting shift in voting bloc loyalties

(D) An election in which a challenging party replaces the incumbent party

6. Which of the following is an accurate comparison of Democrats and Republicans?

	DEMOCRATS	REPUBLICANS
(A)	Lost the Solid South in a regional realignment	Lost much of the support of African American voters
(B)	Constitute the majority party in the Mountain West	Became a strong party after the election of Franklin Roosevelt
(C)	Have stronger support among Asian Americans	Have stronger support among younger voters
(D)	Believe the law should forbid abortions	Support abortion rights

FREE-RESPONSE QUESTIONS

Concept Application

1. Michigan Representative Justin Amash announced Thursday that he was leaving the GOP [Republican Party] after growing "disenchanted" and "frightened" by party politics . . . [and said] that he would remain in Congress as an independent.

"Modern politics is trapped in a partisan death spiral, but there is an escape," said Amash . . . "Most Americans are not rigidly partisan and do not feel well represented by either of the two major parties. In fact, the parties have become more partisan in part because they are catering to fewer people, as Americans are rejecting party affiliation in record numbers."

—Reporter Max Berman, NBCNews.com, 2019

Based on the scenario above, respond to A, B, and C below:

(A) Describe an action Congress could take to address the concern in the above scenario.

(B) In the context of this scenario, explain how the action described in part A might affect the electorate.

(C) In the context of this scenario, explain how a structural barrier may challenge Amash's political success as an independent.

Quantitative Analysis

1968 Democratic Primary Election and National Convention Votes

Presidential Candidate	Percent of Primary Vote	State Primaries Won (14 Total)	Convention Delegate Votes (First Ballot)
Hubert Humphrey	2.2%	0	1756¾
Eugene McCarthy	38.7%	6	601
Robert Kennedy	30.6%	4	0
George McGovern	0%	0	146½
Others	28.5%	4	100

More than 7 million people voted in 14 state primaries, about 23 percent of the Democratic votes in the November general election.

2. Use the information graphic above to answer the questions.

   (A) Identify the candidate who received the highest percentage of primary election votes.

   (B) Describe the difference in one candidate's vote total in the primary elections and the same candidate's votes at the convention.

   (C) Draw a conclusion about the difference identified in part B.

   (D) Explain how the information in the table led to alterations in party nomination process.

CHAPTER 17

Interest Groups

Topics 5.6–5.7

Topic 5.6 Interest Groups Influencing Policy Making

PMI-5.E: Explain the benefits and potential problems of interest-group influence on elections and policy making.

PMI-5.F: Explain how the variation in types and resources of interest groups affects their ability to influence elections and policy making.

Topic 5.7 Groups Influencing Policy Outcomes

PMI-5.G: Explain how various political actors influence public policy outcomes.

Source: Getty Images

Members of a Brooklyn electrical workers union (IBEW Local 3) rally during a contract dispute.

Interest Groups Influencing Policy Making

"By a faction, I understand a number of citizens ... united and actuated by some common impulse of passion, or of interest, adversed to the rights of other citizens, or to the ... aggregate interests of the community."

—James Madison, *Federalist No. 10, 1787*

Essential Question: What are the benefits and potential problems of interest-group influence on elections and policy making?

At any level of government, people differ on the question of how to shape the law and the delivery of government services. Some citizens naturally become part of formal groups based on their common beliefs. James Madison and other founders expressed concern about factions, groups of "interested" people motivated by the pursuit of wealth, religious beliefs, or alliances with other countries. Today, these special interests are known as interest groups, or lobbies, and are concerned with corporate profits, workers' rights, the environment, product safety, or other issues. They are linkage institutions because they connect citizens to government and provide organizations through which citizen voices can be heard. Historic and recent accounts of bribery, scandal, and other unethical behavior have shaped the public's impression of these groups. Yet, the First Amendment guarantees the right of special interests to operate and express opinions.

Benefits of Interest Groups

Since Madison wrote *Federalist No. 10* (see Topics 1.2 and 1.3), United States political beliefs have developed into a complex web of viewpoints, each seeking to influence government at the national, state, and local levels. The nation's constitutional arrangement of government encourages voices in all three branches of government and at all three levels. This **pluralism**, a multitude of views that ultimately results in a consensus on some issues, has intensified the ongoing competition among interests to influence policy. Yet, the competition ensures distribution of political power to all and not just the elite and powerful.

The three separate and equal branches of government, Madison argued in *Federalist No.10*, would prevent the domination and influence of factions or interests. The American system of federalism, however, with policymaking bodies in multiple branches within state and federal governments, has created many access points and thus encouraged the rise of interest groups. Modern interest groups have become adept at influencing policies in all three branches. Within each branch there are people and entities—individual members of Congress, a president's appointed staff, agency directors, and scores of federal courts—that have helped to increase the influence of special interest groups.

The division of powers among national and state governments has also encouraged **lobbying,** applying pressure to influence government, not only in Washington but also in every state capital. The term evolved from the last place citizens could access and hopefully convince lawmakers before they voted—the lobby outside the House of Commons, Congress, or the local city council room.

State governments are based on the federal model: within each state branch are a multi-member legislature, state agencies, and various courts, all of which provide targets for interest groups. County and city governments also make important local-level decisions on school funding, road construction, fire departments, water works, and garbage collection. Many of the national interest groups, such as the Fraternal Order of Police or national teachers' unions, have local chapters to influence local decisions. Thus, interests have an incentive to meet not only with national and state legislators but also with mayors, county administrators, and city council members. **BIG IDEA** Multiple actors and institutions interact to produce and implement possible policies. Interest groups must compete in the marketplace of ideas just as products must compete in a free enterprise system. This competition tends to increase democratic participation, since people cannot take for granted that their interests will be considered. Interest groups also devote time and resources to creating practical solutions to real problems and have the power to get their solutions accepted. In exercising those benefits, interest groups also educate the public and use their resources to mobilize support for their point of view. They draft legislation and work with lawmakers and government agencies to see it put into law.

Some interest groups represent broad issues, such as civil rights or economic reform. Others, such as those focusing on eliminating drunk driving or preserving gun rights, represent very specific or narrow interests. Both types form in response to changing times and circumstances and both demonstrate the benefits of interest groups—their ability to have their voices heard, gain support for their position, and influence government policies and elections. Interest groups, along with the protest movements that sometimes brought them into being, form with the goal of making an impact on society and influencing policy.

Source: Wikimedia Commons

Chicago public school teachers went on strike in October 2019. Schools closed for 11 days during the 15-day strike by the 25,000 members of the Chicago Teachers Union (CTU). Issues that prompted teachers to act were length of contract, salary increases, class size, and preparation time.

Drawbacks of Interest Groups

Interest groups have many benefits but have also been the subject of much criticism. President Woodrow Wilson (1913–1921) often expressed his frustration over the tactics used by lobbyists. "Washington has seldom seen so numerous, so industrious, or so insidious a lobby," he once lamented when corporations opposed his tariff bill. "The newspapers are being filled with paid advertisements calculated to mislead the judgments of public men …"

In the 1930s, Senator Hugo Black (D-AL) investigated one utility company's 1930s lobbying effort, as recounted by Kenneth Crawford in *The Pressure Boys*. Senator Black became suspicious when very similarly worded letters opposing a bill to regulate electric utilities began to flood Capitol Hill. Black exposed the scheme that a gas and electric company had paid a group of telegraph messengers to persuade Pennsylvania citizens to send telegrams opposing the bill to their member of congress. The company provided the talking points for the messages. One congressional member received 816 of these telegrams in two days, mostly from citizens with last names that began with *A*, *B*, or *C*. As it turned out, names had been pulled from a phone book starting from the beginning.

"The lobby has reached such a position of power that it threatens government itself," an outraged Senator Black said in a radio address. To Black's dismay, it turned out that the utility company had done nothing illegal, and this tactic continues today with email and social media. Interest groups send members and supporters legislative alerts when an issue of concern arises. Along with the alerts they send sample messages for supporters to use as a base for writing their own messages, although many just send the sample message. Some cell phone apps will even fax the message to a person's representatives.

Another potential problem is that interest groups by definition promote the interests of their members over more general interests. When groups pull in many different or completely opposite directions, compromise becomes challenging and gridlock can result. This phenomenon of multiple competing interest groups is called *hyperpluralism*. In such a situation, a form of elitism can also develop. Groups with more power and resources are more likely to achieve their goals than groups with smaller memberships or limited funding, putting interest groups on an uneven playing field in the marketplace of ideas.

This lack of resources for smaller groups is intensified by another issue in what is known as the **free-rider** problem. Groups that push for a collective benefit for a large group inevitably have free riders. The free-rider problem limits the group's potential because not all those benefitting help pay the bill.

Relationships between interest groups and government representatives develop, deepen, and expand over time, so the inequality of resources and access widens even more.

Iron Triangles and Issue Networks

As you read in Topic 2.12, **iron triangles** are the bonds among an agency, a congressional committee, and an interest group. The three entities establish relationships that benefit them all. Bureaucrats benefit by cooperating with congressional members who fund and oversee them. Committee members benefit by listening to interest groups that reward them with campaign donations.

For example, an iron triangle exists to influence policy in favor of those of retirement age. In this relationship, the American Association of Retired Persons (interest group) works with the Subcommittee on Aging (congressional committee) and the Social Security Administration (government agency) to fund, create, and oversee policy that affect seniors.

Source: United States Senate

The Special Committee on Aging holds hearings to learn about issues brought to them from AARP and other special interests. In this photograph, Senator Elizabeth Warren (D-MA) and Chairman Bill Nelson (D-FL) hear testimony during he 113th Congress on ID theft and fraud affecting senior citizens.

Issue networks are also collectives with similar goals, but they have come together to support a specific issue and usually do not have the long-term relationships that characterize iron triangles. If and when their issue of common concern is resolved, the networks break up. Issue networks often include a number of different interest groups who share an opinion on the issue at hand but may have strongly differing opinions on other matters. For example, religious interest groups and some civic organizations might have differing views on abortion or same-sex marriage, but they may agree on the importance of health care for children living in poverty and work together to advance that cause.

Exerting Influence

Once an issue has been brought to the surface, the education of both voters and legislators can begin. Interest groups use many different channels to educate the public and legislators about their concerns. With enough public support, interest groups can help draft legislation to support their cause. This process requires ongoing relationships with lawmakers and others in government. To keep up the pressure on legislators to produce the desired result, interest groups mobilize their members and the public to take to the streets in demonstrations or make phone calls or in-person visits to representatives.

Interest groups use a variety of techniques to exert influence. The most common form of activity for those who have access is **direct lobbying** of legislators. Groups also try to sway public opinion by issuing press releases, writing op-ed articles for newspapers, appearing as experts on television, and purchasing print and TV advertising. They also mobilize their membership to call or write members of Congress or state legislators on pending laws or to swing an election.

Lobbying Legislators

The term *lobbying* came into vogue in the mid-1600s when the anteroom of the British House of Commons became known as "the lobby." **Lobbyists** were present at the first session of the U.S. Congress in 1789.

Access to Washington, DC Lobbyists work to develop relationships through their contacts who have access to government officials. Through these contacts, they monitor legislators' proposed bills and votes. Lobbyists assess which lawmakers support their cause and which do not. They also help draft bills that their congressional allies introduce and find which lawmakers are undecided and try to bring them over to their side. "Influence peddler" is a derogatory term for a lobbyist, but influencing lawmakers is exactly what lobbyists try to do.

Political scientists use data to evaluate the growing influence of interest groups on U.S. politics. For example, the tobacco industry went to great lengths to hide information about the dangers of smoking. Campaign donors from the tobacco industry used their influence and money to try to prevent lawmakers from taking action to protect the public, but they failed. In 2009 the Family Smoking Prevention and Tobacco Control Act was signed into law, which gave the FDA greater authority to regulate the tobacco industry. Statistics like those below were partly responsible for motivating lawmakers to create the law.

Practice: Use the table below to answer the questions that follow.

ANNUAL CIGARETTE SMOKING-RELATED MORTALITY IN THE UNITED STATES, 2005–2009			
Disease	**Male**	**Female**	**Total**
Cancer			
Lung cancer	74,300	53,400	127,700
Other cancers	26,000	10,000	36,000
Subtotal: Cancer	**100,300**	**63,400**	**163,700**
Respiratory Diseases			
Pneumonia, influenza, tuberculosis	7,800	4,700	12,500
COPD (lung disease that restricts airflow)	50,400	50,200	100,600
Subtotal: Respiratory Diseases	**58,200**	**54,900**	**113,100**
Secondhand Smoke			
Lung cancer	4,374	2,959	7,333
Coronary heart disease	19,152	14,799	33,951
Subtotal: Secondhand Smoke	**23,526**	**17,758**	**41,284**

Source: cdc.gov

1. What conclusions can be made from the information presented in the table?

2. What information would make the table more useful to lawmakers as they crafted the 2009 law?

3. What information might the tobacco industry want shown to defend their product?

4. How could this data have been presented in a different visual format to convey the information more clearly?

Give and Take Lobbyists want access to legislators, and Congress members appreciate the information lobbyists can provide. Senators and House members represent the individual constituents living in their districts. Sometimes so-called special interests actually represent large swaths of a given constituency. A lobbyist for a defense contractor that sells fighter jets to the Pentagon represents her company but might also speak for hundreds of plant workers. Democracy purists argue that a lawmaker should disregard a heavily financed influence peddler, but most members of Congress recognize the useful byproduct—the resources lobbyists offer.

For example, imagine a North Carolina representative has a meeting with a tobacco lobbyist, who is concerned about a pending bill that further taxes and regulates the sale of cigarettes. The tobacco company sees the bill as dangerous to its bottom-line profits.

The lobbyist presents the legislator with the results of an opinion poll—an expensive endeavor—that shows 57 percent of registered voters in his district oppose the bill. The lobbyist also points out that the tax increase will lead to a rise in black market sales. The lobbyist then hands the lawmaker a complete report at the end of the meeting. Could the poll or report be bogus? Probably not.

Lobbyists have an agenda, but they are generally looking to foster a long-term relationship with lawmakers in which credibility is key. "[T]hey know that if they lie, they lose," Congressman Barney Frank (D-MA) once declared. "They will never be allowed to come back to this office." Imagine further that the following day the lawmaker meets with a representative from the American Heart Association. He provides a medical research study about cigarette prices as a deterrent to new smokers. He also provides poll results from a nationwide survey on smoking in public places.

The elected official has now spent only a couple hours to obtain valuable information with no money spent by his office. With that information, he can represent more of his constituents while considering attitudes and factors across the country. "I help my boss the most," declared one congressional staffer, "when I can play the good lobbyists off each other."

ACTIVITIES OF LOBBYISTS TO EXERT INFLUENCE
Insider strategies: quietly persuading government decision makers through exclusive access
Outsider strategies: public efforts to influence policy with such things as lawsuits or get-out-the vote drives
Client interaction: informing clients, discussing strategy
Legislative activity: providing information/researching bills/drafting bills
Social media: monitoring congressional activity, targeting outreach
Implementation: testifying on bills/filing amicus curiae briefs
Electoral activity: advertising, making PAC donations
Other activity: meetings, business development/media commentary, etc.

What different skills must congressional lobbyists have?

Key Targets and Strategizing No one is more effective in lobbying a legislator than another lawmaker. In the early stages of a legislative fight, influential members of Congress, especially those serving on key committees, become interest group targets. Some legislators are especially influential, so lobbyists target them first.

To what degree do lobbyists move legislators on an issue? Little evidence exists to show that lobbyists actually change legislators' votes. Most findings do not prove lobbyists are successful in "bribing" legislators. Also, lobbyists tend to interact mostly with those members already in favor of the group's goals. So the campaign contribution didn't bring the legislators over to the interest group; the legislator's position on the issue brought the interest group to him or her.

Researcher Rogan Kersh conducted a two-year study of corporate lobbyists. "I'm not up here to twist arms and change somebody's vote," one lobbyist told him in a Senate anteroom crowded with lobbyists from other firms, "and neither are most of them." These lobbyists seem more concerned with waiting, gossiping, and rumor trading. A separate study conveyed that lobbyists want information or legislative intelligence as much as the lawmakers do. "If I'm out playing golf with some congressman or I buy a senator lunch, I know I'm not buying a vote," one lobbyist declared before recent reforms. The lobbyist is simply looking for the most recent views of lawmakers in order to act upon them. Kersh tabulated congressional lobbyists' legislative activities. A lobbyist attempting to alter a legislator's position occurred only about 1 percent of the time.

Resources

The types and resources of interest groups affect their ability to influence elections and policy. For example, nonprofit interest organizations fall into two categories based on their tax classification. The **501(c)(3)** organizations, such as churches and certain hospitals, receive tax deductions for charitable donations and can influence government, but they cannot lobby government officials or donate to campaigns. By comparison, **501(c)(4)** groups, such as certain social welfare organizations, can lobby and campaign, but they can't spend more than half their expenditures on political issues. Available resources also affect the ability of groups to influence policy. Well-funded groups are usually able to wield more power and to have greater access to government decision makers than groups with fewer resources.

Research and Expertise Large interest groups have created entire research departments to study their concerns. Mothers Against Drunk Driving wanted to know, "How many lives would be saved if government raised the drinking age from 18 to 21?" The American Bar Association pondered, "What kind of a Supreme Court justice would nominee Clarence Thomas make?" These are the kinds of questions that members of Congress also ask as they contemplate legislative proposals. During the fact-gathering phase of lawmaking, experts from these groups testify before congressional committees to offer their research findings. Since they represent their own interest, researchers and experts from interest groups and think tanks will often focus on the positive aspects of supporting their desired outcomes.

Campaigns and Electioneering As multiple-term congressional careers have become common, interest groups have developed large arsenals to help or hinder a legislator's chances at election time. Once new methods—TV ads, polling, direct mail, and marketing—determined reelection success, politicians found it increasingly difficult to resist interest groups that had perfected these techniques and that offered greater resources to loyal officials.

A powerful interest group can influence the voting public with an **endorsement**—a public expression of support. The Fraternal Order of Police can usually speak to a lawmaker's record on law enforcement legislation and financial support for police departments. The NRA endorses its loyal congressional allies on the cover of the November issue of its magazine, printed uniquely for each district. Groups also rate members of Congress based on their roll call votes, some with a letter grade (A through F), others with a percentage. Americans for Democratic Action and the American Conservative Union, two ideological organizations, rate members after each congressional term. Creating "scorecards" or ratings are also a way interest groups can keep their members engaged or linked to the government process.

Grassroots Lobbying When an interest group tries to inform, persuade, and mobilize large numbers of people they are **grassroots lobbying**, which is generally an outsider technique. Originally practiced by the more modest citizens and issue advocacy groups, such as students marching against the war in Vietnam, grassroots techniques are now increasingly used by Washington-based interests to influence officials. Mobilizing opposition or support to legislation can be the primary goal of a grassroots campaign.

In 1982, soon after Republican Senator Bob Dole and Democratic Representative Dan Rostenkowski introduced a measure to withhold income taxes from interest earned on bank accounts and dividends, the American Banking Association went to work encouraging banks to persuade their customers to oppose the measure. *The Washington Post* called it the "hydrogen bomb of modern day lobbying." Banks used advertisements and posters in branch offices; they also inserted flyers in monthly bank statements mailed out to every customer, telling them to contact their legislators in opposition to the proposed law. Banks generated nearly 22 million constituent communications. Weeks later the House voted 382–41, and the Senate 94–5, to oppose the previously popular bipartisan proposal.

Framing the Issue When the debate over the Clean Air Bill of 1990 began, *Newsweek* asked how automakers could squash legislation that improved fuel efficiency and reduced both air pollution and America's reliance on foreign oil. A prominent grassroots consultant reasoned that smaller cars—which would be vital if the act were to be successful—would negatively impact child safety, senior citizens' comfort, and disabled Americans' mobility. Opponents of the bill contacted and mobilized senior organizations and disability rights groups to create opposition to these higher standards. What was once viewed as an anti-environment vote soon became a vote that was pro-disabled people and pro-child.

Use of Media Television and telephones, combined with email and social media use, have encouraged grassroots lobbyists and issue advocacy groups. Depending on their tax classification, some groups cannot suggest a TV viewer vote for or against a particular congressperson. So instead they provide some detail on a proposed policy and then tell the voters to contact members of Congress to express their feelings on the issue. Such ads have become backdoor campaigning. They all but say, "Here's the congressperson's position. You know what to do on Election Day."

The restaurant industry responded rapidly to a 1993 legislative idea to remove the tax deduction for business meals. Everyday professionals conducting lunchtime business in restaurants are able to write off the expense at tax time. As Congress debated changing that deduction, special interests acted. The National Restaurant Association (sometimes called "the other NRA") sponsored a television ad that showed an overworked server-mother: "I'm a waitress and a good one. But I might not have a job much longer. President Clinton's economic plan cuts business-meal deductibility. That would throw 165,000 people out of work. I need this job." Opposition to eliminating the tax benefit no longer came from highbrow, lunchtime dealmakers but instead from those wanting to protect hardworking servers, cooks, and dishwashers. At the end of the ad, the server directed concerned viewers to call a toll-free number. Callers were put through to the corresponding lawmaker's office with the push of a button. The use of television helped the "other NRA" successfully defeat the bill.

Interest groups increase their chances of success when they reach the masses, but they also target opinion leaders, those who can influence others. Rather than mobilizing large numbers of people, interest groups and their lobbyists will narrowly target opinion leaders and individuals who know and have connections with lawmakers. This more limited approach to shaping opinion is known as **grasstops** campaigning. Some lobbyists charge $350 to $500 for getting a community leader to communicate his or her feelings to a legislator in writing or on the phone. They also set up personal meetings between high-profile constituents and members of Congress.

Grasstops lobbying sometimes shifts public opinion in the desired direction; for example, it might cherry-pick selected opinions that create an artificial view, sometimes called "Astroturf." This deceitful tactic can give the appearance that people are concerned about an issue when, in reality, a powerful interest group is behind the false impression.

Congressional lobbyists sometimes also use grassroots techniques in tandem with their Washington, DC, operations. Once they determine a legislator's anticipated position, especially if it is undecided, lobbyists can pressure that congressperson by mobilizing constituents in his or her district. Interest groups can use their website and emails to alert members their help is needed. The interest group will provide messages and talking points so their members can easily create a factual letter to send to their representative. With email, this technique has become easier, cheaper, and more commonly used than ever before. With the click of a mouse, interest group members can forward a message to a lawmaker to signal where they stand and how they will vote. Such organizing has also become commonplace on social media. Lobbyists are also developing ways to mine social media for data so they can create highly targeted outreach.

REFLECT ON THE ESSENTIAL QUESTION

Essential Question: *What are the benefits and potential problems of interest-group influence on elections and policy making? On separate paper, complete the chart below.*

Benefits of Interest Groups	Drawbacks of Interest Groups

KEY TERMS AND NAMES

501 (c) (3)	grasstops
501 (c) (4)	iron triangles
direct lobbying	issue networks
endorsement	lobbying
free-rider	lobbyist
grassroots lobbyingt	pluralism

Groups Influencing Policy Outcomes

"We run hard-hitting independent issue ads on television and radio that expose [politicians who] . . . raise taxes, increase regulations, and expand the role of the government. NO politician wants to be the feature of one of our ads."

—Club For Growth, Official Website, 2020

Essential Question: How do various political actors influence public policy outcomes?

"Agitate, educate, legislate!" were the watchwords of the Women's Christian Temperance Union, an influential anti-alcohol interest group around the turn of the 20th century, neatly summarizing the ways in which many interest groups spread their influence and use it to bring about change. Interest groups have come a long way since their proliferation in the Progressive Era and after a post-World War II boom. They agitated through public demonstrations, like the 1965 Selma, Alabama, march in search of the franchise. They educated the citizenry on the need to preserve the environment. And they have mobilized on health care, firearms, and workplace safety laws.

Many interest groups are now professionalized, well-funded, and well-oiled machines. They provide opportunities for citizen participation in the political arena. Social movements have spawned multiple interest groups seeking to address similar causes. Others oppose each other and duel on the issues as they influence the shaping of policy.

Growth of Interest Groups

Interest groups arose in response to the changes in the United States as the nation developed from a mainly agrarian economy to a manufacturing nation. Immigrants arrived on both coasts, bringing a wide variety of viewpoints into the country. Factory workers banded together for protection against their bosses. War veterans returning from armed conflicts looked to the government for benefits. Women and minorities sought equality, justice, and the right to vote. Congress began taking on new issues, such as regulating railroads, addressing child labor, supporting farmers, and generally passing legislation that would advance the nation. As democracy increased, the masses pushed to have their voices heard.

Broad Interests of Labor Unions

One interest group that represented a broad issue is the American Federation of Labor (AFL), organized in 1886 under the leadership of Samuel Gompers. The AFL's most useful tool was the labor strike—skilled workers banded together and refused to work until the company met their demands. Labor unions also entered the political arena and pushed for legislation that protected workers against unhealthy and hazardous conditions. Labor unions have been instrumental in achieving new state (and sometimes national) laws addressing the 40-hour workweek, employer-sponsored health care, family and medical leave, an end to child labor, and minimum wages.

Growth of Labor Unions The power of labor organizations reached new levels in the 1950s. In 1955, the AFL merged with the Congress of Industrial Organizations (CIO), a large union composed of steelworkers, miners, and unskilled workers. The AFL-CIO became the leading voice for the working class and is now comprised of 57 smaller unions. Union membership peaked in 1954 with roughly 28 percent of all households belonging to unions. In 1964, the nation's largest truckers' union, the Teamsters, signed a freight agreement that protected truckers across the country and increased the union's power.

After a decline in manufacturing started a decline in union membership in the 1960s, union organizers turned to the public sector. Between 1958 and 1978, public sector union membership more than doubled, from about 7.8 million to 15.7 million. Union membership remained high until the early 1980s. Today, about 13 percent of households, or about 7 percent of American workers, belong to organized labor and benefit from union influenced state laws that allow collective bargaining for such public employees as teachers, firefighters, and police.

Business Response to Labor Growth Businesses soon organized in response to the growing labor movement so they could gain influence for their positions. Manufacturing and railroad firms sent men to influence decisions in Washington. As more and more influential "lobby men" roamed the Capitol, these interests became known as the "third house of Congress."

The number of **trade associations**, or interest groups made of businesses within a specific industry, grew from about 800 in 1914 to 1,500 in 1923. By 2010, that number had grown to more than 90,000.

The National Association of Manufacturers (NAM) was founded in 1895 to advocate for manufacturers' interests. NAM pushed for the creation of the U.S. Chamber of Commerce, which formed in 1912, and its members include many local chambers of commerce in cities across the country, as well as private firms and individuals. Heavily financed, the NAM and the Chamber became deeply involved in politics.

The U.S. Chamber of Commerce is among the larger and more influential interest groups in Washington, DC, and seeks to protect business interests. It opposed the Affordable Health Care for America Act and spent more than $16 million to elect senators who would support a competing plan more favorable to the health insurance companies that were Chamber of Commerce members. It has also opposed government action on climate change. It supported the American Recovery and Reinvestment Act of 2009, sometimes called the stimulus bill, which provided government money to businesses to preserve jobs and improve the nation's infrastructure. The U.S. Chamber of Commerce has been the top spender on lobbying for many years. In 2017, the organization spent more than $1.4 billion to help promote the interests of its members. In contrast, organized labor spent only $46 million, most of it in support of the interests of public sector and transportation employees.

Social Movement Interests

The Progressive Era (1890–1920) was a fertile period of American reform. The growing population and rise in immigration resulted in a push for greater levels of democracy and policies to assist the average citizen. The push for a women's suffrage amendment was growing. African American leaders and compassionate northern intellectuals sought to ease racial strife in both the South and the North. The Woman's Christian Temperance Union wanted to eliminate consumption of alcohol. Many believed that the nation's cities had become overcrowded, filthy denizens of vice, and various groups formed to clean them up.

Progressive Era Amendments The ratification of three amendments—the Sixteenth, Seventeenth, and Nineteenth—contributed to interest group growth and activity. The **Sixteenth Amendment** (1913) empowered Congress to tax individual incomes, which enhanced the national treasury and encouraged groups to push for more services. The **Seventeenth Amendment** (1913) empowered citizens to elect their U.S. senators directly, replacing the old system in which state legislators and party caucuses picked the senators. Senators now had to consider the views of all voters, not just the elites. The **Nineteenth Amendment** (1920) guaranteed women the right to vote, doubling the potential voting population. Civic-minded women drew attention to urban decay, child labor, alcoholism, and other humanitarian concerns.

PROGRESSIVE ERA INTEREST GROUPS		
Group	Purpose	Founded
Veterans of Foreign Wars	To secure rights for military veterans	1899
National Association for the Advancement of Colored People	To advocate for racial justice and civil rights	1909
Urban League (originally called Committee on Urban Conditions Among Negroes)	To prevent discrimination, especially in northern cities	1910
U.S. Chamber of Commerce	To unify businesses and protect commercial affairs	1912
Anti-Defamation League	To stop bigotry and defamation of Jewish people	1913
American Farm Bureau	To make farming more profitable; to secure farmers' benefits	1919
American Legion	To assist war veterans, service members, and communities	1919
League of Women Voters	To assure good government	1920
American Civil Liberties Union	To guarantee free speech, separation of church and state, and fair trials	1920

After World War II, civil rights and women's equality, environmental pollution, and a rising consumer consciousness were the focus of leading social movements. Backing for these causes expanded during the turbulent 1960s as citizens began to rely less on political parties with general platforms and more on interest groups addressing broad issues but working toward very specific goals. Interest groups tied to social movements cannot match the financial resources of the Chamber of Commerce or even unions to lobby policymakers, but they have another tool to help sway opinion—grassroots movements.

Civil Rights The National Association for the Advancement of Colored People (NAACP) and the Urban League were founded in 1909 and 1910, respectively, to seek racial equality and social fairness for African Americans. In the 1950s and 1960s, these groups experienced a dramatic rise in membership, which increased their influence in Washington. NAACP attorneys worked tirelessly to organize black communities to seek legal redress in the courts. In addition to filing cases to challenge unfair laws, the NAACP worked tirelessly to defend wrongly accused African Americans or to assure justice in criminal cases. They still do today.

The Urban League worked to increase membership to enhance its influence. Additional civil rights groups surfaced and grew. The Congress of Racial Equality (CORE) was founded at the University of Chicago and became instrumental in the nonviolent civil disobedience effort to desegregate lunch counters. Reverend Martin Luther King's Southern Christian Leadership Conference (SCLC), an organization of leading black southern clergymen, began a national publishing effort to create public awareness of racist conditions in the South.

The Student Nonviolent Coordinating Committee (SNCC) was a leading force in the dangerous Freedom Rides to integrate interstate bus lines and terminals. Whether in the courts, in the streets, or on Capitol Hill, most changes to civil rights policy and legislation, especially the Civil Rights Act of 1964 and the Voting Rights Act of 1965, resulted from these organizations' efforts.

Women's Movement A growing number of women entered public office in the mid-20th century. Federal laws began to address fair hiring, equal pay, and workplace discrimination. The 1963 Equal Pay Act and the 1964 Civil Rights Act addressed occupational equality but left unsettled equal pay for equal work and a clear definition of sex discrimination.

Leading feminist Betty Friedan wrote *The Feminine Mystique* in 1963 and formed the National Organization for Women (NOW) in 1966. NOW had 200 chapters by the early 1970s and was joined by the National Women's Political Caucus and the National Association for the Repeal of Abortion Laws (NARAL) to create a coalition for feminist causes. The influence of these groups brought congressional passage of the Equal Rights Amendment (which failed in the state ratification battle) and Title IX (1972), which brought more focus and funding equality to men's and women's school athletics. They also fought for the *Roe v. Wade* (1973) Supreme Court decision that prevented states from outlawing abortion. (See Topic 3.10 for more on women's rights.)

Environmental Movement As activists drew attention to mistreatment of African Americans and women, they also generated a consciousness about the misuse of our environment. Marine biologist Rachel Carson's best-selling book *Silent Spring* (1962) criticized the use of insecticides and other pesticides that harmed birds and wildlife. Her title referred to the silence resulting from the death of birds, long the harbingers of springtime cheerfulness. Organizations such as the Sierra Club, the Wilderness Society, and the Audubon Society expanded their goals and quadrupled their membership.

In 1963 and 1964, Congress passed the first Clean Water Act and Clean Air Act, respectively, in part through the efforts of the environmental groups. The years of disregard of pollution and chemical dumping into the nation's waterways reached a crisis point in 1969 when Cleveland's Cuyahoga River was so inundated with chemicals that it actually caught on fire. This crisis led to even stronger legislation and the creation of the Environmental Protection Agency in 1970. Also in 1970, Earth Day became an annual event to focus on how Americans could help to preserve the environment.

In 1980, environmental interest groups celebrated the creation of the Superfund under the Comprehensive Environmental Response, Compensation, and Liability Act (CERCLA). The Superfund taxes chemical and petroleum companies and puts the revenue into a trust fund to be used for cleaning up environmental disasters. The first disaster to use Superfund resources was at Love Canal in New York, an abandoned canal project into which a chemical company had dumped 21,000 tons of hazardous chemicals between 1942 and 1953, putting the health of residents in the area at risk. (See Topic 1.9 for more on the Love Canal.)

Source: Massachusetts Department of Environmental Protection

The Shpack Landfill in Attleboro and Norton, Massachusetts was the site of a Superfund cleanup effort to remove hazardous waste materials, including low-level radioactive waste.

Consumer Movement Consumers and their advocates began to demand that manufacturers take responsibility for making products safe. No longer was *caveat emptor* ("let the buyer beware") the guiding principle in the exchange of goods and services. In 1962 President Kennedy put forth a Consumers' Bill of Rights meant to challenge manufacturers and guarantee citizens the rights to product safety, information, and selection. By the end of the decade, Consumers Union established a Washington office, and activists formed the Consumer Federation of America. With new access to sometimes troubling consumer information, the nation's confidence in major companies dropped from 55 percent in 1966 to 27 percent in 1971.

Ralph Nader emerged as America's chief consumer advocate. As early as 1959 he published articles in *The Nation* condemning the auto industry. "It is clear Detroit is designing automobiles for style, cost, performance, and calculated obsolescence," Nader wrote, "but not for safety." In 1965 he published *Unsafe at Any Speed*, an exposé of the industry, especially General Motors' (GM) sporty Corvair. To counter Nader's accusations, GM hired private detectives to tail, discredit, and even blackmail him. When this effort came to light, a congressional committee summoned GM's president to testify and to apologize to Nader. In 1966, Congress also passed the National Traffic and Motor Vehicle Safety Act, which, among other things, required seat belts in all new cars.

After the financial crisis of 2008–2009, consumer interest groups united under an umbrella organization called Americans for Financial Reform which helped pressure lawmakers to create the Consumer Financial Protection Bureau. Its responsibilities include regulating debt and collection practices, monitoring mortgage lending, investigating complaints about financial institutions, and obtaining refunds for consumers.

Groups and Members

Interest groups fall into a handful of categories. These consist of institutional (corporate and intergovernmental groups), professional, ideological, member-based, and public interest groups. There is some overlap among these. For example, business groups want to make profits, but they also have a distinct ideology when it comes to taxation and business regulation. Likewise, citizens groups have members who may pay modest dues, but these groups mostly push for laws that benefit society at large.

Institutional Groups

Institutional groups break down into several different categories, including intergovernmental groups, professional associations, and corporations.

The U.S. system of redistributing federal revenues through the state governments encourages government-associated interest groups. Governors, mayors, and members of state legislatures are all interested in receiving funding from Washington. The federal grants system and marble cake federalism increase state, county, and city interest in national policy. Governments and their employees—police, firefighters, EMTs, sanitation workers, and others—have a keen interest in government rules and regulations that affect their jobs and funding that impacts their salaries. This interest has created **intergovernmental lobby**, which includes the National Governors Association, the National League of Cities, and the U.S. Conference of Mayors, all of which have offices in the nation's capital.

Unlike labor unions that might represent tradesmen like pipefitters or carpenters, **professional associations** typically represent white-collar professions. Examples include the American Medical Association (AMA) and the American Bar Association (ABA). They are concerned with business success and the laws and practices that guide their trade. The AMA endorsed the 2010 Affordable Care Act. The ABA rates judicial nominees and testifies before Congress about proposed crime bills. Police and teachers' unions, such as the Fraternal Order of Police or the National Education Association, are often associated with the labor force, but in many ways, they fall into this category.

The Business Roundtable, formed in 1973, represents firms that account for nearly half of the nation's gross domestic product. During this time, new conservative **think tanks**—research institutions, often with specific ideological goals—emerged and old ones revived. The American Enterprise Institute and the Heritage Foundation, among other policy institutes, countered the ideas and policy coming from liberal think tanks and progressive foundations.

Some think tanks are associated with universities, even though their funding comes entirely from corporations, philanthropic foundations, and private individuals. For example, the Mercatus Center at George Mason University in Virginia was founded to promote free market ideas and solutions in higher education with the backing of billionaire Libertarian Charles Koch and other free market proponents.

As writer John Judis explains, in 1971, only 175 businesses registered lobbyists in Washington. By 1982, there were 2,445 companies that had paid lobbyists. The number of corporate offices in the capital jumped from 50 in 1961 to 500 in 1978 and to 1,300 by 1986. By 1978, 1,800 trade associations were headquartered in the nation's capital. Today, Washington has an army of lawyers and public relations experts whose job it is to represent corporate interests and lobby the government for their corporate clients.

Professional Organizations

Most groups have a defined membership and member fees, typically ranging from $15 to $40 annually. (Corporate and white-collar associations typically charge much higher fees.) When groups seek to change or protect a law, they represent their members and even nonmembers who have not joined. For example, there are many more African Americans who approve of the NAACP's goals and support their actions than there are actual, dues-paying NAACP members. There are more gun advocates than members of the National Rifle Association (NRA). These nonmembers choose not to bear the participation costs of time and fees but do benefit from the associated group's efforts—the free rider problem. (See Topic 5.6 for more on the free rider problem.)

To encourage membership, interest groups offer incentives. **Purposive incentives** are those that give the joiner some philosophical satisfaction. They realize their money will contribute to some worthy cause. If they donate to an organization addressing climate change, for example, they might feel gratified that their contribution will help future generations. **Solidary incentives** are those that allow people of like mind to gather on occasion. Such gatherings include monthly organizational meetings and citizen actions. Many groups offer **material incentives**, such as travel discounts, subscriptions to magazines or newsletters, or complimentary items such as bags, caps, or jackets.

One study found that the average interest group member's annual income is $17,000 higher than the national average and that 43 percent of interest group members have advanced degrees, suggesting that interest group membership has an **upper-class bias**. Though annual membership fees in most interest groups are modest, critics argue that the trend results in policies that favor the higher socioeconomic classes.

As opposed to special interest groups, **public interest groups** are geared to improve life or government for the masses. Fully 30 percent of such groups have formed since 1975, and they constitute about one-fifth of all groups represented in Washington.

In 1970, Republican John Gardner, who was President Lyndon Johnson's Secretary of Health, Education, and Welfare, took what he called the biggest gamble of his career to create Common Cause. "Everybody's organized but the people," Gardner declared when he put out the call to recruit members to build "a true citizens' lobby." Within six months Common Cause had more than 100,000 members. The antiwar movement and the post-Watergate reform mindset contributed to the group's early popularity. Common Cause's accomplishments include the Twenty-sixth Amendment to grant voting rights to those 18 and over, campaign finance laws, transparent government, and other voting reforms. More recently, the group pushed for the 2002 Bipartisan Campaign Reform (McCain-Feingold) Act and the 2007 lobbying regulations in the Honest Leadership and Open Government Act, which called for public disclosure of lobbying activities and limits gifts for Congress members. Today, Common Cause has nearly 400,000 members and 38 state offices.

With money from a legal settlement with General Motors, Ralph Nader joined with other consumer advocates to create Public Citizen in 1971. He hired bright, aggressive lawyers who came to be known as Nader's Raiders. In 1974, *U.S. News and World Report* ranked Nader as the fourth-most influential man in America. Carrying out ideals similar to those that Nader had emphasized in the 1960s—consumer rights and open government—Public Citizen tries to ensure that all citizens are represented in the halls of power. It fights against undemocratic trade agreements and provides a "countervailing force to corporate power." Nader went on to create other watchdog organizations, such as the Center for Responsive Law and Congress Watch, to address the concerns of ordinary citizens who don't have the resources to organize and lobby government.

Single-Issue and Ideological Groups

Some interest groups form to address a narrow area of concern. Two **single-issue groups**—focused on just one topic—of note are the National Rifle Association (NRA) and the American Association of Retired Persons (AARP).

The National Rifle Association (NRA) is the "single-issue" group most associated with narrow interest lobbying. The NRA has gone from post–Civil War marksmen's club to pro-gun Washington powerhouse, especially in the last 30 years under the leadership of lobbyist Wayne LaPierre. Its original charter was to improve the marksmanship of military soldiers. After a 1968 gun control and crime law, the NRA appealed to sportsmen and Second Amendment advocates. Its revised 1977 charter states that the purpose of NRA is "generally to encourage the lawful ownership and use of small arms by citizens of good repute." In 2001 *Fortune* magazine named the NRA the most powerful lobby in America. The NRA appeals to law enforcement officers and outdoorsmen with insurance policies, discounts, and its magazine *American Rifleman*. The group holds periodic local dinners for "Friends of the NRA" to raise money. The annual convention provides a chance for gun enthusiasts to mingle and view the newest firearms, and attendance reaches beyond 50,000 gun enthusiasts.

The NRA endorses candidates from both major political parties but heavily favors Republicans. From 1978 to 2000 the organization spent more than $26 million in elections; $22.5 million went to GOP candidates and $4.3 went to Democrats.

Breakdown of Political Spending by the NRA, 1998-2017

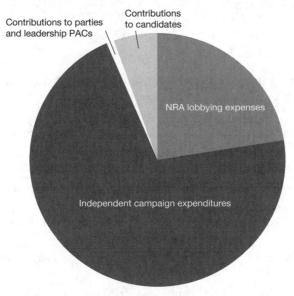

Contributions to parties and leadership PACs

Contributions to candidates

NRA lobbying expenses

Independent campaign expenditures

Source: Center for Responsive Politics

In what category of spending does the NRA expect to see the greatest return on investment?

The American Association of Retired Persons (AARP) has the largest membership of any interest group in the nation. AARP has twice the membership of the AFL-CIO, its own zip code in Washington, and its own registered in-house lobbyists. Its magazine has the largest circulation of any monthly publication in the country. People age 50 and over can join for $16 per year. The organization's main concerns are members' health, financial stability and livelihood, and the Social Security system. "AARP seeks to attract a membership as diverse as America itself," its web site claims. With such a large, high voter-turnout membership, elected officials tend to pay close attention to AARP.

You have already read about a number of **ideological groups**—interest groups formed around a political ideology. On the liberal side of the ideology spectrum are groups such as the NAACP and NOW. On the other end of the spectrum, conservative ideological interest groups include the Christian Coalition and the National Taxpayers Union.

One of the more active groups today is the American Civil Liberties Union (ACLU) which formed after World War I to counteract government's authoritarian interpretation of the First Amendment. At that time, the federal government deported radicals and threw dissenters of the war and the military draft in jail. Guaranteeing free expression became the ACLU's central mission. In 1925, the organization went up against Tennessee state law to defend John Scopes' right to teach evolution in a public school.

Over the following decades, the ACLU opened state affiliates and took on other civil liberties violations. It remains very active, serving as a watchdog for free speech, fair trials, and racial justice. The ACLU has about half a million members, about 200 attorneys, a presence on Capitol Hill, and chapters in all 50 states.

ACLU ACTION IN SUPREME COURT		
Year	Case	Outcome
1962	Engel v. Vitale	Outlawed New York's state-sponsored school prayer
1967	Loving v. Virginia	Ended state laws against interracial marriage
1969	Tinker v. Des Moines	Overturned student suspensions for protesting Vietnam War
1971	New York Times Co. v. US	Prevented government prior restraint of news publication
1997	Reno v. ACLU	Internet speech gained full First Amendment protection
2003	Lawrence v. Texas	Overturned state laws against same-sex intimacy

The ACLU has represented clients or filed amicus briefs in the above cases.

Interest Group Pressure on Political Parties

Political parties and interest groups are both linkage institutions, creating connections between people and government. Political parties and interest groups also have connections between them. Some interest groups align with political parties that share their ideology and goals by endorsing candidates in that party and encouraging their membership to vote for those candidates. However, interest groups can also exert pressure on political parties in areas of disagreement, and the result can be an official party ideology shift in the direction of the interest group pressure.

Republican Party's Pull to the Right Several examples in recent history show the power of interest groups to influence policy positions of political parties. For example, as early as 1940, the Republican Party declared in its platform, "We favor submission by Congress to the States of an amendment to the Constitution providing for equal rights for men and women." With that statement, Republicans were the first party to endorse the Equal Rights Amendment (ERA) after Congress proposed submitting it to the states for their ratification in 1972. By 1980, however, the Republican platform expressed a different stance to the ERA: "We acknowledge the legitimate efforts of those who support or oppose ratification of the Equal Rights Amendment." What happened during the eight years between those statements to shift the Republican position?

Phyllis Schlafly (1924–2016) was a lifelong Republican, playing an active role in the party and even running for office. She founded a conservative interest group, now called the Eagle Forum, in 1972, but refocused her energy on stopping the Equal Rights Amendment by founding the interest group STOP ERA (STOP stands for "Stop Taking Our Privileges"). By this time the ERA had won overwhelming support in Congress and ratification of 30 of the required 38 states. Schlafly's organization took the position that the ERA would disadvantage women—that it would deprive them of certain spousal rights, require them to serve in the armed forces and in combat, force them to use unisex bathrooms—and eventually lead to same-sex marriage. Against the backdrop of the Supreme Court's 1962 ban on school prayer in *Engel v. Vitale* (see Topic 3.2) and the legalization of abortion in *Roe v. Wade* in 1973 (see Topic 3.9), women from a variety of backgrounds, especially conservative and Christian, feared that their traditional values were under attack, and they feared the consequences of the ERA that Schlafly predicted.

Source: Florida Memory Project, State Archive of Florida

A solemn group of anti-ERA women line the wall of the Florida Senate Rules Committee room in Tallahassee, where standing room only was available. The Senate Rules Committee defeated, then tabled consideration of, the Equal Rights Amendment, virtually killing the bill for the 1979 session.

The anti-ERA movement gained so much strength that the Republican Party could not ignore its influence, and it withdrew its support for the ERA from its platform. STOP ERA and other anti-ERA interest groups, including Concerned Women for America, Women for Constitutional Government, the John Birch Society, and Daughters of the American Revolution, carried out well-organized efforts and were successful in halting the ratification of the amendment and at the same time in pulling the Republican Party toward more conservative policy positions.

In a similar way, after President Obama's Patient Protection and Affordable Care Act passed in 2010, the Tea Party ("Tea" stands for "Taxed Enough Already") movement appeared on the scene to combat it and other government spending considered to be handouts to undeserving people. A number of interest groups arose as a result of this movement, and they helped elect conservative replacements for more moderate Republicans at every level of government. Once again, the Republican Party was pulled to the right as a result of pressure from interest groups.

Democratic Party's Push to the Left The Democratic Party has experienced a similar shift in policy positions. Until the 20th century, it was more conservative than the Republican Party (the party of Abraham Lincoln) and was opposed to civil rights. However, during the administration of Franklin D. Roosevelt in the 1930s and 1940s, African Americans aligned with the Democrats. During the administration of Lyndon Johnson in the 1960s, powerful interest groups such as NAACP exerted pressure for progress in civil rights legislation, and the Democratic Party welcomed more African American and other minority voters, as well those favoring the ERA and opposing war. Its policy positions became more liberal in the party's shift to the left.

Other interest groups have also greatly influenced the Democratic Party. In 1984, the National Organization for Women (NOW) made its first-ever presidential endorsement when it endorsed Democratic candidate Walter Mondale, and the Democratic Party made history by nominating Geraldine Ferraro as his runningmate, the first woman to be nominated for vice president by a major party. In 1985, EMILY's List was founded to help Democratic women to office. (EMILY stands for "Early Money Is Like Yeast," referring to the importance of securing donations early in a candidate's campaign in order to ensure donations later as well, to help a campaign rise as yeast makes dough rise.) Its first victory was the election of Senator Barbara Mikulski of Maryland, who became the longest-serving woman in the history of Congress. EMILY's List has gone on to help many Democratic women, including women of color and gay women, get elected. These strong associations between women's interest groups and the Democratic Party influenced the party's stand on women's issues.

The Sierra Club, a large environmental interest group, also carries influence with the Democratic Party. Many of its resources go to lobbying for environmental protection, and nearly all of its super PAC money goes to Democratic candidates. Super PACs can make unlimited independent contributions as long as the committee is not directly advocating for a candidate. (See Topic 5.11 for more on PACs.)

In Topic 2.1, political institutions were defined as government organizations that make, enforce, or apply laws. Interest groups try to exert influence on all three functions of political institutions. Political scientists divide interest groups into one or more categories to better understand their influence. For example, some are categorized as single-issue groups, focused on one narrow topic. Others are categorized as ideological groups, formed around a political ideology.

Practice: Read the mission statements of these interest groups and determine if the group is best categorized as a public interest group, a single-issue group, or an ideological group. If you choose ideological group, also identify which political ideology it will appeal to most (conservative, liberal, or other).

1. **American Association of Retired Persons**—AARP enhances the quality of life for all as we age. We champion positive social change and deliver value through advocacy, information, and service.

2. **National Organization for Women**—Since our founding in 1966, NOW's purpose is to take action through intersectional grassroots activism to promote feminist ideals, lead societal change, eliminate discrimination, and achieve and protect the equal rights of all women and girls in all aspects of social, political, and economic life.

3. **Common Cause**—Common Cause is a nonpartisan, grassroots organization dedicated to upholding the core values of American democracy. We work to create open, honest, and accountable government that serves the public interest; promote equal rights, opportunity, and representation for all; and empower all people to make their voices heard in the political process.

Ethics and Reform

Lobbyists work for many different interests. The Veterans of Foreign Wars seeks to assist military veterans. The Red Cross, United Way, and countless public universities across the land employ lobbyists to seek funding and support. Yet the increased number of firms that have employed high-paid consultants to influence Congress and the increased role of PAC money in election campaigns have given lobbyists and special interests a mainly negative public reputation. The salaries for successful lobbyists typically outstrip those of the public officials they seek to influence. Members of Congress and their staffs can triple their salaries if they leave Capitol Hill to become lobbyists. This situation has created an era in which careers on K Street—the noted Washington street that hosts a number of interest group headquarters or lobbying offices—are more attractive to many than careers in public service. Still, old and recent bribery cases, lapses of ethics, and conflicts of interest have led to strong efforts at reform.

Scandals Bribery in Congress, of course, predates formal interest groups. In the 1860s Credit Mobilier scandal, a holding company sold low-priced shares of railroad stock to members of Congress in return for favorable votes on pro-Union

Pacific Railroad legislation. A century ago, *Cosmopolitan* magazine ran a series entitled "Treason in the Senate" that exposed nine senators for bribery. In the late 1940s, the "5 percenters," federal officials who offered government favors or contracts in exchange for a 5 percent cut, went to prison. Over the years, Congress has had to pass several laws to curb influence and create greater transparency.

CONGRESSIONAL ACTS ON LOBBYING
• Federal Regulation of Lobbying Act (1946)
• Lobbying Disclosure Act (1995)
• Honest Leadership and Open Government Act (2007)

The high-profile cases of congressmen Randall "Duke" Cunningham and lobbyist Jack Abramoff created headlines in 2006 that exposed lawlessness taking place inside the lawmaking process and the effects of elitism. Cunningham, a San Diego Republican representative, took roughly $2.4 million in bribes to direct Pentagon military defense purchases to a particular defense contractor. That contractor, a California organization with more power, resources, and influence than its competitors, supplied Cunningham with lavish gifts and favors such as cash, a Rolls-Royce, antique furniture, and access to prostitutes. He was convicted in 2006.

A more publicized scandal engulfed lobbyist Jack Abramoff, whose client base included several Native American casinos. He was known to trade favors—fancy dinners, golf trips to Scotland, lavish campaign contributions—for legislation. He pled guilty in January 2006 to defrauding four wealthy tribes and other clients of nearly $25 million as well as evading $1.7 million in taxes, and he went to jail.

Recent Reform Congress responded with the Honest Leadership and Open Government Act (HLOGA) in 2007. New rules banned all gifts to members of Congress or their staff from registered lobbyists or their clients. It also banned members from flying on corporate jets in most circumstances and restricted travel paid for by outside groups. The 2007 law also outlawed lobbyists from buying meals, gifts, and most trips for congressional staffers. Lobbyists must now file expense reports quarterly instead of twice a year. The new law also requires members to report the details of any **bundling**—raising large sums from multiple donors for a candidate. Lobbyists who bundle now have to report it if the combined funds equal more than $15,000 in any six-month period. Also, for the first time ever, lobbyists who break ethics rules will face civil and criminal penalties of up to $200,000 in fines and five years in prison.

Revolving Door However, the HLOGA had loopholes that have been repeatedly exploited. One relates to the matter of the **revolving door**—the movement from the job of legislator to a job within an industry affected by the laws or regulations. Many officials leave their jobs on Capitol Hill or in the executive branch to lobby the government they departed. Some members of Congress take these positions after losing an election. Others do so because they can make more money by leaving government and working in the private sector. These former lawmakers already have influential relationships with members of Congress.

A Public Citizen study found that half the senators and 42 percent of House members who left office between 1998 and 2004 became lobbyists. Another study found that 3,600 former congressional aides had passed through the revolving door. The Center for Responsive Politics identified 310 former Bush and 283 Clinton appointees as lobbyists working in the capital. As of late 2019, 356 former members of Congress serve as registered lobbyists.

Interest groups by definition promote the interests of their members over more general interests. When groups pull in many different or completely opposite directions, compromise becomes impossible and gridlock can result. This phenomenon is called hyperpluralism.

In such a situation, a form of elitism can also develop. Groups with more power and resources are more likely to achieve their goals than groups with smaller memberships or more limited funding, putting interest groups on an uneven footing in the "marketplace of ideas."

The challenges created by powerful interest groups have led some critics to wish to silence their voices. However, these critics need look no further than the First Amendment to understand why this cannot be done. Interest groups are legal and constitutional because the amendment protects free speech, free association, and the right to petition the government. In response to escalating lobbying efforts over the years, however, Congress began in 1946 to require lobbyists to register with the House or Senate. The Supreme Court upheld lobbyists' registration requirements but also declared in *United States v. Harriss* (1954) that the First Amendment ensures anyone or any group the right to lobby.

REFLECT ON THE ESSENTIAL QUESTION

Essential Question: *How do various political actors influence public policy outcomes? On separate paper, complete the chart below.*

Groups Exerting Influence	Influence on Public Policy

KEY TERMS AND NAMES

bundling	revolving door
ideological groups	Seventeenth Amendment (1913)
intergovernmental lobby	single-issue groups
material incentives	Sixteenth Amendment (1913)
Nineteenth Amendment (1920)	solidary incentives
professional associations	think tanks
public interest groups	trade associations
purposive incentives	upper-class bias

CHAPTER 17 Review:
Learning Objectives and Key Terms

TOPIC 5.6: Explain the benefits and potential problems of interest-group influence on elections and policy making. (PMI-5.E)

Explain how the variation in type and resources of interest groups affects their ability to influence elections and policy making. (PMI-5.F)

Function of Interest Groups (PMI-5.E.1)	**Influence of Interest Groups** (PMI-5.E.2 & 5.F.1)
free-rider	501 (c) (3)
iron triangles	501 (c) (4)
issue networks	direct lobbying
pluralism	endorsement
	grassroots lobbying
	grasstops
	insider strategies
	lobbying
	lobbyist
	outsider strategies

TOPIC 5.7: Explain how various political actors influence public policy outcomes. (PMI-5.G)

Interest Groups' Influence on Policy Making (PMI-5.G.1 & 2)	**Interest Groups' Influence on Political Parties and Elections** (PMI-5.G.3)
ideological groups	bundling
intergovernmental lobby	revolving door
material incentives	trade associations
professional associations	Nineteenth Amendment (1920)
public interest groups	Seventeenth Amendment (1913)
purposive incentives	Sixteenth Amendment (1913)
single-issue groups	
solidary incentives	
think tanks	
upper-class bias	

CHAPTER 17 Checkpoint:
Interest Groups

Topics 5.6–5.7

MULTIPLE-CHOICE QUESTIONS

1. Which of the following is true regarding interest groups?

   (A) Interest groups do not draft legislation.

   (B) Most U.S. citizens join interest groups.

   (C) The free-rider problem limits the group's resources.

   (D) Interest groups form iron triangles with executive branch agencies and the courts.

2. The National Association for the Advancement of Colored People (NAACP) learns that a local prosecutor has charged an African American teen with assault and armed robbery. The organization has reason to believe the defendant has been wrongly charged for the crime. The defendant has little money but much support in the local area. Which of the following course of action will the NACCP likely take?

   (A) Meet with state legislators to change the laws that define assault and robbery

   (B) Talk to the judge in this case and offer a donation to his reelection campaign

   (C) Defend the accused teen in court

   (D) Petition the governor for a pardon

Questions 3 and 4 refer to the cartoon below.

Source: Nick Anderson, Cartoonist/Group

3. Which statement reflects the perspective of the cartoonist?

(A) Interest groups working together improve legislation.

(B) Health care reform has been threatened by special interests.

(C) Special interests make surgically precise changes to proposed policy.

(D) Government involvement in health care is unwise.

4. Which activity would an interest group most likely employ to influence the legislative reform effort depicted in cartoon?

(A) Filing suits in court

(B) Lobbying of congressional staffers

(C) Campaign donations

(D) Electioneering

5. Which interest group action would most influence rulings in the courts?

(A) Rating senators and representatives based on roll call votes

(B) Directly lobbying House and Senate members

(C) Filing an *amicus curiae* brief

(D) Purchasing an ad in a newspaper

6. Which of the following is an accurate comparison of public interest groups and special interest groups?

	Public Interest Groups	Special Interest Groups
(A)	The National Rifle Association is a good example	Funded by government subsidies and taxes
(B)	Include trade organizations and/or labor unions	Active in the national capital, but not the state capitals
(C)	Address policy concerns that impact the nation at large	Have a unique membership and try to shape policy with those members in mind
(D)	Engage directly in electoral politics	Include interest groups like Public Citizen and Common Cause

FREE-RESPONSE QUESTIONS

Concept Application

1. "Most Nevadans don't have a choice. We don't get to decide how much our health care costs go up. No one's asking us if older Americans should be charged five times more for coverage than everyone else. And it's not our decision if Congress cuts Medicaid, leaving millions of seniors without the care they need . . . Just one vote could be enough to stop this bill. And Senator Heller, that vote is yours. Call Senator Heller today. Tell him to vote NO on the healthcare bill."

—AARP Radio Ad, June 20, 2017

After reading the above scenario, respond to A, B, and C below:

(A) Describe the purpose of the interest group's radio ad.

(B) In the context of such radio ads, explain why the ad will likely help the AARP accomplish its goal.

(C) Explain one factor that could prevent the AARP from acheiving its policy goals.

Quantitative Analysis

Types of Interest Groups, 1959 and 1995

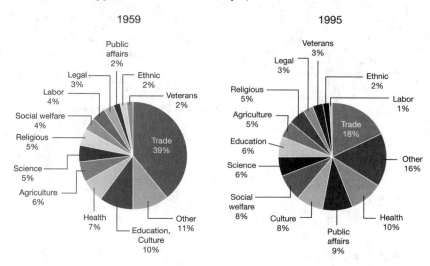

2. Use the information graphic above to answer the questions.

(A) Identify the largest interest group type in both 1959 and 1995.

(B) Describe a difference between one interest group category from 1959 and 1995.

(C) Draw a conclusion about that difference.

(D) Explain how the data in the illustration may affect interest group influence on policymaking.

CHAPTER 18

Elections

Topics 5.8–5.9

Topic 5.8 Electing a President

PRD-2.A: Explain how the different processes work in a U.S. presidential election.

PRD-2.B: Explain how the Electoral College facilitates and/or impedes democracy.

Topic 5.9 Congressional Elections

PRD-2.C: Explain how the different processes work in U.S. congressional elections.

Source: Getty Images

Voters wait in line at their polling place to have their registrations confirmed before casting their votes.

Electing a President

"Vote for the man who promises the least; he'll be the least disappointing."
—Bernard Baruch, in *The New York Times*, 1960

Essential Question: How do different processes work in a presidential election, and does the electoral college facilitate and/or impede democracy?

Every four years in November, millions of Americans go to the polls to cast a vote for the American president and other offices. Sometimes a candidate will win in a landslide with a strong margin and claim victory before sunset. Sometimes close elections require careful vote counting, and a victor is not declared for days. In November 2016, United States citizens, through the nation's complex electoral system, elected Donald Trump president. **BIG IDEA** Popular sovereignty, individualism, and republicanism are important considerations of U.S. laws and policymaking and assume citizens will engage and participate.

The Constitution includes broad statements regarding voting and elections. Article I empowers Congress to set the date for federal elections. Article II explains the Electoral College and the basics of the system for electing the president. The Twelfth Amendment, ratified in 1804, altered the procedure so that electors cast separate ballots for the presidential and vice presidential candidates. In the time since the framing and the 1804 change, federal statutes, state law, and political party customs have shaped the overall path to the presidency.

Road to the White House

The U.S. presidential race is more complex and more involved than any other election. The road to the White House is long and arduous, with layers of rules and varying state election laws. A presidential campaign requires two or more years of advance work to make it through two fierce competitions—securing the party's nomination and winning a majority of states' electoral votes. Before presidential hopefuls formally announce their candidacy, they test the waters. Most start early, touring the country and making television appearances. Some author a book, typically a memoir that relies heavily on their political philosophy. As the election year approaches, announced and unannounced candidates compete in the **invisible primary** (sometimes called the media primary or the money primary), as public opinion polls and comparisons of fundraising abilities begin to tell the score long before the first states have voted.

Incumbent Advantage Phenomenon

An **incumbent** president—one already holding the office—seeking a second term has a much easier time securing the nomination than a challenger because of the **incumbent advantage phenomenon**—the ability to use all the tools of the presidency to support candidacy for a second term. At the end of a president's second term, the field opens up again for candidates since the president has served as long as he or she can.

Although being an incumbent does not guarantee reelection, the rate of reelection is high, about 80 percent. The list below shows some of the factors in the incumbent advantage phenomenon.

ELECTORAL ADVANTAGES OF INCUMBENT PRESIDENTS
• Already well known, having been in the national spotlight for four years
• Has four years of experience and a record to evaluate the president's performance
• Commands the "bully pulpit" and can use his position to get messages out to the American people
• Already proven he or she can win a national election
• Has a network of campaign contributors who can raise a large amount of money
• Has a network of campaign staff and volunteers with voter outreach
• Already seen as "presidential," a perception that other candidates have to earn

Primaries and Caucuses

To win the presidential nomination, candidates must first win state **primary elections** or caucuses. Technically, citizen-voters in these contests cast votes for delegates to attend the party's national convention. With their vote, the citizen-voters advise those delegates whom to nominate at that national convention. The Republican and Democratic rules for nomination differ, but both require a majority of votes by the appointed delegates at the convention. To win the nomination, candidates must win the requisite number of these state contests from January into the summer.

Types of Primaries Today, most states hold a primary election. For years, the closed primary was standard. In a **closed primary**, voters must declare their party affiliation in advance of the election, typically when they register to vote. The **open primary**, used by about half of the states today, allows voters to declare party affiliation on election day. Poll workers hand these voters one party's ballot from which they select candidates.

The rarest primary is the **blanket primary.** California and other western states pioneered the blanket primary, which allows voters to cast votes for candidates in multiple parties. In other words, voters can cast a **split ticket**, picking Republicans in some races and Democrats in others. California voters instituted a nonpartisan primary in 2010. This new runoff system includes all candidates—both party members and independents. The top two vote-getters, regardless of party affiliation, compete for office in the general election. The quest for inclusiveness created a unique dynamic that caused the press to dub it the "jungle primary" because the winners emerge through the law of the jungle—survival of the fittest without regard to party.

A few states use **caucuses** to nominate presidential candidates. Since 1976, the Iowa caucuses have taken place before any other state nominating elections. Caucuses differ from primary elections. Across Iowa, rank-and-file party members meet at community centers, schools, and private homes where they listen to endorsment speeches, discuss candidates, and then finally cast their vote before leaving the caucus. In comparison to standard elections, caucuses are less convenient and more public. This two-hour commitment makes attendance hard for some, especially those who might have to skip work. Others dislike the public discussion and the somewhat public vote (voters usually cast a vote at a table set aside for their candidate). So, those who do show up at caucuses tend to be more dedicated voters who hold strong opinions and often fall on the far left or far right of the ideological spectrum, thus causing more liberal or more conservative figures to win the delegates from those states.

In 2020, the Iowa caucuses left Democratic Party members confused and frustrated. The process was plagued by issues with a new reporting app and reporting errors and took nearly a month to declare a winner. The confusion led some to consider whether the Iowa caucus should be replaced by a traditional primary.

New Hampshire typically follows Iowa on the primary schedule. Candidates travel the state and hold town hall forums. They campaign in grocery stores and on the streets of relatively small New Hampshire towns. During this time, the voters actively engage these presidential candidates. When asked hhis or her opinion on a particular candidate, a typical New Hampshire voter might respond, "I don't know if I'm comfortable with him; I've only met him twice."

This contest has such great influence that candidates cautiously frame their primary election night speeches to paint themselves as front-runners. In 1992, the news came to light that Bill Clinton had been part of a sex scandal when he was governor of Arkansas, but he survived his diminished poll numbers to earn a second-place spot in New Hampshire. During his speech late that night, Clinton confidently referred to himself as "The Comeback Kid." This sound bite made its way into headlines that gave the impression that Clinton had actually won the New Hampshire primary.

Iowa and New Hampshire receive immense national attention during their primaries. Campaign teams and the national media converge on these states well in advance of election day. Hotels and restaurants fill with out-of-state customers, bringing massive revenues. Politically, these states hold more influence than those that conduct their elections much later. This reality has brought on **front-loading**—states scheduling their primaries and caucuses earlier and earlier to boost their political clout and to enhance their tourism. Iowa and New Hampshire have followed suit and leapfrogged those other states to continue to be first and second. The national party committees have also shaped and influenced the schedule, and for the foreseeable future, those states will begin the contests.

Candidates then travel an uncertain path through several more states, hoping to secure enough delegates to win the nomination. In recent years, South Carolina has followed New Hampshire and has served as a barometer for the southern voting bloc. More conservative GOP primary voters will now impact that nomination, and the large African American voting bloc will influence the Democrats' quest. A few weeks later, several states coincidentally hold primaries on **Super Tuesday** (so known because of the large number of primaries that take place on that day), when the race narrows and voters start to converge around fewer, or perhaps just one nominee.

According to a Pew study, since 1980, voter turnout in presidential primaries has ranged from 15 to 30 percent of the voting-eligible population. In 2016, about 57.6 million primary voters, or about 28.5 percent of the estimated eligible voters, voted in Republican and Democratic primaries.

Party Conventions

The national party conventions have become less suspenseful in modern times because the nominees are determined long before the convention date. Both parties have altered rules and formulas for state delegation strength.

States determine their convention delegates in different ways and hold them to different rules. Some states give their delegates complete independence at the convention. Some presidential primaries are binding on "pledged delegates." Even in those cases, states differ on how these delegates are awarded. Some operate by congressional district. Some use a statewide winner-take-all system, and some use proportional distribution for assigning delegates. For instance, in a **proportional system**, if Candidate A receives 60 percent and Candidate B receives 40 percent of the popular primary vote, the state sends the corresponding percentage of delegates for each candidate to the national gathering. The parties at the state and national level change their rules at least slightly every election cycle. The Democrats' use of superdelegates— an unelected delegate who can support any candidate—also leaves room for uncertainty in the process.

When assigning superdelegates, Democrats take into account the strength of each state's electoral vote and compare it to the record of how the state has cast votes for Democratic candidates in past general elections. Republicans place more value on the number of GOP representatives in Congress from those states and whether states have cast their electoral votes for Republican presidential candidates. In other words, Democrats give more delegates to *large* states, while Republicans give extra delegates to *loyal* states. Democrats have also instituted the idea of *fair reflection* to balance delegates by age, gender, and race in relation to the superdelegates or party elders.

The General Election

The **general election** season starts after party nominations and kicks into high gear after Labor Day. Candidates fly around the country, stopping at key locations to deliver speeches. As the public and press begin to compare the two major party candidates, the issues become more sharply defined. Different groups and surrogates (spokespersons) support each candidate and appear on television. The major party candidates debate, usually in three televised events over the course of several weeks. The vice presidential candidates usually debate once. Major newspapers endorse a candidate in their editorial pages. The media's daily coverage provides constant updates about which candidate is ahead as measured by public opinion polls and campaign funding. By November, candidates have traveled to most states and have spent millions of dollars.

Where candidates spend those millions depends on where they have the best chance to influence outcomes. Republicans and Democrats live in all 50 states, but in some states, Republicans have a long history of being victorious, while in others, Democrats often win. The patterns have changed in the last generation, but in recent times, the so-called "red states," those in which Republicans usually win, and "blue states," those in which Democrats usually win, have remained fairly constant.

However, some states have a less predictable pattern. They are known as **swing states** because the victories swing from one party to another in different elections. Candidates concentrate their campaign resources in those states. While they travel to most of the states meeting with wealthy donors to raise money, they focus on swing states by holding campaign events and spending advertising money.

Republican, Democratic, and Swing States 2004–2016

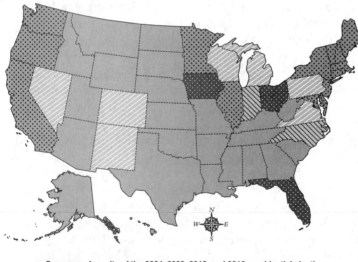

If you were managing the campaign for a Republican presidential candidate in the 2020 election, in what states would you spend most of your television advertising budget? Why? If you were managing the campaign for a Democratic presidential candidate for the same election, which states would you be targeting with your advertising money? Why?

Summary of results of the 2004, 2008, 2012, and 2016 presidential election:

- States carried by the Republicans in all four elections
- States carried by the Republicans in three of the four elections
- States carried by each party twice in the four elections
- States carried by the Democrats in three of the four elections
- States carried by the Democrats in all four elections

Electoral College

The **Electoral College** system is both a revered and a frustrating part of the presidential election because it shapes a presidential candidate's strategy. The system to elect the president has several features. The "college" is actually a simultaneous gathering of **electors** in their respective capital cities to vote on the same day. The framers devised this system to temper public opinion and to allow the more informed statesmen to select a consensus president. State and federal law as well as party custom also affect the process. Each state receives the same number of electors (or electoral votes) as it has members of Congress; however, these electors cannot be U.S. senators or representatives.

Originally, the Constitution provided that each elector cast one vote for each of his or her top two choices for president. The winner became president and the runner-up became vice president. The Twelfth Amendment (1804) altered the system so that electors cast one vote for president and another for vice president. To win, candidates must earn a majority of the electoral votes. Since the **Twenty-third Amendment** (1961), Washington, DC, adds three electoral votes. This brings the vote total to 538: 435 to align with the House total, plus 100 to match the total Senate seats, plus the three for DC. The candidate who earns 270 electoral votes, a simple majority, will become president. If no presidential candidate receives a majority, then the U.S. House of Representatives votes for president by delegations, choosing from among the top three candidates. Each state casts one vote for president, and whichever candidate receives 26 states or more wins. The Senate then determines the vice president in the same manner.

ELECTORAL VOTE WINNERS WHO LOST THE POPULAR VOTE	
1824	John Quincy Adams
1876	Rutherford B. Hayes
1888	Benjamin Harris
2000	George W. Bush
2016	Donald Trump

Winner-Take-All

Today, most states require their pledged electors (people already committed to a party's ticket) to follow the state's popular vote. Besides, electors are typically long-time partisans or career politicians who are ultimately appointed by the state party. The candidate who wins the **plurality** of the popular vote (the most, even if not the majority) in a given state will ultimately receive all of that state's electoral votes. This is known as the **winner-take-all** system. Only Nebraska and Maine allow for a split in their electoral votes and award electors by congressional district rather than on a statewide basis.

In early December, electors meet in state capitals and cast their votes. The ballots are transported to Washington in locked boxes. When Congress opens in January, the sitting vice president and Speaker of the House count these votes before a joint session of Congress. Since most states now require their electors to follow the popular vote, the electoral vote total essentially becomes known on election night in November. Television media coverage typically shows a U.S. map with Republican victories depicted in red and Democratic victories in blue. Soon after popular votes are tabulated, losing candidates publicly concede and the winner gives a victory speech. The constitutionally required procedures that follow—states' electors voting in December and the Congress counting those votes in January—thus become more formal ceremonies than suspenseful events.

Five times in American history, the winner of the popular vote did not win the electoral vote. Hillary Clinton's loss to Donald Trump in 2016 is the most recent example. This possibility has led some to criticize the Electoral College system. Others see the process as a way to ensure balance and to guarantee that a consensus candidate becomes president. Gallup has found that more than 60 percent of those polled want a constitutional amendment to change the electoral system, while only about 33 percent want to keep it in its current form. A proposed constitutional amendment to scrap the system and replace it with a popular vote has been offered repeatedly in Congress for years.

BENEFITS OF THE ELECTORAL COLLEGE	DRAWBACKS OF THE ELECTORAL COLLEGE
• States retain their importance in electing the president.	• One candidate can win the popular vote and not win the electoral vote.
• Candidates must campaign and seek votes in most states rather than only heavily populated states.	• Electoral vote strength is higher per capita in smaller states.
• The practice guarantees a consensus president with broad support.	• The winner-take-all system discourages those who voted for the runner-up.
• States retain power if the election goes into the House and Senate.	• If the election goes to the House and Senate, these delegations can vote independently of their states.

THINK AS A POLITICAL SCIENTIST: *ARTICULATE A DEFENSIBLE CLAIM*

In the argument essay that you write on the AP® exam, one of the directions is to "Respond to the prompt with a defensible claim or thesis that establishes a line of reasoning." Remember, a claim is a statement about which people may disagree that can be supported by facts or evidence.

Every four years, millions of citizens participate in the democratic process of choosing the president of the United States. The founders established the process for choosing the president, and, for the most part, this process has worked as originally designed. Yet, some people still question if the way the nation chooses its executive leader truly reflects the intention of the framers.

Practice: Based on information from Topic 5.8, make a claim that addresses the prompt below. Also, list evidence from the topic that would support your claim.

Explain the degree to which the process of nominating presidential candidates and electing a president of the United States is democratic.

REFLECT ON THE ESSENTIAL QUESTION

Essential Question: *How do different processes work in a presidential election, and does the electoral college facilitate and/or impede democracy? On separate paper, complete the chart below.*

Processes That Facilitate Democratic Presidential Elections	Processes That Impede Democratic Presidential Elections

KEY TERMS AND NAMES

blanket primary	open primary
caucuses	plurality
closed primary	primary election
Electoral College	proportional system
front-loading	split ticket
general elections	Super Tuesday
incumbent	swing states
incumbent advantage phenomenon	Twenty-third Amendment (1961)
invisible primary	winner-take-all system

Congressional Elections

"We also have to be reminded they weren't part of a presidential campaign, Lincoln and Douglas were running for the Senate."
—Bob Schieffer, CBS's *Face the Nation*, 1996

Essential Question: How do different election processes work in congressional elections?

Congress has set federal elections to occur every two years, in even-numbered years, on the Tuesday after the first Monday in November. Congressional and presidential terms begin the next January. Each state has a slightly different method for congressional candidates to get their names on the ballot, but typically a number of signatures are required and some fees apply. In most states, a candidate must first win one primary election to earn the right to run as the party nominee. The candidate must follow both federal and state law. State governments have drawn congressional districts to maximize party control and, in the process, have contributed to preserving congressional seats for members for long tenures. Much has changed about congressional elections since the notable 1858 Lincoln-Douglas contest, but those debates and the focus on that Senate election shows how important they can be.

Congressional Elections

All House seats and one-third of Senate seats are up for election every two years. Federal elections that take place halfway through a president's term are called **midterm elections**. Midterm elections receive a fraction of the media attention, and usually fewer voters cast ballots. However, the 2018 midterm elections had 53 percent of eligible voters participate, representing an 11-point jump from 2014. The Council of State Governments reports that since 1972, voter turnout in midterm elections is on average 17 points lower than in presidential elections. Yet, in terms of policymaking, these campaigns are important and deserve attention.

To compete in a modern campaign for the U.S. House or Senate, a candidate must create a networked organization that resembles a small company, spend much of his or her own money, solicit hundreds of contributions, and sacrifice many hours and days. Senator Sherrod Brown (D-OH) explains that a candidate "must hire a staff and make wise use of volunteers . . . craft a cogent, clear message . . . budget carefully in spending money on mail, radio, television and printed material . . . and be able to successfully sell the product—himself—to the public and to the media." Large campaigns divide these tasks into several categories, such as management, public relations, research, fundraising, advertising, and voter mobilization.

The Advantage of Incumbency

Even more so than presidential candidates, the incumbent in congressional elections has an advantage over a challenger. With rare exception, a congressional incumbent has a stronger chance of winning than the challenger.

The incumbent's financial and electoral advantage is so daunting to challengers that it often dissuades viable candidates from ever entering the race. House incumbents tend to win reelection more than 90 percent of the time. Senators have an incumbency advantage too, but theirs is not quite as strong. Incumbents capitalize on their popularity and war chest, showering their districts with mail and email throughout the congressional term. During campaign season, they purchase commercials and load up their district with yard signs while ignoring their opponent and sometimes refusing to take part in public debates.

Incumbents have several built-in advantages. Name recognition is a powerful factor. For two or more years, congressional incumbents have appeared in the news, advocated legislation, and sent newsletters back to constituent voters. Nine out of ten voters recognize their House member's name, while fewer than six out of ten recognize that of the challenger.

Incumbents nearly always have more money than challengers because they are highly visible and often popular and they can exploit the advantages of the office. They also already have a donor network established. **Political action committees (PACs)**, formal groups formed around a similar interest, donate heavily to incumbents. PACs give $12 to an incumbent for every $1 they donate to a challenger.

Party leaders and the Congressional Campaign Committees (see Topic 5.3) realize the advantage incumbents have and invariably support the incumbent when he or she is challenged in a primary. In the general elections, House representatives receive roughly three times more money than their challengers. Challengers receive a mere 9 percent of their donations from PACs, while House incumbents collect about 39 percent of their receipts from these groups.

A substantial number of incumbents keep a small campaign staff or maintain a campaign office between elections. Officeholders can provide services to constituents, including answering questions about issues of concern to voters, such as Medicare payments and bringing more federal dollars back home.

Certainly not all incumbents win. A bad economy will decrease incumbents' chances, because in hard economic times, the voting public holds incumbents and their party responsible. Regardless of the condition of the economy, the president's party usually loses some seats in Congress during midterms, especially during the president's second term. The 2018 midterm elections illustrate these points with Democrats gaining a majority in the House by winning 41 seats. Based on results from five recent midterm elections, the president's party lost an average of 26.4 House seats and 3.6 Senate seats.

THINK AS A POLITICAL SCIENTIST: *SUPPORT THE ARGUMENT USING RELEVANT EVIDENCE*

When writing an argument essay, make a clear and direct claim. Support your claim with facts and evidence. The more evidence you can present, the stronger the argument will be.

Congressional elections take place every two years—all House members and one-third of the Senate. Members of Congress, especially in the House, have to devote a significant amount of time to campaigning and strategizing how to win the ever-pressing next election.

Practice: Use details and evidence from Topic 5.9 to support the following claim.

Because of the incumbency advantage, Congressional members should be limited to a certain number of terms.

During presidential election years, congressional candidates can often ride the popularity of their party's presidential candidate. When a Democrat presidential candidate wins by wide margins, fellow Democratic congressional candidates down the ballot typically do well also. This is called the **coattail effect**.

Districts and Primaries

Legislative elections in several states have resulted in one-party rule in the statehouse. When drawing congressional districts for the reapportionment of the U.S. House, these legislatures have gerrymandered congressional districts into one-party dominant units. (See Topic 2.3.) This situation dampens competitiveness in the general election. In 2016, only 33 House races, less than 10 percent, were decided by 10 points or less. Nearly three-quarters of all House seats were decided by 20 points or more.

These "safe" districts make House incumbents unresponsive to citizens outside their party, and they have shifted the competition to the primary election. Several candidates from the majority party will emerge for an open seat, all trying to look more partisan than their competitors, while one or two sacrificial candidates from the minority party will run a grassroots campaign. When House incumbents do not act with sufficient partisan unity, candidates will run against them, running to their ideological extreme.

Gerrymandering Has Made Most Seats Safe

In the past 25 years, the number of congressional districts considered competitive has plunged from 103 to about 25. The high number of "safe seats" has allowed more extremists to get elected.

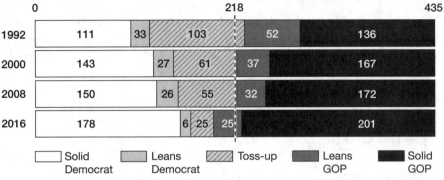

Source: FiveThirtyEight, Cook Political Report

REFLECT ON THE ESSENTIAL QUESTION

Essential Question: *How do different election processes work in congressional elections? On separate paper, complete the chart below.*

Processes Affecting Congressional Elections	Impact of Processes

---

KEY TERMS AND NAMES

coattail effect

midterm elections

political action committees (PACs)

CHAPTER 18 Review:
Learning Objectives and Key Terms

TOPIC 5.8: Explain how the different processes work in a U.S. presidential election. (PRD-2.A)

Explain how the Electoral College facilitates and/or impeded democracy. (PRD-2.B)

Processes That Impact Presidential Elections (PRD-2.A.1)		Role of Electoral College (PRD-2.B.2)
blanket primary	open primary	Electoral College
caucuses	plurality	general elections
closed primary	primary election	proportional system
front-loading	split ticket	swing states
incumbent	Super Tuesday	Twenty-third Amendment (1961)
incumbent advantage phenomenon	invisible primary	winner-take-all system

TOPIC 5.9: Explain how the different processes work in U.S. congressional elections. (PRD-2.C)

Processes that Impact Congressional Elections (PRD-2.C.1)

coattail effect	political action committees (PACs)
midterm elections	

CHAPTER 18 Checkpoint:
Elections

Topics 5.8–5.9

MULTIPLE-CHOICE QUESTIONS

1. To win the Electoral College, a presidential candidate must
   (A) Win more popular votes than any other candidate
   (B) Win the plurality of popular votes in all states
   (C) Win a majority of electoral votes
   (D) Win a plurality of electoral votes

Questions 2 and 3 refer to the table below.

CALIFORNIA PRESIDENTIAL PRIMARY ELECTION RESULTS, 2016 (TOP FIVE VOTE-GETTERS)					
Democrat	**Total Votes**	**Percent**	**Republican**	**Total Votes**	**Percent**
Hillary Clinton	2,745,302	53.1	Donald Trump	1,665,135	74.8
Bernie Sanders	2,381,722	46	John Kasich	252,544	11.3
Willie Wilson	12,014	0.2	Ted Cruz	211,576	9.5
Michael Steinberg	10,880	0.2	Ben Carson	82,259	3.7
Roque De La Fuente	8,453	0.2	Jim Gilmore	15,691	0.7
Total Democratic Votes	5,158,371	100	Total Republican Votes	2,227,205	100

***Democrats use a proportional system for allocating delegates, and Republicans use a hybrid system (winner-take-all if candidate receives more than 50% of the votes statewide).
Source: California Secretary of State

2. Which of the following statements is reflected in the data in the table above?
   (A) All the Democratic delegates would be awarded to Bernie Sanders.
   (B) More voters participated in California's Republican primary than in the state's Democratic primary.
   (C) John Kasich would receive a proportional number of delegate's votes.
   (D) Donald Trump would receive all the state's Republican delegates.

3. Based on the data in this table, which statement is accurate?

(A) Because California holds the first primary election, this outcome will have great impact on subsequent primary elections.

(B) The outcome of this state election will have no impact on which candidates receive their party nominations.

(C) The winning nominee will choose the second-place candidate as his or her vice-presidential running mate.

(D) Donald Trump earned a greater percentage of Republican delegates than Hillary Clinton earned Democratic delegates.

4. Which of the following is an accurate comparison of congressional and presidential elections?

	CONGRESSIONAL	PRESIDENTIAL
(A)	Are conducted at three-year intervals	Are conducted every four years
(B)	Have lower turnouts than presidential elections	Are decided by the Electoral College
(C)	Occurs every two years	Second-highest vote-getter in primaries becomes vice presidential candidate
(D)	Are determined by a national popular vote	Have candidates who compete for federal matching money

5. Which type of primary election provides the greatest choice for voters?

(A) Blanket primary

(B) Open primary

(C) Closed primary

(D) Caucus

6. One month before the general election, the local incumbent congressional candidate is leading in the polls by 13 points and has plenty of campaign funds in his war chest. Which advice will a campaign manager or consultant likely give this candidate?

(A) Recommend a campaign of negative television attack ads against his opponent

(B) Suggest the candidate refuse any more donations for the campaign

(C) Encourage the candidate to hone his message to his base without alienating moderate voters

(D) Recommend a series of televised debates with his chief opponent

FREE-RESPONSE QUESTIONS

Concept Application

1. "Rep[resentative]-elect Alexandria Ocasio-Cortez [D-NY] and . . . activist groups on the left aren't content with a Democratic-controlled House: They are determined to move the party to the left. 'Long story short, I need you to run for office,' Ocasio-Cortez said Saturday . . .

   'All Americans know money in politics is a huge problem, but unfortunately the way that we fix it is by demanding that our [Democratic] incumbents give it up or by running fierce campaigns ourselves,' . . .

   The incoming congresswoman's chief of staff, Saikat Chakrabarti, a co-founder of Justice Democrats, was blunter.

   'We need new leaders, period,' he said on the call. 'We gotta primary folks.'"

   —Reporter Alex Thompson, *Politico*, 2018

   After reading the scenario, respond to A, B, and C below:

   (A) Describe the electoral process in the passage above.

   (B) Explain how the process described in part A will impact incumbency advantage.

   (C) In the context of the scenario, explain what may result from the approach Chakrabarti suggests.

Quantitative Analysis

PAC Expenditure Totals According to Political Party in the 2014 Congressional General Election

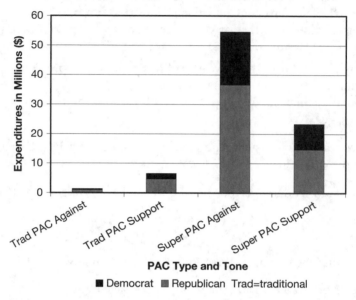

Source: Federal Election Commission

2. Use the information in the graphic above to respond to the tasks below.

   (A) Identify the most common category of PAC expenditures.

   (B) Describe a difference between PAC spending that is in support of a candidate and PAC spending that is against a candidate.

   (C) Draw a conclusion about the cause of that difference.

   (D) Explain how the information in the chart may influence the public's view of Congress.

CHAPTER 19

Campaigns

Topics 5.10–5.11

Topic 5.10 Modern Campaigns

PRD-2.D: Explain how campaign organizations and strategies affect the election process.

Topic 5.11 Campaign Finance

PRD-2.E: Explain how the organization, finance, and strategies of national political campaigns affect the election process.

Source: Getty Images

Senator Bernie Sanders (I-VT) speaks at a UNC-Chapel Hill campaign rally for the 2020 Democratic presidential nomination. Unlike other candidates, Senator Sanders relied on small donations for his campaign because he believes that corporate money plays too large a role in electing candidates.

5.10

Modern Campaigns

"Television has replaced the political party."
—Arthur Schlesinger, *Time* Magazine, 1988

Essential Question: How do campaign organizations and strategies affect the election process?

When citizens decide to run for political office, whether for county constable or president of the United States, they must consider many factors and push through a challenging path. This path includes a public examination of them, their past, their spouse, their religion, their resume, and their ideology. Candidates for office must create and manage a campaign organization of staff and volunteers to connect with the voters. They spend months traveling their districts and states campaigning. They also employ a strategy that targets certain voters, shapes their ad campaign, defines their opponent, and affects the election process. A campaign of any size requires hiring a political consultant or more staff. The average U.S. House race spends more than $1 million each cycle, and competitive Senate races in a large state can require candidates to raise and spend upwards of $30 million. Acquiring such large sums necessitates events such as fancy and expensive fundraising dinners to build strong relationships with interest groups.

Campaign Organization

Competitive candidates must work with and, at times against, their own party leaders and organizations. Outside interest groups and PACs can assist or derail a candidate's chances to win the election. The effort to bring in money is constant and necessary to persuade voters with their message through advertising. Most candidates will assemble a team of professionals that coordinate their events, talk to the press, develop strategy, conduct voter outreach, and design television and web ads.

Candidate's Committee

In most campaigns, from the presidential down to the county-level, a candidate will form a committee and file for candidacy with the appropriate governmental offices. In a presidential race, a leadership team that has experience in presidential politics will likely form around each candidate. In more local elections, the committee is made up of friends and family. The officially listed treasurer of the campaign has the legal responsibility to report donations, expenses, income, and receipts to the Federal Election Commission (FEC) or state authority.

Party Organizations

Alongside any candidates wearing a party label is the party itself. National, state, and local party organizations will get involved in electioneering, spend money, and mobilize members. Usually, though, when it sees a competitive primary with two or more strong candidates, the party stays out. But sometimes the party sees who the favorite is and endorses that person. Having the support of a party organization is a game changer in political campaigns, because with these relationships come a sharing of information, member email lists, donor connections, and ad costs.

More often than not, party organizations put resources toward re-electing an incumbent, because that is usually a safe bet. However, the party may choose not to endorse and instead allow voters to make that decision. The party leadership may not always be in agreement with the candidate about how to handle or manage the campaign, and intraparty friction can occur. Official or *ad hoc* party organizations include the local Republican Club or the state Democratic Party Committee.

Congress has four committees that primarily work to elect their members to the House and Senate. (See Topic 5.3 for more on Congressional Campaign Committees.) One of those committees is the Democratic Congressional Campaign Committee (DCCC), the Democrats' national party headquarters. Democratic House members lead this committee, but talented and hard-working staffers do the real work in campaigning and coordinating with their chosen candidates. They are the ones who will have their sleeves rolled up, circled around a table, highlighting the marginal or toss-up districts where they will spend on advertising, and the safe districts where they will not spend.

In 2017, the DCCC created a program that trained more than 14,000 new Democratic activists in less than two years. It then deployed DCCC organizers to 38 of the most vulnerable Republican-held House districts. In 2016, the DCCC provided financial backing to 28 House candidates. In 2018, that number rose to 65. As Luke Mullens has reported, the DCCC can play favorites and with intensity. "Despite the DCCC's lip service to grassroots outreach," says Mullens, "the party bosses back in Washington still dictate who gets on the ballot."

Outside Groups

Both longstanding and sometimes temporary groups engage in electioneering and can have a strong effect on the election process. The most obvious examples are political action committees (PACs), such as the National Rifle Association (NRA). Standing interest groups run ads, donate to candidates, hold rallies, and impact the vote. (See Topic 5.11 for more on PACs.) Also, a 527 organization is a tax-exempt group that can raise unlimited funds from individuals, corporations, and labor unions for the purpose of influencing policy or elections.

Fundraising

Since the government has tracked campaign spending, cash that has flowed through federal elections has skyrocketed. Few candidates finance their own campaigns, while most rely on the party organization and thousands of individual donors for contributions. The size of a candidate's **war chest**, or campaign fund, can play a role in determining the outcome of the election. The campaign for financial resources begins long before the campaign for votes. Fundraising allows candidates to test their chances. Those who can gather funds begin to prove a level of support that makes them viable. In more competitive districts with strong media markets, that number will rise. To raise the required cash over a two-year period, candidates dedicate about one-fourth of their campaign schedule to making personal phone calls to wealthy donors and holding high-dollar formal fundraisers. Campaigns bring in headline speakers, sometimes a former president or other political celebrity, and charge the legal maximum for entrance and a seat near the main attraction.

Senate candidates, because they are running statewide and may attract wealthier opponents, begin raising money much earlier than House candidates and devote more time to soliciting cash. Contributions by PACs to congressional candidates, who have a considerably smaller budget than presidential candidates, are essential to successful campaigns. Often, PACs will donate to an incumbent due to their likelihood of winning the election.

The internet became a campaign and fundraising tool in the 1990s. By 2002, 57 percent of all House candidates and virtually every Senate candidate used the web or email to gather funds. This type of solicitation is free, compared with an average of $3 to $4 for every direct mail request.

By the Numbers

Typical House Candidate Campaign Budget

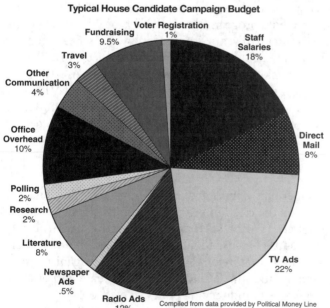

Source: Paul S. Herrnson, Congressional Elections, 2008

What do the numbers show? What are the chief expenses in a House campaign? What portion of a candidate's expenditures are for marketing/showcasing the candidate? What percent goes to support staff or some type of research?

Compiled from data provided by Political Money Line (www.politicalmoneyline.com/), 2016

Campaign Strategies

How candidates develop their strategies depends on the geographic location in which they are running, their experience and background, and what issues they want to put front and center in their campaign. They usually develop a slogan, a logo, a recognizable font and color for their signs and bumper stickers, and an advertising campaign. They target particular voting blocs to build a base of support and mobilize members of their coalition to get to the voting booths.

Professional Consultants

Winning elections requires the expertise of professional consultants. These may include a campaign manager, a communications or public relations expert, a fundraiser, an advertising agent, a field organizer, a pollster, and a social media consultant. The campaign profession has blossomed as a consulting class has emerged. Staffers on Capitol Hill, political science majors, and those who have worked for partisan and nonprofit endeavors also overlap with political campaigns. Entire firms and partisan-based training organizations prepare energetic civic-minded citizens to enter this field that elects officials to implement desired policy.

One such professional is strategist Corry Bliss. In 2016, at age 35, Bliss was entrusted to run the Republicans' Congressional Leadership Fund PAC and oversee a $100 million effort to assure Republicans get elected to the House and Senate. In the top GOP circles, Bliss is viewed as one of the party's most influential political operatives. Bliss entered campaign work and had success in Virginia elections. Now the Leadership Fund frequently sends him from DC to a faltering campaign as a fixer.

Showcasing the Candidate

Most voters, like most shoppers, make their decision based on limited information with only a small amount of consideration. For this reason, electronic and social media, television, and focus groups are essential to winning an election. A candidate's message often centers on common themes of decency, loyalty, and hard work.

Polling results can help candidates frame their message. Polling helps determine which words or phrases to use in speeches and advertising. Campaigns occasionally use tracking polls (see Topic 4.5) to gain feedback after changing campaign strategy. They may also hold focus groups. Incumbents also rely on constituent communication over their term. Candidates also keep an eye on internet blogs, listen to radio call-in shows, and talk with party leaders and political activists to find out what the public wants. Campaigns set up registration tables at county fairs and on college campuses. They gather addresses from voter registration lists and mail out promotional pieces that highlight the candidate's accomplishments and often include photos of the candidate alongside spouse and family. Campaigns also conduct robocalls, automated mass phone calls, to promote themselves or to denounce an opponent.

A typical campaign is divided into three segments: the biography, the issues, and the attack. Successful candidates have a unique story to tell. Campaign literature and television ads show candidates in previous public service, on playgrounds with children, on a front porch with family, or in church. These images attract a wide variety of voters. After telling the biography, a debate over the issues begins as voters shop for their candidate. Consultants and professionals believe issues-oriented campaigns motivate large numbers of people to come out and vote.

Defining the Opponent Candidates competing for independent voters find it necessary to draw sharp contrasts between themselves and their opponents. An attack phase begins later in the race, often motivated by desperation. Underdogs sometimes resort to cheap shots and work hard to expose inconsistencies in their opponent's voting records. Campaigns do opposition research to reveal their opponent's missteps or any unpopular positions taken in the past. Aides and staffers comb over the *Congressional Record*, old interview transcripts, and newspaper articles to search for damaging quotes. They also analyze an opponent's donor list in order to spotlight special-interest donations or out-of-state money.

Debates As the election nears, candidates participate in formal public debates, highly structured events with strict rules governing response time and conduct. These events are risky because candidates can suffer from gaffes (verbal slips) or from poor performances. Incumbents and front-runners typically avoid debates because they have everything to lose and little to gain. Appearing on a stage with a lesser-known competitor usually helps the underdog. For races with large fields, the organizations sponsoring the debates typically determine which candidates get to participate. Their decisions are sometimes based on where candidates stand in the polls.

Television Appearances The candidate's campaign team also strategizes about appearances on television, either in news coverage or in a commercial. Veteran Democratic speechwriter and campaign consultant Bob Shrum laments, "Things are measured by when a campaign will go on television, or if they can and to what degree they can saturate the air waves."

Candidates rely on two forms of TV placement: the news story and the commercial. A news story is typically a short news segment showing the candidate in action—touring a factory, speaking to a civic club, visiting a classroom, or appearing at a political rally. Candidates send out press releases announcing their events, usually scheduled early enough in the day to make the evening news. This is free media coverage because, unlike expensive television commercials, the campaign does not have to pay for appearing in the news. The most expensive part of nearly any campaign is television advertising. The typical modern campaign commercial includes great emphasis on imagery, action-oriented themes, emotional messages, negative characterizations of the opponent, and quick production turnaround.

NUMBER OF TELEVISION COMMERCIALS BY CANDIDATE 2016 PRESIDENTIAL ELECTION		
Candidate	Ads Sponsored by Candidate's Campaign	Ads Sponsored by Pro-candidate Groups
Donald Trump	120,447	44,153
Hillary Clinton	404,704	112,896

A candidate's appearance on camera can influence voters more deeply than words. For instance, in the first televised debate in 1960, John F. Kennedy's youthful, handsome, and charming demeanor was a stark contrast to Richard M. Nixon's frail appearance after a recent hospital stay for an infection. Many who watched the first debate considered Kennedy the "winner" of the debate, while those who listened to the debate on the radio clearly thought Nixon sounded much better. Kennedy won the election.

Social Media

Just as Kennedy became the first "television president" because he used the medium so well, Barack Obama is often called the first "social media" president. His campaign, especially for reelection in 2012, spent years on research and development to create complex programs that could link data available through social media and the party's own paper records in a precise and highly efficient voter outreach program. Digital ad costs were also much lower than those of television ads. For about $14.5 million, Obama's campaign bought YouTube advertising that would have cost $47 million on television.

Many supporters gave the Obama campaign permission to access their connections on social media, which were then cross-checked in the campaign's vast data repository. Rather than asking supporters to share an Obama ad with all their connections, the campaign told supporters to do so only in key states or with a certain demographic. Since people are much more likely to trust the outreach of a friend than the outreach of a political volunteer, this strategy won many votes for Obama. Since then, parties try to develop the most efficient social media strategies to gather data for targeted outreach.

Despite the positive aspects of connectedness and free or low-cost advertisement on social media, there is a negative side. Facebook and Twitter, in particular, ran thousands of "dark ads" during the 2016 election. **Dark ads** are anonymously placed status updates, photos, videos, or links that appear only in the target audience's social media news feeds but not in the general feeds. They are created to match the personality types of their audience to the message and to manipulate people's emotions—especially anger or fear—in order to sway their votes. Facebook and Twitter have both promised to provide more transparency to voters regarding this strategy.

Connecting to voters via social media has become essential in campaigning. For a fee, Facebook offers consultants to political groups to help reach voters, much as they offer consulting connections to a corporation to sell cereal or dog food. As Trump's key digital campaign manager, Brad Parscale, explained on

60 Minutes, the Trump team took Facebook's offer of help; the Clinton team did not.

The Facebook platform and technology allow campaigns to micro target—identify by particular traits and criteria—independent voters who could be persuaded and learn what might persuade them. Perhaps an intense, issues-oriented ad would sway their opinions, or maybe the color of a button on a website might enhance the chances for a donation. Marketers use psychographics—profiles of a person's hobbies, interests, and values—to create image-based ads that would appeal to certain personalities. Different personality types will see different ads.

THINK AS A POLITICAL SCIENTIST: *USE REASONING TO ANALYZE EVIDENCE AND JUSTIFY A CLAIM*

A growing number of people use social media platforms. Political campaigns have used this trend as an opportunity to connect with more potential voters in inventive ways. The use of technology and social media to reach voters is likely to continue in even more creative ways over time. Political scientists look at the effect that social media have on voter behavior.

Practice: Study the information in the graphs. Read the question below, and then use information from the graphs to develop a claim in response to the question. Then, choose three pieces of evidence from the graphs and/or from Topic 5.10 to support your claim.

To what extent has the increase in the use of social media strategies had an impact among all demographic groups recently?

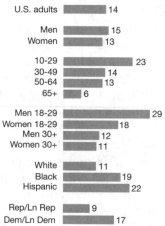

Roughly three-in-ten younger men changed their views on an issue because of socia media

% of U.S. adults who say they changed their views on a political or social issue because of something they saw on social media in the past year

U.S. adults	14
Men	15
Women	13
10-29	23
30-49	14
50-64	13
65+	6
Men 18-29	29
Women 18-29	18
Men 30+	12
Women 30+	11
White	11
Black	19
Hispanic	22
Rep/Ln Rep	9
Dem/Ln Dem	17

The 2016 Presidential Campaign

The unusual 2016 presidential campaign is perhaps the worst example to study for understanding norms and trends in voting, campaigns, and elections. More than 20 candidates brought an intense intraparty contest in both major parties, set a new record for money spent, sparked attempts to manipulate election rules to stop an unconventional candidate, and took the candidates down in the mud like no other public campaign in memory.

The General Election Campaign

As the post-convention campaign began, a late August poll showed perhaps the widest gap between the candidates, Democrat Hillary Clinton with 45 percent to Republican Donald Trump's 33 percent. That gap narrowed. The candidates' respective poll averages from September through Election Day had Clinton outpolling Trump by only 45.5 percent to 42.2 percent.

An Ugly Campaign

What followed was what many termed "a race to the bottom." Trump continued his unconventional and, to many, unstatesmanlike approach to campaigning. He won support among many middle-class workers who responded well to his America First ideology and the concern he expressed for average working persons who may have lost their jobs as industry steadily declined.

By early October, Clinton's campaign had spent $145 million on TV commercials to Trump's $32 million. Trump, however, received an estimated $200 million in free media. Top cable news reporters stood by at his rallies awaiting his grand entrance and anticipating some shocking behavior or pronouncement that would boost ratings. Meanwhile, his "Make America Great Again" message resonated with those who felt shut out by traditional politicians.

Meanwhile Clinton took a jab at some of Trump's supporters, referring to them as "a basket of deplorables." Trump strategists were able to turn the comment into another liberal elite's uptown view of Middle America.

An October surprise came with the release of a decade-old *Access Hollywood* video of Trump on a hot mic bragging about how he could have his way with women, kissing and grabbing them. When this news broke, he apologized before quickly pointing to Bill Clinton's dalliances, affairs, and aggressions toward women, suggesting that Hillary enabled this behavior. He invited Bill Clinton's past accusers to the next televised debate to turn the spotlight on the former president's behavior. The campaign had sunk to a new low.

The Vote

When citizen voters cast their popular votes on Tuesday, November 8, and such states as North Carolina, Florida, and Ohio went for Trump, the Clinton team became very nervous. Into the late evening and early morning, Trump won Pennsylvania, Wisconsin, and by the closest of margins, Michigan. In the final tally, Trump won 306 electoral votes to Clinton's 232. However, Clinton's large-margin successes in states like New York and California took her over the top in the national popular vote. Once states counted provisional and absentee ballots, Clinton had 3 million more votes than Trump. She received 48 percent of the national total, he received 46, and the minor party candidates split the remainder. But with the winner-take-all system and the razor-thin victories in the Rust Belt (parts of the Northeast and Midwest where industry is in decline), Trump took the Electoral College. In his 2:45 a.m. victory speech, the president-elect said in a partially scripted and partly ad-libbed address, "Now it's time for America to bind the wounds of division; have to get together. To all Republicans and Democrats and independents across this nation, I say it is time for us to come together as one united people."

REFLECT ON THE ESSENTIAL QUESTION

Essential Question: *How do campaign organizations and strategies affect the election process? On separate paper, complete the chart below.*

Organizations and Strategies That Affect the Election Process	Influence of Organizations and Strategies

KEY TERMS AND NAMES

dark ads

war chest

Campaign Finance

"There are two things that are important in politics. The first is money and I can't remember what the second one is."

—attributed to Senator Mark Hanna, on presidential campaigns, 1896

Essential Question: How does the organization, finance, and strategies of national political campaigns affect the election process?

Winning an election requires a political campaign to first make voters aware of a candidate and then to persuade the same voters that he or she is the best choice. That takes money. Mark Hanna, politico and campaign manager for President William McKinley certainly knew this as well, whether he publicly made the above statement or not. Candidates today require everything from bumper stickers and yard signs to a full-time staff and televised commercials.

Campaign Finance

The quote from Mark Hanna illustrates that politicians realize money is at the heart of politics. The entanglement of money and politics reached new levels when people with unscrupulous business practices became fixtures in the political process in the late 19th century in an effort to influence and reduce the federal government's regulation of commerce. The bulk of today's relevant campaign finance regulations, however, came about much later—in the early 1970s—and other laws and Supreme Court decisions followed.

Federal Legislation on Campaign Finance

In 1971, Congress passed the **Federal Election Campaign Act (FECA)**, which tightened reporting requirements and limited candidates' expenditures. In spite of this law, spending in the 1972 presidential race between Richard Nixon and George McGovern reached $91 million. The public soon realized how much money was going through the campaign process and how donors had subverted the groundbreaking yet incomplete 1971 act. Congress responded with the 1974 amendment to the FECA.

The Federal Election Commission

The 1974 law prevented individual donors from giving more than $1,000 to any federal candidate and prevented political action committees from donating more than $5,000 in each election (primaries and general elections are each considered "elections"). It capped the total a candidate could donate to his or her campaign and set a maximum on how much the campaign could spend. The law created the **Federal Election Commission (FEC)** to monitor and enforce the regulations. It also created a legal definition for political action committees (PAC) to make donations to campaigns, declaring that they must have at least 50 members, donate to at least five candidates, and register with the FEC at least six months in advance of the election.

The FEC has structural traits to help it carry out several responsibilities. The president appoints the FEC's board of commissioners to oversee election law, and the Senate approves them. This commission always has an equal number of Democrats and Republicans. The FEC requires candidates to register, or file for candidacy, and to report campaign donations and expenses on a quarterly basis. A candidate's entire balance sheet is available to the government and the public. The site www.fec.gov has a database that allows anyone to see which individuals or PACs contributed to the candidates and in what amounts.

KEY PROVISIONS OF THE 1974 FEDERAL ELECTION CAMPAIGN ACT

- Limited an individual's contributions to $1,000 per election
- Limited a candidate's own contribution to $50,000 per election
- Defined and regulated donations of political action committees (PACs)
- Created a voluntary public fund to assist viable presidential candidates

---

One of the first challenges to FEC law came with the case of *Buckley v. Valeo*. In January 1975, a group of conservatives and liberals joined New York Senator James Buckley to overturn the Federal Election Campaign Act (FECA) in the courts. They argued that the early 1970s law unconstitutionally limited free speech. The Court upheld the law's $1,000 limit on individual donations and the $5,000 limit on political action committee (PAC) donations, claiming such limits did not violate free speech guarantees. However, the Court also ruled that Congress cannot limit a candidate's donation to his or her own campaign nor can it place a maximum on the overall receipts or expenditures for a federal campaign. With the *Buckley* ruling, Congress and the Court ultimately reached consensus that unlimited donations make for unfair elections.

Even after the ruling in *Buckley*, however, television advertising and money became more important in campaigns as interest groups, politicians, and lawyers found loopholes in the law. The FECA covered only money going directly to and from a candidate's treasury. If a non-candidate wanted to spend money to influence an election—for example, to buy a radio ad for or against a candidate—there were no limits. **Hard money**, a donation given directly to a candidate, could be traced and regulated. But **soft money**, a donation to a party or interest group, was not tracked. Therefore, the party could flood a congressional district with television ads that paint the opponent in a bad light, causing large, ultimately untraceable spending on electioneering at the end of a campaign. Unsurprisingly, soft money spending escalated.

Bipartisan Campaign Reform Act

This situation brought greater attention to soft money's influence on elections and highlighted how much that influence was able to subvert the spirit of the 1970s reforms. Senators John McCain (R-AZ) and Russ Feingold (D-WI) had pushed for greater campaign finance regulations since the mid-1990s. After some modification, the **Bipartisan Campaign Reform Act (BCRA)** of 2002, also known as the McCain-Feingold Act, finally passed the House with a 240–189 vote and the Senate with 60–40 vote, and President Bush signed it. The act banned soft money contributions to the national parties, increased the limits on hard money donations to $2,000 from individuals (with future adjustments for inflation), $5,000 from PACs, and $25,000 from the national parties per election cycle. The law also placed an aggregate limit on how much an individual could donate to multiple candidates in a two-year cycle. Since then, the limit has been raised to $2,700 per individual.

The BCRA prohibited PACs from paying for electioneering communications on radio or TV using campaign treasury money within 60 days of the general election and 30 days of a primary. To clear up who or what organization is behind a broadcasted advertisement, the McCain-Feingold law also requires candidates to explicitly state, "I'm [candidate's name] and I approve this message." That statement must last at least four seconds.

Though the law was dubbed bipartisan, the vote in Congress and the reaction to the law has been somewhat partisan, with more Democratic support than Republican. It was challenged immediately by then-Senate Majority Whip, Mitch McConnell (R-KY), in the courts and largely upheld. The 2010 case of *Citizens United v. Federal Election Commission (FEC)*, however, overturned key parts of the law.

MUST-KNOW SUPREME COURT CASES: *CITIZENS UNITED V. FEC* (2010)

The Constitutional Questions Before the Court: Does the 2002 Bipartisan Campaign Reform Act's (McCain-Feingold Act) donation disclosure requirement violate the First Amendment's free speech clause, and is a negative political documentary that never communicates an expressed plea to vote for or against a candidate subject to the BCRA?

Decision: No and Yes for Citizens United, 5:4

Before *Citizens United*: *Buckley v. Valeo* (1976) upheld the limits on campaign contributions from individuals ($1,000) and PACs ($5,000) but ruled that candidates could contribute unlimited funds from their own money to their campaigns. It also ruled that there was no limit on total revenue or expenditures for campaigns.

Facts: The BCRA prevented corporations or nonprofit agencies from engaging in "electioneering communications," primarily TV and radio campaign ads, 60 days before the general election. In 2008, the conservative group Citizens United produced *Hillary: The Movie*, a critique meant to derail Hillary Clinton's chance for the presidency. The law prevented the film's airing, regarding it as "electioneering communications," but the group appealed to the Supreme Court. The opportunity to broadcast the movie had passed by the time the Court issued its ruling, which has had a dramatic impact on campaign financing.

Reasoning: The Court ruled that part of the BCRA violated the First Amendment's free speech clause and that corporations, labor unions, and other organizations could use funds from their treasuries to endorse or denounce a candidate at any time, provided ads are not coordinated with any candidate. The majority opinion reasoned that the limitations amounted to censorship.

The Court reasoned further that just because a PAC or any entity entitled to free speech supports a candidate via advertising, that candidate does not necessarily owe anything to that PAC. There's no assumption that the donation is buying a favor from the candidate, which in any event is already criminal and punishable by statute.

The Court's Majority Opinion by Mr. Justice Anthony Kennedy, joined by Chief Justice John Roberts and Justices Antonin Scalia, Samuel Alito, and Clarence Thomas: The law before us . . . makes it a felony for all corporations—including nonprofit advocacy corporations—either to expressly advocate the election or defeat of candidates or to broadcast electioneering communications within 30 days of a primary election and 60 days of a general election. . . . These prohibitions are classic examples of censorship. Were the Court to uphold these restrictions, the Government could repress speech by silencing certain voices at any of the various points in the speech process. . . . If [this part of the law] applied to individuals, no one would believe that it is merely a time, place, or manner restriction on speech. Its purpose and effect are to silence entities whose voices the Government deems to be suspect.

Speech is an essential mechanism of democracy, for it is the means to hold officials accountable to the people. . . . The right of citizens to inquire, to hear, to speak, and to use information to reach consensus is a precondition to enlightened self-government and a necessary means to protect it. . . .

For these reasons, political speech must prevail against laws that would suppress it, whether by design or inadvertence. . . .

We find no basis for the proposition that, in the context of political speech, the Government may impose restrictions on certain disfavored speakers. Both history and logic lead us to this conclusion.

Since *Citizens United*: In 2014, in *McCutcheon v. FEC*, the Supreme Court ruled that the limit on how much a donor can contribute over a two-year election cycle was unconstitutional. To stay within that limit, the plurality of the Court argued, donors who could afford to give the maximum amount to a number of candidates would have to rule out some candidates and causes they might also wish to support. In that way, the Court ruled, their freedom of expression was unconstitutionally limited.

Political Science Disciplinary Practices: Analyze and Interpret Supreme Court Decisions

As you analyze the ruling in *Citizens United v. FEC* (or any other court case or law), compare it to other related cases or laws. Identify specific categories for comparison. If you are comparing Supreme Court cases, for example, the categories for comparison might include the constitutional principle at stake, the facts of the case, the decision, the makeup of the court, the historic time of the decision, and dissenting opinions, among others. Creating these specific and relevant categories will help you sharpen the comparisons you make.

Apply: Complete the activities below.

1. Describe the facts of the *Citizens United v. FEC* case and the congressional regulation at issue.

2. Describe the claim the group Citizens United made about BCRA.

3. Explain how the Court's reasoning in *Citizens United* led to its ruling.

Impact of Citizens United

Debates over free speech and competitive and fair elections have increased since *Citizens United*. Free speech advocates, libertarians, and many Republicans view most campaign finance regulations as infringements on their freedoms, so they hailed the ruling. Others agreed with President Obama when he criticized the ruling at his 2010 State of the Union address as a decision that would "open the floodgates to special interests."

In addition to allowing ads by outside or soft money groups immediately before an election, the Court's ruling also allowed for unlimited contributions to these groups from individual citizens and other organizations. This **dark money** has penetrated political campaigning, causing a lack of transparency about where the money originates. Even though political ads must express who is behind them, determining exactly where the money ultimately comes from is hard to do.

"*Citizens United* changed the culture at the same time that it changed the law," according to Zephyr Teachout, Fordham University law professor and author of *Corruption in America*. "Before *Citizens United*, corporate or individual money could be spent with a good enough lawyer. But after *Citizens United v. FEC*, unlimited corporate money spent with intent to influence was named, by the U.S. Supreme Court, indispensable to the American political conversation."

The ruling also concentrates who dominates the political discussion. Five years after the ruling, the Brennan Center at New York University found that of the $1 billion spent, about 60 percent of the donations to PACs came from 195 people or couples. More recently, an analysis by OpenSecrets.org found that during the 2016 election cycle, the top 20 individual donors gave more than $500 million to PACs. The 20 largest organizational donors also gave a total of more than $500 million to PACs. And more than $1 billion came from the top 40 donors. About one-fifth of political donations spent in all federal elections in 2016 came from dark money sources.

In the 2016 election cycle, special interests spent at least $183.5 million in dark money, up from $5.2 million in 2006. Of that, liberal special interests spent at least $41.3 million, or 22.5 percent; conservatives spent most of the remaining amount.

Though Democrats are more prone to use *Citizens United* as a rallying cry against corporate special interests, Democrats have also benefitted from the ruling. As Sarah Kleiner of the Center for Public Integrity pointed out, ". . . many Democrats have . . . taken full advantage of the fundraising freedoms *Citizens United* has granted them." Candidate Hillary Clinton, especially, "benefited from a small army of super PACs and millions of dollars in secret political money." More specifically, in 2016 the Clinton presidential campaign received 18 percent of its contributions, about $220 million, from such sources, whereas Trump received 12 percent of his overall contributions, or roughly $80 million, from PACs.

THINK AS A POLITICAL SCIENTIST: *EXPLAIN HOW A REQUIRED SUPREME COURT CASE RELATES TO A FOUNDATIONAL DOCUMENT*

The required Supreme Court case of *Citizens United v. FEC* (2010) lifted limits on corporate funding in political broadcasts established in the Bipartisan Campaign Reform Act (BCRA) of 2002. The Court ruled that the limits violated the First Amendment's right to free speech. A previous case, *Buckley v. Valeo* (1976), upheld the Federal Election Campaign Act (FECA) that placed limits on campaign contributions from PACs. The foundation for both cases and the government's concern over the influence of "factions" can be traced back to *Federalist No. 10.*

Practice: Read the excerpt from James Madison's *Federalist No. 10,* and explain how it could be used as justification for the concerns about PACs and campaign finance.

". . . as each representative will be chosen by a greater number of citizens in the large than in the small republic, it will be more difficult for unworthy candidates to practice with success the vicious arts by which elections are too often carried; and the suffrages of the people being more free, will be more likely to center in men who possess the most attractive merit and the most diffusive and established characters.

. . .

Hence, it clearly appears, that the same advantage which a republic has over a democracy, in controlling the effects of faction, is enjoyed by a large over a small republic,—is enjoyed by the Union over the States composing it. Does the advantage consist in the substitution of representatives whose enlightened views and virtuous sentiments render them superior to local prejudices and schemes of injustice? It will not be denied that the representation of the Union will be most likely to possess these requisite endowments. Does it consist in the greater security afforded by a greater variety of parties, against the event of any one party being able to outnumber and oppress the rest? In an equal degree does the increased variety of parties comprised within the Union, increase this security. Does it, in fine, consist in the greater obstacles opposed to the concert and accomplishment of the secret wishes of an unjust and interested majority? Here, again, the extent of the Union gives it the most palpable advantage."

Types of PACs

Campaign finance laws define several different types of political action committees, distinguished by how they are formed, how they are funded, and how they can disperse their funds. Some also have different limits on the donation amount from individuals per year or election.

Connected PACs Corporations, labor unions, and trade organizations are not allowed to use money from their treasuries to influence elections. However, they are allowed to form **connected PACs**—political action committees funded separately from the organization's treasury through donations from members—and make limited campaign contributions in that way. Connected PACs are also known as Separate Segregated Funds (SSF) because of the way the money is separated from the sponsoring organizations' treasuries. They cannot solicit donations from anyone who is not a member of the organization.

Nonconnected PACs These political action committees have no sponsoring organization and often form around a single issue. They can solicit funds from anyone in the general public, and they can make direct donations to candidates up to limits set by law. Like the connected PACs, nonconnected PACs must register with the FEC and disclose their donors.

Leadership PACs are a type of nonconnected PAC. They can be started by any current or former elected official and can raise money from the general public. Though the money cannot be used to fund the officials' own campaigns, funds in a leadership PAC can be used to cover travel and other expenses for other candidates.

Super PACs These are the newest kind of political action committee, whose creation resulted from the Supreme Court ruling in *Citizens United v. FEC* and the U.S. District Court ruling in *Speechnow v. FEC*, both cases decided in 2010. The *Citizens United* ruling opened the door for unlimited donations to and spending by large PACs, as long as the don't formally coordinate or communicate with the candidate's campaign. The *Speechnow* ruling determined that those contributions to Super PACs should have no limit placed on them.

TYPE	FORMED BY	REQUIREMENTS	DONATION LIMITS	EXAMPLE(S)
Connected PAC (SSF—Separate Segregated Funds)	Corporations, labor unions, trade groups	Can collect contributions only from their members; can donate directly to candidates	Strict	Coca-Cola Company Nonpartisan Committee for Good Government KochPAC
Nonconnected PAC	No sponsoring (connected) organization	Can collect from general public; can donate directly to candidates	Strict	National Rifle Association Emily's List

(continued)

TYPE	FORMED BY	REQUIREMENTS	DONATION LIMITS	EXAMPLE(S)
Leadership PAC (type of nonconnected)	Current or former elected official	Can collect from general public; can donate directly to candidates	Strict	Leadership Fund (Mitch McConnell)
Super PAC (independent expenditure-only committee)	Anyone	Can collect from anyone; cannot coordinate with candidates	No limits	Vote Latino Super PAC Cryptocurrency Alliance Super PAC

Four years after *Citizens United*, the court addressed campaign finance again in *McCutcheon v. FEC* (2014). McCutcheon, a generous donor to candidates across the nation, questioned multiple points of law, especially the FEC's aggregate limit of donations. While upholding the maximum contributions for individual candidates or committees, the ruling in *McCutcheon* removed the limit imposed by BCRA on how much an individual could donate to multiple candidates in a two-year cycle. This change greatly increased the popularity of the joint fundraising committee (JFC)—a coordinated fundraising effort of a number of candidates and committees. Rich donors can now write just one large check (more than $1 million depending on how many candidates and committees are in the JFC). The contributions are then shared among the members of the JFC according to their own agreement.

These changes affected political parties in several ways. First, state party committees are often members of JFCs, so they received a share of the contributions. Once the money was in their coffers, there was no law against returning a sizable amount of it to the national committees. Through this process, the political parties worked around their limits on hard money and once again had more control of campaign donations and thereby influence on candidate choice and election results. Second, the unofficial structure of the party has changed from a top-down vertical organization to more of a horizontal network. Although the joint fundraising committees and Super PACs are not officially part of the party, they are key players in campaigns, so the political party has become part of a web of actors, dependent on elements outside of the party for funds.

Essential Question: *How does the organization, finance, and strategies of national political campaigns affect the election process?* On separate paper, complete the chart below.

Factors in Campaign Finance	Influence of Factors

KEY TERMS AND NAMES

Bipartisan Campaign Reform Act (2002)
Citizens United v. Federal Election Commission (2010)
connected PACs
dark money

Federal Election Campaign Act (1971)
Federal Election Commission (FEC)
hard money
soft money
Super PACs

CHAPTER 19 Review:
Learning Objectives and Key Terms

TOPIC 5.10: Explain how campaign organizations and strategies affect the election process. (PRD-2.D)

Benefits and Problems with Campaigns (PRD-2.D.1)

dark ads   war chest

TOPIC 5.11: Explain how the organization, finance, and strategies of national political campaigns affect the election process. (PRD-2.E)

Government Limits on Campaign Finance (PRD-2.E.1)	Influence of PACs (PRD-2.E.2 & 3)
Bipartisan Campaign Reform Act (2002)	connected PACs
Citizens United v. Federal Election Commission (2010)	hard money
dark money	soft money
Federal Election Campaign Act (1971)	Super PACs
Federal Election Commission (FEC)	

CHAPTER 19 Checkpoint:
Campaigns

Topics 5.10–5.11

MULTIPLE-CHOICE QUESTIONS

1. Which agency monitors campaign spending and provides that information to the public?

   (A) Federal Election Commission

   (B) Internal Revenue Service

   (C) Federal Bureau of Investigation

   (D) Office of Management and Budget

Questions 2 and 3 refer to the passage below.

[Candidate Mitt] Romney arrived in Denver on Monday night, after one final mock debate. In Denver he held a rally at which he received the endorsement of John Elway, the celebrated former quarterback of the Denver Broncos. His campaign was having trouble calibrating expectations. . . . The day before the Denver debate, Romney got another confidence booster when he got a call from George W. Bush. Don't worry, Bush told him. You'll do just fine. . . .
On the morning of the debate, Obama and his advisers met for a final critique session before flying off to Denver. His advisers knew they were sending him into . . . [this debate] unfocused and with an uncertain strategy.

—Dan Balz, author, *Collision 2012: Obama v. Romney*, 2012

2. With which of the following statements would the author most likely agree?

   (A) Endorsements are what help candidates in a debate.

   (B) As long as a former president is on your side, you will win.

   (C) Romney had more confidence and focus entering the debate than Obama.

   (D) A candidate's debate performance is the key factor in winning a presidential election.

3. Which of the following statements is most accurate about debates, the media, and elections?
   (A) For voters with a party affiliation, the debates are important in voter choice.
   (B) Debates are not watched by many voters.
   (C) Debates allow candidates to fully discuss issues and policy possibilities.
   (D) Debates are often avoided by incumbents and front-runners.

4. The Bipartisan Campaign Reform Act
   (A) Lowered limits on soft money
   (B) Lowered limits on hard money
   (C) Raised limits on soft money
   (D) Raised limits on hard money

5. Two weeks before election day, an average of several independent polls shows that local Democratic congressional candidate, Henry Smith, an incumbent with 8 years in office, is leading against his challenger, 55 to 44 percent. He has $400,000 in his campaign treasury. Which of the following will Smith likely do?
   (A) Donate to fellow Democratic congressional candidates in swing districts
   (B) Begin a negative advertising campaign against his opponent
   (C) Invite his opponent to debate him on television
   (D) Open another campaign office

6. Which of the following is an accurate trend in modern campaigns?
   (A) There has been an increased dependence on political consultants.
   (B) With new forms of media, costs have dropped.
   (C) The duration of election cycles has shrunk.
   (D) The Supreme Court has nearly erased free-speech rights with federal limitations.

Concept Application

The following is from a news report during the 2016 presidential campaign.

1. "I confess to having supported the ACLU position in *Buckley*. As the corrosive effects on democracy of uncontrolled campaign spending became increasingly clear, however, I joined several former ACLU leaders . . . in opposing the organization's campaign finance position [on *Citizens United* that the Bipartisan Campaign Reform Act limited free speech]. We have argued . . . that spending massive amounts of money during an election campaign is not "pure" speech when the spending level is so high that it drowns out competing voices . . . ; that a compelling interest in equality justifies preventing wealthy speakers from buying up an unfair proportion of the speech . . . that massive campaign spending by 'independent' entities poses a serious risk of postelection corruption; and that corporations lack the attributes of conscience and human dignity that justify free-speech protection."

—Burt Neuborne, *The Nation,* March 21, 2012

After reading the scenario, respond to A, B, and C below:

(A) Describe the political behavior that has resulted from the *Citizens United* ruling, according to the author.

(B) In the context of the scenario, explain how the behavior described in part A affects elected officials.

(C) In the context of the scenario, explain how the effect on elected officials can be influenced by linkage institutions.

Quantitative Analysis

Total TV Ad Spending by State
(2012 Presidential Campaign)

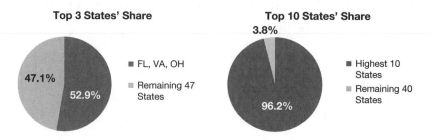

2. Use the information graphic on the previous page to answer the questions.
   (A) Identify the percent of ad spending in the top three states.
   (B) Describe the difference in spending in the top three states and the top ten states.
   (C) Draw a conclusion about the reasons for that difference.
   (D) Explain how the data in the chart reflects a principle of electoral politics.

SCOTUS Comparison

3. In June 1985, the Michigan Chamber of Commerce wanted to run a newspaper ad in support of a candidate in the special election to fill a vacant seat in the Michigan House of Representatives. Although the organization had a separate political fund, it wanted to use money from its general treasury to pay for the ad. However, the Michigan State Campaign Finance Act prohibited the use of general treasury funds for political purposes. The Michigan State Chamber of Commerce argued that it was a "nonprofit ideological corporation" and, as such, should not be bound by the Michigan law, which it argued suppressed the Chamber's constitutional rights. A Michigan court upheld the application of the law; an appeals court reversed that decision, and the case came before the U.S. Supreme Court.

   In 1990, in *Austin v. Michigan Chamber of Commerce,* the Supreme Court once again reversed, upholding the Michigan law that prohibited corporations from spending general treasury funds for political purposes. The Court disagreed with the designation of the organization, noting that most of its members were corporations. It reasoned further that since corporations are allowed to make political expenditures through their separate political funds, their constitutional rights were not unduly burdened.

   (A) Identify a similarity between *Austin v. Michigan* (1990) and *Citizens United v. FEC* (2010).
   (B) Given the similarity identified in part A, explain why *Citizens United v. FEC* led to a different holding than the holding in *Austin v. Michigan.*
   (C) Describe an action the Michigan Chamber of Commerce could take to minimize the effect of the ruling.

CHAPTER 20

The Media

Topics 5.12–5.13

Topic 5.12 The Media
PRD-3.A: Explain the media's role as a linkage institution.

Topic 5.13 Changing Media
PRD-3.B: Explain how increasingly diverse choices of media and communication outlets influence political institutions and behavior.

Source: Wikimedia Commons

President Trump, Dr. Deborah Birx, and other members of the Coronavirus Task Force address the media in the Rose Garden of the White House in March 2020. At these daily briefings, President Trump used the media to share information with the public on the government's response to the pandemic.

The Media

"Were it left to me to decide whether we should have a government without newspapers, or newspapers without government, I should not hesitate a moment to prefer the latter."

—Thomas Jefferson, letter to a friend, 1787

Essential Question: How does the media function as a linkage institution?

Soon after Johannes Gutenberg created the printing press, reporting and commenting on government became commonplace. In late colonial America, pamphleteers and newspaper editors printed ideas that helped bring about the American Revolution. The media have since evolved from those hard-copy publications intended for elite audiences to instant reporting and citizen interaction via the Internet. Governments have a love-hate relationship with the press, because journalists and commentators can affect public opinion, government operation, and policy. In fact, the media wield power that rivals that of the three branches of government. For that reason, the media are often referred to as the "Fourth Estate" of government. They have the power to influence society and politics almost as effectively as government itself.

Media as a Linkage Institution

In 1734, New York writer and publisher John Peter Zenger faced an American colonial court on a charge of seditious libel. Zenger had criticized the royal governor in his weekly *New York Journal*, an illegal action at the time. Zenger's attorney argued that the truth, which was not a legitimate defense under the English law, should be an absolute defense. The jury agreed and found Zenger not guilty. This radical verdict marked the beginning of an American **free press**—an uninhibited institution that places an additional check on government to maintain honesty, ethics, and transparency—later enshrined in the First Amendment.

No matter what form it takes, the free press serves to link citizens to their government. Newspapers and television report on citizens' concerns and what their government does. Web-based news organizations provide constant updates as news develops. Social media has become a chief way for citizens and government to exchange information. All media ultimately help shape how people engage with government, including voting, and government actions.

The Traditional Press

Colonial newspapers served a major function during the American Revolution. Later, they fostered a spirit of unity for the new nation's course. However, only large cities could maintain a regular newspaper and most were only four pages and printed weekly. The first daily paper did not appear until 1784.

President Washington and Secretary of the Treasury Alexander Hamilton created *Gazette of the United States*, a newspaper to convey Federalist ideas. Thomas Jefferson's followers responded by publishing the *National Gazette*. The warring political factions debated and sometimes attacked each other through these publications. These publications strengthened the relationship between the party in power and the leaders of the press.

The partisan press ceased to dominate national media as newspapers expanded their circulation and national news organizations came into being. The 1860 opening of the Government Printing Office (GPO)—a permanent federal agency to print government publications—broke the patronage relationship between government and publishers. The GPO prints only government documents, not news stories or editorials.

In 1833, the *New York Sun* became the first successful and affordable daily newspaper. The paper cost one penny per copy and was sold at outdoor city markets. It consisted primarily of human-interest stories and recipes, which were what the average reader desired. Government activity no longer dominated the front pages. Additional similar papers began to thrive as America's readership grew and newspaper owners sought a mass audience.

The telegraph altered communication even further. In 1841, Congress funded inventor Samuel Morse's telegraph line from Washington to Baltimore. In 1848, New York's leading editors gathered to finalize plans for a formal news organization, the Associated Press (AP). By pooling resources, the editors could gather, share, and sell the news beyond their respective cities. Using the expanding telegraph lines, reporters could send information quickly from anywhere in the world to AP headquarters in New York where editors shaped the story and send it out across the nation.

During its first year, the AP covered a presidential campaign, a women's rights convention, and other national stories. It established **news bureaus**, or offices beyond a newspaper's headquarters, in Albany, New York, and Washington, DC. Because it wrote for a national audience in so many different newspapers, the AP standardized unbiased reporting in order to appeal to a range of customers. Today, other wire services such as United Press International and Reuters compete with the AP, but they all follow the same standards of reporting.

Investigative Reporting

In the early 20th century, Washington became a common dateline—the locale listed atop an article in a newspaper. Dispatches from the capital described such major news stories as the progress of the pure food and drug legislation, government efforts at trustbusting, and the controversy over railroad rates.

Progressive Era journalism fostered integrity in reporting and a publication's ability to create real change. **Investigative reporting** became a new genre, as reporters dug deep into stories to expose corruption in government and other institutions. Reporter Ida Tarbell wrote a damaging exposé of John D. Rockefeller's Standard Oil monopoly. Writer Lincoln Steffens and photographer Jacob Riis revealed the tragic conditions in cities. These journalists changed the national mindset to bring about reforms. For example, breaking up monopolies became easier once the public was aware of the harsh and sometimes illegal business practices some industries used. Newspapers served as a link between citizens and their government by reporting situations that called for new legislation.

President Theodore Roosevelt shared the progressive spirit of these investigative journalists, though he did not always appreciate how they threatened his image or that of the United States. He dubbed the journalists muckrakers, a pejorative term that compared them to "the man with the muck rake" in the novel *Pilgrim's Progress*. They were too busy looking down and stirring up filth to gaze upon the stars. Lincoln Steffens proudly reflected on the label years later, "The makers of muck . . . bade me to report them."

National Political News

New media have emerged recently, profoundly influencing how citizens receive news. Yet, national newspapers such as the *Washington Post, Wall Street Journal, New York Times,* and *USA Today* remain influential, even if they have had to adapt to new modes of delivery. These newspapers continue to set the tone for national reporting.

For decades, magazines such as *Time, Newsweek,* and *U.S. News and World Report* dominated in-depth news coverage with middle-of-the-road perspectives. Other magazines cover national and international politics with a particular editorial slant. Some of the more liberal publications—*The New Republic, The Nation*, and *The Progressive*—have been around since the Progressive Era. Others, like *National Review* and *The Washington Times*, attract a conservative readership.

LEADING IDEOLOGICAL POLITICAL MAGAZINES	
Liberal	**Conservative**
The Nation	National Review
The New Republic	Human Events
The Progressive	The Washington Times
Mother Jones	American Spectator

New Communication Technologies

In the 20th century, radio and television both emerged as powerful new communication technologies. Citizens became fascinated with headlines and brief reports coming to them through the air. Broadcast stations developed news departments to shape an industry that competed with—and later surpassed—print media in terms of news consumers.

Radio Radio first appeared shortly after World War I. The concept of a **broadcast network**—broadcasting from one central location to several smaller stations called **affiliates**—was in full force by the 1930s. Early newscasts included readings from *Time* magazine and news dramatizations featuring narrators and voice-over artists playing the parts of world leaders.

Radio journalism transitioned into more fact-based reporting as journalists moved from print to broadcast media. Edward R. Murrow was a key pioneer of this style. In 1940, Murrow broadcast from a rooftop in London in the midst of the Second World War, reporting on Germany's massive bombing efforts. Film of the war appeared in movie theaters at the time, but, as Murrow biographer Bob Edwards put it, "Newsreel footage of the Blitz is in black and white; Ed's radio reports were in color." By the end of World War II, Murrow's voice was the most familiar in radio.

Television In the postwar period, broadcast companies shifted efforts toward television. By 1951, six years after the end of the Second World War, 10 million American homes had a television. Networks worked to develop news departments, and they covered the 1948 Democratic and Republican conventions. Presidential contenders highlighted their credentials in front of the television cameras. Citizens were introduced to candidates for a live look at the individuals vying for each party's nomination. How a politician looked on television suddenly mattered.

Over the next few years, the **Big Three networks** of ABC, CBS, and NBC set the tone for television journalism that is still largely followed today. These networks began to create in-depth programming that examined national affairs, international relations, and the lives of celebrities.

Edward R. Murrow moved from radio to television in 1951 to host *See It Now*, a precursor to the weekly CBS news show *60 Minutes*. Murrow exposed Senator Joseph McCarthy by presenting examples of McCarthy's abusive tactics toward alleged American communists, which ultimately helped bring about McCarthy's downfall. Citizens trusted the voice—and now the image—of a reliable reporter over an aggressive and corrupt politician. Television journalism had asserted itself as a watchdog, which made it an even more influential medium and strengthened its linkage function.

In 1960, Senator John F. Kennedy became one of the first politicians to use the power of television to his advantage. The televised presidential debates between Kennedy and his opponent, Vice President Richard Nixon, began a new era of campaigning. More of those who viewed the debates on television felt Kennedy won, while a majority of those who listened to the debates on the radio saw Nixon as the winner. Once elected president, Kennedy proved a master of the medium, working with reporters and holding the first televised live press conferences.

In 1980, Atlanta TV station owner Ted Turner created the **Cable News Network (CNN)**. Americans suddenly had access to national news 24 hours a day. Cable companies added MSNBC and the Fox News Channel in the mid-1990s. These three cable news networks changed television news from a daily cycle with an evening peak to a fluid cycle with updates and analysis on the hour. This "narrowcasting" appeals to a specific audience, while the more common broadcasting is intended for the mass public.

This change explains why President Bill Clinton's White House affair with Monica Lewinsky was so widely reported and why previous presidential affairs were not. Veteran White House reporter Helen Thomas noted how news reporting changed in the wake of the Lewinsky scandal: "Although gossip was also rampant about previous presidents, it remained just that—gossip—and reporters did not attempt to verify it."

Today, Fox, MSNBC, and CNN lead in viewership of cable TV news channels, though others like Bloomberg and BBC America also compete. Viewership of the top three cable channels peaked in 2008 at 4.3 million viewers per evening and has declined somewhat as more channels are offered and as people turn to the Internet for news and entertainment. The Pew Research Center reported in 2016 that about 3.1 million combined viewers tune into those channels nightly. Though viewership has dropped, ad revenues for these channels have steadily increased.

The original Big Three's (CBS, NBC, and ABC) 30-minute evening news broadcasts still lead as America's key venue for political news consumption, hovering between 23 to 25 million combined viewers each night. Though local TV news has lost some of its audience over the past decade, it still has more viewers than the chief national networks or cable TV channels. More Americans turn on the local news for traffic and weather than the national news for politics.

The Internet

The U.S. military created the Internet as a tool to connect its vast network of computers. The technology became generally available to the public in the early 1990s. It is now an ever-present source of news, information, and entertainment.

In the early days of the Internet, journalists and news-savvy citizens scoffed at news traveling across the web. But major news magazines, dailies, and other traditional media outlets have now followed their audience to the Internet. While some people still receive a daily subscription of their favorite printed newspaper, the newsprint rolling off the presses for home delivery has decreased drastically. Today, nearly all Americans (93 percent) rely on the Internet somewhat to get their news. People under 30 have made the web their preferred news source. Pew reports about 38 percent of people primarily get their news from a digital platform, versus about 20 percent from print.

Internet news sources can be divided into those outlets that were "born on the web," and "legacy" news sources. In the first category, websites such as *Huffington Post* and *Politico* are setting the standards for online political reporting. These and other digital media organizations, such as Yahoo News and BuzzFeed, have spent millions to bring well-known print and TV journalists into their ranks.

Meanwhile, traditional news outlets like the *New York Times* and the *Washington Post*, the legacy sources, have developed strong and popular Internet platforms for reporting. These organizations have turned to digital platforms to compete and remain afloat financially. Promoting digital versions of their newspapers has helped ease the transition from print to digital somewhat, though the number of full-time journalists has dropped from almost 55,000 in 2007 to just under 24,000 in 2015.

The shift from print to electronic journalism and the intense competition to "scoop" competitors in a fast-paced news environment has sped up publishing, shortened stories, enabled sloppy reporting, and caused journalists to seek out anything unique on an almost hourly basis to grab attention. This shift has not only encouraged sensationalism, but it also has increased the number of errors and after-story corrections.

Social Media Advances

In 2004, Harvard student Mark Zuckerberg launched Facebook, originally a campus social networking site that has since grown into a multibillion-dollar corporation that engages as many as 400 million users daily worldwide. Competitors and other social media sites soon followed until social media became a primary vehicle for a vast number of Americans to consume their news. In 2018, about 86 percent of 18-to 29-year-olds used social media, and about 34 percent of senior citizens did. .

This social media interaction between consumers and news outlets has encouraged the outlets to use social media to their advantage. Even the Big Three networks now have a strong social media presence. News outlets engage readers online, allowing direct conversations between journalists and consumers. Consumers also use social media to help organize newsworthy events, such as the nationwide Women's March in January 2017 and the student-organized March for Our Lives in March 2018. Social media therefore plays an increasingly large role in shaping news presentation and consumption.

By the Numbers

Television and Online News Consumption, 2016–2017

% of U.S. adults who <u>often</u> get news on each platform

57% Television 50
19-point gap
7-point gap
Online 43
38%
25% Radio 25
20% Print Newspapers 18

2016   2017

Source: Pew Research Center

What do the numbers show? From what media platform do Americans often obtain news the most? What portion of citizens often obtain news via the Internet? What percentage often read a printed newspaper?

Roles and Influence

The Fourth Estate has established itself as an institution in the United States, protected by the First Amendment and intertwined with government and politics. The media partially sets the agenda, grades candidates in campaign season and government performance year-round, and shines light on problems they believe government should address.

Keeping Score

Before an election, reporters update readers and viewers nonstop on the ups and downs of competing candidates. This **horse-race journalism** leads reporters to overly discuss who is leading and who is falling behind in the campaign. As a result, this **scorekeeper** role causes the media to over-emphasize public opinion polls, mainly because these numbers tend to change day to day, while it tends to ignore or under-report candidates' complex proposals or the examining of intricacies of pending legislation. Candidates' ideas, policies, or biographies remain static, so once those are reported, they are no longer newsworthy. And, poll results are simple measures that viewers can understand in short news segments.

As scorekeeper, reporters track other political successes and failures beyond election season. The scorekeeping continues after an election by examining an elected official's approval rating or by crediting or blaming the successes and failures of government proposals and programs. This constant—often circular—style of reporting also causes media outlets to turn political events into popularity contests, rather than contests in which voters make decisions based on candidate qualifications and platforms.

Gatekeeper

Much more is happening in the world than can fit into a 30-minute broadcast or in the front section of a newspaper. The news media therefore act as a **gatekeeper** by setting their own news agenda by determining what is newsworthy and therefore deciding what information the public will receive. What the media decide to publish directly influences the issues people regard as important. What the public learns through the media will encourage citizens to contact their member of Congress, write letters to the editor, and assemble in support of a cause.

For example, a 2017 news story that implicated powerful filmmaker Harvey Weinstein as a sexual assault offender sparked a movement for women to speak out against sexual aggression and assault. Before, such accusations may have resulted in powerful people in the film industry scoffing at them or ending the accuser's movie career. As the media accurately portrayed these women as victims, the news spread quickly and encouraged additional victims (recent and old) to make similar accusations. With what became the #MeToo Movement, the press had directly or indirectly facilitated an organized effort to stop sexual aggression in the workplace.

In political or other arguments, opposing or alternate perspectives need to be addressed to show why the supported view, despite opposition, is still the stronger one. Argument provides several ways to address opposing or alternate perspectives: refutation, concession, and rebuttal. Refutation is proving a statement or point to be wrong through reasoning. Concession is admitting a statement or position is correct in some ways. Rebuttal is to contradict a statement or a point with facts and evidence.

Practice: Study the graphic below. Then provide a refutation, concession, or rebuttal to the claim stated below the graphic.

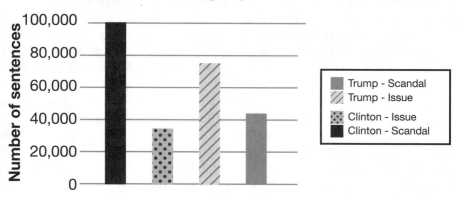

2016 Election Coverage, by Number of Sentences

Claim: The media coverage of negative topics leading up to the 2016 presidential election provided an unfair advantage to the eventual winner, Donald Trump.

Digging for the Truth

Keeping an eye on government or industry is part of the press's function as a **watchdog**. Investigative reporters look for corruption, scandal, or inefficiency. In fact, Congress may not even decide to address an issue until after the press has brought it to the public's attention.

Recently, the Pulitzer Prize for Investigative Journalism, the industry's top honor, was awarded to journalists who investigated the flood of opioids into West Virginia counties with the highest overdose rates in the nation, causing a series of state laws to be passed in October 2018 to address the drug problem. Also, the media has drawn the attention of the public to the responsibility of the state of Florida for violence and neglect toward mental patients in state hospitals, and a rigged system orchestrated by doctors and the denial of benefits to coal miners with black lung disease.

The media's watchdog approach was strengthened during and after the Vietnam War. Unlike the patriotic press corps during prior wars, journalists stationed in Vietnam began to question information the United States military and diplomats presented. Television images brought the war into citizens' living rooms, and journalists did not hold back on showing the tough realities of the war. Roughly 10 American journalists were assigned to Vietnam in 1960. By 1968, about 500 full-time correspondents representing print, television, and radio were in South Vietnam. NBC Vietnam Bureau Chief Ron Steinman said "We listened, hoping to discover a kernel of truth in a fog of lies." The reporting from Vietnam helped inspire the mass protests against the war that eventually led to U.S. withdrawal. In early 1968, after a trip to Vietnam, CBS anchor Walter Cronkite—known as the "most trusted man in America"—closed the evening news with an opinionated report that had big consequences. "We have been too often disappointed by the optimism of American leaders, both in Vietnam and Washington, to have faith any longer in the silver linings they find in the darkest clouds." President Lyndon Johnson, commander in chief at the time, reportedly remarked that if he had lost Cronkite, he had also lost America.

As the conflict in Vietnam waned, President Nixon sought reelection. *Washington Post* reporters Bob Woodward and Carl Bernstein served as watchdogs by uncovering the Watergate burglary scandal. In 1972, while reporting on a burglary of the Democratic National Committee office in the Watergate Hotel, Woodward and Bernstein eventually discovered that the burglars stole information in order to help Nixon's reelection campaign. These investigative reporters kept the story alive throughout a congressional investigation and the eventual resignation of the president.

The media skepticism that grew out of these events solidified what has become an **adversarial press** in the U.S.—where reporters continually question government officials, their motives, and their effectiveness.

REFLECT ON THE ESSENTIAL QUESTION

Essential Question: *How does the media function as a linkage institution? On separate paper, complete the chart below.*

Changes in Media Coverage of Politics	Impact of Media on Elections

---

KEY TERMS AND NAMES

adversarial press

affiliates

Big Three networks

broadcast networks

Cable News Network (CNN)

gatekeeper

horse-race journalism

investigative reporting

news bureaus

scorekeeper

watchdog

Changing Media

"The new tools of social media have reinvented social activism . . . making it easier for the powerless to collaborate, coordinate, and give voice to their concerns."

—Malcom Gladwell, *The New Yorker*, 2010

Essential Question: How do increasingly diverse choices of media and communication outlets influence political institutions and behavior?

Media have continued to advance in the new millennium. The press covers and interacts with all three branches of government, providing political reporting to citizens. The media provide a great diversity of choices to reach citizens from different walks of life and with different depths of concern. The reporting and commentary that comes out of various outlets also shape citizens' views of politics, government, and policy. Increased media options, ideologically oriented programming, and consumer-driven media decisions have shaped the media landscape. Information coming and going at such a fast pace and through so many platforms has called into question how much the media can be trusted. The fact-checking industry has emerged from the lack of credibility in some news outlets.

Media and the Three Branches

Various types of media coverage—objective reports on the three branches, breaking news, election coverage, and commentary—influence political participation and policy as they inform the public to make educated decisions and sometimes sway parts of the public to their way of thinking.

Political Reporting

Government and its leaders have always been topics of interest to the press and the public. Much coverage takes the form of objective **political reporting**, standard "just-the-facts" types of stories. This reporting began in the age of growing newspapers and national news services trying to reach broad audiences. An honest, unbiased approach separated the trusted reporter from one with an ideological agenda. It still does today. Front-page stories and investigative pieces usually follow this model, yet some political reporting can include other genres, such as profiles, op-eds, and critical "hit pieces." The public sometimes finds it hard to distinguish between objective reporting and biased commentary.

Using media is an efficient and free way for government officials to make announcements, test the popularity of ideas (sometimes called "trial balloons"), or assist in operating the government. Politicians try to interact with the press in a way that paints themselves and the government institutions they run in a positive light. The press's ability to influence public opinion has always kept government officials on their toes, and the sometimes adversarial relationship between journalists and government officials creates a rift between the two. Though candidates and officeholders cannot do without the press, an unfavorable headline can sometimes make or break an official's reputation. Today, an unfortunate snapshot or video clip suddenly available on YouTube can ruin a politician's career.

This dynamic has created a love-hate relationship between the government and the press. Candidates and officeholders will frequently contact reporters to offer up a news story about themselves, their platforms, or their new programs. In reality, such efforts by politicians may be nothing more than public relations campaigns. Depending on the day's events and how much news is happening, a reporter may be grateful for the easy story that will result in a "puff piece" highlighting the positive side of a politician on the front page.

Reporters sometimes have their own agenda or bias, and how they present information in **sound bites**—short excerpts edited from a longer remark that are especially vivid in presenting an issue—can have drastically different effects on the public depending on how they are worded, so politicians take great care in providing the press with the typically eight-second sound bite they want to carry their message. President Trump declared the investigation into his campaign's ties to Russia as the "greatest political hoax in American history." Bernie Sanders encapsulated his main message into the phrase "The top 1/10 of 1 percent now owns almost as much wealth as the bottom 90 percent." Jeffery Scheuer, New York University professor and author, writes, "The sound bite culture . . . is a society that thrives on simplicity and disdains complexity."

A politician or his communications chief may deem a reporter as hostile and not return calls if the reporter seems to be painting the politician in a bad light. This tenuous and sometimes confusing relationship between government and media influences how the Fourth Estate covers the three branches of government.

Congress and Press Coverage

The House of Representatives voted during the first Congress to open its doors to the public and the press. In the late 1800s, many reporters preferred to cover Congress instead of the White House. In the 1950s, Americans became familiar with Congress during Senator McCarthy's televised committee hearings and in the 1970s during the Watergate hearings.

Congressional stories include members' roles on committees and in the legislative process—these are typically technical story lines, not easily conveyed in short headlines or brief TV news segments. Two traditional print outlets that cover Congress, *Roll Call* and *The Hill*, have gained national popularity with their websites. Large newspapers and most TV news services have at least one Capitol Hill correspondent.

In the late 1970s, the cable industry created **C-SPAN**—the Cable Satellite Public Affairs Network—a privately funded, nonprofit public service. Cable and satellite affiliates pay fees that in turn fund the network. C-SPAN began covering the House in 1979. The Senate decided to allow cameras into its chamber in 1986, which gave rise to C-SPAN 2. Congress owns and controls the cameras in the two chambers, but C-SPAN receives the feed and can broadcast House and Senate floor debates. When Congress is not holding debate in its respective chambers, the network covers committee hearings, seminars at university campuses and think tanks, public meetings, and political rallies.

Presidents and Press Coverage

News organizations provide significant media resources to cover the president. The press delves into the president's domestic policy, relations with fellow policymakers, the first family, and interactions with other world leaders. Beyond the regular 100 or so top reporters who might cover the president daily, in person, another 2,000 have White House press credentials. Some travel on *Air Force One* (the president's plane) or on the chartered press plane that follows it.

John F. Kennedy did the first live televised press conferences in the early 1960s and developed a positive relationship between the chief executive and the media. By the end of President Richard Nixon's term in 1974, the dynamic between president and press had changed drastically. Nixon's paranoia, complicated by the release of the Pentagon Papers and the Watergate scandal (see Topic 2.4), pitted him directly against the press. He had offending reporters' phones tapped, his vice president spoke publicly about "disloyal" reporters, his Department of Justice tried to subpoena reporters' notes, and a White House aide threatened antitrust lawsuits against TV networks if they did not let more conservatives on the air. Like President Donald Trump, who tweeted that the press is the "enemy of the people" in 2019, Nixon was quoted as saying "The press is the enemy" repeatedly to Secretary of State Henry Kissinger.

In recent times, a full-time White House press secretary has served the president. The press secretary holds regular press conferences. The White House controls these media events. TV networks and wire services get preferential seating, as do the other major news outlets, such as the *New York Times* and the *Washington Post*. The more senior reporters are called on first, and the press secretary typically signals the close of the session by calling on the senior wire service reporter.

A press conference, at which presidents appear at a podium to field questions, occur less frequently than press briefings, usually only a few times each year. In their first year, Presidents George W. Bush, Barack Obama, and Donald Trump held 19, 27, and 21 overall press conferences, respectively.

Donald Trump's candidacy and his first year in office led to tense relationships with the press. While on the campaign trail, Trump encouraged crowds at his rallies to rough up reporters. From his inauguration onward he and his team have misled and battled with the press.

Media coverage of President Trump's initial year reflected some of the adversarial relationships between the president and the press by tending to include more stories on personality, character, and leadership than on policy. The Pew Research Center found that two-thirds of the coverage during his first year concentrated on the president's political skills, immigration policies, appointees, U.S.-Russia relations, and health care. President Trump at first held a few briefings and discontinued this custom entirely on March 11, 2019. After the outbreak of the COVID-19 virus, President Trump appeared at regular press conferences and resumed press briefings.

Courts and Press Coverage

The press covers crime, lawsuits, courtroom activity, and appeals court decisions. The Sixth Amendment requires that trials be public and thus makes regular press coverage possible. At the national level, major newspapers and television news typically assign a legal affairs correspondent to cover the Supreme Court and high-profile trials throughout the country. Viewers often see footage of a trial from the state level, especially one involving celebrities or a horrific crime. In the federal courts, however, cameras are generally not allowed. Instead, pastel drawings depicting courtroom people and events usually appear on screen during TV news coverage or on a website.

Attempts to bring cameras into the Supreme Court for increased understanding and transparency will likely fail. For every person who sees court coverage on C-SPAN gavel-to-gavel, the late Justice Antonin Scalia once warned, "10,000 will see 15-second take outs on the network news, which, I guarantee you, will be uncharacteristic of what the court does."

Political Analysis

A form of journalistic expression that explores and provides opinions on a topic in depth is called **political analysis**. This form offers explanations on topics, usually by experts, which help readers understand complex subjects. Political analysis is valuable as a way to educate news consumers on likely causes, effects, and implications of proposed legislation, court rulings, or budget proposals. Experts examine the topic from a variety of angles but do not include their own opinions on the subject.

For example, in 2014, there was discussion in the Senate about a constitutional amendment to limit campaign contributions that would have undone both *Citizens United v. FEC* and *Buckley v. Valeo*. (See Topic 5.11.) No one expected the amendment to come into being, but it provided an opportunity to reexamine the extremely complex issues intertwined in those cases. Mark Schmitt, New America's Director of Political Reform, wrote an analysis in the *Washington Post* of the amendment's likely effects. Pieces such as these provide important information and explanations for engaged citizens who want to take seriously the consequences of government actions.

New America is a think tank that "does not engage in research or educational activities directed or influenced in any way by financial supporters," according to its website, so its political analysis is likely objective. Other think tanks, however, have strong ideological bases, such as the liberal Center for American Progress and conservative Heritage Foundation. Analysis from such think tanks would likely have a biased perspective.

Political Commentary

As journalism developed in the 20th century, it made distinctions between fact and opinion. In print newspapers, the front pages offered more of an Edward R. Murrow-style of objectivity. **Editorials**—those opinionated articles that reveal the publication's view—soon appeared on a distinct editorial page or section of the newspaper. These still appear in printed publications and online today. Editorials have no by-line or author listed, as a team of editors often draft these articles which represent the official position of the newspaper. Additionally, similar opinionated articles with an author listed appear on the opposing page to allow other opinions. These **op-eds** also appear online written by professional journalists and citizens as guest columns. On these pages a reader will find endorsements of political candidates in campaign season and praise and criticism of government officials.

On television news broadcasts, similar customs developed. Though the vast majority of minutes are devoted to straight news, newscasters and newsroom editors occasionally go on the air and read their written **commentary** as the word "Commentary" appears on the screen, meaning opinion and interpretation rather than "just-the-facts" reporting.

As more media outlets have appeared on cable TV and online, these distinct lines dividing news and commentary have blurred. Though the solid wall between newsrooms and editorial departments remains in the offices at some news outlets, in other places the wall between what is fact and what is opinion is not as strong or obvious. A 2018 Pew study found that the public has difficulty distinguishing between news statements of fact from those of opinion. People who considered themselves more digitally savvy could more easily discern fact and opinion than those who considered themselves politically aware.

Ideologically slanted websites and TV channels compete with and are often as powerful and present as those following traditional standards of journalism. Born-on-the-web ideological outlets and cable TV networks hire partisans, political strategists, and former Congress members and give them prominence on their web pages and in their studios. Many columns and blogs are not clearly labeled as "opinion," and thus the non-discerning reader may not immediately realize the voice of an ideological extremist and may accept those views as if they were coming from the old-guard reporter dedicated to objectivity. CNN's *Anderson Cooper 360,* for example, often showcases commentators on each side of the political spectrum, competing not only to express their political goals but perhaps also for a more-permanent position with the network or a higher-paying offer from another channel. In other words, their statements are unlikely to be purely objective.

Cable networks have employed more and more commentators, in part because of so many expanded outlets, but mainly to draw particular audiences. The basic news can be presented in only so many ways, but commentators often have their own colorful personalities or backgrounds that serve to draw viewers looking for something different.

"Make politics boring again," says Noah Rothman in the conservative *Commentary* magazine. His bland solution might help Americans have a realistic understanding of governmental functions and would allow the press to neutralize politicians who incite controversies that exacerbate tensions. He admits, however, that his approach "would murder a lucrative industry that has turned societal divisiveness into a sport."

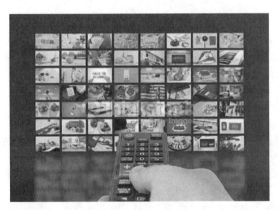

Media consumers have more choices than ever before as a result of producers appealing to niche markets. These often one-sided media outlets have also popped up in new media through podcasts, streaming content on YouTube, and social media outlets such as Twitter. The line between traditional journalistic content and uninformed citizen editorialization is often blurred.

Media Ownership and Bias

The increasingly diverse options presented by so many media outlets have altered how citizens rely on the media. The around-the-clock demand for information has created a fast-paced, competitive market of outlets. They constantly vie for readers, viewers, and consumers, becoming increasingly partisan in their efforts to do so. As a result, demand for more media content also encourages the growth of media outlets with a specific political agenda and a targeted audience—a concept known as **narrowcasting.**

The rapid surge of new media outlets has therefore altered the political landscape. The 1987 lifting of the **Fairness Doctrine**—a former federal policy that required radio and television broadcasters to present alternative viewpoints—has allowed media outlets more leeway and freedom in what they air. For many years, the news media had the reputation of liberal bias; however, in the last two decades conservative alternatives have increased in popularity. For example, Sinclair Broadcast Group, reaching 40 percent of American households, is known for its conservative slant. Cable television has given birth to a variety of outlets that have altered news delivery to specialized audiences. The Internet has also created seemingly endless choices. All of these changes have redefined the roles and relationships between media and citizens.

For example, conservative radio talk show host Rush Limbaugh emerged as a national conservative voice and gained a strong following in the early 1990s. One reason he succeeded was because he created a sense of community among people already inclined to agree with one another. By 2008, this pioneer of the new medium had as many as 20 million listeners. Over the same period, **talk radio**—those syndicated political shows that air at stations coast-to-coast—grew apace and became a common way for Republicans to get political news. Without the Fairness Doctrine, there was no need to provide other viewpoints to challenge the community's beliefs, which became self-reinforcing on both the right and left. Left unchecked, both ideologies have experienced an increase in the extreme views expressed by some members of the media.

Media Ownership

In 1934, Congress passed the Federal Communications Act, which created the **Federal Communications Commission (FCC)**. The FCC regulates electronic media, and it has authority over the content of radio, television, wire, and satellite broadcasts. It also regulates ownership by attempting to prevent monopolies. In 1941, for example, the FCC forbade NBC from operating two networks. NBC sold one of its two networks, which led to the establishment of ABC. In the last years of the 20th century, the popularity of cable news exploded, the Internet became a viable news source, and the entire landscape of media ownership changed.

Though Ted Turner and CNN invented cable news in general, the **Fox News Channel (FNC)**, under the media empire of Rupert Murdoch, drastically altered it when it started in 1996. As media critic David Folkenflick claims in his book *Murdoch's World*, "No other news organization has done more in recent years to reshape that terrain than Fox." The time was ripe for an alternative news channel. The Republicans had gained control of Congress. A longstanding conservative disdain for the media had reached a new zenith.

Folkenflick shows that the news at Fox is presented in ways "that reflect and further stoke a sense of grievance among cultural conservatives against coastal elites." Since its early days, the motto "Fair and Balanced" has suggested that the other networks are not and Fox is here to correct that. Another catchphrase, "We Report, You Decide," suggested that the others—the liberal media elite—are indoctrinating viewers.

The risk paid off. After September 11 and the initial years of the George W. Bush presidency, Fox took the number one slot as the most watched cable TV news channel and it has never lost it.

A 2014 study showed that Fox had edged out the Big Three networks as the "most trusted" news overall, though not likely due to Fox's journalistic standards. Right-leaning citizens from that sample consistently backed

Fox News, while moderates and liberals chose from a variety of other not-conservative networks as the most trustworthy. Self-described conservatives trusted Fox by 48 percent. Among self-described liberals, the Big Three led as most trusted, with CNN and PBS essentially tied for second.

Impact of Ownership This market fragmentation has only encouraged network owners to find more potential viewers to turn to their channel. For those presenting political news while in search of profits—competing for viewers in order to attract advertisers—Fox, CNN, and MSNBC have each gone further away from objectivity and have revealed their bias. Studies show that 24-hour news channels actually show little substantive news, repeat sensational stories throughout the day, and have reporters talk about their story as much as traditionally reporting on it. The journalistic drive to answer the hard questions is spotty. The regular newscasters and anchors tend to ignite tempers, employ sarcasm, stoke fear, and conduct their presentations with a sense of moral righteousness. Sometimes their partisan guests deliver ad hominem attacks.

Politically savvy citizens in search of more than what the main networks offer turn to their choice of cable media, especially during election season. Most Americans still watch the evening Big Three, but during campaign season, many Americans say they turn to one or more cable channels for election coverage. In 2016, all news channels advanced in the ratings. Fox led all basic cable networks with an average of 2.5 million viewers during its prime-time lineup, up 36 percent from the previous year. CNN went up 77 percent to 1.3 million viewers and MSNBC increased at the same rate to 1.1 million.

As Pew Research Center confirms, "Those on the right and left have significantly different media diets." In a study done in late 2016, Pew found about 40 percent of Trump voters relied on Fox News as their "main source" for news. Clinton voters, on the other hand, listed CNN as their main source, but only 18 percent did so. MSNBC was second, and Fox didn't make it into the top ten for Clinton voters.

Fox viewers include a high number of self-described conservatives, 60 percent. Meanwhile both CNN and MSNBC viewers claimed to be split with roughly one-third conservative, liberal, and moderate.

Media Bias

With the explosion of niche cable networks and online news sources, there is no longer any doubt as to whether bias in the media exists. Now, it is merely a question of where it is and which way it leans. In fact, bias has become essential to the business model of several news outlets. Meanwhile, the **mainstream media**, or the collection of traditional news organizations, still operates an objective news model. Conservative critics have called the media liberal for nearly two generations, and researchers have found liberal tendencies in the media both in its membership and in its delivery. But to understand bias in the media, one has to ask, "Which media are you talking about?"

Traditional Bias Label The media have been accused of a liberal bias since the early 1970s, when the press hounded President Nixon. But that is a simplistic characterization that circumvents the real challenges of measuring bias. Today, with thousands of national reporters for every entity from Fox News to the *Huffington Post*, a sound method to determine the question of bias is challenging. One measurement is to examine the professionals who report the news. Overwhelmingly, national reporters who shape political coverage vote with the Democratic Party, and they have for some time. A 1972 poll showed that 70 percent of reporters voted for Democrat George McGovern in the presidential election. A 1992 election study discovered that 89 percent of reporters voted for Democrat Bill Clinton, who received only 43 percent of the popular vote.

Studies that examine ideological slants also find that leading news outlets describe Republican and Democratic officials differently. David Brady and Jonathan Ma found that the *New York Times* and the *Washington Post* tend to treat liberal senators as cooperative bipartisans and to malign conservative senators. Their study saw a distinct difference in favorable or unfavorable adjectives that preceded "liberal" or "conservative" in their reporting. These outlets too often painted liberal senators as bipartisan lawmakers and iconic leaders of a noble cause but portrayed conservatives as hostile, combative, and out of the mainstream.

In a different study of 20 major print and TV news outlets, researchers found that only two leaned conservative, Fox News and *The Washington Times*, but the other 18 ranged from slightly to substantially left of center.

Contemporary Bias While professional journalists may still strive for objectivity, the increasing choices of media driven by writers and broadcasters of different ideological persuasions have, in some cases, made objectivity a minor concern at best. Slanted media predated the Internet, but now legacy outlets—*The New Republic*, *Slate*, and *Salon* on the left; *National Review* and *The Washington Examiner* on the right—mesh with other news sites, and readers may or may not discern source bias as they read their stories. Newer, born-on-the-web outlets, such as *Red State* or *Huffington Post*, are noticeably ideological. They and the nightly cable broadcasts provide diametrically opposite presentations and narratives of the same basic stories.

One Pew study at the end of the 2012 presidential election found President Obama received far more negative than positive coverage on Fox. About 46 percent of Fox stories on Obama were negative, while only 6 percent were positive (the remainder being neutral). The same study found MSNBC was harsher on Republican nominee Mitt Romney, with 71 percent of election stories negative and only 3 percent positive. Another study found that 90 percent of the evaluative statements made about President Trump on the ABC, CBS, and NBC nightly news from September 1 to November 30, 2017, were negative. Based on the viewership differences and where citizens are going to get their information online, people on the left and right have distinctly different information streams from those of people with mixed political beliefs.

Meanwhile, as "news sources" are playing fast and loose with journalistic norms, citizens are communicating more frequently via the Internet, and people are choosing more selectively what they read. People of like mind are supplying one another with a tailored diet of news and commentary that only confirms what they already believe. While the exercise of First Amendment rights allows people to read or not read what they want, the self-reinforcing and isolated loop of "news" is not helpful in developing consensus policy or in finding the best solutions for America's problems, nor is it helpful in understanding the alternative viewpoints.

 THINK AS A POLITICAL SCIENTIST: *EXPLAIN HOW REQUIRED SUPREME COURT CASES APPLY TO SCENARIOS IN CONTEXT*

Nearly all of the cases that make it to the Supreme Court have far-reaching effects on the country, which can make their rulings very divisive. Certain cases highlight the nation's ideological divide. That divide can be fueled by the media's sometimes biased presentation of the cases and other related issues. How would today's media and its often slanted coverage present some of the required Supreme Court cases that you have studied if they were ruled and reported on today?

Practice: Review the cases listed below. If that case was ruled on by the Supreme Court today, explain how a conservative-leaning media outlet and a liberal-leaning outlet would differ in their description of the Court's decision.

United States v. Lopez (1995). See Topic 1.8.

Engel v. Vitale (1962). See Topic 3.2.

Tinker v. Des Moines Independent Community School District (1969). See Topic 3.3.

Gideon v. Wainwright (1963) See Topic 3.8.

Roe v. Wade (1973). See Topic 3.9.

Media and Democratic Debate

Scholar and political expert Cass Sunstein calls the phenomenon of people remaining in echo chambers of their own creation "cyberpolarization." He believes public life would be better served if people relied on what he calls "the general interest intermediary," streams of information from those traditional, objective outlets. Without these, the level of political knowledge of citizens is reduced, and the result is a decline in the quality of public debate. At least four factors affect the quality of public debate and level of political knowledge: increased media choices, ideologically oriented programming, consumer-driven media and technology, and the credibility of news sources.

Increased Media Choices

In 1960, the average American home received three television stations. By 2014, Nielsen Research estimated that the average had risen to nearly 200. Evening news telecasts on the Big Three networks changed very little from Presidents Kennedy to Clinton. Viewers could expect the time slots around the dinner hour and before bedtime to be reserved for news broadcasts. But the explosion of cable news channels and their wide variety of programming have given consumers many more choices for their time in front of the TV.

While at one time viewers were regularly exposed to the news no matter what channel they tuned to, now they can choose to watch entertainment of a seemingly endless variety instead. Studies have shown that while some people use the increased amount of news broadcasting to try to deepen their understanding of politics, others simply tune out news and politics by choosing to watch entertainment. This situation creates a gap not only in political knowledge but also in political participation because people with greater political knowledge turn out to vote more than people with less political knowledge. Public debate is diminished by the uneven distribution of political knowledge.

Ideologically Oriented Programming

Fox News is by far the most-watched cable news channel, outpacing its liberal competitors CNN and MSNBC by a significant margin. The ideologically oriented programming on cable news channels has made the outlets a subject of great interest to political scientists, who ask a number of questions about their influence on voters and public debate. How much influence do the ideologically oriented news programs actually have on viewers, especially if viewers are attracted to a channel because they already share that channel's ideology?

Ideological Shifts in Cable News

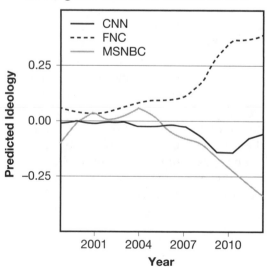

Source: Adapted from Martin and Yurukoglu 2017

Researchers Martin and Yurukoglu studied evolving liberal or conservative slants of CNN, FNC, and MSNBC based on broadcast transcripts and word connotations. The higher the score, the more conservative the slant.

A 2017 study by Emory University political scientist Gregory Martin and Stanford economist Ali Yurukoglu found that Fox News has a sizable influence on viewers' political attitudes, which in turn influence how they vote. They estimate that if Fox News hadn't been on the scene, John Kerry would likely have won the 2004 presidential election instead of George W. Bush.

They also found that CNN tried to develop its political ideology to match it to the maximum number of viewers it could attract, while Fox took a different approach. The political views of Fox are more conservative than those of their viewers, but Fox has had the effect of shifting their viewers' attitudes to the right. Fox is more successful at persuasion than the other cable news outlets and in this way is a major political agent.

As people are drawn to ideologically oriented programming, they demonstrate **confirmation bias,** the tendency to seek out and interpret information in a way that confirms what they already believe. They have no incentive, then, to consider opposing views, and yet the clash of ideas is vital for democratic debate and the democratic process. Scholar and political expert Cass Sunstein writes, "Unplanned, unanticipated encounters [of ideas] are central to democracy itself. Such encounters often involve topics and points of view that people have not sought out and perhaps find quite irritating—but that might nevertheless change their lives in fundamental ways."

Consumer-Driven Media and Technology

Confirmation bias is evident on social media as well, where more than 60 percent of Americans get news. On Facebook, for example, people exchange political links and memes in a circle of like-minded friends, in the process reinforcing their own and other group members' beliefs and even accepting as true statements that have been proven false as long as they fit in with their beliefs.

While people are creating their own "bubbles" for information sharing, usually without critical evaluation, professionally trained journalists are being laid off and printing presses are shutting down. Reliable, ethical news outlets are disappearing. Cities that once had multiple newspapers that kept one another in check as they competed to provide the best news possible may typically now have only one newspaper.

Information outlets—newspapers, television stations, and radio stations— have always had to make decisions about what issues to cover, exercising their gatekeeper function. They considered what issues they believed would be most important to their consumers and assigned their resources to cover those issues accordingly. They always had to attract readers or go out of business. In today's highly competitive media environment, however, consumer-driven media has entered a new dimension. **Consumer-driven media** are those media whose content is influenced by the actions and needs of consumers. Ultimately, these media outlets are businesses, and profit drives their actions. The desire to attract the most consumers and, in turn, make the most profits influences the way media present issues or events.

Now news companies and tech companies figure out what the average consumer will click on and generate stories from there. In other words, the role of gatekeeper has been passed on from experienced journalists to average web surfers. Responsible news outlets still try to balance the forces of genuine newsworthiness and popular interests. But in the competitive media world, too often the citizen-gatekeepers, perhaps more interested in the Kardashians than foreign policy, have become the gatekeepers. When more trivial topics are covered at the expense of serious issues, the level of political knowledge and public debate declines.

Continuously monitored ratings provide similar data for television news stations, which now have to compete with not only other news stations but also a wide array of other programming—including on-demand services such as Netflix and Amazon Prime Video. Some analysts believe the hunger for ratings contributed to Donald Trump's rise to the Republican presidential nomination among a field of experienced politicians. As journalist and Fox contributor Michael Goodwin explains, at first the media treated Donald Trump's candidacy as a publicity stunt, until "television executives quickly made a surprising discovery; the more they put Trump on the air, the higher their ratings climbed." Cable news shows started devoting hours to simply pointing the cameras at Trump as he gave off-the-cuff speeches at his rallies. By one estimate, Goodwin notes, Trump received so much free airtime that if it had been purchased, it would have cost $2 billion.

Managers of legacy news organizations are changing their business model and operating differently to survive. "Dependence generates desperation," laments Franklin Foer, former editor at the New Republic. "A mad, shameless chase to gain clicks through Facebook, a relentless effort to game Google's algorithms," has altered the role of one of progressive journalism's century-old magazines. When Google changes an algorithm—such as the rules by which autocomplete fills in possibilities after a user enters a few words to start, or the rules determining the order in which search results appear—web traffic can change significantly, benefiting some media companies and hurting others. In this way, tech companies can influence the ethics and ethos of an entire profession.

Credibility of News Sources

While Americans have more media choices and more control over what information to seek, consumers are simultaneously sent information from people with an agenda: friends and family who are of like mind, media sources with the goal of gaining more clicks, political groups trying to impact public opinion, or foreign adversaries trying to stoke the flames of discord or to influence an election. The result is an era of dubious credibility and impulsive clicks.

Pew discovered that when citizens access political news digitally, they go to a news organization's website 46 percent of the time. Social media is the second most frequently used source, 31 percent of the time; 20 percent go through a search engine such as Google; and 24 percent seek out news links after receiving email alerts from a news organization or friend. Those who independently go to a reliable news organization are more likely to get credible information.

Consumers are not always as responsible in their consumption of news as an informed and engaged citizenry would require. For example, this same Pew study found that citizens who received an article via social media could recall and name the original news outlet only 56 percent of the time. Another finding was that fully 10 percent cited "Facebook" as the news outlet, when of course Facebook is not a news outlet at all.

If indeed this is an era of consumer-driven media, then consumers demanding credibility and objectivity would have influence in the content news outlets provide. Author Clay Johnson in *The Information Diet* compares consumers' intake of news to their consumption of food and argues that the problem is not that people consume too much information but rather that they take in too much "junk" information. Just as people have to consciously make choices about healthy eating, they need to make responsible choices about news consumption. He advocates for education in media literacy so people can develop the critical evaluation skills needed to make informed choices about information.

REFLECT ON THE ESSENTIAL QUESTION

Essential Question: *How do increasingly diverse choices of media and communication outlets influence political institutions and behavior? On separate paper, complete the chart below.*

Media that Influences Political Participation	Influence of Media

---

KEY TERMS AND NAMES

commentary	Fairness Doctrine
confirmation bias	mainstream media
consumer driven media	narrowcasting
C-SPAN	op-ed
editorials	political analysis
Federal Communications Commission (FCC)	political reporting
	sound bites
Fox News Channel (FNC)	talk radio

CHAPTER 20 Review:
Learning Objectives and Key Terms

TOPIC 5.12: Explain the media's role as a linkage institution. (PRD-3.A)

Media's Role in Connecting People to Government (PRD-3.A.1)	**Media's Influence in Elections** (PRD-3.A.2)
affiliates	adversarial press
Big Three networks	horse-race journalism
broadcast networks	gatekeeper
Cable News Network (CNN)	scorekeeper
free press	watchdog
investigative reporting	
news bureaus	

TOPIC 5.13: Explain how increasingly diverse choices of media and communication outlets influence political institutions and behavior. (PRD-3.B)

Media's Influence on Politics (PRD-3.B.1)	**Media Bias** (PRD-3.B.2)	**Media and Democratic Debate** (PRD-3.B.2)
commentary	Fairness Doctrine	confirmation bias
C-SPAN	Federal Communications Commission (FCC)	consumer-driven media
editorials	Fox News Channel (FNC)	talk radio
op-eds	mainstream media	
political analysis	narrowcasting	
political reporting		
sound bites		

CHAPTER 20 Checkpoint:
The Media

Topics 5.12–5.13

MULTIPLE-CHOICE QUESTIONS

Questions 1 and 2 refer to the passage below.

Shortly after Richard Nixon resigned the presidency, Bob and I were asked a long question [which] we answered with a short phrase that we've used many times since to describe our reporting on Watergate and its purpose and methodology. We called it the "best obtainable version of the truth." It's a simple concept for something very difficult to get right because of the enormous amount of effort, thinking, persistence, pushback, removal of ideological baggage and the sheer luck that is required, not to mention some unnatural humility. Underlying everything reporters do in pursuit of the best obtainable version of the truth, whatever our beat or assignment, is the question "what is news?" What is it that we believe is important, relevant, hidden, perhaps, or even in plain sight and ignored by conventional journalistic wisdom or governmental wisdom?

I'd say this question of "what is news" becomes even more relevant and essential if we are covering the president of the United States. Richard Nixon tried to make the conduct of the press the issue in Watergate, instead of the conduct of the president and his men. We tried to avoid the noise and let the reporting speak.

—Reporter Carl Bernstein, White House
Correspondents Dinner, 2017

1. Which of the following statements best summarizes Bernstein's views?

   (A) Journalists' egos often get in the way of determining what stories to cover.

   (B) For a variety of reasons, most journalism is unfortunately shallow.

   (C) Reporters use professional judgment about what to cover as they filter out a variety of distractions and follow the facts.

   (D) Partisan spokespersons color the facts and are not reliable sources of information.

2. Which of the following reasons likely explains why Bernstein thinks the question of "what is news" is especially important when covering the president?

(A) The question of "what is news" is easier to determine when covering Congress than the president.

(B) The president can use the bully pulpit to assert his interpretation of events.

(C) The Freedom of Information Act provides access to virtually unlimited presidential documents.

(D) News reports about the president help increase a newspaper's circulation.

3. During political campaigns before an election, the news media is said to cover the campaigns like a horse race. Which of the following statements best explains the reason for this analogy?

(A) The press constantly compares candidates' poll numbers like the positions of horses in a race.

(B) The results of an election, like the results of a horse race, can't be known until it's over.

(C) The candidates are groomed and trained for the campaign just as racehorses are groomed and trained for a race.

(D) As gatekeepers, members of the press officially begin the horse race.

4. Which of the following is an accurate comparison of objective news and commentary?

	OBJECTIVE NEWS	COMMENTARY
(A)	Includes factual accounts of events and people	Includes opinions of experts or people with political goals
(B)	Includes endorsements as long as they are on the editorial pages	Is less common today than in the past and found in fewer places
(C)	Is delivered by the guests on a talk show	Avoids criticizing government or government officials
(D)	Is a hallmark of talk radio after the removal of the Fairness Doctrine	Is usually found on the front pages of traditional newspapers

Questions 5 and 6 refer to the infographic below.

Main Sources of News for Voters in 2016
% of voters who named___as their "main source" for news about the 2016 campaign

ALL VOTERS	TRUMP VOTERS	CLINTON VOTERS
Fox News* 19%	Fox News* 40%	CNN* 19%
CNN* 13	CNN 8	MSNBC 9
Facebook 8	Facebook 7	Facebook 8
Local TV 7	NBC 6	Local TV 8
NBC 5	Local TV 5	NPR 7
MSNBC 5	ABC 3	ABC 6
ABC 5	CBS 3	New York Times 5
NPR 4	Local radio 3	CBS 5
CBS 4		NBC 4
New York Times 3		Local newspapers 4
Local newspapers 3		Fox News 3

Source: Pew Research Center 2016

Only those news outlets reaching 3% or higher are listed.

5. Which statement accurately reflects the information presented in the above infographic?

   (A) More Clinton voters watched CNN than any other outlet for their campaign news.

   (B) Trump voters tended to watch a wider variety of news outlets than Clinton voters.

   (C) One of the Big Three led in viewership when voters were asked what they watched for election news.

   (D) For election news viewing, CNN ranked highest in all three categories.

6. What conclusion can you draw from the data in the information graphic?

   (A) Fox News built its viewership on its reputation for credibility.

   (B) Fox News targets conservatives as their niche audience.

   (C) Trump voters tend to rely more on print journalism than television.

   (D) Social media play a very small role in getting election news.

FREE-RESPONSE QUESTIONS

Concept Application

1. "For it seems now more certain than ever that the bloody experience of Vietnam is to end in a stalemate . . . To say that we are mired in stalemate seems the only realistic, yet unsatisfactory, conclusion. On the off chance that military and political analysts are right, in the next few months we must test the enemy's intentions, in case this is indeed his last big gasp before negotiations. But it is increasingly clear to this reporter that the only rational way out [of the Vietnam conflict] then will be to negotiate, not as victors, but as an honorable people who lived up to their pledge to defend democracy, and did the best they could."

   —Anchorman Walter Cronkite, CBS News Broadcast, 1968

   After reading the scenario, respond to A, B, and C below:

   (A) Describe the type of reporting delivered in this televised broadcast.

   (B) In the context of the passage, explain how the type of reporting in part A may influence citizens.

   (C) In the context of the passage, explain how the media serves as a linkage institution.

Quantitative Analysis

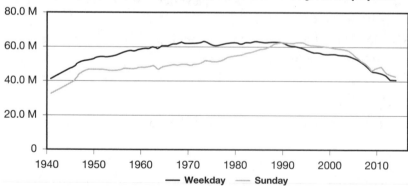

Total Estimated Circulation for U.S. Daily Newspapers

2. Use the information graphic to answer the questions.

   (A) Identify a decade when Sunday circulation peaked.

   (B) Describe a similarity in weekday and Sunday circulation.

   (C) Draw a conclusion about that similarity.

   (D) Explain how newspaper circulation as shown in the graphic demonstrates the changing media landscape.

UNIT 5: Review

The chapters in Unit 5 have explored how political parties, interest groups, campaigns and elections, and the media are conduits to voters and democracy. If it weren't for parties, elections, interest groups, and the press, many American voices would never be heard, and fewer citizens would understand government. Political parties, very broad coalitions, choose candidates and try to place them into office. Countless people also have more narrow interests, and they coalesce to create interest groups. These groups represent everyone from police officers to Wall Street financiers. Many form political action committees (PACs) and develop relationships with lawmakers. The pluralist theory holds that many interests are better than few and that they create opposing political forces and operate as a check and balance outside the Constitution. Because winning elections takes so much money and public effort, the government has passed laws to properly and fairly administer elections. Most notably, the Congress created the Federal Election Commission to monitor campaign finance limits.

The media report on government, help set a national agenda, and often give their opinions. They have gone from party-financed printed publications to a fast-paced, interactive platform. Language or image choices can heavily enhance or ruin candidates or stop a policy idea. Since the Supreme Court has ruled that government has no right to prior restraint, the freedom of the media to express a wide range of ideas is guaranteed.

MULTIPLE-CHOICE QUESTIONS

1. Which of the following statements about interest groups and lobbying is true?

   (A) Lobbying is protected by the Fourth Amendment.

   (B) Lobbyists spend most of their time persuading lawmakers to change their political views.

   (C) A Capitol Hill lobbyist's most precious asset is access.

   (D) Free riders rarely benefit from interest group activity.

2. Which of the following is an accurate comparison of challengers and incumbents?

	CHALLENGERS	INCUMBENTS
(A)	Tend to win in a bad economy	Raise and spend less money
(B)	Have an easier time raising money because of their fresh appeal	Are viewed skeptically because they have an open voting record
(C)	Have generally fewer resources than incumbents	Have resources that help support their candidacy
(D)	Mainly use federal matching money	Coordinate with Super PACs

Source: CartoonStock.com

3. Which of the following might result if the public came to hold similar opinions as the artist of this political cartoon?

(A) Creation of a federal agency that examines campaign advertising before it is aired

(B) A law that prevents groups from criticizing candidates with advertising

(C) A change in law that allows greater coordination between super PACs and candidates

(D) Greater awareness by voters of the veracity of political advertising

4. Which of the following court cases is most relevant to the topic of the cartoon?

(A) *Tinker v. Des Moines*

(B) *Citizens United v. Federal Elections Commission*

(C) *Shaw v. Reno*

(D) *Engle v. Vitale*

5. Which of the following statement best summarizes the voter registration process in the United States?

(A) Voter registration is a national process that is uniform among the states.

(B) States can require citizens to register to vote as much as one year in advance of an election.

(C) Voter registration helps assure accuracy in the election outcomes.

(D) Efforts to ease registration have dramatically increased voter turnout.

Questions 6 and 7 refer to the graphic below.

Pathways to Online News

Twice a day for one week, online news consumers were asked **if they got news in the past two hours.**

When they did, average % of the times they got it through...

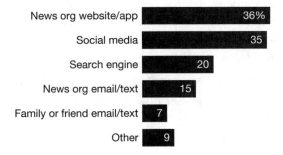

Note: Respondents were asked about the news they got on their main topic in each instance. Numbers add to more than 100% because respondents could report using more than one pathway in each survey.

Source: Pew Research, 2016

6. Which option accurately describes the information presented in the graph on the previous page?

    (A) Most people obtain news online mostly through a news organization's website.

    (B) More Americans are getting news through social media than by television.

    (C) Most Americans use Google, Bing, or other search engines to find relevant news stories.

    (D) Texts from family and friends are what most often lead people to online news.

7. Which of the following is a reasonable conclusion based on the data in the graph?

    (A) Americans prefer watching video to reading text for their news.

    (B) Consumers of news online are not necessarily receiving news from news organizations.

    (C) Email will soon be the main way news outlets deliver news.

    (D) Search engines provide an unbiased index to the news.

8. Around 9:30 p.m. on election day, 75 percent of the precincts in the congressional district have reported their vote totals. The Democrat candidate has 46 percent of the vote so far, and the Republican candidate has 53 percent. A local news station calls the election and lists the Republican candidate as the winner. Which of the following actions will the Democrat candidate most likely take?

    (A) Concede the election and congratulate the victor.

    (B) Wait until more votes are counted before conceding the race.

    (C) Call for an investigation, because 25 percent of the vote is unaccounted for.

    (D) Criticize the media for a biased call.

9. The media and the government have a "love-hate" relationship. Which of the following statements best reflects that label?

    (A) Ratings and sales for news outlets greatly fluctuate over time.

    (B) Reporters and the media dislike federal regulations but enjoy the public broadcasting grants.

    (C) Most partisan viewers enjoy a cable news network that aligns with their beliefs and don't like the others.

    (D) Politicians are often unsatisfied with what journalists print or broadcast but still need journalists on their side.

Questions 10 and 11 refer to the passage below.

I'm 27 years old, and I'm a lobbyist . . . While [older lobbyists] are throwing down $1,000 in the hope of grabbing a member's ear for five minutes at a fundraiser, I'm in the Fairgrounds outside Nationals Park, having a beer with some friends before first pitch. Inevitably, many of those friends are [Capitol] Hill and administration staffers—people I roomed with in college or met last weekend at a friend's birthday party. The most useful strategies I develop often comes out of these kinds of off-campus interactions with staffer friends. When we start nerding out over possible bill co-sponsors at our monthly poker game, for instance, we know we don't have to filter our ideas—which means we can be more open, bold and innovative.

—Lobbyist Mickey Leibner, *Roll Call*, 2013

10. What type of interest group activity does this author most likely engage in?

   (A) Electioneering

   (B) Grassroots lobbying targeted at voters

   (C) Filing cases in federal court

   (D) Direct lobbying of legislators

11. With which statement would this author most likely agree?

   (A) Political donations are the key to accomplishing policy goals.

   (B) Connecting with congressional staff is valuable in developing policy strategy.

   (C) The information-for-access game is a bad one.

   (D) Policymaking should take place in the halls of government, not in casual settings.

12. Which of the following party types most align with the Progressive and American Independent parties?

   (A) Ideological party

   (B) Splinter party

   (C) Realigning party

   (D) Economic protest party

Concept Application

The following passage is from *National Review*.

1. "Joe Biden is a gaffe-prone 75-year-old Washington veteran—who is exactly what Democrats need. The suburbs have turned against Republicans, but Donald Trump's working-class base [will] . . . define the 2020 election. The play for Democrats should be obvious: Make a serious appeal to Trump's voters, take back the Blue Wall states of Wisconsin, Michigan, and Pennsylvania, and win the presidency. In other words, go with Joe Biden . . . .

    Biden still talks of himself as a scrappy kid from Scranton . . . No one calls him "Middle Class Joe," as he likes to refer to himself. Yet, he has roots in the Democratic party of yore that had a solid base among working-class whites . . . [and he is] as close as the contemporary national Democratic party gets to a working-class match for the Great Lakes states that Trump stole from it in 2016. . . . Democrats need to win all three of Wisconsin, Michigan and Pennsylvania to take back the White House. Even if they pick off 2016 red states Arizona and Georgia, they still need Michigan or Pennsylvania to get over 270."

    —Rich Lowry, "Trump Should Fear Uncle Joe,"
    National Review, 2018

    After reading the scenario, respond to A, B, C below:

    (A) Describe a voting constituency in the scenario.

    (B) In the context of the scenario, explain why that voting constituency in Part A is valuable to the candidate.

    (C) Explain how competition for a voting constituency might impede democracy.

Quantitative Analysis

Spending of Federal Lobbying, 1998–2014

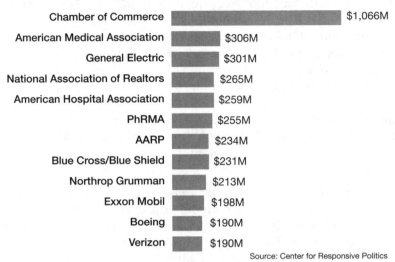

Chamber of Commerce	$1,066M
American Medical Association	$306M
General Electric	$301M
National Association of Realtors	$265M
American Hospital Association	$259M
PhRMA	$255M
AARP	$234M
Blue Cross/Blue Shield	$231M
Northrop Grumman	$213M
Exxon Mobil	$198M
Boeing	$190M
Verizon	$190M

Source: Center for Responsive Politics

2. Use the information graphic above to answer the following questions.

   (A) Identify the PAC/group that spent the most on federal lobbying.

   (B) Describe a similarity or difference between interest group spending on federal lobbying.

   (C) Draw a conclusion about that similarity or difference in spending.

   (D) Explain how the data in the chart will impact the role of the iron triangle in policymaking.

SCOTUS Comparison

3. The 2002 Bipartisan Campaign Reform Act included an aggregate financial limit that a donor can give to candidates for federal campaigns across the board. The overall limit, like the individual limits, were occasionally recalibrated to adjust for inflation. Shaun McCutcheon, an avid Alabama political donor, gave to the Republican Party, other Republican committees, and several GOP candidates. He wanted to continue donating to other candidates in increments under the individual limit but could not due to the aggregate limit. He and other plaintiffs sued the Federal Elections Commission arguing that the aggregate limit was a violation of his constitutional rights and failed to serve a substantial governmental interest with such a prohibitively low limit.

In *McCutcheon v. Federal Elections Commission* (2014), the Supreme Court held that the aggregate limit did little to address the corruption concerns the law was intended for, while it limited participation in the democratic process. The total limit forces a donor to choose which interests or issues to support and advance in a given election. The Court ruled that the government interest in combating corruption cannot unnecessarily curtail constitutional rights.

(A) Identify the constitutional clause that is common to both *McCutcheon v. Federal Elections Commission* (2014) and *Citizens United v. Federal Elections Commissions* (2010).

(B) Based on the constitutional clause identified in Part A, explain why the differences in the facts of the case nonetheless led to similar rulings.

(C) Describe an action Congress could take to respond to the Court's ruling.

You have developed a claim or thesis statement that takes a defensible position and lays out a line of reasoning (see page 257), gathered evidence to support it (see page 390), and stitched your ideas together by using reasoning to show how your evidence supports your claim (see page 489). While at this point the essay may seem complete in your mind, it still lacks a vital part of a strong argument: addressing opposing or alternative perspectives. *Opposing perspectives* are those that argue on one side or other of the basic pro and con positions. Since few if any issues have only two sides, responding to *alternative perspectives*—those that present a different angle or viewpoint rather than a simple "yes" or "no"—is another aspect of an effective argument. Three main approaches help you accomplish this requirement.

- Refutation—Showing conclusively how opposing or alternative views are wrong
- Concession—Admitting that parts of the opposing argument may have merit but showing how, overall, your position still prevails
- Rebuttal—Arguing against an opposition by showing its weaknesses

Suppose you have developed an argument based on the following claim: "A free press is essential to democracy because the founders recognize the media plays an important role in keeping government and its leaders accountable to the citizens." You have supported your claim with evidence from a foundational document, the Constitution, citing the First Amendment's guarantee of freedom of the press. You also pointed to the role investigative reporters have played in uncovering wrongdoing in the government using Watergate as an example. You've used reasoning to explain how your evidence supports the claim (for example, "If the press had not revealed the Watergate scandal, free, fair elections might have been weakened, threatening democracy").

To fulfill the requirements of the prompt (and any good argument), you need also to consider opposing or alternative perspectives and show why yours is better. To do so, ask what other positions people hold on this topic and examine why they hold those views. When you understand them better, you can refute, concede, or rebut them. For example, you might identify opposing views that focus on the unreliability of many news sources and the low level of critical viewing skills among news consumers that dilute the value of a free press. You might counter this argument in several ways:

- Refute it by arguing that there are actually many reliable news sources and that consumers can be educated to find and use them
- Concede that those observations are true but then point out that governments that censor the press are known for authoritarian rule rather than democratic rule.
- Rebut them by showing that those observations disregard the guarantees of the First Amendment.

Having thought through and responded to opposing or alternative perspectives, you may now wish to modify your thesis statement to reflect the bigger picture you have taken into account. A stronger, revised thesis statement would be:

"Despite legitimate questions about the accuracy of some news stories, a free press is essential to democracy, because through its news coverage, the media helps to keep government and its leaders accountable to citizens."

Often in your claim you can introduce the idea that you have considered and rejected opposing views by using such words and phrases as *although, despite, while it is true that*, and *while*, saving the presentation of your position for the second part of the sentence (underlined in the above example).

Application: As you complete the argument essay below, be sure to identify and address opposing or alternative perspectives through refutation, concession, and rebuttal.

For current free response question samples, check the College Board's website.

Argument Essay

4. Regulations on radio, television, and other broadcast media have waxed and waned. Develop an argument that evaluates whether federal broadcast regulations are necessary for an informed citizenry.

   Use at least one piece of evidence from one of the following foundational documents:

   - Article I of the Constitution
   - First Amendment to the Constitution
   - *Federalist No. 10*

   In your response, you should do the following:

   - Respond to the prompt with a defensible claim or thesis that establishes a line of reasoning.
   - Support your claim with at least TWO pieces of specific and relevant evidence
     - One piece of evidence must come from one of the foundational documents listed above.
     - A second piece of evidence can come from any other foundational document not used as your first piece of evidence, or it may be from your knowledge of course concepts.
   - Use reasoning to explain why your evidence supports your claim or thesis.
   - Respond to an opposing or alternative perspective using refutation, concession, or rebuttal.

Think Tank:
Making a Civic Connection

Think tanks are research organizations that work alongside government and political policies, institutions, and issues. For the AP® Government and Politics course, the AP® USGOPO student community, including you, will take on the study of political science in making a civic connection. "Students are provided with an opportunity to engage in a political science research or applied civics project," states the College Board's CED. The project can involve participation in nonpartisan service-learning opportunities and internships, or it can involve close observations of government-related activities. The Think Tank Project provides the student an opportunity to engage in a sustained, real-world activity that will deepen their understanding of course content. This project also helps students develop disciplinary practices to succeed on the exam.

You have developed these skills throughout this course as you analyzed and interpreted foundational documents and Supreme Court cases, completed the Think as a Political Scientist activities, and answered the questions at the end of each chapter and unit.

The project must connect with the course framework and must culminate with your presentation of findings. Think broadly as you consider topics and project ideas, and think openly as you begin to consider your presentation format. Projects can range from an explanation of how local city government works presented in multimedia format to a competent and persuasive letter to the editor seeking to alter public policy on an issue of importance to you or your community.

Local educators and school officials will govern which project types and subjects are acceptable. Your AP® Government teacher will guide the research and presentation process and determine the scope and timing based on your interests, available resources and transportation, and the community's political climate. Your teacher will assist you in choosing topics and will give you feedback so you can refine them. Projects can be group-based or individual, also determined by your teacher, but in either case, they should involve or end with a formal presentation to an actual audience.

A good project will apply course concepts to actual political issues, institutions, people, procedures, interactions, and/or policymaking. The key is choosing an appropriate issue or inquiry. What question or questions are you ultimately asking? Whether researching and writing a traditional research paper or scripting and cutting a digital documentary, what question are you trying to answer? Like a political scientist, you might answer a conceptual question, or like a citizen activist, you might shine light on a specific issue, work on persuading others, or even institute or change a policy.

The project must:

- Connect course concepts to real-world issues
- Demonstrate disciplinary practices
- Present or communicate findings in an authentic way

Think Local

The College Board has included a Project Guide in the Course and Exam Description available on the College Board website. (See pages 131–137 of CED for project ideas.) The guide encourages students to submerge themselves into real-world observance of and interaction with government. This activity could be as simple as becoming involved in a local municipal government meeting or interviewing local public officials. Find the local governments in your community. Visit your local county or city government websites and determine what responsibilities each entity covers, what services it provides. What actions, plans, or concerns do they have? How do they spend taxpayer money? Attend one or more meetings and interview official(s) involved.

In addition to local, county, and state governments, organized nonprofit agencies interact with government regularly. Linkage institutions, such as public sector labor unions (police, firefighters, teachers, for example) are somewhat accessible and would assist your understanding of their role. National and local interest groups concerned about the environment, civil rights, and taxpayer burdens have local chapters that regularly interact with government. Television reporters and community newspaper journalists engage with government and policy daily. Interacting with these professionals would enhance your understanding of the media.

Connect and engage with local real-world experts. For example, if looking into an upcoming or past election, think about interviewing a local elections official, party chair, field staffer, or precinct captain living around the corner to get an authoritative, real-world perspective. If your government-based or political topic involves events or people from the past, connect with a local historian or visit the local history section of your library for ideas and information.

Activities and Sources for Thinking Local

- Attend meeting(s)
- Conduct interview(s)
- Contact your city council members, county commissioner, or state representative
- Collect and study local news articles, video clips, and radio segments/podcasts
- Examine local government publications online and at your public library
- Read the minute books from a local governing body

Think National

Though you may live far from Washington, DC, the institutions of national government have never been more accessible. You can monitor your elected members of Congress and examine their voting records. You can listen to audio of the Supreme Court's oral arguments days after they occur. The National Archives, the Library of Congress, the executive departments and agencies all have an abundance of information, documents, and ways to connect via their websites. National research organizations and think tanks offer documents, data, and secondary sources online at no charge. Events from hours ago are archived online, whether in a summary of a White House press briefing at the *Washington Post's* site or full-length videos of committee hearings at C-SPAN's video library. Additionally, though the federal government is headquartered in the nation's capital, government buildings and operations exist throughout the country and beyond. Within miles of your high school, you can likely find a federal agency building, U.S. courthouse, or military base.

National politics is worthy of deeper analysis to understand and connect with the course content and concepts. American presidential elections with differing dynamics are well documented with primary sources. Think of political personalities—Speakers of the House, Supreme Court justices, and White House chiefs of staff who have been involved in the policymaking arena. A thorough look into their experiences and interactions with other branches and the public would facilitate your practice with the skills and reasoning of this course. On a national scale, a thorough look into the passage of landmark legislation, a pivotal presidential decision, or a Supreme Court ruling could be interesting and engaging.

Activities and Sources for Thinking National

- Interview an officer of the federal courts or a federal branch employee
- Research a database of national newspapers
- Contact your member(s) of Congress, an executive agency, or federal court
- Examine the *Congressional Record*, presidential speeches/briefings, and Court rulings
- Attend a portion of a trial or public hearing
- Study reports from reliable think tanks
- Read books and other secondary sources from public libraries
- Explore the National Archives website
- Visit presidential libraries' websites

Think Numbers

Collecting and analyzing data is essential in the study of political science. Think about election data, budget expenditures, census data, polling and survey results, roll call votes in Congress or at the local city council, and other quantifiable measures that could help you answer your question(s). If numbers are your chief source, be sure to round out your statistical findings with other narrative information to understand your findings and to give your presentation context.

Statistics and reports with measurements rely on a technical language that goes with explaining stats. Assertions and qualifications, precise language, and apples-to-apples comparisons are necessary when dealing with stats whether you are writing a paper, creating a slide presentation, or narrating a digital broadcast. So when you present an analysis of figures, use proper language to explain your findings.

Activities and Sources for Thinking Numbers

- Conduct an original survey/measure public opinion on a topic or issue
- Examine polling data from Gallup, Pew Research Center, or other organizations
- Obtain and review local reports, surveys, and budgets
- Collect and compare statistics from government agencies (Census Bureau, FEC, OMB, for example)
- Explore election data and methods of statisticians at such organizations as fivethirtyeight.com

As you research your project, consider the source of all the information you have acquired. The following checklists will guide you as you evaluate your information sources and distinguish reliable from unreliable news sources.

Checklist for Evaluating Books

- What is the publication date? Is the book likely to be up-to-date??
- Is the author a recognized expert? See if other people frequently cite this author.
- Who is the publisher? Major publishers, including university presses and government agencies, are likely to be reputable sources.

Checklist for Evaluating News Articles from News Organizations

- When was the article published? Is it up-to-date?
- What are the author's credentials?
- Does the magazine or newspaper appeal to a special interest group that may have a biased viewpoint on the subject?

Checklist for Evaluating Websites

- If you receive a link through social media, consider the views of the person or organization that sent it. What bias might that sender have?
- Identify the top-level domain name. Is the site maintained by a for-profit company (.com) that might be trying to sell something? Is it an educational institution (.edu), which tends to be more reliable, or an independent organization (.org)? If it is an organization, is it one whose name you recognize? Be aware that ".org" sites are often owned by nonprofit organizations that may support a particular cause.
- If the website contains an article, is it signed? If not, you should be skeptical of its credibility.
- Do the language and graphics avoid sensationalism?
- Has the site been recently updated?

Verify information by finding corroboration in a number of sources. Some errors may be obvious, but unless you check the facts and find an agreement about them among sources, you might miss some bias, misinformation, and outright untruths.

Think Presentation

You will share your findings with others—classmates, a governing body, or other citizens—so plan for a real-world audience and consider appropriate presentation formats. Some findings will be statistical, so creating your own charts and graphs may be necessary. If you are trying to generate a discussion in the process, perhaps an interactive blog would be useful.

Ideas for Thinking Presentation

- In-person presentation with oral, visual, and Q & A component
- An informative or persuasive documented website
- A published Op-Ed, letter to the editor, or article
- A display for a political science fair
- A regular, interactive blog for a defined period
- A detailed, supported letter to a government official
- An analysis of media coverage with embedded video or audio clips
- Interview(s) of public official(s)
- A documentary film
- A report on a public action as part of a community organizing effort
- Research paper or portfolio on an issue
- An ad campaign/series of advertisements

Practice Exam

Section 1

Multiple-Choice

1. Which element of the Electoral College system causes some people's votes to be discounted?

   (A) Variation in electoral votes per state

   (B) Winner-take-all system

   (C) The closed primary

   (D) The Australian ballot

2. Which of the following is an accurate comparison of the Articles of Confederation and the U.S. Constitution?

	Articles of Confederation	Constitution
(A)	Supported by arguments made in *The Federalist*	Reserves powers to the state governments
(B)	Declared and listed reasons for a political break from Great Britain	Included a bill of rights in its original form
(C)	Created a loose union of states, each receiving one vote in Congress	Proposed in 1787, sets up a framework for national government
(D)	Allowed the United States to raise national troops and fund a war	Was ratified by the 13 states within one year after written

3. Two citizens are arguing over the role and influence of the many organized interest groups that try to influence public policy. The first citizen suggests that interest groups should be limited. The second suggests that since there are so many groups looking to influence policy from so many different perspectives, these competing groups will bring about more acceptable policies. The second citizen believes in which type of political model?

   (A) Elitist model

   (B) Direct democracy model

   (C) Politico model

   (D) Pluralist model

Questions 4 and 5 refer to the map below.

Legal Drinking Ages, 1975

Source: U.S. Department of Transportation

4. Which of the following accurately describes the information in the map?

   (A) States with a legal drinking age of 18 were clustered together in one region.

   (B) Most states in the Northeast were among those with the lowest drinking age.

   (C) Federal laws on drinking and driving caused the differences displayed in the map.

   (D) The West Coast states maintained different ages for different beverages.

5. Which of the following constitutional principles or policies best explains the information in the map?

   (A) The amendment process

   (B) National supremacy

   (C) Congress's commerce power

   (D) Federalism

6. Due to Supreme Court rulings, public schools can no longer conduct morning prayer, and they must respect students' right to nondisruptive symbolic speech. Also, local police must warn arrested suspects of their right to remain silent. The Court has established these policies through which process?

(A) Prior restraint

(B) Judicial restraint

(C) Selective incorporation

(D) Plea bargaining

Questions 7 and 8 refer to the graph below.

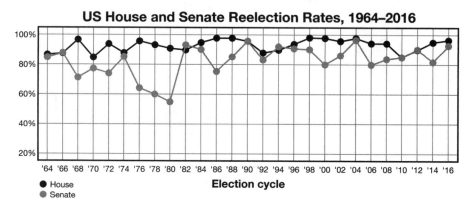

US House and Senate Reelection Rates, 1964–2016

● House
● Senate

Source: Center for Responsive Politics

7. Which of the following statements is reflected in the data in the line graph?

(A) Congressional incumbents win reelection a majority of the time.

(B) Incumbent success was at the lowest point in both houses in 1990.

(C) Voter turnout for both houses was at a high point in 2004.

(D) House incumbents rarely win at rates above 80 percent.

8. Which of the following is a chief cause for the trend shown in the line chart?

(A) Unbiased, nonpartisan drawing of congressional districts maintains this trend.

(B) Different campaign finance rules apply to incumbents and challengers.

(C) Incumbents do not need to raise as much money as challengers.

(D) Citizens are familiar with incumbents, who use their office for outreach.

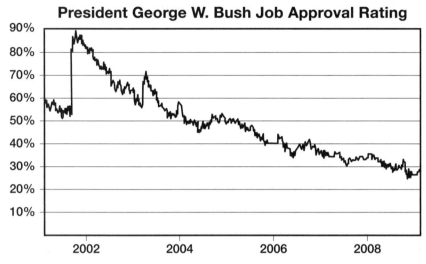

President George W. Bush Job Approval Rating

Source: The Presidency Project, UCSB

9. Which of the following accurately describes the information presented in the chart above?

   (A) George W. Bush had a better approval rating than most presidents.

   (B) George W. Bush had an approval rating below 50 percent during his second term.

   (C) George W. Bush had his best approval rating during the lame duck period.

   (D) George W. Bush's approval rating reached a peak in his second term.

10. Which of the following was a likely consequence of the trend illustrated in the graph?

   (A) President Bush's political party lost the 2008 presidential election.

   (B) President Bush's honeymoon period came at the end of his term.

   (C) President Bush used his second term to forward his policy agenda.

   (D) President Bush's approval rating actually made it easier for him to govern.

11. A member of the president's Cabinet disagrees strongly with the president on how executive branch policy should be carried out and has publicly expressed those views. Which of the following outcomes will likely happen?

(A) The president will reassign the official to another Cabinet position.

(B) The president will remove the official with the Senate's approval.

(C) The president will remove the official from his or her administration.

(D) The president will have the remainder of the Cabinet vote to remove or keep the official.

12. Which of the following statements is an accurate interpretation of the law on obscene speech in America?

(A) Governments cannot outlaw obscene materials as long as the material has a warning label.

(B) Governments cannot limit speech, and therefore cannot ban obscene speech.

(C) Speech thought to be obscene is not protected unless it can meet established standards of value.

(D) Restrictions on obscene speech are uniform throughout the United States.

13. Which of the following best supports an argument that the national news media is a liberal-leaning institution?

(A) The Democratic Party tends to win more elections due to media coverage.

(B) A high percentage of the media are self-described Democrats or vote more often for Democrats.

(C) Corporations run the media, and most corporate executives are Democrats.

(D) More journalists donate to the Republican Party than to the Democratic Party.

14. Which of the following actions may Congress take to limit the president's power?

(A) Refuse to spend money that the president has allotted

(B) Override a presidential veto with a two-thirds vote

(C) Name new Cabinet secretaries from the opposite political party of the president

(D) Raise taxes on the president's supporters

Questions 15 and 16 refer to the political cartoon below.

"I'm not so sure about this 'life, liberty and pursuit of happiness' bit. Whaddya say we look at some polling numbers first?"

Source: cartoonstock.com, cartoon by Tim O'Brien

15. The central message of this political cartoon is best summarized by which of the following statements?

   (A) The founders drew their ideas by sampling public opinion.

   (B) The founding principles of "Life, liberty, and the pursuit of happiness" were negotiable.

   (C) The founders were more concerned about reelection than about separating from Britain.

   (D) The founding principles are more enduring than public opinion.

16. What implication does the cartoon convey about today's government officials?

   (A) They over-consider polls when determining their messaging.

   (B) They take seriously the concerns of the public and shape policy accordingly.

   (C) They are powerful, small groups of people who make important decisions in secret.

   (D) They would rather be true to the founding principles than popular with voters.

17. Which of the following is an accurate statement about the necessary and proper clause?
    (A) The clause has allowed Congress to bar guns near schools after *United States v. Lopez* (1995).
    (B) The clause has often been used by Congress to overrule Supreme Court decisions.
    (C) The clause has empowered Congress to act in a flexible manner to carry out its expressed powers.
    (D) The clause has mainly been used to return authority to the states in contested laws.

18. Which of the following sequences accurately follows the impeachment and removal process as outlined in the Constitution?
    (A) The Senate votes to accuse the official; the House determines if the charges warrant removal.
    (B) The House accuses an official; the Senate judges and decides whether to remove the official.
    (C) The Cabinet, by a majority vote, impeaches the president out of office; the Senate convicts or acquits.
    (D) The Justice Department impeaches the official; the Supreme Court convicts or acquits.

19. Which of the following best describes Congress's use of the commerce clause over time?
    (A) Congress has used it to protect workers and the environment.
    (B) Congress has been denied much of its commercial regulatory authority by Supreme Court rulings.
    (C) Congress can legislate only on products that cross state lines.
    (D) Congress has used its commerce power sparingly and there are few federal commercial laws.

20. Which of the following statements about the Declaration of Independence is accurate?
    (A) It provides a legal and moral justification for rebellion.
    (B) It sets forth the new system of national government.
    (C) American colonists unanimously agreed to it.
    (D) It was drafted in 1787 and eventually ratified by the states.

Questions 21 and 22 refer to the graph below.

Equal Employment Opportunity Commission (EEOC) Complaints Filed, 2016

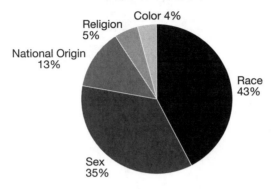

Source: EEOC, 2016. 91,503 total complaints

21. Which of the following is an accurate statement based on the data in the pie chart?

    (A) Discrimination based on weight is covered under EEOC rules.

    (B) Discrimination based on national origin is at the highest point in the nation's history.

    (C) Discrimination based on race and sex are the most common complaints.

    (D) Discrimination based on national origin and religion have about the same percent of complaints.

22. Which of the following is a reasonable conclusion based on the information in the chart?

    (A) Despite some legislative protection, people of color and women still face widespread discrimination.

    (B) Enforcing racial equality and equality of the sexes is a reserved power.

    (C) Government employers cannot discriminate in hiring and firing, but private employers can.

    (D) A majority of these complaints were justified and punished.

Questions 23 and 24 refer to the table below.

Opinions about Legalizing Marijuana Use			
% who say marijuana should be...	Legal	Illegal	DK
	%	%	%
Total	61	37	3
Men	64	33	3
Women	57	41	3
White	62	36	2
Black	71	25	4
Hispanic	52	44	4
College grad+	65	32	3
Some college	65	32	3
HS or less	54	43	2
Republican	43	55	2
Democrat	69	28	3
Independent	65	32	3
White Evangelical Protestant	38	60	2
White mainline Protestant	64	33	2
Catholic	52	45	4
Unaffiliated	78	20	2

Oct. 25–30, 2017. DK=Don't Know
Note: Figures may not add to 100 because of rounding.

Source: Pew Research Center

23. Which of the following statements reflects the data in the chart?
   (A) Most religious groups tend to have the same opinion about legalizing marijuana.
   (B) A higher percentage of women than men want to legalize marijuana.
   (C) Less educated citizens favor legalization more than well-educated citizens.
   (D) More people want marijuana to be legal than illegal.

24. Based on the information in the table, which of the following is implied?
   (A) Democrats would be more likely to support marijuana use than Republicans.
   (B) White Evangelical Protestants have the strongest pro-legalization views.
   (C) African Americans and Hispanics believe in legalizing at the same levels.
   (D) Women favor legalizing marijuana for medical, not recreational, purposes.

Questions 25 and 26 refer to the passage below.

It looked like I was going to win the popular vote, maybe by a significant margin. There was some comfort in that fact. It meant that a majority of Americans hadn't embraced Trump's "us versus them" campaign, and that despite all our troubles more people chose our platform and vision for the future. I had been rejected—but also affirmed. It was surreal . . . . I'd been saying since 2000 that the Electoral College gave disproportionate power to less populated states and therefore was profoundly undemocratic. It made a mockery of the principle of "one person, one vote."

—Hillary Clinton, *What Happened*, 2017

25. Which of the following statements best summarizes candidate Hillary Clinton's argument?
   (A) The Electoral College system impedes citizen participation.
   (B) The Electoral College system is the constitutional way to elect a president.
   (C) The Electoral College advantages mainstream candidates.
   (D) The Electoral College disadvantages states with large populations.

26. Based on this passage, with which of the following statements would Clinton most likely agree?
   (A) The Electoral College is at odds with the Voting Rights Act of 1965.
   (B) The Electoral College is at odds with a principle established in *Shaw v. Reno*.
   (C) Congress should initiate a constitutional amendment altering the Electoral College.
   (D) The winner-take-all system should be adopted by all 50 states.

27. In a primary election for the U.S. House of Representatives, a citizen votes for a candidate whose record she has studied carefully. What model of voting is she using?

    (A) Rational-choice

    (B) Prospective

    (C) Retrospective

    (D) Party-line

28. Which of the following is true about super PACs?

    (A) They can collect limited donations from members of their organization and donate directly to candidates.

    (B) They can collect donations from the general public up to a limit and donate directly to candidates.

    (C) They can collect donations from the general public and can donate directly to candidates with no limits.

    (D) They can collect donations from the general public with no limits but cannot coordinate with candidates.

29. Which of the following statements most accurately reflects voter trends in U.S. congressional midterm elections?

    (A) Voter turnout in midterm elections is higher than in presidential elections.

    (B) The president's party typically loses seats in Congress during a midterm election.

    (C) Incumbents in the House of Representatives have about a 50 percent chance of reelection.

    (D) The closest races are in safe districts.

30. Which of the following best defines judicial activism?

    (A) The demands on judges to increase their caseload and issue more rulings

    (B) Rulings based on the assumption that judges can make policy as well as interpret it

    (C) The efforts of judges to actively lobby Congress for increased funding for their staffs

    (D) Judges refusing to remove themselves from cases in which they have a conflict of interest

Questions 31 and 32 refer to the passage below.

> In republican government, the legislative authority necessarily predominates. The remedy for this inconveniency is to divide the legislature into different branches; and to render them, by different modes of election and different principles of action, as little connected with each other as the nature of their common functions and their common dependence on the society will admit. It may even be necessary to guard against dangerous encroachments by still further precautions. As the weight of the legislative authority requires that it should be thus divided, the weakness of the executive may require, on the other hand, that it should be fortified.
>
> —James Madison, *Federalist No. 51*, 1788

31. What constitutional principle does Madison address in the above passage?
    (A) Bicameralism
    (B) Federalism
    (C) Freedom of speech
    (D) Due process

32. Which of the following statements is most consistent with Madison's views in the passage?
    (A) A three-branch design makes the legislature a safe branch.
    (B) The president should be on the same level as the legislature.
    (C) Checks in the lawmaking process limit the legislature's power.
    (D) The commander in chief should create most of the laws.

33. Which of the following is an accurate comparison of the Fourteenth and Fifteenth Amendments?

	Fourteenth Amendment	Fifteenth Amendment
(A)	Established that states had to assure residents equal protection	Assured states could not deny citizens the right to vote based on color or race
(B)	Abolished slavery	Assured states could not deny women the right to vote
(C)	Gave Congress the power to enforce voting rights	Assured citizenship to all persons born in the United States
(D)	Required businesses to serve all citizens regardless of race or heritage	Prevented states from determining voting rights without federal preclearance

Questions 34 and 35 refer to the infographic below.

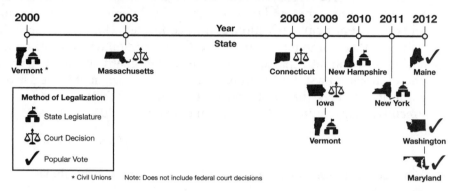

State Legalization of Same-Sex Marriage

34. Based on the infographic, which of the following statements is most accurate?

(A) Same-sex marriage was legalized nationally within a decade after Massachusetts legalized it.

(B) Popular vote was the common method for legalizing same-sex marriage early on.

(C) Strong majorities approved same-sex marriage in states that legalized through ballot measures.

(D) The last five states that legalized same-sex marriage used more representative methods than the first five states.

35. Which of the following constitutional clauses is followed in the legalization of same-sex marriage?

(A) Commerce clause

(B) Necessary and proper clause

(C) Free exercise clause

(D) Equal protection clause

36. A local police officer searched a person's car on a slight suspicion and happened to find the person possessed an illegal gun. The person never consented to a search, nor did the officer obtain a warrant. Which of the following might prevent the gun from being introduced as evidence in a trial?

(A) The doctrine of selective incorporation

(B) The exclusionary rule

(C) *Stare decisis*

(D) Failure to read Miranda rights

Questions 37–39 refer to the graph below.

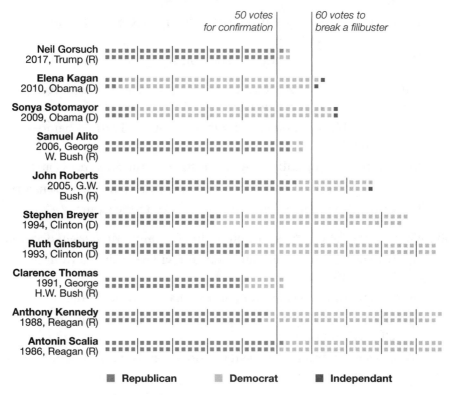

Total Senate Votes for Confirmation (by Party) Supreme Court Justices

Source: Washington Post, 2017

37. Based on the infographic, which of the following is an identifiable trend?

(A) Several justices received confirmation votes from only one party.

(B) Senators from the president's party vote to confirm nominated justices more than senators from the opposing party.

(C) Intense partisan voting on Supreme Court nominees was more common two decades ago than it is now.

(D) Decisions of justices confirmed by party-line votes have generally not aligned with views of the party that confirmed them.

38. What conclusion can you draw from the information in the graphic?
    (A) Each senator has to vote yes or no on a confirmation.
    (B) Republicans controlled the Senate when Justice Kagan was confirmed.
    (C) Justice Kennedy appealed nearly equally to Republican and Democratic senators.
    (D) Controversy surrounding Justice Ginsburg led to a close vote.

39. Which of the following strategies might a president follow to receive greater support for Supreme Court nominees?
    (A) Using public opinion polls for judges' approval ratings before naming them
    (B) Naming ideologically moderate justices to the Supreme Court
    (C) Broadcasting party-supported television ads to influence senators
    (D) Nominating more women and minorities to the Court

40. Which of the following is a result of the *Gideon v. Wainwright* decision?
    (A) Evidence acquired without a warrant will be excluded from the defendant's trial.
    (B) No state can prevent a woman from having an abortion.
    (C) Police must tell arrested suspects that they have a right against self-incrimination.
    (D) States must provide indigent or poor defendants with public defense attorneys.

41. How can public opinion polling affect political participation?
    (A) Random samples leave too many people out of the poll.
    (B) It contributes to "horse-race" journalism so voters don't engage with the real issues.
    (C) Confirmation bias makes people vote for candidates whose policies align with their own.
    (D) It predicts results so accurately that there's little need for an actual election.

42. Which of the following groupings constitutes an "iron triangle"?
    (A) Executive agency, congressional committee, interest group
    (B) President, House majority leader, Senate majority leader
    (C) Interest group, Senate majority leader, House majority leader
    (D) Executive department, House majority leader, president

43. Which of the following statements about the federal government and economic policy is true?

(A) Supply-side economics requires more taxes in order to increase government services.

(B) The secretary of the treasury holds the power of the purse.

(C) The House Budget Committee chair initiates the budget process each year.

(D) The Federal Reserve Board uses monetary policy to aid the health of the economy.

44. A Congress member and several other sponsors are ready to introduce a bill into the legislative process. The bill is designed to reduce tax rates on people with lower incomes. In which committee will these House members introduce their bill?

(A) Finance Committee

(B) Budget Committee

(C) Ways and Means Committee

(D) Welfare Committee

45. Which of the following is an accurate comparison of how the legislative branch and the executive branch can influence the federal courts?

	Legislative Branch	Executive Branch
(A)	Withholding or decreasing judges' salaries	Issuing executive orders to override Court decisions
(B)	Pressuring justices to resolve matters a certain way	Giving advice and consent on judicial decisions
(C)	Impeachment and removal of judges who behave improperly	Implementation of decisions through administrative bureaucracy
(D)	Refusing to carry out judicial decisions	Setting jurisdiction between federal and state courts

46. Which of the following principles protects a citizen from imprisonment without the government taking certain prescribed steps?

(A) Substantive due process

(B) *Stare decisis*

(C) Procedural due process

(D) Selective incorporation

47. Which of the following is a fair criticism of the federal bureaucracy?
    (A) Overlapping bureaucratic authority can cause wasteful spending and duplication.
    (B) Senior-level bureaucrats keep their jobs because they cannot earn comparable salaries working elsewhere.
    (C) After Congress creates a bureaucratic agency, it has little influence on how that agency operates.
    (D) The bureaucracy does not rely on experts in their fields to formulate regulations.

48. Which of the following would most likely be in violation of the Twenty-Fifth Amendment?
    (A) The president-elect asks to delay his inauguration until January 22.
    (B) The president writes and uses his own oath of office rather than saying the words in the Constitution.
    (C) The president refuses to sign or veto a bill without giving reasons for his refusal.
    (D) The president puts his secretary of defense in charge of the executive branch while he undergoes a medical procedure.

49. Which of the following is an accurate statement regarding congressional leaders?
    (A) The House speaker and the Senate whip have about the same amount of power and influence within their respective chambers.
    (B) The vice president breaks a tie vote in the Senate.
    (C) The vice president regularly presides over and casts votes in the Senate.
    (D) The minority and majority whips focus primarily on fundraising for the party.

50. Which of the following is an accurate comparison of state and local governments to federal government with respect to jurisdiction over national elections?

	State & Local Governments	Federal Government
(A)	Endorse candidates once they have filed for office	Certifies statewide vote totals once votes are fully counted
(B)	Monitor campaign donations and expenditures	Determines the type(s) of ballots to be used in federal elections
(C)	Define campaign donation limits from political action committees	Sets a national standard for voter-identification laws
(D)	Administer elections and designate voting districts	Enacts voting legislation to enforce constitutional suffrage amendments

51. A Republican president has nominated a federal judge for an opening on a U.S. Court of Appeals. A number of senators, including Republicans, have declared that they do not support the nominee. The Democratic minority leader has publicly opposed the nomination. Which of the following scenarios will likely occur?

    (A) The House of Representatives will withdraw the nomination.

    (B) The Senate will likely vote to confirm the nominee.

    (C) The president will withdraw the nomination

    (D) The Senate will hold additional nomination hearings.

52. An interest group's political action committee has donated to Representative Jones's campaign, yet Jones has signaled she opposes a proposed bill that the same interest group favors. Which of the following actions is the interest group most likely to take?

    (A) Create and air negative ads about Representative Jones

    (B) File an *amicus curiae* brief in court against Representative Jones

    (C) Ask for the donation to be returned to the political action committee

    (D) Ask to meet with the representative to explain and persuade her to vote otherwise

53. Which of the following is true regarding the public's perception of Congress?

   (A) A House member's individual approval rating is usually higher than Congress's approval rating.

   (B) Most Americans see Congress as hardworking, ethical, and responsive to people's needs.

   (C) Congress's approval rating tends to be higher than that of the president.

   (D) The public appreciates the bipartisan spirit in Congress that brings people together.

54. Which of the following is an accurate comparison of traditional media and new media?

	TRADITIONAL MEDIA	NEW MEDIA
(A)	Radio and television stations are licensed and regulated by the federal government.	Cable stations and Internet news platforms appeal to niche markets.
(B)	Print media usually provides shorter and simpler stories than broadcast media.	Cable news tends to be objective and uphold high journalistic standards.
(C)	Local newspapers as a practice do not endorse candidates for office.	Social media is a reliable news source.
(D)	National broadcast networks typically endorse the Democratic presidential nominee.	Cable television networks blossomed with the development of wire services.

55. Which of the following best describes a frequent source of contention between the executive branch and the legislative branch?

   (A) Appointment of Cabinet secretaries

   (B) Determining the federal budget

   (C) Homeland Security

   (D) Voter ID laws

Concept Application

1. "If trends continue . . . Mr. Trump will win or come very close to winning by the convention in July. If party forces succeed in finagling him out of the nomination, his supporters will bolt, which will break the party. And it's hard to see what kind of special sauce . . . would make them come back in the future. If [he] is given the crown in Cleveland [at the national convention], party political figures, operatives, loyalists, journalists and intellectuals . . . sophisticated suburbanites and . . . donors will themselves bolt. . . .And again it's hard to imagine the special sauce— the shared interests, the basic worldview—that would allow them to reconcile with Trump supporters down the road."

—Peggy Noonan, *Wall Street Journal*, March 5, 2016

After reading the scenario, respond to A, B, and C below:

(A) Describe the nomination process referred to in the scenario.

(B) In the context of the above scenario, explain how the process described in part A can be affected by interactions with the media.

(C) In the context of the scenario, explain what citizens can do to affect the impact of the interactions between elections and the media.

Quantitative Analysis

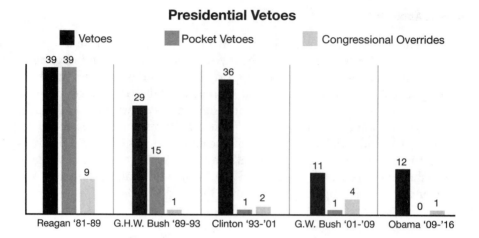

Presidential Vetoes

■ Vetoes　　　■ Pocket Vetoes　　　☐ Congressional Overrides

- Reagan '81-89: 39, 39, 9
- G.H.W. Bush '89-93: 29, 15, 1
- Clinton '93-'01: 36, 1, 2
- G.W. Bush '01-'09: 11, 1, 4
- Obama '09-'16: 12, 0, 1

Source: The American Presidency Project, University of California, Santa Barbara

2. Use the bar graph above to answer the questions.

   (A) Identify the president who rejected the most laws through vetoes.

   (B) Describe a similarity or difference in the use of the veto as illustrated in the chart.

   (C) Draw a conclusion about that similarity or difference.

   (D) Explain how the information represented in the graph demonstrates checks and balances in the lawmaking process.

3. The Alabama legislature passed laws (1978–1982) that authorized the state's public school teachers to set aside time to conduct a moment of silence for individual students to pray or meditate. Ishmael Jaffree, on behalf of his children who were students in the Mobile, Alabama, schools, filed suit against school and state officials, namely Governor George C. Wallace, seeking to stop such religious observances and "maintaining or allowing the practice of regular religious prayer services or other forms of religious observances" during the school day.

In Jaffree's case, *Wallace v. Jaffree* (1985), the Supreme Court held in a 6:3 decision in favor of Jaffree that Alabama law and this practice were not only a deviation from the state's duty to maintain neutrality toward religion but represented an affirmative endorsement of religion and clearly lacked any secular purpose.

(A) Identify the constitutional clause that is common to both *Wallace v. Jaffree* (1985) and *Engel v. Vitale* (1962).

(B) Based on the constitutional clause identified in part A, explain why the facts of *Engel v. Vitale* led to a similar holding as the holding in *Wallace v. Jaffree*.

(C) Describe an action that citizens who disagree with the holding in *Wallace v. Jaffree* could take to limit its impact.

4. Federal judges serve what are referred to as "life terms." Develop an argument to explain whether the existing term of office for members of the federal judiciary is suitable for interpretation of American law.

   Use at least one piece of evidence from one of the following foundational documents:

   - *Federalist No. 51*
   - *Federalist No. 78*
   - The Constitution

   In your response, you should do the following:

   - Respond to the prompt with a defensible claim or thesis that establishes a line of reasoning.
   - Support your claim or thesis with at least TWO pieces of specific and relevant evidence
     - One piece of evidence must come from one of the foundational documents listed above.
     - A second piece of evidence can come from any other foundational document not used as your first piece of evidence, or it may be from your knowledge of course concepts.
   - Use reasoning to explain why your evidence supports your claim or thesis.
   - Respond to an opposing or alternative perspective using refutation, concession, or rebuttal.

Sourcebook

Source: National Archives

The Declaration of Independence, the Constitution, and Bill of Rights are now permanently housed in the Rotunda for the Charter of Freedom at the National Archives Museum in Washington, DC. This image is of the Constitution.

The Declaration of Independence

IN CONGRESS, JULY 4, 1776

The unanimous Declaration of the thirteen United States of America

[1] When in the Course of human events it becomes necessary for one people to dissolve the political bands which have connected them with another and to assume among the powers of the earth, the separate and equal station to which the Laws of Nature and of Nature's God entitle them, a decent respect to the opinions of mankind requires that they should declare the causes which impel them to the separation.

[2] We hold these truths to be self-evident, that all men are created equal, that they are endowed by their Creator with certain unalienable Rights, that among these are Life, Liberty and the pursuit of Happiness. — That to secure these rights, Governments are instituted among Men, deriving their just powers from the consent of the governed, — That whenever any Form of Government becomes destructive of these ends, it is the Right of the People to alter or to abolish it, and to institute new Government, laying its foundation on such principles and organizing its powers in such form, as to them shall seem most likely to effect their Safety and Happiness. Prudence, indeed, will dictate that Governments long established should not be changed for light and transient causes; and accordingly all experience hath shewn that mankind are more disposed to suffer, while evils are sufferable than to right themselves by abolishing the forms to which they are accustomed. But when a long train of abuses and usurpations, pursuing invariably the same Object evinces a design to reduce them under absolute Despotism, it is their right, it is their duty, to throw off such Government, and to provide new Guards for their future security. — Such has been the patient sufferance of these Colonies; and such is now the necessity which constrains them to alter their former Systems of Government. The history of the present King of Great Britain is a history of repeated injuries and usurpations, all having in direct object the establishment of an absolute Tyranny over these States. To prove this, let Facts be submitted to a candid world.

[3] He has refused his Assent to Laws, the most wholesome and necessary for the public good.

[4] He has forbidden his Governors to pass Laws of immediate and pressing importance, unless suspended in their operation till his Assent should be obtained; and when so suspended, he has utterly neglected to attend to them.

[5] He has refused to pass other Laws for the accommodation of large districts of people, unless those people would relinquish the right of Representation in the Legislature, a right inestimable to them and formidable to tyrants only.

[6] He has called together legislative bodies at places unusual, uncomfortable, and distant from the depository of their Public Records, for the sole purpose of fatiguing them into compliance with his measures.

[7] He has dissolved Representative Houses repeatedly, for opposing with manly firmness his invasions on the rights of the people.

[8] He has refused for a long time, after such dissolutions, to cause others to be elected, whereby the Legislative Powers, incapable of Annihilation, have returned to the People at large for their exercise; the State remaining in the mean time exposed to all the dangers of invasion from without, and convulsions within.

[9] He has endeavored to prevent the population of these States; for that purpose obstructing the Laws for Naturalization of Foreigners; refusing to pass others to encourage their migrations hither, and raising the conditions of new Appropriations of Lands.

[10] He has obstructed the Administration of Justice by refusing his Assent to Laws for establishing Judiciary Powers.

[11] He has made Judges dependent on his Will alone for the tenure of their offices, and the amount and payment of their salaries.

[12] He has erected a multitude of New Offices, and sent hither swarms of Officers to harass our people and eat out their substance.

[13] He has kept among us, in times of peace, Standing Armies without the Consent of our legislatures.

[14] He has affected to render the Military independent of and superior to the Civil Power.

[15] He has combined with others to subject us to a jurisdiction foreign to our constitution, and unacknowledged by our laws; giving his Assent to their Acts of pretended Legislation:

[16] For quartering large bodies of armed troops among us:

[17] For protecting them, by a mock Trial from punishment for any Murders which they should commit on the Inhabitants of these States:

[18] For cutting off our Trade with all parts of the world:

[19] For imposing Taxes on us without our Consent:

[20] For depriving us in many cases, of the benefit of Trial by Jury:

[21] For transporting us beyond Seas to be tried for pretended offences:

[22] For abolishing the free System of English Laws in a neighboring Province, establishing therein an Arbitrary government, and enlarging its Boundaries so as to render it at once an example and fit instrument for introducing the same absolute rule into these Colonies

[23] For taking away our Charters, abolishing our most valuable Laws and altering fundamentally the Forms of our Governments:

[24] For suspending our own Legislatures, and declaring themselves invested with power to legislate for us in all cases whatsoever.

[25] He has abdicated Government here, by declaring us out of his Protection and waging War against us.

[26] He has plundered our seas, ravaged our coasts, burnt our towns, and destroyed the lives of our people.

[27] He is at this time transporting large Armies of foreign Mercenaries to complete the works of death, desolation, and tyranny, already begun with circumstances of Cruelty & Perfidy scarcely paralleled in the most barbarous ages, and totally unworthy the Head of a civilized nation.

[28] He has constrained our fellow Citizens taken Captive on the high Seas to bear Arms against their Country, to become the executioners of their friends and Brethren, or to fall themselves by their Hands.

[29] He has excited domestic insurrections amongst us, and has endeavored to bring on the inhabitants of our frontiers, the merciless Indian Savages whose known rule of warfare, is an undistinguished destruction of all ages, sexes and conditions.

[30] In every stage of these oppressions we have petitioned for redress in the most humble terms; our repeated petitions have been answered only by repeated injury. A Prince, whose character is thus marked by every act which may define a Tyrant, is unfit to be the ruler of a free people.

[31] Nor have We been wanting in attentions to our British brethren. We have warned them from time to time of attempts by their legislature to extend an unwarrantable jurisdiction over us. We have reminded them of the circumstances of our emigration and settlement here. We have appealed to their native justice and magnanimity, and we have conjured them by the ties of our common kindred to disavow these usurpations, which would inevitably interrupt our connections and correspondence. They too have been deaf to the voice of justice and of consanguinity. We must, therefore, acquiesce in the necessity, which denounces our Separation, and hold them, as we hold the rest of mankind, Enemies in War, in Peace Friends.

[32] We, therefore, the Representatives of the United States of America, in General Congress, Assembled, appealing to the Supreme Judge of the world for the rectitude of our intentions, do, in the Name, and by Authority of the good People of these Colonies, solemnly publish and declare, That these united Colonies are, and of Right ought to be Free and Independent States, that they are Absolved from all Allegiance to the British Crown, and that all political connection between them and the State of Great Britain, is and ought to be totally dissolved; and that as Free and Independent States, they have full Power to levy War, conclude Peace, contract Alliances, establish Commerce, and to do all other Acts and Things which Independent States may of right do. — And for the support of this Declaration, with a firm reliance on the protection of Divine Providence, we mutually pledge to each other our Lives, our Fortunes, and our sacred Honor

---

1. Describe the perspective, or point of view, of the authors of the Declaration of Independence and the philosophical assumptions underlying their argument.

2. The key claim in the Declaration of Independence—the claim on which the revolution was based—is in the second paragraph. Identify that claim and describe it in your own words.

3. What role do the facts "submitted to the candid world" play in the argument?

4. What is the purpose in the argument of paragraph 31, beginning with "Nor have we been wanting . . ."?

5. Describe the final claim of the Declaration of Independence.

6. An implication is a conclusion that can be drawn even if it is not stated directly. Identify the implications of the argument in the Declaration of Independence about the nature of the new government. Even though the new government was not yet formed, what implications about its political principles, processes, institutions, and behaviors does the Declaration of Independence suggest?

The Constitution of the
United States of America

Note: *The passages that have been amended or superseded have been struck out. In sections with more than one paragraph, paragraph numbers have been added in brackets to help you locate passages easily.*

PREAMBLE

We the people of the United States, in order to form a more perfect Union, establish justice, insure domestic tranquility, provide for the common defense, promote the general welfare, and secure the blessings of liberty to ourselves and our posterity [descendants], do ordain [issue] and establish this Constitution for the United States of America.

ARTICLE I. CONGRESS

Section 1. Legislative Power All legislative powers herein granted shall be vested in a Congress of the United States, which shall consist of a Senate and House of Representatives.

Section 2. House of Representatives

[1]   The House of Representatives shall be composed of members chosen every second year by the people of the several states, and the electors [voters] in each state shall have the qualifications requisite [required] for electors of the most numerous branch of the state legislature.

[2]   No person shall be a representative who shall not have attained to the age of twenty-five years, and been seven years a citizen of the United States, and who shall not, when elected, be an inhabitant of that state in which he shall be chosen.

[3]   ~~Representatives and direct taxes shall be apportioned among the several states which may be included within this Union according to their respective numbers [population], which shall be determined by adding to the whole number of free persons, including those bound to service for a term of years [indentured servants], and excluding Indians not taxed, three-fifths of all other persons.~~ The actual enumeration [census] shall be made within three years after the first meeting of the Congress of the United States, and within every subsequent term of ten years, in such manner as they shall by law direct. The number of representatives shall not exceed one for every thirty thousand, but each state shall have at least one representative; ~~and until such enumeration shall be made, the State of New Hampshire shall be entitled to choose three, Massachusetts eight, Rhode Island and Providence Plantations one, Connecticut five, New York six, New Jersey four, Pennsylvania eight, Delaware one, Maryland six, Virginia ten, North Carolina five, South Carolina five, and Georgia three.~~

[4]   When vacancies happen in the representation from any state, the executive authority [governor] thereof shall issue writs of election to fill such vacancies.

[5]   The House of Representatives shall choose their Speaker and other officers; and shall have the sole power of impeachment.

Section 3. Senate

[1]   The Senate of the United States shall be composed of two senators from each state, ~~chosen by the legislature thereof~~, for six years; and each senator shall have one vote.

[2]   Immediately after they shall be assembled in consequence of the first election, they shall be divided as equally as may be into three classes. The seats of the senators of the first class shall be vacated at the expiration of the second year, of the second class at the expiration of the fourth year, and of the third class at the expiration of the sixth year, so that one-third may be chosen every second year; and if vacancies happen by resignation, or otherwise, during the recess of the legislature of any state, the executive [governor] thereof may make temporary appointments until the next meeting of the legislature, which shall then fill such vacancies.

[3]   No person shall be a senator who shall not have attained to the age of thirty years and been nine years a citizen of the United States, and who shall not, when elected, be an inhabitant of that state for which he shall be chosen.

[4]   The vice president of the United States shall be president of the Senate, but shall have no vote, unless they be equally divided [tied].

[5]   The Senate shall choose their other officers, and also a president pro tempore [temporary presiding officer], in the absence of the vice president, or when he shall exercise the office of president of the United States.

[6]   The Senate shall have sole power to try all impeachments. When sitting for that purpose, they shall be on oath or affirmation. When the president of the United States is tried, the chief justice [of the United States] shall preside; and no person shall be convicted without the concurrence of two-thirds of the members present.

[7]   Judgment in cases of impeachment shall not extend further than to removal from office, and disqualification to hold and enjoy any office of honor, trust, or profit under the United States; but the party convicted shall nevertheless be liable and subject to indictment, trial, judgment, and punishment, according to law.

Section 4. Elections and Meetings of Congress

[1]   The times, places, and manner of holding elections for senators and representatives shall be prescribed [designated] in each state by the legislature thereof; but the Congress may at any time by law make or alter such regulations, except as to the places of choosing senators.

[2] The Congress shall assemble at least once in every year, ~~and such meeting shall be on the first Monday in December,~~ unless they shall by law appoint a different day.

Section 5. Rules and Procedures of the Two Houses

[1] Each house shall be the judge of the elections, returns, and qualifications of its own members, and a majority of each shall constitute a quorum to do business; but a smaller number may adjourn from day to day, and may be authorized to compel the attendance of absent members, in such manner, and under such penalties, as each house may provide.

[2] Each house may determine the rules of its proceedings, punish its members for disorderly behavior, and with the concurrence of two-thirds, expel a member.

[3] Each house shall keep a journal of its proceedings, and from time to time publish the same, excepting such parts as may in their judgment require secrecy; and the yeas [affirmative votes] and nays [negative votes] of the members of either house on any question shall, at the desire of one-fifth of those present, be entered on the journal.

[4] Neither house, during the session of Congress, shall, without the consent of the other, adjourn for more than three days, nor to any other place than that in which the two houses shall be sitting.

Section 6. Members' Privileges and Restrictions

[1] The senators and representatives shall receive a compensation for their services, to be ascertained [fixed] by law and paid out of the treasury of the United States. They shall in all cases except treason, felony [serious crime], and breach of the peace [disorderly conduct], be privileged [immune] from arrest during their attendance at the session of their respective houses, and in going to and returning from the same; and for any speech or debate in either house, they shall not be questioned in any other place.

[2] No senator or representative shall, during the time for which he was elected, be appointed to any civil office under the authority of the United States, which shall have been created, or the emoluments [salary] whereof shall have been increased, during such time; and no person holding any office under the United States shall be a member of either house during his continuance in office.

Section 7. Lawmaking Procedures

[1] All bills for raising revenue shall originate in the House of Representatives; but the Senate may propose or concur with amendments as on other bills.

[2] Every bill which shall have passed the House of Representatives and the Senate shall, before it becomes a law, be presented to the president of the United States; if he approve, he shall sign it, but if not, he shall return it, with his objections, to that house in which it shall have originated, who shall enter the objections at large on their journal, and proceed to reconsider it. If after such reconsideration two-thirds of that house shall agree to pass the bill, it shall be sent, together with the objections, to the other house, by which it shall likewise be reconsidered, and, if approved by two-thirds of that house, it shall become a law. But in all such cases the votes of both houses shall be determined by yeas and nays, and the names of the persons voting for and against the bill shall be entered on the journal of each house respectively. If any bill shall not be returned by the president within ten days (Sundays excepted) after it shall have been presented to him, the same shall be a law, in like manner as if he had signed it, unless the Congress by their adjournment prevent its return, in which case it shall not be a law.

[3] Every order, resolution, or vote to which the concurrence of the Senate and House of Representatives may be necessary (except on a question of adjournment) shall be presented to the president of the United States; and before the same shall take effect, shall be approved by him, or, being disapproved by him, shall be repassed by two-thirds of the Senate and House of Representatives, according to the rules and limitations prescribed in the case of a bill.

Section 8. Powers of Congress The Congress shall have power:

[1] To lay and collect taxes, duties, imposts, and excises, to pay the debts and provide for the common defense and general welfare of the United States; but all duties, imposts, and excises shall be uniform [the same] throughout the United States;

[2] To borrow money on the credit of the United States;

[3] To regulate commerce with foreign nations, and among the several states, and with the Indian tribes;

[4] To establish a uniform rule of naturalization [admitting to citizenship], and uniform laws on the subject of bankruptcies throughout the United States;

[5] To coin money, regulate the value thereof, and of foreign coin, and fix [set] the standard of weights and measures;

[6] To provide for the punishment of counterfeiting the securities and current coin of the United States;

[7] To establish post offices and post roads;

[8] To promote the progress of science and useful arts by securing for limited times to authors and inventors the exclusive right to their respective writings and discoveries;

[9] To constitute tribunals [establish courts] inferior to [lower than] the Supreme Court;

[10] To define and punish piracies and felonies committed on the high seas and offenses against the law of nations [international law];

[11] To declare war, grant letters of marque and reprisal, and make rules

concerning captures on land and water;

[12] To raise and support armies, but no appropriation of money to that use shall be for a longer term than two years;

[13] To provide and maintain a navy;

[14] To make rules for the government and regulation of the land and naval forces;

[15] To provide for calling forth the militia to execute [carry out] the laws of the Union, suppress insurrections [rebellions], and repel invasions;

[16] To provide for organizing, arming, and disciplining [training] the militia, and for governing such part of them as may be employed in the service of the United States, reserving to the states respectively the appointment of the officers, and the authority of training the militia according to the discipline [regulations] prescribed by Congress;

[17] To exercise exclusive legislation in all cases whatsoever, over such district (not exceeding ten miles square) as may, by cession of particular states, and the acceptance of Congress, become the seat of government of the United States, and to exercise like authority over all places purchased by the consent of the legislature of the state in which the same shall be, for the erection of forts, magazines [warehouses for explosives], arsenals, dockyards, and other needful buildings; and

[18] To make all laws which shall be necessary and proper for carrying into execution the foregoing powers, and all other powers vested by this Constitution in the government of the United States, or in any department or officer thereof.

Section 9. Powers Denied to the Federal Government

[1] ~~The migration or importation of such persons as any of the states now existing shall think proper to admit shall not be prohibited by the Congress prior to the year 1808; but a tax or duty may be imposed on such importation, not exceeding ten dollars for each person.~~

[2] The privilege of the writ of habeas corpus shall not be suspended, unless when in cases of rebellion or invasion the public safety may require it.

[3] No bill of attainder or ex post facto law shall be passed.

[4] No capitation [head] or other direct tax shall be laid, ~~unless in proportion to the census or enumeration herein before directed to be taken.~~

[5] No tax or duty shall be laid on articles exported from any state.

[6] No preference shall be given by any regulation of commerce or revenue to the ports of one state over those of another;

[7] No money shall be drawn from the treasury, but in consequence of appropriations made by law; and a regular statement and account of the receipts and expenditures of all

public money shall be published from time to time.

[8] No title of nobility shall be granted by the United States; and no person holding any office of profit or trust under them shall, without the consent of the Congress, accept of any present, emolument, office, or title, of any kind whatever, from any king, prince, or foreign state.

Section 10. Powers Denied to the States

[1] No state shall enter into any treaty, alliance, or confederation; grant letters of marque and reprisal; coin money; emit bills of credit; make anything but gold and silver coin a tender [legal money] in payment of debts; pass any bill of attainder, ex post facto law, or law impairing the obligation of contracts, or grant any title of nobility.

[2] No state shall, without the consent of the Congress, lay any imposts or duties on imports or exports, except what may be absolutely necessary for executing its inspection laws; and the net produce [income] of all duties and imposts, laid by any state on imports or exports, shall be for the use of the treasury of the United States; and all such laws shall be subject to the revision and control of the Congress.

[3] No state shall, without the consent of Congress, lay any duty of tonnage, keep troops or ships of war in time of peace, enter into any agreement or compact with another state or with a foreign power, or engage in war unless actually invaded or in such imminent [threatening] danger as will not admit of delay.

---

1. Identify four relevant categories for comparing the house and the Senate, and explain the similarities and differences within those categories.

2. Explain the reasons for the differences between the House and Senate. What did the framers accomplish with these structures?

3. Explain the significance of the difference between the powers of Congress described in Article I, Section 8, paragraphs 1–17 and the power described in Article I, Section 8, paragraph 18.

ARTICLE II. THE PRESIDENCY

Section 1. Executive Power

[1] The executive power shall be vested in a president of the United States of America. He shall hold his office during the term of four years, and, together with the vice president, chosen for the same term, be elected as follows:

[2] Each state shall appoint, in such manner as the legislature thereof may direct, a number of electors, equal to the whole number of senators and representatives to which the state may be entitled in the Congress; but no senator or representative, or person holding an office of trust or profit under the United States, shall be appointed an elector.

[3] ~~The electors shall meet in their respective states, and vote by ballot for two persons, of whom one at least shall not be an inhabitant of the same state with themselves. And they shall make a list of all the persons voted for, and of the number of votes for each; which list they shall sign and certify, and transmit sealed to the seat of the government of the United States, directed to the president of the Senate. The president of the Senate shall, in the presence of the Senate and House of Representatives, open all the certificates, and the votes shall then be counted. The person having the greatest number of votes shall be the president, if such number be a majority of the whole number of electors appointed; and if there be more than one who have such majority, and have an equal number of votes, then the House of Representatives shall immediately choose by ballot one of them for president; and if no person have a majority, then from the five highest on the list the said House shall in like manner choose the president. But in choosing the president, the votes shall be taken by states, the representation from each state having one vote; a quorum for this purpose shall consist of a member or members from two-thirds of the states, and a majority of all the states shall be necessary to a choice. In every case, after the choice of the president, the person having the greatest number of votes of the electors shall be the vice president. But if there should remain two or more who have equal votes, the Senate shall choose from them by ballot the vice president.~~

[4]   The Congress may determine the time of choosing the electors, and the day on which they shall give their votes; which day shall be the same throughout the United States.

[5]   No person except a natural-born citizen, ~~or a citizen of the United States at the time of the adoption of this Constitution,~~ shall be eligible to the office of the president; neither shall any person be eligible to that office who shall not have attained to the age of thirty-five years and been fourteen years a resident within the United States.

[6]   ~~In case of the removal of the president from office, or of his death, resignation, or inability to discharge the powers and duties of the said office, the same shall devolve on the vice president, and the Congress may by law provide for the case of removal, death, resignation, or inability, both of the president and vice president, declaring what officer shall then act as president, and such officer shall act accordingly, until the disability be removed, or a president shall be elected.~~

[7]   The president shall, at stated times, receive for his services, a compensation, which shall neither be increased nor diminished during the period for which he shall have been elected, and he shall not receive within that period any other emolument from the United States, or any of them.

[8]   Before he enter on the execution of his office, he shall take the following oath or affirmation: "I do solemnly swear (or affirm) that I will faithfully execute the office of President of the United States, and will, to the best of my ability, preserve, protect, and defend the Constitution of the United States."

Section 2. Powers of the President

[1]   The president shall be commander in chief of the army and navy [all the armed forces] of the United States, and of the militia of the several states, when called into the actual service of the United States; he may require the opinion in writing of the principal officer in each of the executive departments upon any subject relating to the duties of their respective offices; and he shall have power to grant reprieves and pardons foroffenses against the United States except in cases of impeachment.

[2]   He shall have power, by and with the advice and consent of the Senate, to make treaties, provided two-thirds of the senators present concur; and he shall nominate, and, by and with the advice and consent of the Senate, shall appoint ambassadors, other public ministers and consuls, judges of the Supreme Court, and all other officers of the United States whose appointments are not herein otherwise provided for and which shall be established by law; but the Congress may by law vest the appointment of such inferior officers as they think proper in the president alone, in the courts of law, or in the heads of departments.

[3]   The president shall have power to fill up all vacancies that may happen during the recess of the Senate, by granting commissions which shall expire at the end of their next session.

Section 3. Duties and Responsibilities of the President

He shall, from time to time, give to the Congress information of the state of the Union, and recommend to their consideration such measures as he shall judge necessary and expedient [advisable]; he may, on extraordinary [special] occasions, convene both houses, or either of them, and in case of disagreement between them with respect to the time of adjournment, he may adjourn them to such time as he shall think proper; he shall receive ambassadors and other public ministers; he shall take care that the laws be faithfully executed, and shall commission [appoint] all the officers of the United States.

Section 4. Impeachment

The president, vice president, and all civil officers of the United States, shall be removed from office on impeachment for, and conviction of, treason, bribery, or other high crimes and misdemeanors [offenses].

---

1. On September 8, 1974, President Gerald Ford issued former President Richard Nixon "a full, free, and absolute pardon" for any wrongdoings while he was president, especially in relation to the Watergate scandal. Describe the executive power Ford used to accomplish this act and the relationship of that

power to the duty outlined in Section 3 to "take care that the laws be faithfully executed."

2. Compare the powers of the president with those of the legislature, and explain how those differences affect the government.

ARTICLE III. THE SUPREME COURT AND OTHER COURTS

Section 1. Federal Courts The judicial power of the United States shall be vested in one Supreme Court, and in such inferior [lower] courts as the Congress may from time to time ordain and establish. The judges, both of the Supreme and inferior courts, shall hold their offices during good behavior, and shall, at stated times, receive for their services a compensation, which shall not be diminished during their continuance in office.

Section 2. Jurisdiction of Federal Court

[1] The judicial power shall extend to all cases in law and equity arising under this Constitution, the laws of the United States, and treaties made, or which shall be made, under their authority; to all cases affecting ambassadors, other public ministers, and consuls; to all cases of admiralty and maritime jurisdiction; to controversies to which the United States shall be a party; to controversies between two or more states, between a state and citizens of another state, ~~between citizens of different states,~~ between citizens of the same state claiming lands under grants of different states, and between a state, or the citizens thereof, and foreign states, citizens, or subjects.

[2] In all cases affecting ambassadors, other public ministers, and consuls, and those in which a state shall be a party, the Supreme Court shall have original jurisdiction. In all the other cases before mentioned, the Supreme Court shall have appellate jurisdiction, both as to law and fact, with such exceptions and under such regulations as the Congress shall make.

[3] The trial of all crimes, except in cases of impeachment, shall be by jury; and such trial shall be held in the state where the said crimes shall have been committed; but when not committed within any state, the trial shall be at such place or places as the Congress may by law have directed.

Section 3. Treason

[1] Treason against the United States shall consist only in levying [carrying on] war against them, or in adhering to [assisting] their enemies, giving them aid and comfort. No person shall be convicted of treason unless on the testimony of two witnesses to the same overt [open; public] act, or on confession in open court.

[2] The Congress shall have power to declare the punishment of treason, but no attainder of treason shall work corruption of blood or forfeiture except during the life of the person attainted.

1. Based on Article III, under what jurisdiction did the Supreme Court hear the cases that are required for this course? Explain how the cases reached the Court.

2. Compare the process for settling disputes between states outlined in the Articles of Confederation with the process outlined in the Constitution. Draw a conclusion about the purpose of the plan for the courts outlined in the Constitution that was lacking in the plan in the Articles of Confederation.

ARTICLE IV. INTERSTATE RELATIONS

Section 1. Official Acts and Records
Full faith and credit shall be given in each state to the public acts, records, and judicial proceedings of every other state. And the Congress may, by general laws, prescribe the manner in which such acts, records, and proceedings shall be proved, and the effect thereof.

Section 2. Mutual Obligations of States

[1]   The citizens of each state shall be entitled to all privileges and immunities of citizens in the several states.

[2]   A person charged in any state with treason, felony, or other crime, who shall flee from justice and be found in another state, shall, on demand of the executive authority of the state from which he fled, be delivered up, to be removed to the state having jurisdiction of the crime.

[3]   ~~No person held to service or labor in one state, under the laws thereof, escaping into another, shall, in consequence of any law or regulation therein, be discharged from such service or labor, but shall be delivered up on claim of the party to whom such service or labor may be due.~~

Section 3. New States and Territories

[1]   New states may be admitted by the Congress into this Union; but no new state shall be formed or erected within the jurisdiction of any other state; nor any state be formed by the junction [joining] of two or more states, or parts of states, without the consent of the legislatures of the states concerned as well as of the Congress.

[2]   The Congress shall have power to dispose of and make all needful rules and regulations respecting the territory or other property belonging to the United States; and nothing in this Constitution shall be so construed [interpreted] as to prejudice [damage] any claims of the United States, or of any particular state.

Section 4. Federal Guarantees to the States
The United States shall guarantee to every state in this Union a republican form of government, and shall protect each of them against invasion; and on application of the legislature, or of the executive (when the legislature cannot be convened), against domestic violence [riots].

1. Describe ways in which the United States government can "guarantee to every state in this Union a republican form of government."

2. Much of the remaining conflict related to Article IV centers on family law issues. For example, the legal adoption of a child by unmarried partners in one state is not recognized in another state that does not allow unmarried partners to adopt. Based on the example of *Obergefell v. Hodges* (2015), what might be necessary to make such adoptions uniformly recognized?

ARTICLE V. AMENDING THE CONSTITUTION

The Congress, whenever two-thirds of both houses shall deem [think] it necessary, shall propose amendments to this Constitution, or, on the application of the legislatures of two-thirds of the several states, shall call a convention for proposing amendments, which, in either case, shall be valid, to all intents and purposes, as part of this Constitution when ratified by the legislatures of three-fourths of the several states, or by conventions in three-fourths thereof, as the one or the other mode [method] of ratification may be proposed by the Congress; provided that no amendment which may be made prior to the year 1808 shall in any manner affect the first and fourth clauses in the ninth section of the first article; and that no state,

without its consent, shall be deprived of its equal suffrage in the Senate.

1. Describe the steps in one of the legal processes for amending the Constitution.

2. Describe the steps in another legal process for amending the Constitution.

ARTICLE VI. MISCELLANEOUS PROVISIONS

Section 1. Public Debts All debts contracted and engagements [agreements] entered into before the adoption of this Constitution shall be as valid [binding] against the United States under this Constitution as under the Confederation.

Section 2. Federal Supremacy This Constitution, and the laws of the United States which shall be made in pursuance thereof, and all treaties made, or which shall be made, under the authority of the United States, shall be the supreme law of the land; and the judges in every state shall be bound thereby, anything in the Constitution or laws of any state to the contrary notwithstanding.

Section 3. Oaths of Office The senators and representatives before mentioned, and the members of the several state legislatures, and all executive and judicial officers, both of the United States and of the several states, shall be bound by oath or affirmation to support this Constitution; but no religious test shall ever be required as a qualification to any office or public trust under the United States.

ARTICLE VII. RATIFICATION

~~The ratification of the conventions of nine states shall be sufficient for the establishment of this Constitution between the states so ratifying the same.~~

Done in convention, by the unanimous consent of the states present, the 17th day of September, in the year of our Lord 1787, and of the independence of the United States of America the twelfth. In witness whereof we have hereunto subscribed our names.

Signed by
George Washington
[President and Deputy from Virginia]
and 38 other delegates

---

1. Explain the reasons the Constitution, in contrast to the Articles of Confederation, made the federal government the "supreme law of the land."

2. The absence of a religious test was a matter of debate in many state ratification conventions. At the 1788 convention in Massachusetts, Theophilus Parsons expressed his views: "But what security is it to government, that every public officer shall swear that he is a Christian? Sir, the only evidence we can have of the sincerity and excellency of a man's religion, is a good life—and I trust that such evidence will be required of every candidate by every elector. That man who acts an honest part to his neighbor, will most probably conduct honorably towards the public." has the electorate lived up to Parsons's expectations? Provide an example to explain your position.

AMENDMENTS TO THE CONSTITUTION

Note: The first ten amendments to the Constitution, adopted in 1791, make up the Bill of Rights. The year of adoption of later amendments (11 to 27) is given in parentheses.

Amendment I. Freedom of religion, speech, press, assembly, and petition

Congress shall make no law respecting an establishment of religion, or prohibiting the free exercise thereof; or abridging [reducing] the freedom of speech or of the press; or the right of the people peaceably to assemble, and to petition the government for a redress [correction] of grievances.

Amendment II. Right to bear arms

A well-regulated militia being necessary to the security of a free state, the right of the people to keep and bear arms shall not be infringed [weakened].

Amendment III. Quartering of troops

No soldier shall, in time of peace, be quartered [assigned to live] in any house without the consent of the owner, nor in time of war, but in a manner to be prescribed by law.

Amendment IV. Searches and seizures

The right of the people to be secure [safe] in their persons, houses, papers, and effects [be-longings] against unreasonable searches and seizures shall not be violated; and no [search] warrants shall issue but upon probable cause, supported by oath or affirmation, and particularly describing the place to be searched, and the persons or things to be seized.

Amendment V. Rights of the accused; property rights

No person shall be held to answer for a capital or otherwise infamous crime unless on a presentment or indictment of a grand jury, except in cases arising in the land or naval forces, or in the militia, when in actual service in time of war or public danger; nor shall any person be subject for the same offense to be twice put in jeopardy of life or limb; nor shall be compelled in any criminal case to be a witness against himself; nor be deprived of life, liberty, or property without due process of law; nor shall private property be taken for public use without just compensation.

Amendment VI. Additional rights of the accused

In all criminal prosecutions [trials], the accused shall enjoy the right to a speedy and public trial by an impartial [fair] jury of the state and district wherein the crime shall have been committed, which district shall have been previously ascertained by law; and to be informed of the nature and cause of the accusation; to be confronted with the witnesses against him; to have compulsory process for obtaining witnesses in his favor; and to have the assistance of counsel for his defense.

Amendment VII. Civil suits

In suits at common law where the value in controversy shall exceed twenty dollars, the right of trial by jury shall be preserved, and no fact tried by a jury shall be otherwise reexamined in any court of the United States, than according to the rules of the common

law.

Amendment VIII. Bails, fines, and punishments

Excessive bail shall not be required, nor excessive fines imposed, nor cruel and unusual punishments inflicted.

Amendment IX. Rights not listed

The enumeration [listing] in the Constitution of certain rights shall not be construed to deny or disparage [weaken] others retained by the people.

Amendment X. Powers reserved to the states and people

The powers not delegated to the United States by the Constitution, nor prohibited by it to the states, are reserved to the states respectively, or to the people.

1. Describe the philosophical and political assumptions underlying the provisions in the Bill of Rights.

2. On the basis of the Ninth and Tenth Amendments, describe the powers the states and the people have in the federalist system.

Amendment XI. Suits against states (1798)

The judicial power of the United States shall not be construed to extend to any suit in law or equity, commenced or prosecuted against one of the United States by citizens of another state, or by citizens or subjects of any foreign state.

Amendment XII. Election of president and vice president (1804)

[1]   The electors shall meet in their respective states, and vote by ballot for president and vice president, one of whom at least shall not be an inhabitant of the same state with themselves; they shall name in their ballots the person voted for as president, and in distinct [separate] ballots the person voted for as vice president; and they shall make distinct lists of all persons voted for as president, and of all persons voted for as vice president, and of the number of votes for each, which lists they shall sign and certify, and transmit sealed to the seat of the government of the United States, directed to the president of the Senate.

[2]   The president of the Senate shall, in the presence of the Senate and House of Representatives, open all the certificates, and the votes shall then be counted; the person having the greatest number of votes for president shall be the president, if such number be a majority of the whole number of electors appointed; and if no person have such majority, then from the persons having the highest numbers not exceeding three on the list of those voted for as president, the House of Representatives shall choose immediately, by ballot, the president. But in choosing the president, the votes shall be taken by states, the representation from each state having one vote; a quorum for this purpose shall consist of a member or members from two-thirds of the states, and a majority of all the states shall be necessary to a choice. And if the House of Representatives shall not choose a president whenever the right of choice shall devolve upon them, before the fourth day of March the next following, then the vice president shall act as president, as in the case of the death or other constitutional disability of the president.

[3]   The person having the greatest number of votes as vice president shall be the vice president, if such number be a majority of the whole number of electors appointed; and if no person have a majority, then from the two highest numbers on the list, the Senate shall choose the vice president; a quorum for the purpose shall consist of two-thirds of the whole number of senators,

and a majority of the whole number shall be necessary to a choice. But no person constitutionally ineligible to the office of president shall be eligible to that of vice president of the United States.

Amendment XIII. Abolition of slavery (1865)

Section 1. Slavery Forbidden
Neither slavery nor involuntary servitude [compulsory service], except as a punishment for crime whereof the party shall have been duly convicted, shall exist within the United States, or any place subject to their jurisdiction.

Section 2. Enforcement Power
Congress shall have power to enforce this article [amendment] by appropriate [suitable] legislation.

Amendment XIV. Citizenship and civil rights (1868)

Section 1. Rights of Citizens All persons born or naturalized in the United States, and subject to the jurisdiction thereof, are citizens of the United States and of the state wherein they reside. No state shall make or enforce any law which shall abridge the privileges or immunities of citizens of the United States; nor shall any state deprive any person of life, liberty, or property, without due process of law; nor deny to any person within its jurisdiction the equal protection of the laws.

Section 2. Apportionment of Representatives in Congress
Representatives shall be apportioned among the several states according to their respective numbers, counting the whole number of persons in each state, excluding Indians not taxed. But when the right to vote at any election for the choice of electors for president and vice president of the United States, representatives in Congress, the executive and judicial officers of a state, or the members of the legislature thereof, is denied to any of the male inhabitants of such state, being twenty-one years of age and citizens of the United States, or in any way abridged, except for participation in rebellion or other crime, the basis of representation therein shall be reduced in the proportion which the number of such male citizens shall bear to the whole number of male citizens twenty-one years of age in such state.

Section 3. Persons Disqualified from Public Office No person shall be a senator or representative in Congress, or elector of president and vice president, or hold any office, civil or military, under the United States, or under any state, who, having previously taken an oath, as a member of Congress, or as an officer of the United States, or as a member of any state legislature, or as an executive or judicial officer of any state, to support the Constitution of the United States, shall have engaged in insurrection or rebellion against the same, or given aid or comfort to the enemies thereof. But Congress may, by a vote of two-thirds of each house, remove such disability.

Section 4. Valid Public Debt Defined The validity [legality] of the public debt of the United States, authorized by law, including debts incurred for payment of pensions and bounties [extra allowances] for services in suppressing insurrection or rebellion, shall not be questioned. But neither the United States nor any state shall assume or pay any debt or obligation incurred in aid of insurrection or rebellion against the United States, or any claim for the loss or emancipation [liberation] of any slave; but all such debts, obligations, and claims shall be held illegal and void.

Section 5. Enforcement Power The Congress shall have power to enforce, by appropriate legislation, the provisions of this article.

Amendment XV. Right of suffrage (1870)

Section 1. African Americans Guaranteed the Vote The right of citizens of the United States to vote shall not be denied or abridged by the United States or by any state on account of race, color, or previous condition of servitude [slavery].

Section 2. Enforcement Power The Congress shall have power to enforce this article by appropriate legislation.

---

1. All three "Reconstruction Amendments"—the Thirteenth, Fourteenth, and Fifteenth— conclude with an "Enforcement of Power" section. Explain how this differs from the necessary and proper clause in Article I, Section 8.

2. The Fourteenth Amendment, especially its due process clause, has been called the "Second Bill of Rights." Explain the effect of the Fourteenth Amendment

on incorporation of the Bill of Rights.

Amendment XVI. Income taxes (1913)

The Congress shall have power to lay and collect taxes on incomes, from whatever source derived, without apportionment among the several states, and without regard to any census or enumeration.

Amendment XVII. Popular election of senators (1913)

[1] The Senate of the United States shall be composed of two senators from each state, elected by the people thereof, for six years; and each senator shall have one vote. The electors [voters] in each state shall have the qualifications requisite for electors of the most numerous branch of the state legislatures.

[2] When vacancies happen in the representation of any state in the Senate, the executive authority of such state shall issue writs of election to fill such vacancies: Provided, that the legislature of any state may empower [authorize] the executive thereof to make temporary appointments until the people fill the vacancies by election as the legislature may direct.

[3] ~~This amendment shall not be so construed as to affect the election or term of any senator chosen before it becomes valid as part of the Constitution.~~

Amendment XVIII. Prohibition (1919)

Section 1. Intoxicating Liquors Prohibited ~~After one year from the ratification of this article, the manufacture, sale, or transportation of intoxicating liquors within, the importation thereof into, or the exportation thereof from the United States and all territory subject to the jurisdiction thereof, for beverage purposes is hereby prohibited.~~

Section 2. Enforcement Power ~~The Congress and the several states shall have concurrent power to enforce this article by appropriate legislation.~~

Section 3. Conditions of Ratification ~~This article shall be inoperative unless it shall have been ratified as an amendment to the Constitution by the legislatures of the several states, as provided in the Constitution, within seven years from the date of the submission hereof to the states by the Congress.~~

Amendment XIX. Women's suffrage (1920)

[1]   The right of citizens of the United States to vote shall not be denied or abridged by the United States or by any state on account of sex.

[2]   Congress shall have power to enforce this article by appropriate legislation.

Amendment XX. Presidential and congressional terms (1933)

Section 1. Terms of Office The terms of the president and vice president shall end at noon on the 20th day of January, and the terms of senators and representatives at noon on the 3d day of January, of the years in which such terms would have ended if this article had not been ratified; and the terms of their successors shall then begin.

Section 2. Convening Congress The Congress shall assemble at least once in every year, and such meeting shall begin at noon on the 3rd day of January, unless they shall by law appoint a different day.

Section 3. Presidential Succession If, at the time fixed for the beginning of the term of the president, the president-elect shall have died, the vice president-elect shall become president. If a president shall not have been chosen before the time fixed for the beginning of his term, or if the president-elect shall have failed to qualify, then the vice president-elect shall act as president until a president shall have qualified; and the Congress may by law provide for the case wherein neither a president-elect nor a vice president-elect shall have qualified, declaring who shall then act as president, or the manner in which one who is to act shall be selected, and such person shall act accordingly until a president or vice president shall have qualified.

Section 4. Selection of President and Vice President The Congress may by law provide for the case of the death of any of the persons from whom the House of Representatives may choose a president whenever the right of choice shall have devolved upon them, and for the case of the death of any of the persons from whom the Senate may choose a vice president whenever the right of choice shall have devolved upon them.

Section 5. Effective Date ~~Sections 1 and 2 shall take effect on the 15th day of October following the ratification of this article.~~

Section 6. Conditions of Ratification ~~This article shall be inoperative unless it shall have been ratified as an amendment to the Constitution by the legislatures of three-fourths of the several states within seven years from the date of its submission.~~

Amendment XXI. Repeal of prohibition (1933)

Section 1. Amendment XVIII Repealed The eighteenth article of amendment to the Constitution of the United States is hereby repealed.

Section 2. Shipment of Liquor into "Dry" Areas The transportation or importation into any state, territory, or possession of the United States for delivery or use therein of intoxicating liquors in violation of the laws thereof is hereby prohibited.

Section 3. Conditions of Ratification ~~This article shall be inoperative unless it shall have been ratified as an amendment to the Constitution by conventions in the several states, as provided in the Constitution, within seven years from the date of the submission hereof to the states by the Congress.~~

Amendment XXII. Limiting presidential terms (1951)

Section 1. Limit Placed on Tenure No person shall be elected to the office of the president more than twice, and no person who has held the office of president, or acted as president, for more than two years of a term to which some other person was elected president shall be elected to the office of the president more than once. ~~But this article shall not apply to any person holding the office of president when this article was proposed by the Congress, and shall not prevent any person who may be holding the office of president, or acting as president, during the term within which this article becomes operative from holding the office of president or acting as president during the remainder of such term.~~

Section 2. Conditions of Ratification ~~This article shall be inoperative unless it shall have been ratified as an amendment to the Constitution by the legislatures of three-fourths of the several states within seven years from the date of its submission to the states by the Congress.~~

Amendment XXIII. Suffrage for Washington, D.C. (1961)

Section 1. D.C. Presidential Electors The district constituting [making up] the seat of government of the United States shall appoint in such manner as the Congress may direct: A number of electors of president and vice president equal to the whole number of senators and representatives in Congress to which the district would be entitled if it were a state, but in no event more than the least populous state; they shall be in addition to those appointed by the states, but they shall be considered, for the purposes of the election of president and vice president, to be electors appointed by a state; and they shall meet in the district and perform such duties as provided by the Twelfth Article of amendment.

Section 2. Enforcement Power   The Congress shall have power to enforce this article by appropriate legislation.

Amendment XXIV. Poll taxes (1964)

Section 1. Poll Tax Barred   The right of citizens of the United States to vote in any primary or other election for president or vice president, for electors for president or vice president, or for senator or representative in Congress, shall not be denied or abridged by the United States or any state by reason of failure to pay any poll tax or other tax.

Section 2. Enforcement Power   The Congress shall have the power to enforce this article by appropriate legislation.

Amendment XXV. Presidential succession and disability (1967)

Section 1. Elevation of Vice President   In case of the removal of the president from office or his death or resignation, the vice president shall become president.

Section 2. Vice Presidential Vacancy   Whenever there is a vacancy in the office of the vice president, the president shall nominate a vice president who shall take the office upon confirmation by a majority vote of both houses of Congress.

Section 3. Temporary Disability   Whenever the president transmits to the president pro tempore of the Senate and the Speaker of the House of Representatives his written declaration that he is unable to discharge the powers and duties of his office, and until he transmits to them a written declaration to the contrary, such powers and duties shall be discharged by the vice president as acting president.

Section 4. Other Provisions for Presidential Disability

[1]   Whenever the vice president and a majority of either the principal officers of the executive departments or of such other body as Congress may by law provide, transmit to the president pro tempore of the Senate and the Speaker of the House of Representatives their written declaration that the president is unable to discharge the powers and duties of his office, the vice president shall immediately assume the powers and duties of the office as acting president.

[2]   Thereafter, when the president transmits to the president pro tempore of the Senate and the Speaker of the House of Representatives his written declaration that no inability exists, he shall resume the powers and duties of his office unless the vice president and a majority of either the principal officers of the executive department or of such other body as Congress may by law provide, transmit within four days to the president pro tempore of the Senate and the Speaker of the House of Representatives their written declaration that the president is unable to discharge the powers and duties of his office. Thereupon

Congress shall decide the issue, assembling within 48 hours for that purpose if not in session. If the Congress, within 21 days after receipt of the latter written declaration, or, if Congress is not in session, within 21 days after Congress is required to assemble, determines by two-thirds vote of both houses that the president is unable to discharge the powers and duties of his office, the vice president shall continue to discharge the same as acting president; otherwise, the president shall resume the powers and duties of his office.

Amendment XXVI. Vote for 18-year-olds (1971)

Section 1. Lowering the Voting Age
The right of citizens of the United States, who are 18 years of age or older, to vote shall not be denied or abridged by the United States or by any state on account of age.

Section 2. Enforcement Power The Congress shall have power to enforce this article by appropriate legislation.

Amendment XXVII. Congressional pay (1992)

No law, varying the compensation for the services of the Senators and Representatives, shall take effect, until an election of Representatives shall have intervened.

Bibliography

Books

Aberback, Joel D. and Bert A. Rockman. In t*he Web of Politics: Three Decades of the U.S. Federal Executive.* Washington: Brookings Institution Press, 2000.

Acheson, Dean. *Present at the Creation: My Years in the State Department.* New York: Norton, 1969.

Allen, Jonathan and Amie Parnes. *Shattered: Inside Hillary Clinton's Doomed Campaign.* New York: Crown, 2017.

Alter, Jonathan. *The Promise: President Obama, Year One.* New York: Simon and Schuster, 2010.

Alterman, Eric. *What Liberal Media? The Truth About Bias in the News.* New York: Basic Books, 2003.

Alvarez, R. Michael and John Brehm. *Hard Choices, Easy Answers.* Princeton: Princeton University Press, 2002.

Asher, Herbert. *Polling and the Public: What Every Citizen Should Know.* Washington: Congressional Quarterly Press, 2004.

Balz, Dan. *Collision 2012: Obama vs. Romney and the Future of Elections in America.* New York: Viking, 2013.

Balz, Dan and Haynes Johnson. *The Battle for America 2008: The Story of an Extraordinary Election.* New York: Viking, 2009.

Becker, Carl L. *The Declaration of Independence: A Study in the History of Political Ideas.* New York: Vintage Books, 1970.

Bowen, Catherine Drinker. *Miracle at Philadelphia.* Boston: Little, Brown and Co., 1966.

Bowling, Kenneth R. and Donald R. Kennon eds. *The House and Senate in the 1790s: Petitioning, Lobbying, and Institutional Development.* Athens: Ohio University Press, 2002.

Brown, Sherrod. *Congress from the Inside.* Kent, Ohio: Kent State University Press, 2004.

Caesar, James W., Andrew E. Busch, and John J. Pitney, Jr. *Defying the Odds: The 2016 Elections and American Politics.* Lanham, MD: Rowan and Littlefield, 2017.

Chernow, Ronald. *Alexander Hamilton.* New York: Penguin, 2004.

Cigler, Allan J. and Burdettt A. Loomis eds. *Interest Group Politics.* Washington: CQ Press, 2002.

Clinton, Hillary Rodham. *What Happened.* New York: Simon and Schuster, 2017.

Clyburn, James E. *Blessed Experiences: Genuinely Southern Proudly Black.* Columbia: University of South Carolina Press, 2014..

Crawford, Kenneth G. *The Pressure Boys: The Inside Story of Lobbying in America.* New York: J. Messner, 1939.

D'Antonio, Michael. *A Consequential Presidency: The Legacy of Barack Obama.* New York: Thomas Dunne Books, 2016.

David, Paul T., Ralph Goldman, and Richard Bain. T*he Politics of National Party Conventions.* New York: Vintage Books (Brookings Institute), 1964.

Edwards, Bob. *Edward R. Murrow and the Birth of Broadcast Journalism.* Hoboken, NJ: John Wiley and Sons, 2004.

Elkins, Stanley and Eric McKitrick. *The Age of Federalism: The Early American Republic,* 1788 to 1800. New York: Oxford University Press, 1995.

Fauntroy, Michael K. *Republicans and the Black Vote.* Boulder: Lynne Rienner Publishers, 2007.

Frank, Nathaniel. Awakening: *How Gays and Lesbians Brought Marriage Equality to America.* Cambridge: The Belknap Press of Harvard University Press, 2017.

Gillespie, Nick and Matt Welch. *The Declaration of Independents: How Libertarian Politics Can Fix What's Wrong with America. New York: Public Affairs, 2011.*

Goldberg, Bernard. Bias: *A CBS Insider Exposes How the Media Distort the News.* Washington: Regnery Publishing, 2002.

Goldman, Ralph M. *The Democratic Party in American Politics.* New York: Macmillan Company, 1966.

Goldstein, Kenneth M. *Interest Group Lobbying, and Participation in America.* Cambridge, UK: Cambridge University Press, 1999.

Gould, Lewis. *The Most Exclusive Club: A History of the Modern United States Senate.* New York: Basic Books, 2005.

Gray, David. *The Fourth Amendment in an Age of Surveillance.* New York: Cambridge University Press, 2017.

Fleischer, Ari. *Taking Heat: The President, the Press, and My Years in the White House.* New York: William Morrow, 2005.

Halperin, Mark and John Heilemann. *Double Down: Game Change* 2012. New York: Penguin Press, 2013.

   Game Change: Obama and the Clintons, McCain and Palin, and the Race of a Lifetime. New York: Harper, 2010.

Hamilton, Lee. *How Congress Works and Why You Should Care.* Bloomington: Indiana University Press, 2004.

Herrnson, Paul S. *Congressional Elections: Campaigning at Home and in Washington.* Washington: CQ Press, 2000.

Jensen, Merrill. *The Articles of Confederation: An Interpretation of the Social-Constitutional History of the American Revolution, 1774-1781.* Madison: University of Wisconsin Press, 1959.

Judis, John B. *The Paradox of Democracy: Elites, Special Interests and the Betrayal of Public Trust.* New York: Pantheon, 2000.

Kaiser, Robert G. *So Damn Much Money: The Triumph of Lobbying and the Corrosion of Government.* New York: Knopf, 2009.

Kelly, Kate. *Election Day: An American Holiday, An American History.* New York: Facts on File, 1991.

Ketchum, Ralph. *The Anti-Federalist Papers and the Constitutional Debates.* New York: New American Library, 1986.

Krent, Harold J. *Presidential Powers.* New York: New York University Press, 2005.

Labunski, Richard E. *James Madison and the Struggle for the Bill of Rights.* Oxford: Oxford University Press, 2006.

Lazarus, Edward. *Closed Chambers: The Rise, Fall, and Future of the Modern Supreme Court.* New York: Penguin Books, 1998.

Mann, Thomas and Norman Ornstein. *The Broken Branch: How Congress Is Failing America and How to Get It Back on Track.* New York: Oxford, 2006.

Marlin, George J. *The American Catholic Voter: 200 Years of Political Impact.* South Bend, IN: St. Augustine Press, 2004.

Medoff, Rafael. *Jewish Americans and Political Participation.* Santa Barbara, CA: ABC-CLIO, 2002.

Newport, Frank. *Polling Matters: Why Leaders Must Listen to the Wisdom of the People.* New York: Warner Books, 2004.

Nichols, David. *A Matter of Justice: Eisenhower and the Beginning of the Civil Rights Revolution.* New York: Simon and Schuster, 2007.

Nichols, Tom. *The Death of Expertise: The Campaign Against Established Knowledge and Why it Matters.* New York: Oxford University Press, 2017.

Nixon, Richard. *The Memoirs of Richard Nixon.* New York: Grosset and Dunlap, 1978.

Patterson, Bradley H. *The White House Staff: Inside the West Wing and Beyond.* Washington: Brookings Institution Press, 2000.

Piven, Frances Fox, Lorraine C. Minnite, and Margaret Groarke. *Keeping Down the Black Vote: Race and the Demobilization of American Voters.* New York: The New Press, 2009.

Rehnquist, William. *The Supreme Court.* New York: Vintage Books, 2001. Remeni, Robert V. The House. New York: Harper Collins, 2007.

Safire, William. *Safire's New Political Dictionary.* New York: Random House, 1993.

Schlesinger, Arthur M., Jr. *The Imperial Presidency.* Boston: Houghton Mifflin, 1989.

Sorenson, Theodore C. *Kennedy.* Old Saybrook, CT: Konecky & Konecky, 1965.

Steinman, Ron. *Inside Television's First War: A Saigon Journal.* Columbia: University of Missouri Press, 2002.

Storing, Herbert. *What the Antifederalists Were FOR."* Chicago: University of Chicago Press, 1981.

Sunstein, Cass R. *#republic: Divided Democracy in the Age of Social Media.* Princeton: Princeton University Press, 2017.

Teachout, Zephyr. *Corruption in America: From Benjamin Franklin's Snuff Box to Citizens United.* Cambridge: Harvard University Press, 2014.

Thomas, Helen. *Watchdogs of Democracy? The Waning Washington Press Corps and How It Has Failed the Public.* New York: Scribner, 2006.

Tocqueville, Alexis de. *Democracy In America.* Chicago: University of Chicago Press, 2002. Toobin, Jeffrey. The Nine: Inside the Secret World of the Supreme Court. New York: Anchor, 2008.

Tribe, Laurence and Joshua Matz. *Uncertain Justice: The Roberts Court and the Constitution.* New York: Henry Holt, 2014.

Van Cleve, George William. *We Have Not A Government: The Articles of Confederation and the Road to the Constitution.* Chicago: University of Chicago Press, 2017.

Waldman, Michael. T*he Second Amendment: A Biography.* New York: Simon and Schuster, 2014.

Whitcover, Jules. *Party of the People: A History of the Democrats.* New York: Random House, 2003.

White, Theodore. *The Making of a President 1960.* New York: Atheneum, 1961.

Wood, Gordon S. *The Creation of the American Republic, 1776-1787.* Chapel Hill: UNC Press, 1998.

Woodward, C. Vann. *The Strange Career of Jim Crow.* New York: Oxford University Press, 2002.

Articles

Abello, Cristina. "Changes in Store at the FCC." T*he News Media and the Law.* Winter 2009.

Alterman, Eric. "Bush's War on the Press." T*he Nation.* May 9, 2005.

Baker, Peter. "The Education of a President." *New York Times.* October 12, 2010.

Basinger, Scott, and Maxwell Mak. "The Changing Politics of Federal Judicial Nominations." *Congress and the President, vol. 37.* 2010.

Beckel, Michael and Russ Choma. "Decision Helped Romney Neutralize Obama's Fundraising Advantage." *Open Secrets <www.opensecrets.org>.* October 30, 2012.

Biskupic, Joan. "Ellis Island: This Land is Whose Land?" *Washington Post.* January 11, 1998, and May 27, 1998.

Bogost, Ian. "Obama Was Too Good at Social Media." *The Atlantic.* January 6, 2017.

Bottum, Joseph. "There is No Catholic Vote." *The Weekly Standard.* November 1, 2010.

Brand, Rachel. "Judicial Appointments: Checks and Balances in Practice." *Harvard Journal of Law and Public Policy.* Volume 33, Number 1.

Brill, Steven. "On Sale: Your Government." *Time.* July 12, 2010.

Carney, Eliza Newlin. "K Street's Sea Change." National Journal. September 22, 2007.

Casey, Winter. "Why They Lobby." National Journal. May 31, 2008. "Everything You Need to Know about the Voter ID Controversy." *The Week.* October 25, 2014.

Chamberlain, Craig. "Will White House Continue to Use Photos as a Social Media Tool?" *Illinois News Bureau.* December 20, 2016.

Cole, David. "Privacy 2.0: Surveillance in the Digital State." *The Nation.* April 16, 2015.

Conway, Kelly. "Primary Polling Problems: Can Horse Race Coverage Alter Results?" *Brown Political Review.* March 9, 2016.

Cornell, Saul. "Half Cocked." *The Journal of Criminal Law and Criminology. Vol. 106, No. 2.* 2017.

Eilperin, Juliet. "Here's How the First President of the Social Media Age has Chosen to Connect with Americans." *Washington Post.* May 26, 2015.

Elliot, Philip, "The GOP's Inside Man." *Time.* December 25, 2017.

Farber, Daniel A. and Anne Joseph O'Connell. "The Lost World of Administrative Law." *Texas Law Review.* Vol. 92: 1137. 2014.

Filisko, G.M. "Gun War: Congress Has Been Silent on Guns, But States Haven't, So Change is on the Horizon." *ABA Journal.* May 2017.

Fisher, Daniel, "Bureaucrats May be the Losers if Gorsuch Wins a Seat on Supreme Court." *Forbes.* Jan. 26, 2017.

Foer, Franklin. "When Silicon Valley Took Over Journalism." *The Atlantic.* September 2017.

Fox, Justin and Stuart V. Jordan. "Delegation and Accountability." *The Journal of Politics.* Vol. 73, No. 3, July 2011.

Garrow, David. "The Once and Future Supreme Court." *American History.* February 2005.

Goldmacher, Shane. "Four Years Later." National Journal. June 8, 2014.

Goodwin, Michael. "The Collapse of Fair-Minded Journalism." *USA Today Magazine* September 2017.

Grant, Rebecca. "Marie Newman vs. The Democratic Machine." *The Nation.* August 12, 2019.

Gray, C. Boyden. "Congressional Abdication: Delegation without Detail and Without Waiver." *Harvard Journal of Law & Public Policy.* Winter 2013.

Greenberg, David. "Spinning With Obama." *Dissent.* Fall 2015.

Groseclose, Tim and Jeffery Milyo. "A Measure of Media Bias." Stuart Kallen ed., Media Bias. San Diego: *Greenhaven Press*, 2004.

Guiliano, Paola and Antonio Spilimebergo, "Growing Up in a Recession." *Review of Economic Studies.* November 2013.

Guldon, Bob. "Mr. X Speaks: An Interview with George Kennan." Foreign Service Journal. February 2004.

Huffman, Jim, "What the Supreme Court's Decision in Arlington v. FCC Means for America." *Daily Caller.* May 22, 2013.

Jackson, Jannie, Peter Hart and Rachel Coen. "The Media are Biased Against Conservative Economic Policies."

Stuart Kallen ed., *Media Bias.* San Diego: *Greenhaven Press*, 2004.

Johnson, Fawn. "The End of No Child Left Behind." National Journal. October 29, 2011.

Jost, Kenneth. "Revising No Child Left Behind." CQ Researcher. April 16, 2010. "Voting Controversies: Are U.S. Elections Being Conducted Fairly?" Congressional Quarterly Researcher. February 21, 2014.

Klein, Daniel B. and Charlotta Stern. "By the Numbers: The Ideological Profile of Professors." The Politically Correct University. Washington: *AEI Press*, 2009.

Kleiner, Sarah. "Democrats Say Citizens United Should Die. Here's Why That Won't Happen." Time. August 31, 2017.

Kohler, Peter. "The Unfairness of the 'Fairness Doctrine.'" *The Masthead.* Spring 2009.

Lewis, Charles. "Why I Left 60 Minutes." Politico Magazine. June 29, 2014..

McLeod, Ethan. "Will the GOP-Led Congress Further Loosen Gun Restrictions?" *CQ Researcher.* July 17, 2017.

Meyerson, Harold. "California's Jungle Primary: Tried it. Dump it." *Los Angeles Times.* June 21, 2014.

Mullens, Luke. "Flip or Flop: The DCCC Will do Whatever it Takes to Win." Mother Jones. November/December 2018.

"New American Center," *Esquire.* November 2013.

Rendell, Steve. "The Fairness Doctrine: How We Lost It, and Why We Need it Back." Extra! January/February 2005.

Rothschild, David. "Understanding How Polls Affect Voters." *Huffington Post.* October 26, 2012.

Smock, Raymond W. "The Institutional Development of the House of Representatives, 1789– 1801."

Sohoni, Mila. "A Bureaucracy If You Can Keep It." Harvard Law Review. November 2017.

Thrall, A. Trevor and Erik Goepner. "Millennials and U.S. Foreign Policy: The Next Generation's Attitudes Toward Foreign Policy and War (and Why They Matter)." Cato Institute, 2015.

Turley, Jonathan. "The Rise of the Fourth Branch of Government." *Washington Post.* May 24, 2013.

Underwood, Julie. "The Privacy of a Student's Backpack." *Kappan.* October 2017.

Unger, Ross. "Boss Rove." *Vanity Fair.* September 2012.

"Voting Trends by Age Group." *Congressional Digest.* January 2017.

Walker, Jesse. "Beyond the Fairness Doctrine." Reason. November 2008.

Wolfensberger, Donald R. "The Return of the Imperial Presidency?" *The Wilson Quarterly.* Spring 2002.

Reports

American National Election Study (ANES). Stanford University, University of Michigan, and the National Science Foundation, 2014.

Congressional Research Service.

_____ An Introduction to Judicial Review of Federal Agency Action. December 7, 2016.

_____ Congressional Research Service. *An Introduction to Judicial Review of Federal Agency Action.* December 7, 2016.

_____ *Declarations of War and Authorizations for the Use of Military Force: Historical Background and Legal Implications.* March 17, 2011.

_____ *Lobbying Reform, Background and Legislative Proposals, 109th Congress.* March 23, 2006.

_____ *Membership of the 115th Congress: A Profile.* March 14, 2014.

_____ *Women in Congress: Historical Overview, Tables, and Discussion.* April 29, 2015.

Democratic National Committee. Moving America Forward: Democratic National Platform. 012.

Gans, Curtis. *African-Americans, Anger, Fear and Youth Propel Turnout to Highest Level Since 1960.* American University. December 17, 2008.

_____ Testimony Before Senate Rules Committee. March 11, 2009.

Klein, Daniel B. *By the Numbers: The Ideological Profile of Professors.* American Enterprise Institute Conference. November 14, 2007.

Pew Research Center. *Digital News Fact Sheet.* August 7, 2017.

_____ *How Americans Encounter, Recall and Act Upon Digital News.* February 9, 2017.

_____ *Local TV News Fact Sheet.* July 13, 2017.

_____ *The Future of Free Speech, Trolls, Anonymity and Fake News Online.* March 29, 2017.

_____ *Trump, Clinton Voters Divided in Their Main Source for Election News.* January 18, 2017.

U.S. Elections Project. *America Goes to the Polls 2016: A Report on Voter Turnout in the 2016 Election.*

U.S. Office of Personnel Management. *Biography of an Ideal: A History of the Federal Civil Service.* 2003.

_____ *A New Day for the Civil Service.* Fiscal Year 2010 Annual Performance Report. 2011.

_____ *Sizing Up the Executive Branch Fiscal Year 2016.* June 2017.

Films

Casino Jack and the United States of Money. Magnolia Home Entertainment, 2010.

The Most Dangerous Man in America: Daniel Ellsberg and the Pentagon Papers. First Run Features, 2009.

The War Room. Criterion Collection, 1994.

Index